JOSEPH CHAMBERLAIN
AND LIBERAL REUNION

STUDIES IN POLITICAL HISTORY

Editor: Michael Hurst

Fellow of St John's College, Oxford

1. Joseph Chamberlain

JOSEPH CHAMBERLAIN
and Liberal Reunion

❧❦❧

The Round Table Conference
of 1887

❧❦❧

by
MICHAEL HURST
Fellow in Modern History and Politics,
St John's College, Oxford

LONDON: Routledge & Kegan Paul
TORONTO: University of Toronto Press
1967

First published 1967
in Great Britain by
Routledge & Kegan Paul Ltd
and in Canada by
University of Toronto Press

Printed in Great Britain by
Richard Clay (The Chaucer Press) Ltd
Bungay, Suffolk

To

Beatrice, Katrina and Elizabeth

(But for whom this book would have been written much
sooner)

CONTENTS

PLATES

Plates are reproduced by kind permission of the National Portrait Gallery (Nos. 1–8) and Radio Times Hulton Picture Library (No. 9).

PREFACE

WRITING history should be like constructing some intricate machine, the delicately wrought parts of which must occupy just the right position, be exactly of the appropriate size and shape and weigh what the designer allowed for. However highly trained the historian's mind he will doubtless fall short of this utopian concept to some extent, distorting in one place and omitting in another, with the result that his work would only just pass muster if transformed by some magic process into the world of engineering. Bad historians' efforts would probably turn out as disgracefully as a car with the axles in the correct position on one side and coming through the coachwork on the other.

All too often, even when trying to apply Ranke's triple test of spotting the general trend of events, singling out the telling illustrative detail and comprehending the intricacies of human personalities, historians fail to evaluate the weight of different factors with anything approaching exactitude and, what is worse, resort to highly impressionistic judgments based on what by the highest standards is lamentably incomplete evidence. It was not for nothing that Ranke argued for comprehensive presentation of the story. Without it his triple test was bound to function no more efficiently than a lame duck. None of the departments of historical study can have more examples of harmful treatment than assessments of personalities, though that of general trends must run it very close indeed. According to Lord David Cecil, Sir Keith Feiling engaged his enthusiastic interest in history by blowing the 'Whig interpretation of history sky high'. Honoured worthies of the 'leftist' pantheon with the standing of Pym and Hampden were dubbed 'typical examples of the sharp politician type'. Leaving aside the point of why men should be described as typical of a type, and not questioning the ability of Sir Keith to put up an excellent case for his point of view, the fact remains that in such a statement is a wealth of power for good or evil to be used on students of history by those in positions of influence. Joseph Chamberlain is commonly regarded as a 'sharp politician type'; Gladstone considerably less so. What was the truth of the matter? To find an answer a thorough enquiry is called for. Without it let men hold their peace, or hedge themselves round with 'ifs' and 'buts'.

By taking a limited subject, collecting all the available evidence of significance upon it, and, at the risk of being charged with conflation, presenting the whole of a short but complicated story, an attempt has been made to practise what has been preached in the two preceding paragraphs. If the degree of sin remains great and the experiment has failed, it will not be for want of trying.

The *Times Literary Supplement* reviewer of A. J. P. Taylor's new *Oxford History of England* volume, 'English History, 1914–1945', described the author as a 'gadfly'. All he meant was that everyone in the book, of whatever doctrinal affiliation and of whatever social status, had stood in danger of criticism. But there was praise as well as blame. Why then a gadfly and not a 'balmfly'? All A. J. P. Taylor had done was to distribute moral and political rewards and punishments. Perhaps his approach was unduly moralising, but the aim and object of any good historian should be fundamentally the same, albeit without the Quaker gloss! Issues, their details and the men involved in them have to be presented: 'beauty spots', 'warts' and all. That much is surely self-evident?

There are plenty of 'beauty spots' and 'warts' in this book. Perhaps the most interesting fact from the human point of view to emerge most forcibly is the wide measure of similarity between statesmen and politicians widely regarded as poles apart. What might be termed the 'Partisans'' interpretation of history can probably be held responsible for what is, after all, far from a reasonable assumption of dissimilarity even allowing for variations of temperament in individuals. The disgruntled citizen is constantly dismissing public men as 'all the same', or 'all as bad as each other', yet plumps like an unreflecting sheep for the argument of some devotee that Doe was, or is, quite a different proposition from Roe. And this, not only in the matter of policies or moral worth, but in the sphere of professional techniques.

Individual leaders were bound to dominate this story. The parties and electorate looked to them for direction. It would be unfair to say, however, that 'grass root' and intermediate stage influences have not received their due. The only thing is that they have been treated of in relation to their effect upon leadership. And why not indeed, given the contemporary structure of politics?

Foreign affairs and the state of the British economy do not receive more than passing attention in what follows. The reason is that neither the one nor the other played any real part in determining the mutual relations between the Liberal and Radical Unionists and either the Conservative government or the Gladstonian Liberal opposition. The Unionist alliance and Liberal disunion hinged on other things— things explained as the story unfolds.

United Kingdom domestic concerns had all but crowded out foreign affairs during the 1886 general election campaign and nothing happened to reverse this trend in the succeeding months. Admittedly, Salisbury's desire to endear himself to the French by sweet words and to consolidate the British position in Egypt unobtrusively when their guard was dropped remained unsatisfied while Randolph Churchill stayed in the Cabinet. It was also true that the same minister blocked his chief's plans for tackling Russia over Bulgaria and the security of the notorious Straits. But his resignation, instead of aggravating these complications, swept them right away. Hartington, Goschen and the bulk of Liberal Unionist parliamentarians were only too pleased to see Salisbury's ideas come to fruition in the Mediterranean Agreements of February and March 1887. What slight doubts Chamberlain did have counted for little or nothing in determining his political decisions, strategic or tactical, and almost invariably found no expression, except in the odd remark to Dilke. Such near indifference facilitated his relations with both Conservatives and Hartingtonians on the Unionist side and Liberals of most shades among the Home Rulers. Preoccupation with internal problems was for the time being the rule for an overwhelming proportion of Gladstonian and Unionist Liberals, whether or not they were politically active in the fullest sense. A situation bound to result in a virtual free hand for their leaders over external matters and an ignoring of the disagreements about them potentially so important to the Left. Its being out of office and not having to take actual foreign affairs decisions meant the situation glided on undisturbed, even for most Radical Unionists, faced with having to back the Conservative government.

Although economic conditions in Ireland were going from bad to worse at the end of 1886 and played a crucial part in shaping political developments generally, those in Britain itself took a distinct turn for the better. Nor was it a rapidly passing phase. The recovery was to last well into 1890. By the time Churchill went prices had shown distinct signs of rising and higher imports and exports boded well for the future. Investments too had already shot up, with the result that a note of quiet optimism had crept into trade reports. Yet politics did not turn upon the new-found prosperity of many vital sectors of the economy. What influence it did have was so tenuous as hardly to be noticed and almost always purely negative. That is, the government avoided having to face a worse crisis because of it, but failed to gain any noticeably increased support. Working class discontent and the longstanding adherence to Gladstone by the majority of the poor were not to be destroyed by a little amelioration. In the agricultural sector, where conditions continued to be depressed, there were no desertions to the Home Rule and 'reformist' side worth mentioning. Indeed, the paradox was that just then events generally were tending to strengthen rather than weaken Salisbury's position among the

PREFACE

landowners and their labourers. A preponderance of the former were
ardent Unionists dead set against widespread reform, and a growing
number of the latter had come to feel let down by Gladstone's preoccupation with Home Rule and Irish agrarian woes. Distress in the
Scottish Highlands provided Chamberlain with another much needed
stumping ground and Gladstonian caution played into his hands.
Nevertheless, it would be true to say that neither prosperity nor adversity affected political conditions profoundly one way or the other.
Hence they could be dealt with in brief.

Of course, this in no way challenges the basic fact that long term
economic conditions had played an immense part in shaping British
politics. That much is clear from what was said above about amelioration. But for most purposes, in this book, the matter has had to be
taken for granted. Lengthy discussion of it would have meant having
chapter upon chapter before coming on to the particular events
analysed here.

'One should always play fairly . . . when one has the winning cards.' (Mrs Cheveley: *An Ideal Husband*, Act One)

INTRODUCTION

⸻━━━◆◆◆━━⸻

'In my Father's house are many mansions,'
St. John xiv. 2

HAD Herbert Gladstone[1] been asked to define the Liberalism current during his father's leadership, the words of this quotation would have provided a telling first sentence for his answer. At no point between 1868 and 1894 did the Liberal party become monolithic in doctrine or organisation. Opinions ranging from the cautious moderation of patrician Whiggery to the rip-roaring and whole-hogging Radicalism based on the big cities had their devotees occupying 'mansions' throughout these crucial years. The general trend was for the Whig ones to become less populated while those in Radical hands gradually filled up to bursting point, especially after Gladstone's adoption of Home Rule in 1885–6 led to a substantial exodus of right wingers. But sadly depleted though the moderates were, there remained in the persons of Spencer,[2] Granville[3] and Kimberley[4] enough Whig influence near the 'throne' to preserve an important flavour in the pot-pourri of British reformist politics.

Domestic conditions within the great 'house' had never been easy, The G.O.M. himself was usually able to discipline any troublemakers, or, if not, to cajole them into a cooperative mood. The Home Rule

[1] Herbert J. Gladstone (1854–1930) was the Liberal leader's youngest child. As M.P. for West Leeds from 1880 until 1910 he played an important part in Liberal party affairs. He flew the Hawarden Kite in December 1885 and was Chief Whip 1899–1906. After serving as Home Secretary 1905–10 he became a viscount and went out to South Africa as Governor-General until 1914.

[2] The 5th Earl Spencer (1835–1910), twice Lord Lieutenant of Ireland (1868–74 and 1882–5) and Lord President of the Council in the third Gladstone ministry of 1886.

[3] The 2nd Earl Granville (1815–91), Foreign Secretary 1880–5 and Colonial Secretary in the third Gladstone ministry of 1886. He had earlier held various ministerial posts and was joint leader of the Liberal party with Hartington during Gladstone's 'retirement' of 1875–80. As they were cousins the Whigs felt very snug.

[4] The 1st Earl of Kimberley (1826–1902), served as Secretary for India in the third Gladstone ministry. Like Granville he had already occupied several responsible positions in Cabinets, but unlike him lived to become a member of the fourth and last of Gladstone's administrations.

B   1

affair was the one vital exception. Even so, the amount of energy required for running affairs would have been way beyond all but the most exceptional men. Of these, of course, the party was fortunate in having a most notable example at its head. Yet it must be admitted that his authority had stood periodically in need of reinforcement and finally crumbled away. First had come the build-up after his 'unmuzzling' in 1865[1] and the formation of the 1868 ministry, followed by fairly widespread disillusionment, electoral defeat in 1874 and his retirement from the leadership the next year. From then until 1880 came the second build-up of prestige, culminating in the Midlothian campaigns, electoral victory and return to the leadership. The five-year interval had left him 'unmuzzled' once more. The process proved one of considerable gain for his party. Absence made the public heart grow fonder, all the more so, as it was of a very special sort. Being absent from the leadership meant being present in the country once the Bulgarian crisis dragged him away from scholarship. Unhappily, repetition was not restricted to success. Disillusionment soon set in, severely aggravated by the situation in Ireland and the masterly direction of the Nationalist cause by Parnell. Until 1885 Gladstone had not been challenged in any sustained way from within the leadership of the party. No one seriously disputed his being the nation's leading Liberal. His prestige remained immense. What had changed was the degree to which the Whigs and Chamberlain were prepared to play the game of follow my leader. Quarrels between Hartington, the Whig leader, and Chamberlain, the white hope of Radicalism were drowned by the Home Rule flood.[2] When Gladstone had voluntarily abandoned command a decade before, his inherent strength as a public figure had preserved for him the fee simple of the 'house'. His worthy successors, Hartington and Granville, had been mere tenants-at-will. The facility with which he had resumed control demonstrated that. Now, while the fee simple was still vested in him, the 'house' ceased to be the sole zadruga of Liberalism. Many of the Whig 'mansions' became well nigh empty. Some were even bolted and barred. The fine Birmingham Radical dwelling, once the abode of bustling men, stood deserted, full of bitter echoes. Out of the nightmare of 1885–6 came what appeared to be a third 'unmuzzling'. This time, however, things

[1] On the 18th July 1865 Gladstone began his speech to a vast audience in the Free Trade Hall, Manchester, with the words: 'At last, my friends, I am come among you, and I am come among you "Unmuzzled".' J. Morley, *Life of Gladstone*, Vol. II, p. 146.

[2] In 1883 the *Fortnightly Review* (Vol. XXXIV) carried an article entitled 'The Future of the Radical Party'. Many commentators tended to assume that internecine rows inside the Liberal party would lead to an eventual split on strictly domestic issues. As the title of the article shows, one component part of Liberalism was openly referred to as a 'party'. So were the Whigs or 'Moderates'.

were different. Gladstone himself was feverishly eager to use his defeat in the election of 1886 as an opportunity to crusade for Home Rule. The new Radical majority in the 'house' insisted other things be considered too. They agreed with their leader over Home Rule, but still demanded several pounds of 'constructionist' and 'faddist' flesh. Gone was anything like a real balance of forces over which the G.O.M. could lord it. Almost as soon as the Liberal Unionist secession took place his thoughts turned to the subject of reunion. Home Rule was all very well, but a 'house' divided against itself was a tragedy which might be blamed on him. Imbalance meant that 'unmuzzling' led to swallowing things he of all people found singularly distasteful.

To the one great series of efforts to make the 'house' a home for Liberal Unionists and Gladstonians alike many contributed. Its failure can be attributed to many factors. One of them was Gladstone's new way of being 'unmuzzled'. Morley and the new Radical ascendancy made sure Gladstone realised which were the truly powerful 'mansions'. Nor were they alone, for Parnell and his cohorts stood at their back. Public recognition of the true state of affairs came with the 'Newcastle Programme' of 1891. In its items may be seen the extent to which Gladstone had become a partner in power—a mere 'mansion' dweller in what was at last gradually ceasing to be his own 'house'. The conveyance of his fee simple was a long and painful process, vastly accelerated after the Lords' rejection of the second Home Rule Bill of 1893. His final years of office from 1892 to 1894 were not ones of power. He might have remained the 'People's William', but was ceasing to be the party's centre of power. He was at the end not even a partner—simply a figurehead. The man who had once been almost bigger than the Liberal party had lived to see it become infinitely bigger than him. Ironically, Gladstonianism had at last proved it could flourish without Gladstone.

The power structure of these classic processes has to be laid bare before the full significance of the reconciliation attempt to which this book is principally devoted can be appreciated. Part of the general context of Liberal activity was, of course, made by forces directly opposed to it. Of these, the Conservative and Irish Home Rule parties were by far the most vital to the matters now under consideration and must necessarily loom large in what follows. No political party or its leaders can escape completely from their past. Many factors once important may not be relevant to a later situation, but belief that they are, held by those who remember previous experiences, often makes them equally or more vital in a crisis as other, directly inherited, or newly pertinent ones. The place of the subjective in history can all too easily be underestimated. Usually, most of the principal participators

3

in events consciously revere the past as a guide to future wisdom and suffer frequent disappointment. But sometimes the subjective is acted on unconsciously and men indulge prejudices the origins of which elude them. Nor is this all, for there are strong elements of continuity in most periods of up to half a century in British political history of recent times, primarily because of the absence of bloody revolutions inaugurating fundamental changes in the structure of the state. So, not only were Gladstone, Salisbury, Hartington, Chamberlain, Parnell and their respective henchmen being influenced by the irrelevant past in tackling the problems of 1886 and 1887, but by the past that was still the real present. New factors were visible to some and invisible to others. Had statesmen been as adept in the discovery of them as historians the world would have had a vastly different story to tell. How relevant factors of the old subjective and objective types fit in together and with those intrinsic importance derived solely from the actual events of the crisis can only be properly understood by taking the mechanism of events to pieces. This is where the power structure comes in.

When the Conservative party split in 1846 over Corn Law repeal, and two-thirds of its members in the House of Commons stuck out for agricultural protection, there began a period of confusion in party alignments that was only to end with the great Liberal victory of 1868. It was the triumph of a new party and a new Gladstone. Peel had faced what might be termed an anti-Conservative front as an Opposition. Derby had initially done likewise. After 1865, there was a rapid change and this Front gave way to a fully-fledged political party by the time the country went to the polls three years later. The *sine qua non* in this metamorphosis was the new Gladstone. He it was who had gone to the masses, imposed unity and rebuilt 'Palmerston Mansions' into the magnificent 'house' over which he presided. Immediately after his defeat at Oxford University in July 1865 he had sped north to Lancashire, painfully aware that education was not, from a progressive viewpoint, synonymous with enlightenment. Addressing six thousand people in Manchester's Free Trade Hall, he had declared: 'At last, my friends, I am come among you, and I am come among you "unmuzzled" '.[1] This was the first 'unmuzzling' and led to a marked acceleration in the courtship between the man who had once been the hope of the 'stern unbending Tories' and the British democracy. Léon Blum once claimed that 'pour animer les masses, il faut montrer aux masses que vous êtes des animateurs'[2] Gladstone had long anticipated him in the preaching of this doctrine, and had himself set an unequalled example. His activities in South Lancashire,

[1] See p. 2, note 1.
[2] J. Joll, *Intellectuals in Politics: Blum, Rathenau, Marinetti*, p. 33.

for which he was elected the third member following this memorable speech, constituted the first minor climax in the build-up that was to prove so profitable in 1868. The disappointment at Oxford had given added stimulation to his quest for by-passing Palmerston's objections to reform. In a moment of self-revelation he stated the key to his position was that his opinions had gone one way and his 'lingering sympathies' the other. Rejection by his own university dealt those sympathies a body blow.

Until 1868, the Whigs had always enjoyed an ultimate ascendancy among anti-Conservatives. No Radical or progressive group had ever succeeded in wresting from them the real initiative in any left-wing or centre government. Palmerston had emerged as the true gainer after the Aberdeen coalition ended. Even the formidable Peelites had failed to break the Whig spell. The explanation lies in the social system and the width of the franchise. The first gave tremendous advantages to the Whig leadership and their hangers-on. The second was a reflection of this. The Reform Act of 1832 had enfranchised those sections of the propertied classes previously excluded from political influence.[1] Whiggery appealed more to the voters than anything to its left. Indeed, it can be argued that but for the split in their ranks the Conservatives would have established an almost unbreakable political control over the political system as it stood. A peaceful transition into democracy was probably much easier on account of their quarrels, for the Whigs invariably kept their ears to the popular ground and exploited the situation in order to keep up a flow of moderate reforms calculated to tie all other progressives, however unwillingly, to their coat tails. So thorough-going was their success that Conservatives found it necessary to advocate parliamentary reform from the late 1850s before standing any chance of breaking out of the barbed wire entanglement Russell and Palmerston had set up around them. By the early sixties, however, the political pressure from behind the Radicals began again to play the part the Chartists had filled back in the 1840s. Many Radicals, Cobden included, had never really favoured democracy in the fullest sense of the term. They had simply assumed the working classes would back them against reactionary interests like the Church of England, the landowners and the House of Lords. Others went further, but still envisaged that any franchise extension would stop short of universal male suffrage. Yet others were true democrats and to these the masses crowded for encouragement. Their admission as non-voters into organisations devoted to Radical politics gave them hope that their problems could be solved through the means offered by the existing system of government. Of such bodies

[1] For a full discussion of franchise questions in this period see C. Seymour, *Electoral Reform in England and Wales.*

the Birmingham Liberal and Radical Association, founded in 1865, was to become by far the most celebrated. For a decade or more Palmerston's own special brand of personal jacobinism had stood him in good stead. Vented against crowned heads abroad and pomposity at Windsor, it made him appear not only a 'Friend of the People', but one of them. This was all very well when economic circumstances seemed permanently set fair. With a change for the worse, Palmerston's little trick quickly wore thin with the majority of the non-electors. Whatever the electors thought of him, there was an opportunity for any determined man to establish himself with the masses. And before long a considerable slice of them would acquire the vote. Franchise extension was part of both Whig and Conservative policy, however unwillingly it had been included. Whoever ruled the masses would soon rule the country. In 1865 Palmerston had just won the election. Arrayed against the solid phalanx of Derby–Disraeli Conservatism the congeries of groups around and behind the old premier looked uncommonly anaemic. They needed a blood transfusion from the 'People'. When Palmerston died before the year was out the way was clear for change, but when it came the Whigs would be the greatest losers. They would cease to control the 'Left'. The Conservatives might have been the more frightened of the two parties, but they had no ascendancy to forfeit. The three years after 1865 were the swansong of Whiggery as Palmerston had known it. Russell became king again, but Gladstone was mayor of the palace.

In the build-up, first to the Second Reform Act of 1867 and then to the 1868 election, Gladstone found his feelings and the popular mood chimed in well together.[1] As an established minister of considerable experience and standing; a member of the upper-middle class married into the aristocracy; an orator of the first class; a man of superb education and culture; and an unequalled pedlar of public morality, he stood a much better chance than his nearest rival for popular favour, Bright, in coming out on top. At the beginning of his

[1] In an article entitled 'Gladstone's Whips and the General Election of 1868' to be found in the *English Historical Review* (referred to hereafter as the *E.H.R.*) for 1948, Mr A. F. Thompson discusses the financial difficulties in the Liberal party resulting from sulks among the Whig aristocracy. Nevertheless, as he himself points out (p. 193, note 1) 'In their own particular spheres of influence of course the magnates usually returned men upon whom the party could rely: their refusal to help the whips caused inconvenience rather than electoral disaster'—an imperative commentary upon the situation of 1868. Although the Conservative headquarters had £100,000 at its disposal and the Liberal headquarters a mere tenth of that sum, the comparison gives a most misleading picture of the resources with which the two parties fought the election. All in all the Liberals were quite well placed to organise and exploit the feeling in their favour.

public life he had had to face the dilemma of reconciling his rigid principles and firm intellectual convictions with the suppleness required of a practical politician. What most intelligent and sensitive men knew at once he had to learn by experience. But as an apt pupil he eventually acquired the knack of operating successfully in the art of the possible, and saw that 'jam' tomorrow would be the usual result of his reforming endeavour. He also came to realise how very enjoyable the prospect of 'jam' could be. Gradually his bigotry in religion had given way to tolerance as he came to understand morality counted as well as theology—at least in this world. Gradually, too, his contempt for the masses had changed into trust and admiration with the realisation they were willing to accept his lead and refrain from excessive demands. It was in this spirit that he approached the frustration heaped upon his Peelite zeal for useful reforms, public saving and the banishment of abuses. He drank in a deal of Whiggery and Radicalism, embracing belief in equality before the law and accommodation of popular clamour, but never for one moment thought in terms of leading from behind. In all he did was an indomitable will to prevail. In capturing support he more than took a leaf out of Palmerston's book. Moral fervour, sympathy with oppression and the plethora of anathemas launched against those opposing the things he desired most created in the minds of the masses the conviction that he was the 'People's William'. There were, as might have been expected, deep cleavages of opinion between him and most of those he impressed on a wide range of topics. The vast majority never came to see this fact, nor that his great strength as head of the Liberal 'house' lay in his sharing to some extent the outlook of all the 'mansions'. The strength of his hold on the popular imagination cannot be overstressed. It is as relevant to 1885, 1886 and 1887 as to 1865, 1866 and 1867. Equally vital was his awareness of its existence. If ever a man believed he spoke from a position of strength it was Gladstone.

The Second Reform Act of 1867 established a one-legged democracy in Britain. The borough constituencies were in future to be based on a very wide franchise giving the working and lower-middle classes a majority of the electorate. The pressure from them had actually led to a greater change than most anti-Conservatives and Conservatives had wanted. Defeat of anti-Conservative reform schemes had brought in a Conservative government. Initially, Disraeli tried to meet the demand for franchise change by a Bill embodying the principle that while many would now be equal, some should be more equal than others. In other words, swamping new voters with plural voters drawn exclusively from the propertied classes. This Gladstone and Bright refused to tolerate, and when at the eleventh hour Disraeli decided to outbid them, the result was a borough electorate of a fairly democratic kind. This did not mean Gladstone suffered any setback in his build-up, and the electoral system under the new scheme actually provided him with exactly the sort of advantages he needed for prevailing over the whole anti-Conservative front and galvanising it into a working Liberal party.

As a large section of the middle class still felt it had some way to go before achieving the amount of political power and influence that was its due, Gladstone found it possible to retain considerable support in that quarter. There were defections from the right of the Palmerstonian groups as the new elections approached, but their change of heart was largely hidden because of the vast increase in the electorate. On balance the loss was a blessing in disguise, for those Whigs and Moderates in the Commons—the Adullamites—who had opposed reform were thereby weakened within the anti-Conservative front, and Lowe, their leader, soon came to heel. Like Peel in 1834 he decided to grin and bear it. The assumption that all manner of social reforms dear to the hearts of the working class would follow 1867, just as they would have the implementation of the Chartists' 'Six Points', kept Gladstone's following intact among the poor, and consequently reduced still further the extent of Whig and Moderate influence. For the moment the Irish immigrant vote was an added source of strength on the left wing side, though in Ireland itself the 1868 Act, a paltry measure, had little or no effect either way. On the other hand, the county constituencies remaining undemocratic preserved the Whigs and Moderates to an extent which even at the moment of victory in 1868 enabled Gladstone to hold the balance of power and be a real master in his 'house'. Then, too, although the urban franchise was roughly quadrupled, the effect of the change was lessened by the retention of the two-member system of representation, which encouraged Whiggery to stand its ground, benefit from Conservative caution in sometimes running only one candidate and exploit the hankering after compromise among the floating voters.

Given the build-up of Gladstone's ascendancy and the open horror of wide electoral reform expressed by numerous Whigs and Conservatives, Derby's description of the 1867 Act as 'A leap in the dark' seems more poetic than accurate. Before anything was done to extend the 1832 settlement the national electorate in borough and county seats taken together had grown enormously through the increase in national wealth. Gladstone, Bright and a considerable section of the Radicals had perhaps got some advantage from this and were confident a further change down the income scale would ensure their future. Conservatives, on the other hand, had lost out on the first development at the hands of all sections of the Front arrayed against them and regarded the future with grave misgiving. Disraeli's sudden change of plan infuriated Salisbury and Carnarvon not so much because of its amorality in sacrificing principle as because principle was based on what they considered the best interests of traditional Conservatism. Disraeli himself thought he had secured a master stroke in 'Dishing the Whigs' and hoped to succeed accordingly in the ensuing elections. As, therefore, everyone claimed to know where they were going, why is darkness thought relevant, however wildly they leapt? Certainly disagreement over destinations and Disraeli's miscalculation were no arguments in favour of using the word. Disagreement was not all that widespread among politicians and, though Disraelian heresy had some appeal in the Conservative parliamentary party, it never took root in the country.

Confident of victory, Gladstone fought the 1868 election with only a modest borrowing of Radical clothing and thus gave the Conservatives an opening for further opportunism. Their candidate in Birmingham came out for granting the Trades Unions all they desired in the way of legal rights and far-reaching reforms in housing conditions. Working-class candidates were actively canvassed by Lord Sandon for some seats in Lancashire. The plan came to nothing, but not through want of trying, and even with their usual type of candidate, the Conservatives waged a certain amount of blatant anti-middle-class war upon the Liberal sections of the employers in the cotton industry. They got some reward, especially where the old anti-Catholic and anti-Hibernian line was played up as well. The 'democracy' was in a raw state and bound to some extent to bear out Proudhon's dictum that 'Universal suffrage is counter-revolution'. Happily for the Liberals there was an abundance of reformist rawness already under their control. The commonsense conclusion that if Palmerston could win in 1865, *a fortiori* Gladstone could in 1868 was thoroughly borne out. 'Peace, Retrenchment and Reform' meant many things to different people. Such, however, was the enthusiasm of the moment that all the leftists, apart from some Whigs and a handful of Radicals, united behind their new leader. What disenchantment there was did not have any profound effect. Sometimes, even, it proved a blessing in disguise. For example, Whig sulks about 1867 might have led to parsimony and non-cooperation over central funds, but the very inaction in London of a powerful right wing group made the task of formulating policy all the easier and in the constituencies there was a very different state of affairs. The Whigs showed themselves most anxious to return their particular members as part of the Liberal parliamentary party. Where Liberals of different shades were competing against each other, Gladstone generally profited, for the party's strength was so great that one or other of them won and all accepted him as leader. Applegarth called upon him to support Mundella against Roebuck in Sheffield and received an answer describing interference as something 'beyond the line of duty'[1] Radical or Whig, it was all one to Gladstone. Roebuck was a distasteful Palmerstonian, yet Mundella had criticised Forster's plans for education. Whichever was returned would prove a nuisance in some way. Whichever was returned, Sheffield would have another Liberal member. Meanwhile, in the circumstances of the time, their rivalries enhanced Gladstone's authority. Diversity, too, maximised the appeal to the electorate. The sort of 'Peace, Retrenchment and Reform' represented by Whiggery differed in degree and sometimes in kind from that espoused by other sections. The dual constituency system favoured harnessing two different sections and scooping up support from all possible quarters. Where the new triple constituency plan was in operation, the chances were of increase, despite the idea behind it of benefiting Conservative minorities in the big cities.[2] In Birmingham Radicalism swept the board, but its success in landing all three seats was not a freak due to tricks of organisation. Without a large and eager majority, its ascendancy would have been impossible to acquire. Whiggery played a feeble rôle in the town and Conservatism, though militant, was simply doomed to a humiliating minority status.[3] Another advantage the Liberals were quick to exploit was the pusillanimity all too common among urban Conservatives in the south. Opportunism was far from being a universal religion in the Carlton Club, particularly, of course, among the anti-Disraelian faction. W. H. Smith found himself the sole Conservative in the borough of Westminster—a situation bound to play into Whig hands, and therefore into Gladstone's.[4] All the influential Liberal sections were united on the issue of Ireland. Its established church was to be

[1] W. H. G. Armytage, *A. J. Mundella, 1825–1897: The Liberal Background to the Labour Movement*, p. 60.

[2] The triple constituency plan consisted of giving the electors two votes wherewith to elect three M.P.s.

[3] This is not to say that superlative organisation played no part in securing the continuance of the Liberal and Radical monopoly of the town's representation. The main means of success is generally described as follows: 'Each elector was told which two of the three Liberal candidates he as an individual should vote for'. This implies there was a very exact calculation made over the whole constituency. In fact things were a little more rough and ready. The arrangements were made on a ward basis. All Liberals in any one ward receiving exactly the same instruction. Hence the left had had to have quite a lead over the right for such an approximate method to work. Of course, there is no telling what the caucus might have achieved had the challenge been greater, but its performance has often been overrated and the record should be put right.

[4] Viscount Chilston, *W. H. Smith*, p. 58.

disestablished and its land system reformed. With these grand designs the cracks were to be papered over. They served the same purpose as anti-clericalism was so often to do for the French 'Left'. To revert to the image of the 'house' and the 'mansions', they were the stucco Gladstone had persuaded all his friends to adopt for the exterior of the Liberal 'house'. He was to value this stucco far beyond its useful life.

Had Disraeli won this election perhaps Lowe and company might not have stuck to their 'mansion', but he had not and the problem therefore never arose. The power structure of Palmerston's time passed into oblivion, and with it, for a time, the whole idea of deserting to the Conservatives so prevalent before the Second Reform Act among the more right-wing Whigs and Moderates. The election of 1868 had remade the political scene. No Liberal leader now needed to think as Palmerston had done as to how the Conservatives could be kept small enough to be kept out of effective control and yet large enough to impose discipline upon the anti-Conservative front. The 'strange doings' he had forecast would accompany Gladstone's leadership were about to begin in earnest. Not that they were all that strange for a Whig with a capacity for keeping abreast with the needs of the time. One of the greatest pitfalls an historian has to avoid is the tendency to treat men as of the same age throughout their public life. Palmerston was over eighty when he died. His principles had not so much changed as atrophied, and he was no longer applying the same touchstones to public affairs he had used in his prime. The long period of quiet in preceding decade accelerated the atrophy. Nevertheless, at one time, though always erring on the cautious side in domestic affairs, he would have subscribed for the most part to what Lord Holland once explained about what many regarded as the chief article of the Whig political creed. Speaking in clear and forceful terms, he declared:

We are well aware that the privileges of the people, the rights of free discussion, and the spirit and letter of our popular institutions, must render—and they are intended to render—the continuance of an extensive grievance, and of the dissatisfaction consequent thereupon, dangerous to the tranquillity of the country, and ultimately subversive of the authority of the State. Experience and theory alike forbid us to deny that effect of a free constitution; a sense of justice and a love of liberty equally deter us from lamenting it. But we have always been taught to look for the remedy of such disorders in the redress of grievances which justify them, and in the removal of the dissatisfaction from which they flow—not in restraints on ancient privileges, not in inroads on the right of public discussion, nor in violations of the principles of a free government.

To this tradition Gladstone had ultimately attached himself in the early 1860s. Redress of grievances, not seeing things through the eyes of those he was assisting thus became, and indeed remained his forte.

Long after he had ceased to be an obscurantist with a closed mind, complaints that he remained one with the spoken and written word were echoing loudly round the country. Added to which, a maddening unpredictability aroused widespread belief in his disingenuousness. At this stage in his career this feeling was well-nigh groundless. So great was his study of problems that his study of people never developed to anything like the extent Disraeli's did. The great differences between himself and the bulk of his nonconformist supporters over some aspects of policy affecting religion were not deliberately covered up by him during the 1868 election campaign. Admittedly, he practised a line of 'No enemies on the Left' and outstripped Grey, Russell and Palmerston in its application. But his proceedings were much more intuitive and the appeal he exerted did away with much of the necessity to keep his ear to the 'People's' ground. He was an infinitely more powerful leader than they had been—and something else besides—a preacher. When he entered upon his first ministry any deception there was tended to that of himself rather than the masses. His mood appealed and things were presumed without evidence. Much of the subsequent disappointment in nonconformist and working class trade union circles was self-induced, and almost all the rest derived from accidental misunderstanding. This is not to say Gladstone lacked cunning and the capacity to calculate political advantages for himself. He often applied these qualities, but mostly in the executive and legislative spheres. As he was to remark much later, he was an 'old parliamentary hand'. On the stump he took much of the adulation he inspired for granted and, like many a religious man before and since, enjoyed the feeling of being on the side of the angels. 'The great thing,' he enthused, 'is to be right'.[1]

There was, nevertheless, something singularly complicated about the formulation of his Liberal political principles. This much is proved by his talk of 'lingering sympathies'. Complications also arise because of the particular mode he employed, albeit inherent in his temperament, for presenting an issue to the public. For the historian this latter is particularly dangerous as it might well lead, or rather has led, to frequent misjudgments based on the self-estimation offered to posterity by the Liberal leader himself. Closer examination reveals

[1] John Morley remarked of Gladstone: 'I am convinced that the more that is known about Mr Gladstone the greater he will appear.' C.R.L.F. (C. R. L. Fletcher), *Mr Gladstone at Oxford, 1890*, p. 3. Most men took strongly for or against the G.O.M. without any but the highly obvious evidence.

him as a vehemently moderate, not a moderately vehement man. Morality there is, but often burning at a belated hour. All discussion is bound to contain some elements of sheer inaccuracy because of the impossibility of seeing right into the mind of so complicated a human being, be he alive, let alone dead.

The long evolution from the High Toryism of his youth to the moment of the first 'unmuzzling' had meant recanting things the vast majority of his followers had never thought of championing. Observed data not imagination seem to have driven his mind to Liberalism against the initial preference of his emotions. Once in the anti-Conservative front these underwent a shift in the direction of self-justification and defence. After 1865 Liberalism increasingly became a matter of justification by faith as well by works, for at the outset a deal of utility had motivated his actions. Political 'progress' had been a *pis aller* taken to secure the implementation of efficient government, equality before the law in things not related to the franchise and foreign and colonial policies of the 'Smaller England' variety, including good works for suffering Christians and nationalities 'rightly struggling to be free' (though in this a good deal of selectivity was to be found). During the years of his supremacy there can be little doubt the 'lingering sympathies' were frequently consigned to the back of his mind. When they did re-emerge it was after dinner, not in the course of official business, except perhaps where this concerned the Church of England. Probably the greatest factor in the profound intellectual process leading away from 'Church and State' to the 'Union of Hearts' approach of 1886 was the conviction that only through change could there be any lasting conservation. In other words, Gladstone's principles, far from atrophying grew so as not to recognise themselves. He had become a Liberal because he was convinced that Liberalism was the only intelligent Conservatism—something the Whigs had proved again and again since 1688. The unusually intense way in which this view was acquired meant, however, that he ended up with a Liberalism all his own. Newman's acceptance of Roman Catholicism was similar and also resulted in a peculiarly personal version of the faith. Two such incorrigible individualists could hardly have been expected to entertain flat orthodoxy, but the painfully thorough examination of the issues involved produced a heightening of their separate identity. The statesman was to find happiness in his new home, the churchman unease and belated honour. With the one, 'lingering sympathies' sank to the level of nostalgia. With the other they remained a constant worry. He found that to be 'right' was not in itself enough for spiritual contentment. By staying in the Church of England after the Gorham shock of 1850 Gladstone both preserved his political prospects and ensured a happy balance of outlook when his politics gravitated to the left. Convinced of the genuine Catholicity of the English Established Church, yet contented with its practical adherence to liberty of conscience, he could feel constantly in the right. Cooperation with wholehearted Protestants in the cause of reform seemed safe and desirable, even when the actual steps taken deprived the Anglicans of privileges. To liberate nonconformists and Roman Catholics from what they considered disabilities was not in his eyes a recognition of the possibility they might be theologically in the right. There was no question but they were in error. All he believed in was their right to be wrong. Temporalities did not matter to him where their material quantity went beyond the real needs of the Anglican communion. There was therefore no harm in scrapping them. Spiritual certainty undoubtedly gave him great strength in political life. Joined with academic and social distinction, it made calm assessments of national needs and a willingness to entertain the idea of change much easier to entertain. A firmly anchored man cares little for the raging of the seas. Much additional power accrued to him through the especially electric nature of his working recipes in politics. The extra force of histrionics raised him still higher. In an age heading towards democracy offence given at Windsor or in an aristocratic drawing-room was an ephemeral setback. What counted was popular reaction and the tactics of indignation were as ambrosia to a large section of the British electorate. Even in Ireland they had periods of triumph. The Whigs had been 'The Friends of the People'. Palmerston admittedly got some way beyond that, but Gladstone far outstripped him. Much of what he said in public was 'Greek' to his vast audiences. That did not matter twopence. Without anything approaching mutual comprehension, there grew up strong bonds between the Liberal leader and the 'People' during the first build-up, which were never seriously damaged to the last. The Liberal party was what finally changed the power balance. When the first ministry began Gladstone was regarded by the left wing sections of the masses as more than a 'Friend'. He was a possession—'The People's William'. But, for all that, a possession they obeyed.

The precise factors governing the formulation of the policies applied or advocated by Gladstone defy adequate definition. When Mr Joll writes of his being a man who 'was never afraid to put moral and intellectual issues squarely before the people, in the confidence that they would understand and support him',[1] he is ignoring the question of timing, so important in politics and so carefully handled by this particular man. What was expediency and what true principle is a problem he simply leaves out of account, yet, obviously, it is of

[1] Joll, *op. cit.*, p. 21.

central importance. Certainly, Gladstone regarded politics as the art of the possible, though just what was possible he tended to rate higher than most men. Nevertheless, the distinction between the possible and the expedient cannot be overstressed. As a born demagogue, he was bound to influence men. He did so as a Pericles not a Cleon, trying to appeal to the better instincts of humanity. From his basic beliefs and a keen desire to pursue them there was no hope of distracting him. It was in doing the right thing at the right time that the difficulty lay. As with General Staffs, so with him, grand strategies once formulated might have to be tucked away for some time. Their sudden emergence at opportune moments gave rise to the charge of pursuing expedient tactics for immediate success, and the moral intensity dominating the presentation only tended to heighten suspicion. Why, it was asked, if the plan had been thought of before, had Gladstone been silent, cryptic or equivocal on the subject it concerned? Surely something of such moral urgency could not possibly have been put on one side for one moment had it been properly thought out? Another complication was Gladstone's lack of a sense of proportion in dealing with comparatively minor matters. All tactical manoeuvres tended to be put on a level with the vital issues and the significance attached to the seemingly endless supply of fervour consequently dropped. If things clearly done for a momentary advantage received the full treatment, anything similarly dealt with became tarred with the brush of expediency. Even the 'house' and 'mansions' position brought some discredit when ideas long advocated by Liberal Radicals were suddenly adopted after a sustained period of snubs. So too did the watering down of reformist schemes to harmonise with Whig objections. As head of his 'house', Gladstone had to personify the resultant of its forces. As this included his own exercise of influence, his gyrations seldom involved going against his own inner convictions during the first ministry, however much this was to change later on. In several aspects of policy, and especially over foreign affairs, the working classes submitted to what they were ready to regard as his better judgment. The 'Smaller' and 'Little Englanders' remained a minority on the left, but became, under his direction, a ruling one. When the outcome of party consultation was contrary to the leader's considered opinion and this was known, his falling in with it gave rise to unkind comment. Undoubtedly, a strong desire for unity played an important part in shaping party policy. Memories of the anti-Conservative front were to have their influence up into the 1880s. The attraction exercised over him by the aristocratic idea also played a big part in helping to consolidate joint operations by 'mansions' in the interests of the 'house'. Probably personal considerations played their part here, though not in any seriously undesirable way. What penchant Gladstone had towards mixing in high society was balanced by a genuine concern for the masses, whom he regarded as 'deserving' *per se*. The actual form of the help offered might not have corresponded with the innermost desires of the recipients, but there was no mistaking the sincerity behind it. As with Newman, blind spots over housing, lighting and drainage did not mean a deficiency in Christian charity.

Naturally enough, politics being a live thing, no strategy was taken out of cold storage and applied without especial attention to the exact conditions of the day. Adaptation to suit new surroundings could be called intelligent variation or base expediency according to the standpoint of the commentator. Only the most uncharitable would dismiss all compromise as sin. No party leader can hope to become an absolute dictator and still remain a convincing purveyor of liberal ideas, apart from the practical obstacles almost certain to arise in a body like the Liberal party with its wide spectrum of opinions. Some elements of Gladstonianism were bound to have found but a lukewarm response from its founder, and this is surely no discredit to him? Within the 'house' the Radical cause could prosper and the Whig cause make graceful concessions without too much scuffling in the corridors. The local Solomon was there to arbitrate and endowed with qualities no one came near to rivalling until well on into the 1880s. Until 1865, Palmerston and Russell on the right, and Cobden and Bright on the left, had filled the rôles of organs and organisers of the anti-Conservative front. Afterwards the whole task fell indubitably to one man and the power structure of Liberalism had him as its apex sending out the dominant messages in the inevitable two-way movement of ideas to and from Westminster.

The legend of Gladstone and Disraeli is no legend at all. The influence both exercised on their respective parties was immense, but that of the former went far beyond anything achieved by the latter. And this despite the simpler doctrinal structure in the Conservative camp. Whereas the one stood head and shoulders above everyone else in his party as his first government took office, the other was initially an expert on trial. Gradually the position changed as the Conservative disappointment and recrimination over the election results gave way to a sustained glee as Gladstone's mistakes were exploited to practical advantage. Disraeli's tactical skill ended most talk of probation and on his assuming power in 1874 there was no doubt as to who made the running in the new cabinet. Comprehensive criticism of Liberalism and all its works provided a useful keynote for Conservative speakers. Maximum flexibility and minimum responsibility exercised an irresistible appeal over a party so familiar with yet so unreconciled to the political wilderness. 'Mind you, no policy' was an injunction most supporters welcomed with a knowing wink. Disraeli made no bones among his inner circles about his aims and methods. Real standstill Conservatism was out of the question. The task was to make inevitable changes, yet to act in ways likely to frustrate their full effect in sectors where old conditions had remained dear to reactionary hearts. Some social reforms affecting living conditions for the working classes were unreservedly espoused, not only for their intrinsic merit, but because of the electoral benefit likely to accrue from them. Basically, however, there can be no doubt that even at its 'Young England' stage Disraeli's Radical Toryism had had a mild species of counter revolution intertwined with its praiseworthy humanitarianism, and long before the sixties a strong and subtle dose of opportunism had become added. To escape from the barbed-wire entanglement laid by the anti-Conservative front and sustained by the new Liberal party, Disraeli set out to make anything he said about domestic affairs exciting at home and anything about foreign and colonial affairs impressive both at home and abroad. His blatant playing of politics over the second Reform Act had not paid off. Henceforward he nurtured Conservative fortunes with the same inspired caution adversity had rapidly taught him to apply to his own personal advancement. Using daring where sheer initiative would have sufficed he cultivated those possessed of power. After 1867 this meant more than it had, but he had realised this too late. Men with influence, not men who might acquire it had received his attention. A bird in the Lords was worth any number in the unenfranchised towns —or so he had thought. Gladstone had sought influence early as a means of pursuing his genuine legislative and administrative plans. His mission always reached the level of something as important as the pacification of Ireland. Disraeli's was usually negative. 'Dishing the Whigs' remained a great dream with him.

Another Conservative weakness had been bad relations with the Crown. Here Disraeli excelled himself and backed up the imperialism he blared forth in the Crystal Palace speech with a mighty symbol. But this is to anticipate somewhat. Before Gladstone's ministry began, the sapping of Windsor had not got very far. After it ended Disraeli found there was practically nothing left for him to do. The Queen was only too ready to fall in with his notions of working for a popular monarchy. Strangely enough, though he scarcely understood the type of elector who responded ecstatically to Gladstone's campaigning and was himself far from being in the same category as a campaigner, his grasp of certain fundamental elements in the popular outlook like nationalism, anti-Catholicism and anti-Hibernianism was quite exceptional. Making capital out of these factors by what were in fact traditional methods was all very well, yet yielded rather moderate results. It remained for Lord Randolph Churchill to come along in the 1880s as the super-salesman of Tory Democracy before the creation of a 'National' party to oppose the 'People's' party came to bear rich fruit. The 'Nation versus People' battle was not fully joined while the 'Nation' lacked a first-class demagogue.

Gladstone was a Liberal, Disraeli a Conservative. One had missions, the other the zest to survive. One took pains with fallen women, the other contented himself, at least in the earlier years, with mistresses. Were they then utterly different? Was the mutual dislike based on the clash of opposites? Unravelling inborn and environmentally created aspects of character is an impossible task. Certainly the young High Church Tory Gladstone had an outlook widely divergent from that of the young Tory Radical Jew. Without doubt these two very different individuals became even more opposed to one another because of the course their political lives took in the period before the Repeal of the Corn Laws. What followed simply aggravated the process. The story can be told in two words—security and insecurity.[1] Opportunity and promotion on the one side has to be contrasted with frustration, victimisation and anguish on the other. The quest to follow the dictates of his convictions drove Gladstone to thwart and oppose the Conservative and rightmost Whig portion of the noble 'phalanx of the great families' and the 'great many' who 'still' spoke up for them. With Disraeli it was quite the opposite. For him that phalanx came to represent the way to salvation. Having to make his way to an extent Gladstone did not, led to his adopting a nauseating parvenu snobbery. A man virtually one of the 'People' through being a Jew, cut himself off from it as an individual, however much his perspicacity revealed about what the masses felt and thought. Baptism had made success in public life possible not probable, despite his talents. Conformism to the aristocratic Conservative groups had provided his opportunity. Once in their employ it became his business to guarantee there would be crowds to 'speak up' for them. Yet, the very trend away from the democracy in his own inner self militated against a brilliant execution of the task. The greatest political agent of modern British political history had de-

[1] In his essay on 'The Rise of Disraeli', to be found in *Essays in British History* (presented to Sir Keith Feiling): edited by H. R. Trevor-Roper (Foreword by Lord David Cecil), R. Blake maintains that much of Disraeli's insecurity was self-induced. Maybe, but it was still insecurity. It would, however, be foolish, bearing in mind the conditions of nineteenth-century Britain, to suppose that Disraeli's origins did not place him in some insecurity once he began to try and make a big name for himself in public life. Doubtless he would have felt few disadvantages as an obscure citizen, but that is not really a fair test. Quietism had long been the refuge of countless second-class citizens and had got them nowhere.

veloped the psychology of a principal. That is why there were never any Disraelian 'unmuzzlings'—no Midlothians in the cause of Tory Democracy. The great Liberal election victory of 1880 reflected this failure to 'sell' 'Crown and Constitution' at the grass roots and marked what was perhaps the zenith of Gladstone's pull with the common people and the last occasion when left wing support among the middle and upper classes remained virtually intact.

For the Conservatives the occasion provided a traumatic experience. Two rival schools of thought among them produced two different methods of combating the dangers of doom. Churchill and other lively sparks prescribed a bid to capture enemy voters of all classes, but especially those of the town masses by a dose of right wing Midlothianism. Patriotism and reform were to be peddled in what was later termed the spirit of General Booth. Sir Stafford Northcote, the staid leader of the Commons Conservatives pronounced in favour of bidding for the Whig vote by quiet yet persistent exposure of Liberal 'excess'. Neither approach was wholly well-conceived, but both obtained a certain amount of success. By July 1886 Salisbury had begun his second ministry. Instead of dying away the Conservative party had found a way to survival and even substantial expansion. That way was connected in several respects with the character and career of Joseph Chamberlain and his radical Liberal associates.

The legend of Gladstone and Chamberlain was a truly classic saga, although quite wrongly overshadowed at times by the preoccupation of so many with Disraeli, or even Churchill. Much of the underrating has stemmed from the fact that so much of the origin and development of the story went on inside the 'house'. Chamberlain, a Unitarian screw manufacturer, entered parliament for Birmingham in 1876 at the age of forty.[1] He was already an experienced and eminent provincial politician with the reform of his adopted city very much a personal achievement and a bid for Nonconformist control of the Liberal party behind him. Like Cobden and Bright before him, he had sought by concentrating on a narrow field in national politics in the late sixties and early seventies to drive through a major reform of fundamental importance, both for its own sake and for the other major reforms likely to prove its sequels. And who could deny that public elementary education was and is basic to the development of a sophisticated and mobile society? The instrument forged to carry on the task was the National Education League, and it was as its representative, seeking to scrap the essentially compromise measure

[1] One French author has compared him with Dick Whittington. Presumably Jesse Collings (for whom see p. 32 note 2) was his cat. J. Condurier de Chassaigne, *Les Trois Chamberlains*, p. 2.

advocated by Forster and herald in a system of free, compulsory and secular instruction that Chamberlain first clashed with Gladstone. The conflict was highly symbolic for the future, but only for the immediate and long term parts of it. Once the rash of Nonconformist resentment had subsided and the Conservatives had actually won a general election outright the centre and left of the Liberal party became almost reconciled. Gladstone's retirement did much to accelerate the process, for with Hartington and Granville leading in the Commons and Lords respectively, Whiggery appeared to have regained an influence lost during the Gladstonian build-up of 1865–8. Once at Westminster, Chamberlain soon placed himself at the head of a new bid to outflank both Whiggery and Conservatism. Gladstone was inevitably involved, having returned to the political arena through the efforts of the 'Little and Smaller Englander' groups during the Eastern Question crisis of 1876. Pique had led him into the position of a partial Cincinnatus, whereby he remained in the Commons. Hence a return from Hawarden to become *de facto* leader was all too easy to bring off, once a reluctance to set aside his books had been overcome. The political methods he had done so much to develop were already being supplemented by something new as to scale if not as to nature. The celebrated platform stumping was to Chamberlain's mind rather like a gigantic gas leak—good stuff going to waste. It had to be piped, and an extension of organisations like the Birmingham Liberal and Radical Association would, he considered, do the trick. So the national caucus was born. Organisation at the grass roots would in future ensure that the enthusiasm of the vast swirling and excited Liberal election meetings was put to good use. That way too, Whig committees and cabals could possibly be swept aside and the People's party become controlled by the 'People' in general and the Nonconformists in particular. Where the National Education League had failed, the National Liberal Federation should succeed. With a left wing organisation to push Gladstone on and encourage him in being 'unmuzzled' Chamberlain had visions of rapid reform and a permanent seal being set upon the alliance of the centre and left 'mansions' inside the Liberal 'house'. He was to be disappointed, though this was far from apparent until the dust had settled after the election of 1880.

On 31st May 1877 Gladstone spoke at an immense gathering in support of the N.L.F. at Bingley Hall, Birmingham. Quite mistakenly, Granville had assumed he would refuse to go, but, as one author says: 'The great demonstration . . . reflected a desire on the part of both Chamberlain and Gladstone to remake the party in their own terms.'[1] Writing to Granville at this time, Gladstone showed no

[1] R. T. Shannon, *Gladstone and the Bulgarian Agitation 1876*, p. 270.

traces of having any distasteful memories about Chamberlain dating
from the education rows. On the contrary he is positively enthusiastic
about his able and resourceful ally. The Radical is appraised as 'a
man worth watching and studying, of strong self-consciousness under
most pleasing manners and I should think of great tenacity of purpose: expecting to play an historical part, and probably destined to
it'.[1] Eight years later Granville's assessment would most probably
have been correct. The part Chamberlain conceived that he was destined to play in history was by that time far from being to his leader's
taste. Sure enough force of circumstances had placed Gladstone, not
Hartington or Granville, at the head of the 1880 Liberal ministry,
and Chamberlain entered the Cabinet as President of the Board of
Trade. None the less, the sequel proved extremely frustrating to the
Radical and to some extent even to Gladstone. It was in their differing reactions to the situation that the seeds of trouble lay. But, of
course, those reactions were themselves merely symbolic of pro-
founder things.[2] The centre and left of the Liberal party may have
been allied, yet were far from fused. Matters inside the 'house'
thwarted Chamberlain's hopes. The Whigs could not command a
Liberal ministry: they could dominate a Cabinet so far as numbers
went. In consequence reforms Radicals and Irish Nationalists treated
as urgent were put off to the Chatsworth Kalends, or proposed in an
emasculated form. Lamentable mishandling of foreign and related
colonial policies also took their toll. Chamberlain gradually swung
round towards the 'Big England' school of thought, albeit in a singular way. This was not all that surprising. Much of his experience at
this time was a learning and digesting process. Intense concentration
on domestic issues and the predilections of his upbringing had tended
to lead him into accepting a Gladstone view of the outside world and
what it meant to the United Kingdom. Politicans, indeed statesmen,
often have either unclear, or largely stereotyped views upon matters
outside their range of experience and immediate interest. The 1880
Chamberlain was just such a one. The Chamberlain of 1885 was quite
a different kettle of fish. As the ministry dragged on and Gladstone
gradually yet perceptibly lost authority in parliament and the country,
Chamberlain rocked the party boat constantly and resolutely.[3] The
more he learned the more confident he became. Being the man he was

---

[1] Shannon, *op. cit.*, p. 274.

[2] Even so, as late as May 1882 Queen Victoria regarded Chamberlain as Gladstone's 'evil genius'. G. E. Buckle (Editor), *The Letters of Queen Victoria*, 2nd
Series, Vol. III, p. 298. This view was regarded as sufficiently important for
quotation in Arthur Ponsonby's *Henry Ponsonby: Queen Victoria's Private
Secretary. His Life from his Letters*, p. 191.

[3] What was termed his 'biting sarcasm' aggravated the process not a little. The
Rev. W. Tuckwell, *Reminiscences of a Radical Parson*, p. 35.

the process was rapid. From being a big frog in a little Birmingham pond he had long ago moved on to being a big frog in a medium-sized Radical and Nonconformist one. Now he undoubtedly aspired to being a very large frog in the large lake at Westminster. Gladstone might well have turned his mind to La Fontaine, but there was no need for Chamberlain to crave for the dimensions of an ox, Gladstone himself was only a huge frog. Then, too, the N.L.F. appeared to be going from strength to strength among the active and enthusiastic centre and left Liberals. That large numbers of the less forceful of the former hung back seemed of scant moment. Euphoria tended to seize hold of Chamberlain precisely at the point when caution would have paid him handsome dividends. Instead of cultivating Gladstone he spoke in hectoring tones. Instead of cajoling the Whigs he addressed them in terms of increasing virulence. Frustration led to loss of temper and more extremism, whereas it should have taught him to walk warily. Manners may not make men, but ill manners can go a long way towards unmaking them. While his obvious talents and command of the left caused him to be talked of as Gladstone's very probable successor, his general beliefs and behaviour as they developed during this ministry put him into Hawarden's Black Books Certainly, the G.O.M. was partly jealous of so gifted a parliamentarian and minister and disliked the idea of anyone growing as big as himself. Old men do not forget the future. Even so, policy differences of note had emerged between the two men and disagreement over method and the future complexion of the Liberal party were profound.

Chamberlain's very calibre was bound to disturb any party leader. His pushing qualities were also somewhat out of place in the ruling circles of the 1880s. Here, however, was an element of irony, for Gladstone himself was constantly upsetting Society by his intensity of manner and dictatorial habits. As a younger man he had been more than insufferable on occasions. Still, there was a saving grace. As Granville once assured the Duchess of Manchester, Gladstone was not as bad as he seemed.[1] And, from her viewpoint this was true. Were there not his 'lingering sympathies', transferred from Conservatism to the Whig sections of his adopted party? Unfortunately for him, everyone, whether friend or foe, could see that Chamberlain was every bit as bad as he seemed and more. The leader had an over-mighty subject on his hands—one without the background of education and training 'desirable' in the would-be governors of the United Kingdom. Subordinate provincial figures, or secondary and tertiary

[1] Lord Granville to the Duchess of Manchester, 3rd February 1869. Devonshire Papers, 340, Add. MS. For the Duchess of Manchester see below, Chapter II, p. 72, note 2.

parliamentary characters like Mundella,[1] Stansfield[2] and company could safely be patted on the back. Get near Chamberlain and he would soon be giving his companion an encouraging caress, be he none other than 'Mr Gladstone'. While too gentlemanly to echo Disraeli's remark that Chamberlain 'looked and spoke like a cheese-monger', Gladstone must sometimes have thought something very similar. On the policy side Chamberlain's open and avowed aim of destroying the Whigs shocked his leader to the core. 'Lingering sympathy' demanded the Liberal party preserve social and doctrinal variety—so did a species of the liberalism the old man had taken so long to imbibe. This very appeasement of Hartington and his men aroused contempt and suspicion in Chamberlain. Contempt because of the premier's apparently limited authority and will to prevail. Suspicion because appeasement inevitably led to a standstill or a slowing down. Personality and policy differences interacted in such a way as to ruin all chances of cooperation and intimacy between the two men. Intellect prompted mutual admiration. Both found it impossible, however, to sustain any conviction on the point when so much was at stake.[3]

Gladstone had purported to see 'the hand of God manifest' in the 1880 election result.[4] Chamberlain saw what he regarded as the process of democratic destiny in the two outstandingly important pieces of legislation accomplished by the second Gladstone ministry—the Third Reform Act of 1884 and a Redistribution Act passed in 1885. Beside them matters like the second Irish Land Act of 1881 appeared almost paltry. Under a two-legged democracy the Radicals felt they could carry all before them. Now that large urban areas not in borough seats and the countryside generally were to enjoy a wide franchise and the discrepancies in the sizes of constituency electorates had been significantly reduced, upper class cliques, whatever their material and organisational resources, were to Chamberlain's mind fair game for annihilation. Remaining bugbears such as those connected with the residue of electoral qualification restrictions, the registration laws and the failure to bring about exactly equal electoral

[1] A. J. Mundella (1825–97) was M.P. for Sheffield 1868–85 and for the Brightside division of that city from 1885 until his death. In the short-lived third Gladstone ministry he held the Presidency of the Board of Trade.

[2] J. Stansfeld (1820–98) had been President of the Local Government Board 1871–4. His campaigns against the Contagious Diseases Act and for women's suffrage made him well known. At the time of the 'Round Table' conference he was M.P. for Halifax.

[3] Occasionally Gladstone paid tribute to Chamberlain in public even after the Home Rule quarrel, declaring him the best debater in the Commons. G. Melly, *Recollections of Sixty Years—1833–1893*, p. 66.

[4] W. L. Arnstein, *The Bradlaugh Case: A Study in Late Victorian Opinion and Politics*, p. 2.

districts, not to mention the plural voting problem seemed almost nothing.[1] After all, what effect had these obstacles had on stopping the march of the N.L.F. and Radical Liberalism in the large boroughs? Not only would seat rationalisation limit what force they did have, but the flood of new and grateful voters in the county seats, when joined with borough enthusiasm, would make any factor favouring static or reactionary forces look nothing short of silly. So ran his thoughts and the list of reforms, known unofficially as the 'Unauthorised Programme' on which he fought the 1885 election constituted an attack both on Conservatism and Whig Liberalism.[2] A by-product of such an act was a challenge to Gladstone's leadership and the chances of any intimacy between the two men receded still further. That the leader had virtually been asking for the moon, or rather that the whole of the Liberal part of the earth should acknowledge his assessment of what was good for it as the solely right and proper one, made a considerable difference to the development of the situation. Had the Radicals waited until he gave the word to advance and had the Whigs grinned and borne it whatever its meaning Liberal unity would have been a good deal healthier than it actually was. But one man, even Gladstone, could not manage this gigantic task of control. The groups of men involved were far too headstrong and wayward, and their mutual exasperation and past restraint a powerful factor making for an end to forbearance. Nor was Gladstone at a peak of influence. Until his authority was challenged out and out over the Home Rule issue challenging him did not arouse the full force of rank and file support built on the emotional experiences of the 1860s and 1870s. Consequently, Chamberlain exaggerated the extent of the leader's decline of authority inside the party at the same time as he was blatantly optimistic about the Radical future. Instead of realising much of his success derived from association with Gladstone and that the N.L.F. drew most of its life blood from masses inspired by the spirit of Midlothian, he thought it a personal and policy achievement. 'A man and measures' was his subconscious motto. Little did he know that for most Gladstone not himself was the 'man', and some

[1] Since this text was written this point of the remaining electoral bugbears has been more fully developed by N. Blewett in his article 'The Franchise in the United Kingdom, 1885–1918', *Past and Present* 1965.

[2] The 'Unauthorised Programme' came out in book form during July 1885. Most of it had been published piecemeal beforehand, but as a unity it made a considerable impact. Chamberlain provided a new preface and, needless to say, also the formulator of the main contents. There were nine chapters, dealing respectively with an introduction to the problems under review, machinery of government, measures to be proposed, the housing of the urban poor, the agricultural labourer, religious equality, free schools, taxation and finance, and local government and Ireland.

of his proposed measures had been fathered on to the party leader. Chamberlain was too theoretical by half, despite his business genius, and failed to cotton on to the force of the irrational in politics when it reflected a failure on the part of the electors to absorb fact. His realisation of and remedy for this came only in his Unionist phase after the Liberal split of 1886.

As the borough election results of 1885 were to show the assumption of a rosy Radical future was partly ill-founded. Conservatives and Whigs alike had hit back to some effect.[1] Both the Churchill and Northcote tactics for championing 'Crown and Constitution' worked some impressive wonders. The more so when supplemented with economic and religious factors. Fair Trade and defence of the Church of England were not to be sneezed at as preservers and extenders of Conservative support. Then too there was the foreign and colonial policy aspects of discontent. These Salisbury exploited in good measure. Most surprising of all was the Fox–North element in the situation. Parnell had instructed his Irish Nationalist supporters in British constituencies to vote Conservative, except in a small number of specified cases.[2] Concentrated as they were in urban areas the Irish proved defectors from the Liberal cause of no small significance, and this facet of the situation was to prove of paramount importance. When the election results were complete, it was clear that the Conservatives and Irish Nationalists combined equalled the Liberals. Gone were the palmy days of 1880.

Whig and Moderate Liberalism spoke up for itself very effectively during the election campaign. Merit as well as privilege was to the forefront and Hartington cast aside lethargy with an abandon and zest few realised he possessed. Moreover, while the N.L.F. was powerful as never before in the boroughs, its hold on many constituency parties did not extend to pushing out the Whig or centre parliamentary candidate. While in the counties many advantages lay with the Whigs and centre over selecting candidates, in spite of the wider franchise. With everything over bar the shouting fully-fledged Chamberlain-type Radicals made up not more than a third of the parliamentary Liberal party. Lord Richard Grosvenor and the

[1] For some useful material on Chamberlain's conduct of his campaign and the reactions to it see C. H. D. Howard's article, 'Joseph Chamberlain and the Unauthorised Programme'. *E.H.R.* 1950.

[2] C. H. D. Howard in his article 'The Parnell Manifesto of 21 November, 1885 and the Schools Question' *E.H.R.* 1947, argues that education issues, stressed by the Roman Catholic clergy in Britain more than Home Rule, pushed the Irish vote into the Conservative camp in 1885. Why the same arguments about education and its influence had not applied previously and, if they did so in 1885, failed to persist in 1886 is not explained. For some criticisms of the article see V. A. McClelland, *Cardinal Manning*, pp. 188–9.

Liberal Central Committee could therefore claim that the N.L.F. and the Radicalism of its Birmingham base had overstated its claim to speak for Liberal Britain.

The word 'Britain' is used advisedly, for not a single Liberal candidate won an Irish constituency. What had caused such a revolution, and why had the Irish voters in Britain been so effectively and rapidly persuaded to throw over quite a long tradition of supporting Gladstone? The answer is simple. Well before the Third Reform Act let loose the full effect of Catholic Irish public opinion upon the parliamentary scene, Parnell had succeeded in forming an Irish Nationalist party on thoroughgoing Home Rule lines.[1] The strategy as opposed to the tactics of this party could be summed up in the two words 'Independent Opposition'. Nevertheless, large sections of the Liberal party had regarded Irish Nationalist aspirations in the social, economic and even political spheres with considerable friendship and, although on some matters like the Bradlaugh case, Parnell ultimately worked wholeheartedly with Northcote and Churchill, there was a working Liberal–Irish Nationalist agreement of mutual support on general day-to-day political problems. Needless to say, these did not include the *raison d'être* of the Irish Nationalists—Home Rule. Yet the Radical leaders Chamberlain and Dilke were mindful of Parnell's feelings on this score. Well before the 1885 election though, this particular flirtation was over and both men agreed with Gladstone when he asked the electorate for a majority independent of the Irish Nationalists, so that the whole Irish issue could be settled free from parliamentary blackmail. How and why the Radical–Irish Nationalist rupture came to pass is crucial for everything that followed.

Chamberlain's conviction about the Irish question was fundamentally similar to that of Michael Davitt.[2] It was that the undemocratic nature of government in Britain willy nilly maintained the undemocratic nature of government in Ireland. Now the former thought the Third Reform Act would sweep oligarchy away and destroy the one big obstacle in the way of cordial relations between Protestant Britain and the Catholic Irish majority. This is where he and Davitt parted company. At the same time Chamberlain did see there would be great practical advantages in devolving considerable administrative duties upon a locally selected National Council in Ireland, so

---

[1] The best account of how this came about is *Parnell and his Party, 1880–1890*, by C. C. O'Brien.

[2] This much emerges from T. W. Moody's article, 'Michael Davitt and the British Labour Movement, 1882–1906'. *Transactions of the Royal Historical Society*, 1953. Davitt never became conscious of the fact and very probably never formulated his thoughts with anything like the precision and clarity of Chamberlain. Nevertheless, he certainly accepted nationalism as a second best to democracy and looked with favour upon British working men.

while being a centralist and imperialist in the sense of believing in a United Kingdom parliamentary structure for Britain and Ireland, he urged precisely such a scheme on the Gladstone Cabinet in May 1885 in the belief that Parnell would accept it as a final political settlement.[1] A mild dose of coercion was to go alongside it to reassure the weaker brethren. Gladstone was willing enough, but the Whig Cabinet majority would have none of it. Chamberlain fumed, but he fumed still more when Parnell, despite his 'Independent Opposition' principles, let himself be bought over by the Conservatives with promises of no coercion and hints of future cooperation. Things had come to a pretty pass when the second Gladstone ministry was ejected from office in June 1885 by a Conservative–Irish Nationalist lobby pact.

Three vital points concerning Chamberlain emerge here. The first is that if National Councils had been what Parnell regarded as Home Rule, the Conservative sirens would not have allured him. The second is that Chamberlain regarded himself as having been double-crossed by Parnell and never forgave him. That the facts were otherwise he was totally unaware. Hence the truth had no relevance in judging his acts, however much it is relevant to Parnell's. Captain O'Shea had misled Chamberlain and thus, unwittingly, initiated a piece of political revenge for Parnell's stealing his wife that was to lead on to the personal revenge of five years later. The third is that this scheme was the limit to which Chamberlain was really willing to go in order to appease the Irish Nationalists.

Home Rule in the sense it was generally understood went way beyond the idea behind the National Council scheme.[2] The central core

[1] For full accounts of just how matters went in this matter see C. H. D. Howard (Editor) 'Documents Relating to the Irish Central Board Scheme, 1884–1885; *Irish Historical Studies*, 1953; and C. H. D. Howard (Editor), *Select Documents XXI. Joseph Chamberlain, W. H. O'Shea and Parnell, 1884, 1891–1892*; *Irish Historical Studies*, 1962. (Referred to hereafter as *I.H.S.*)

[2] W. R. W. Stephens in *The Life and Letters of Edward A. Freeman* at p. 292 writes: 'The great object of a large number of articles and letters which he (i.e. Freeman) wrote upon the subject (i.e. Home Rule) from 1885 to 1890 was to show first of all what the proper meaning of Home Rule was.' His efforts were very necessary, but not altogether successful. L. P. Curtis, Jnr. in his *Coercion and Conciliation in Ireland, 1880–1892: A Study in Conservative Unionism*, uses the term Home Rule in a loose fashion and he is by no means alone in this. Freeman's own definition is both succinct and accurate. For him it was 'the relation of a dependency to a superior power when the dependency had the management of its own internal affairs, but had to follow the lead of the superior power in all other matters. It thus differed alike from complete union and complete separation.' Clearly no National Council scheme went this far. Sir Henry Lucy in his *Nearing Jordan*, p. 132, provides an excellent example of how the terminology had got seriously confused. 'The first Home Rule Bill,' he wrote, 'was drafted by Mr. Chamberlain in collaboration with Sir Charles Dilke, and in collusion with

of Irish Nationalist Home Rule doctrine was that a united Ireland should have national parliament. Its powers were to be as numerous and wide as the British could be persuaded or forced to concede. The National Council on the other hand would have been no more than a glorified form of municipal government with narrowly circumscribed powers dealing with secondary and tertiary matters. In all probability the Protestant North-East would have had a big say inside an Ulster Provincial Council. At a time when no part of the United Kingdom had even county government such a suggestion was bound to appear relatively extensive to British electors and enormous confusion later reigned as to what exactly any proposals had to contain before they came within the category of Home Rule. Chamberlain's own subsequent gyrations made matters worse, many men confusing his initial and ultimate positions with the tergiversations at the height of the crisis and concluding they all added up to the same thing and that the Radical Unionist position was essentially hypocritical. Of the tergiversations more below—here all that need be demonstrated is the comparatively modest nature of Chamberlain's pet solution to Irish political problems.

While he doubtless drew immense satisfaction out of thwarting both Parnell and Gladstone it is certain his opposition to Home Rule was quite genuine. The era of democracy had not arrived with the 1885 election, but it must surely be on its way. Ireland would soon have its social and economic and all but one of its political grievances tackled by the imperial parliament. So Chamberlain's thoughts ran and the grooves dictating their course were profound and long-established. By nature he was a great amalgamator and monopoliser. In business he had created for his firm a virtual control of screw manufacturing in the Birmingham district. In local government absolute control of the Birmingham Corporation had enabled him to put through immense reforms with comparative ease. The same conviction that only mastery could secure success had been behind the foundation both of the National Education League and the National Liberal Federation. Smallholdings may seem at first sight a contradictory tendency, but that was not so. They were to be the means of breaking an opponent and could easily be organised as a group to ensure a permanent eclipse of the landed aristocracy. Maybe to Chamberlain the businessman the small unit would have been anathema. To Chamberlain the Radical the small economic unit in the countryside promised political monopoly. Home Rule struck him

Mr. Parnell. It was wrecked by Lord Hartington, a curious concatenation of circumstances in view of the momentous changes, in two cases tragic, that befell these four men within the narrow space of twelve months.' Quite clearly he is referring to the 'National Councils' scheme and not to what could have been accurately described as Home Rule.

28

as a wasteful aberration, for which there was no excuse once Westminster was willing to grant justice. He denied that the feeling of national identity uppermost in countless Irish Nationalists' minds justified the splitting up of the United Kingdom at the parliamentary level, especially as Parnell wanted to exclude Irish members from Westminster. For Chamberlain Home Rule spelt ultimate separation. The self-made man in him made him suspicious and watchful.

The term 'self-made' is easily misunderstood. Chamberlain had started off neither penniless nor without backing. On the contrary, within west midland nonconformity and the business community connected with it he occupied the position of a young quasi-aristocrat, married into a comfortable family twice and cut a great dash in local society. This aristocracy was nevertheless provincial and he a mere member of it. In the conditions of the 1860s and 1870s it was an aristocracy of outsiders. Conservatism and Whiggery, dominated by the 'establishment' of the time had much of their own way. First Chamberlain made himself into a great business and political force in the west midlands. From manufacturer he rose to tycoon. From aspiring Radical to political boss. The process begun, he took the spirit of an unapologetic and aggressive nonconformist Radicalism into parliament and then into the Cabinet, never forgetting to secure his path of retreat and prepare for the next advance. For the first time Radicalism proper had a representative of superlative ability near the very top of affairs. The journey from the screw factory to the Cabinet room had been long. He had made the steam to carry him along. In that sense he was a 'self-made' man, or perhaps we ought to say 'statesman'.

Suspicion and lack of an easy confidence were major considerations in making Chamberlain jib at Home Rule. His contretemps with Parnell only went to heighten it still further. Experience during the second Gladstone ministry had brought out what Harcourt somewhat colourfully called the 'jingo' in him. A sense of imperial pride therefore merged with his feelings of insecurity to push him irrevocably into a unionist conviction he never modified within himself. Then, too, there was the progressive in him, the dislike of the Roman Catholic Church and a fear for Irish Protestants that seemed by the 1880s to have evaporated in Gladstone. Business matters too would be safer under the Westminster umbrella. Throw in pride and obstinacy and the picture is complete.

Proud Chamberlain certainly was. Having once taken up the National Council scheme he was not the man lightly to drop it in the face of the opposition from those he disliked. Pride led on to obstinacy. The will to prevail in his cause moved him powerfully into

29

action. A man who can drown the sorrow of losing two wives in rapid succession has steel in his soul. At the 1885 elections Ireland was one of several vital issues. Chamberlain never became so immersed in cows, acres and school boards as to forget its significance.

Because he had become openly and seriously at odds with Parnell, it was easy enough for him to find common ground with Hartington in denying the possibility of Home Rule being willingly granted by a Liberal Cabinet. It was to be a time of ironies. Both had reckoned without their 'Chief', just as he reckoned without them in coming to the conclusion that Home Rule must be granted. Chamberlain–Hartington relations improved as the election campaign revealed the falsity of the supposition that electoral change would lead to Chamberlain becoming to Gladstone what Gladstone himself had been to Russell in 1865. In periods of left wing party decline or embarrassment the right wing elements of left wing parties are usually in a better position for appealing to the erring floating vote. This Chamberlain came belatedly to see. Just at the moment therefore when the Radical–Whig clash had reached its climax the seeds of future accord between the Whigs and Chamberlain and those Radicals putting him before Gladstone in their estimation were sown.

Gladstone's response to the Conservative–Irish Nationalist flirtation had been characteristic, so was his answer to electoral frustration. The one convinced him Home Rule would have to come and the other persuaded him that the Conservatives were the ones to put it through.[1] Premature disclosure of his views on the general issue in mid-December 1885 had the effect of revealing how many leading Liberals of all shades of opinion were opposed to satisfying Parnell's demand and providing the Conservative government with a grand opportunity of playing the 'Crown and Constitution' card against the Liberals yet again.[2] Needless to say, they rejected the generous oppor-

[1] Writing of the summer of 1885 Hammond and Foot remark at p. 167 of their *Gladstone and Liberalism*: 'Gladstone was by now wholly preoccupied with the Irish question, so far as a man of such multifarious interests could ever be preoccupied with one single subject.' This was *a fortiori* true six months later. Dilke was referring to British politicians as a whole when he remarked: 'When we are thinking about Ireland, which is very commonly the case, we are apt to forget all else, and both our relations with foreign Powers and those with our dependencies drop into the background.' Sir C. W. Dilke, *The Present Position of European Politics*, p. 10. He came very near the truth, though domestic issues survived better than external ones and the electorate ensured they loomed increasingly large on the political scene once the Home Rule Bill of 1886 was defeated.

[2] The premature disclosure was dubbed the 'Hawarden Kite'. It was thought by many that Gladstone had actually inspired it as a means of testing out public reactions while he sat tight in his home at Hawarden Castle. A letter from Sir Edward Hamilton to Herbert Gladstone, dated 7th January 1886 suggests this was not so. See Add. MS. 45990, f. 1. While Herbert Gladstone was responsible for the leakage he would appear to have acted off his own bat. In London the

tunity to please the Irish Nationalists and reverted to their traditional 'Orange' rôle. Gladstone was left with the task of carrying through his idea. At this point he showed himself a master of tactics. But so too did Chamberlain. The old man managed to eject the minority Conservative government on the issue of smallholdings—an especial nostrum of Chamberlain's—without Home Rule having been discussed. He followed this up with forming a government ostensibly aimed at an enquiry as to what the Irish situation demanded. A mere handful of Liberal M.P.s had voted with the Conservatives—many had abstained or absented themselves. Almost the whole Whig phalanx now declined to join the new administration.[1] Not so Chamberlain, nor Trevelyan.[2] The former had learned a few lessons from the 1885 election and now had an infinitely more realistic idea of the influence he wielded. The latter had always known how the masses felt about Gladstone. They played their cards well, resigning at the end of March on details of an actual Home Rule scheme. From January to July Chamberlain claimed that his objections to the Gladstone scheme were not of principle, but of detail. There was, moreover, a highly unpopular Land Bill introduced at the same time. Chamberlain knew he was safe enough in pursuing this course. It would preserve his authority in Birmingham—the essence of full political survival—and never be exposed conclusively as humbug. If Gladstone surrendered there was the Ulster issue to get over. Neither Chamberlain nor Churchill were necessary to arouse feelings in the 'Six Counties'.[3] Then the Lords stood as an obstacle, making sure Home Rule could not be implemented without a general election, Gladstone was likely, whatever Schnadhorst thought, to lose quite decisively in Britain. New Irish Nationalist support would not be of much use to

Conservative *Standard* published the news; in the provinces the *Leeds Mercury*. According to John St Loe Strachey in his autobiography, *The Adventure of Living*, p. 182, the *Standard* was Gladstone's favourite newspaper. He would therefore have been likely to look at it before its rivals. But that is about all. Herbert Gladstone's own account of the affair is to be found in his book *After Thirty Years* at pp. 306–16. Charles Mallet has some interesting information to offer on the subject in his *Memoir* of Herbert Gladstone at pp. 118–23. The correspondence of Gladstone and Granville about it is to be found in the *Political Correspondence of Mr. Gladstone and Lord Granville, 1876–1886*, edited by Miss A. Ramm, Vol. II at pp. 415–17.

[1] Some mistakenly associate the Liberal Unionist revolt almost exclusively with Whiggery. For example, Dr G. Goodman called his article on the Liberal split and its consequences 'Liberal Unionism: The Revolt of the Whigs'. It was published in *Victorian Studies* for 1959.

[2] See p. 34, note 2.

[3] It was pointed out by G. M. Young in his essay on Gladstone that in the volume of the G.O.M.'s writings on Ireland—a book of 370 pages—Ulster receives but two passing mentions. One is a quotation from Castlereagh. G. M. Young, *Today and Yesterday*, p. 29.

him then, for the anti-Home Rule M.P.s would be certain to command almost half the House of Commons and very likely a large and independent majority. Gladstone himself had always appreciated the Lords point as fully as Parnell himself. But Chamberlain was saved such prolonged anxiety over what Gladstone would do. Relations had not been improved by the way the leader had handled Chamberlain at the outset, when the latter had aspired to the Colonial Office. 'Oh! A Secretary of State' was hardly the language to use on Chamberlain. The same awkwardness surrounded the situation which arose after he had taken on the Local Government Board.[1] An attempt was made to cut the salary offered to Jesse Collings,[2] who was to act as second-in-command. Harcourt had to mediate. Had he only known how much more Joe-sweetening he would have on his plate before another year had passed! Failure to introduce substantial local government reforms also upset Chamberlain, but the die was secretly cast. Things reached a climax at the end of March when Gladstone replied unfavourably to Chamberlain's acid tests on the 'details'. Less than a month later the Birmingham Liberal and Radical Association stood by their local leader against their national leader. The programme was—'Home Rule—yes! Exclusion of Irish members—no!' Bright's name was then invoked to a meeting of Liberal and Radical M.P.s. The N.L.F. rejected its Birmingham leadership and stood by Gladstone, but Chamberlain carried on. His base was secured for the moment and Whig and Conservative support impressive. Provided he appeared, or could plead that he was an unwilling rebel, Gladstone could be defeated in the Commons and the future take care of itself. Birmingham Radical Unionism developed therefore on its own. Those like Trevelyan and Heneage, who resigned with Chamberlain, were dragged in his wake. Sympathisers in the nation at large looked to him for a lead.

Quite different was the foundation and development of Whig Liberal Unionism.[3] Almost immediately it was clear that Gladstone could not be restrained and would insist on trying to convince them he was 'right' a strong barricade was set up in the Whig wing of the

[1] G. M. Young again commented with a telling penetration: 'He (i.e. Gladstone) never understood why Chamberlain should spend the money of the Birmingham ratepayers on "fine schools" for the children of the poor: he never understood why England worshipped Gordon.' Young, *op. cit.*, p. 29. The gulf yawned between the two statesmen on domestic and imperial matters.

[2] Jesse Collings (1831–1920), was a very close friend of Chamberlain's and at this time Liberal M.P. for the Bordesley division of Birmingham. Together they had run and were running the 'Three Acres and a Cow' campaign. At the time of the split Collings became a prominent Radical Unionist and afterwards the prime mover in the Radical Unionist bid for widespread support among farm labourers.

[3] See Goodman, *op. cit.*

great Liberal house.[1] 'Hartington Mansions' was its new name. Rank and file rebellions in the constituencies stopped little in parliament. The Whig wing was in any case something of a skeleton army. Many 'moderate' voters had already supported the Conservatives in 1885.[2] The officers, however, were very much alive and haunted even more effectively than the dead. Hartington headed a formidable group of M.P.s. Like Chamberlain he was careful to make clear he was not ratting to anybody or thing to which he had previously been opposed. After a much criticised joint meeting at 'Her Majesty's Theatre' in the Haymarket in mid–April, he played very safe and was at pains to stress his consistency on Irish matters with Gladstone's earlier Irish policy and the genuineness of his Liberal politics. Unlike Chamberlain, the Whigs began to organise on a national scale before the second reading debate on the Home Rule Bill. Some M.P.s of the left and right were taken back to Gladstone by his withdrawal of the Land Bill and the proposal to use the second reading vote as one on the principle alone. But Gladstone himself admitted in a moment of ill-temper that the latter was no more than a delaying tactic and a few M.P.s changed sides yet again.

Three unionist parties then faced Gladstone in June 1886—the Conservative, the Whig Liberal Unionist, and the Radical Liberal Unionist. Salisbury, aged fifty-six and lately prime minister, headed the first from the House of Lords. In the Commons his principal lieutenant was Churchill, thirty-seven years of age and Secretary of State for India in the late Salisbury administration. The second had Hartington, heir to the Duke of Devonshire as its leader. Fifty-two and technically a bachelor, he had risen to such heights of oratory and displayed such energy over the Home Rule issue that anyone knowing him of old could scarcely believe he was the same man. While Secretary for War during the Sudan crisis his inert behaviour

[1] Many Liberal Unionists of the right were much influenced by fixed ideas on constitutional practice. Pamphlets like A. B. M'Grigor's 'The British Parliament, Its History and Functions' were highly popular with them.

[2] One of the attitudes prevalent among them is well summed-up by some words of Theobald Pontifex in Samuel Butler's *The Way of all Flesh*: 'What is this horrid government going to do with Ireland.' The 'horrid government' being, of course, Gladstone's third ministry. See H. Ausubel, *The Late Victorians: A Short History*, p. 75. The Home Rule threat had a powerful effect in Ulster. See D. C. Savage, 'The Origins of the Ulster Unionist Party, 1885–1886', *I.H.S.* 1961. An aggravating factor for right wing Liberals during the third Gladstone ministry was the Railway Rates question. It occupied a position in some ways similar to that of the Maynooth Grant issue for many Conservatives in 1845. While the article 'The Railway Rates Question and the Fall of the Third Gladstone Ministry' by W. H. G. Armytage (*E.H.R.* 1950) is in some respects inaccurate, its main arguments are sound enough and are not invalidated by what P. M. Williams says in 'Public Opinion and the Railway Rates Question in 1886' (*E.H.R.* 1952).

had become a byword. His new party abounded in lieutenants of all ages. Goschen was the ablest of the middle-aged and Albert Grey the most zealous of the younger brood.[1] Among the Radical Unionists Chamberlain stood out as their one great figure. In fact his party was rather like a tadpole with him as its head. A month from his fiftieth birthday, with ten years of experience in parliament, he was really the man of the hour. With Bright's help he became 'The Man who Killed Home Rule'. For many of his former Radical allies who had admired and envied him so intensely he was 'The Judas from Birmingham'. But this was not all. To the Conservatives and Whigs he was still a Cleon among men and potentially an overmighty friend. Trevelyan, aged forty-seven, they cared little about.[2]

Mass defections had left the Gladstonian Liberals short of front bench talent. Gladstone, now in his seventy-seventh year, was as prominent in his band as Chamberlain among the Radical Unionists. Harcourt now became deputy leader and John Morley his main aide. The former was nearly sixty, the latter forty-seven. The one was chancellor of the exchequer in the third ministry, the other secretary for Ireland. The new Liberal-loving Parnell would very soon be forty. He and his numerous lieutenants had never held office!

These are the men round which the web of events discussed below was spun. These are the men whose wisdom and errors made up the stuff of politics and showed how much more history is than a thing of 'forces' unconnected specifically with particular individuals in particular situations.

EXPLANATORY NOTE

At frequent intervals during this book mention is made of houses in which individuals prominent in the story often resided. On p. 35 is a list of them for the convenience of the reader.

[1] Albert G. Grey (1851–1917) was the eldest son of General Grey, second son of the 2nd Earl Grey and secretary to Queen Victoria. He was currently Liberal M.P. for Tyneside, but was defeated in the 1886 general election when standing as a Liberal Unionist. From 1884 to 1885 he served as unpaid secretary to H. C. E. Childers, Chancellor of the Exchequer in the second Gladstone ministry. In 1894 he succeeded his uncle, becoming the 4th Earl Grey. From 1904 to 1911 he served as Governor-General of Canada with considerable distinction. His personality was exceptionally pleasing.

[2] George O. Trevelyan (1838–1928) sat at this time as Liberal member for the Border Burghs. Until his resignation he served as Secretary for Scotland in the third Gladstone ministry. When standing as a Liberal Unionist in the 1886 general election he was narrowly defeated. In 1880 he had published his *Early History of Charles James Fox* and was a historian of some note, though his uncle, Lord Macaulay, and his son, G. M. Trevelyan, were more distinguished members of the profession.

Resident	*House*
Salisbury	Hatfield House (Hertfordshire)
Hartington	Chatsworth House (Derbyshire)
Chamberlain	Highbury (Birmingham, Warwickshire)
Trevelyan	Welcombe (Warwickshire)
Gladstone	Hawarden Castle (Flintshire)
Harcourt	Malwood House (Hampshire)
Morley	95, Elm Park Gardens (London)
Spencer	Althorp Park (Northamptonshire)

I

THE POWER STRUCTURE OF UNITED KINGDOM PARTY POLITICS AFTER THE HOME RULE SPLIT OF 1886

＊＊＊

'Who is on my side? Who?' 2 Kings ii. 32.

THINK. I beseech you, think well, think wisely, think not for a moment but for the years that are to come before you reject this bill.'[1] These concluding words of Gladstone's last speech on his first Irish Home Rule Bill were intended to rivet the thoughts of those about to vote for or against it on to the rights and wrongs of the Irish question. For him, history and current affairs alike pointed inexorably in the direction of the 'aye' lobby. For the overwhelming number of his party matters were much more complicated. The grand ecstasy of moral rectitude and the compelling simplicity of historical truth had made their mark, but the leader's admonishment could not drive considerations of the Liberal future out of sight. Whether they liked it or not, home ruler, unionist and the hitherto uncommitted Liberal members had to face not only the moment but the years that were to come in terms of British party

[1] Hansard, Vol. CCCVI, Col. 1240. J. Morley, *Life of Gladstone*, Vol. III, p. 338. For an interesting letter to the press, aimed at bringing over waverers and written by a Gladstonian Liberal M.P., see F. A. Channing, *Memories of Midland Politics, 1885–1910*, pp. 66–67, and *Daily News*, 7th June 1886.
Tuckwell regarded the pace at which Gladstone moved with considerable distaste, declaring: 'To declare the necessity of Home Rule was well, to force it on was madness.' Tuckwell, *op. cit.*, p. 65. In May 1886 the *Nineteenth Century* carried an article by Matthew Arnold entitled 'The Nadir of Liberalism'. Tuckwell stuck to Gladstone, Arnold became a Liberal Unionist, yet both alike felt the times were out of joint for Liberalism. On the other hand in the June issue of the *Nineteenth Century* there appeared 'Morley and Gladstone and the Irish Bill: A Nonconformist View' by J. Guinness Rogers—an article of aid and comfort for the G.O.M. The *Nineteenth Century*, May and June 1886, Vol. 19.

politics. 'Think well, think wisely'—very few would have denied the need for reflection, yet altruism was hardly the paramount sentiment.

Whatever sort of conclusion anyone previously in doubt eventually accepted, the time for thinking it out was remarkably short. Immediately after Gladstone had finished, the division on the crucial second reading was taken and the government defeated by thirty. The 8th June 1886 dawned with the Liberal party fully split. Not even the most devoted wishful thinker could explain away the fact that no fewer than ninety-three Liberal members elected less than a year before had repudiated their leader and voted with the Conservatives.[1] Almost exactly forty years before, Peel had lost some two-thirds of his Conservative party on the Corn Law Repeal issue. Gladstone had now lost just under one-third of the Liberals over a more fundamental proposal. Two hundred and twenty-nine men had remained faithful and enabled him to face the future with some hope. Allowing for the changes in the nature of the party system arising out of the vast extensions of the franchise, his score was perhaps not so much more impressive than Peel's. However, this was scarcely the point because the practical effect was so different. There could be no doubt that he could continue as leader of the Liberal party despite the sizeable secession.

At a specially convened Cabinet meeting the government decided to ask for an immediate dissolution of parliament. Apart from Gladstone's confidence that the electorate would grasp the essential justice of his scheme, the advice of Schnadhorst, Secretary of the National Liberal Association, was of a highly optimistic nature. He was convinced the Liberal vote of 1885 would remain substantially intact and be joined by the Irish vote lately cast for the Conservatives as part of Parnell's successful bid to hold the balance. Had this rosy view been borne out by events, Gladstone's position would have been infinitely more advantageous than before his parliamentary defeat. Indeed, the secession of the Liberal and Radical Unionists had itself already eased his general difficulties. With the

[1] A discussion of the relative strengths of the Chamberlainite and Hartingtonian elements among the dissidents is to be found in *Historical Journal*, 1964, M. C. Hurst, 'Joseph Chamberlain, the Conservatives and the Succession to John Bright, 1886–89'.

It was the opinion of Henry, later Sir Henry Lucy, that the Liberal Unionist revolt would prove 'futile' without the participation of Chamberlain, despite 'the united effort of the hereditary Radical (i.e. Bright) and the born Whig (i.e. Hartington)'. Viscount Milner, J. A. Spender, Sir H. Lucy, J. Ramsay Macdonald, L. S. Amery, *Joseph Chamberlain: His Life and Work*, p. 120.

F. W. Hirst regarded Bright as the man who had done most 'damage' to the Home Rule cause. Sir Wemyss Reid (Editor), *The Life of William Ewart Gladstone*, p. 709.

vote taken, the basic argument on Home Rule as he understood it was over, bar a little shouting within the Liberal party; and, what is more, the balance in the House of Commons was no longer held by Parnell and his Irish Nationalists. If a victory had followed at the polls his hold on the Liberal, or, as many now called it, the Gladstonian Liberal party would have been more than consolidated and, even had Parnell again held the balance, there would have been every reason to suppose a sustained period of good behaviour towards Hawarden and its work. The most supervening of these reasons would have been the inevitable set-to with the House of Lords and the certainty of serious trouble in Ulster when the Home Rule cause was again pursued in the House of Commons. Without any Nationalist hold on the balance the liberation afforded by the second reading defeat would simply have been augmented and room for manoeuvring against opponents substantially increased.

Events shattered the immediate hopes of the Home Rule camp. Not only were there three hundred and sixteen Conservatives as opposed to a hundred and ninety-one Gladstonian Liberals returned to the new House of Commons, but seventy-eight Liberal and Radical Unionists in addition to the eighty-five Nationalists led by Parnell. On the face of it the secessionists stood an excellent chance of calling the tune whether inside or outside a Unionist administration. By turning down Lord Salisbury's offer to serve under him and declining to join in a coalition with the Conservatives, Lord Hartington avoided the appearance of being swayed by Irish considerations alone and seemed likely to satisfy those Radical Unionists around Chamberlain whose opposition to Gladstone over Home Rule made them ever more anxious to pursue the cause of domestic reform. For Gladstone, a Conservative government constantly prodded into activity by a Liberal and Radical Unionist party, which had survived the rigours of a general election, made an alarming prospect. The argument that as most Liberal and Radical Unionists had owed their electoral survival to Conservative aid and would not therefore be in any position to press home their claims was not basically sound if applied to the particular situation of 1886.

That situation could not be accurately assessed in terms of House of Commons seats and votes cast alone. A man's label in parliament often presented a very unreal picture of the actual state of opinion in his constituency. This was widely true of Conservatives as well as Liberal and Radical Unionists, and sometimes applied to Gladstonians. The crux of the problem lay in what made up the thing referred to as 'the actual state of opinion'. Broadly speaking, two majority views then current in Britain were not always easily reconciled. They were the belief that domestic reform should be continued at a reasonable pace and the feeling that the Union with Ireland should be maintained. Many were afflicted with subscribing to both majorities simultaneously and found it difficult either to choose between, or reconcile them, according to their place in the political spectrum. Conservatives usually had few problems, or rather no more than they had in the past. The lot of the progressive Conservative had seldom been easy and it could be argued that, the Home Rule crisis having caused a Liberal split, the new situation with Liberal and Radical Unionist allies was a welcome change for the better; that, far from complicating matters, it simplified them. Only a minority of Liberals could have said the same. In the general election of 1885 a mere handful of Liberal candidates had declared for Home Rule.[1] Maybe a few more might have done so had Parnell's

[1] An analysis of the election addresses issued by successful Liberal candidates in the 1885 general election reveals that a mere six were at that time full Home Rulers. Devonshire Papers, 340. 1938.

Although Gladstone's experts had assured him the Home Rule issue would sweep the country for his party in the general election of 1886 (see G. W. E. Russell, *Fifteen Chapters of Autobiography*, p. 279, for a conversation the author had with the Liberal leader), he was partly motivated in seeking a dissolution by feelings of pride. When the Queen demurred to a dissolution so soon after the last, he argued for it on grounds of convenience, but then later remarked to a colleague: 'If we did not dissolve, we should be showing the white feather.' G. W. E. Russell, *William Ewart Gladstone*, p. 257. That approval of the course he took was not general is proved by the contents of Appendix I. Many, like Richard Cadbury, saw no problems in a sudden espousal of Home Rule (see Helen Alexander, *Richard Cadbury of Birmingham*, pp. 294-7), but hosts of others took the split so seriously as to let it affect their social relations. Lady St Helier tells in her *Memories of Fifty Years* at p. 243, how Home Rule Liberals came rapidly to be 'virtually ostracised by their friends and relations' and the pleasant occasions like the dinner for Queen Victoria's birthday at Gladstone's house on 29th May 1886, where 'very many who are in opposition on Irish Bills' were among the forty guests became extremely rare events. See *The Diaries of John Bright*, p. 544. For many electors abstention seemed the only way out. The domestic programmes apparently championed by both Gladstone and Chamberlain in the recent past had held and still held their real interest. Hence many thought it a time to 'Wait and See'. (Russell on Gladstone, p. 258. M. K. Ashby, *Joseph Ashby of Tysoe, 1859-1919*, pp. 117-18). Actual rank and file defections were often due to mixed motives. For example, G. B. Hertz in his *The Manchester Politician, 1750-1912* at p. 75 argues that both Gladstone's past Egyptian policy and Home Rule 'brought about the strong Conservative preponderance in the Parliamentary representation of Manchester between 1886-1906'. Surely not a complete explanation, but nevertheless not without value? Anti-Hibernianism stirred up in 1885 must certainly have played its part as well as numerous events after the Liberal party came near to dropping orthodox and vigorous espousal of Home Rule in 1894. (See J. A. Jackson, *The Irish in Britain*, p. 128.) Estimates of the Liberal Unionist impact have sometimes been inflated. In his recent book, *The Habit of Authority*, A. P. Thornton overestimates the electoral victories of the new

tactics been different, but the overall picture would not have been appreciably changed. The very restricted form of Irish self-government championed by Chamberlain and Dilke earlier that year and sometimes loosely dubbed 'Home Rule' had commanded considerable approval, yet was no longer of any real relevance at the time of the open quarrel and electoral civil war. Loyalty to Gladstone, hatred and distrust of the Conservatives and the conviction that domestic reform could only come for sure and in an agreeable form from the left impelled countless voters to pocket their dislike of the Irish and the Home Rule idea and still back Gladstonian Liberal candidates. This was all the more straightforward if they happened to be men with grievances of one kind or another. Among Liberals these were in any case bound to be numerous. In a left wing party this was only to be expected. At a general election therefore, when all the issues have of necessity to be considered simultaneously, Gladstone was bound to benefit from the way the large majority of Liberals ordered their political priorities. Others reasoned differently and arrived on the dissident side. The more radical of them thought reform could still be obtained, albeit from the Conservatives, by means of deftly applied pressure. The rest, some of whom were barely distinguishable from Conservatives, tended to be drawn from the more affluent sectors of society and found themselves able to face the possibility of a temporary stoppage in domestic reform with equanimity. This did not mean in most instances that they had no stomach at all for further change, but only that their ordering of priorities placed defence of the Union to the fore.

There was too a third category of former Liberal voters whose influence on the power structure of politics was to prove very profound. This consisted of the deliberate abstainers—the men who found ordering their priorities too difficult, or having ordered them disliked the result too much to take it to a practical level. Then again there were the disenfranchised voters—those deprived of a chance to give an answer to Gladstone's appeal because their local member was returned unopposed. Whereas in 1885 only thirteen Liberals and ten Conservatives had enjoyed this advantage. No fewer than forty-

party in Scotland (see p. 271). In fact not 14, but 42 Gladstonian Liberals won seats in the 1886 general election there. (For a good account of events in Scotland see D. C. Savage, 'Scottish Politics, 1885–1886', *Scottish Historical Review*, 1961.) Organisationally there were *some* significant signs of the times taking Britain as a whole. Whereas the Primrose League had a rocketing membership at this time (Janet H. Robb, *The Primrose League, 1883–1906*, p. 58) that of the National Agricultural Labourers' Union dropped ominously. (J. Collings and Sir J. L. Green, *Life of Jesse Collings*, p. 153.) The counties let Gladstone down badly in the general election of 1886 and the Conservatives were the prime gainers.

two Liberals, twenty-four Liberal and Radical Unionists and eighty-six Conservatives did so in 1886. Untested voters were an unknown quantity up to a point and contributed towards the feeling of uncertainty later played on to such effect by Chamberlain in his campaign to extract reforms from the Salisbury government. British members of parliament of almost every shade had to face some elements of doubt and uncertainty whenever they raised the domestic reform and Irish questions. By its very nature politics includes a substantial element of the kaleidoscopic. The new alignment of forces and the profundity of the big issues connected with it increased the tempo of shifts in the power pattern. Salisbury once remarked that a general election, unlike a legal proceeding, does not admit of a clear answer being given by the deciding authority to separate questions. Nevertheless, once the election is over public opinion can pronounce on each issue individually with much greater effect. The fact that parliaments deals with proposals more or less *seriatim* guarantees this. By and large, at the outset, the government and its allies enjoyed their maximum strength when pronouncing on Irish matters and their minimum over purely domestic reform. Chamberlain and his following determined to change this, both for their own and the country's sake. Unionism was to have a strong front on the domestic as well as the Irish issues. The Gladstonians on the other hand were equally intent upon selling 'Justice for Ireland' and playing up any domestic grievances in an attempt to win back Unionist Liberals and Radicals, win over former abstainers and build up support among the untried. The Conservatives began by constructing a ministry and carefully sounding out the ground. Many were fearful of the price to be paid for maintaining the Union, while some saw the new situation as one offering a unique opportunity for dishing Gladstone and making sure 'Tory Democracy' had a prosperous future. Of this latter group the most prominent and influential was Lord Randolph Churchill.

At thirty-seven he occupied positions few politicians ever reach however long their public service. As the Leader of the House of Commons and Chancellor of the Exchequer in the new Salisbury administration, he was well placed to attempt the implementation of a reform programme, particularly because of his friendship with Chamberlain and the need to propitiate Radical Unionist and floating voters. In the course of a few years the Churchill mystique had grown to impressive proportions among the local Conservative associations. When Northcote was deliberately trying to woo moderate Liberalism away from Gladstone, convinced by the 1880 general election results that this was the only sure way to regain office for the Conservatives, Churchill had been the prime mover in a brilliant guerilla war against the Liberals in and out of parliament. His small group, rapidly dubbed the 'Fourth Party', had soon assumed an importance out of all proportion to its numbers and reverted to the notion favoured by Disraeli in 1867 that a direct appeal to the masses was the better means of flourishing in the future. Through a resourceful use of wide backing in the National Union of Conservative Associations, his considerable gifts as a parliamentarian and the lively sense of fear his possible enmity aroused in the hearts and minds of the party leadership he had battered a way towards the top. The whole process had been accelerated by the sympathy Salisbury, as Conservative leader in the Lords, had felt with him over Northcote's pusillanimity. A successful tenure of the India Office during the first Salisbury administration had strengthened his overall position and the feeling, even among his hordes of enemies, had been that the Conservative gains in the 1885 general election owed not a little to him and his approach.

When Salisbury took office then, Unionist progressives cheered and standstillers and reactionaries groaned to see Churchill's promotion. Their responses were not entirely sound. Unlike Chamberlain, Churchill was not a genuine believer in developing and making a lasting political force out of the mass support of a party. Being at heart a thorough devotee of the concept of aristocratic rule he had conceived of the National Union, not as the mainstay of any authority he might have acquired, but as something to use on the way to the top. As he once told Rosebery, 'Tory Democracy' was aimed at making the 'democracy' Tory and persuading it to place its trust in the 'aristocracy'. Now of course men like Chamberlain subscribed to the general idea of leadership in public life, yet with several vital differences. They craved for an aristocracy of merit and, although confident most of it would be drawn from the higher reaches of the professions and business, did not rule out the possibility of recruits arising from the most intelligent working men. At this time too, all but the merest handful assumed these recruits would be happily accommodated within the folds of the Liberal party. Churchill on the other hand wished for an essentially static society with the newly powerful urban voters drawn in behind the aristocracy of birth. The definition of aristocracy and quality was purely pragmatic, although allowing for accretions of membership due to worldly success and the gradual rise to eminence from the parvenu status of the new rich. That the economic amelioration he favoured and the general trend of events made such a view of things unreal does not affect the fact that Churchill subscribed to and was governed by it. Unfortunately for him, a strong tendency to arrogance pushed him still further in the same direction. Instead of building up the National Union to a thing of real power, he let it lapse into ineffectiveness once his place in the sun had been reached and enjoyed. No alternative source of influence had been acquired through creating a large following in the House of Commons. The truth was that Churchill depended on the figure cut by Chamberlain with his government colleagues, even at the very time they took on office, more than on any power he could himself independently muster to push forward any reform schemes. In reality he was largely alone in his party—voluntarily having renounced the generation and use of power at its base and completely unable to master the personnel at its apex. The narrow class for whom he was basically striving rejected his unorthodox methods and offensive masterfulness. The cause of change largely depended upon how Salisbury and the bulk of the Cabinet judged the political situation. If they opted for stonewalling on domestic issues, then Hartington would be largely responsible, for he it was who had the decision to make or break them in parliament within his grasp. Without his consent no big decisions for a standstill policy could or would be taken. From a purely parliamentary viewpoint, Chamberlain could be ignored, especially if Hartington approved.[1]

Chamberlain saw that both Gladstone and Parnell stood to gain a great deal from any static condition in domestic affairs. The more the British electorate fumed about its own particular discontents the more support would grow for the Gladstonians. The more they grew in influence the more Gladstone would be able to push his

---

[1] Hurst, *op. cit.*, and M. C. Hurst, *Joseph Chamberlain and West Midland Politics, 1886–95, passim.*

Lord George Hamilton quite rightly stressed the importance of Radical Unionism: 'Outside Birmingham and the big towns in its locality the actual voting power of the Liberal Unionists was small.' He went on, however, to pinpoint the main strengths of Liberal Unionism as a whole: 'Their leaders were the pick of the old Gladstonian party and their powers of speech and writing were considerable.' Lord G. Hamilton, *Parliamentary Reminiscences and Reflections, 1886–1906*, p. 30. Chamberlain's position in the post-split years was very similar to that of Léon Blum after the failure of his Popular Front governments in France. As Blum himself put it on 7th June 1938: 'We must accept the fact that power is held by others, even if they do not entirely satisfy us, because we prefer to see them there rather than someone else; because we know the dangers of political instability. Our difficulties will start again because we are acting in the midst of inextricable events, because we are caught between a society we cannot yet destroy and a society we cannot yet construct.' Joll, *op. cit.*, p. 49. But 'Our Joe' was made of sterner stuff than Blum and, as A. J. Balfour remarked: 'the new Parliamentary Era then began.' A. J. Balfour, *Chapters of Autobiography*, p. 222. The seriousness of Chamberlain's defection has been underlined by D. Southgate in his *The Passing of the Whigs, 1832–1886* at p. 418. He writes: 'Then came Home Rule. The Liberal party lost its incubus, but also its practical-minded demagogue'.)

Home Rule scheme. This in turn would lead Parnell to stick even more closely to the alliance with the G.O.M. in the hope of a government collapse, a Liberal and Radical Unionist eclipse and a reintroduction of the Home Rule proposals without the encumbrance of an unpopular Land Bill. Inside the Gladstonian fold the leader's prestige was beyond challenge. Nevertheless, the split had been the occasion for a virtual policy takeover by the Radicals of the National Liberal Federation. 'Constructionism' and nonconformist specialities would have to receive at least his outward blessing in future as the price for pursuing the Home Rule cause. Perhaps the major strength of the Liberal party under Gladstone had always been the way in which practical reform ideas had been elevated to the level of moral axioms. Along with the zest for change had gone the feeling of righteousness and a passion for the liberty of the individual. Home Rule fitted this pattern of emotional response and there can be little doubt of the enormous obstacle to Unionism maintaining its ground it presented once the initial attitudes already discussed ceased to monopolise men's minds. When Bevin spoke of a 'bleeding heart' running away with a 'bloody head', he was referring to Lansbury, yet the phrase applies very well to the outlook of countless Liberals, Gladstonian and Unionist alike, when facing up to the logic of Home Rule and Unionism. Denial of Parnell's demands would probably entail coercion at a comparatively early stage. For many Gladstonians this prospect destroyed all vestiges of anti-Irish prejudice and for many Unionists, especially those of the more radical sort, created a situation where their hearts pulled one way and their heads another. Which won depended very largely on the individual quirks of each man or woman. This illogicality among left-wing Unionists was also common among the abstainers at the 1886 general election, as the by-election history of the next few years was to prove. When parliament met on 5th August the traditional sympathy for the underdog had hardly begun to operate, but Conservative and Liberal and Radical Unionist members needed no instruction on it as a potential threat. After all, some of them would be among those affected by it. Any farsighted Conservative prime minister at this time should therefore have been prepared for a fairly extensive series of reforms in Britain and Ireland and anxious to avoid any coercion measures in the latter for as long as circumstances permitted. Only by the use of such practical and emotional balm could the Unionist cause prosper against a left-swinging Gladstonianism in which 'bleeding hearts' had things more their own way than before the split. Only by such balm could Liberal and Radical Unionism remain intact and stand a chance of appealing to former abstainers.

A deceptive calm reigned in Ireland. The Nationalist cause had suffered a serious check in parliament and in the British elections. For the time being the only sensible course for Parnell to follow was one of continued support for Gladstone. There was no telling how well the Unionist parties would get along together and any aggressive move on the Irish agrarian front could only have the initial effect of consolidating their friendship, however much any Conservative resort to coercion as the disorder continued put left Unionism into disarray. In Ulster too the Protestant community was sitting tight and hoping it could continue to be 'right' without having to 'fight', though fight it would if need be. British moral and military authority prevented the simplification of Irish politics into a straight 'Orange' versus 'Green' antagonism from proceeding beyond the stage of an agonised still life. Without a restraining hand violence would certainly have broken out frequently at a local level where Nationalist and Unionist lived side by side. Had Home Rule passed the Commons the likelihood of well-prepared and widely organised 'Orange' resistance would have been vastly increased. No Churchill was required to rouse the Ulstermen into militant activity, for back in 1883 Northcote had been treated to a generous dose of demonstrations of a highly excited character.[1] The Gladstonian claim that the North-East of Ireland had been artificially aroused through the unscrupulous exaggerations of British Unionist politicians does not bear any serious examination. Chamberlain was undoubtedly right to stress the Ulster problem before and after the vote on the second reading of the Home Rule Bill and Churchill was more the reflector than the creator of political, social and religious passion. If Churchill is to be condemned at all, it must be for aggravating and failing to dampen down unconstitutional trends, not for bringing them into being. Unionist victory at the polls in any case saved him from having to reap the whirlwind and even if Gladstone had won renewed confidence nothing in Ulster would have needed to go beyond the preparatory stage unless the Lords were routed. Unionists living in the strongly Nationalist centre, south and west naturally felt badly exposed. If the Conservative government survived and prospered, their safety and political future would be assured. Should it falter and fall, they would have no alternative but to reconcile themselves to the plans of a Gladstonian administration backed by Parnell, unless, of course, they left for Britain. In any event the elimination of the local Liberals at the polls and the enrolment of virtually all their following under the Liberal and Radical Unionist banner meant that Gladstone's approach to the Irish question was freed from at least one embarrassing complication.

[1] A. Lang, *Sir Stafford Northcote, First Earl of Iddesleigh*, Vol. II, pp. 249–55.

The first post-election move of any real note was made by Salisbury, who called the Conservative parliamentary party together at the Carlton Club on 27th July and explained the why and wherefore of his dealings with Hartington.[1] He spoke of how he had offered to support even a purely Liberal and Radical Unionist administration and of how Hartington had declined, preferring to have a Conservative government with Liberal and Radical Unionists in alliance, so long as there was agreement on basic policy. Although parliament was to meet within ten days the government had not at that point decided on an exact plan as to timing. A few days later it opted for completing a short session in the ordinary way and avoiding one in the autumn. Parliament would then reassemble early in 1887 when detailed policies could be produced. Quite rightly, the Gladstonians regarded all this as an attempt to hide the lack of a real policy for Ireland, but made little fuss on the 5th August when Speaker Peel found himself unanimously elected, new writs for by-elections caused through ministerial appointments were issued, and parliament adjourned for a fortnight. Later that day Hartington addressed the Liberal and Radical Unionist parliamentary parties at Devonshire House. In a speech of some length he explained why he had declined to undertake the formation of a ministry with or without the Conservatives, while at the same time offering Salisbury general support, and expressed the hope that Liberalism would soon be reunited on a unionist platform. This latter point was doubtless thrown in for propaganda purposes and to ease the path of Chamberlain and his Radical Unionists. Certainly it paid rapid dividends, for when Hartington sat down Chamberlain got up and, after expressing entire agreement with the former's projected political strategy, declared himself willing to accept his leadership from then on. Reunion was much in his mind and he went out of his way to stress the 'feelings of unmixed pleasure' which any satisfactory Liberal reunion would arouse in him.[2] To underline the essential oneness of Liberals he and the other Liberal and Radical Unionist ex-ministers intended to sit upon the front opposition bench with the Gladstonians. Typically, though, he provided for a stronger bargaining position *vis-à-vis* the G.O.M. by promising amalgamation between the Liberal Unionist Association and his new Radical Unionist organisation based on Birmingham. Salisbury's line of letting sleeping dogs lie for the next few months had come as a considerable relief to many present, and during the subsequent discussion scarcely a word was uttered about what sort of aid and comfort should be given to the Conservatives. No controversial proposals were to be brought forward in the short

[1] *The Times*, 28th July 1886.
[2] *The Times*, 6th August 1886. *Annual Register*, 1886, p. 257.

forthcoming session, hence the need for formulating tactics just did not arise.

Under different circumstances Gladstonian taunts about evading the issues might well have wrought some havoc. As it was they fell quite flat. Any new government had to be allowed to find its feet and come to grips with the nature of the situation. So ran the Unionist argument and, despite the criticisms Unionists had themselves levelled against Gladstone for delay earlier that year, the general public response was charitable. Openings for a Gladstonian onslaught were therefore slight and Salisbury looked like getting the benefit of numerous doubts from those keen for change. Not that Unionism was altogether free from immediate inconvenience. Chamberlain in particular was under constant pressure, and the first of several severe embarrassments destined to rush in upon him that autumn arose over the East Birmingham by-election, caused by Matthews' appointment as Home Secretary.[1] At the general election the Conservatives had demanded and received the right to contest the seat with Chamberlain's blessing against the retiring member, Alderman Cook, whose adherence to Gladstone put him at odds with the controlling interest in the local Liberal caucus. Matthews had won by a narrow majority, owing to the scrappy nature of Radical Unionist support, and the possibility of a second contest with the political balance so delicately poised sent shivers down the backs of the Highbury party.[2] Things at one time looked very awkward, for Cook thought fit to announce he would be standing again. At the general election the support given him by the Rev. R. W. Dale,[3] the city's prime advocate of Home Rule with the Irish members retained at Westminster and the man to whom Chamberlain owed most in the Home Rule crisis, and the weighty approving authority of the *Birmingham Daily Post* had been blurred through their wide advocacy of the Unionist cause elsewhere. Now there might be a bald exposure of Unionist rifts. Cook adopted what was then Chamberlain's ostensible Irish Policy—an Irish parliament subordinate to that of the United Kingdom, the retention of the Irish members at Westminster, and opposition to the Land Bill—and thus placed him in a position of acute discomfort. Though they were later to admit the East Division to be Radical at heart, the Conservatives' immediate concern was to secure the safe return of a Minister on the '*beati possidentes*' rule. Chamberlain having been as good as his word, the National Radical Union had joined the Liberal Unionist Association on the very day of his announcement at Devonshire

---

[1] Henry Matthews (later Lord Llandaff), 1826–1913.

[2] Highbury was Joseph Chamberlain's house in the southern suburbs of Birmingham.

[3] For the Rev. R. W. Dale, see Chapter II, p. 70 note 2.

House.[1] About the same time Gladstone told Harcourt that Chamberlain's acts, not words, were the real test of his desire for compromise.[2] He never said a truer thing. The link at the national level with the Whig Unionists showed which way the wind was blowing, and it blew harder in the same direction when Churchill wrote to Chamberlain on 9th August. The latter's plight can be summed up well by the description given long before of a dissident figure in another sphere: 'Mr. Wesley, like a strong and skilful rower looked one way while every stroke of his oar took him in the opposite direction.'[3] Present tactics dictated the strokes of Chamberlain's oar and his nostalgic looks made no difference. The noble lord's letter sounded a forceful note: 'The re-election of Matthews is *almost vital* to me and I feel sure that if other things are equal you will stretch a point in my favour.'[4] Not content with this plea for an act of grace, he sent again the same day, using the vanity of his friend as a weapon against the doctrinal chaos that friend had done so much to engender:

> I really feel rather guilty of having unintentionally added to your difficulties, but in all these cases the bold and frank course is generally the safest. Surely, Schnadhorst . . . Kitson and Co. have delivered themselves into your hands by their defiant and impertinent manifesto, published in this morning's papers? I don't think you can silently put up with that. Besides your joining the Liberal Unionist Association along with Collings has attracted naturally much remark, and will not such action be rather incongruous with the negative attitude in the East Birmingham contest? This much arises clear and plain out of all that is doubtful and dark in Birmingham politics. If Matthews wins the credit goes to you, it is your victory; if he loses, it is Schnadhorst's victory and a pretty hulloo balloo they will raise.[5]

This prodded him into throwing his full weight against Cook, whom he outmanoeuvred by having brother Arthur Chamberlain publish a letter in the local press. In it the differences between the Chamberlain and Cook views on a 'subordinate parliament' were quite effectively explained, though another more solid factor simultaneously helped to secure Matthews an unopposed return. Gladstonian canvassing figures showed a Unionist victory certain, and *The Times* was not slow to stress the fact.[6] It looked as though the

---

[1] *The Times*, 5th August 1886.

[2] A. G. Gardiner, *Life of Sir William Harcourt, 1827–1904*, Vol. II, pp. 4–5.

[3] B. Gregory, *Sidelights on Conflicts in Methodism*, p. 54.

[4] Churchill to Chamberlain, 9th August 1886. First letter, Chamberlain Papers, JC5/14/21.

[5] Churchill to Chamberlain, 9th August 1886. Second letter, Chamberlain Papers, JC5/14/22. Sir James Kitson was prominent in the N.L.F. and the leading Gladstonian Liberal in Leeds.

[6] *The Times*, 12th August 1886.

Chamberlain pull outweighed the squeamishness of Dale, Bunce (Editor of the *Birmingham Daily Post*) and a goodly proportion of the Radical Unionist members of the Birmingham Liberal Association. Perhaps the local leader was going to find that, as for Gladstone in the national field, most difficulty was coming from 'officers' rather than 'men'. Nevertheless, success in politics often depends not simply upon doing the right thing, but on doing it at the right time. The unopposed return came too late to prevent a quickening of bad feeling between the two wings of Unionism. Conservatives felt their allies had been grudging in political aid, none too sure in their adherence to national agreements, and hopelessly unsound, if not completely at sea, on the Home Rule issue in failing to face the Irish Nationalists with an absolute negative.[1] On Chamberlain's own admission, as late as the summer of 1887, 'Many of the rank and file among the Unionists were uneasy and anxious to know what were really the points of difference' between themselves and the Gladstonians.[2] In August 1886 their unease and anxiety can only have been as great, or even greater. Addressing his constituents at this time Matthews showed himself especially keen to allay these fears.[3] Apparently Gladstone had assured one of his numerous correspondents that it was an 'open question' whether, if 'this folly' were to persist, 'the thing' might not 'in the end contribute to repeal'.[4] The 'folly' was, of course, Unionism and the aim of the letter a heightening of Liberal and Radical Unionism 'unease and anxiety' and the creation of alarm among recent abstainers. The 'old parliamentary hand' was evidently up to his tricks and had to be exposed. Matthews had struck a shrewd blow for all Unionists by speaking out and Chamberlain had good reason to be grateful.

In their 'defiant and impertinent manifesto' Messrs Kitson and Schnadhorst, along with the other members of the Emergency Committee of the National Liberal Federation, admitted that 'the result of the election had not realised the expectations of those who hoped that the country would recognise the necessity of a change in the relations of England and Ireland'. They could hardly have done any other. But the initial note of humility soon gave way to bold claims and self-justification. The future, they claimed, was most promising. Gladstone had received the continued support of the 'vast majority' of the Liberal vote in Britain and the dissidents favouring half measures for Ireland constituted the smallest party in the House of Commons. Only when the Irish question was settled could

---

[1] Hurst, *Joseph Chamberlain and West Midland Politics, 1886–95*, p. 39.
[2] Chamberlain to W. H. Smith, 12th August 1887. Hambledon Papers.
[3] *Annual Register*, 1886, p. 258.
[4] *Ibid.*

the Liberal party continue with its 'ordinary work' and so 'the pretensions of the dissentient minority to impose their views on the majority' could not be defended or accepted. An all-out effort would therefore be made to win back dissentients and abstainers alike.[1] All this afforded the Liberal and Radical Unionists scant comfort indeed. Here was no veiled peace offer but the trumpets of war, blown with a noisy provocation. Yet it could be seen as making a din to keep flagging spirits in the Gladstonian camp up to the mark of initial enthusiasm. Just how difficult it was for N.L.F. people to press forward at that juncture, whatever the internal strains events like the East Birmingham by-election set up among Unionists, can easily be seen from the speech made by Salisbury at the Lord Mayor of London's customary dinner, where, as the new prime minister he was able to elucidate his position and intentions.[2] The soundness of his arguments was almost beside the point. What really mattered was the type of emotionalism with which they were charged. Before sympathy with the Irish Nationalist underdog had had time to reach serious proportions the appeal he made on 18th August was bound to go down to some effect with large sections of all classes of the British public. He played on the fact that Unionism had drawn its electoral support from a full social spectrum, claiming that far from contemporary politics being a matter of the 'classes' against the 'masses', differences of opinion were largely based on regional variations. Passing rapidly over his favourite topic of foreign affairs, he turned to the Irish question and pronounced the government's first duty to be 'freeing the loyal people of Ireland from the constraint that is exercised upon them'. An independent government for Ireland was out of the question. The whole concept had been rejected in an 'emphatic' and 'unequivocal' manner by the only relevant tribunal—the electorate of the United Kingdom. Patriotism was the central theme of this keynote speech and included a variation on the underdog idea well calculated to have a wide appeal—that of sympathy for the fellow countryman in distress, oppressed by a 'foreign' and 'disloyal' element within our very own frontiers. Radical Unionists and recent abstainers could not lightly remain deaf to it.'[3]

The next day, very soon after parliament had assembled, Granville in the Lords and Gladstone in the Commons called upon the government to announce their Irish policies. A short message from the Queen had only contained a statement to the effect that the Commons would be called upon to vote the estimates previously presented by the defunct Gladstone Ministry. Irish, imperial and foreign affairs had all suffered an identical neglect. The G.O.M. bore his defeat

[1] *The Times*, 18th August 1886.
[2] *The Times*, 19th August 1886.   [3] *Ibid.*

well. His speech on this occasion showed the full distinction of statesmanship besides the carping self-righteousness of the experienced
partisan. Along with sincere advice about the need to produce some
solution to current Irish difficulties before the winter hardship renewed agrarian agitation and made likely a 'No Rent' manifesto
went a jibe about coercion. If special measures were not necessary
now, what had been the point of the Conservatives' request for them
eight months before? The government was to be congratulated for
not planning an immediate coercion move, but the abandonment of
repression must mean the Home Rule cause was getting nearer to
success.[1] Gladstone baulked became Gladstone the 'handiest' of
'parliamentary hands'. A new Leader of the House like Churchill
might easily have mismanaged the situation by becoming too heated
in reply. Happily for the government nothing of the kind occurred.
As one authority put it: 'He managed to be discreet without dulness
and aggressive without bitterness.'[2]

Official policy appeared at once constructive and non-committal.
Land, public order and local government were to be treated separately as part of the bid to get away from the Gladstonian concept of
Ireland as a distinct national entity. Nobody could justly dismiss the
plan as mere negation. The working of the existing land legislation
was to be enquired into by a Royal Commission with terms of reference designed to produce recommendations for its extension and
improvement. Another such Commission was to be used for

[1] Hansard, Vol. CCCIX, Cols. 1044–60. Despite the promise of and the actual
letting off of numerous parliamentary fireworks, one Liberal ex-minister found the
new session 'a wearying round of duty to constituency and constituents'. He was
Hugh C. E. Childers (1827–96), newly elected M.P. for South Edinburgh and recently Home Secretary in the third Gladstone ministry. See Lt.-Col. S. Childers,
The Life and Correspondence of the Rt. Hon. H. C. E. Childers, p. 267. Perhaps he
was bored waiting for the fulfilment of Herbert Gladstone's prophecy: 'there is
reasonable expectation that both Lord Hartington and Mr Goschen will come
round to Mr Gladstone's views and Mr Chamberlain . . . could not consistently
oppose it'. *Quarterly Review*, July–September 1886, p. 277. Or, as some unkindly
pointed out, Childers was now in receipt of a pension of £2,000 per annum and
might have felt his career was at its close. *Quarterly Review*, October–December
1886, p. 548. As a zealous Home Ruler he might, of course, have been inwardly
alarmed by the speech of Patrick Ford, as reported in the *Irish World* on 22nd
May 1886, in which Mr Gladstone's Home Rule Bill was described as certain to
originate 'strong separatist feelings in Ireland'.

[2] *Annual Register*, 1886, p. 263. When Churchill resigned Bright wrote in his
diary: 'that Churchill should have been leader is an astounding fact'. *Bright's
Diaries, op. cit.*, p. 548. On 24th September 1886 Churchill wrote to Sir A. Borth-
wick, proprietor of the *Morning Post*, Conservative M.P. for South Kensington
and later Lord Glenesk: 'The party is a splendid one; such materials Dizzy never
had to work with. With luck, constitutional principles ought now to hold their
own for many years.' R. Lucas, *Lord Glenesk and the Morning Post*, p. 314.

examining ways and means of making the most of Ireland's economic resources. To cope with disorders in the disturbed portions of Connaught and Munster, Sir Redvers Buller had been entrusted with a special mission of pacification. He was to be directly responsible to the Chief Secretary. Over local government 'equality, similarity, and simultaneity' were the fundamental aims. Definite proposals for the whole United Kingdom were promised as a means of setting up 'a genuinely popular system of local government'.[1] However derisive the reception given the programme by the Irish Nationalists, Liberal and Radical Unionists were relatively well satisfied. All the numerous amendments to the Address suffered rejection by majorities varying from seventy-five up to a hundred and twenty-five and twelve days of haggling brought the opposition few tactical or moral advantages. Parnell's own amendment, relating to heavy fall in Irish agricultural prices and the likelihood of numerous evictions and social disorder was defeated by three hundred and four to a hundred and eighty-one, with forty-six Liberal and Radical Unionists among the majority. Chamberlain spoke out strongly against Parnell because acceptance of his amendment would have been tantamount to throwing over the government. But although he declared himself ready to await the development of Salisbury's policy, he was most uneasy about the prospects in store for him and the Radical Unionists generally if affairs in Ireland did get out of hand and coercion became necessary for the maintenance of law and order. While nothing happened before the session was prorogued by commission on 25th September to suggest any widespread Liberal and Radical Unionist recantation, considerable heart searchings had been occasioned by Parnell's Tenant Relief Bill, introduced on the 10th and given a second reading debate on the 20th and 21st. Only thirty-one Liberal Unionists voted with the Conservatives to defeat it, and one, J. W. Barclay, the member for Forfarshire even lent his support to the Gladstonians and Parnellites.[2]

It was not as though much resentment was felt against Churchill

---

[1] Full announcements as to government policy were made by Salisbury in the House of Lords (Hansard, Vol. CCCVIII, Cols. 55–70) and Churchill in the House of Commons (Hansard, Vol. CCCVIII, Cols. 113–33. The Queen's Speech appears in Hansard, Vol. CCCVIII, Cols. 20–1. A full list of business tackled in this short session appears in H. W. Lucy, *A Diary of the Salisbury Parliament, 1886–92* on p. 7.

Sir Redvers Buller (1839–1908) had entered the army in 1858 and served in the Chinese war of 1860, the Red River expedition, the Ashanti and Kaffir wars, the Zulu war (in which he won the V.C.), the Egyptian war and the Sudan expedition. Later he was to be in command at Aldershot and in Natal. He led the forces which relieved Ladysmith.

[2] Chamberlain abstained. See J. L. Garvin, *The Life of Joseph Chamberlain*, Vol. II, pp. 268–9, for two letters from Chamberlain to Hartington, on the 7th and 9th September 1886, explaining the former's attitude to Parnell's Bill. Garvin

for conceding the time for a Bill dangerous to their party's solidarity without as much as a word to Hartington or Chamberlain.[1] As was made perfectly clear at the time, the decision was a tactical move designed to minimise obstruction on the estimates and all Unionists could see only advantages springing from that. The actual contents of the proposal provoked the real trouble. Besides having been shown in draft to the Gladstonian leadership and approved of in principle by the G.O.M. himself, they undoubtedly went some way towards tackling a problem no progressive could conscientiously ignore, whatever his position on Home Rule. Their kernel was the notion that 'the land court should have power to suspend eviction proceedings on payment of half the rent'.[2] According to C. C. O'Brien, the defeat of the Bill did not prevent it from serving a useful purpose—that of declaring an emergency.[3] This Chamberlain and company were only too quick to recognise—hence the sharpness of their reaction. That many of the clauses were badly drafted, that the Gladstonians were not very enthusiastic in their support and that Gladstone disapproved altogether of some items was no real comfort. Before its full contents were known, Chamberlain had, on 7th September, warned Hartington that he would find himself unable to oppose the measure if it contained provisions previously and publicly adopted by the Highbury camp.[4] Far better in that case, he thought, for the whole Radical Unionist group to stay away. Hartington and the Whig Unionists should do the same and deny Gladstone the pleasure of seeing a rift

merely printed extracts. The originals are Devonshire Papers, 340. 2042 and 340. 2043.

J. W. Barclay had attempted to bring down the first Salisbury ministry in January 1886 by proposing the Irish system of the 'Three F's' set up by the second Irish Land Act be introduced into Britain. Though Hartington voted for the Conservatives the move attracted little notice and the rôle of executioner was in fact left to Jesse Collings, who moved the fatal 'Three Acres and a Cow' amendment to the Address. Goschen's biographer remarks that afterwards Barclay became 'a steady member of the Liberal Unionist party'. A. D. Elliot, *Life of Lord Goschen, 1831–1907*, Vol. II, p. 12. Maybe he did, but he had a few flings first, of which the vote noted above was one. It was not the last. See Chapter VI, p. 271, note 4. Other Liberal Unionists were far from happy. Peter Rylands, the Radical Unionist M.P. for Burnley had been ill and W. S. Caine, the Radical Unionist M.P. for Barrow-in-Furness and Liberal Unionist whip wrote to him as follows: 'There is nothing either to bring you up or to pair you for. Parnell's Bill is the only thing and we don't intend to bring our men up for it. Chamberlain couldn't vote for it, and Hartington probably will; so we let everybody do as he likes as the Government are quite safe without us.' W. S. Caine to P. Rylands, 10th September 1886. L. G. Rylands (Editor), *Correspondence and Speeches of Peter Rylands, M.P.*, Vol. II, p. 372.

[1] See Hurst, 'Joseph Chamberlain, the Conservatives and the Succession to John Bright, 1886–89', *Historical Journal*, 1964, p. 75.

[2] C. C. O'Brien, *Parnell and his Party, 1880–90*, p. 201.   [3] *Ibid.*

[4] Chamberlain to Hartington, Devonshire Papers, 340. 2042.

in the party's ranks he would certainly try to exploit at the earliest opportunity. The government would win anyway and had, after all, proceeded without consultation. Returning to the point two days later, he tried to have his cake and eat it. After inveighing against the folly of Liberal and Radical Unionists responding to the challenge in different ways, he was extremely anxious the government should not give an iota of ground to Parnell, otherwise the Irish Catholic masses would never be weaned away from belief in the efficacy of agitation. Apparently he had come round to the opinion that, apart from the exigencies of the Irish question, there was a much bigger issue involved, altogether separate from the actual merits and demerits of the Bill. Abstention with the government sure to win was to him a heaven-sent way out of his dilemma. The general predicament of Liberal and Radical Unionism had been brought home to him, not only by the current situation in the House of Commons, but by what his Birmingham henchmen were pouring into his ears. Powell Williams[1] had been the latest of these to pronounce and the effects can be seen in what he told Hartington two days later

'Our great difficulty,' he complained, 'is that in order to preserve the Union we are forced to keep the Tory government in power; that every time we vote with them we give a shock to the ordinary Liberal politicians outside, and, if we do it too often, we shall be completely identified with the Tories and shall lose all chance of recovering the lead of the Liberal party. Our real policy is never to vote with the Tories unless they are in danger and to vote against them whenever we can safely do so. This policy would be the best for them as well as for us, for if we lose our hold on Liberal opinion we can bring them no strength on critical occasions. The result of any other course will be that what I may call your section will gravitate to the Tories and be absorbed by them, while mine will make their peace with the Gladstonians'.[2]

By this time Hartington had decided to vote with the government, despite what his lieutenant termed 'the impolicy of such a course'.[3] The actual provisions of Parnell's Bill had turned out far less moderate than he had originally expected them to be. Nevertheless, unlike Chamberlain, he attempted to follow a constructive and progressive path, urging Salisbury on 10th September to adopt such parts of the Bill as the Irish administrators thought desirable.[4] Pride was not the 'forte' with him that it was with 'our Joe'. Nasty though the whole affair was for Radical Unionists, their leader cannot be acquitted of

[1] Radical Liberal Unionist M.P. for Birmingham South and a great organiser for Chamberlain's pet schemes, great and small alike.
[2] Chamberlain to Hartington, 9th September 1886. Devonshire Papers, 340. 2043.
[3] *Ibid.*
[4] Hartington to Salisbury, 10th September 1886. Salisbury Papers.

all blame over it. His fault here was in wanting to fight too many battles at once. The keen sense of priorities, which had served him and was to serve him so well, had temporarily become somewhat numbed. Parnell was in a strongly entrenched position with the Irish peasantry already and Chamberlain exaggerated the effect of showing Parnell any goodwill. In any case, amelioration might come from agitation, but, if thoroughgoing, could undermine more than encourage such a mode of political warfare. Gladstone too was well placed with his followers, yet stood to lose support, if Chamberlain played his cards aright, much more easily than Parnell. Moreover, the British Liberal was infinitely the more potent and dangerous enemy. His support could expand at the Unionists' expense in ways the Irish Nationalist's could not. The first priority therefore should have been his containment prior to an onslaught and the course proposed by Hartington was well-chosen for these purposes. He found an important ally in the chief secretary, Hicks Beach, but failed to rope in either Churchill or Matthews.[1] Salisbury was able therefore to overrule a lone subordinate and take a purely negative line. That he failed to fall in with Hartington does not, however, exonerate 'Our Joe' from having indulged in some rather sloppy tactical thinking. Perhaps the profound dislike he felt for Parnell had confused his mind.

One of the disadvantages of foresight in a statesman is proneness to suppose a given series of events will unfold more quickly than in fact it does. Chamberlain often fell victim to this in the course of his public life and not unnaturally also tended to regard his lifeline— Birmingham and the west midland fiefs—as though it was the be all and end all of everything. Seeing the strategy Gladstone was already trying to adopt and being well appraised of the dangers abounding in his home base, he overestimated the fluidity of politics at the time Parnell's Bill was before the House of Commons. The 'old parliamentary hand' was suffering under no such delusion. Like the Russian Tsar before him he was relying on the devilish operations Général Février had in store. Immediately after speaking on Parnell's amendment to the Address he had published a pamphlet on the Irish issue divided, like the Irish people, into two main parts.[2] The first dealt with 'The History of an Idea' and the second with 'Lessons of the Elections'. Without waiting to see public reactions he set out for a tour of Bavaria, confident he could be temporarily spared from the scene. The actual vote on Parnell's Bill, taken after his return, bore out the contention that things were quieter. Only two-hundred and

---

[1] Lady V. A. Hicks Beach, *Life of Sir Michael Hicks Beach* (*Earl St. Aldwyn*), Vol. I, p. 284. Sir W. S. Churchill, *Lord Randolph Churchill*, Vol. II, p. 219.
[2] W. E. Gladstone, *The Irish Question*.

sixty-six Conservatives voted against and a hundred and twenty-two Gladstonian Liberals for it. Even the Irish Nationalists had a few absentees. In these circumstances, even allowing for Radical Unionist abstention and revolt, the low Liberal and Radical Unionist vote on the government side falls into a better perspective. Things were not as bad for the dissentients as Chamberlain supposed and nothing had happened by the end of the session to suggest Barclay's little fling was going to be widely emulated in or out of parliament. The paramount mood of the Gladstone pamphlet was one of reasoned appeal and the tactic one of *Reculer pour mieux sauter*.

Part one was something of an apologia spliced with a strong element of certitude. First he maintained his 'language and conduct', 'governed by uniformity of principle', had 'followed the several stages by which the great question of autonomy for Ireland' had been brought 'to a state of ripeness for practical legislation'. Then he listed the three vital conditions 'under which alone he considered Home Rule possible'. 'Hope that Parliament could serve as a passable legislative instrument for Ireland' had to be at an end. The plan had to be 'the unequivocal and constitutional demand of the Irish members' and 'unaccompanied by any danger to the unity and security of the empire'. And there had to be 'the possibility of dealing with Scotland in a similar way in circumstances of equal or equally clear desires'. Turning to the charge of having 'sprung' Home Rule upon both the Liberal leadership and party, made against him by numerous Liberal and Radical Unionist spokesmen, he argued there was no duty incumbent upon any Minister to reveal every idea in his mind, even to Cabinet colleagues. 'What is true,' he conceded, 'is that I had not publicly, as in principle, condemned it, and also that I had mentally considered it.' Finally, he sought to prove how when the belief in the policy had first come to him it had not been 'the unequivocal demand of Ireland' and had lacked precise definition; how until the foundation of Isaac Butt's movement the choice had been one between repeal and removal of grievances; and how the pressure for constitutional change had mounted to the level of 1885 when he had singled out the Irish question as 'ripe for legislation' and likely to push every other issue into the background for some time to come.[1]

In part two a cold douche of frankness was followed by a honeyed attempt to minimise differences between Gladstonian Rome and Liberal Unionist Canterbury. Although admitting the dissentients had carried away what he estimated as two-sevenths of the Liberal party, Gladstone attempted to delineate this in more striking terms by adding that, whereas five-sixths of his peers had defected, not more than one in twenty of Liberal working men had followed suit.

[1] *Ibid.*, Part One.

Nor was that all, for three of the four national regions of the United Kingdom had embraced the Home Rule cause, leaving only England against. The salvo delivered, he proceeded to try and prove that a continuance of the split was rather pointless. The Liberal and Radical Unionists were already 'pledged to immediate and large concession; many of them on such a scale that they give to their idea the name of Home Rule, declaring themselves favourable to its principle, and only opposed to the awkward and perverse manner in which it was handled by the late Administration'. The Nationalist cause could 'hardly fail to receive more life and more propulsion from the hands of those who have been its successful opponents in one of its particular forms'. Here was a bold attempt to get round the Chamberlain section at the very least. The oblique reference to the ill-effects of a repressive policy showed the G.O.M.'s cunning had not dropped in quality, but his next move outshone all his previous points. As the Land Bill had, he was sure, been the most important single cause of his defeat, it was only right and proper for him 'explicitly to acknowledge that the sentence' which had 'gone forth for the severance of the two measures is irresistible, and that the twinship' which had 'been disastrous to the hopes of Ireland', existed no longer. 'At the same time, the partnership between enemies of Home Rule and enemies of the Land Bill', which had 'brought about this result' would now, he hoped, 'be dissolved.'[1] As an essay in apologetics the pamphlet was open to serious challenge, as a political *ballon d'essai* it fell flat. The bad points hindered rather than helped and the good ones had either been used before or, as over the Land Bill, guessed at by all but the boneheaded. His general political behaviour at this time proved Gladstone appreciated the season was one for marking time. Why then he published anything is not easy to understand, unless the need to jettison the Land Bill by a pronouncement *ex cathedra* struck him as something demanding immediate implementation. Getting it out of the way in a quiet interval would facilitate any reunion moves which might be made if the situation in Ireland deteriorated, and he was certain this was inevitable.

Salisbury was a singularly good judge of matters relating to power, provided, of course, his information was complete and accurate. Perhaps because the conduct of foreign affairs had made him tend to concentrate unduly upon the demands of the moment, or perhaps because of a strong preference for making the minimum of change when events permitted, he used the calm of August and September to assert the authority of Conservatism. Knowing full well the moderate majority in the Liberal Unionist party would not desert him were he to reject their counsels over Parnell's Bill, he had spurned a constructive

[1] *Ibid.*, Part Two.

57

rôle pending the reports of his Royal Commissions and order restorer. The possibility that circumstances might outstrip their pace did not seem to lose him the sleep Chamberlain and even Hartington were missing all too regularly. Progressive forces like Churchill and to some extent Hicks Beach within the Cabinet, with the help of dissentient Liberalism outside, had secured a promise of 'jam tomorrow' on Ireland and Britain, but in that order. And what was promised for the latter was by no means extensive. Chamberlain was bound to be on tenterhooks about the future for self-interested and for altruistic reasons. Political survival and the numerous reform causes close to his heart naturally dictated a course of endless prodding from him and the Radical Unionist group. Pressure from a very influential right wing and the numerous conservative causes he had at heart produced a strong sales resistance in the prime minister.

The great counter-attack whereby Chamberlain built for himself the renewed chance of a political career on a firm basis was in its most incipient stages at the end of September 1886. There is then a danger of overestimating the influence he was then able to bring to bear and of ante-dating the closer relationship between the Cabinet and Radical Unionism, unless this is borne constantly in mind. Immediately after the split he had felt 'it was the duty of the Liberal Unionist leaders in the first place to exhaust every possibility of reconciliation, and to satisfy themselves that no occasions could or would be made by the Gladstonian leaders which would remove the objections to Mr Gladstone's Home Rule Bills'.[1] Now it had become a question of substituting the word 'Bill' for 'Bills', after the publication of Gladstone's pamphlet, but his position was otherwise the same. Nothing had so far taken place to offer any real prospect of widespread domestic reform and, as yet, the influence Churchill could wield in Cabinet for creating it remained unknown. The prime minister, prompted by his Chief Whip, Akers-Douglas, and his Chief Agent, Captain Middleton, tended to doubt the reality of Chamberlain's power and therefore to discount him then and for the future.[2] However, Lord Randolph was already bandying his name about in Cabinet in much the same way as mothers threaten children with the bogey man to ensure good behaviour. So much so that, before long, some indulged in wild overestimations and assumed him all-powerful over Churchill, if not in the country as a whole.[3] In fact there was rarely, if ever, any truly slavish consultation by the latter, and the

[1] J. Chamberlain, *A Political Memoir, 1880–92*, C. H. D. Howard (Editor), p. 277.

[2] Hurst, *Historical Journal, 1964*, p. 74.

[3] Viscount Chilston, *Chief Whip*, p. 100. Churchill to Chamberlain, 24th December 1886. Chamberlain Papers, JC5/14/27. J. L. Garvin, *Joseph Chamberlain*, Vol. II, p. 275.

business of Parnell's Bill shows that sometimes there was no inter-communication whatever. This is not to say that the influence of the one man over the other was not considerable; after all, it was to a large extent invited. But being so, it was subject, with a man of Churchill's temperament, to rejection without notice. Perhaps the best indication of the true nature of the relationship is given by a public political indiscretion committed at Dartford by Churchill soon after the Parnell debate. It was received in silent horror by most colleagues, who saw there the baneful influence of 'Birmingham', yet it was in fact embarked upon independently of his mentor. The two had not been in regular communication just then ('I have not troubled you with letters lately, as I have been really hustled, and I knew you would write to me if you were dissatisfied with anything') and Churchill had not pressed for any 'good talk' before going off to what he airily termed 'a damned political demonstration in Kent'.[1] But, while not 'made' with 'Birmingham' wares, he was in a way the precursor of all out anti-Gladstonian counter-attack politics, taking what steps he thought necessary for Unionist popularity from the Chamberlain armoury, while retaining some initiative for the Conservatives even in a way distasteful to them.

Often in history important forces lay immobilised for want of a release point. When Churchill set off for his 'damned political demonstration in Kent' the deep and widespread desire for domestic reform was in almost that position. There was little or no immediate force of circumstances operating to oblige Salisbury to fill the government shop with a fair range of reformist goods. In some respects, because of the smallness of their numbers, the Radical Unionists could be discounted so far as parliament was concerned and the charge that they were mere window dressing to give the Unionist alliance a bogus air of reforming respectability seemed not altogether without substance. Chamberlain and Churchill both realised the potentially explosive nature of such a situation and the latter's bid to obviate it was a bold and farsighted gamble. On 2nd October at Dartford the crowds heard the crystal clear message of reforming Unionism. Besides Ireland, parliamentary procedure and retrenchment, Lord Randolph discussed and outlined reforms concerned with freehold plots and allotments of land for the agricultural labourer, the law of tithe, land transfer problems, the local government question and local taxation.[2] Quite a budget, even for a chancellor of the exchequer, and

---

[1] Churchill to Chamberlain, 23rd September 1886. Chamberlain Papers, JC5/14/24. Churchill coupled to his programme of domestic reform one of generosity abroad. The Balkan peoples should, he maintained, receive their freedom. R. C. K. Ensor, *England, 1870–1914*, p. 173.

[2] Churchill, *op. cit.*, Vol. II, pp. 164–5.

one calculated to put Chamberlain and his men in fine fettle. Five days later the Radical Unionist leader felt able to board ship for a visit to Greece and Turkey that was to keep him away until 13th December with a 'song in his heart'. Churchill had tried to whistle up the wind all the Unionist reformers had needed so badly and Chamberlain was confident he would succeed. The precise nature of what the former had in mind to do had certainly been communicated to his friend, very probably quite some time before, in view of their lack of recent interchange of letters and failure to hold frequent têtes-à-têtes. The day before Dartford, Chamberlain was fairly bubbling over with high spirits during a visit to Dilke, who recorded:

> Chamberlain called and gave me an interesting picture of the political state. He seemed to think that he could keep Mr Gladstone out for life, and was persuaded that Randolph would give him all he wanted and leave Hartington and Salisbury in the lurch. Randolph had promised him to have an anti-Jingo foreign policy, leaving Turkey to her fate, and to pacify Ireland with the National Councils scheme, modified into two Councils, or into Provincial Councils, to suit Ulster; and Churchill had also promised him procedure reform—that is, a sharper closure—and a three-acres-and-a-cow policy for England.[1]

On the very day of Dartford the *Morning Post* sported an article 'representing Churchill's democratic views'.[2] All seemed set fair at home, whatever was going to happen on the sea.

Chamberlain was not alone in taking things easy. Quite unperturbed by Chaplin's protest against his closure project, Churchill took a leaf out of Gladstone's book and hastened to Germany for three weeks. On his return the first public gathering requiring his presence was the Bradford conference of his old friends the National Union of Conservative Associations. To them, on 26th October, he made no fewer than three separate speeches.[3] The first was a eulogy of the Liberal Unionists.

> So long as we continue to receive from the Liberal Unionists that independent, but still at the same time very loyal support, which they gave us in the last session of Parliament, so long, I submit to you, they have a right to the same support, and even to more support than that which they obtained from us in the last election.[4]

[1] S. Gwynn and G. M. Tuckwell, *The Life of the Rt. Hon. Sir Charles Dilke Bt., M.P.*, Vol. II, p. 265.

[2] *Morning Post*, 2nd October 1886.

[3] *The Times*, 27th October 1886.

Henry Chaplin (1841–1923) was Conservative M.P. for Sleaford and an ardent protectionist. In Salisbury's first ministry he had been Chancellor of the Duchy of Lancaster. In the second he became President of the Board of Agriculture in 1889. Eventually he was made a Viscount.

[4] *Ibid.*

After reiterating the Dartford line on foreign policy, he ladled out compliments to Jesse Collings and all he stood for, stuck to his latest pronouncements on the closure, painted a rosy picture of the state and prospects of Ireland and earnestly hoped that British 'constitutional principles' would achieve rapid popularity across the Irish Sea. Chaplin again protested against the closure proposal, but the noble lord remained undaunted. Chamberlain's camp could rest well-content over their Cabinet friend, but, three days before, the 'Plan of Campaign' had been publicly launched through an article in 'United Ireland'.[1] Hicks Beach's endeavours to stave off a new full scale agrarian agitation had failed. Undoubtedly the impossible behaviour of landlords of the Clanricarde ilk had contributed towards this outcome, but the really supreme motive power behind it was genuine and ubiquitous agricultural distress.[2] Prices had reached an alarmingly low level. Without a Coercion Act the government was going to be considerably hampered in facing the new turn of events, with one its British support stood to drop, or waver, or remonstrate. No coercion until the last possible minute was therefore dictated by practical needs at home whatever the individual preferences of Cabinet ministers. Chamberlain's holding operation looked like being threatened, but there was a chance the Irish peasants would overreach themselves and deprive the Gladstonians of any added advantage in the tactical struggle until such time as coercion was actually embarked upon by the government. Strong sections of the Gladstonians immediately experienced a nervous reaction to the latest developments in Ireland, yet for the most part maintained an outward calm. On 4th October five Irish deputations paid homage at Hawarden, one bringing an address from four hundred thousand Irish women and the rest bearing the freedoms of Clonmel, Cork, Limerick and Water-

[1] *United Ireland*, 23rd October 1886. C. C. O'Brien summed up the 'Plan': 'Tenants on each estate were "to consult together and decide by resolution on the amount of abatement (i.e. of rent) they will demand"; should that abatement be refused, the proferred rent was to be handed over to a managing committee elected by the tenants themselves and used for the benefit of the evicted. National League branches might cooperate in bringing the tenants on each estate together, and the league itself should guarantee the Estate Fund, but the actual struggle was to be carried out not by the league but by the tenants on each estate. This procedure would make it more difficult, under the Coercion Act, which was now foreseen, to suppress the league. At the same time it gave the new movement an unofficial character, which should be helpful to the leadership of the parliamentary party in its dealings with the liberals.' C. C. O'Brien, *op. cit.*, p. 202.

For further discussion of the 'Plan' see Sir J. O'Connor, *History of Ireland, 1798–1924*, Vol. II, pp. 123–5.

[2] Conditions on the estates of Lord Clanricarde are graphically described in W. S. Blunt, *The Land War in Ireland*, pp. 63–5. The last Marquess of Clanricarde, though a Liberal Unionist, was one of the least liberal landlords in Ireland. His name was a byword for bad treatment of tenants.

ford. In reply the G.O.M. praised the temperance and moderation of the Irish Home Rule movement—a move that can only be regarded as a hint as anxious as it was strong.[1] On the surface, however, the Gladstonian Liberal party throughout Britain usually took up a strongly militant attitude towards its opponents throughout the months of October and November, and most of December. At the Scottish Liberals' conference at Glasgow on 30th October and that of the National Liberal Federation at Leeds four days later, Home Rule and a thoroughgoing 'constructionist' programme received most enthusiastic endorsements.[2] The process continued hot and strong in Labouchère's and John Morley's speeches some weeks later,[3] and at another conference, held in Leicester, about the same time an encomium upon Home Rule was the sole topic for discussion.[4]

What conciliatory feelings there were tended to be expressed *sotto voce*, or in thick and almost opaque wrappings. Gladstone himself was awake to the dangers of a possible emotional backlash about the split, if the party continued to mark time and the consequences of defeat dampened the ardour among ambitious and impatient men. There was, moreover, a grave risk that hardship would lead to Irish Nationalism getting out of hand and nothing much would have to happen before the half-hearted began to raise a song and dance, perhaps in full view of the general public. Already, Rosebery and Fowler had expressed a vague dissatisfaction and such a thing could all too easily spread. Still, difficult though some aspects of the situation were, the Gladstonian party was holding together well and enjoyed a relatively easy relationship with the Irish in parliament. The same could not be said of the government and some of its allies. Embarrassments merely continued for the Liberal and Radical Unionists. They began in earnest for the government.

Chamberlain's absence in the eastern Mediterranean did not bring Birmingham politics to a standstill. When the annual municipal elections took place in November only four out of sixteen wards were contested, but, instead of following the general election pattern of Radical Unionist–Conservative cooperation, the parties tried to carry on as though the 'Hawarden Kite' had never flown. Liberal

[1] *The Times*, 5th October 1886.

[2] *The Times*, 1st November 1886, for the Scottish Liberal conference. See also P. W. Clayden, 'England under Coalition', pp. 136–7, *The Times*, 4th and 5th November 1886, for reports of and comments upon the National Liberal Federation conference at Leeds.

[3] Labouchère spoke at Manchester on 24th November 1886. *The Times*, 25th November 1886; Morley at Hawick on the 29th November and Edinburgh on 2nd December 1886. *The Times*, 30th November 1886 and 3rd December 1886.

[4] This conference was held on 25th November 1886. *The Times*, 26th November 1886.

faced Conservative in the traditional way and the latter won in two wards. In one because of the personal character of their candidate and in the other because of the Liberal split. Even where the Liberals held the seats, the Conservatives gained ground when their opponent was a Gladstonian. The pattern was clearly one of Conservative gain from the split. Substantial numbers of Liberal and Radical Unionists were either voting against their own Liberals of the Gladstonian sort, or staying at home in disgust. This certainly made for an easing of Conservative frustration in one way, yet there was always the danger that increased municipal representation would whet their parliamentary appetites. Chamberlain had also to be careful that more opposition councillors did not give Schnadhorst the opportunity of convincing Radical Unionists that their creed might be the Trojan horse for bringing reaction to the seats of power in the citadel of reform. Overall the situation within 'Joe's' base remained one of considerable tension.[1]

When a parliamentary seat fell vacant at Brighton a little later it was Hartington's turn to feel the pinch. Conservative and Liberal Unionist leaders generally had regretted Goschen's general election defeat at East Edinburgh and Brighton seemed to offer an excellent opportunity for bringing him back into the House of Commons. Goschen consented to stand on condition he could be a Liberal Unionist candidate and sit on the Liberal side of the chamber if elected. As the seat was previously held by a Conservative, the local Conservative Association insisted he should be a full-blown ministerialist. The Liberal Unionists being unable to win unaided and Goschen being unwilling to comply with the Conservatives' terms, the situation became one of stalemate. He therefore declined to stand and both Unionist sections then hopefully offered their backing to Trevelyan, only to find he too was difficult. In fact he turned them down flat, refusing to represent even the Liberal and Radical Unionists because of their divided attitude on the alternative to Gladstonian Home Rule.[2] The whole affair provided both Salisbury and Hartington with a minor headache at a busy time and consumed an amount of their attention out of all proportion to its inherent importance. Nevertheless, it was of an especially irritating nature for the latter, because nothing could have illustrated better the heterogeneous character of the Liberal Unionist party and tended to lower any respect felt for it at Hatfield more decisively. Little things often

---

[1] Hurst, *Joseph Chamberlain and West Midland Politics, 1886–95, passim.* For H. H. Fowler see Chapter II, p. 119, note 2.

[2] *Annual Register*, 1886, pp. 296–7. Goschen to Hartington, Autumn 1886. Devonshire Papers, 340. 2057. Goschen to Hartington, 5th November 1886. Devonshire Papers, 340. 2059.

have big effects. Proceedings at the party's conference early in December could hardly be said to have erased the impression the Brighton incident had made.[1]

Ironically enough, it was exactly at this time that a powerful dose of Liberal and Radical Unionist pressure might have had a crucial effect on the shape of government policy and the future career of Lord Randolph Churchill. Cabinet meetings from the beginning of November on had largely been consumed by a virtually lone battle waged by the chancellor of the exchequer to secure implementation of his 'Unauthorised' Dartford and Bradford Programme. By the beginning of December discord had reached some intensity and on the 8th Salisbury had assured the City of London Conservatives that their party was as Conservative as ever, claiming that the points on which it differed from its allies were in 'the background'.[2] A month before at the Guildhall the same sangfroid had been evident in his approach to the Irish question. 'Speculation in politics' should, he thought, be stopped among the Nationalist masses. What the Irish people needed was 'a steady course of honest government'. While not excluding legislation, he was convinced there should be as little of it as possible and such as was undertaken would best be tackled with the minimum of haste and 'with as much caution and prudence' as the government could 'command'.[3] Small wonder that Churchill's head soon became sore with a wall of such magnificent brick against which to bang his hot head. Speaking at Melksham on 15th December, Walter Long, President of the Local Government Board, revealed the amazing gulf between the Dartford–Bradford idea of local government reform and the plan the Cabinet majority had in its mind to propose. As described, the new country councils would be representative, but representative of 'all interests connected with the land'. In other words the aristocracy and gentry were to have built in advantages to prevent 'wanton extravagance with public money'. Wide the powers of the new bodies might be, but their use was to be hedged about with a generous helping of 'discretion'. Meanwhile 'the democracy' was to be soothed by the proliferation of allotments.[4] Measures like the arrest of some Irish Nationalist members and the seizure of rent paid to them instead of to the landlords attracted a good deal of attention away from this notable example of the Conservatives being as Conservative as ever. Its contents were not, none

[1] 7th December at Willis's Rooms, London. *The Times*, 8th December 1886.
[2] *The Times*, 9th December 1886.
[3] *The Times*, 10th November 1886.
[4] *Annual Register*, 1886, pp. 302–3. Walter Long (1854–1924) was Conservative M.P. for East Wilts and Parliamentary Secretary to the Local Government Board. Subsequently he became a contender for the Conservative leadership and was made a Viscount.

the less, lost on the Liberal and Radical Unionists. This was not just a matter for Chamberlain and the leftists. The whole party was in trouble. Compared with the earlier official announcements of government policy, Long's speech was literally reactionary. Hartington may not have been one of the world's leading thirsters after change, but this sort of thing would not do for him.

Out to luncheon at Dilke's on the 17th, Chamberlain really let himself go.[1] It had been the profoundest and most alarming disappointment for him to find things going so badly within the Unionist camp shortly after returning to this country. Long's speech had been the last straw. As almost always, his prime concern was domestic policy for Britain. The great arguments about foreign affairs which had taken up so much of Salisbury's public speeches and dragged in Churchill at a Cabinet level were well nigh nothing in his eyes compared with matters like local government reform. Nor did he mind coercion, except for the emotional upsets it would bring on in countless Liberals, irrespective of their alignment on Home Rule. So great was his fury about the local government proposal that he was positively anxious to defeat Salisbury on it, failing severe modifications 'to suit his policy'.[2] Churchill was not so lucky. His grouses ranged over almost the whole spectrum of government policy. And on procedure, local government, foreign policy and economy he was finding an almost complete absence of support. Only after his draft budget had been shown to the Cabinet on the 18th did the quarrel become concentrated on economy and this was to serve him ill when the climax of the trouble arrived. As a last desperate bid for his own way, he tried on the tack which had sometimes worked before—that of resignation.[3] Salisbury leapt at it and on the 23rd all the world knew he was out.

Back in October the Dartford speech had led Rosebery to assure one of his friends: 'Randolph will be out, or the Cabinet smashed up, before Christmas'.[4] He had been right with a mere two days to spare. Two issues have to be separated here—the personal and the policy aspects of the ensuing crisis. Salisbury was quite adamantly against a compromise with Churchill, but, as things turned out,

[1] Gwynn and Tuckwell, *op. cit.*, p. 265.
[2] *Ibid.*
[3] Ostensibly the Cabinet row was about the projected Service Estimates, but the world guessed, and rightly, that it had been more broadly based. A tentative compromise on Local Government, arrived at in November 1886, had been ruined through Hicks Beach—the Chief Secretary for Ireland—having opposed the Irish part of the plan. Salisbury to Cranbrook, 28th November 1886, gives details of what had been proposed. Cranbrook Papers, East Suffolk and Ipswich County Records, HA 43/L/T501/263, Box 13.
[4] R. R. James, *Lord Randolph Churchill*, p. 274.

perfectly prepared to modify his reactionary views to secure the blocking of a Home Rule victory. Most of the policy subsequently pursued by the government reeked of Dartford not of Melksham. Churchill's going may itself have been one of the reasons for this, but that was the limit of his effect on the frantic to'ing and fro'ing that ended in Hartington declining to replace Salisbury, or enter a coalition, or change his original position in any way, except to promise the Conservatives support even if Chamberlain defected. Goschen, as the new chancellor of the exchequer, was his New Year's present to the government and the government's to him was an assurance on policy intentions handed over through Goschen as an earnest of respectability. Before it was given Goschen declined to be handed over and anyway insisted upon being described as a Liberal Unionist. Salisbury had to swallow what a local Conservative Association had recently been able to refuse.[1]

Right-wing Conservative opinion had been dead against any sort of Hartington government, but the price paid for keeping an exclusive hold on office had meant evacuating the Melksham line. Churchill's resignation had given Hartington a lever he had previously lacked. The government had substantial Commons representation and could generally blackmail the Whig majority of the Liberal Unionist parliamentary party into giving them support by playing up the Home Rule threat. But no government can be run without competent Ministers and Hartington was able to provide a truly heavyweight replacement when its paramount Commons personality gave up office. He was, moreover, able to provide the replacement without inconvenience to himself. Though the undertakings on policy were given to Goschen, Hartington and his colleagues clearly needed them too. Merely staying out of the government and shunning coalescence with the Conservatives would not in itself be anything like enough to preserve Hartington's pull in Gladstonian, floating voter and Radical Unionist circles. To enter a relatively progressive coalition without Chamberlain would be considerably less dangerous than supporting a purely Conservative government wedded to Melkshamism. Being able to provide Goschen had provided a strong means for twisting Salisbury's arm. Then too the impotence of the Whigs in the face of Chamberlain's immediate reaction to Churchill

---

[1] Salisbury to Queen Victoria, 2nd January 1887. Letters of Queen Victoria, 3rd Series, Vol. I, p. 247. F. W. Hirst described Goschen's 'progress to Conservatism' as 'very rapid'. This is rather unfair as he had declined to serve under Gladstone since 1880 on the ground that he regarded the policies to be pursued as too progressive and made a great deal of fuss about the conditions upon which he would join the Salisbury ministry. One of his conditions was that he should be described as a Unionist not a Conservative. See Sir Wemyss Reid (Editor), *The Life of William Ewart Gladstone*, p. 711.

going—a bid for a reunion conference with the Gladstonians—was an added source of strength *vis-à-vis* the government. In the previous summer Hartington had refused to head a purely Whig Liberal Unionist or coalition administration for fear Chamberlain would gravitate back to Gladstone.[1] Now he had done so for the same reasons plus a convincing piece of evidence his fears were well-founded. Churchill's resignation made Salisbury need Hartington so much more. Could it not be said then that whereas Churchill forgot Goschen when playing up Salisbury, Salisbury forgot Hartington when playing up Churchill? The sacrificing of Churchill created the basic conditions enabling Chamberlain to regard life as a Radical Unionist as just about tolerable though he did not think so at the time and the Conservatives struggled long against the logic of events. But this is to jump too far ahead. Even Goschen's consent to take the Chancellorship of the Exchequer, given on 2nd January 1887, lies well on in the sequence of events the cumulative process of which created the ready response in important Gladstonian circles to Chamberlain's apparent zeal for Liberal reunion. Our main business is with these events and to them we must now go.

[1] B. Holland, *Life of the Duke of Devonshire, 1833–1908*, Vol. II, pp. 169–70.

II

IN WHICH LORD RANDOLPH CHURCHILL RESIGNS AND JOSEPH CHAMBERLAIN PUTS FORWARD A PROPOSAL

'Pride goeth before destruction and a haughty spirit before a
fall.' Proverbs xvi. 18.
'A word spoken in due season, how good is it.' Proverbs xv. 23.

ELEVEN days after Goschen accepted the Treasury the first of
three meetings, styled the 'Round Table Conference', took place
between Chamberlain and Trevelyan on the one hand and Harcourt,
Herschell and Morley on the other. The aim was to explore the
possibilities of Liberal reunion. No undisputed account exists of why
and how the effort ever came to be made and what the motives of the
participants and their backers really were. As things turned out
'roundness' proved an elusive quantity in all senses and most of the
evidence on this singularly complicated affair must be subjected to
searching analysis.

The split had hardly taken place before leaders on both sides were
expressing strong desires for reunion. Given the circumstances of
mid-1886 nothing could have come of them. It was far too early for
anyone on either side genuinely to reconsider the position on the
basic question dividing them. True remorse, frustration and doubt
were reserved for the future. Yet that future did not prove long in
coming, for in October Lord Rosebery followed up Gladstone's
virtual abandonment of Land Purchase with an appeal to Liberals
to give practical shape to the growing desire for conciliation.[1] This

---

[1] 19th October 1886, at Newcastle-upon-Tyne Liberal Club. He argued that the
high abstention rate at the recent general election indicated the country was
'asking for time to make up its mind'. The Marquess of Crewe, *Lord Rosebery*,

plea was not perhaps especially noteworthy, coming from one so notoriously addicted to polish rather than to spit, but there is no denying the significance of the moves made by other party leaders.

Non-radical Gladstonians, except for Spencer and the G.O.M. himself, tended to underestimate the differences between themselves and the Liberal Unionists. They interpreted their own willingness to compromise on Home Rule as the way to complete reconciliation. But even had this been justified, and it is doubtful whether it was,

Vol. I, pp. 280–1. Speaking at Manchester during that general election, Gladstone had singled out Rosebery as 'the man of the future'. *Ibid.*, p. 278. R. R. James, *Rosebery*, p. 194.

As early as 20th July 1886 Harcourt wrote to Chamberlain: 'Mr Gladstone . . . has expressed repeatedly a strong desire to take the course which would best conduce to the reunion of all sections of the party.' Harcourt to Chamberlain, 20th July 1886. Chamberlain Papers, JC5/38/10. Approaching Chamberlain on a personal note Harcourt went on to declare: 'The great majority of Liberal Unionists were and are nearly as hostile to your views as to those of Mr Gladstone.' But, in any case, '*after your migration*, he could not have accepted your alternative without altogether alienating the Parnell party, and to make a proposal which they could not accept was and always will be futile'. Here were words Harcourt would have done well to remember later on. *Ibid.* On 2nd August 1886 Gladstone sent his famous letter to Harcourt about deeds being the true test of Chamberlain's professions of goodwill. He added: 'Next to the Irish Question I desire to do everything for the reunion of the party, though with doubts whether this can be effected until Ireland is out of the way, and therefore with a disposition to mislike *prima facie* whatever may seem like a plot to gain time and unity to prolong our present embarrassments. As in the case of Ireland, so in the matter of reunion, I am above all things determined not to be personally an obstacle in the way of what is good.' A. G. Gardiner, *The Life of Sir William Harcourt, 1827–1904*, Vol. II, p. 5. Soon after making his speech Rosebery left for the East. Before going he sent Chamberlain a letter of goodwill. He had in fact called upon him while he was out intent upon wishing Chamberlain as nice a trip as he was hoping for himself. As Chamberlain left Britain early in October, so Rosebery probably wrote this letter before making his Newcastle speech. The two men had been exchanging views on foreign and internal affairs. Rosebery to Chamberlain. Undated, but October 1886, JC5/61/4. Another letter of goodwill from someone formerly fairly close to him reached Chamberlain before his departure. Guinness Rogers made a generous gesture. Although very unlike Rosebery and in no way a rival of Chamberlain's for leadership among Liberals (see J. W. Robertson Scott, *The Story of the Pall Mall Gazette*, p. 283) he was a man of no mean influence and on relations of 'perfect understanding' with the Rev. R. W. Dale. (See J. Guinness Rogers, *Autobiography*, p. 215.) Although expressing deep dissatisfaction with Gladstone—a dissatisfaction shared by numerous Radical nonconformists—over the 1885 election campaign, he stuck to the G.O.M. over Ireland, but hoped men wanting essentially the same things in domestic affairs would not long remain divided. Meanwhile nonconformists were being sacrificed. 'Lord Randolph Churchill seems ready to conciliate everybody but Dissenters. Well, we can wait till the storm has blown over.' Rev. J. Guinness Rogers to Chamberlain, 4th October 1886. Chamberlain Papers, JC6/42/I. The Rev. J. Guinness Rogers (1822–1911) was an eminent Congregationalist and Gladstonian Liberal in his sympathies. For Lord Herschell see p. 74, note 1.

they did not call the party tune. An admission of this was the central point of a letter from Harcourt to Spencer on 4th October.[1] It ran:

> ... I agree, however, seriously with Rosebery that it is highly desirable for the next two months we should abstain from any demonstration on Irish questions which might give colour to the belief that we were endeavouring to fan the flames. Of course, our party cannot be restrained from speaking their own mind, but I am clear that the ex-Cabinet Ministers ought not to lead in this matter.

All the more important then when an ex-Cabinet Minister, often to the fore on the Irish issue and undeniably a Radical, made a move in Chamberlain's direction. It was made by approaching Dale, whose little 'u' Unionism and powerful standing in Birmingham marked him as an obvious though none the less brilliant choice. The ex-Minister was Morley. He suggested some sort of meeting, preferably dinner, and seemed anxious to move systematically and fast. 'It is possible that some good and it is certain that no ill would result to the Commonwealth if we occasionally met in these trying times. If you come on Monday next, 25th, by any happy chance you would find your old confederate Schnadhorst here.'[2] Morley wrote on the 18th and a week was the least time he could in all politeness expect Dale to take over arranging a London visit.

It could be argued that, far from being a move towards Chamberlain, this was an attempt to lure away from him during his absence the man, who, apart from Bright, had done more than any other to preserve his local pre-eminence and political prospects. Schnadhorst happened to be not only Dale's 'old confederate', but Chamberlain's deadly enemy, and in an excellent position to know about the smouldering discontents among some of the Birmingham Liberals. Morley's later actions do not bear this out, and while it is possible that his motives changed, the balance of probabilities is against thinking so. Even assuming malice, Dale's character, the certainty of exposure and the strong disapproval of colleagues bent on peace must surely have acted as deterrents against indulging it?

Many had interpreted the statement on Land Purchase in Gladstone's pamphlet on the 'History of an Idea and Lessons of the Elections' as more than a simple abandonment of Land Purchase.[3] And

[1] Harcourt to Spencer, 4th October 1886. Spencer Papers.
[2] Morley to Dale, 18th October 1886. Dale Papers. R. W. Dale, D.D., LL.D. (1829–95) had been a Congregational minister in Birmingham since 1853. He was a fast friend of Chamberlain. For his part in helping secure Birmingham for Liberal Unionism, see Hurst. *op. cit., passim.*
[3] See Chapter I, pp. 55–57.

with justice, because after an acknowledgment that the Land Bill
had been the largest single factor in the defeat of his policy, he went
on: 'the sentence which has gone forth for the severance of the two
measures is irresistible, and . . . the twinship, which has been for the
time disastrous to the hopes of Ireland, exists no longer. At the same
time, the partnership between enemies of Home Rule and enemies
of the Land Bill, which has brought about this result, will now, we
may hope, be dissolved.' Clearly this, published at the end of August,
was at least an attempt to regain the support of some Radical
Unionists and perhaps something by way of a peace feeler. Though
if it was, peace was to be on his terms, as the original Land Bill had
been abandoned before the crucial vote of 8th June and he had just
reaffirmed adhesion to 'the basis and principle' of his Home Rule
policy. There was no serious response and as time passed even
Chamberlain seemed relatively satisfied, contenting himself with
abstention on Parnell's Tenants' Relief Bill already described.

Liberal differences were bound to be aggravated by the launching
of the Plan of Campaign on 23rd October.[1] Liberal and Radical
Unionists generally felt justified in their stand against Home Rule.
Events seemed to prove Irish nationalism was 'marching through
rapine to the disintegration of the Empire'.[2] While for Gladstonians
both proper approval and full disavowal were out of the question.
They thus fell between two stools, not only appearing to Unionists as
conniving in the Plan, but to the extreme Nationalists as at best
a source of lukewarm and untrustworthy support. Such was the
trend of developments as the N.L.F. prepared for its first post-split
national conference.

At a gathering of some of the Gladstonian leaders at Hawarden
held just before this Leeds conference it was decided no reunion call
would be made to the 'dissidents'. Instead, there was simply to be a
moratorium over baiting and abuse. Harcourt and Morley definitely
echoed Gladstone's opinions when stressing this before the assembled
delegates of the N.L.F. Nevertheless, these same delegates did so
more tellingly by reaffirming that any Irish settlement had to satisfy
the Nationalist party and include a legislature for coping with those
affairs a future parliament decided lay within its province. The
'Federation' appeared to be in fine spirits, having, according to its
president acquired the membership of a hundred new associations
since Chamberlain's quarrel with the majority. That 3rd November
saw renewed and increased personal allegiance given to Gladstone
and a deepening hostility develop towards criticism of him. Ironically

[1] See Chapter I, p. 61, note 1.
[2] Gladstone at the Cloth Hall, Leeds, on 7th October 1881, had used these
words in his great attack upon Parnell. *The Times*, 8th October 1881.

enough it was accompanied by the adoption of a heavy dose of that very 'constructionism' the leader had hated so in the 'Unauthorised Programme'. Chamberlain had left his mark, and Gladstone was having to pay a high price for Home Rule resolution and hero-worship alike.[1]

On 5th November Hartington reported to his mistress:

> There was not much in Harcourt's and Morley's speeches at Leeds; but they will evidently be as factious as they can, and I hear that the G.O.M. says that they must turn out the Government before Easter. I have got out of my visit to St Alban's and the Nottingham Committee.[2]

Apparently his erstwhile collaborators would have to rely on souls less attuned to distrust for the success of their non-baiting policy, and, what is more, hold a few more conferences before driving him into frenzied organisational activity. The comment on Gladstone is, of course, gossip. Even so, it would be foolish to dismiss it as false or distorted. Hartington seldom failed to smell out the truth. If it was true there can be no doubt of Leeds having had a remarkably rapid effect on Gladstone's attitude towards reunion. What way lay open to him for getting the government 'out before Easter' except through that?

Other evidence too points to this. Five days later Hartington, again to his mistress, is saying that: 'The G.O.M. has written a letter to Lord Wolverton which I think will not help to conciliate the Liberal Unionists, and I hope will make things easier for us at our Conference.'[3] Three days after that this letter appeared in the *Specta-*

[1] *The Times*, 4th November 1886. Gladstone's dislike of 'Constructionism' tended to wilt before his hopes on the Home Rule question and the charge put so brutally by John Bright: 'You've broken up the Liberal party.' Tuckwell, *op. cit.*, p. 69. The new spirit of liveliness so evident in Welsh Liberal and Radical politics since the general election of 1886 found ample expression in the demands for Welsh disestablishment made before the Leeds conference and satisfied at it. See K. O. Morgan, *Wales in British Politics, 1868–1922*, pp. 76–8.

[2] Hartington to the Duchess of Manchester, 5th November 1886. Devonshire Papers, 340. Add. MS. Louise Fredericke Augusta, wife of the 7th Duke of Manchester (1832–1911), was the second daughter of Count von Alten of Hanover. After the death of her husband freed her from legal entanglements and the death of Hartington's father, the 7th Duke of Devonshire, freed him from embarrassments, they were privately married on 16th August 1892. She died following a cerebral haemorrhage suffered at Sandown Races.

[3] Hartington to the Duchess of Manchester, 10th November 1886. Devonshire Papers, 340. Add. MS. Conciliation of the Liberal Unionists was not the only possibility of political 'ententeisme' under consideration, or so it would appear from a letter from Herbert Gladstone to Henry Labouchère, dated 7th November 1886. It ran:—'I return Parnell's letter and agree with your comments on it. I can't help thinking that Healy and Randolph Churchill have some understanding between them; for H. appears less keen for an arrangement with us. He is, however, quite right I think, from his own point of view, to avoid working with us until he

tor.[1] Its main idea was the prospect of reunion if the 'dissidents' could bully the government into adopting a positive Irish policy, and Hartington proved wrong in thinking a generally hostile reaction would follow. Many Radical Unionists were waiting for just such a sign, but Gladstone was then and probably always hoping to win back those about whom Hartington was right. Did they not represent much that was good in Liberalism? Good not only in itself, but in comparison with Leeds 'Constructionism'. While the argument of a letter to Harcourt on 16th November was open to question, the message leaves no doubt that Gladstone had been made painfully aware that politics should not always be Ireland, if the 'Bilious Brigade' of the N.L.F. was not to push all before it. He confided:

... Randolph, by taking up the Liberal Programme, has, as was expected, caused a *superfoetation* of Radical ideas on our side. I do not know how you view this. I will not break with the 200 (the Federation) or the Radical section of them if I can help it. But I am rather old to put on a brand new suit of clothes.[2]

The fact that he could not regain the Whig and Moderate Unionists did not mean he was not hoping to, nor that he was unwilling to pay a price.

Before Leeds there can be no doubt he was sticking fully to Home Rule. Perhaps his current approach was best summed up by Fowler at the conference itself when he appealed for 'dissidents' to return because Gladstonians were equally anxious to maintain the supre-

knows what his party may expect from us. He is, in my opinion, wrong in believing that my Father will be obliged to retire, though it is natural that he should fear this.

'I think our position is improving.' It is clear 'the only alternative to Home Rule is the revival of the C.A. and Coercion in Ireland and at Westminster. When the Whigs see that moderate nostrums are impossible' they will probably come 'direct to Home Rule. Of one thing I am really glad: that we have had no negotiations of any kind with the Parnellites. In regard to the practical question negotiations could not have improved our position and in regard to the party they would have been fatal. Your idea of sending a good man to Ireland to counteract the mischievous rubbish in the "Times" was an excellent one.' Herbert Gladstones papers. Add. MS. 46016. f. 123. Labouchère (1831–1912) was Gladstonian Liberal M.P. for Northampton and, some thought unsuitably, owner-editor of the weekly Radical newspaper *Truth*. Both he and Herbert Gladstone were inclined to excitability, but the contents of this letter do very probably mirror quite accurately the nervousness felt at Hawarden about the effect of having unduly close relations with the Irish Nationalists and the inconvenience that was likely to stem from caution in this direction.

[1] *Spectator*, 13th November 1886. The 2nd Baron Wolverton (1824–87) had been the Liberal Chief Whip 1872–3 and Postmaster-General in the third Gladstone ministry.

[2] Gardiner, *op. cit.*, Vol. II, p. 12.

macy of the imperial parliament and the integrity of the empire. In other words the mixture was as before, yet wrapped in the Union Jack. But things were much changed. He was facing the possibility of Home Rule having to be postponed indefinitely if Hartington matched up to his wishful thinking. On the very same day—13th November—as the *Spectator* revelation Herschell spoke of the need for reunion at Bristol.[1] Taking the line of sweet reason he argued that all Liberals believed in some form of self-government for Ireland and none in endangering national security. Their quarrels arose over the degree of self-government and the degree of security required before it could be given. Irreconcilable principles were not at stake. Here again, no sympathy came forth from Chatsworth. Far from contemplating matters of degree Hartington waxed almost enthusiastic on the 18th at the prospect of a large and successful Liberal Unionist conference, and, revising his former contempt for Gladstone's move, judged it rather more on its effect than intention.

> I saw some private letters from Mr G. since I wrote to you, still harping on the same thing; and evidently thinking that he will succeed in making a split between us and the Government if they do not bring in their Local Government of Ireland Bill at once next Session. I really think he is beginning to get a little doting; but he has written no letters and made no speeches this week, which is a comfort.[2]

It was of course true that Gladstone wished to divide the Liberal Unionists and the government, yet it was also true that by offering what in effect was the indefinite postponement of Home Rule he was challenging all liberal Liberal Unionists to re-examine their *raison d'être*. Hartington's reaction was to regard the move as the knavery of a self-righteous old fool and to resent the likely, and as it happened, the actual response of some Radical Unionists. Granville might lament broken social contacts. Hartington continued to meet everyone he had ever truly wanted to have near him. Gladstone certainly wanted Liberal reunion, and on 13th November that must have been his paramount intention. Because that intention had the effect of bothering Hartington, through disturbing what to him was a welcome working arrangement with the Conservatives, he adopted an unpleasant tone.

Before he was obliged to meet Radical Unionist pressure by putting pressure in turn upon the government, another move had been made by Gladstone on the 23rd in the form of a memorandum privately

[1] *Observer*, 14th November 1886. *The Times*, 15th November 1886. Baron Herschell (1837–99) had been Lord Chancellor in Gladstone's third ministry and was a man noted for his highly conciliatory disposition.

[2] Hartington to the Duchess of Manchester, 18th November 1886. Devonshire Papers, 340. Add. MS.

circulated to his leading colleagues.[1] Intensifying the trend of the Wolverton letter, he now proposed joint Liberal Unionist–Gladstonian talks, First, to secure the adoption of Liberal policy in British legislation; and, second, to further the solution of the Irish issue by prodding the government into producing its measures for local government. He saved his face over making such a great concession by stating that neither side would abandon its views on Home Rule; begged the question somewhat by stating the government might well produce a measure good in itself, although assuredly inadequate; and opened up an almost infinite range of possible discussion by saying it should deal with any other 'points or details' those taking part might opt for. The representatives coming together should be—and here he used a formula later taken up by Chamberlain—two or three thorough Liberals from either side 'who had not been deeply or sharply involved in the controversy'.

Not content with a blueprint, he sent to Granville a list of the 'thorough Liberals' he wished to participate. They were: Derby, James and Bright for the Liberal Unionists and Herschell, Kimberley and Whitbread for the Home Rulers.[2] Rosebery was a desirable

[1] Memorandum by Gladstone, 23rd November 1886. Gladstone Papers, Add. MS. 44179, f. 189. Already on 17th November Morley reported to Harcourt that Gladstone believed the Liberal Unionists were 'in a hole' over the postponement of Irish reform. Morley to Harcourt, 17th November 1886. Harcourt Papers. But Harcourt did not draw undue comfort from such a thought. As he warned Gladstone and Morley alike, 'logic' might not prevail. Harcourt to Gladstone, 17th November 1886. Gladstone Papers, Add. MS. 44200, f. 180. Harcourt to Morley, 20th November 1886. Copy. Harcourt Papers. To the latter he expressed the hope that an 'intermediate measure' would be produced to deal with the Irish issue. Home Rule was such a bore. The difficulty was as to when it should be proposed. Harcourt to Morley, 20th November 1886. Copy. Harcourt Papers. Replying to Harcourt the next day, or the day after, Morley took comfort from Rosebery's approval of the proceedings at Leeds, yet seemed to regard the prospect of serious trouble arising over in Ireland with very mixed feelings. Morley to Harcourt, 21st (or 22nd) November 1886. Harcourt Papers. For his part Harcourt was content to live in the present and expressed more interest in how Hartington was allegedly being used to contain Churchill and the possible excitements at the forthcoming Liberal Unionist conference. Harcourt to Morley, 23rd November 1886. Copy. Harcourt Papers.

[2] Gladstone to Granville, 23rd November 1886. Granville Papers, P.R.O. 30, 29, 29A. The 15th Earl of Derby (1826–93), son of the Prime Minister and formerly Foreign Secretary under Disraeli. He had been a Conservative until 1880, but served as Colonial Secretary in the second Gladstone ministry from 1882. Sir Henry James (1828–1911), later Lord James of Hereford, had served as Attorney-General in the second Gladstone ministry and declined to become Lord Chancellor in the third. He was currently Liberal Unionist M.P. for Bury. John Bright sat for Central Birmingham. Fortunately for Chamberlain, he had not listened when the S.D.F. leader H. M. Hyndman had attempted to persuade him to have Bright withdraw from Birmingham in 1885 so that Hyndman might oppose Churchill. See C. Tsuzuki, *H. M. Hyndman and British Socialism*, pp. 70–1.

candidate, but absence abroad put him out of the question. There was, as one might have expected from an 'old parliamentary hand', another good hard practical end in view besides the desire to dish the Radicals. Gladstone was an old man in even more of a hurry. What could not be got round in the foreseeable future had to be worked with—at least until conditions changed. Getting the government 'out before Easter' involved reunion. Reunion then was intended to wean the Hartingtonians away from Salisbury, not only for their inherent worth and counterbalancing of 'constructionism', but for their voting power in the Commons without which no fourth Gladstone ministry could be formed, short of an unlikely victory in a general election no one wanted. The great difficulty was that the memorandum plan made Whig and Moderate Liberal Unionist response still less likely than the Wolverton letter.

Granville liked the idea of negotiating.[1] He did not like the arbitrary selection of negotiators, arguing reasonably enough that Gladstone was in no position personally to nominate plenipotentiaries and that even if Hartington consented it was extremely unlikely Derby, James and Bright would quietly do as they were told. Though Hartington did press the government to produce its Irish measures, Granville quite rightly said he would never pledge himself to do so, and saw no hope of reconciliation, given Gladstone's point on keeping principles for and against Home Rule, unless such a step was taken. Granville ended by putting Gladstone into an awkward position. Only if Hartington wanted reunion could talks be of considerable value, and then they would have to be between the two leaders, aided by one or two assistants. All this put Gladstone about a good deal. His reply turned down a direct approach to Hartington on the ground that it would end in his own discomfiture and prove a waste of time.[2] Instead, Granville might well approach Bright, who was now discovered to be independent of Hartington and James and an avoider of the House when he—Gladstone—was there. But Granville had known his man and how much reunion would have to be in appearance at least a good imitation of Liberal Unionist surrender. Within hours of writing this to Granville on 27th November the G.O.M. was saying very different things in letters to Campbell-

Samuel Whitbread was the grandson of his famous namesake and sat for Bedford as a Gladstonian Liberal. All his efforts had been strongly in favour of compromise before the split took place and he was the originator of the idea that a vote for the Second Reading of the Home Rule Bill should merely be taken as an approval of its grand central principle.

[1] Granville to Gladstone, 26th November 1886. Gladstone Papers, Add. MS. 44179, f. 194.

[2] Gladstone to Granville, 27th November 1886. Granville Papers, P.R.O. 30, 29, 29A.

Bannerman[1] and, believe it or not, to Granville himself![2] With the government likely to proceed with coercion, talks with the Liberal Unionists would not be useful at the moment and the Gladstonians could play a waiting game. A game for the winning cards before fair play could begin in another more active entertainment. In this manoeuvring lay the keynote of the whole process leading up to and including the 'Round Table Conference'—ambivalence.

Meanwhile the Wolverton letter had been having an effect and on the 25th Hartington was worried. A talk with Churchill had revealed that the government did not 'seem to intend to bring in any Local Government Reform Bill for Ireland next Session'.

> This would give the Gladstonians a great handle; and it will be difficult for me to keep all our Liberal Unionists in order. But I think they would stand it if the Government would bring in a good Bill for England and would say that they would have one on the same principles for Ireland as soon as they could. But if they say that they will do nothing for Ireland we shall have a bad time. I do not think that things look well in Ireland. The organised resistance to rent seems to be growing; and it is in a form which is very difficult to deal with.[3]

He was therefore anxious to have the meeting with Salisbury Churchill had urged upon him. So anxious in fact that it took place that day. Reporting to Hicks Beach the next day that Hartington had begun by pressing for an Irish local government Bill next session, Salisbury revealed how at his meeting with Churchill, just mentioned, the Liberal Unionist leader had been equally urgent. 'He was certain that Gladstone's efforts would be directed to compelling us to produce our Irish policy, and that if we gave no promise to do so during the Session the opinions and the pledges of a great number of his men would force them to vote against us.'[4] Hartington had laid it on pretty thickly. Only one Liberal Unionist had actually voted against the government on Parnell's Bill in September and the language he himself employed to his most intimate friend suggests abstentions rather than fullblown rebellion. Still, Radical Unionism was a mercurial force and he could take no chances. When Salisbury explained the difficulties about English local government he demurred to postponement of the District Councils issue, but was prepared to

[1] Gladstone to Campbell-Bannerman, 27th November 1886. Campbell-Bannerman Papers, Add. MS. 41215, f. 25.

[2] Gladstone to Granville, 27th November 1886. Granville Papers, P.R.O. 30, 29, 29A.

[3] Hartington to the Duchess of Manchester, 25th November 1886. Devonshire Papers, 340. Add. MS.

[4] Salisbury to Hicks Beach, 26th November 1886. Hicks Beach Papers, STALDP. PCC/69.

withdraw his objection if the Irish Bill emerged first, labouring once more the point about Gladstone's aims and the contingent nature of the government majority. Most important of all Chamberlain thought, an Irish Bill would 'put an end to the current suggestion that' the government 'had some sort of Home Rule Bill in reserve' and 'bring the Unionist and Separatist parties again face to face with each other: and the air would be much clearer after the Separatists had been beaten once again'.[1] Salisbury hoped Hicks Beach might see his way to consent, especially as Hartington had said a settlement of Ireland first would avoid unfavourable comparison with what would inevitably be the more liberal English measure.[2]

As if this were not enough to blow the G.O.M.'s daydreams of well-meaning Whigs and Moderates sky-high, two of the chosen three Liberal Unionists pronounced adversely on reunion as he conceived of it, and of these Bright hardly possessed the moral courage to act even had he wanted to. When refusing Hartington's request to speak at the forthcoming Liberal Unionist conference he moaned:

> I could say nothing without seeming to attack Mr Gladstone. [This would only widen the breach unnecessarily, and for nothing.] The course taken by Mr Gladstone since the close of the Session has astonished me and given me great trouble. His speaking and writing, and especially his reception of the Irish delegation seem to me to have driven him so far in a wrong course we can have no hope of any more moderate policy from him. . . . Mr Gladstone is leading the bulk of the Liberal party in support of the men who are the authors of the desperate struggle which is now being waged between the owners and occupiers of land in Ireland; his voice is not heard on behalf of peace and moderation.[3]

That was on the 28th, the day before Morley made a speech at Hawick without mentioning the 'Plan of Campaign'. A little later, on 3rd December James delivered his cold douche in a letter to Gladstone's friend MacColl.[4] There is an air of genuine puzzlement about it. He says: 'I share with you the desire to preserve the unity of the Liberal party, but I do not gather from your letter what practical step should be taken to procure that most desirable result. There is a great gulf between us I fear. You believe in Home Rule—I do not.' These were

[1] *Ibid.*   [2] *Ibid.*

[3] Bright to Hartington, 28th November 1886. Devonshire Papers, 340. 2075. Bright thought Gladstone's mind had become 'seriously unhinged'. The G.O.M. had mutual feelings, declaring that Bright's reason had become 'seriously affected'. A. M. W. Stirling, *Victorian Sidelights*, pp. 224–5.

[4] G. W. E. Russell (Editor), *Malcolm MacColl: Memoirs and Correspondence*, pp. 375–6. Malcolm MacColl (1838–1907) was an Anglican clergyman of High Church proclivities. These he combined with an ardent Liberalism and thus was eminently suited for the rôle of friend to Gladstone. His works included books on Turkey and Armenia. The accord was close!

men uninterested in the indefinite postponement of Home Rule. Only its complete abandonment would suffice. They saw through Gladstone's long term plans even if they did scant justice to his willingness to tone them down for both idealistic and tactical reasons. Neither accepted the split with the same smug resignation as their leader, but both were uncompromising Unionists, however much one played about with compromise formulae there was no getting away from that. Neither was optimistic about the future. Bright's pessimism is obvious and James admitted to MacColl that his dire forecasts of the fate of the Liberal Unionists were probably correct. Yet neither emulated Gladstone and made a virtue of necessity. James's parting shot on parliamentary affairs reveals the bitterness harboured by one of the most generous of men.

> If Mr Gladstone's Bill had been withdrawn before the Second Reading Division, no dissolution would have occurred, and then ample time would have been given to consider a fitting measure by men who had not made a rigid record of their positive views upon the principle of Home Rule.[1]

If MacColl ever told Gladstone this, he might well have lamented how late he had conceived of his test for deciding who should bring Liberals together.

There is no evidence as to whether or not Dale had met Morley and Schnadhorst on 25th October, but it is certain that he met Morley at least before 26th November. On the 24th, or 25th the interview was reported by Morley to Harcourt in some detail.[2] It had lasted three hours and had involved a mutually frank exchange of views. Dale had disclaimed any recent news from Chamberlain and described how he and his Birmingham associates had decided to delay 'a little meeting . . . to grope for a basis of union about Irish policy' until Chamberlain's return from abroad. Morley had approved. According to his account, Dale's current proposal was rather fanciful. Gladstone was to say: 'The rejection of the Land Bill by the country has taken the linchpin out of the machinery of the Home Rule Bill and has fatally deranged the working of our plan; therefore, we are open to the consideration of any other plan which, say Hartington may produce, and I (Mr G.) will if possible, support it.' Still more startling was the means by which this Hartington plan was to be carried through Parliament. 'This might involve the standing

---

[1] *Ibid.*

[2] Morley to Harcourt, Undated. Harcourt Papers. Harcourt replied to this letter on the 26th November 1886 and had written another to Morley three days earlier, in which no mention is made of Dale. Harcourt's habit of replying to Morley's communications by return suggests Morley's undated letter was written on the 24th November at the latest.

aside of Mr Gladstone' and Morley 'from an administration, yet', with the G.O.M.'s goodwill, Harcourt 'and the others might join a Hartington government and Mr Gladstone would get out of his disgrace of leaving a divided party'. 'There's a bit of ingenious politics for you,' Morley told Harcourt, 'But Mr Gladstone has a great respect for Dale and I shall tell him of it.' The reply was typical: 'I confess I laughed outright at Dale's "Eirenikon". A plan which is to dispense with Mr G. and yourself is not, I think, one which is likely to commend itself to what remains of the Liberal party.'[1] No less typical were the concluding remarks of each letter. Morley ended: '*My notion*, if you care for it—is that the first business next January, as it was last, will be *coercion*; that blessed word will give a new shake to the kaleidoscope and all the present talk will prove to be perfectly idle.'[2] Harcourt, as follows:

'I think you will find Mr G. ready to waive his own plan and take an intermediate one *de bene esse*. But as I told him, the difficulty is, who is to propose it? The Unionists are *pas si bête*. They will stand on a simple *non possumus* to Mr G.'s plan. I suppose your anticipations of coercion rest on Irish information, which I do not possess, though I observe the "Times" is much less positive than it was on the subject of the tranquillity of the country.'[3]

Surprisingly enough, neither alluded to the great convenience Birmingham, and above all Chamberlain, would find in Dale's scheme. The worthy divine was taken very much at his own face value. In a letter to him of the 28th, Morley makes quite clear his own good faith and Dale's firm alignment with Birmingham Liberal Unionism.[4] After thanking him for an enclosure Morley goes on:

The difficulty in the way of the notion we talked about the other day is that nobody will propose it. We cannot—even if we were ultimately to accept. Now Chamberlain will not, because he is content with things as they are. Who then? The pretty evident approach of coercion will make a good deal of difference in the situation. It will not be easy for your friends to keep the present attitude of mere *non possumus*. I hope that we shall soon meet again.[5]

In other words Morley is hoping any coercion proposals will help towards reunion rather than render it superfluous. Maybe some news of Hartington's concern had leaked out and made Gladstone anxious to exploit any Radical Unionist rumblings and attempt a

[1] Harcourt to Morley, 26th November 1886. Copy in the Harcourt Papers.
[2] Morley to Harcourt, Undated. Harcourt Papers, see p. 79, note 2.
[3] Harcourt to Morley, 26th November 1886. Copy in the Harcourt Papers.
[4] Morley to Dale, 28th November 1886. Dale Papers.
[5] *Ibid.*

cornering of the whole Liberal Unionist party for talks on a 23rd November basis. Second thoughts could always have undermined his confidence in the coercion boomerang, and a growing fixation over reunion have dimmed past hatreds. Anyhow, whatever the reason, he was more than content that Morley continue his initiative through Dale to the point of meeting Chamberlain. Only something substantial could have brought this about.

Morley switched from backstage approaches to public campaigning on 29th November. Speaking at Hawick, he contrived to ignore the 'Plan of Campaign' and yet make Ireland his topic. The government, he claimed, ought to have adopted Parnell's amendment to the Address giving the Land Courts power to stay ejectments where three-quarters of the rent was paid and circumstances had made impossible payment of the rest. Churchill was inconsistent in promising 'simultaneous' local government reforms for England, Scotland and Ireland, and then saying the Irish measure ought not to be hurried on, and in claiming the government would place local works in the hands of the Irish people, only to allow Salisbury at the Guildhall to declare that Ireland needed good administration rather than new laws. Such were the two main points Morley had to make, and very apposite they were. On that very day Salisbury wrote to Hicks Beach reporting Hartington had dropped his insistence on priority for an Irish local government Bill. Apparently the concession had been obtained from him 'by Rothschild at Randolph's instance—the latter taking the very strongest possible objection to the proposal'. The plan now was that 'an Irish Local Government Bill be promised in the Queen's speech after the English and Scotch'.[1] Morley would appear to have been right over Churchill, yet that was a comparatively minor offset to the disadvantage of Hartington's change of plan. Forlorn though the chances had always been of getting all sections of the Liberal Unionists to talks, they were now, had Morley only known it, well

---

[1] *The Times*, 30th November 1886. The issues of Scottish Disestablishment and Home Rule had come well to the fore north of the Border during November. Consequently, Morley had been able to push unpleasant matters like the 'Plan' into the background with comparative ease. Down in London no such conditions prevailed and Liberal Unionists, James among them, were keenly critical of Gladstone and all his works. See Morley to Harcourt, 17th and 18th November 1886. Copies. Harcourt Papers. On 9th December 1886, Sir Henry Campbell-Bannerman told J. Bryce he could best express his opinion as to 'Scotch Home Rule by saying nothing about it', though he thought 'it would come'. He intended to 'play both the Priest and the Levite both to Home Rule and the Crofter'. Campbell-Bannerman to Bryce, 9th December 1886. Bryce Papers. For J. Bryce see Chapter III, p. 122, note 6.

The whole disestablishment issue in Scotland is well dealt with in *The Liberal Party and the Scottish Church Disestablishment Crisis* by J. G. Kellas. See *E.H.R.* 1964.

nigh nil. If the Whigs and Moderates had decided to brave any Radical Unionist tantrums there was no bringing them under pressure, and pressure alone would make them talk. While galling for Gladstone such a situation was meat and drink to Morley, who at heart pined for none besides wayward Radicals.

In a second speech at Edinburgh, on 2nd December, he compared the government to a blind man led by two very lively dogs with very different conceptions of the route; claimed the need for Scottish local government reform was not at all like the Irish need for Home Rule; sympathised with Disestablishment in Scotland; excused himself from treating of the 'Plan of Campaign' as being soon *sub judice* and anyway an Irish concern; and most important, insisted that 'to give Ireland a separate Legislature, and yet not to give her a separate Executive, dependent on that Legislature, would be to mock her with the hope of reforms which need never be carried out'.[1] Brave words, and the last were to prove highly crucial in the next three months.

From Granville's comments on Morley's northern tour it might appear that all was well in the Gladstonian camp. He wrote to Spencer: ' ... how good I thought your speech. So are the two Morley has just made, especially the Edinburgh one. It is a great political comfort having such a man with us.'[2] Gratifying though a Whig bouquet to a Radical might be, there were other Whigs and other Radicals in the Home Rule camp, and with them much despondency, confusion and disagreement. The speech of Spencer's, to which Granville referred, was nothing if not woeful. He had told a regional conference at Leicester, on 25th November, that Home Rule should be tried because all else had failed. Fowler had been even worse, admitting Gladstonians were in a fog and enjoining them to stick together until it lifted.[3] On the 24th, at Manchester, Labouchère had sent cold shivers down the spines of countless Gladstonians by

[1] *The Times*, 3rd December 1886.

[2] Granville to Spencer, 3rd December 1886. Spencer Papers. Sir Edward Hamilton shared this enthusiasm. His diary for 2nd December 1886 reads: 'J. Morley is the most active of the Gladstonians; he is now giving forth in Scotland. His speeches are certainly very satisfying; and he often puts in finished and clear language points which one wants to put and argue oneself.' Nevertheless, he noticed the avoidance of the 'Plan of Campaign' and pronounced the latest Nationalist tactic 'wholly indefensible'. Sir Edward Hamilton's Diary, 2nd December 1886, Add. MS. 48645, p. 45. Hamilton (1847–1908) was private secretary to Gladstone 1873–4 and 1880–5. At this time he was Principal Clerk in the financial branch of the Treasury. In 1902 he became Permanent Financial Secretary to the Treasury. Six years later he was made a Privy Councillor. Also on 2nd December Chamberlain wrote to Dilke from Corfu about Balkan policy. Gladstone's Bulgarian agitation of 1876 had, he declared, been as 'gigantic' a 'mistake' as his present Home Rule policy. Chamberlain to Dilke, 2nd December 1886. Dilke Papers, Add. MS. 43888, f. 85.

[3] See Chapter I, p. 62, note 3.

extolling a programme of extreme Radicalism. Nothing short of Home Rule, presumably *au Gladstone*, he said, would satisfy Ireland or England.[1] Gladstone himself was not always so absolutely certain. As early as 16th November his doubt about the 'England' part emerged in a letter to Harcourt.[2] He wrote that he favoured an 'intermediate measure' of an inherently good kind and would like to know how the Nationalists would regard it. Needless to say, he was not abandoning an ultimate measure. Unionists would simply enjoy stay of execution, not reversal of the sentence. Developments *vis-à-vis* the Liberal Unionists stimulated him into sending Morley and Spencer to interview Parnell on 7th December, the day of the Liberal Unionist conference. The unfortunate pair were charged with finding out the Irish leader's reactions to the idea of 'a small measure as a step to his ultimate demands, in order to reunite the Liberals'.[3] It was hardly surprising that he rejected it out of hand, saying, 'such a course would be repudiated by the active men in his party'.[4] Desire for reunion had certainly led Gladstone a long way from reality, on the left as well as on the right. Parnell disapproved on tactical grounds of the 'Plan of Campaign', but none the less grinned and bore it. He wanted Home Rule as sincerely as anyone, and was certainly not going to fight against his own men for something he did not want when he had proved unwilling to risk fighting them over something he did want. It was sheer wishful thinking on Hartington's part to write: 'If things could only have been kept quiet in Ireland this winter, Home Rule might have died out.'[5] But the G.O.M. was tending towards the same fault in supposing Parnell could, or would, give a favourable response.

[1] See Chapter I, p. 62, note 3.
[2] Gladstone to Harcourt, 16th November 1886. Harcourt Papers. On 29th November Morley reported to Harcourt how much Gladstone felt the prospect of coercion transformed the political scene. The Liberal Unionists would feel bound to press yet harder for a reform programme to be produced by the government and be still more vulnerable to Gladstonian pressure. He spelt out Gladstone's reunion talks plan in full detail, as if to prove the party was ready to move in for the kill of full-blown Liberal Unionism. But the Liberal Unionists were blooming in some august quarters. Sir Edward Hamilton estimated Brooks's Club was two-thirds anti-Gladstonian and his companion there that day, Henry Brand, regarded the Hartingtonians as the only politicians who were not 'dishonest opportunists'. Sir Edward Hamilton's Diary, 6th December 1886, Add. MS. 48645, p. 47.
[3] Morley to Gladstone, 7th December 1886. Gladstone Papers, Add. MS. 44255, f. 134. Spencer to Granville, 8th December 1886. Granville Papers, P.R.O. 30, 29, 22A.
[4] *Ibid.* According to Morley, Parnell looked 'very ill and worn'. F. H. O'Donnell, *A History of the Irish Parliamentary Party*, Vol. II, p. 218 See the sketch of Parnell in Lord Bryce's *Studies in Contemporary Biography*, pp. 227–49.
[5] Hartington to the Duchess of Manchester, 1st December 1886. Devonshire Papers, 340. Add. MS.

Hartington regarded the Liberal Unionist conference with appre-hension. However large the company and however great its enthu-siasm final judgment would depend upon him—the leader of the party. On 1st December he grumbled characteristically:

My speech has not made much progress. . . . It will be a very difficult one to make; and I am afraid that things are not looking so well in Ire-land. The anti-Rent movement seems at last to have been making pro-gress; and the prosecution of Dillon will probably have to be followed by others which may cause great excitement, and I should not wonder if the Government had to ask for some kind of Coercion as soon as Par-liament meets. Then there will be a tremendous row and nobody can tell how it will go . . . [and] there will be plenty of people who will say that if Mr Gladstone had been listened to there would have been no disturb-ance.[1]

In the immediate future it was Dillon who happened to provoke further opposition to the 'anti-Rent movement' in England—just what the Gladstonians most dreaded. So if Gladstone, Hartington and Morley were all correct in forecasting coercion would be the scourge of the government, this did not prove that the 'Plan' would not be the scourge of the opposition. At Castlereagh, on 5th December, Dillon spoke of 'the day of reckoning' after Home Rule came in.[2] Hardly a sentiment in tune with the Gladstonians' promise of an 'oblivion of the past', and people were quick to notice it. Among them was Lord Kilcoursie, none other than the Gladstonian member for South Somerset. Liberal Unionists must have drawn great comfort from a letter he wrote to the *Daily News*, published on the morning of 7th December, the day of their conference.[3] Condemning Dillon's speech it declared that if it could be taken 'as the settled and deliberate opinions of the Irish party, as well as an exposition of its future policy', then the writer would find himself unable to vote again for Home Rule. Parnell as an outsider had feared this sort of thing would happen, and when he was afraid Unionists could be glad.

Like Gaullism after it, Liberal Unionism required a sustained state of high nationalist excitement for its lasting success. Maintenance of the Union not only drew together highly various brands of Liberals, but served as an effective rallying cry for missionary work in the constituencies. By the end of 1886 many leading members were

[1] *Ibid.*
[2] *Annual Register*, 1886, p. 298. John Dillon (1851–1927) was the son of the 'Young Ireland' leader, J. B. Dillon, Irish Nationalist M.P. for East Mayo and a lieutenant of Parnell's. From 1896–9, however, he was to become the Anti-Parnellite leader.
[3] *Daily News*, 7th December 1886. On the death of his father in December 1887 he succeeded to the Earldom of Cavan, but as an Irish peer could go on sitting in the House of Commons.

regretting the decision not to go all out to create a fully separate party. Some had always wanted a bold course. A conference in London seemed the best way of bringing supporters from all over the United Kingdom into contact with their leaders and with one another. Eight hundred delegates assembled on 7th December and heard or gave speeches representative of all views and regions, yet at the end a friendly commentator felt able to describe the party as 'a regiment of officers without common soldiers, and with little prospect of finding any rank and file'.[1] An impression like this undoubtedly arose from the great part played by the most right wing elements, but there were incidents which should have modified in part such a sweeping and simple-minded judgment.

Hartington began by reading out communications from Bright (a letter of 28th November) and Chamberlain (a newly arrived telegram) —scarcely men without a following of common soldiers, and lacking the 'prospect of finding any rank and file'. The telegram was of supreme importance in the political context of the day. It ran:

> Regret my absence from England prevents my attendance tomorrow. While Separatists maintain defeated programme organisation of Liberal Unionists is a necessary duty. The speech of Lord Herschell at Bristol fairly states the problem. If the Gladstonian Liberals sincerely desire reunion they should invite both sections of the party to a free conference as to the extent and character of reforms which can safely be granted to Ireland, without reference to the discarded scheme of the late Government. Our opposition is confined to the defeated policy. If that be frankly abandoned we are ready to discuss any safe scheme, but must first have assurance that the old plan, or one equally objectionable will not again be proposed. Agreement on this cardinal point a necessary preliminary to any joint action. Failing this responsibility of division rests with Separatists.[2]

Response from the conference majority ranged from cool to hostile, yet to the moderate Gladstonians, Radical Unionists and the vast number of abstainers in the recent general election it appeared in quite a different light. These men and women were seeking a catalyst for reunion and this might well be it. Following an avalanche of Whiggery Trevelyan made an impassioned speech hoping for rapid reunion, and had he too not been abroad, Caine would certainly have supported him. Chamberlain's own absence was highly un-

---

[1] Henry Sidgwick. See A. and E. M. Sidgwick, *Henry Sidgwick: A Memoir*, p. 463. Henry Sidgwick (1838–1900) was one of the many prominent intellectual figures of the time attracted to Liberal Unionism. At the time he expressed this opinion he held the Professorship of Moral Philosophy at Cambridge. See Bryce, *op. cit.*, pp. 327–42.

[2] *The Times*, 8th December 1886.

fortunate, as it left the Radical Unionists leaderless at a crucial point in relations with the public and the Gladstonians.

In his presidential address Hartington sounded an altogether different note—one most delegates liked. The Conservative alliance was essential for the defence of the Union and had to go on. Gladstone's plan for prodding the government into producing their Irish policy through the joint efforts of the Home Rule and Unionist Liberals together should be rejected. He did not want the government to produce a Home Rule scheme 'or any substitute for it'. Liberal Unionist Liberalism would find Conservative legislation quite progressive and could itself influence its ally further in the same direction. The National League was doing exactly what it had been expected to do with 'outrage, disorder, assassination and dynamite', but that should not modify the Unionist stand. Gladstone should denounce the 'Plan of Campaign', otherwise all Liberalism would stand condemned. Unionist Liberals would regret this as much as Gladstonians. These were his main points, all delivered in that inimitable style.[1] 'You do manage somehow,' wrote his sister, 'to speak out so clearly and truly, and yet keep clear of personal bitterness.'[2] This had been especially difficult to do when elaborating on Gladstone's reunion probe, because it involved direct mention of specific persons besides the G.O.M. Herschell was singled out for praise. His approach would make reunion both desirable and possible. On the other hand Harcourt and Morley clearly did not share it and had publicly underlined the need for a separate Irish parliament and executive. There was not therefore 'the slightest ground for hoping' the two Liberal sections could work together. Instead, similar local government should be granted by the present government to all three countries. Armed with this commonsense logic and an unassailable social preeminence Hartington seemed almost too big to be blamed for anything. Possession of a quasi-Gulliver was obviously a first-rate political weapon, albeit of a defensive variety. Small wonder then that ministers had invoked the Queen's aid to prevent his going off on a visit to India. No one could speak with such authority for the Liberal Unionist majority, nor ward off so well proposals unpalatable to the Conservatives.

There followed a veritable spate of oratory directed either to a devotion to the Union, or the existing social order; a spate continued at the subsequent banquet until Trevelyan's turn came round. Hartington was followed by Selborne, whose attitude towards the split can be summarised by an adaptation of Whistler's remark on leaving

[1] *Ibid.*
[2] Lady Francis Egerton to Hartington, 9th December 1886. Devonshire Papers, 292. 248.

the R.B.A.: that the Liberals had gone and the Home Rulers remained.[1] In a somewhat condescending tone he appealed to Spencer for condemnation of Irish anarchy and urged all to read Dicey's *England's Case Against Home Rule*. Why, he asked, was Gladstone encouraging demands for Scottish and Welsh Home Rule when he had declared his Irish scheme to be final.[2] Perhaps more to the point was the strong support for Hartington's line from George Dixon, Radical Unionist member for Edgbaston, Birmingham. Admittedly, his Radicalism savoured of Bright rather than Chamberlain, yet he was reckoned a Chamberlainite and might have been expected to echo his master's voice. Instead he seemed to go out of his way to stress how very indulgent the party must be to the government to ward off the dread prospect of Gladstone's return to power.[3] Another even more radical Radical Unionist, T. W. Russell, concentrated, as an Ulster member could have been expected to do, on the 'Plan of Campaign' and the approval given it by Archbishop Walsh.[4] Yet another, Mrs Fawcett, talked of the Union and national existence, but not of reunion.[5] The Duke of Westminster and Lord Northbrook followed with suitably Hartingtonian sentiments.[6] Aid and comfort for the Conservatives abounded.

When Goschen made the principal speech at the banquet—'The Unionist Cause'—proceedings took another shift to the right—or so it appeared. After claiming Hartington was 'practically in power', he went on to claim that having formed to defend the Union, the Liberal Unionists had to go on to do not only that, but also to maintain 'the integrity of society' and 'the structure of the social fabric'. This was to be done by fighting anarchy. Invitations to join what he termed the 'Gladstone–Parnell–Labouchère–Dillon–O'Brien party'

[1] When Whistler and some of his associates left the R.B.A. he declared that the artists were going and the British remained. Lord Selborne definitely thought of the Liberal Unionists as the cream of the pre-split Liberal party.

[2] *The Times*, 8th December 1886. For Lord Selborne see Chapter III, p. 122, note 1.

[3] *Ibid*. George Dixon (1820–98) was Radical Unionist M.P. for Edgbaston, Birmingham. He had been one of the initiators of the National Education League.

[4] *Ibid*. T. W. Russell was Radical Unionist M.P. for South Tyrone and famous as a land and temperance reformer. Archbishop Walsh (1841–1921) had been appointed to the Dublin Primacy in 1885. His writings covered subjects as diverse as the Land Acts and Gregorian music, and his best known piece of political activity that against Parnell at the time of the latter's divorce case.

[5] *Ibid*. Mrs Millicent, later Dame Millicent Fawcett, *née* Garrett (1847–1929), was the widow of the Radical Henry Fawcett and a pioneer in the campaign for women's rights. In 1889 she became President of the Women's Unionist Association.

[6] *Ibid*. The 1st Duke of Westminster (1825–99), Lord Lieutenant of Cheshire and a prominent racehorse owner. The 2nd Lord Northbrook (1826–1904) had been First Lord of the Admiralty in Gladstone's second ministry.

he dismissed as preposterous, maintaining that the Liberal Unionists alone could salve the reputation of Liberalism for wise and necessary reform. As a financier he chose as the crowning horror of Gladstonianism the certainty of Irish bankruptcy under the impact of Home Rule. It is, of course, arguable that Goschen said nothing more conservative than Hartington. Both had praised the Conservative alliance, repudiated reunion and condemned the 'Plan of Campaign'. Nevertheless, previous reputation, present turn of phrase and future action all point towards supposing he meant something more conservative. Derby certainly went further in this direction. He was surprised at the 'tolerance, not to call it encouragement' with which many Gladstonian politicians regarded the 'Plan of Campaign', and feared the 'undisguised socialism' worked for in Ireland would all too soon be worked for in Britain.[1] Then came a speech which did not slam the door right in Gladstone's face; that of Henry James. Needless to say it was very cautious and moderate. Not so cautious and so moderate, however, as to preclude a spirit of genuine enquiry. Like his letter to MacColl the speech made everything depend on the future. Unlike the letter it contained no element of acerbity. Where the Liberal Unionists ended up, he declared, would depend on the actions of the Gladstonian leaders. In other words, he was honest enough to say in public that he thought there was no place for a truly independent third party in British politics. A cool appraisal of the general position in the constituencies told him that. He was also bold enough to add that the Liberal Unionists, and by that he meant the majority, could go either rightwards to a more modern Conservatism, or leftwards to a purged Gladstonianism. Gladstone was to make much of this slight encouragement.[2]

James can have done little to prepare the delegates for Trevelyan's contribution. Although lacking the anti-Gladstonian militancy and arrogance of the Chamberlain telegram, there was no mistaking the general agreement with its policy. An anti-Irish rather than an anti-Gladstonian outburst, it decried both Irish nationalism and agrarian outrage. He wanted Gladstone to see that the majority of Englishmen would never accept such things and that the best course for Britain, Ireland and the Liberal party lay in a moderate policy of reform upon which Liberal Unionists and Gladstonians could reunite.[3]

Only a very wishful thinker could have seen in these differences of approach signs of the imminent disintegration of the party. Obviously,

[1] *Ibid.* William O'Brien (1852–1928) was joint leader with Dillon of the 'Plan of Campaign'. He was not in Parliament at this point, but later sat as an Irish Nationalist for East Cork. As editor of *United Ireland* his influence was considerable.
[2] *Ibid.*   [3] *Ibid.*

it had a militant and electorally vital left wing wedded to the idea of Irish political and social reform. There were, too, differences of stress between the other sections of the right and centre as to how the Irish problem should be tackled. But the arguments were about how to wear their Unionism, not as to whether it should be worn. The ultimate stand on the power of London stuck out a mile both in Chamberlain's telegram and Trevelyan's speech. Expressing the desire for reunion did not mean any abandonment of their fundamental position to get it. Both Radical Unionists had higher hopes than James, and infinitely higher hopes than Hartington, of a change in the Gladstonian aims. Hopes, however, are not policies, and this applied with even greater force to the pious yearnings of Goschen, Derby and others of that ilk. Whatever the differences on Unionist doctrine, those on Liberalism loomed larger. Yet what real chance was there of a 'Gentlemen's' government with Chamberlain, Churchill and the N.L.F. forcing the national political pace? Goschen and Derby were living in a 'Players'' world, and came to realise it. Hartington realised it already. Hence he can be counted along with James as a man of the centre—a playing 'Gentleman'—although his inner proclivities lay with Goschen and even the orthodox Conservatives. Fact played havoc with faction in the Liberal Unionist party and made its relative unity secure.

Dissatisfaction abounded. Naturally enough, when a party contained such disparate views. Whereas most of the Unionist press saw in the conference a fine display of confidence in the government, or a welcome rebuttal of Gladstone's feelers by insistence that 'Hawarden should come to' Hartington, the *Birmingham Daily Post* deplored the negative line of blind opposition to Home Rule and support for the Conservatives.[1] It did not proceed though to call for a pilgrimage to Hawarden. *The Times*,[2] *Standard*,[3] and *Daily Telegraph*[4] all thought Chamberlain's telegram illustrated only too clearly the impossibility of reunion between the two sets of Liberals while the Gladstonians remained full Home Rulers. The last journal went so far as to claim Chamberlain had shown agreement with Hartington and was refusing to follow Gladstone's suggestion that the government be forced to produce an Irish programme by joint Liberal pressure.[5] Again Bunce put a different stress on the situation, seeing in the telegram the one really positive feature of the whole conference, and hoping a reconciliation would be strongly pressed for as soon as possible.[6] Being

[1] *Birmingham Daily Post*, 8th December 1886.
[2] *The Times*, 8th December 1886.
[3] *Standard*, 8th December 1886.
[4] *Daily Telegraph*, 8th December 1886.
[5] *Ibid*.
[6] *Birmingham Daily Post*, 8th December 1886.

out of step with Chatsworth did not mean rushing off to join the Hawarden column. Birmingham had grumbled from the very beginning, and, while there was even the faintest chance of Gladstone repenting, wanted to appear prepared for a compromise. After all, Provincial Councils, retention of the Irish representation, special treatment for Ulster and their like were all Brummagem ware. A compromise was likely then to be a grand opening for Chamberlain and his men to be proved right; and what followed from that but renewed prospects of the succession to Gladstone. Nor must local tensions be left out of account in assessing Bunce's pronouncements. The pitched battle between Liberal Unionists and Gladstonians in Birmingham had yet to be fought. An undivided Liberal Association under a Chamberlainite leadership meant a fluid situation with the controlling group partially on the defensive. The press was a powerful means of keeping trouble within safe limits, and it cost nothing to please many waverers by friendliness to Gladstone joined to a radical Liberal Unionism. People in two minds like to feel their dilemma is in fact a logical position.

Privately the Cavendish family took pride in the conference. On 8th December the Duke of Devonshire recorded in his diary: 'The Unionist Liberals' meeting appears to have been a great success. Cavendish seems to have made an admirable speech, perhaps a better one than he ever made before.'[1] And Hartington himself seemed quite bucked for once, reporting: 'Everybody seems much satisfied with it all.'[2] He had apparently had 'to leave a good many things out'; what, will never be known, but nothing as it turned out to prevent James pronouncing it his best speech ever. The experience of receiving thanks from Churchill must have been quite exhilarating to a one-time 'boa constrictor'.[3] Chamberlain can hardly have been pleased with the cool reception given to his telegram. Nevertheless he had the benefit of the approval of those wanting reconciliation, if they were prepared to believe in his *bona fides*, and freedom from any public accusation by any responsible Gladstonian leader that he had come to favour pure negation. So smug were the general Liberal Unionist reactions and claims to influence that Salisbury was much at pains to point out how the government's policy had been and would be not

---

[1] Diaries of the 7th Duke of Devonshire, 8th December 1886. Devonshire Papers.

[2] Hartington to the Duchess of Manchester, 10th December 1886. Devonshire Papers, 340. Add. MS.

[3] Churchill had compared Hartington to a boa constrictor during a speech at Manchester on 6th November 1885 in the course of the general election campaign. The Whig leader had a short time before contumaciously refused an invitation to 'come over and join us' (i.e. 'me' = Churchill). R. R. James, *Lord Randolph Churchill*.

only its own, but truly Conservative. 'The Conservatives,' he told the City Association on 8th December, 'are as Conservative as ever.' Differences with the Liberal Unionists were in the background. 'The straightforwardness and simplicity of intention with which we have been met by Lord Hartington and those who follow him have made cooperation with them a very easy task indeed.'[1]

For Gladstonians genuinely anxious for reconciliation the conference was an affair of some importance. Would Hartington, as the *Daily Telegraph* put it, go to Hawarden for the sake of reunion, or would he compel it to go to him?[2] Or, and this was what moderate opinion generally desired, would hope be held out of a compromise? Their disappointment was intense and sometimes bitter. On the evening of 7th December, acting in the heat of the moment, MacColl wrote to Gladstone:

> I have just been reading the speeches at the Liberal Unionist meeting this afternoon. My impression is that they will help the cause of Home Rule. These men have no policy except coercion. They have gone back from their former professions at the last two General Elections. Their only policy is to say 'ditto, ditto' to a Tory Government, provided that Government will act a little more despotically. No power of sophistry will make their position defensible or even intelligible at the next dissolution. Those who may think it desirable to keep a Tory Government in office will vote for a Tory. Those who think it desirable to have a Liberal Government in office will vote for a Gladstonian Liberal.[3]

Hartington's 'reproach' that Gladstone had been silent on the 'Plan of Campaign' was condemned as 'cool' and Bright's letter as 'impudent'. MacColl fumed on:

> Where was he [i.e. Bright] when you were supporting in September a policy which would have made the 'Plan of Campaign' impossible? . . . I hope you will not for the present be induced to break your silence. The Liberal Unionists . . . deny you the right to wait for the Government's policy. I hope you will disappoint them.

Then follows a note of wistful caution:

> But I wish you could find means of warning the Irish against the most imprudent language attributed to Dillon as to 'a policy of revenge'.[4]

Here we see, and shall again and again, the Gladstonian dilemma of trying to win moderates for a policy not truly satisfying to extremists.

Most of those aiming at reconciliation now tended to echo what the *Daily News* had said after Herschell's Bristol speech, that the Liberal Unionists had not ever really said reunion was desirable, nor

[1] *The Times*, 9th December 1886.
[2] *Daily Telegraph*, 8th December 1886.
[3] Russell, *op. cit.*, pp. 129–30.   [4] *Ibid.*

responded to moves to bring it about.[1] MacColl made no mention of Chamberlain's telegram. Harcourt agreed with the general interpretation given to it by the Unionist press, expressing his view to Morley in characteristic terms. It was he claimed: 'nasty without being strong. Being interpreted it meant he (Chamberlain) was open to any plan so long as Mr G. ate dirt.'[2] Spencer took exception to it,[3] and Morley doubted the good faith of the Herschell reference and the apparent readiness for a conference.[4] He did, however, admit that Chamberlain's approach was markedly different from that of the conference majority, whose general position was like that of the Conservatives. Hartington's sole comment on the subject reeks of cynicism. Writing to his father on 10th December he said:

I have heard, but I don't know whether there is any truth in it that Mr G. is much impressed by Chamberlain's message and intends to accept his suggestion for a . . . Conference with all his conditions. If he does it can only be a move and to put me in a difficulty, for no agreement is likely to come out of it. . . .[5]

Once more, past experience of Gladstone and apprehension over Chamberlain's long-term plans had misled him. His informant was almost certainly Brett, in a letter of the previous day. 'I hear,' he wrote, 'that Mr G. is much impressed by Chamberlain's suggestion of a Conference, and is strongly inclined to propose one, upon the terms offered. This is upon high authority and I have no doubt about the truth of it myself.'[6] He was quite right. Morley had already complained to Spencer about Gladstone's readiness 'to humble himself in the dust'.[7] Reunion was all very well in itself, but there was a world of difference between discreet advances through Dale and a brash, almost frantic, call for a conference. Moreover, Morley realised how much more likely a compromise with Chamberlain was.

[1] *Daily News*, 15th November 1886.

[2] Harcourt to Morley, 9th December 1886. Copy in the Harcourt Papers. An extract is to be found in Gardiner, *op. cit.*, Vol. II, p. 19. Sir Edward Hamilton recorded on 9th December that the 'Liberal Unionist demonstration' had 'gone off with great éclat'. He thought Chamberlain had gone abroad expressly to be out of the way that autumn. Diary of Sir Edward Hamilton, Add. MS. 48645, pp. 48–9.

[3] Spencer to Granville, 11th December 1886. Granville Papers, P.R.O. 30, 29, 22A.

[4] Morley to Gladstone, 9th December 1886. Gladstone Papers, Add. MS. 44255, f. 141.

[5] Hartington to the Duke of Devonshire, 10th December 1886. Devonshire Papers, 340. 2066.

[6] Viscount Esher, *Extracts From Journals, 1880–1895*, pp. 167–8.

[7] Spencer to Granville, 8th December 1886. Granville Papers, P.R.O. 30, 29, 22A. See also Harcourt to Morley on the subject. Gardiner, *op. cit.*, Vol. II, p. 19.

Yet his leader still nourished hopes of an arrangement with Harting-ton's section.

Granville, Spencer, Harcourt and Herschell agreed with MacColl and Morley. On 9th December Granville told Spencer: 'The Unionist meeting was a success in one sense, but it has thrown an immense responsibility on Hartington. He appears to have some suspicion of this. But the others are like the Duc de Gramont in /70. It will be the Tories who will carry Home Rule after all.'[1] The next day he con-tinued in the same vein, saying Herschell's speech read to him 'like a surrender' and that 'whether that was so or not' he 'felt sure . . . Hartington's allusion was founded on that construction'.[2] Spencer himself was even more definite about the uselessness of any move for general reconciliation with the 'dissentients'.

> I do not [he insisted], believe in reunion at present and I think it bad policy to appear to wish for it by negotiation. It is too early for this; we must see what the Government are going to do first. This may pinch some of the dissentients. I suppose by the appeal in today's 'Times' to Chamberlain that they think J. C. will be shirking? if any exceptional legislation is proposed. If we attempt to reunite on compromise we shall estrange Parnell and put him in the position of 'going beyond his letter'.[3]

Harcourt, to whom this had been addressed, answered the next day:

> The situation is no doubt a bad one, but it will not be improved by our taking up an abject position. There was a time when a conciliatory attitude on the part of Mr G. would have been well and useful, but that is a long time ago; I feel sure that the Unionists have only one creed and that is *delenda est Hawarden*. For, as I think the most politic and dignified course is to keep quiet and to await events. If Ireland can be governed on the system which the present Government believe and in-sist, they are right and we are wrong. No doubt the country would prefer not to give Home Rule if they can help it. But if the old system breaks down as it has done before, and, as we believe, it will do again, we shall be proved to have been in the right. But nothing we can *say* now will affect that issue.[4]

Herschell was perhaps more discouraged than anyone else, thinking 'reconciliation' was 'at present out of the question'.[5] Harcourt dis-missed Hartington's compliments of Herschell as 'only spoken *in odium tertii*',[6] and Herschell himself had turned quite savagely upon

---

[1] Granville to Spencer, 9th December 1886. Spencer Papers.
[2] Granville to Spencer, 10th December 1886. Spencer Papers.
[3] Spencer to Harcourt, 13th December 1886. Harcourt Papers.
[4] Harcourt to Spencer, 14th December 1886. Spencer Papers.
[5] *Ibid.*
[6] *Ibid.*

a Liberal Unionist, who praised his temper. 'It is a pity you did not imitate it,' he had snapped.[1]

All three senior men were very worried about the 'Plan of Campaign'. Granville recommended a somewhat tortuous course of action. 'Surely our part is to be quiet. When obliged to speak to deprecate violence and allegedly to support reform of procedure, and complain strongly of coercion without remedial accompaniment, but not to go as far as obstruction to oppose it.'[2] Spencer broke a speaking engagement in Wales when the government moved against Dillon. 'I should have been in a hopeless position,' he told Harcourt, 'just now, before the case is developed, having (though under different circumstances) acted on the same lines now adopted by the Irish Government.'[3] Harcourt himself agreed with Spencer and had 'abounded to Morley in that sense—that we must have nothing to do with the present agrarian tactics of Dillon & Co.'[4] To have done so would have spoilt the advantages expected to accrue from government resort to coercion. Among which, of course, the most important were electoral gains and a better bargaining position *vis-à-vis* the 'dissidents' over the reunion issue. Yet could they escape from a dilemma any more than the government and its allies? Spencer had argued that compromise would upset Parnell just then, and therefore compromise must not be sought.[5] The Gladstonians were thus tied to the Irish Nationalists, and thereby willy-nilly involved in any discredit arising from the 'Plan of Campaign'. The government might well have its troubles because some of its supporters quailed before the logic of Unionism and found the prospect of coercion totally unpalatable. But if coercion strengthened the Home Rule case, would not compromise and inevitable row with Parnell become increasingly out of the question? In such a situation only '*delenda est Chatsworth*', with Hartington eating dirt, could be the policy. Moreover, the most Radical Gladstonians, like Labouchère had not hesitated to champion the 'Plan', aggravate relations with all Liberal Unionists still further, and risk men like Kilcoursie going over to the other side. Yet the Irish question never became the sole concern of the British electorate, and the two Liberals most aware of this were Gladstone and Chamberlain.

Although the G.O.M. misjudged the mood of the Liberal Unionist conference, there was more to his move than 'remorse at having

[1] Morley to Gladstone, 12th December 1886. Gladstone Papers, Add. MS. 44255, f. 142.

[2] Granville to Spencer, 9th December 1886. Spencer Papers.

[3] Spencer to Harcourt, 13th December 1886. Harcourt Papers.

[4] Harcourt to Spencer, 14th December 1886. Spencer Papers.

[5] Spencer to Harcourt, 13th December 1886. Harcourt Papers. Gardiner, *op. cit.*, Vol. II, p. 19.

divided the party', or the feeling that 'time was against him'. Time was against Liberal unity. The Harcourt idea of the Gladstonians biding their time assumed the Irish question alone interested the electorate and divided the 'dissidents' from the true faith. At best it could apply only to the Radical Unionists, and at worst, and with the 'plan' this was likely, not even to them. All the Radical Unionists, except Trevelyan, were men of a combative spirit. Few would view any increase in Parnellite power as a signal for surrender. Compromise on Chamberlainite lines would be ruled out by Parnellite power, whether or not Harcourt wanted it. Could it not have been then that Gladstone wished to bring all Liberal Unionists back to the fold for the British reasons already examined and for an Irish reason too— 'The Plan of Campaign'? What had appeared of medium importance in November, appeared absolutely vital by 8th December, the day Gladstone started his next reunion approach. Estate after estate was falling prey to the attack of agrarian 'revolutionaries'. Constitutional Home Rulers could best control extreme Irishmen by commanding the strength to offer a scheme of self-government. Reunion on a compromise he thought would create that strength. That most Liberal Unionists would only consider reunion on a unionist platform; that Chamberlain's group alone was eager for a conference and possessed little parliamentary as opposed to electoral strength; and that any compromise would be bound to be rejected by extreme Nationalists and very probably by Parnell—these were inconvenient trifles beneath the notice of the 'old parliamentary hand' in a mood of mission.

Gladstone tended to adopt towards the Liberal Unionist party the attitude of a self-confident wooer, interpreting a major rebuff as an invitation to show further attentions. His attitude to Chamberlain and Hartington showed what little impact the past year had made upon him. Dismissing the one as 'contemptuous as usual', and the other as 'a bull in a china shop', he placed enormous stress on the fact that only just over half of the Liberal Unionist parliamentary party had been at the conference.[1] As the party's supporters were loosely organised they could be won over on a *modus vivendi* programme, or, a common opposition to coercion unaccompanied by 'Liberal political legislation for Ireland'.[2] James was singled out as the instrument for success. On 8th December he urged Granville to get Herschell to sound out James about the Liberal Unionist view on reconciliation.[3] Replying on the 10th, Granville poured cold water on the whole idea,

[1] Gladstone to Ripon, 9th December 1886. Ripon Papers, Add. MS. 43515, f. 45.
[2] *Ibid.*
[3] Gladstone to Granville, 8th December 1886. Granville Papers, P.R.O. 30, 29, 29A.

forwarded Gladstone's letter to Spencer and told him the purport of the reply.[1] Unless Gladstone telegraphed him to proceed he was disinclined to write to Herschell, whose speech read to him like a surrender. Whether it was or not, Hartington had interpreted it that way. Both the 'dissidents'' and Salisbury's speeches made an approach to the former more difficult than before, because it would seem to made through alarm at their effect. Canvassing on the subject had been restricted to Spencer and Wolverton, both of whom saw great difficulties in the way, and Morley was believed to be of the same mind.[2] As far as he could see Salisbury had said he was not going to prepare remedial legislation for Ireland immediately, and had been fortified in that course by encouragement from the 'dissidents'. Spencer was asked to telegraph in the event of his disagreeing with Granville's conclusions. He did not.

Pride again made Gladstone draw back. He neither insisted with Granville, nor acted himself. Hartington had at last gone abroad on the 10th, though only for a month in France and Italy. James was most unlikely to take any step in his absence and had in any case told Granville it was quite out of the question—at least for the time being. His deep affection for Gladstone was not going to lead him into any quixotic and futile gestures. All this fussing in the face of disagreement from the principal Gladstonian henchmen aroused considerable irritation in those gentlemen. Spencer was foremost in expressing it: 'Mr G. is ready to grovel in the dust to bring about reunion, either from remorse at having divided the Party, or because he feels time is against him.'[3] An unjust, but understandable comment, it summed up excellently the exasperation felt when the leader indulged in useless manoeuvrings. Wolverton took the calmest view, simply deprecating an approach to the Liberal Unionists because it could be taken as a sign of weakness and lower party morale.[4] Like his col-

[1] Granville to Gladstone, 10th December 1886. Gladstone Papers, Add. MS. 44179, f. 204.

[2] Ibid.

[3] Spencer to Harcourt, 13th December 1886. Harcourt Papers. Gardiner, op. cit., Vol. II, p. 19.

[4] Wolverton to Granville, 11th December 1886. Granville Papers. P.R.O. 30, 29, 22A. Wolverton to Granville, 15th December 1886. Granville Papers, P.R.O. 30, 29, 28A. Harcourt and Morley had corresponded regularly during these days. On the 9th December 1886 Harcourt had hoped Gladstone would not be provoked by the Liberal Unionist meeting into a downright condemnation of its sponsors. Harcourt to Morley, 9th December 1886. Copy. Harcourt Papers. The next day Morley replied, expressing himself dissatisfied with the Liberal Unionist meeting. Chamberlain would soon be standing all by himself. Morley to Harcourt, 10th December 1886. Harcourt Papers. Both sent off letters on the 13th. Morley reported on his meeting with Parnell and on Herschell's clash with a 'Liberal Unionist'. Morley to Harcourt, 13th December 1886. Harcourt Papers. Harcourt

leagues he saw there was not the slightest chance of a response from Hartington.

Just as all this was boiling up Morley began the activity which was to make him the chief actor in Gladstone's bid to reconcile all anti-Conservatives. On 12th December he had another meeting with Parnell, who while quite prepared to support an Irish local government Bill, was, not surprisingly, totally opposed to its being regarded as in any way a substitute for Home Rule. He was not going at this stage to embrace Chamberlainite notions of County, Provincial and National Councils in place of the real thing. Still Gladstone persisted in his latest heart's desire, and at last seemed prepared for the supreme sacrifice—a speech by him, calling for reconciliation. Both Morleys thought this highly undesirable unless a favourable response was assured beforehand. John Morley knew one would not be forthcoming from the Hartingtonians, and that left Gladstone's *bête noire*—Chamberlain. The Dale connection could be used to ascertain his attitude and how much the telegram had represented a sincere and considered opinion. Yet whatever it was, Gladstonians generally would be against such a speech for the same reasons as Wolverton disliked the James scheme, and some were opposed to any compro-

for his part said the real crux about Ireland was whether or not it could be governed without Home Rule—his old argument in favour of Gladstone. Chamberlain might be in a difficult position, but that he would embrace' coercion and Gladstone's plan for an 'intermediate scheme' to settle Ireland struck Harcourt as useless as no one supported it. Salisbury's speech he saw as a 'slap in the face for Randolph'. Harcourt to Morley, 13th December 1886. Copy. Harcourt Papers. Harcourt had invited Morley to Malwood and Morley had accepted for after Christmas. On that same 13th Harcourt extended an invitation to Chamberlain and Collings. The former was heartily welcomed back and a joke made about how Collings had described Home Rule as a matter of 'administrative details' a mere twelve months before. Harcourt to Chamberlain, 13th December 1886, JC5/38/12. Two days before, Alfred Milner, formerly secretary to G. J. Goschen and now a Liberal Unionist organiser, received from his friend G. von Bunsen a letter in which Gladstone's Home Rule scheme was described as '*the* plan and the *only* plan for a lasting cure' for Ireland. G. von Bunsen to Milner, 11th December 1886. Milner Papers. Writing his diary on the 12th, Sir Edward Hamilton shared Harcourt's view of the Salisbury speech. It had been a 'Tory' effort, designed 'To take the taste of some of R. Churchill's unorthodox statements out of Tory mouths'. Diary of Sir Edward Hamilton, Add. MS. 48645, p. 51. He concluded that on the left Gladstone's position was 'getting more and more difficult' on account of automatic association with the 'Plan of Campaign'. *Ibid.* Chamberlain had come home on the 13th and on the following day promised to see Dilke as soon as he had settled down. The process must have been quickened on the 15th when a letter arrived from Bradlaugh, in which that redoubtable man went out of his way to deny having wished to abuse Chamberlain in a recent public pronouncement. It should be remembered that he had always received 'Joe's' support when it had been most needed. Chamberlain to Dilke, 14th December 1886. Dilke Papers, Add. MS. 43888, f. 87. Bradlaugh to Chamberlain, 15th December 1886. Chamberlain Papers, JC8/4/2/16.

mise at all. Arnold Morley, the Chief Whip, dreaded the consequences of an ill-considered 'Let us be friends' appeal.[1]

Chamberlain had become something of a mystery man since the autumn. His absence abroad and tortuous approach to the question of how much local authority he really wanted the Irish to have put him in what most people regarded as this most uncharacteristic category. Morley's contacts with Dale had not led to direct exchanges of views with the Radical Unionist leader. They were no more than means of stimulating goodwill in the mind of one very much in possession of his ear. That communications between the two Birmingham men had not been regular in the previous weeks is clear from the fact that Dale's invitation to Chamberlain to address the Central Nonconformist Committee, sent on 3rd November, was not forwarded abroad and remained unanswered until 14th December, the day after his return.[2] Apparently, Dale had been asked to secure Chamberlain for a Liberation Meeting and he now accepted with advice as to its timing. A plea for delay was based on the desire not to throw 'our shot away' at an inappropriate moment, when 'the public mind is absorbed either in the Irish question, or the state of foreign affairs'. He continued: 'I think that at any moment an opportunity may arise for striking an important blow in connection with the Disestablishment movement; but it will be necessary to watch carefully for the proper time. I know of no other question on which it would be possible to unite the advanced section of the Liberal party.' Next came a suggestion obviously aimed at minimising friction inside the Unionist camp. 'Should the meeting when it is held be directed to the general question of Disestablishment, or confined to the more urgent one of the Welsh Church?' There was no apparent desire for an urgent meeting with Dale. He merely mentioned that they would 'probably' have an opportunity to discuss this and other questions before Christmas, when his stay in Birmingham would end. The main part of the letter ends with a gloomy assessment of the political situation:

> The state of Liberal politics at the present time is almost enough to make one despair. Mr Gladstone has wrecked the Liberal Party, and I greatly fear we are in for a prolonged period of reaction. I am convinced that another General Election would give the Tories a clear and decisive

---

[1] Arnold Morley to Gladstone, 17th December 1886. Gladstone Papers, Add. MS. 44253, f. 46. The son of Samuel Morley (1809–86), who had flirted with Liberal Unionism in the first months of 1886, Arnold subsequently became Postmaster-General in the fourth Gladstone ministry. He sat as Gladstonian M.P. for East Nottingham.

[2] Dale to Chamberlain, 3rd November 1886. Chamberlain Papers, JC5/20/13. Chamberlain to Dale, 14th December 1886. Copy. Chamberlain Papers, JC5/20/57.

majority. The Counties are absolutely lost to us and there will be further heavy losses in the boroughs. For this Mr Gladstone is primarily to blame, but at the same time nothing can exceed the unwisdom of the present managers of the Home Rule section of the Liberal Party.[1]

On this showing Morley was going to have to overcome considerable 'contempt' before getting down to brass tacks over reunion. If Welsh disestablishment was Chamberlain's ideal for achieving it, no self-respecting Gladstonian would consider the project further. The letter as a whole is surely attempting to argue that things should go on as they are? The Conservatives are on top and nothing can be done about it for some time. Questions of Irish and foreign policy militate in their favour. The full disestablishment dose must wait and meantime why not limit activity to the Welsh issue? To do so makes the conflict secondary, and a possible score for Radical Unionism with important electoral consequences. Certainly, it seems that on arrival home Chamberlain lived fully up to Morley's judgment as being 'content with things as they are'. Why should he not have been when, as Brett said, Churchill and Natty Rothschild seemed 'to conduct the business of the Empire in great measure, *together*, in consultation with Chamberlain'?[2] He could not lead the Liberals while Gladstone remained in public life, or even alive. Moreover, 'reaction' held few terrors for Radical Unionism if it added up to the Dartford and Bradford programme. Was not the word thrown in to pander to Dale's prejudices? After all, it must be admitted the letter was a very tactful one all round. Two things only could upset the applecart, trouble in Birmingham and the defeat of Churchill in the Cabinet.

For some reason the letter to Dale did not go straight off. In the meantime local and national political intelligence must have acted with some force on Chamberlain's mind.

Since writing the above [he added in a postscript] I have decided to address my constituents on the 5th January. Previously to making any public declaration, I should like to talk over the situation with my Liberal colleagues in the representation of Birmingham, and I have asked them (Mr Bright excepted, as he is away from Birmingham) to dine here on Monday next at 7.30 p.m. Will you join us? You are in the

[1] Chamberlain to Dale, 14th December 1886. Copy. Chamberlain Papers, JC5/20/57.

[2] Reginald Brett to Hartington, 3rd October 1886. Esher Papers. Reginald B. Brett (1852–1930) had been Hartington's private secretary from 1878 until 1885, and had sat from 1880 until 1885 as Liberal M.P. for Penryn and Falmouth. In the 1885 general election he contested Plymouth unsuccessfully as a Liberal and never stood for the Commons again. Rosebery made him Secretary to the Office of Works in 1895 and from then on he never looked back, becoming Permanent Secretary to the War Office in 1900. Baron Rothschild (1840–1915) was a Liberal Unionist and brother-in-law to Rosebery.

confidence of all of us and we should be glad of your advice and opinion.[1]

There is perhaps some reason for supposing national factors were troubling him more than they otherwise would have done because of their effect on the Birmingham scene. Instead of remaining at home until Christmas he went off almost immediately to London. There, though a coercionist, he made out to someone later in touch with Morley that he was not. Now horror of coercion was well-developed in Birmingham and the Gladstonians knew just how to exploit it. He must too have found out soon after arrival that Churchill had been defeated in the Cabinet on the English and Irish local government issues. On the 17th he vented his anger on this to Dilke, yet did not seem to worry about coercion or foreign policy.[2] Even so, it was probably the prospect of coercion which had occasioned his sudden move to address his constituents, albeit three weeks hence. Churchill did not write urging him to speak out on local government until the 19th, but was at pains to stress all might yet be well and urged moderation of tone.[3] Chamberlain also told Morley's informant that he was going to do nothing to endanger either the government's existence or the unity of the Liberal Unionist party, although determined to work for the abandonment of the coercion plan. Home Rule would be thought to be kept under control and the government in office for two or three years.[4] It would seem then that while he was still hoping all would go well in Cabinet and that Salisbury would take note of his refusal to compromise on local government, things in Birmingham had reached a serious pitch. Had the crisis been a truly national one Bright would certainly have been brought into the conclave. With three weeks to play with Chamberlain would have made arrangements to obtain his views and told Dale he was going to do so. Bright was rather aloof from the split in Birmingham and not at all hated by the Gladstonians. On the contrary, whether or not he deserved it, all local Liberals looked on him with something like affection. Age, ill-health and a general passivity kept him out of provincial difficulties.

Chamberlain's telegram to the Liberal Unionist conference expressed a genuine desire for reunion, however unlikely its accomplishment on his terms might be. His anti-coercionism was simply window dressing to fend off trouble in his base. A concern for Liberal reunion was natural enough in one who hoped to lead the

---

[1] Chamberlain to Dale, 14th December 1886. Copy. Chamberlain Papers, JC5/20/57.

[2] Gwynn and Tuckwell, *op. cit.*, Vol. II, p. 265.

[3] Garvin, *op. cit.*, pp. 272–3.

[4] Morley to Gladstone, 18th December 1886. Gladstone Papers, Add. MS. 44255, f. 146.

party, but that could hardly come about if he had lost his grip on Birmingham and with it most of his power to influence politics. Just as before he had to trim, and that meant lies.

Though Morley had long been working up to an approach, Harcourt got in first, with an invitation to Malwood.[1] Chamberlain replied on 15th December in a friendly and light-hearted spirit.[2]

Your letter and invitation have given me great pleasure. Although retired from politics, I am gratified to find that I am not quite forgotten and that, in the midst of your absorbing struggles, you can still find time to think of the poor exile 'returning from a foreign strand'. As you have rightly concluded, I have lost all touch with present domestic controversies, but I should indeed rejoice to join you in historical researches and enquire into the morality of the Norman Conquest, or the blackguardly treatment of Boadicea. Alas, the prospect is too fair. I find all sorts of engagements, chiefly personal and private, awaiting me, and I do not think I can leave Birmingham, except for a flying visit which I am paying to London tomorrow, until I go up for the Session. But I do owe you a visit to Malwood and there is no debt which I could repay with greater pleasure, whenever a convenient opportunity arises. I expect to have plenty of leisure next year, and perhaps even you may find it possible to devolve the cares of leadership on Osborne Morgan—or Labouchère—or whoever else may be the heir apparent to that honour, and then we can run down to the Forest for a Saturday and Sunday and 'babble of green fields'.

Reading between the lines it is easy to see that Chamberlain, with Birmingham very much on his mind, was seriously exercised by the direction national affairs were taking, and entertained a lively fear of Labouchère and the new Radicals. Politics was not the 'still life' many Liberals of both sections desired. Reunion would not lead to a restoration of the *status quo ante*. Events had moved on, making Chamberlain into a Liberal of the left-centre because men of the Labouchère stamp refused to envisage compromises on matters like disestablishment where he saw they would have to be made. Their very distance from office and responsibility encouraged their natural proclivities. They now hated him and would shun his leadership if reunion came about. And on that very issue their attitude was as unhelpful as Goschen's. Friends had to be fostered wherever they could be found and Harcourt was a good one. The Malwood visit had therefore to be kept, like the Liberation meeting, for a vitally strategic moment.

Whatever was going to happen, a strengthening of Radical

---

[1] Harcourt to Chamberlain, 13th December 1886. Chamberlain Papers, JC5/38/52.

[2] Chamberlain to Harcourt, 15th December 1886. Harcourt Papers.

Unionism strengthened Chamberlain. If Churchill was thwarted in the Cabinet, extra pressure from the left Unionists could well save the day for reform. If not, the larger Chamberlain's following the better chance he stood of making any reconciliation talks with the Gladstonians undertaken alone into a serious proposition. An exchange between equals they would never be, but there are times when a 'Good little un' with an important electoral draw could be of vital assistance to the best of 'Big uns'. Local government was his main immediate concern, yet the coercion bogey loomed larger on 15th December. To a man of resource the local crisis offered an opportunity. If 5th January was to be the time for soothing Birmingham Radical Unionists of a squeamish disposition, why should it not be given a wider significance and soothe others of like feelings, Radical Unionists, floaters and former abstainers? On 4th December Trevelyan had invited him to a meeting at Hawick, planned for the 8th or 15th of January.[1] He now reciprocated and Trevelyan straightaway accepted with some enthusiasm.

> I shall gladly attend the Radical Unionist gathering. Being out of Parliament, my steering is rather delicate just now; for I do not care to come in except for a *Liberal* seat, as I never should be compatible in any other. I agree with your general views on Ireland, and the pleasure it gives me to have you at Hawick is greater than I can say.[2]

The presence of the second most important Radical Unionist, a non-Birmingham figure, along with the sectional leader transformed prospects considerably. What would at best have been a west midlands affair acquired a national character.

While Chamberlain was in London Dale took the initiative and wrote again to Morley. He urged that Chamberlain be offered an olive branch. Morley told Gladstone on the 18th, describing the letter as 'strong and very good', but his optimism must have been shaken by what his London informant had told him.[3] Nevertheless he mentioned none of this in the very warm reply sent off that same day to Dale, restricting himself to a note of nostalgia.[4] 'When you speak of the hopes you once had of the good that Chamberlain and I might do together for the country you recall what until a year ago was the great dream of my life. Things do not look as if your hopes and my dream were likely to come true.' Having deplored the outbreak of

[1] Trevelyan to Chamberlain, 4th December 1886. Chamberlain Papers, JC5/70/18.
[2] Trevelyan to Chamberlain, 16th December 1886. Chamberlain Papers, JC5/70/19.
[3] Morley to Gladstone, 18th December 1886. Gladstone Papers, Add. MS. 44255, f. 146.
[4] Morley to Dale, 19th December 1886. Dale Papers.

mutual recriminations, he went on: 'Nothing would be easier to me than to banish all sense of grievance from my mind'; but ended with a non-committal platitude: 'I don't know . . . that I have any more to say—whether he and I are destined to work together again in the future no man can tell. But I at least wish not to forget our comradeship in the past.' Dale could at least be pleased, however, that his mood was answered and Morley had not gone back on his earlier moves. Indeed, being a cunning man, Morley had spiced the letter with exactly the sort of sentiment to which he knew Chamberlain would be likely to succumb. Dale would, he supposed, show it to his friend and lead to the first crucial step towards reunion being taken by the Radical Unionists. Events did not move that well for Morley. He got a letter from Chamberlain, on the 21st, but it was one of personal greetings sent with a present of oysters, and written at the same time as similar letters in previous years.[1] It is well-nigh certain Chamberlain wrote after seeing or hearing about Morley's letter. Monday, 19th, had been the date of the dinner party at Highbury. Absence of any correspondence from Chamberlain to Dale recounting its proceeding suggests he was there, and if this was so, he certainly would not have omitted to raise the matter of Morley and his letter. Chamberlain's cunning more than matched Morley's. He was not going to make the first move unless absolutely forced, and things had not yet reached that pitch.

> I do not like to discontinue an old custom [he cooed], and have therefore ventured to send you my usual humble tribute of Birmingham oysters. Pray overlook the Unionist flavour, which you may possibly detect in them and believe that they are accompanied by my sincere and hearty wishes for your health and happiness and personal prosperity. I am sorry that all the interests that we have so long had in common have been, by the relentless hand of fate, relegated to a dim and distant future; and that we are probably doomed to spend the rest of our lives in a fruitless discussion of the only subject on which we differ. May the controversy carry with it as little bitterness as is compatible with the weakness of our nature and the strength of our convictions![2]

Sincere no doubt, but 'devilish clever'. It evaded yet answered the decoy letter. Evaded, by avoiding mention of it and making no move.

[1] Chamberlain to Morley, 21st December 1886. Copy. Chamberlain Papers, JC5/54/691. The Gladstonian leadership had been pooling opinions on the situation and on 21st December Harcourt wrote to Gladstone telling him Spencer had sent on the crucial packet of letters and laying out his general assessment of the situation once again. It would, he thought, be no practical good approaching either the Hartington, or the Chamberlain party of Liberal Unionists. Both were in an irreconcilable humour; much better therefore to wait upon events. Parnell he professed to find as inexplicable as usual. Harcourt to Gladstone, 21st December 1886. Gladstone Papers, Add. MS. 44200, f. 186.

[2] *Ibid.*

Answered, by sending goodwill and stressing the width of their agreement. Behind the nonchalance lay a serious purpose, yet it was to be achieved at the price of a struggle for position. This Chamberlain meant to win.

So overcome was Morley by all this and so keen his curiosity, that he quite gave the game away. Thanking Chamberlain by return of post, he remarked: 'As it happens, no later than Sunday last, I wrote in reply to a letter from Dale something which I rather thought he might show you on Monday evening.' And then comes some fishing for information: 'But I believe the opportunity did not arise. I am not sorry—for as it is, we see that the other had something of the same sort in his mind.'[1] This would not appear to have been quite honest. He was surely doing no more than trying either to arouse Chamberlain's interest if Dale had not spoken out, or to get an admission of a lukewarm response if he had. Still, whatever his motive, he came very much to the point. 'I have often thought it a pity that we had not had a plain conversation together, as to the personal matters between us. . . . The future is too obscure for anticipation. Nothing can ever happen to me so painful, so miserable, as the events of this year.'[2] Here is a hint that a personal talk could lead to bigger things. That Morley was in fact sorry because, as far as he could judge, Chamberlain was still in the dark as to his attitude is perfectly clear from what he wrote to Dale on 22nd December. So is his fear lest the affair leak out.

> I had a very kind letter from Chamberlain this morning (of which, however, I do not wish you to speak to any third person). In reply I told him that I had written to ask you to send him my letter—as if your notion, if you should see fit. When you come to town again pray let us meet.[3]

Provided events worked for Chamberlain as they had done here, his prospects during any contact that might take place with the Gladstonians looked like being remarkably bright.

The brighter they were the better. The local government row in the Cabinet might end to his and Churchill's satisfaction, but the more feasible an arrangement with the Gladstonians became, the more effective a final threat of desertion accompanied by a statement of the situation would become. Chamberlain had always to try so to manage affairs that he could move in either direction—Conservative–Hartingtonian or Gladstonian at a moment's notice. So while he wanted reunion on his terms he had to use any move towards it as part of a power game inside the Unionist alliance. This alliance would have to serve his purposes until the very day of reunion, if it ever came, otherwise his bargaining position would be substantially

[1] Garvin, *op. cit.*, p. 276.   [2] *Ibid.*
[3] Morley to Dale, 22nd December 1886. Dale Papers.

104

reduced. He sometimes tended to forget a good hand could be overplayed and, though himself objecting to the proposed checks and restrictions in the County Councils Bill, Lord Rothschild warned him on the 19th that Salisbury 'if driven too hard might jib'.[1] Chamberlain remained unimpressed, insisting that an undemocratic scheme would do 'unbelievable mischief'.[2] What this meant in terms of his own actions is not clear. Nevertheless, Brett thought it necessary to add his warning and advice on the 22nd.[3]

> It appears that J. Morley knows of your strong objection to the County Government Bill and some hopes are already shaping themselves into prophecies that the Union of the Unionists will shortly end. Perhaps this feeling acting upon Lord Salisbury has brought about a desire of re-arrangement of the Bill. . . . However, I understand that two things are important. Firstly, that you should not appear to threaten Lord Salisbury, as he is not at present strong enough to disregard the right wing of the party, and that any semblance of yielding to pressure would weaken him still more. Secondly, that it would be useful to the Alliance that you should be the first publicly to point out the dangers—such as they are— of extravagance in the new local bodies, dangers greater than exist in the towns; and further that the remedy does not lie in fancy franchises and ex-officio members, but in the control of the Central Government, and in self acting interdependent laws. This 'little rift' is by no means so serious as the crevasse which exists in the Gladstonian camp.

To Brett then, method was all. He expected an outcome pleasing to the left Unionists, planning to tell Hartington: 'Chamberlain's attitude is so determined that the Government will be forced to reconsider their decision, unless they abandon the policy of maintaining the unity of the Unionist party.'[4] Gladstonian knowledge of the 'little rift' did Chamberlain no harm so long as the Conservatives would do something to keep him. Indeed, a crisis could illustrate how high a price the G.O.M. would have to pay to detach him. Morley was the one to find out about Churchill's defeat in Cabinet. Naturally, he told his leader both about this and his exchange with Chamberlain.[5] Ignorance of Dale's talk to Chamberlain led him into saying the latter had acted entirely on his own initiative and in good faith.

Signs of what Brett called the 'crevasse' in 'the Gladstonian camp' were not wanting. The new Radicals defended the 'Plan of Campaign' and so went clean contrary to what we know Gladstonian majority opinion to have been. Professor Stuart, speaking at Darlington, declared that even if there was illegality, moral justice lay at the

---

[1] Garvin, *op. cit.*, p. 273.   [2] *Ibid.*
[3] Brett to Chamberlain, 22nd December 1886. Copy. Esher Papers.
[4] Brett to Hartington, 24th December 1886. Devonshire Papers, 340. 2068.
[5] Morley to Gladstone, 23rd December 1886. Gladstone Papers, Add. MS. 44255, f. 149.

bottom of it. Just as Quakers had sometimes defied laws to which they took objection, Dillon and his friends were fighting the injustices of the Irish land system.[1] Stansfeld was less extreme in his statements, yet they added up to an open avowal of sympathy with the 'Plan'.[2] Mundella ventured into Chamberlain's 'Grand Duchy' on 22nd December and told an audience at Wednesbury that Liberals hated all illegality, but would not be deterred from fighting for justice by the accusation that they condoned crime.[3] 'Crevasse' was a strong word for Brett to have used—too strong in fact. Gladstone had enormous prestige and influence, especially on the Irish question. This cannot be doubted in view of what happened whenever any policy change was effected. Many Radicals would eat their words rather than go against him. Mundella, for instance, practically worshipped the ground he walked on. Just three days before the Wednesbury speech he had written describing a visit to Hawarden:

> The G.O.M. is really grand at home. He lives in a house of books. His library is immense; and as for diligence and method, they surpass belief. His knowledge is the *widest*, the minutest, the most accurate that any man probably ever possessed. I shall never forget my visit. I had him alone the whole time, Mrs and Miss Gladstone being the only two persons in the house. It was like living in another world for its intellectuality, abounding knowledge and wonderful prescience. I felt myself a very dry sponge, so I absorbed all I could in the time I was with him.[4]

Rebels were not made of such stuff. Trouble there would undoubtedly be if reconciliation talks began, but even Labouchère would not go so far as directly to challenge his leader's authority. His guns would be trained on the Liberal Unionist representatives. By provoking them into breaking off relations the same object could be attained. Gladstone's aims would be then sapped rather than stormed. But for every Labouchère there would be several Mundellas. Morley was undoubtedly right in thinking that with Chamberlain's friendly attitude the 'way is now open, if the time should come for *pour-parlers*'.[5]

It did, for on the day he wrote these words to Gladstone came the news of Churchill's resignation. Chamberlain's balancing act was suddenly brought into jeopardy. Practically speaking he had seen this as never voting 'with the Tories, unless they are in danger', and voting

[1] *Annual Register*, 1886, p. 301. Professor Stuart was Gladstonian Liberal M.P. Hoxton, Shoreditch. In 1875, at the age of thirty-two he had been appointed to the Chair of Mechanisms and Applied Mathematics at Cambridge.
[2] *Annual Register*, 1886, p. 302.
[3] *The Times*, 23rd December 1886.
[4] Mundella to Messrs. Leader, 19th December 1886. Mundella–Leader Papers.
[5] Morley to Gladstone, 23rd December 1886. Gladstone Papers, Add. MS. 44255, f. 149.

'against them whenever we can safely do so'.[1] The scope for putting this into operation had been limited because of the brief nature of the parliamentary Session. On Parnell's Bill he had contented himself with abstention. Still, these plans genuinely represented a firm conviction. By 'we' he meant the whole Liberal Unionist party, which he wished to preserve intact. Although Hartington had rejected Salisbury's overtures for a coalition, he had not obliged by falling in with this interpretation of his function. Chamberlain had not, however, let the desire for party unity force him to abandon it. Even abstention on a matter like Parnell's Bill emphasised his independence of the government and helped preserve the Radical Unionists' morale. Faced with a choice between keeping in step with Hartington and maintaining his hold on Radical Unionism he had to opt for the latter—his lifeline. How could he ever lead a reunited Liberal party if all the Radicals lost confidence in him before reunion was accomplished? Ostensibly the Cabinet row was about projected Service Estimates, but the world guessed, and rightly, that it had been more broadly based. Chances of reform seemed to have dwindled overnight and Chamberlain did immediately that which his basic aims and dire necessity left him no alternative but to do—namely, made the now famous speech at Birmingham appealing for Liberal reunion. He had in any case to make two speeches. The conclave at Highbury had decided that the situation demanded the bringing forward of the prospective address to his constituents from 5th January, to 23rd December; and, what was more, that he should on the same day enter into 'frank parley'[2] with his Divisional Council, many of whose

---

[1] Chamberlain to Hartington, 9th September 1886. Devonshire Papers, 340. 2043. Much to Queen Victoria's annoyance the news reached her from a newspaper—*The Times*. For the monarch's part in politics at this stage see F. Hardie, *The Political Influence of Queen Victoria, 1861–1901*, Chapter 2. Sir Edward Hamilton thought Churchill was 'The "Joe" of the Conservatives'. 'They (i.e. Churchill and Chamberlain) have both taken what appears to be for the moment suicidal steps; but they are both too clever by half to strand themselves permanently.' The resignation had been like 'a thunderbolt from a tolerably clear sky'. Sir Edward Hamilton's Diary, 23rd December 1886, Add. MS. 48645, p. 65. Akers-Douglas, the Conservative Chief Whip, wrote to W. H. Smith, destined to replace Churchill as Leader of the Commons and currently Secretary of State for War, that many of Churchill's 'particular friends' thought his behaviour 'insane'. Akers-Douglas to W. H. Smith, 24th December 1886. Viscount Chilston, *W. H. Smith*, p. 227. Akers-Douglas proved a shrewder judge than Hamilton on this occasion. Lord Cranbrook, Salisbury's Lord President of the Council, found Churchill's explanation of why he had resigned unconvincing. A. E. Gathorne Hardy, Editor, *Gathorne Hardy, 1st Earl of Cranbrook: A Memoir*, p. 280. A. J. Balfour later commented about Churchill: 'He rarely took advice. Even more rarely did he take good advice. Though admirable with subordinates, with equals he was difficult and sometimes impossible.' Sir J. A. R. Marriott, *Modern England, 1885–1945: A History of My Own Times*, p. 33.

[2] Garvin, *op. cit.*, p. 277.

members disagreed strongly with his Irish policy. After all, with sympathy mounting for evicted Irish tenants among Liberals of all shades, he had to make a determined attempt at disentangling himself from the Conservatives, or risk an explosion among a restive '2000' and complete discredit in Radical eyes.

Municipal election results had if anything aggravated the local restiveness. Modest Conservative gains had given the Schnadhorst section another argument: might not Radical Unionism be the means for bringing reaction to the seats of power in Birmingham—the citadel of reform? Had not Liberal Unionism generally given a reactionary government security of tenure? Churchill had certainly gone at an awkward time; and gone without giving Chamberlain warning. With him went not only the chief force for reform, but 'Our Joe's' only friend in the Cabinet. Great hopes had been pinned on him from the outset, the Dartford–Bradford programme merely serving as a pleasant confirmation of what was anyway in store. On 19th September, Chamberlain had exulted to Hartington: 'R. Churchill's statement about Local Govt. Board and Public Works looks as though the Govt. had determined to accept National or Provincial Councils'.[1] Just a day before Dartford he exuded the same self-confidence to Dilke, who recorded in his diary:

> He seemed to think that he could keep Mr Gladstone out for life, and was persuaded that Randolph would give him all he wanted and leave Hartington and Salisbury in the lurch. Randolph had promised him to have an anti-Jingo foreign policy, leaving Turkey to her fate, and to pacify Ireland with the National Councils scheme, modified into two Councils, or into Provincial Councils, to suit Ulster; and Churchill had also promised him procedure reform—that is, a sharper closure—and a three-acres-and-a-cow policy for England.[2]

Defeat for Churchill had warned him all this might after all be difficult to come by, but, as was natural in a man of his sanguine temperament, he had hoped the setback would prove temporary, especially if he thundered off stage. Now that was out of the question and he found himself thundering on stage. Stirring up trouble rather than trying to soothe it down, as he would undoubtedly have done had Churchill remained at the Exchequer. A temporarily thwarted Churchill was a very different kettle of fish from no Churchill at all. Within the Unionist alliance he was alone as never before. His dealings with the government, if any, would now have to be through Hartington. As long ago as 22nd October Hicks Beach had pointed out that the Cabinet 'would have some considerable difficulty in

[1] Chamberlain to Hartington, 19th September 1886. Devonshire Papers, 340. 2051.
[2] Gwynn and Tuckwell, *op. cit.*, Vol. II, p. 265.

communicating with Joe C.'[1] Churchill had destroyed the only way found for overcoming it.

Before it was destroyed, of course, Churchill had told him enough for the resignation to be rightly interpreted. At least, up to a point. For who was to know that a great game was being played by a Minister intent upon a quick victory; that he expected strong Liberal and Radical Unionist pressure to be brought upon Salisbury; and that the result of this was supposed to be that the Prime Minister would 'take a broad view of the situation'?[2] Nevertheless, Chamberlain's speech was something of a bull's eye, making him the national cynosure. Very shrewdly, it was the one to the Divisional Council that he chose as his principal vehicle. Equally shrewdly, he did not make it until the discontented had aired their views, asked their questions and received more than their fair share of his notorious and irresistible charm. His subjects were the ministerial crisis and the future of the Liberal party, and he went much further than the determined disentangling opted for by the conclave. Churchill was a Liberal unbeknown to himself. 'I confess it seems to me possible— I fear it is probable—that the old Tory influences have gained the upper hand and that we may be face to face with a Tory Government whose proposals no consistent Liberal will be able to support.'[3] Caution of language could not, and was not intended to hide a firm threat to go further than disentanglement into downright opposition. Then began his invitation to the Gladstonians.

> It seems to me that they have a great and perhaps a final opportunity . . . we Liberals are agreed upon ninety-nine points of our programme; we only disagree upon one. . . . We are agreed, I say, upon I believe every important point of Liberal policy as affecting England, Scotland and Wales. Do you not think that these three countries have some claim upon us? Do not you think they have a right to put pressure upon their leaders to do those things upon which we are agreed? . . . But I go further than that. I say even upon Irish matters, when I look into the thing, I am more surprised at the number of points upon which we are agreed than at the remainder upon which for the present we must be content to differ. . . . Without solving this land question Home Rule is impossible; and I believe that if you solve it, Home Rule will be unnecessary. . . .[4]

The crux of his speech was expressed most dexterously, the sort of compromise he suggested corresponding closely to his particular ideas on Ireland.

[1] Lord Stalbridge to Hartington, 22nd October 1886. Devonshire Papers, 340. 2056. Stalbridge was formerly Lord Richard Grosvenor, but recently the Chief Whip of the nominally united pre-split Liberal party.
[2] Garvin, *op. cit.*, p. 275.
[3] Garvin, *op. cit.*, p. 278.   [4] *Ibid.*

I believed it was possible to devise a plan—I have never doubted it—I am convinced now that, sitting round a table and coming together in a spirit of compromise and conciliation, almost any three men, leaders of the Liberal party, although they may hold opposite views upon another branch of the question, would yet be able to arrange some scheme which would fulfil the conditions I have laid down, which would not involve unnecessary or unfair risk to the British taxpayer, and yet would make in a short time the Irish tenant owner of the land he cultivates. . . . Even upon this question of local government, the difference recedes if you come to think of it. We are all agreed, I imagine, as to the nature of a plan to be applied to England and Scotland. We are all agreed to apply it in principle at all events, with such alteration of detail as may be necessary, to the sister country of Ireland. We are prepared, none more so than I, to decentralise the system of administration which is known as Dublin Castle. . . . Is it not possible now once more that we may make an honest attempt, if not to agree upon every point, at least to agree upon this—that we will proceed to carry out all those vast changes, all those important reforms upon which there is no difference; and that we will leave it to time and to experience and to free and frank discussion to say whether when we have accomplished all these we shall not go one step farther in the direction of the views of those who now unfortunately are our opponents? . . .

Having plied his audience copiously with sweet reason, he ended by playing his strongest card—local sentiment.

My life is bound up in Birmingham; all its institutions, its prosperity, its politics have been my care and principal thought for the whole course of my political life. I know its people. Your faces, if not your names, are familiar to me. As I walk through the streets I seem to gather instinctively the minds of the people.[1]

Quite a masterpiece in its way, it swept the board. 'A large part of his audience had been full of refractory feelings when the meeting began. When it ended, they all dispersed in a melted and fraternal mood.'[2] Why had it happened? This excoriating man, attacker of established people as much as of established ideas, had, simply by speaking harshly of the traditional foe and amicably of the Gladstonians, suggesting his own ideas provide a basis for Liberal reunion, gently depreciating the Irish policies of Gladstone and saying he loved Birmingham, won a substantial victory. How substantial few present at the Ellen Street Board School quite realised, but Chamberlain was of their number. Garvin's opinion that Chamberlain knew 'about as little as may be of self-conscious psychology' is surely tommy-rot? Rarely can a political leader have been so acutely aware of the sort of audience he was facing. It could be played on like an old

[1] Garvin, *op. cit.*, p. 279.   [2] *Ibid.*

violin if one only knew how, and he did. The effect might not have been permanent, but he was always able to bring off a repeat performance. A trimmer's rôle in modern politics has vast drawbacks. Generally, like Goschen, he is quite unable to muster a mass following, cannot therefore easily stir the people in times of moment, and depends on personal contacts. Such a man is often overborne in crises under an oligarchy, let alone a democracy. Chamberlain was no trimmer in the usual sense of the word. His political position on the lefter-most wing of Unionism was never in doubt. He was not, to use Goschen again, a man who could without much effort belong to either great party. Yet he was *par excellence* the one leading statesman in December 1886 whose adherence to his side was in doubt. So left wing was he on domestic issues, and even on Irish ones barring Home Rule, that Conservatives and Gladstonians alike tended to regard him as virtually a law unto himself. This speech was really an effort directed towards making sure that that was literally true. He spoke out as the nation's leading Independent, for that is what he was rather than a trimmer. His bargaining position *vis-à-vis* Gladstone appeared very poor in face of Churchill's resignation. It looked as though the government might not mind his breaking with them and that destroyed the delicate balance working in his favour, which was described above. No one could say, however, that the speech indicated he had anything but a bargain in mind. There was no impending trip to Canossa. All that had changed was the tone. Chamberlain was later to say he regarded the speech as a sequel to the telegram of 7th December.[1] Gladstone considered that contemptuous in tone. The same could not be said of the speech, despite its bold independence. Certainly, every word of it was seriously meant, even the sentiment at the end. Very often in politics truth turns to one's advantage. Is not honesty said to be the best policy? Chamberlain was killing three birds with one stone. First, he was bidding to keep his hold on the base making independence a reality. Only a man with a substantial and concentrated public support can be a serious independent political force. Second, he was making known his displeasure to the government. If it wanted him as part of an active Unionist alliance things would have to change. If it did not, then his attack did no harm that was not already done. Third, he was trying to keep alive his chances of succeeding Gladstone by responding to Morley's approach through Dale. All three aims interacted one upon the other.

A successful local meeting meant aim number one was attained for the immediate future, and it was the immediate future that was going to affect the remaining two aims first. What Birmingham had dictated fitted in fairly well with what Chamberlain himself wanted

[1] In a letter to Churchill of 3rd January 1887. Churchill, *op. cit.*, p. 268.

to do. He had not, as things turned out, played the hypocrite over coercion. We do not know that he was intending to before the Churchill issue put it into the background, but he would certainly have made conditions and was making out to some at any rate that he opposed it. Now he dealt in generalities when attacking the government, and concentrated on explaining his way to reunion. As it stood about halfway between the government and Gladstone his case seemed convincing. Labouchère's taunt that, along with Churchill, Chamberlain ignored the power of the 'machine' was sadly wide of the mark.[1] Things were just the other way round. Precisely because he recognised this power he wooed his local caucuses with great care. Indeed, he cherished them. There were occasions, like 21st April, when he had differed from the caucus so seriously that complete frankness would have been politically suicidal.[2] He had under these circumstances to wheedle out of it a decision at once clear and flexible. Clear to please the caucus. Flexible to enable him to go quietly on his way while appearing to adhere to the agreed policy. Generally, however, tergiversation was unnecessary and he 'made' the caucus decision. That he could do so was a tribute to the loving care bestowed on local concerns. Washing one's clean linen in public was in the Radical tradition and he had raised it to a fine art.

Trevelyan did not witness it this time after all, yet no Conservative leader needed persuading that the meeting was of national importance. Matters no longer stood as they had on the 16th. Chamberlain seemed belatedly to be echoing what Morley had claimed at Leeds in November: 'You will not get a bounteous affluence of fresh water into the Tory pump by the simple act of fitting it with a brand-new Radical handle, kindly lent for the occasion by a friend from Birmingham.'[3] Emotionally it was highly satisfying for the Radical Unionists to hear that the lending might be coming to an end. More so for some than any concrete move towards the Gladstonians. Naturally the Gladstonian minority of the nominally united Association could not feel like this, but Radical Unionism and its hangers-on called the tune. Moving away from the Conservatives without adopting full Home Rule was exactly what Chamberlain was offering. For the government his speech meant nothing less than 'Heads I win, Tails you lose'. Gambling on the success of this approach, he had indulged his feelings, though not beyond the limits of the power a local paramountcy could bring. He knew that if local Conservatism grew restive all the Liberals would act together against them. The East Birmingham by-election had strained the Radical Unionists'

[1] Churchill, *op. cit.*, pp. 253–4.
[2] See Hurst, *Joseph Chamberlain and West Midland Politics, 1886–95, passim.*
[3] Garvin, *op. cit.*, p. 272. *The Times*, 4th November 1886.

Unionism to its limits and renewed hostilities with the former foe would come as a relief. All but a small bitter core of the Gladstonians would have welcomed a diversion from Liberal disunity and hoped right wing animosity would jolt Chamberlain into seeing still more of the light. While this remained true it was a factor to be exploited. However weak his parliamentary or national bargaining position became he could speak from a secure base. From it he would try to create the influence he wanted. Meanwhile his course was clear. The Conservatives had to be shaken from the Disraelian concept of 'Mind you, no policy'. The Gladstonians to be lured from Parnell by the prospect of reunion, a thing Chamberlain wanted if that came about. The first was the easier proposition, given his recipe.

Garvin claims Chamberlain restated precisely his 'position before the rejection of the Home Rule Bill'.[1] If he means immediately before, the facts do not support him. There was no mention on 23rd December of the ideas dominating the speech of 21st April. Indeed, 'Home Rule' would be 'unnecessary' provided the land question was solved. Parnell was offered nothing beyond National and Provincial Councils. Thus the point that 'The persuasive appeal that others shall be conciliatory comes from one who himself does not budge an inch'[2] carries even more weight than its author supposed. It involved 'postponement of Gladstonian policy to a future to which Gladstone will not belong'.[3] In March Chamberlain had expressed his long-term hopes quite clearly:

> . . . in time the situation will clear. Either Mr Gladstone will succeed and get the Irish question out of the way, or he will fail. In either case he will retire from politics and I do not suppose the Liberal Party will accept Childers, or even John Morley as its permanent leader.[4]

Gladstone had failed and had not retired. The Irish question remained his passion and blocked the implementation of the 'Unauthorised Programme' by a Radical dominated Liberal party. Nor had Chamberlain been correct in thinking the future depended on Gladstone alone. Many Radicals liked the Irish alliance and would move heaven and earth to get him to reconsider should he decide on retirement. Labouchère had told Dilke in November:

> It looks as though Chamberlain will be the scapegoat. At present his going over bag and baggage to the Whigs has utterly disgusted the Radicals. As long as Gladstone lives things will go on fairly with us, but after—the deluge. The Radical M.P.'s are regretting your not being in, as they would have accepted you as the leader.[5]

[1] Garvin, *op. cit.*, p. 279.   [2] *Ibid.*   [3] *Ibid.*
[4] Chamberlain to Arthur Chamberlain (his brother), 8th March 1886. Chamberlain Papers, JC5/11/5.
[5] Gwynn and Tuckwell, *op. cit.*, p. 264.

Perhaps this disgust might be overcome with the support of the many Liberals of the centre and right, who had come to esteem 'The Man from Birmingham', but the great question remained—how and when? While Gladstone still led it might be argued that reunion could only come about through a Chamberlain surrender. Yet if this was so, did Morley's moves mean nothing? The speech assumed they did not, and there was too another point to bear in mind. Most Gladstonians did not want to grant Home Rule unless they could help it. A statesman who appeared to offer both reunion and a compromise solution stood to gain much in their eyes. Even an abortive reunion appeal would probably prove profitable in future. All the more so if couched in the right tone. In the past Chamberlain had done himself considerable harm by the manner of his utterances. Many took more exception to this than to the actual matter. Gladstone could never have been in any doubt about the enmity borne him by the Queen. Knowledge, experience and a profound concern for the constitution combined prevented him from hitting back, except for an occasional sarcastic remark in Cabinet. Such was the discretion the situation demanded. Chamberlain had not been so wise and attacks on Gladstone, however justified, had simply boomeranged. Now he restrained himself and accordingly gained ground.

He had exploited the apparent Conservative desertion of the Dartford–Bradford programme to overcome difficulties within his base. Trusting to this success he had bid for the best of all worlds just when his bargaining position seemed at its worst. Whatever happened, he could not straightway lose more than was already lost. Morley might withdraw under the new conditions, but it was only sensible to try him out, especially if no basic commitment was betrayed in doing it.

Short though the government crisis was, Chamberlain had moved to within sight of the 'Round Table' before Goschen finally said 'yes'. Some assumed him largely responsible for Churchill's conduct; men as near the centre of things as Hartington and W. H. Smith among them. 'It looks rather suspicious,' remarked the former, 'that Chamberlain has just got back and that Randolph has had an interview with him,' yet an unfailing caution prompted a doubt. 'But it is no use making guesses and in a day or two I suppose I shall know more.'[1] Smith voiced his views with much greater certainty:

He dined with Joe on Friday and that I think settled it, for after trying for two hours on Monday to beat me down, he told me, quite in a friendly way, that he should resign, and he let out frankly that his 'rapprochement' was towards Joe rather than any other politician of the

[1] Hartington to the Duchess of Manchester, 23rd December 1886. Devonshire Papers, 340. Add. MS.

present day; and unless they quarrel we shall see the two working together.[1]

Both were wrong on the main point. Chamberlain's first letter after the bombshell was to Churchill. Its contents and general tone reveal a genuine surprise over what has happened. 'Whew! The cat is among the pigeons with a vengeance. My sympathies are entirely with you, and I think you may rely on my cordial cooperation, if it can be of any value.' Then comes a reference to his speech. It hardly suggests abject despair. 'I have to speak tonight, and must express my first thoughts on what is an entirely changed situation. I wish I was able to communicate with you beforehand, but if you have any wishes or ideas as to immediate action let me know.'[2] Had the resignation created a real desire to rejoin Gladstone at the price of considerable sacrifice, he would surely not have revealed such a fluid attitude and invited suggestions from a leading Conservative, albeit a rebel one? 'If necessary,' he adds, 'we will arrange a meeting, and I will run up to London again', and then comes the crux of his message: 'The Government is doomed, and I suspect we may have to re-form parties on a new basis. You and I are equally adrift from the old organisations.'[3] Churchill's feelings on 'rapprochement' were shared.

A little later on the same day Chamberlain was chaffing Brett: 'What do you think of the "little rift" now? Salisbury is a bold man and is no doubt prepared for all the consequences. The old combination is irretrievably smashed. I hardly know what new ones may be possible in the future.'[4] Here are the private thoughts of a man whose mind is far from made up. The conviction that the government cannot last is not matched by any clear idea of what is to come next. Hunting with the Gladstonian hounds and running with the Conservative hare has to continue—with a difference. The hare has to be forced to run in a more progressive direction. For this no one seemed a better ally than Churchill. In or out of the Cabinet he appeared to be the stick with which to beat Salisbury. Hartington had neither the personality nor the inclination for the job. Both Churchill[5] and Brett[6] wrote approving the Birmingham speech and, replying to the former on 26th December, Chamberlain revealed both his optimism and the rôle he intended the two of them should play. While admit-

[1] W. H. Smith to Akers-Douglas (Conservative Chief Whip), 24th December 1886. Chilston, *op. cit.*, p. 100.

[2] Churchill, *op. cit.*, p. 252.

[3] *Ibid.*

[4] Chamberlain to Brett, 23rd December 1886. Journals and Letters of Reginald, Viscount Esher, Ed. M. V. Brett, Vol. I, p. 129.

[5] Churchill to Chamberlain, 24th December 1886. Chamberlain Papers, JC5/14/27. Garvin, *op. cit.*, p. 275.

[6] Brett to Chamberlain, 23rd December 1886. Copy. Esher Papers.

ting: 'You will have a hard time to go through. Your case will be mine almost exactly, and I can tell you it is a bitter pilgrimage which is in prospect. The party tie is the strongest sentiment in this country —stronger than patriotism or even self-interest,' he still claims: 'But it will all come right in the end for both of us.' He then assumes that Churchill 'will maintain an independent position', for 'in that case you will be a power that your party cannot ignore'.[1] Perhaps Labouchère was only too right to insist that 'Joe' was 'no good' to the rebel Conservative.[2] The Birmingham base brought Chamberlain the security making possible the maintenance of an 'independent position'. Churchill had no base to nurse, unless it were also Birmingham where he was the darling of the Joe-hating Conservatives. His chances of building anything up there were slight. Before resigning he had worked with Chamberlain. Now he almost depended upon him for an alliance if he wished to exert true influence on a national scale. Chamberlain meant to use him, whereas in fact Churchill needed aid. The Birmingham leader would not, as soon as he realised this, encourage the growth of the Randolph cult within his own area, and there was too the certainty that official Conservatism would frown upon it. There was going to be so such thing as a truly 'independent position' of any real worth for Churchill, not least because of Chamberlain.

Nevertheless that was what 'Joe' temporarily had in mind for them both and, what is more, inclined to think: 'It might be the best thing now under all the circumstances' for Hartington 'to form a Coalition Government' he—Chamberlain—'could not join'. 'The majority in the Cabinet', were 'rampant Tories and if they' carried 'on by themselves there must come a crash and a dissolution', and, though he did not mention it, a grave threat to the 'independent position' he enjoyed and for the moment wanted Churchill to enjoy.[3] The Conservative leaders might be committed to the Dartford–Bradford programme, but current events did not point to a faithful application of it. A coalition would be a 'sufficient answer for Liberal Unionists to make to the charge of turning Tories' and 'much easier to support Hartington than Salisbury, who is identified with narrow and aristocratic Conservatism'.[4] The existence of a coalition would have made

---

[1] Churchill, *op. cit.*, pp. 252–3.   [2] Churchill, *op. cit.*, p. 254.
[3] Chamberlain to Edward Heneage, 26th December 1886. Chamberlain Papers, JC5/41/22. Heneage, although a Whig, had joined Gladstone's third ministry and resigned along with Chamberlain and Trevelyan in March 1886. His post—the Chancellorship of the Duchy of Lancaster—gave a good indication of the ceiling of his abilities and importance, but he was a useful recruit to Liberal Unionism and kept his seat at Great Grimsby at the 1886 general election. He lost it, however, in 1892. Ultimately he became a peer.
[4] *Ibid.*

Chamberlain much more a 'man of the centre' on the Home Rule issue, with vastly better prospects of occupying an 'independent position' in the judgment of the public. And it was just from that public that he needed to win the approval that would take him beyond a holding of his own to a position where he could launch out and bid again for the Liberal leadership. He was in any case on his own. The important thing was that this should become so apparent no one could possibly miss it.

For the time being he occupied a position *vis-à-vis* Gladstone in terms of parliamentary support rather like that of Tito and Khrushchev, and had to 'Use the barbarians to control the barbarians'. He was not then to know that Hartington would stymie his quest for separateness by refusing coalition for fear of losing him and his following, nor that Gladstonian success in by-elections would provide him quite a powerful alternative to Churchill as leverage upon the Conservatives. Nor was he fully aware that many Conservatives disliked Churchill's demagoguery and intrigue more than his policies, that Salisbury deliberately waited to be squeezed for concessions knowing he would ultimately grant much of what the Liberal Unionists asked, and that Hicks Beach had the day before confessed 'to much doubt whether the country can be governed nowadays, by persons holding opinions which you (Salisbury) and I should call even moderately Conservative'.[1] All he knew was that running with the Conservative hare had to be re-established on acceptable terms, that every issue on which Unionists and Home Rulers clashed took the Liberal sections further from one another, that this was bad for him, that at best Morley's approach might mean reunion and at worst provide a good means of bringing the Conservatives to reason and Birmingham to heel. He did not expect the best. 'My speech,' he told Churchill, 'has fluttered the dovecotes tremendously, and my correspondence shows that many of the Gladstonians are very uncomfortable and anxious to come to terms. But I do not believe that there will be any practical result. Mr Gladstone does not give way on the main point—neither will I.'[2]

Not content with his victory of the 23rd, he decided to press it home in readiness for another meeting which was to take place on 5th January, the date originally fixed for the first. The secret of success on the 23rd had partly consisted in making out that the 'independent position' could be ended. The audience had wanted some emotional relief and the hostile minority had been fobbed off by hopes of reunion. We know Chamberlain was not at all sanguine in reality. Reality had, however, to be given a good push into the background

[1] Hicks Beach to Salisbury, 25th December 1886. Salisbury Papers.
[2] Churchill, *op. cit.*, p. 253.

for the sake of local politics. Circumstances dictated one of the famous Highbury dinners to arrange how things should go. With the leading figures in unison nothing was likely to go wrong at the meeting. As early as the 24th Dale wrote congratulating Chamberlain on his speech and saying he and Harris could dine on either the 3rd or 4th of January.[1] Choosing the 3rd, probably to give himself the more room to manoeuvre, Chamberlain replied on the 26th, implying they would be *à trois*.[2] This was not to be, for at the same time he was making sure Collings would make it a quartet. The form of his invitation suggests a certain amount of unease about the political menu. 'Dale and Harris are coming ... to dine ... and talk about the Liberal Association. Will you come and protect me?'[3] Collings had but a day or two before been sounding out Trevelyan at Welcombe. He found a thorough approval of Chamberlain's speech together with an equally thorough distaste for battle. Nor did the visit buck up any courage.[4] On Christmas Day Trevelyan was clearly trying to back out of his long-standing promise to visit Birmingham on 5th January:

> ... though I am anxious otherwise to get back North I should very much like to hear you at Birmingham, if it is to be no later than the 5th. I do *not* want to go about making speeches, both on account of being out of Parliament and from the peculiarity of the situation; but I should value the opportunity of showing the very strong personal and political feeling I have about you on an occasion when it is natural to do so. Would you send a line by an early post to say whether this would suit you as I shall have some arrangements to make.[5]

Chamberlain sent one by the earliest post available, replying in the sense Trevelyan wanted. A silent Trevelyan would be worse than no Trevelyan at all. Without a speech who could tell how strong his 'personal and political feeling' was? There had to be no risks taken over the 5th. On the 27th, much relieved and as full of armchair fight as ever, he wrote: 'I have something of the same feeling myself about coming on the 5th, and, if you have the same feeling it is pretty sure

[1] Dale to Chamberlain, 24th December 1886. Chamberlain Papers, JC5/20/14.

[2] Chamberlain to Dale, 26th December 1886. Copy. Chamberlain Papers, JC5/20/58.

[3] Chamberlain to Collings, 26th December 1886. Copy. Chamberlain Papers, JC5/16/18. William Harris had been a vice-president of the National Liberal Federation from its foundation until the defeat of the Chamberlainite group over the Home Rule Bill in May 1886. After the reunion attempt failed he slowly drifted back to Gladstone, finding coercion and inadequate reform unacceptable.

[4] Trevelyan to Chamberlain, 25th December 1886. Chamberlain Papers, JC5/70/20.

Welcombe was Trevelyan's house near Stratford-upon-Avon.

[5] *Ibid.*

to be correct: so I will not come and it is better not.'[1] This incident was to go down in black letters in the Highbury annals and colour subsequent events more than Trevelyan at least suspected. With his going out and Collings coming in the stage was set for the next round of securing the base.

Still, one had to think ahead, above all over matters impinging on the west midlands. Fowler of Wolverhampton had prudently congratulated 'Joe' on his speech.[2] He was the secondmost important of the Gladstonians 'sick of the strife and hopeful of reunion' to do so, and everything called for a prompt and reassuring reply. Chamberlain made it in the spirit of a true leader on that very busy 26th December.

> Thanks. Throughout this bad business I have specially noted your fairness and moderation towards former associates and friends. Would that others had been like minded! I have now done my part and can do no more. I fancy that if any advantage is to be taken of the situation, it must be by the wise and temperate men of the party—those who have done nothing to embitter the controversy—using their influence with the leaders of both sections and compelling an agreement.[3]

Fowler was one of the men whom he thought 'could be brought to put pressure on Hawarden'. He was also one of the few Gladstonians upon whom pressure could be put. Birmingham could be used for aggressive purposes even at a time when there was not, to Chamberlain's mind, any chance of 'R. Churchill's returning to the Government'.

[1] Trevelyan to Chamberlain, 27th December 1886. Chamberlain Papers, JC5/70/21.

[2] H. H. Fowler (1830–1911), later Lord Wolverhampton, was a moderate Gladstonian of Wesleyan background. He had held minor office before the split and became President of the Local Government Board in 1892 under Gladstone and Secretary for India under Rosebery in 1894. His ministerial career ended in 1910, two years after he took a peerage.

[3] Chamberlain to Fowler, 26th December 1886. Copy. Chamberlain Papers, JC5/31/9.

III

THE RECEPTION OF
THAT PROPOSAL

———◆◆◆———

'Repent ye, for the kingdom of heaven is at hand.'
St. Matthew iii. 2.

REACTIONS to the speech had been fast, furious and amazingly varied. Most, however, shared one thing in common—a refusal to take it at its face value. The Conservative leadership generally assumed the worst. For all their past abuse of him they underestimated his pride and desire to dominate, and misunderstood the means he was employing to attain long-term ends. Salisbury was quite sure what was involved. 'Chamberlain has evidently made up his mind to leave us,'[1] he told Hartington, and placed his faith in the parliamentary cohorts of moderate Liberal Unionism. The smallness of Radical Unionist representation alone enabled him to take up this 'good riddance to bad rubbish' attitude. No one on the Commons Front Bench echoed it, though Smith seemed to accept Chamberlain's loss as a *fait accompli*. His 'friends' might all be 'staunch', but he knew legislative concessions would accompany a coalition; Chamberlain or no Chamberlain. 'With such a combination Salisbury will swallow a far more Liberal Local Government Bill and even Allotments, that I am sure of.'[2] With his past experience of the Whigs Chamberlain could hardly have expected to see affairs quite in the same light. What he miscalculated on was the Whig belief in his power and the widespread feeling that Liberal Unionists were all Liberals together: that the caucus was better than the Carlton. Hicks Beach came nearer the mark in appreciating the existence of the 'independent position'.

[1] Salisbury to Hartington, 24th December 1886. Devonshire Papers, 340. 2070.
[2] W. H. Smith to Akers-Douglas, 24th December 1886. Chilston, *op. cit.*, p. 100.

120

... it is clear from his late speech that Chamberlain will hold himself and his following free to oppose us in all matters which formerly divided Radicals from Conservatives, and in questions such as those on which our recent differences have arisen (expenditure, local government, allotments, etc.) he will be assisted by R.C., who could I think draw off not a few of our party with him.[1]

Wrong on Churchill's drawing power, he was right in seeing Chamberlain's pronouncement for what it was—a shift from the policy explained to Hartington on 9th September, but not a complete about turn.

Liberal Unionists displayed an even greater diversity of opinion. Hartington himself did not pronounce on the speech as such, but a little later on dismissed the mutual offering of olive branches as 'a sort of game among them which is to have the best of it; and they all want to show that *they* are not the obstacles to reconciliation'.[2] This slow moving and cynical aristocrat thought: 'Chamberlain is very clever and, I daresay, he will be able to take care of himself.'[3] Meanwhile one intemperate correspondent had informed him:

I suppose he [Chamberlain] wishes to make it almost impossible for you to join the Government by representing it as so retrograde and reactionary that even a Conservative inclined to Liberalism is obliged to leave it; and if this is the case how would it be possible for a strong Liberal as yourself to have anything to do with it.[4]

Such ideas were extremely wide of the mark and Colonel Hozier was already speculating to Goschen on the 24th as to the size of the majority a coalition was likely to have over a Churchill–Chamberlain–Gladstone combination. 'I do not think that it would be much more than thirty, or that a dissolution would much strengthen us.'[5] Goschen confessed himself nonplussed: 'Chamberlain's speech is against the Unionists though he may contend it is in favour of the Union. His offer of reconciliation and his backing of Churchill are also awkward factors. It is difficult to see light in any direction.'[6]

[1] Hicks Beach to Salisbury, 25th December 1886. Salisbury Papers.
[2] Hartington to the Duchess of Manchester, 5th January 1887. Devonshire Papers, 340. Add. MS. See also K. (Mrs) Courtney's Diary, 23rd and 24th December 1886. Courtney Papers, XXIII.
[3] *Ibid.*
[4] H. A. Lascelles to Hartington, 24th December 1886. Devonshire Papers, 340. 2069.
[5] Hon. A. D. Elliot, *Life of Lord Goschen, 1831–1907*, Vol. II, p. 104. Col. H. M. Hozier was at this time Secretary of the Liberal Unionist Association. Subsequently he was awarded the K.C.B. Many remember him as author of *The Seven Weeks' War.*
[6] Goschen to Leonard Courtney, 27th December 1886. G. P. Gooch, *The Life of Lord Courtney*, p. 271. Courtney (1832–1918) was at this time Liberal Unionist M.P. for Bodmin.

Selborne too drew 'no favourable omen' from the speech,[1] but anyone supposing it meant *delenda est Chatsworth* fell into the same error as the intemperate correspondent namely that Chamberlain was unutterably opposed to a coalition and would fight it, once in being, with might and main. He told Heneage straight out that though unable to join he 'might readily support it'.[2] To suppose he meant to prevent Hartington from joining by encouraging him to do so not only assumes a subtlety excessive even for Highbury, but goes clean against the evidence. Moreover, Chamberlain was admittedly reckless, yet seldom to the point of folly. Dale contented himself with simple rejoicing,[3] while Trevelyan gushed helplessly:

> The Gladstonians must see that it is their only chance of retreating from their terribly false position to come to terms with you. Your telegram to the Unionist gathering was the only real solution. The great bulk of the respectable Gladstonians, and of those who would be glad to come back to office some day, must recognise that it is the only way out of the business.[4]

Like Hartington, Courtney struck a caustic note. Opposed to coalition, except in 'extremity', he suspected the speech was an attempt to delineate Gladstone as the great obstacle to reunion and Chamberlain as its foremost exponent. To this was added a doubt as to whether the bulldog would conform to type: 'Everyone says Mr Chamberlain *can't* give way to Mr Gladstone, but no one says he *won't*.'[5] Bright tactfully decried coalition, but was otherwise silent.[6]

From the top of one of the most carefully constructed fences ever

[1] Selborne to Hartington, 25th December 1886. Devonshire Papers, 340. 2071. The first Earl of Selborne (1812–95) had been Lord Chancellor 1880–5 in Gladstone's second ministry. An ardent Anglican, he was the author of several works on ecclesiastical affairs and Christian worship. As a prominent Whig and anti-Home Ruler he followed Hartington after the split. His heir, Lord Wolmer, was a prominent Liberal Unionist, married to a Cecil, and M.P. for Petersfield.

[2] Chamberlain to Heneage, 26th December 1886. Copy. Chamberlain Papers, JC5/41/22. Gardiner, *op. cit.*, p. 24, proves Morley had heard of these sentiments.

[3] Dale to Chamberlain, 24th December 1886. Chamberlain Papers, JC5/20/14.

[4] Trevelyan to Chamberlain, 27th December 1886. Chamberlain Papers, JC5/70/21. Sir Edward Hamilton thought Chamberlain had been truly more conciliatory and believed he and Churchill would 'cast in their lot together and form an "Opportunist" party'. Churchill would not at any rate 'be forgiven by the Conservatives in a hurry'. This was an unusually straightforward interpretation of events and, incidentally, foreshadowed the abortive moves soon to be made by Chamberlain and Churchill towards founding a so-called 'National' party. Sir Edward Hamilton's Diary, Add. MS. 48645, p. 67.

[5] K. (Mrs) Courtney's Diary, 26th January 1887. Courtney Papers, XXIII.

[6] Bright to Hartington, 28th December 1886. Devonshire Papers, 340. 2075. The sentiment in favour of Scottish Home Rule, which Harcourt and Morley had noted in November had at this time been worrying James Bryce. In a letter to him of 28th December 1886 Gladstone pooh-poohed the 'threat'. 'Notwithstanding your fears,' he declared, 'I cannot think the Scotch will largely bite at such a bait

known in our history Brett pronounced both volubly and shrewdly. His approval of the speech was given despite the belief that the government was going to 'fall to pieces irretrievably'[1] under its impact, coming so close as it did to the Churchill resignation. Perhaps this was because he thought: 'Chamberlain distinctly holds out the olive branch' meant 'Chamberlain is going to contrive a compromise'. After all, he was one of the very many Liberals who prized party unity above everything: certainly, in his case, above Gladstone's leadership. With these views he was bound to hope Hartington would decline to lead or join a coalition, but wisely abstained from volunteering advice on the subject.

Most Gladstonians got no nearer to giving Chamberlain's speech an accurate interpretation. Whether they liked him or not seemed to make no difference. Significantly, the tone had a bigger impact than anything else, though great stress was put on the shift from a demand for the dropping of Home Rule in the telegram of 7th December to a request that it be indefinitely postponed. He was about to help perform a miracle, spring some nasty trick, surrender, or end his career an utter failure, according to the attitude held towards him. Gladstone had apparently taken developments with a packet of salt, regarding Chamberlain as a new Machiavelli. 'We stand mid-way in his estimation between the Government plus Churchill and the Government minus Churchill.'[2] He hoped Hartington would consent to a coalition and so help clear the ground. Churchill would not be readmitted and Goschen alone be no more good to the Conservatives than Bright's pills for an earthquake. Whatever happened, the Home Rule cause would be furthered. There should not now be any

as a cut and dried plan of Home Rule. My correspondence, which is large, in no way leads me to expect it.' On 8th December Campbell-Bannerman had been equally confident about the immediate situation only, saying: 'I have no strong feelings either way. I think it will come; but to press it now will only bedevil other things. Some of our best people, I hear, are very strong about it.' Perhaps Gladstone was living for the moment, though his general mood was one of optimism. Also in his letter of 28th December he wrote: 'What a political Saturnalia we have got. It is hard to foresee the upshot. But I think that whatever the form progress will be marked on the Irish Question; even if Randolph were to patch it up and go back again "refurbished" in Disraeli's phrase.' Gladstone to Bryce, 28th December 1886. Bryce Papers. Campbell-Bannerman to Bryce, 8th December 1886. Bryce Papers. James Bryce (1838–1922) was an Ulsterman, brilliant scholar and writer, and Gladstonian Liberal M.P. for Aberdeen. Subsequently British ambassador in Washington, he was created a Viscount in 1914.

[1] Brett to Hartington, 24th December 1886. Devonshire Papers, 340. 2068.
[2] Gladstone to Harcourt, 30th December 1886. Gardiner, *op. cit.*, p. 25. The absence of Herbert Gladstone in India between the beginning of December 1886 and the end of February 1887 removed at least one potent anti-Chamberlain voice from Hawarden at a crucial time. As it happened, however, this did not prove material to the situation.

approaches made to the Liberal Unionists. The speech was certainly of great importance, but as with Arabi Pasha, Chamberlain's time was not yet. The G.O.M. wanted to see just how isolated the man he feared most could become. As ever there was no real understanding of his subject. Whereas 'Joe' saw coalition as a possible salvation, his former leader thought only in terms of laying him low; and assumed isolation meant a politician had willy nilly to get on the run. Not for the last time, he underestimated the man from Birmingham and the forces of his locality. Of course, all this represented a change of tune by the old Machiavelli. After the Liberal Unionist conference rumours of his readiness to accept the Chamberlain telegram were rife, and it would appear that his first fine careless rapture following the speech urged him in the same direction. Brett regaled Hartington with the details: 'Mr G. is burning with ardour—difficult to restrain —for denunciation of the "plan of campaign" and for a "Conference" with the Unionists.'[1] Reflection restored 'balance' and 'realism'. The process was speeded on by the activities of Morley. Even Gladstone's pity for Hartington was marred by the feeling that 'it serves him right'.[2]

Ironically, Morley the initiator of the moves through Dale was the least sympathetic to the response he had himself evoked. Though 'much inclined for a rejunction of forces', he held back 'from a large concession', or indeed, any meaningful concession whatever. 'Mind,' he assured Courtney, 'whatever you hear about other people, I shall stand firm to my guns.'[3] Any conference then in which he might become involved was not likely to result in disarmament. Almost certainly the eagerness for reunion reported by Brett to Hartington on the 24th was that communicated to him by Morley on the 20th, three days before the Chamberlain speech. This being so, his statement to Courtney is much more understandable. He regarded the speech as second only in importance to Churchill's resignation and thought the two events would lead to Gladstone being 'back in office before the New Year is very old'.[4] In his mood of exultation he judged concessions should come from Chamberlain and Parnell. 'If he [Chamberlain] can be got to advance, and if Parnell were moderate in the sense of his last conversation with me, there might be some chance of daylight.'[5] Apparently there was to be some disarmament —but not by the Gladstonians! The chances of this coming to pass were slight. Morley himself admitted the Birmingham speech represented nothing but a change of tone and Brett 'understood' on the

[1] Brett to Hartington, 24th December 1886. Devonshire Papers, 340. 2068.
[2] Gladstone to Morley, 25th December 1886. Morley, *op. cit.*, p. 365.
[3] Gooch, *op. cit.*, p. 271.   [4] Esher, *op. cit.*, p. 171.
[5] Morley to Gladstone, 24th December 1886. Gladstone Papers, Add. MS. 44255, f. 152.

29th that there was 'no chance of Parnell agreeing to a compromise', adding: 'Knowing your sentiments, I see that reunion is therefore postponed.'[1] The Irish position was stressed to Chamberlain at the same time: 'I *know* that all "accommodation" with Parnell is now impossible. You will appreciate the bearing which this fact has upon others.'[2] Morley must have appreciated it too. A letter to Dale on the 24th is almost one of goodbye. 'I quite understand the delicacy of the moment. I have just the same sense of pain at any motion myself. We must trust to time the healer. Whatever course events may run I shall always be grateful for your kind offices and friendly mind upon this occasion.'[3] At the back of his mind there was always the nagging thought that Chamberlain was 'foxing'. It must have been one of his regular gusts of anti-Chamberlainism which prompted one of the strangest statements of the whole history of the 'Round Table' affair. Soon after the 'olive branch', when Gladstone was hoping for reconciliation, Morley blurted out to Brett his fears that Hartington's joining Salisbury 'would leave the Liberal Party, and consequently the destinies of the country, in the hands of those in whom the public have no confidence. He said there was no one with whom he had so often agreed, and under whom he would sooner serve than' the Whig leader, described as 'the strongest bulwark we have against all the socialist doctrines'.[4] What else could have promp-

---

[1] Brett to Morley, 29th December 1886. Esher Papers.

[2] Brett to Chamberlain, 29th December 1886. Esher Papers. On that very day Chamberlain had penned what now seems a most remarkable letter to Dilke. The crucial portion ran: 'There is no secret as to Parnell's letters. They prove him to be a liar, but I do not know that they have any other interest just now.' Chamberlain to Dilke, 29th December 1886. Dilke Papers, Add. MS. 43888, f. 90. Which particular letters these were is impossible to say. Nevertheless, they seem to have excited Dilke. Well might Salisbury remark to Sir Henry Holland, also on the 29th, 'The chess-board is in the oddest condition—but it is impossible to guess who will win.' Lady G. Cecil, *Life of Robert, Marquess of Salisbury*, 1880–6, Vol. III, p. 338. Sir Edward Hamilton more than agreed with Gladstone's hopeful outlook. His diary for 30th December 1886 has the following entry: 'There is a distinctly more conciliatory and cheerful tone among Liberals; but how the disjointed atoms are to unite I do not well see, though it is something that conciliation is in the air. I wrote to Mr Gladstone today to put in a word for his not losing the opportunity of listening to any overture that may be made. It is no use disowning Chamberlain as Labouchère does, who is always widening the breach. (That man does untold harm to Mr Gladstone and to the party.) There can be no sacrifice of principle, but there may be some *modus vivendi* forthcoming. Without some compromise political cooperation becomes impossible. Might a reunion with Chamberlain be brought about by some endeavour to settle the land question in Ireland? A settlement would put to the test the not uncommon contention that it is not Home Rule but the land which the Nationalists want.' Sir Edward Hamilton's Diary, 30th December 1886. Add. MS. 48645, p. 70.

[3] Morley to Dale, 24th December 1886. Dale Papers.

[4] Brett to Hartington, 31st December 1886. Devonshire Papers, 340. 2079.

ted this but a fear that Chamberlain would ultimately prevail and the Home Rule issue be pushed into the background? As things hardened against his ex-friend the tune changed. On the 27th he told Gladstone and Spencer quite cheerfully that a coalition would bring disunion to both Unionist parties, but did not go back on his request of three days before not to be the intermediary with Chamberlain, unless his leader deemed it his bounden duty.[1]

Spencer, like Hartington and Smith, suspected Chamberlain and Churchill were hand in glove over the whole business of resignation and 'olive branch'. It was with considerable relief that he learned of Gladstone's about turn on reconciliation. Grand gestures might well have proved highly damaging when dealing with an out and out 'opportunist' like Chamberlain.[2] Not that his response was wholly negative. As he wrote to Granville, it was a great pity the land question could not be settled on its own.[3] Parnell's intransigeance put it out of court if Gladstone was to stand his ground against Unionism. Ripon rather weakly spoke up for reunion provided no sacrifice of principle was called for,[4] and Granville tended to restrict himself to clichés, noting: 'What a Prince of opportunists is Chamberlain' and how useful his cooperation could be.[5] Wolverton subscribed to the Churchill–Chamberlain conspiracy theory;[6] but the chief whip, Arnold Morley, interpreted things quite differently, suspecting Birmingham pressure from Dale and Harris.[7] Small though the concessions offered seemed to be, nothing better was likely at that time. Mundella reacted with characteristic simple-mindedness. 'Chamberlain is *climbing down. Don't discourage him.*'[8] Later he was sure that 'Randolph and his followers will go into fierce opposition if Hartington joins the Government; so will Chamberlain.'[9] One leading

[1] Morley to Gladstone, 24th December 1886. Gladstone Papers, Add. MS. 44255, f. 152. Morley to Gladstone, 27th December 1886. Gladstone Papers, Add. MS. 44255, f. 158. Morley to Spencer, 27th December 1886. Spencer Papers.

[2] Spencer to Granville, 27th December 1886. Granville Papers, P.R.O. 30, 29, 22A.

[3] Spencer to Granville, 26th December 1886. Granville Papers, P.R.O. 30, 29, 22A.

[4] Ripon to Gladstone, 29th December 1886. Gladstone Papers, Add. MS. 44287, f. 67. The 1st Marquess of Ripon (1827–1909) had been 1st Lord of the Admiralty in the third Gladstone ministry. His previous and subsequent ministerial experience was extensive and he had followed up being Grandmaster of the Freemasons in 1870 by a conversion to Roman Catholicism.

[5] Granville to Spencer, 24th December 1886. Spencer Papers.

[6] Wolverton to Gladstone, 24th December 1886. Gladstone Papers, Add. MS. 44349, f. 221.

[7] Arnold Morley to Gladstone, 24th December 1886. Gladstone Papers, Add. MS. 44253, f. 50.

[8] Mundella to Messrs. Leader, 25th December 1886. Mundella–Leader Papers.

[9] Mundella to Messrs. Leader, 29th December 1886. Mundella–Leader Papers.

Gladstonian, in fact the second most important, welcomed the 'olive branch' with unfeigned pleasure. But for his untiring efforts there would very probably never have been any 'Round Table' conference. Once under way much of its life and nearly all of its soul came from him. For Harcourt, as for Brett, party unity was worth a hundred Parnells.

Chamberlain's speech roused Harcourt from something of a depression. Two days before he had reluctantly backed up Granville's pessimism over reunion. 'I do not believe there is any practical good to be done by approaching either the Hartington or Chamberlain party. At present they are in an altogether irreconcilable humour and I see nothing for it but to abide the course of events.'[1] By the 24th, Gladstone, to whom these chastening thoughts were addressed, had assumed an altogether more reserved approach and Harcourt switched into a mood of near ecstasy. To Chamberlain himself he opened both heart and mind.[2]

I read with sincere satisfaction the speech you made last night and which is reported in today's papers. I need not tell you that your temporary separation from some of your former colleagues has been to me a cause not only of political, but of personal regret, and that I hail with the greatest pleasure any prospect of the healing of a breach I have always deplored.

Speaking solely for himself, he had 'an earnest desire to cooperate with' the Radical Unionist 'in any measures which may tend in any way towards a reunion of the Party', and was *prepared in any event to act in that sense*'. Here was a man who both desired a compromise with Chamberlain and thought it within his grasp. Base considerations of the relative bargaining positions were to him the last things to bear in mind. But then, as a lukewarm adherent of Home Rule, a firm friend of most of what Birmingham stood for, and a pliable enough man to look beyond present problems into the future, he entertained priorities repugnant to Gladstone and Morley alike. For some reason the former was spared an ode to Chamberlain. The latter received something of the sort, couched in terms of confident restraint. 'The speech of Chamberlain reported in the papers today seems to me to be as important a factor in the situation as the resignation of Randolph Churchill itself. I am most strongly of opinion that we ought to meet the overtures he makes as far as we can. He has spoken', and here came a tribute to the tone, 'for the first time in what I regard as a real spirit of conciliation and I think we shall be responsible for the irretrievable ruin of the party if we hold him at arm's length.' Quite rightly, he adjudged:

[1] Harcourt to Gladstone, 21st December 1886. Draft. Harcourt Papers.
[2] Harcourt to Chamberlain, 24th December 1886. Chamberlain Papers, JC5/38/53. Garvin, *op. cit.*, pp. 280–1.

THE RECEPTION OF THAT PROPOSAL

The attitude he has taken will, I think, make it almost impossible for Hartington to join Salisbury, who is now put in the position of a re-actionary. I see Tory papers almost give up Hartington and hanker after Goschen, who will do them no good. If we behave like men of sense, Salisbury will go to pot and the lost battle may yet be won.[1]

'If we behave like men of sense': for sense read 'compromise'! Clearly, Harcourt is expecting the Conservatives to crumble when denied a coalition by the Liberal Unionists. He is also hoping that in a new general election the Liberals, with Chamberlain at their side, will gain an independent majority in the House of Commons. Failing a victory of this sort, there will still be a greater degree of unity and time seemingly on the progressive side, if the prodigal is allowed to return partially on his own terms. For, after all, vast numbers of Gladstonians really share his views though abhorring all truck with the Conservatives. Even were Salisbury to avoid a dissolution, the future would be much more promising with 'Joe' than without. The great thing was to get 'Joe', and with sense he could be got.

From these initial responses the developments of the next weeks were to grow. Men on both the Gladstonian and Liberal Unionist sides were to show themselves full of sense and nonsense; abounding in sensibility and insensibility. Over the whole preliminary period leading up to the first session of the 'Conference', on 13th January, some of the basic attitudes described underwent temporary revisions. More frequent were the changes of tactics made to appear in the best possible light to those groups of the population each participant happened to deem most vital. Like Humpty-Dumpty, the Liberal party had had a great fall. The tragedy could not easily be overcome, for men who had parted reluctantly in the first place would not lightly join together again. There was, moreover, until 2nd January chronic uncertainty as to the government's intentions. With these clear, Gladstonian chances became inevitably less bright and Radical Unionism more prone to caution. For nigh on three weeks the real initiative on the Home Rule side lay with Harcourt. While the situation retained any real fluidity even Parnell was partially in his hands. The genuine wish for unity and power felt by most Liberals afforded him this truly impressive advantage. Admittedly, Chamberlain set the ball rolling and Hartington was the fish Gladstone most wanted to catch. Nevertheless, it was Harcourt who constantly injected fresh impetus into the whole affair and acted as the 'honest broker'. A broker preferring domestic reform to Home Rule shares. Through his correspondence and the correspondence it in turn provoked the complicated pattern of manoeuvring can be followed from day to day.

[1] Harcourt to Morley, 24th December 1886. Copy. Harcourt Papers.

Just as Harcourt wrote to Morley on the 24th, so Morley wrote to him. Whereas one letter went straight to the Chamberlain point and treated of the government crisis second, the other did the precise opposite. Nor were the two things equated in value. Indeed, Morley seems to judge Birmingham only in the light of Chatsworth. Confusion will be spread in the Unionist camp, but the resignation of Churchill was the greater event. He sees the situation with a cold and steely eye.

> Of course, he [Chamberlain] does not in substance advance beyond his old position—Land Bill *plus* Local Government. But the tone is altogether different and it looks as if he had begun to realise the weakness of his position. They say that Dale, Harris, Bunce, etc., remonstrated with him upon the telegram and generally urged a more Christian spirit. I confess that I do not feel certain whether he really intends to hold out an olive branch, or only to take up a plausible sort of position before the moderate Unionists.

Rather shyly he tells Harcourt how Chamberlain had sent him greetings for his birthday and of his friendly response, adding, as if to reassure himself, 'I don't suppose that this has any political motive whatever, but it certainly makes things easier for me.'[1] 'Joe' has come quite near to hooking his goodwill, even though doctrinally he remains true to himself. While it is impossible to be sure either way about the birthday move, such a thorough campaigner would certainly leave nothing to chance, as subsequent letters from Collings and Dale to Harcourt were to prove. Albeit temporarily, Morley is sympathetic and his sympathy is heightened by the belief that the Conservatives will collapse if Hartington declines a coalition, the more so with rumour insisting that this would happen. Faced with the seeming prospect of office, the toughest of Gladstone's Home Rule lieutenants thinks of accommodation.

> It looks to my innocent vision as if the situation might by and by come to something of this kind: patch up with J. Chamberlain on basis of land, *plus* Local Councils; Home Rule to be left open for consideration: Mr P. to agree to give time for said consideration, his security being the presence of Mr G. at the helm. There are difficulties no doubt—especially about land, because Mr G. has always protested against leaving the Creditor State face to face with the tenant Debtor. But is J. Chamberlain simply foxing as he did all through the Session.[2]?

Naturally, this suggestion is a mere makeshift with a stay of execution only for the Union implied in it. The 'consideration' would not have to last very long, given Nationalist impatience and Gladstone's mortality. Morley was underestimating both Chamberlain and Parnell

[1] Morley to Harcourt, 24th December 1886. Harcourt Papers.
[2] *Ibid.*

as players of the long-term game. Yet in seeing good in the former his conscience was clear. Had not Gladstone himself, after hearing of Dale's scheme at the end of November, 'expressed a strong wish that if an opportunity offered of making friends with J. Chamberlain' he should 'not let it pass'?

Lewis Harcourt stressed to Brett on 25th December the 'real desire for conciliation' felt at Malwood.[1] His father was grateful for Morley's response to Chamberlain, but irritated by what he termed his 'suspicious character'. Christmas was a fitting season for telling his colleague of the belief that 'from whatever motive' Chamberlain really desired a *modus vivendi* 'with his old friends and if that is really his wish' they would be 'idiots to balk him'. Harcourt agreed with the general impression as to Hartington's intentions, was very satisfied with what he heard of Gladstone's disposition towards Chamberlain, and hoped that this would lead to permission to negotiate with him being granted. There were 'only two people who can seriously affect the situation now, one is Chamberlain, the other is Hartington. With the latter we can do nothing. The former, I think, should be judiciously handled.'[2] This underestimated not only his own importance, but the emotional penchant of Morley and Gladstone's capacity for 'foxing'. Not to speak of Parnell, ready to exploit every ounce of his very considerable strength without a moment's notice. However, it was understandable that in a fit of enthusiasm he should suffer a lapse of judgment, especially when faced with Morley's compromise plan and the news of the 'lubrication' of relations between two erstwhile friends. The general state of euphoria at Malwood was hardly disturbed by what Morley wrote. The spirit of Christmas past loomed powerfully between the lines. For men of sense 'it ought only to be a question of time', and all would be well. Labouchère was 'full of the spirit of mischief—mischief and folly', because of his attitude to Chamberlain, and Parnell might not be all that of a problem. 'It

[1] Lewis Harcourt to Brett, 25th December 1886. Esher Papers. Lewis Harcourt (1863–1922), was the son of W. V. Harcourt. He was not an M.P. at this time, but in the thick of his father's political activities. Between 1905 and 1910 he served as colonial secretary and became a Viscount in 1916.

[2] Harcourt to Morley, 25th December 1886. Copy. Harcourt Papers. Gardiner, *op. cit.*, pp. 19–20. Hartington had the habit of putting things into unanswerable form. What more could be said after he summed up his differences with Gladstone over Home Rule and dismissed any attempts to minimise them with the words: 'Mr Gladstone and I don't mean the same thing'? This splendid clarity which his lack of intellectual subtlety made so easy for him was no mean gift. He was *par excellence* a non-intellectual, and this made H. H. Asquith's comment that when Churchill resigned Hartington was in Rome 'studying antiquities' so telling a piece of irony. Asquith put the words in quotation marks, which points to their having been taken from some pompous newspaper report, Earl of Oxford and Asquith, *Fifty Years of Parliament*, Vol. I, p. 161.

may be that the exigencies of his position may drive him to a semi-irreconcilable position. But he is certainly shrewd enough to know that he will have to take half a loaf to begin with.' Finally, it is clear that a favourable decision had been arrived at over 'Joe's' *bona fides* in his personal approach. 'By the way, if you should be writing to J. Chamberlain better *not* mention the raccommodement betwixt him and me. He's a sensitive man, in spite of all appearance to the contrary.'[1]

On that same Christmas Day Harcourt ventured his first approach to Gladstone about the 'olive branch'.[2] A letter from Hawarden of the day before contained but passing mention of Chamberlain, though full of comment on Churchill, the likelihood of Hartington joining Salisbury and the improved prospects for the Home Rule cause.[3] Although indulging in sustained suspension of disbelief, Harcourt displayed mild signs of guile in his choice of arguments to persuade the G.O.M. Knowing his leader's passion for historical precedents, it was shrewd to compare the current crisis to the break up of the Rockingham ministry and the Fox–Shelburne quarrel. Excited by the prospect of participation in grand events, Gladstone might well be ready to make a grand gesture. Through talking about Hartington, Harcourt works round to the real point of the letter. Both Chamberlain's speech 'and other private indications which have come to my knowledge' lead him to believe he was sincerely conciliatory. Consequently, he felt most strongly that here was an opportunity for reunion. It should be fully exploited, there being no guarantee of a recurrence. 'We ought to go half way to meet him.' Mood concerned Harcourt more than matter.

It is too soon yet to speculate on the details of the basis of reconciliation, but it is a great thing that the *animus revertendi* is there and I think we ought to show that we recognise and welcome it. I think it possible I may see Chamberlain before long and I should be very glad if I had your authority to speak to him in this sense.[4]

Just to make sure the point is carried home Morley's concurrence is mentioned by way of a Parthian shot.

Pens and ink had scant rest on Boxing Day either, for while Harcourt again pressed his views on Morley and Gladstone,[5] Chamber-

[1] Morley to Harcourt, 25th December 1886. Harcourt Papers.
[2] Harcourt to Gladstone, 25th December 1886. Gladstone Papers, Add. MS. 44200, f. 195.
[3] Gladstone to Harcourt, 24th December 1886. Harcourt Papers.
[4] Harcourt to Gladstone, 25th December 1886. Gladstone Papers, Add. MS. 44200, f. 195.
[5] Harcourt to Morley, 26th December 1886. Copy. Harcourt Papers. Harcourt to Gladstone, 26th December 1886. Gladstone Papers, Add. MS. 44200, f. 199. Gardiner, *op. cit.*, p. 20.

lain, directly and indirectly stated his terms.[1] Morley was reassured and urged on. 'I return you Labouchère's letter. He is an imp, with happily little power of mischief, though plenty of will. Let us pay no sort of attention to him.' With Gladstone in 'a jolly mood' the prospects are good. 'Let us go in hot and strong for a compromise with our old friends and not mince matters too much if the thing can be done. After all, the smash of a great party is a great evil and one which it is worth making some sacrifices to repair.'[2] Here is probably the clearest exposition of Harcourt's fundamental aims. Let us get on with being Liberals and get this bore of an Irish question out of the way. Hang the details—unity comes first. Two vital details he was unwise to ignore. Gladstone had certainly sent a 'jolly' letter on the 24th, but it was one thing to be joyous over Churchill and quite another to be so over Chamberlain. A new development could bring a new mood. New factors bring new priorities into play. Nor was the failure to mention the Nationalists a sign of the highest political realism, though to be fair, that vital genuflection to hard fact was made in the letter to Gladstone. This was a bold if somewhat clumsy essay in fabian tactics. Not until Churchill's stand on economy had been discussed at length and Hartington's general intentions turned inside out did the name of Chamberlain obtrude itself upon the scene. Churchill had failed where Harcourt had succeeded. 'But then,' he slyly slips in, soft-soaping for all he is worth, 'I had the good fortune to have the Prime Minister on my side.'[3] Hartington will not join Salisbury or form a government of his own. 'Indeed, I believe that the Liberal Unionists are thoroughly in love with their independent position, in which they conceive they hold the balance and can give the law to both parties, and that they will not consent to depart from it.' Then at last comes the crucial subject, presented as a part of the general upset in politics. 'Chamberlain's speech at all events shows that he is in no mind for a combination with Salisbury in any shape.' Were Hartington to coalesce and he to stand out 'there would be an end of the Liberal Unionists as a party. ... Altogether I think the crisis is a healthy one and that it must lead in its results to the union of our party.' Not that anyone in his senses would have supposed Chamberlain would coalesce, speech or no speech, though his coming advice to Hartington remained a mystery. And why the crisis had to result in Liberal unity is far from clear. Failure to coalesce did not

[1] Chamberlain to Harcourt, 26th December 1886. Harcourt Papers. Chamberlain, *op. cit.*, pp. 235–7. Garvin, *op. cit.*, p. 281. Collings to Harcourt, 27th December 1886. Harcourt Papers. Dale to Harcourt, 27th December 1886. Harcourt Papers.

[2] Harcourt to Morley, 26th December 1886. Copy. Harcourt Papers.

[3] Harcourt to Gladstone, 26th December 1886. Gladstone Papers, Add. MS. 44200, f. 199.

make Hartington a potential Gladstonian, and Harcourt himself admitted that nothing could be done with him. All the wrapping was in vain. The climax has no element of surprise. 'I am all for making the most of Chamberlain's advances and from what J. Morley tells me the leader of the Irish party is not in an unreasonable frame of mind, so that a *modus vivendi* may possibly be found.'[1] Harcourt knew he was on dangerous ground with his chief. This was the second letter sent off into the blue and shows less confidence than the first. With no kind word from Hawarden nothing authoritative could be done and there was at present no word at all. Meanwhile he could only comfort himself with the thought that no news was good news.

Whatever one's opinion of the ideology or methods of Birmingham politics there was no denying their efficiency. At times over-efficiency stood to mar results, and but for Harcourt's 'desire for conciliation' the letters sent to him from Chamberlain, Collings and Dale might have had just this effect. The Highbury 'Eirenikon' was of a markedly different order from Dale's in Novenber. There was no laughing at it. Chamberlain led into his subject gently, clearing up a minor mis-apprehension of Harcourt's connected with attacks on the 'Unautho-rised Programme' of 1885 and thanking him for the 'doughty blow struck in its defence'.[2] Such assistance in time of need had not been and would not be forgotten. Having thus established a suitable *rapport* with his correspondent, he went on to use to the full the advantage afforded him by the influence he could have on Harting-ton's future course of action. As it was common knowledge that the risk of his displeasure and consequences attendant upon it made up the principal reason for the Whig Liberal Unionist leaders' refusal to coalesce with the Conservatives in July, that advantage was no mean one.

> I know [he purred] that Hartington does not mean to hurry home. I assume that when he arrives in London he may want to see me, but till I hear from him I shall remain quietly at home. I confess I have not made up my mind what advice to tender to him, supposing that he should ask it. It must depend in part upon the reception which my appeal for union may meet with from my late colleagues.

With the need for a wooing made clear, he felt able to offer a meeting. The promised visit to Malwood might come off, if the Session were delayed, on the weekend of the 15th and 16th. Knowledge of Har-court's desire for haste apparently impressed him not at all, for he asks: 'In the meanwhile is there anything to be done?' Chamberlain is simply playing hard to get, being well aware that Hartington would

[1] *Ibid.*
[2] Chamberlain to Harcourt, 26th December 1886. Harcourt Papers. Garvin, *op. cit.*, p. 281. Chamberlain, *op. cit.*, pp. 235–7.

have returned long before the 15th of January. Then comes his scheme:

> In strict confidence, and not to be mentioned unless you are able yourself fully to approve and adopt the suggestion, here is my notion. The Land Question in Ireland is the most urgent, whether you have regard to social order or the parliamentary position. If we were all agreed upon a strong land Bill the Irish members must support it. Their constituents would not allow the question to be postponed, for Home Rule or anything else. When I spoke of '3 Liberals round a table' I thought of you, Herschell and Fowler, as the three conspicuous Gladstonians who have done nothing to embitter the differences which have arisen and have shown moderation and fairness throughout. To such a Committee I would gladly submit in detail various suggestions for dealing with the land question. I should have confidence that you at least would not use these confidential proposals in subsequent public discussion, nor take advantage of my frankness and endeavours to come to an agreement in order to accuse me afterwards of inconsistency and double dealing. Land, and Local Government, could doubtless be got out of the way quite easily by this Committee, but 'there appears to be a cardinal difference of opinion between Mr Gladstone and the Liberal Unionist leaders on the subject of an Irish Parliament. I cannot pretend to see my way as yet out of this difficulty, but time and full discussion may work miracles.' Disagreement might cease or at least be brought down to a minimum, though treatment of this all-important topic should begin until settlement had been reached on the other two. In mentioning names my only object is to indicate the nature of the influence that is likely to be most effective. Others might be found as good or better, but I feel that they ought to be chosen among those who have not done anything to accentuate differences.[1]

Personal attacks had struck into this 'sensitive man' and he now stressed that reunion could only take place fully on the political plane. For him 'a temporary effacement' was 'a necessary prelude to any future usefulness', but the dangers for Liberalism would be immense if the dissensions were allowed to continue. If they did continue, he would be forced to change his tactics and organise seriously against Gladstone. Liberal or Radical Unionist Committees would then spring up in every constituency and all Chamberlain cared for in politics would 'be indefinitely postponed'. Should Harcourt think there was nothing in them they were to be consigned to the 'waste paper basket without hesitation'.

This was about the last thing likely to happen, and Chamberlain needed no telling. As a contributor to foreign affairs during the eighties he seldom shone. A rather surprising fact, given that he could produce something as skilful as this letter. It was tailor-made for Harcourt. Party reunion is the thing deeply desired. Men of goodwill

[1] *Ibid.*

can achieve it. Past personal experience has convinced Chamberlain goodwill was often lacking on the Home Rule side. This must not happen again. Not that Chamberlain neglected to be clear about himself. The injured innocent had to have guarantees. His request for confidence suggests he might give away much to reach a 'miracle'. But his 'miracles' are to be dealt with on a sale or return basis. If what he regards as one is rejected by the men of 'goodwill', then he will be at liberty to claim it never happened and must never see the light of day. This is the 'Heads I win, tails you lose' policy in operation. More than that he mentions his own independent deterrent— Liberal and Radical Unionist party organisation. Whatever its striking power in fact, its potential existence was enough to alarm many a man of 'goodwill' including the recipient of the letter. 'Goodwill' itself was a weighted term. It really meant those indifferent to Home Rule. Naturally with such people, above all Fowler, 'miracles' were a lot more possible than with unkind sceptics like Morley, Spencer, Granville or the unspeakable Labouchère; not to mention the G.O.M. The Committee was therefore to consist under this scheme of one ardent Unionist and three lukewarm Home Rulers. Though this was all very clever, it was too clever. Of course the extent of the demands could be lessened as part of a preliminary bargain, but the exclusion of all the convinced Home Rulers only seemed to confirm the suspicions these men were anxious enough to entertain of Chamberlain and all his works. He weakened Harcourt, Herschell and Fowler, and those agreeing with them, just at the time they needed all their strength. A true balance cannot be achieved with false weights, nor is politics run on a 'Think of a number' basis.

While 'Joe' was concocting his little spell up at Highbury, Collings and Dale were brewing up a spot of supporting magic. Both disclaimed inspiration from their leader, but the almost identical terms of their proposals suggests some coordination, and who was better at that than 'Our Joe'? Their timing also was of that quality rarely arising from mere chance. Dale's was the better letter, and deserves considerable attention.[1] Many a nail was hit firmly yet fairly upon the head. The air of detachment gave great weight even to the minor points.

> In past years [he began] you and Mr Chamberlain were very good friends. I think that you had a kindness for him; I know that he had a great kindness for you; nor, as far as I know, have your personal relations been very much disturbed by recent troubles. You are as likely as any of his former colleagues to approach with an open mind the consideration of the speech which he made to his Divisional Council last week.

[1] Dale to Harcourt, 27th December 1886. Harcourt Papers.

I venture, therefore, to ask whether, in your judgment, the time has not come for attempting to draw together the divided ranks of the Liberal Party. This is a question to which I do not expect an answer, but I should like to trouble you with a few reasons for considering it.

I suppose that since the time of Pitt no minister had had the same kind and the same measure of ascendancy over his followers as Mr Gladstone, and, speaking generally, I believe that this ascendancy is unbroken. The enthusiasm with which they stood by him last June and the fury with which they attacked all their Dissentient comrades—with the exception of Lord Hartington who dissented most—may very naturally lead him to conclude that they are passionate supporters of his policy. This, to the best of my belief is contrary to the fact. The allegiance is allegiance to himself; and they attribute to him a policy which he has never accepted.

Take for example the Leeds Conference. The report declared that the demand of the Radical dissentients for the retention of the Irish members at Westminster had been conceded; and whenever I discuss the subject with supporters of Mr Gladstone I find that this concession is always assumed. I need not remind you that if this were really conceded you would have to reconstruct the Bill on lines which might make it acceptable to dissentients like myself, and even to Mr Chamberlain.

It was of the essence of Mr Gladstone's proposal that Ireland should be liberated from liability to a war tax, from liability to any increase in the imperial charges in time of peace, from any share in an increased national debt. But this has never occurred to the enthusiastic supporters of Mr Gladstone's scheme with whom I have had the chance of talking about it; when it is pointed out to them they express their strong opposition; they decline to believe that Mr Gladstone meant it; or—those whose faith is less robust, yield to the proof in the printed Bill, they maintain that he would not have insisted on it.

Frankly, I believe that what the great mass of those who supported you at the polls a few months ago desired—and what they thought they were fighting for—was a Home Rule Bill which retained England, Scotland, Wales and Ireland in one Imperial Parliament *with all that this involves*.

Mr Labouchère is hardly a serious politician, but it may be worth while to say that on addressing a Home Rule meeting in Birmingham ten days ago he had the audacity to assure his audience that the late Government, if the Bill had passed its Second Reading, would of course have kept the Irish representatives at Westminster; and as a necessary consequence of this decision would have abolished the 'tribute'.

That Mr Parnell and his friends understood the Bill and descried it I can well understand, but I do not believe that English Liberals saw what they were doing. They believed that the scheme—in its large outlines—might be applied to Scotland and Wales as well as to Ireland, and when they are asked whether they mean England to bear alone the strain of a great European war they are confounded.

The substance of what I wanted to say is—that in my judgment there is far more of unanimity in the party than appears. Whether it is possible for the leaders to draw together and arrive at some working compromise is a problem which lies far out of the reach of persons like myself. But unless some attempt is made, and made soon, to take advantage of Mr Chamberlain's speech, I think that all chance of settling the Irish difficulty will disappear for some time to come, and the condition of the Liberal Party will become more and more chaotic.

Mr Gladstone's supreme position imposes on him supreme responsibilities. He always said that his Land Bill was necessary to his Home Rule Bill. The Liberal Party refused him the machinery he wanted for the Bill of last summer; can he not say that this compels him to construct the Bill on other lines?

At such a time as this he can hardly fail to take counsel with his former colleagues; your voice I hope will be for peace.

Forgive this long letter. You have always shown me so much courtesy that I thought I might venture to trouble you.

I ought perhaps to say that Mr Chamberlain knows nothing of this letter, and that I have written without instructions from Highbury.[1]

The sorcerer's apprentice had outshone his master. The disclaimer of instructions could have spoilt things, but Dale's reputation for independence and integrity was proof against the odd coincidence. Collings never stood a chance of being taken seriously, disclaimer or no. He never left the background and his writing at all was probably due to 'Joe's' caucusmonger's over-thoroughness. As an unimportant man all he did was all too soon forgotten. Dale was different. Besides being eminent in his own right, he was, Bright excepted, the one Birmingham Unionist commanding respect at Hawarden. His last essay in peacemaking had been unrealistic. This time there was no such mistake. The effect of his letter was deadly serious. In fact it was just what Harcourt needed to try and drive anti-Chamberlain prejudice out of Gladstone's mind at the time when his decision about the reunion negotiations would have to be made. Moreover, Gladstone was perfectly well aware of meriting much of the blame for splitting the party. That a man like Dale was prepared openly to accuse him was bound to make him anxious to appear conciliatory. Not that Dale's armoury was purely ethical. Attacks on the financial provisions of the Home Rule scheme might prove electorally dangerous. Chamberlain had talked of organisation. Dale of the sort of ammunition that organisation could use once in being. At a stretch, it looked as if the most respectable of Unionists in the home of small arms was capable of using political dum-dum bullets.

Before Harcourt had received and digested Collings and Dale, Gladstone belatedly sent him word.[2] The excuse was plausible enough:

[1] *Ibid.*
[2] Gladstone to Harcourt, 27th December 1886. Harcourt Papers.

'My perceptions are slower than yours.' Chamberlain's speech was 'an important event, of which due account must be taken and ought to lead to a *modus vivendi* in the Liberal party'. Mixed motives form one of the least palatable sides of political life. The G.O.M. was suffering from a bad attack of them at this moment. On the one hand, there was the need to reunite the party, both for its own sake and his. So keen a theologian was bound to be acutely conscious of the guilt he had to expiate. Yet peace of mind in one direction could be bought at the price of new worry in another, and Home Rule was more than a matter of conscience. It concerned the party position in the Imperial Parliament and law and order in a substantial part of Ireland. He had then to balance against the need for a *modus vivendi*, not only his conviction that the Nationalists were 'rightly struggling to be free', but the realities of politics as they then stood. Then there was the deep dislike and distrust of Chamberlain and all he represented. Added to which was the present weakness of Radical Unionism. Just as Highbury 'foxed', so did Hawarden. Two reservations sprang to the Liberal leader's mind. First, he thought it his 'own duty to make no binding declarations till' he knew 'who are the Government'. Second, 'that the importance of Chamberlain's speech' lay more in the temper it showed and 'the change from his own position of extreme hostility, than in the plan which, with characteristic facility and rapidity, he has laid down'. The old man could not forebear from sneering at the younger. Jealousy forbade a simple acceptance of the change in tone. An open doubt as to *bona fides* could not then be raised, above all, not with Harcourt. For reasons connected with orthodox finance and political tactics Gladstone would not consent to 'the proclaimed postponement' of a Land Bill. He had declared it to be his 'mode of dealing with the question of social order in Ireland'. Chamberlain should have realised how foolish it was to begin with the impossible. Rather there should be an enquiry as to whether, 'if Home Rule cannot be had at once', an agreed measure of Local Government, accepted by Liberals, Nationalists and Liberal Unionists alike, could be formulated. To clear away any possible doubts as to his own good faith he adds: 'When Morley was last here he told me of a sort of overture he had had from Chamberlain, and I did all I could to encourage him in turning it to account; and spoke emphatically of my own position as meant by me to be in no case an obstacle to national and public good.' *Qui s'excuse, s'accuse* and there follows what is palpable humbug, Gladstone hating Radicalism as he did. 'He was then looking forward to seeing Chamberlain, and is now, I think, confirmed in this intention, which on account of their old friendship and affinity as Radicals seemed to me most appropriate.' What in fact seemed most appropriate was

Morley's touchiness in relations with Chamberlain and the unfailing faith he had in Home Rule. He would serve as a welcome and powerful corrective to any impulsiveness from Harcourt. Though Gladstone says: 'Not that I deprecate Chamberlain's being seen by any one else, and should you see him, I hope there is nothing in this letter which will obstruct your conversation with him', it is difficult to resist the conclusion that he hopes for the precise opposite. And while he plans to pay Chamberlain a 'harmless compliment' in the 'Nineteenth Century', his motives for egging on Morley to see him are clear from the section on local government and the conclusion of the letter: 'I ought to have mentioned my opinion that Chamberlain, though his power of opposing and damaging, especially in debate, is great, has no large following to offer us, nor one of which the quality would make up for defect in quantity.'[1] However justified his distrust of Chamberlain, this comment as to Radical Unionist quality was hardly honest. Chamberlain alone would have been most valuable, but the real aim was to use him for getting back Hartington. This would have suited practically and doctrinally. Yet, three days before, he claimed Hartington could 'hardly avoid joining Salisbury'.[2] Had he any genuine desire then for talks with Chamberlain? Surely not? More than one person was 'foxing'! What 'good' was it, towards which 'on the whole thus far, varied and also ambiguous as are the contingencies opened, the present proceedings' were almost inevitably tending.

Chamberlain's letter did not arrive until the 28th. Immediately, Harcourt set out for London to see Morley. Having talked to him, he sent to both the 'foxes'. The younger one had given him 'supreme satisfaction'. The 'Eirenikon' had in it, 'not only in spirit but in substance', what seemed to him 'a solid basis for reunion'. Would that the proposed discussions had been tried nine months before and the 'present plight' been avoided. 'Short of the most vital principle', all sacrifices must be made 'to repair the ruin of the Liberal party'. It existed 'for something more than Ireland and Irish questions alone'. 'Joe's' point about advising Hartington was well taken. As the 'immediate future depends in a great measure on the line which Hartington will take' and 'he will, of course consult with you. . . . It seems to me therefore of the greatest consequence that you should be as early as possible in possession of' the views of 'your late colleagues'.[3] If 'Joe' will come to see Randolph, why not Harcourt? Tomorrow! 'We are older *pals*.' Harcourt is 'more than willing to be used as a

[1] *Ibid.*
[2] Gladstone to Harcourt, 24th December 1886. Harcourt Papers.
[3] Harcourt to Chamberlain, 28th December 1886. Chamberlain Papers, JC5/38/54.

conduit pipe for the fountains of peace' and he and Chamberlain had 'learned to understand and trust one another'. The G.O.M. had submitted to him the substance of the talks proposals, and very definite advice as to what should be done about them.

> This is a matter [he replied] which brooks no delay, as, of course the tone and spirit in which his definite overtures are met will materially affect what passes between him and Hartington on the return of the latter to England. I have discussed the subject with John Morley this afternoon, and, in agreement with him, I have urged Chamberlain to come to London tomorrow.[1]

Note Harcourt's wisdom in not mentioning Morley to 'Joe'. At a personal interview, the letter went on, 'I may arrive at his real mind in this matter'. How well he knew his man! 'I think it possible, if I see him that I should propose to come down to Hawarden on Thursday, for one night, to talk the matter over with you.' Again he stresses the importance of the opportunity for the Liberal party and concludes: 'If Chamberlain makes reasonable proposals we shall know where we are but at all events, we shall not leave him in a position to say that he came forward to offer terms of agreement which we declined to discuss with him.' (A point that was bound to go home to Gladstone with some force.) 'Discussion is all that he asks at present, but, of course, that cannot take place without your concurrence as to the method on which it is to be conducted and the basis on which it is to proceed. I will let you know whether I think it necessary to intrude on your Xmas repose.'[2]

Morley's suspicions of Chamberlain had been fully rekindled by the suggestion of Fowler as one of the Gladstonians in the reunion talks. The 'Reconciliation' had been but skin deep. Still, friendship apart, it was understandable that an ardent Home Ruler should take alarm when moderates like Harcourt and Herschell were to be accompanied by one he deemed 'practically Chamberlain's creature'.[3] So anxious was he about the whole affair that that very evening he penned Harcourt a note enjoining him most earnestly to stick to the path of caution. 'The more I hear of things, the more do I stick to the point that we ought to be in no hurry publicly to clasp the proferred hand of Chamberlain until we know what he really means.'[4]

'For this knowledge an interview with you and him is indispensable. If he declines that I do not think more ought to be done until we see

---

[1] Harcourt to Gladstone, 28th December 1886. Gladstone Papers, Add. MS. 44200, f. 211.

[2] *Ibid.*

[3] Lewis Harcourt's *Journal*, 28th December 1886. Harcourt Papers. For Fowler's views, see Mrs R. Hamilton, *Life of H. H. Fowler*, Chapter XIII.

[4] Morley to Harcourt, 28th December 1886. Harcourt Papers.

the nature of the new Government in front of us.'[1] Clearly he is afraid that 'Joe' will trick Harcourt, although fully aware of how vital his friend thinks an interview is. Enthusiasm might lead him to excuse a refusal to have it, and Chamberlain was certainly astute enough to know there was plenty of enthusiasm to exploit. From Lewis Harcourt's *Journal* it emerges that Morley is much taken up with the government crisis. He was convinced that Churchill's 'great object' was 'to prevent Hartington from joining Salisbury, in order that Salisbury should take him (R.C.) back on his own terms'.[2] His position was one halfway between Gladstone and Harcourt. Gladstone did not want to do anything by way of public acceptance of the 'olive branch' while the government crisis was unsettled. Harcourt wanted Chamberlain back in the Liberal fold whatever happened between Hartington and Salisbury, and was all for immediate public response. Morley was for that only after Chamberlain had undergone ordeal by interview. Otherwise he would take the Gladstone line. Whether Gladstone had influenced him at all in this we have no means of knowing. Meanwhile Hartington had returned. He dined with Drummond Wolff and Lord Rothschild.[3]

Events did not move quite as quickly as Harcourt wanted. No 'Joe' transpired for a meeting on the 29th, so the Hawarden visit did not take place, but a telegram announced his intention of coming up late that day in good time for one on the 30th.[4] Meanwhile, Harcourt and Gladstone again exchanged views. The one trying all ways to speed reunion.[5] The other busy pouring as much cold water as he dare.[6] After announcing the telegram, Harcourt contradicted completely what he had told Chamberlain the day before. 'I quite agree,' he conceded, 'that the lines of his speech will not serve as a *modus vivendi*, but if the "animus" of making up is present, I think the lines will prove elastic.' Having made his bow to Baal, he proceeded on his usual less elastic line.

The great thing is to ascertain whether he really means *making up* or not, and John Morley and I have agreed on the points on which it is necessary to probe his mind. I confess I am sick of the present civil war in our camp

[1] *Ibid.*
[2] Lewis Harcourt's *Journal*, 28th December 1886. Harcourt Papers.
[3] James, *op. cit.*, p. 306. Sir H. Drummond Wolff was well known as both a politician and diplomat. He had been a member of the notorious 'Fourth Party' during the second Gladstone ministry. At that time he had sat as Conservative M.P. for Portsmouth. Though youthful in spirit he was by far the oldest of Churchill's little band, having been born in 1830. He died in 1908.
[4] Chamberlain to Harcourt, 29th December 1886. Harcourt Papers.
[5] Harcourt to Gladstone, 29th December 1886. Gladstone Papers, Add. MS. 44200, f. 214.
[6] Gladstone to Harcourt, 29th December 1886. Harcourt Papers.

and should be very glad if there were really an opening for a 'safe and honourable peace'.

Labouchère's misdeeds of the past and present alike called forth a hearty condemnation, and Gladstone must have found it rather unnerving to read: 'There is no one for whom I feel a greater personal regard than Chamberlain.' After a promise to forward information about the interview, reunion is abandoned for the spicier subject of Randolph Churchill. At the end the main preoccupation comes up again. 'All the Liberal Unionists are in one accord' that Hartington should not coalesce. 'So the element of doubt may be regarded as dispersed even before his return', the more so as the 'Tories are very indignant with Salisbury for having despaired of going on without' him. 'Hartington is snubbed by the Tories; and the Coriolanus of Birmingham is in a melting mood. Considering what was the state of affairs a fortnight ago, this is surely a great advance?' As if to squash any disagreement with this sentiment there came a P.S. 'Unbeknown to Chamberlain' a letter had arrived from Dale, 'certainly one of the most sincere and influential of all the provincial Liberals'. The contents were 'well worthy of consideration' and reflected 'the opinion of many others'.[1] Gladstone should therefore have the opportunity of perusing them. Well might he wonder on whose side Harcourt really was when he forwarded a Unionist's letter with as good as approbation!

The G.O.M. was already cool. 'It is just as well,' he thought, that he should not be in London. The proceedings there were 'in their nature tentative'. As for Harcourt's visiting Hawarden, he was 'most welcome', though the 'chances of the weather' were bad. A typical way for an old man to say 'keep away'. Nothing is right with Chamberlain. He had not 'sufficiently allowed for the dual nature of the question before him'. First, it had to be considered 'what is fit to be done'; second, 'who is to do it'. Maybe this was a hint to Harcourt to beware of wishful thinking, though he ought to have learned that this was not a season when hints were popular with his deputy. Anyway he let it be known what he expected it would be found that the first question, practically as well as logically was, who are to be the Government? Then Chamberlain had made the mistake of supposing that 'when the power to do harm is great there is a commensurate power to do good. Whereas the useful power is often not a tenth part of the evil one.' Another hint for Harcourt perhaps, yet doubtless genuinely felt about Chamberlain too. Curiously enough, Gladstone never impugns the latter's honesty as much as his intelligence. A favourite way the learned have of trying to write down those they fear. En-

[1] Harcourt to Gladstone, 29th December 1886. Gladstone Papers, Add. MS. 44200, f. 214.

closed was a letter from Illingworth, 'Joe's' old adversary, with 'a tail'[1] about him. So far the only one available from a Gladstonian backbencher on the 'olive branch'. Needless to say, it was not friendly. The more Harcourt plugged away in one direction, the less Gladstone seemed to agree. Coercion was to be the curse of Ireland but the saving of his reputation. Why then worry about reunion when Hartington and an immediate parliamentary majority were placed beyond reach? Gladstone was the egoist of egoists, and although the immediate trend of events did not suit him, he had the self-confidence to think that time was really working for him.

To Dale himself Harcourt announced that he had preached peace to the converted, but appealed for silence, as it was 'not expedient that anything should be known on this matter'.[2] Hopes might rise still further now that 'the Tories—like the stupid party they are— have given' Hartington 'the broad hint to stay away'. So good a man should not be parted with 'if we can help it'. It looked as though Harcourt's fixation about party unity was maybe leading him to err a little too much on the side of optimism, for even if Hartington declined a coalition all experienced observers realised he was not the slightest bit hostile to Salisbury. Had Harcourt heard the current Chamberlain comment on Parnell, he would have still more reason to calm down. What was said to Dilke today might be said in public tomorrow. Yet Parnell had to agree to any compromise solution and any true 'olive branch' should have been offered, at least indirectly, to him as well as the Gladstonians. But then, by Birmingham definitions, he was not a man of 'goodwill'. That evening Chamberlain dined with Churchill and Drummond Wolff. An anti-government rather than a compromise solution gathering, it pointed to a maintenance of union among the progressive Unionists. 'Joe' was profferring his 'olive branch' across, not from the top of the fence.

[1] Gladstone to Harcourt, 29th December 1886. Harcourt Papers. A. Illingworth was to Bradford and its caucus what Kitson was to Leeds and its caucus. He sat as a Gladstonian Liberal for West Bradford and had once been an admirer of and collaborator with Chamberlain.

[2] Harcourt to Dale, 29th December 1886. Copy. Harcourt Papers.

IV

HOW THE GROUND WAS EXPLORED AND PREPARED FOR LIBERAL PARTY REUNION TALKS

——————✦·✦——————

'Cast thy bread upon the waters, for thou shalt find it after
many days.' Ecclesiastes xi. 1.

A T three o'clock the next afternoon he duly went along to Harcourt's house. After a two hour session with Hartington consolidating his links on the right, he now tried to maintain the anti-Home Rule line on the left. Harcourt was unable to extract much from him about what had gone on at Devonshire House. Beyond the statement that he did not think Hartington would join Salisbury after the 'extraordinary change of tone' in the Conservative press of that morning he refused to go. Fortunately, no such reserve marred the general proceedings. Both Chamberlain and Harcourt plunged into the reunion question with no holds barred. From the outset Harcourt let it be understood that he and Morley could in no way throw over Gladstone. Under no circumstances could anything be done without his 'consent and approval'. To this Chamberlain immediately agreed. Harcourt then said it was impossible for the Gladstonian leadership 'in any way to abandon the idea that a legislature was a necessary item in the settlement of Ireland and that this must be one of the questions to be considered by the Committee'. To back this up he read out the relevant passages from Gladstone's letter of 27th December. Chamberlain jibbed a little at this and suggested that the Land and Local Government questions be discussed and settled first. It might, he thought, be unnecessary to discuss Home Rule, but agreed there could be consideration of it once the other two issues were out of the way. Harcourt would have none of it, insisting that it 'must be one of the questions submitted to the Committee' and 'must be included as one of the essential points (in our view) of a settlement'. Naturally, it would be quite open to Chamberlain to say that 'none of the schemes which were submitted to the Committee would meet his views'. Harcourt had come to understand that his bow to Baal had to be permanent if there was to be any real chance of consent to reunion on the Gladstone side. Chamberlain too would have to toe the line. To press home his point Harcourt quoted passages in Chamberlain's speeches and letters of the previous spring about autonomy and a legislative authority for Ireland. He also said it was impossible for the Gladstonians 'to go back from the Leeds Resolution, which declared that the settlement of the question' was to be found 'in some legislative body with power over such affairs as should be declared by Parliament to be specifically Irish'. After a wrangle, Chamberlain at last gave way and agreed Home Rule need not be formally excluded. If desirable it might be discussed. Nevertheless, he was at great pains to stress that though he stood by his 'previous utterances' it was necessary to ensure they should not be misunderstood. As he put it:

I did not think that Ireland could be recognised as a Nation without conceding Separation. Ireland was a Province—as Nova Scotia was a province of Canada and the cardinal difference between Mr G. and myself was that he had treated the question from the point of view of the separate Nationality of Ireland, while I had regarded it from the point of view of a State or Province.

Proper safeguards had, it is true, always accompanied his schemes in the past, and Harcourt wisely did not resist the idea of taking Home Rule last. Otherwise the whole exercise would have been in vain and Chamberlain's 'olive branch' in effect thrown back in his face. Agreement was probable on land and local government. It was not very likely on Home Rule. Why not build up the common ground and thereby help lessen the general importance of differences?

Some talk took place about the composition of the Committee. Harcourt thought there had to be someone on it 'well acquainted with Ireland and the Land Question' and suggested Spencer. Chamberlain 'pursed up his mouth, looked very much displeased and was silent for a long time; then said quite suddenly: "I would much rather have Morley".' Absolutely flabbergasted, Harcourt blurted out: 'Oh, if that is so, so would I.' There the surprises stopped, for, claiming there was need for a financial expert, Chamberlain stuck to Fowler, who had the day before welcomed the 'olive branch' and already begun working for its success. Chamberlain also claimed it as an earnest of good faith that he was to be the sole Unionist on the Committee. When Harcourt asked whether he would like a partner, he 'curled up at once', saying it would not be any use wanting one.

L   145

'There would be some difficulty in getting Hartington to join.' They then discussed what would happen if the Committee effected reunion. Chamberlain thought 'the old Party discipline would be restored and we should be anxious to pick out the Tories at the earliest possible moment'. This went much further than expected and, significantly, no more was heard of self-effacement! Chamberlain next brought off an important piece of bargaining. In return for the cancellation of his Birmingham speech on the 5th January he was promised an official response to the one of 23rd December. To the promise to speak at Hawick for Trevelyan on the 22nd January he adhered.[1]

Lewis Harcourt recorded him as being 'in a very grave and solemn mood, quite unlike anything I have ever seen in him before, with a distinct trace of nervousness and worry, and I could see he was highly strung by the quick pulse which I watched beating in the swollen veins on his temple'.[2] 'Foxing' at that intensity would have taken it out of anybody, but a 'sensitive man' like Chamberlain was bound to find it heavy weather. Hartington saw men that same day from ten in the morning until seven at night; his radical lieutenant only from one to five. Yet there was a world of difference in the operations they each had to face. The Whig had no win-or-lose-all balancing act on hand. 'Joe' had. The Whig had a simple mind and the clearest of consciences. 'Joe' had neither. But his efforts had not been in vain. Harcourt wrote off to Gladstone a glowing report of the proceedings[3] and Morley, however surprised at being suggested, was none the less gratified by it.[4] Yet by any fair test the Gladstonians had more solid grounds for pleasure. The Home Rule issue would be almost bound to come up now and the young 'fox' would then be run dangerously close to earth. He would have to choose some scheme or reject anything approaching true autonomy. Provincial Councils would not wash. The revelation made by Harcourt that Hartington had put off his projected Indian tour owing to the pressure of Liberal Unionist as well as Conservative leaders came to Chamberlain as something of a shock. Not only did it reveal the widespread horror on the right of his

[1] Lewis Harcourt's *Journal*, 30th December 1886. Harcourt Papers. Chamberain, *op. cit.*, pp. 237–9.

[2] *Ibid.*

[3] Harcourt to Gladstone, 30th December 1886. Gladstone Papers, Add. MS. 44200, f. 225. Salisbury was far from being in high spirits on this day. First he told the Queen Hartington's adhesion was unlikely and that this would make it necessary to 'appeal to Mr Goschen'. Salisbury to Queen Victoria, 30th December 1886. Windsor Royal Archives, C38/81. Then he told the poet and journalist Alfred Austin that if Goschen declined the government would be 'driven back upon W. H. Smith—for Beach' seemed 'to think his health an insuperable obstacle and *no one* could replace him in Ireland'. Salisbury to Alfred Austin, 30th December 1886. Alfred Austin Papers.

[4] Lewis Harcourt's *Journal*, 30th December 1886. Harcourt Papers.

influence, but the fact of his being less well informed as to how things really stood in his own camp than the leaders of the Opposition. At that moment it looked as though he would be wise to move towards the Home Rule camp. Evidently he felt the same, for in the second report of the executive of the National Radical Union, published that day it stated: 'With the desire of not widening the inevitable temporary rift in the Liberal party and of cooperating whenever possible with existing Liberal and Radical Associations, efforts have been directed to obtain correspondents, rather than start branches.'[1] Apparently the response of his former colleagues had come up to expectations. For the moment Dale's dum-dum bullets would remain in the arsenal.

Undoubtedly, Harcourt had been tougher than he truly desired over the Home Rule issue because of the combined efforts of Gladstone and Morley. In a note reaching him before Chamberlain's arrival, the latter had hammered home the commitment to Irish self-government, and demanded Spencer be on the Committee.[2] His efforts were largely rewarded when Harcourt put the Gladstonian case to Chamberlain. From Morley too came the quotations for embarrassing the 'enemy' into admitting the crucial point into the discussions. Evidently riled by Harcourt's remarks in conversation as to his good faith, he denied vehemently any hostility to reunion. 'I desire it most strongly,' he chirped, 'and would give up any detail that could be shown not to effect the rest of the matter.' Provided the Leeds Resolution was the starting point 'every detail consequent upon it is open'. Amusingly enough he tried to clinch the argument with the remark: 'Chamberlain himself has within the present year advanced propositions that go as far as our resolution.'[3] The implication being that he was demanding nothing the Radical Unionist had not already conceded. What he lacked in hostility, however, he more than made up for in suspicion. The immense fear his former friend aroused in him comes out again and again during these weeks. It is as though he thinks Chamberlain will simply gobble him up, and if not him, Harcourt, Herschell and, of course, Fowler, should he ever be allowed to reach the Conference table. His pleasure at being invited to participate did not include a greater confidence in Gladstonian success. Lewis Harcourt considered he was 'afraid that when we get into the

---

[1] *Liberal Unionist*, October 1889, p. 41. The Hartingtonians were in a less cooperative frame of mind—just as might have been expected. Steps were taken early in 1887 to found new associations and branches of associations. See, for example, Bagshawe Papers 778 (ii). There Colonel Hozier's correspondence with the Sheffield Liberal Unionists provides a revealing indication of Whig Unionist militancy.

[2] Morley to Harcourt, 30th December 1886. Harcourt Papers.

[3] *Ibid.*

Conference too much will be conceded to Chamberlain'.[1] 'You must remember that I am a Parnellite, which you are not,' was the self-justification-cum-admonition that he threw out to Harcourt that evening. Adding: 'Where Parnell goes, I go.' The reply was the one to expect from a man first and last a Liberal: 'Oh no, you must not use that language; you must say "Where I go, Parnell goes".'[2] Cold comfort for a worried man.

To Gladstone, Harcourt summarised accurately the conclusions arrived at, but omitted the processes involved in coming to them, except for Chamberlain's climb down on the crucial point. Following this, he [Chamberlain] was said to 'propose' that 'a certain number among us should meet him to discuss: 1. Irish Land; 2. Irish Local Government; and 3. What form of Irish Legislature should and could be adopted'.[3] Once more Harcourt was at pains to aver his belief in 'perfect good faith' behind 'the olive branch', judging that 'if we should fail to find a common ground we shall be no worse off than we are now'. Finally, he asked for his leader's sanction for the talks, again repeating that 'the whole discussion would be conducted under your auspices and instructions'. About Hartington's intentions he could offer nothing new. Certainly, from his viewpoint, he was right to repeat over and over again the set piece about Chamberlain's good faith.[4] In his letter to Harcourt, written that morning, Gladstone concluded with the well-known: 'We stand midway in his estimation between the Government *plus* Churchill and the Government *minus* Churchill.' An assessment arrived at when in a mood of 'great tranquillity' in his 'inner self'. So great a tranquillity, indeed, as to give the impression of being slightly out of touch. To say that he would receive accounts of reunion conversations 'with great interest' is surely somewhat detached? Only such an exceptionally well-established party leader like him could afford such a thing. To think Chamberlain was going to London with seeing Churchill as his main object is scarcely intelligent, unless as an attempt to cast aspersions on his good faith in seeing Hartington and Harcourt. In any case it showed the inefficacy of the latter's letters to Hawarden. To claim that one of the things making him feel the 'necessity of caution' was 'the very inadequate sense' Chamberlain seemed to have of 'the inherent difficulties of legislation on the great matters before us' was plain presumption and prejudice, flying in the face of the facts.[5] After all, how could a man who risked the political wilderness on the Home

[1] Lewis Harcourt's *Journal*, 30th December 1886. Harcourt Papers.

[2] *Ibid.*

[3] Harcourt to Gladstone, 30th December 1886. Gladstone Papers, Add. MS. 44200, f. 225.

[4] *Ibid.*

[5] Gladstone to Harcourt, 30th December 1886. Harcourt Papers.

Rule question and thought the matter out more clearly perhaps than anybody, Gladstone included, be said truly to have a 'very inadequate sense' of the difficulties involved? To dismiss Dale as a misser of the point because of one part of his letter and ignore the real force of some of the rest betokens a blinkered mind. Dale might make Gladstone 'sad'. Gladstone must have done the same to Harcourt. Perhaps the birthday celebrations of which the old man complained had had a temporarily numbing effect upon him. Certainly he had shown less self-righteousness in the realisation of his rôle in the party split in recent months than this letter shows, and Harcourt had good grounds for thinking Dale's effort would strike home.

With such a letter in his morning's mail, the last day of 1886 could hardly be said to have begun well. The chances of keeping the bargain with Chamberlain over an official blessing appeared seriously reduced, even though Gladstone had ventured the prophecy, just before letting fly at the hated 'Joe', that 'the crisis' being in the nature of 'a healthy development', 'good' would come out of it.[1] Moreover, in a matter of hours Chamberlain would be crossing the threshold for a second preliminary talk. How could Harcourt be confident he would not be disowned? In these circumstances, could he proceed to act as though everything was sure to go ahead as planned the day before? He decided to take a risk and continue as if nothing untoward had occurred. It was just as well he remained ignorant of the full extent of Gladstone's lack of confidence in him and his works. The speed with which he had gone about responding to Chamberlain had caused his leader considerable alarm an alarm communicated on the 30th December to Granville.[2] Would that he [Granville] were at Harcourt's elbow to keep him in order. Morley was 'solid on his pins' and would not go astray, but unhappily the same could not be said of his friend. At the time of writing, Gladstone did not know that Morley was going to be at that friend's elbow more and more, and would, if the Committee ever met, be a member of it. The situation therefore struck him as all the blacker. How to impose his 'prescription of the moment' and yet avoid blame in the party was not easy to work out. 'Receptivity, tranquillity, patience and caution' were hardly all the rage in the right and centre of the Liberal party.

All told, 31st December was quite an eventful day. Hartington met Salisbury and formally declined to head or participate in a coalition.[3]

[1] *Ibid.*

[2] Gladstone to Granville, 30th December 1886. Granville Papers, P.R.O. 30, 29, 22A.

[3] Salisbury informed the Queen of Hartington's decision. Salisbury to Queen Victoria, 31st December 1886. Editor, Buckle, *op. cit.*, p. 280. So too did Hartington himself. Hartington to Queen Victoria, 31st December 1886. Windsor Royal Archives, C38/92.

Chamberlain went to Harcourt's a second time and continued with arrangements for the reunion talks. The first was something everybody had come to expect. Bar the concluding stitches one side of the crisis was now sewn up, and it was the side responsible for most of the true impetus on the other. Originally, that is to say, for the events beginning with the Birmingham speech had led to a process possessed of a vigorous life of its own. However much Chamberlain might have felt that the new situation suited him, he could not now effect a simple withdrawal. There was a publicly expressed wish for a 'Round Table' to be lived up to, and Radical Unionist forces behind him placing untold hopes upon a successful outcome. Not that he did in fact want to make such a withdrawal. The time was not ripe, nor was Hartington's standing aloof in itself a guarantee that things would be all right. It remained to be seen whether the government minus Churchill was worth his confidence. Unlike Churchill himself, Chamberlain suffered from no illusions about his leader's capacity for progressive politics. A genuinely liberal personality is not necessarily a truly Liberal statesman. Given conditions allowing a real choice, the signal for an abandonment of the talks project would be clear proof that Salisbury was willing to take a fair amount of Radical Unionist advice. Hartington's refusal was a bid to keep Liberal Unionism united. Chamberlain's future actions depended very much on whether this bid would be followed by pressure on the Conservatives for reform legislation.

As he entered Harcourt's house at noon that day his position was stronger than it had been a week before. Now there was no longer any question but that the government would survive. Hartington's refusal was not yet public, but that did not matter. The fact that it would be was all that counted. Unionism had regained its stability. Whereas immediately after Churchill's resignation there was a strong and a weak side in politics, at the end of the year this was no longer true. Both sides were strong. Chamberlain was wanted anyway by the Unionists. The Gladstonians eager for a *modus vivendi* were equally keen for his support and those who loathed him would not be able to resist his coming back to the fold on what basically were their as well as his terms. He had the chance of choosing which side to come down on, provided his timing was shrewd. Right from the beginning he intended to hold firm to his unionism and knew Gladstone would never swallow it, so his choice was never in doubt. The great thing was to create the impression it was. Birmingham would be reassured, the country impressed, and an all-out attack on Gladstone could later be launched with a 'clear conscience'. For the present, the Gladstonians had to be humoured, though not too obviously. Surrender after argument was the tactic called for. One thing and one thing alone made all this possible—the secrecy of the whole proceeding. With that guaranteed he could say anything and later withdraw it with impunity. A wholehearted Home Ruler one day, he could revert to Provincial Councils the next. Hence his request for keeping only Gladstone and Hartington informed of the progress made. It was natural enough to be cautious about any compromise talks because proposals made when peace seems likely may well have to be withdrawn if war is resumed. Harcourt was therefore quite ready to agree. But what Chamberlain actually did to spin out the time was not to arrange a compromise so much as a surrender. This lured Gladstone into giving a reluctant public blessing to what he really thought a dangerous fantasy of Harcourt's. Meanwhile Hartington was given carefully edited versions of what transpired. The one fly in the ointment was Trevelyan. This, however, is to anticipate.

The meeting on the 31st began with Harcourt reading out an extract from his letter to Gladstone 'stating the terms of the arrangement'. Chamberlain at once took issue with the claim that he had 'proposed' to discuss an Irish Legislature. Quite rightly, he insisted he had merely agreed the subject 'need not be formally excluded and might be discussed if thought desirable'. Also the words 'what form of legislature could be granted' should not be taken to imply he 'thought any form of single legislature could safely be conceded'. The farthest concession possible was 'some form of Provincial Assemblies or Councils'. Harcourt was moderate, but 'very stiff', assuring him that he would not be committing himself to anything more than his past speeches and could reject any scheme proposed. In fact, they went over the argument of the day before. Although Harcourt said he could not substitute the words 'legislative body or bodies' or rule out Home Rule because it would look like a 'complete surrender and betrayal of their cause', this was not the real reason. Secrecy would make sure the public remained in total ignorance of what had transpired, if all those involved so desired. The stumbling block was Gladstone. For Chamberlain, having a leader was more a concept than a reality. For Harcourt this was not so, and Gladstone's goodwill was only obtainable if Home Rule was on the agenda. Then, too, Morley had now to be directly considered as a representative and he was insisting that the Leeds resolution be the *sine qua non* of any discussions. The bulk of the Gladstonian party apart, the project would never leave the ground unless Chamberlain caved in. So cave in he did.

The composition of the Committee still worried Harcourt. He now raised seriously what had merely been touched on the day before—the need for Chamberlain 'to have some of his Unionist friends' with him. The 'fox' was in a trap. He could hardly object to having aid and comfort without arousing suspicion in Harcourt's mind, and that he could not afford to do. 'Chamberlain had to consent, though (and his cunning never failed him) he said he thought they might with advantage have come in later, when perhaps some agreement had been already arrived at.[1] Harcourt had suggested Trevelyan, and that was agreed, but the general threat of company made Chamberlain open up a little more about Hartington. Repeating the view that the chances of getting him were remote, he went on to divulge that his leader 'did not at all approve of this idea of a Committee and' had 'told' him that 'he [Chamberlain] was putting himself in the hands of a lot of clever fellows with Gladstone at their back and that he would get the worst of it'.[2] With Trevelyan coming, Chamberlain had grounds for wondering whether he had not been right. Without a real principal and without companions he would have been able to play fast and loose. Even one companion might mar his grand campaign, for secrecy had been intended to operate against everyone except himself and his real intimates. Trevelyan was not a member of the National Radical Union and did not refer to himself as a Liberal Unionist. Anything might happen.

This took an hour. 'At one o'clock' Harcourt 'said he believed John Morley was at the Athenaeum and would Chamberlain like to see him?' Chamberlain 'hummed and hawed, said he had to lunch at Dilke's at two, and perhaps there was not time'. Lewis Harcourt offered to go down in a cab 'to bring John Morley up', and a third surrender took place. It is hard to understand why Chamberlain objected to meeting Morley after having himself suggested he join the Committee. Perhaps to heighten the notion of his fighting all along the line; just conceivably to be wooed the harder. When the young Harcourt brought Morley into the room there was an exchange of New Year greetings between the two Radicals. Harcourt père 'plunged *in medias res* so as to avoid any awkwardness. They were both very obviously shy of one another.' Morley had heard earlier from Brett of Chamberlain's 'pressing Hartington to form a Coalition Government'. His suspicions were having a field day. Once there, however, he concurred in what had been done and promised, along with Harcourt, to write to Gladstone suggesting 'a letter similar in terms to the private letter from him to Harcourt, dated 27th' should be published as the official reply to the 'olive branch'. In response to Chamberlain's complaints about 'the arrogant and unconciliatory

[1] Lewis Harcourt's *Journal*, 31st December 1886. Gardiner, *op. cit.*, pp. 23–4. Chamberlain, *op. cit.*, pp. 239–40.

[2] *Ibid.* For Chamberlain's scorn and distaste for Trevelyan see Granville to Harcourt, 2nd January 1887. Harcourt Papers.

tone of articles in the *Daily News*' both Harcourt and Morley promised efforts to secure a change. 'Subject to Gladstone's approval' the Committee was to meet on 13th and 14th January. Chamberlain was to go down to Malwood late on the second day. The session ended with the moving sight of Chamberlain and Morley going off together in a cab for lunch at Dilke's.[1] Harcourt had advised Morley to accept Chamberlain's characteristically impulsive invitation to Irving's box at the Lyceum that evening. The host himself had pressed hard: 'Hang public opinion! Why should we not be seen together?' was all very well, but even in his impulses 'Joe' tended to work for the king of Birmingham. And his charm could work wonders. Before long Morley found himself admitting that 'Mr G. and all of them recognised that Home Rule in the sense of Mr G's Bill was impossible at present. It might be inevitable in the future but it was not now a practical question.'[2] He even ventured to say that

> Mr G. was much exercised at the idea of going to his grave having just smashed the Liberal Party and was therefore most conciliatory and anxious for reunion. He thought that Home Rule being out of the question during his lifetime he would still have the credit and foresight and patriotism if it came later as he assumed it would, but in the meantime history would deal harshly with him if he did not do his best to prevent the disorganisation and defeat of the Party which had followed him so long.[3]

Morley's suspicions were again temporarily allayed and his judgment thereby impaired. At Dilke's Chamberlain indulged in a lengthy dose of engaging frankness. Dilke recorded:

> Chamberlain and John Morley came in together to lunch, Chamberlain having been asked and Morley not, and it was somewhat startling. Chamberlain thinks that he can get Mr Gladstone by the bait of "Four times Prime Minister" ... Conferences are sitting ... Hartington is crusty at this.'

Morley took it all without turning a hair. Times had certainly changed.[4]

Not everything Brett said could be taken for gospel. His intelligence on the many topics was often a little tall. This time it probably was not, and Morley ought to have pressed Chamberlain about the advice given to Hartington. There would then have been a chance of establishing bad faith before the G.O.M. sent his writ of expedit south. On 26th December Chamberlain had told Heneage he 'might readily support' a coalition.[5] There was certainly some basis of fact to Brett's

---

[1] Gwynn and Tuckwell, *op. cit.*, p. 265.
[2] Chamberlain, *op. cit.*, pp. 239–40.   [3] *Ibid.*
[4] Gwynn and Tuckwell, *op. cit.*, pp. 265–6.
[5] Chamberlain to Heneage, 26th December 1886. Copy. Chamberlain Papers, JC5/41/22.

allegations and he had ready access to Hartington. The news reached Morley within a matter of hours. Now, of course, Chamberlain may have been 'foxing' all round. The statement might simply have been made to prevent any burning of boats to his right. On the other hand, it was in keeping with his innermost thoughts to be against Home Rule at all costs bar one—the cost of his base. Maybe coalition was something he was ultimately prepared to face in order to shore up Unionism to the strength which it needed to carry on, but there can be no doubt as to his relief at Salisbury's being able to do without it. However much time flowed by during the reunion talks it would be easier to sell Birmingham a return to the *status quo ante* than coalition with the Conservatives. Yet why, if fear of a Conservative collapse was the reason he considered supporting a coalition, did he press Hartington to make one as late as 30th December? The only answer fitting the circumstances is lack of confidence. Chamberlain was far less self-assured than he appeared and always liked to minimise risks, while at the same time seeking them out.

Morley the 'realist' in the cab with Chamberlain also slipped from his unusually high 'Parnellite' pedestal in discussing the future of Home Rule. Brett was undoubtedly accurate in reporting him as thinking 'the great obstacle to all compromise in the Irish Question is Parnell's "hurry" lest Mr G. should die, and his determination to make the most of him while he can'.[1] That is to say, in reporting this as his considered opinion. Excited by what seemed the way to a *modus vivendi*, he gave way temporarily to another fit of wishful thinking. For a few hours the Liberal party was all and the Nationalists seen only as a deserving cause to be aided at leisure. Harcourt was exaggerating when he told Gladstone in his report of the second meeting that Chamberlain and Morley had effected a complete reconciliation, but appearances pointed very much in that direction.[2] The more the two men meet, the easier it is to appreciate why, politics apart, their relations were likely to be troubled. Morley felt himself the weaker man, and was dominated. When ideological differences arose the fat was in the fire. There could never be any lasting peace, merely short impulsive spells of mutual confidence, invariably followed on Morley's side by renewed and strengthened feelings of revulsion.

Had Chamberlain seen Harcourt's letter to Gladstone he would have felt a deep satisfaction. His tactic of argue before surrender was

---

[1] Brett to Rosebery, 31st December 1886. Brett, *op. cit.*, p. 133. Esher, *op. cit.*, p. 188. Few would have echoed Brett's comment: 'It really is very amusing.' For an assessment of Parnell see J. Bryce, *Studies in Contemporary Biography*, pp. 227–49. For one of Morley see R. B. Haldane, *An Autobiography*, pp. 95–6. Morley is there adjudged a highly ambitious man essentially unsuited to political life.

[2] Harcourt to Gladstone, 31st December 1886. Copy. Harcourt Papers.

paying handsome dividends. To save him from a 'ticklish position' Harcourt was ready to take great pains.

> Relations with Hartington must be strained and I doubt not that he has seen that the unnatural combination to support a Tory Government could not long be maintained, and therefore he has made up his mind to part company. At the same time, of course, he requires some *management*, as his position is difficult with his own following in the House of Commons and outside, and he must not be placed in a position of absolute surrender in a white sheet. This the proposed conference will obviate.[1]

What a bitter irony it was that the very thing Harcourt saw as the means of drawing Chamberlain into his party Chamberlain himself saw as the excuse for staying out. Morley's news from Brett fell quite flat. Either Harcourt did not believe it, or, while believing it, was so anxious for reunion as to forgive any sign of duplicity in the hope he would eventually land his fish. He certainly put Morley's mind at rest on the point, though maybe the suggestion of having Trevelyan was intended to help keep 'Joe' on the straight and narrow. 'Morley and I agreed,' wrote Harcourt, 'that it would be a good thing, as we were several in number, that Chamberlain should bring in another of his lot, as the more of the dissentients who are parties to the transaction, the stronger the position will be.'[2] Which of the two reasons counted more is not difficult to see. Profound though Harcourt's sympathy for Chamberlain was, it did not extend to saving him from loneliness.

Both sides were now anxious for Gladstone's 'exequatur' and hoped it would arrive the next day.

> It is good to strike while the iron is hot [urged Harcourt, and went on to ask his leader for] something in the sense of your letter of the 27th inst. viz. that you quite agree that the speech of Chamberlain is an important event of which due account must be taken and think it ought to lead to a *modus vivendi* in the Liberal party, and that you would be very glad if a means could be found for bringing about a discussion of the points of difference with a view to arriving at some common understanding, or at least reducing to a *minimum* the points of difference as affecting the whole Irish Question.[3]

Seldom can Gladstone have received such a request since assuming the Liberal leadership. Yet he responded, first with a telegram on New Year's day—'Use *ad libitum* quotation of 27th. Will write. G.';[4] second with a letter not for publication, sent off later that same day;[5] and third, with a letter for publication, written on 2nd January.[6] So

---

[1] *Ibid.* [2] *Ibid.* [3] *Ibid.*
[4] Gladstone to Harcourt, 1st January 1887, No. 1. Harcourt Papers.
[5] Gladstone to Harcourt, 1st January 1887, No. 2. Harcourt Papers.
[6] Gladstone to Harcourt, 2nd January 1887. Harcourt Papers.

ready a response had not been expected, for early on 1st January, when no letter from Gladstone was in his morning's mail, Harcourt wrote post haste to Granville[1] and Spencer.[2] He appealed for their aid in getting the 'exequatur'. Without it the project would come to nothing and he would cease all efforts for reunion. In fact there was no cause for alarm, for after all, what could Gladstone do but bless the plan with the Birmingham 'Coriolanus' in such 'a melting mood'. Refusal would lay him open to charges of indifference to the future good of the Liberal party. Arnold Morley had just told him as much.[3] Moreover, it was not simply a matter of responding to Harcourt's direct appeals. John Morley was speaking with the same voice. Apparently a performance of *Faust* had completed the process of acquiring belief in 'Joe's' good faith. Morley wrote to Gladstone on the 31st December,[4] but next day the enchantment was wearing off a little. He then assured Granville that he doubted whether the coveted *modus vivendi* would emerge, although the talks might well 'soften things' and in any case do no harm.[5] Nor had Wolverton's grumble that most of the really enthusiastic Liberals did not want reunion been addressed to his leader.[6] Receiving it second hand from Granville was not likely to have the same impact on him, and, even if it had, there were more important factors to consider. Anyway, what did Wolverton mean? What constituted a really enthusiastic Liberal? And, what is more, had he not got the good sense to see that the less enthusiastic were those who won or lost electoral battles. The zealots might organise. The non-zealots made up the majority of potential Liberal voters. Naturally enough, Harcourt entertained deep suspicions of some of the real enthusiasts, notably Labouchère and similar 'Joe'-haters. Complaining to Spencer in his appeal for help on New Year's Day, he expressed himself 'a good deal disappointed not to have received an immediate acceptance' from Gladstone, and blamed irresponsible influences. 'I cannot but fear that he is still a good deal under the influences of such evil counsellors as Labouchère, and others who are the principal causes of the mischief that has been already done.'[7] He was wrong. The G.O.M. stood in no need of a Northampton course in 'Joe' hating. Only after seeing the waiting

[1] Harcourt to Granville, 1st January 1887. Granville Papers, P.R.O. 30, 29, 29A.
[2] Harcourt to Spencer, 1st January 1887. Spencer Papers.
[3] Arnold Morley to Gladstone, 31st December 1886. Gladstone Papers, Add. MS. 44253, f. 52.
[4] Morley to Gladstone, 31st December 1886. Gladstone Papers, Add. MS. 44255, f. 165.
[5] Morley to Granville, 1st January 1887. Granville Papers, P.R.O. 30, 29, 22A.
[6] Wolverton to Granville, 30th December 1886. Granville Papers, P.R.O. 30, 29, 28A.
[7] Harcourt to Spencer, 1st January 1887. Spencer Papers.

game was up did he overcome his profound distaste and send Harcourt what he wanted.

His way of going about it was curious. Sending the telegram brought public knowledge of his approval no nearer. Harcourt dashed off a note to Chamberlain on its arrival, describing the wording as 'quite satisfactory'.[1] It showed that the 'spirit of Barkis is willing'. But there was no hiding his disappointment and frustration. 'Of course,' he complained, 'we can *publish* nothing till we have his text.'[2] Nevertheless neither he nor Morley were going to keep mum any longer and chose to treat Gladstone's words as 'complete authority to us *to speak to our friends in the sense of the letter of 27th at once*'.[3] This they proceeded to do, as this letter itself shows. While Harcourt was telling Chamberlain, Morley made it his business to enlighten Childers and Mundella.[4] Of that more later.

In sending the private letter first Gladstone made sure his terms of business would be known by the principal reconciler before either of them committed themselves openly to any reconciliation attempt. In case of last minute disagreement over what was stated, the public letter could be still further delayed. So excessive a caution is certainly curious with the issues already quite clear to both the writer and receiver of the letter. Gladstone must still have fancied Harcourt was a prospective traitor to the Home Rule cause. The presentation was very matter of fact. It began,

> I learn with pleasure the intention of some of my colleagues to confer with Mr Chamberlain and Sir George Trevelyan with the general view indicated by me in a letter of the 27th of December last to you, and again in a friendly spirit consider how far a *modus vivendi* is attainable between the late Government and any of those who resisted their Irish Government Bill.

Then came a definition!

> 2. By a *modus vivendi* I understand a partial agreement without prejudice to what lies beyond it, supplying a plan of present action and prompted by a desire that a wider accommodation may in due season be found practicable.

Like 'Joe', Gladstone wanted an insurance policy. Hence there was an escape clause:

> 3. I conceive that in a conference of this nature, opinions given on one point may materially depend on what is thought as to some other point, and that all who take part are at liberty to resume their previous attitudes, unless in so far as they may arrive at any understanding otherwise.

[1] Harcourt to Chamberlain, 1st January 1887. Chamberlain Papers, JC5/38/55.
[2] *Ibid.*
[3] *Ibid.*
[4] Morley to Harcourt, 1st January 1887. Harcourt Papers.

But, and here 'Joe' is justifiably dragged in, there can be no juggling with the major point at issue.

4. I assume it to be impossible for Mr Chamberlain, as it evidently is for us to recede from the main contention or to do anything in disparagement of it. But it stands to be considered:—(1.) What can we arrange in the way of common action? (2.) How can we handle our differences, or how far can we reserve them, so as not to bring about contention.

Apparently cold storage did not count as juggling. Jam tomorrow was still jam. What followed, however, looked like cutting down the expected amount of common ground.

5. Individually, I do not at this moment see my way as to the construction of a new *Land Purchase Bill*. (*a*) The Ashbourne Act is I believe not nearly exhausted. (*b*) The existence of a widespread desire for purchase in Ireland may be doubtful. (*c*) I do not know how to construct any Bill so good as our Bill *on its financial side*. (*d*) There is also the fear of a needless and useless breach with Ireland. If, however, others find the ground more open than I do, by no means let me stand in the way of their deliberations as to (2.).

The jam tomorrow concept seemed to nag at his mind, for in the next paragraph he played with the idea of securing recognition of the inherent worth of his jam as soon as possible.

6. I put aside all idea of a serious effort to press a plan of Home Rule on our basis under the present circumstances; but leave open the question whether there should, or should not be a vote in its favour; which it would be difficult to decide at the present time.

Turning to the practical application of his principles, he first outlined the contents of a potential *modus vivendi*.

7. As to 1., the *possible* basis for common action seems to me to be (*a*) Some Bill on the lines of a Liberal Local Government for Ireland. It could hardly be proposed I think by us of the main body, but might be accepted and supported without prejudice? It might even be proposed, also without prejudice by a Nationalist? Or, it might be proposed by a Liberal who has resisted us and for whom it would be an expression of his creed? (I assume that the Government do nothing.) (*b*) Bills of Liberal policy on points accepted by the whole party. On motions deemed politic, e.g. public expenditure if so deemed. (*c*) Procedure: to press our own opinions in the sense (*a*) of mere Devolution. (*b*) to clôture by majority. (Some portion of this question might have to be reserved until we know the purport of the Queen's Speech.)

Last was the question of who should be entrusted with these delicate tasks. Here he made no direct attack on Fowler's participation, but contented himself with a pretty broad hint.

8. As to the composition of the conference *ad hoc*. (*a*) I am glad that Sir George Trevelyan is to accompany Chamberlain. (*b*) As this has been a Cabinet matter all along, I should incline to confining it on our side to

say three of the late Cabinet, two of whom should be yourself and Morley. (*c*) If it go beyond the late Cabinet, I should suggest Lefevre[1] as an independent member, who, however, has served in Cabinet. (*d*) There is something to be said in favour of confining it to commoners, or else having some reason of convenience or otherwise in choosing a peer. (*e*) While offering these suggestions, I think it best that the selection for this free and preliminary meeting should be made in London.

At all costs he is determined no odium shall fall on his shoulders and stresses that 'while well-disposed to any really useful measure, and strongly impressed with the necessity of avoiding anything equivocal in our general position', he was 'more anxious for harmony than for activity'. 'Hearty good wishes' and an assurance one would have thought superfluous from a fully sincere man that 'this letter is meant to be useful as far as it may, not to be obstructive' rounded off this magnum opus.[2] Apart, that is, from a P.S. saying that the new *Nineteenth Century* contains a mention of Chamberlain 'meant by me to be friendly'.[3] Did Gladstone realise then that his style was so cryptic as to admit of ambiguity in comparatively simple things? The whole production shows a man in at least two minds—pessimistic and optimistic, obstructive and helpful, disingenuous and straightforward. The first two paragraphs seem curiously formal for parts of a letter to a private individual, especially one so much in contact with him as Harcourt. Of course he realised Morley would see it, yet it was not for publication. Paragraphs 3 to 7 were far too frank to allow that. The initial stiffness wore off, but the mood changes almost from paragraph to paragraph. When a concession has been made he soon seeks to weaken its effect. When an obstruction is brought forward he is anxious to deny its existence or water it down.

Events did not stand still while this was being concocted. Neither Harcourt nor Morley were prepared to let the grass grow under their feet. The former persuaded Morley to tackle the editor of the *Daily News* about its hostility to the 'olive branch'. For the moment he met with success and Chamberlain was reassured: 'You will find the tone of the *Daily News* in future much to your mind.'[4] Morley himself had a horror of being known as a contributor to the paper. The rôle of official interceder did not appeal to him.

> Please note [he pleaded] that I am most urgent that no human soul, save you, your son, Mr G. and the writer should know that I write anything for the *Daily News*. I did not even wish Arnold Morley to know. What happens is that one is held responsible for every word that appears for a year after.[5]

[1] G. J. Shaw-Lefevre (1831–1928). M.P. at this time for Central Bradford. He was out of the Commons during Gladstone's Third Ministry. Created a baron 1906, he took the title Lord Eversley. [2] Gladstone to Harcourt, 1st January 1887, No. 2. Harcourt Papers. [3] *Ibid.* [4] Harcourt to Chamberlain, 1st January 1887. Chamberlain Papers, JC5/38/55. [5] Morley to Harcourt, 1st January 1887. Harcourt Papers.

The main worry, and a justified one, was that his complaints might go unheeded. Time was to show how right he was. For the moment the press problem did not loom large and his energies were largely free to devote to seeing some of the men most closely affected by reunion prospects. Parnell had reacted well to the news that a conference would probably soon take place. 'He seemed quite prepared, for the thing is in the air', but voiced some anxiety, saying: 'When people go into a conference, they are usually ready to give up something.'[1] Morley had quickly pointed out how ultimate authority rested with Gladstone and Parnell seemed satisfied. 'He was very sensible as usual,' was the final verdict on him. 'Very sensible' apparently, because as a keen 'parliamenteer' he was 'thoroughly alive to the scrape in which J. Chamberlain finds himself' and rejoiced accordingly. Childers and Mundella welcomed the reunion project. The one limiting comment to the claim of having first used the phrase *modus vivendi*.[2] The other taking issue with the constitution of the Committee.[3] Though not alarmed by this, Morley does think Fowler's name 'will stir the wrath of Labouchère' as Fowler had gone out of his way to repudiate the views of *Truth* on the talks.

> I must say [comments Morley] that if you could induce J. Chamberlain to mention somebody else, it would disarm a good deal of irritable talk and jealousy. As for the 'financial expert', that is all nonsense; the true reason is that he calculates (from H. Fowler's letter to him after his speech last week) on turning H. Fowler away from you and me. Do be more suspicious.[4]

Undoubtedly, he was partly right!

By the next day Gladstone's authority over Harcourt seemed to be near its limit. Still no publishable authorisation had shown up, so he sent Morley a telegram suggesting a paragraph in the form of a communiqué be put in the papers stating that 'Mr Gladstone attaches much importance to Mr Chamberlain's recent speech and is of opinion that it ought to lead to a *modus vivendi* in the Liberal party'. It should be prefaced by the words: 'We are authorised to state' and sent through *Central News* to the metropolitan and provincial press.[5] In a supplementing letter he explained:

[1] *Ibid.*   [2] *Ibid.*   [3] *Ibid.*   [4] *Ibid.*
[5] Harcourt to Morley, 2nd January 1887. Copy. Harcourt Papers. Writing to Harcourt on 2nd January 1887 Granville said that had Harcourt and Morley not believed in Chamberlain's *bona fides*, he, Granville, would have been afraid the whole move the Radical Unionist leader had initiated was simply intended to 'put himself right with the large body of Liberals, without any prospect of coming to an arrangement'. Granville to Harcourt, 2nd January 1887. Lord Edmond Fitzmaurice, *The Life of Lord Granville, 1815–1891*, Vol. II, pp. 490–1. Meanwhile Sir Edward Hamilton was more sure of himself. He had learnt from Arnold Morley, whom he had bumped into on Charing Cross station on the evening of

This I think would answer the purpose almost as well as a letter from Mr G. and I consider that his telegram of yesterday that we should use the quotation from his letter of the 27th *ad libitum* is a complete authority for such an announcement. It has the advantage that it loses no time and clinches the thing at once.[1]

Not being a naturally patient man, Harcourt must have found the delay almost unendurable and he was especially anxious nothing else should go wrong. Pressure on the press must be maintained. Morley was strongly urged to carry out his intention of ' "bossing" the *Daily News*' and told how to do it. 'I should not mince matters at all, but speak out very plain and put my feet down on Labby. If he squeals, never mind.' And things could be taken beyond mere pressure to direct arrangement of copy. 'Had it occurred to you,' he asked, 'that Dilke might be got to write up the fusion in the *Daily News*— I mean of course in leaders?'[2] More men of 'goodwill' had to be dragged into the fray at once with the risk of Lefevre coming on and Fowler going off the proposed Committee. The balance in favour of the Harcourtian interpretation of events stood in danger of disturbance.

Lord Spencer had no hesitation as to the side on which he should throw his weight. Althorp was offered as a convenient halfway meeting place between Hawarden and London. 'Come any moment,' he told Harcourt, 'and bring anyone, including the great J.C. if you like.' Compared with Gladstone's complicated reactions Spencer's were simplicity itself. 'Well done!' was his verdict on Harcourt's exertions.[3] He agreed entirely with what the latter had written to him about the 'olive branch' and thought excellent results were very possible. In the event of failure rough places would have been smoothed over and the Gladstonians relieved 'of the responsibility of maintaining disunion in our ranks'. While not blind to the difficulties likely to be met, he was sure that

if Chamberlain really wishes for reunion, some *modus vivendi* ought to be found which would be accepted by Parnell and Co. It will not do to alienate Parnell, but if the plan of compromise is skilfully framed so as to be one which Parnell could recommend to his party without appearing

1st January 1887, that negotiations for a rapprochement with Chamberlain were 'afoot', that Chamberlain and John Morley had been together to the theatre and that Chamberlain's having invited Morley to do so was regarded as a conciliatory move. All this he took at its face value. Sir Edward Hamilton's Diary, 2nd January 1887. Add. MS. 48645, p. 73. He also recorded that the editor of the *Daily News* (Lucy) was to be upbraided for giving undue prominence to Labouchère's attacks upon Chamberlain. *Ibid.*, p. 74.

[1] *Ibid.*   [2] *Ibid.*

[3] Spencer to Harcourt, 2nd January 1887. Harcourt Papers.

to sell the Pass, he will see the advantage of getting the question, if not actually settled, put on the highway to settlement.[1]

There is a distinct air of Malwoodian optimism about his approach. The amount of verbal juggling required to satisfy Chamberlain and Parnell was more than even Gladstone could tackle, but the hope of its achievement illustrates well enough the relief with which another Gladstonian leader welcomed a possible means of reuniting his party and easing his conscience. Responding to Harcourt's plea he had written to Hawarden, but thought it superfluous. 'I don't know whether Labouchère has Mr G.'s ear just now, but from what John Morley told me I was afraid that Mr G. was disposed to grovel in the dust to bring about a reunion.'[2] There should therefore be no worries, especially as Chamberlain had agreed to discuss Home Rule. Here was encouragement indeed! But did it contain a revelation of duplicity in Morley? Was he responsible for the G.O.M.'s procrastination and equivocation? For all his suspicion this is highly unlikely. Very probably he caught his leader in a strong reunion mood. The letter of New Year's Day showed the old man found it difficult to arrive at a *via media* on the reunion issue and tended to seing this way and that. Morley never found Home Rule stock low, nor Chamberlain stock high on the Hawarden Exchange, yet views as to tactics varied with rapidity. That the question of moral responsibility for splitting the party weighed heavily with Spencer is fully apparent from what he wrote to Granville that same 2nd January.[3] Refusal to meet Chamberlain would have been a great responsibility. No harm could result from failure. Parnell would naturally have to agree to any scheme, and it was undoubtedly fortunate that the initiative had come from Chamberlain. His fear was that the talks would reveal profound differences of opinion over several basic policies. To Granville he was, of course, absolutely frank. What he told him did not differ in any material particular from what he told Harcourt. There was no question but that he was entirely in good faith. At Hawarden Spencer was regarded as a man of the uttermost reliability. His word carried weight there and Harcourt could be glad that word was for the Committee idea.

When the 'exequatur' finally turned up the day following, it was something of an anti-climax. Apart from a bid to take all the real credit for the reunion idea for himself, the G.O.M. said nothing of a startling nature. 'Having as you may remember spoken in this sense when you were here some weeks ago, I shall not excite your surprise

---

[1] *Ibid.*   [2] *Ibid.*

[3] Spencer to Granville, 2nd January 1887. Granville Papers, P.R.O. 30, 29, 22A.

by retaining the opinion now that some encouragement has been
given to it by an occurrence such as the recent speech of Mr Chamberlain.[1] Harcourt could in fairness claim he was rather surprised by the
whole passage, above all by the claim that it would have been odd
had the writer changed his mind. Nevertheless, he could draw positive comfort from having the letter at last and being able to dispel
harmful rumours.

Despite the delay no one had ever supposed the talks would not
take place. Replying to Harcourt on the 2nd, Chamberlain assumed
Gladstone's letter would come.

> Your letter is more favourable than I could have expected. I know that
> we both feel how much depends on the exact terms of Mr Gladstone's
> public reply to my advances and I am confirmed on reflection that the
> shorter it is the better. The mere fact of the Conference being held,
> when it becomes known, will do a great deal to promote a good feeling
> in the constituencies.

The main aim must be to build up goodwill, and for that reason he
attached

> the utmost importance to the *order* of our friendly discussion. By taking
> first the subjects on which agreement is probable we make any future and
> further proceedings more hopeful, and although I cannot feel sanguine
> at present as to complete accord on the whole of the Irish Question, it
> will be a great point gained to have narrowed the issues and to have
> secured a considerable amount of common ground.[2]

At interviews with Trevelyan and Hartington earlier the same day
the virtues of reunion had been preached, to the converted in one
case and to the unconvertible in the other. Trevelyan agreed to join
the Committee, though everyone spoke as if he had agreed long
before he was asked, and thus betrayed unconsciously what sort of
weight they thought he carried.[3] Hartington again warned Chamberlain his political virtue was in danger and firmly declined his cooperation.[4] In a note sent to Devonshire House some hours before
they met Chamberlain had informed him of Gladstone's telegram to
Harcourt and pressed Hartington to participate.

> I wish you saw your way to join. Not only would you exercise great in-
> fluence on the discussion, but your presence being known would give
> confidence to our friends and silence all rumours as to difference in the
> Liberal Unionist party. Trevelyan, who is with me, and who will join the
> Conference entirely agrees in the above.[5]

[1] Gladstone to Harcourt, 2nd January 1887. Harcourt Papers. Chamberlain,
op. cit., pp. 240–1.
[2] Chamberlain to Harcourt, 2nd January 1887. Harcourt Papers.
[3] *Ibid.*　[4] *Ibid.*
[5] Chamberlain to Hartington, 2nd January 1887. Devonshire Papers, 340.
2084A.

Both men had to be asked. Trevelyan as the next most important Radical Unionist and agreed nominee of the Committee nucleus; Hartington as Liberal Unionist leader. Chamberlain wanted his leader as little as he wanted his co-ideologue. Fortunately for him, Hartington was equally unwilling to come in. His help was for Salisbury alone, and Goschen was just then joining the government.

Gossip was rife about Chamberlain's intentions. Secrecy about what had actually happened on 30th and 31st December had not prevented numerous versions, all 'authentic', from being hawked enthusiastically round the political world. Churchill reproached him bitterly.

> I hear you are meditating surrender to the G.O.M., if you have not already committed yourself. I think you will make a great mistake, if you do. The old man is your mortal enemy and the Labouchère–Parnell lot are dying to make you eat dirt and then laugh at you. This I know, though don't betray me.[1]

'Labby' had obviously been talking—as usual, too much. It was a tribute to Chamberlain's 'foxing' that both Churchill and Labouchère both thought he was in earnest. For the time being rumours of an impending surrender did not matter, for he, like the Hawarden 'Barkis' had to show himself willing. Goschen's joining the government was quite important to it as an efficient organisation but not to the reunion of the Liberals. Hartington had given the administration certainty of life. Goschen simply made it more effective. The Liberal Unionist label he insisted on retaining meant virtually nothing. No other Whig joined him and, as Hartington remarked: 'somehow he seemed to have no influence with the Liberals'; meaning all Liberals. Strangely enough Northbrook of all people was perhaps more promising material to Chamberlain as a reunion Committee man than any other Whig Liberal Unionist leader. He declined to join Salisbury, telling Hartington he had 'no more confidence in Lord Salisbury than in Mr Gladstone'.[2] But Chamberlain wanted no one, least of all the

---

[1] Churchill to Chamberlain, 2nd January 1887. Chamberlain Papers, JC5/14/28.

[2] Northbrook to Hartington, 3rd January 1887. Devonshire Papers, 340. 2086. Lord Lansdowne's first inclination when pressed to join the government by Goschen, Hartington and Salisbury was to accept. Only his duties in Canada, where he was currently Governor-General and a dissolution was in the offing, destroyed his 'first impulse' to say 'yes'. He regarded the offer as 'in some respects a very tempting one'. Being in the Cabinet, re-entering political life in the United Kingdom, pleasing his friend Goschen, for whom he had a strong liking, and returning to his wider family circle were all factors militating for acceptance. See Lord Lansdowne to his Mother, 6th January 1887. Lord Newton, *Lord Lansdowne: A Biography*, p. 43. But liking Goschen was very different from being under his influence and Canada therefore came out on top. Hartington's assessment of Goschen's real pull with other Liberals was correct. It should, of course,

despised Northbrook. As far as possible this was to be his private game. And Northbrook, though not sold on the Conservatives, had no doubt about sticking to Hartington. He was no more than the most promising of an unpromising crew. There was no obligation upon Chamberlain to try him out and therefore he was more than happy to make no approach.

Not everyone shared the Churchill–Morley assessment of his position. On 3rd January, Brett sent Harcourt best wishes for the conference. News of the 'exequatur' had spread like wildfire. 'I think Joe will manage to convert you all. He has got the best of the argument, but a poor supporter in Trevelyan. However, he will be backed up from the outside against the satanic trinity at the other end of the table.'[1] Allowing for the humour, it is clear Chamberlain's 'scrape' had not struck Brett as at all serious. Perhaps, as the most unionist of non-Unionists, he was guilty of wishful thinking. Still more likely he realised 'Joe's' resourcefulness without selecting the right reason for it. Signs of the private game in the *Birmingham Daily Post* that morning should have aroused his detective mind.[2] The paper carried a section purporting to give an accurate account of 'Joe's' real

be remarked that the influence of Hartington and Salisbury would not appear to have been appreciably stronger! On 3rd January 1887 the Duke of Argyll sent a letter to John Bright saying how he had long admired the stand taken by the latter over Home Rule and sympathised with his reluctance to speak out too much against Gladstone. Bright replied on the 9th January 1887, lamenting that any speaking out against Gladstone would necessitate saying extremely harsh things and deploring the government's weakness. He was anxious about the forthcoming conference. Harcourt and Morley would be speaking 'for their chief', but for whom would Chamberlain and Trevelyan be speaking and acting? 'It is not said,' he continued, 'that they have consulted Lord Hartington, and if the result of the conference is to bring Chamberlain and Trevelyan to support Mr Gladstone as against the government on questions apart from Irish affairs, then we may not have a change of government but another dissolution of Parliament and confusion worse confounded.' Gladstone had caused more disorder in politics than any other man who had done so much. He did not see, he added, what more could be done in Irish land reform. Following in Gladstone's footsteps, he had taken to studying Irish history. Wolfe Tone had struck him as more honest than Parnell. Five days later Argyll wrote back, stressing that personal feelings should no longer stand in the way of attacking Gladstone, however painful the process, because of the seriousness of the situation. Eighth Duke of Argyll, *Autobiography and Memoirs*, Edited by the Dowager Duchess of Argyll, pp. 408–9.

The 5th Marquess of Lansdowne (1845–1927) and the 8th Duke of Argyll (1823–1900) had both left office in Gladstone's second ministry because of disagreement about the provisions of what became the Irish Land Act of 1881, giving many Irish tenants the long-desired 'Three F's'—Fair Rent, Free Sale and Fixity of Tenure. Both were ardent Liberal Unionists. On his return from Canada Lansdowne enjoyed a long political career and succeeded Salisbury as Foreign Secretary in 1900.

[1] Brett to Harcourt, 3rd January 1887. Copy. Esher Papers.
[2] *Birmingham Daily Post*, 3rd January 1887.

standpoint over the prospective conference. The subject's first comment was to Harcourt; written as soon as copies became available.

> There is a stupid paragraph in the *Birmingham Daily Post* this morn-
> ing, professing to be by authority. In case it is brought to your notice, I
> will say at once that it is quite inaccurate. I suppose one lie more or less
> does not matter, but I should be sorry for you to think that I was in any
> way compromising the success of our joint efforts at reunion.[1]

This would seem false if the 'foxing' theory is correct, and two further
comments tend strongly to suggest that there was as much in the
incident as met the eye. To Churchill's broadside 'Joe' had an easy
enough reply.

> I do not know yet whether anything will come of negotiations between
> the Gladstonians and the Radical Unionists. I never felt less like 'a
> surrender' in my life, and Labouchère and his crew may put what inter-
> pretation they like on the matter, but they will not be able to show that
> I have advanced one iota from the position of my telegram to the
> Unionist meeting, extended as it was by my speech in Birmingham. The
> future is still obscure to me, but the game is exceedingly interesting at
> this moment.[2]

'Joe' had, however, been stung. The letter is discreetly phrased, yet
betrays a no-compromise attitude. Not to change an iota from 23rd
December does not mean the future is obscure. The other comment
was to Dilke the next day. 'You have of course seen the inspired
account of my position in the B.D.P.'[3] Now no enemy of Chamberlain's could inspire anything in that newspaper, and a friend would
not have acted at any time without consulting him. The inspiration
must have been his own or made with his approval.[4] What irony there
was in the phrase 'one lie more or less does not matter'! Yet why this
particular lie at this juncture? Surely because Churchill's letter made
him think it was dangerous to allow it to be thought he was really in
a 'scrape'? It did not really matter, for a choice of sides was still his.
Even the very nimblest of tightrope walkers sometimes have nerves
and we know from Lewis Harcourt that Chamberlain was under
strain. What was more natural than a reaction of this kind? Not that
he lost his head. With Harcourt so favourable and the Gladstone
telegram sent he took but a small risk. The affair caused no ripples
in London, the denial was believed fully by Harcourt, and did its
work in Birmingham. The private game was a paying game.

[1] Chamberlain to Harcourt, 3rd January 1887. Harcourt Papers.
[2] Churchill, *op. cit.*, pp. 267–8.
[3] Chamberlain to Dilke, 4th January 1887. Dilke Papers, Add. MS. 43888,
f. 93. For a general reference to Chamberlain's admission that all the articles dealing with his position had been inspired by him, see: Gwynn and Tuckwell, *op. cit.*,
p. 267.
[4] See Gwynn and Tuckwell, *op. cit.*, p. 267.

In fact virtually nothing would have discouraged Harcourt that day. He was too busy exploiting the long coveted 'exequatur'. Chamberlain and Morley were sent copies for presentation to the press; Morley, as Harcourt put it, *pro bono publico*.[1] That is to avoid jealousy. Spurred on by enthusiasm the latter went much further than Gladstone would have approved and sent Chamberlain selected extracts from the private letter. To his mind it would prove most beneficial to establish that the letters from Hawarden were 'favourable beyond hope and expectation'. The gesture had only one object: 'to show how complete the good faith and good will of the parties (and especially the principal) is in the whole transaction.' Naturally, the information was to be regarded as *strictly private and confidential*, to be seen by no one besides Chamberlain, and returned to Harcourt 'by next post'.[2] It was to be treated like the letter of the 27th December as something 'which is *read but of which no copy is given or taken*'.[3] (Not surprisingly, a copy was taken.) Paragraphs 1 to 4 were reproduced in full; 5 and 6 were omitted entirely; paragraph 7 was stripped of comment about who should propose the suggested Irish Local Government Bill and the Queen's Speech; paragraph 8 cut down to leave no mention of Lefevre; and the conclusion left intact, apart from the P.S. In a covering letter local government was pushed as the subject with the best claim to the earliest place on the agenda.[4] An honest attempt to stick to Gladstone's inclination. Composition too, on its controversial side, was relegated to the letter. Harcourt operated very smoothly despite his obvious excitement.

> There is only one point on which I must appeal to you to help me [he wrote]. I find that there will be much jealousy and heartburning in our camp if H. Fowler is made one of the Plenipots. There is some bitterness and jealousy felt about him. I don't know why, but so it is. The other Cabinet Ministers down to Lefevre would feel he was put over their heads, and neither Mr G. nor J. Morley affect the nomination, and as far as the management of our people is concerned, it would weaken and not strengthen our hands. Please believe I have good reason for what I say and concede this.[5]

First Morley, then Trevelyan, and now a demand for Fowler not to come. Composition had so far proved unpromising for 'Joe'. It remained to be seen whether he tackled the Fowler point by the withdrawal under protest tactic. There was not much time to think it over. Harcourt asked for a telegram so as to be able to publish all the Committee names 'without delay'.[6]

To Gladstone, Harcourt was over grateful, so relieved was he that the old man had at last played ball.

---

[1] Harcourt to Chamberlain, 3rd January 1887. Chamberlain Papers, JC5/38/56.
[2] *Ibid.*   [3] *Ibid.*   [4] *Ibid.*   [5] *Ibid.*   [6] *Ibid.*

It is a great gratification to me, as I am sure it will be to Morley, to have from you so full a sanction for what we have endeavoured to do. I have no doubt Chamberlain will be more than satisfied with the manner in which you have encountered his overtures, and I feel confident that there will be a sincere feeling of pleasure and relief in the whole party (with the exception of a few mischief makers like Labouchère) on knowing that the watchword of 'Peace' is given out upon your authority.[1]

The old retainer tone scarcely fitted a man of Harcourt's character or background, but that was the effect the G.O.M. seemed to have on many men. Happily, it wore off in the next section of the letter, where he described how he had asked Chamberlain to withdraw the proposal to have Fowler and expressed pleasure that Goschen had joined Salisbury, but returned in part at the end. 'It stands now that our conference is to meet for the first time on the 13th inst. Morley and I shall hope to have your full instructions on the various points, so as to be in possession of your mind and in a position to enforce your wishes on the various heads before that date.' Whether this tone came from contrition after contemplation of a rebellious outburst, or simple euphoria, it hardly became the deputy leader of a great political party.

To Morley, he simply waxed enthusiastic, putting particular stress upon the promising nature of the private letter.[2] After a word about the public letter for the press and the Fowler affair, he plunged into the matter of the draft agenda. 'You will see from Mr G.'s *private* letter to me . . . that he is in a most complying humour; indeed, his seduction is much easier this year; his virtue is not so ferocious, for at that age in both sexes frailty is more common.' Great play was made with paragraph 6. 'What would J.C. give to read this. . . . Ponder on it yourself and consider all it means, and don't "pile up agony", either in the *Daily News* or elsewhere. I thought you were a little unnecessarily *current* on this subject in this morning's *Daily News*.' Commenting on the enclosure of Chamberlain's letter received that morning, he claims to be 'all for humouring him as to order discussion which is not material'. Can it be, however, that Morley is the one more in need of humouring, and on subjects crucially material? On the personal level Harcourt had let it out to Arnold Morley about the *Daily News*.[3] On the political he is at pains to attach Morley more closely to what is happening by making the most of Gladstone's letters, giving him as well as Chamberlain the text for the press, and attempting to lure him down to the New Forest

[1] Harcourt to Gladstone, 3rd January 1887. Gladstone Papers, Add. MS. 44201, f. 14.

[2] Harcourt to Morley, 3rd January 1887. Copy. Harcourt Papers.

[3] See note p. 159, 3.

immediately following the conference sessions. With Chamberlain there too, reunion could be pursued fast and furiously in a more intimate atmosphere. Then there is the comment to Chamberlain about Morley and the press statement. Admittedly Harcourt criticised one to the other, but the contexts point to different motives. To Chamberlain he was at once poking fun at Morley's obvious foibles and making clear publication should come from both sides. Had he thought Chamberlain would have been jealous of Morley, he, Harcourt, could have issued the news from the Gladstonian team. To Morley he was trying to pass off as valueless something rather crucial to the shape of the talks. His confidence is the greater because Gladstone had pointed the way on the question. Yet this was no concession to Chamberlain, harmless or otherwise. Rather was it quite an imposition, belittling the place of land problems on which Chamberlain set such store as possible subjects for agreement.

As the Gladstonians came to realise the talks were near, suspicions of Chamberlain mounted to new heights. Morley was not to be kept calm by a little humouring. His assessment of Labouchère's power remained the same, but party opinion made him reconsider the treatment suitable for that gentleman. 'I don't think it will do at all to put down our foot on Labouchère. Personally he carries no weight, but what he says on this business is what all our staunchest friends are thinking.' Pessimism has rapidly displaced the eager attitude of a few days before. 'I am as anxious as you are to make things easy for Chamberlain. But the chances are 10 to 1 against a *modus vivendi* and then we shall want all our friends: don't let us damp their ardour in the meanwhile.'[1] The awe in which he held 'Joe' was quite remarkable. How could a man supposed to be, according to none other than Morley, in a dreadful 'scrape' constitute such a grave menace to the whole Gladstonian party? The truth was the old fear prompted the thought that he might yet escape and bite back in a state of renewed war. Talks held to cover his surrender could turn out an instrument for inflicting considerable damage on the Home Rule cause. Hence Harcourt's idea of having Dilke write about them in the *Daily News* must not be entertained. 'He will turn his sails too much in the Birmingham direction', so 'I think I will keep my own hand on the "D.N." helm for a few days, if the giant who edits it will let me'.[2] Zealous as ever for his leader's authority and policy, he turned down flat the Harcourt jumping the gun idea, despite having had no word from Hawarden. 'The authoritative paragraph will be in plenty of time when Mr G. tells you what he means.'[3] No news was good news for Morley. As much grass could grow as chose to come up.

[1] Gardiner, *op. cit.*, p. 24.　　[2] *Ibid.*
[3] Morley to Harcourt, 3rd January 1887. Harcourt Papers.

Spencer's first reactions were also wearing off.[1] Granville had much confidence in Morley and that was about all.[2] He had always considered reunion about as obtainable as the Holy Grail. Both had become 'suspicious as to the proposed Board. Herschell is so damned conciliatory; and Fowler (according to Spencer) has some very flabby opinions.' Morley wrote off to Spencer expressing anxiety about the apparent readiness of Herschell, and Harcourt himself, to sacrifice basic principles. And ventured to tell the latter in so many words how little he was to be trusted. 'If I am left in a minority of one on important points (which is a conceivable issue in spite of your well-known love for "Justice for Ireland") it would be a moral triumph for J. Chamberlain.'[3] The next day Spencer put what was now becoming obvious to Granville.[4] If the conference failed, 'Joe' would be strengthened. If he really wanted to rejoin Gladstone a means could be found. If he did not want to surrender nothing much would result and the project would fail. Quite understandably, Spencer just could not believe that in the end there would be a capitulation, however well disguised. By having capitulated, 'Joe' would be in a strong position, provided his return brought him back the leading place on the Gladstonian front bench his abilities merited. Should this become impossible from what happened before he jumped, then the choice he enjoyed on 31st December would no longer be his. Reversion to Unionism or withdrawal from politics would alone remain open to him. But he would have achieved something and this was the point Spencer had in mind. For himself the impression of bad treatment at the hands of the Gladstonians could be wrung out of a failure. That impression had proved invaluable in 1886 and was likely to again. Nowhere more so than in his home base. For his cause of Radical Unionism the chance to say the Gladstonians were unreasonable would be invaluable. Spencer's sense of guilt would make the charge

[1] Morley to Spencer, 3rd January 1887. Spencer Papers.

[2] Granville to Spencer, 3rd January 1887. Spencer Papers.

[3] Morley to Harcourt, 3rd January 1887. Harcourt Papers.

[4] Spencer to Granville, 4th January 1887. Granville Papers, P.R.O. 30, 29, 22A. Sir Edward Hamilton recorded that day how Gladstone considered Goschen's accession to the government would do the Conservative party good, and how the Liberal leader thought 'good may come indirectly more than directly out of Chamberlain's approximations', but did not see his way to agreeing that progress could be made 'through the medium of a Land Purchase Bill', though others might. Sir Edward Hamilton's Diary, 4th January 1887, Add. MS. 48645, p. 76. Goschen's daughter shared Hamilton's views as to the effect of her father's accession to office on the Conservative party. In a letter to Alfred Milner of 5th January 1887 she enthused about it: 'Now I feel we Unionists have a *real* part in the governing of the country and I cannot help hoping that this may be the dawn of a Constitutional party, not a modern Tory or Moderate Liberal, but a combination of what is best in both.' Maude Goschen to Alfred Milner, 5th January 1887. Milner Papers.

seem plausible and therefore damaging to the Home Rule cause.

Chamberlain did not then realise his choice might be slipping away. His tone to Dilke on the 4th January was distinctly jaunty. 'If Morley did send the paragraph to the *Times* he only anticipated me, for I also sent a message to the Press. You will see that the Conference is coming off. Mr G.'s public letter is satisfactory and his private assurances still more completely so.'[1] Undismayed by developments over Fowler, he sent off a telegram withdrawing his suggestion. With a promising line being taken at Hawarden he felt well able to do without this particular insurance policy. Fowler could be tapped for useful information just the same. Chamberlain told Harcourt: 'we can call him in as a witness if necessary' and proceeded to take a step towards doing so. Fowler was asked:

> Did you sketch out some plan of Irish Land Purchase for the late Cabinet, based on Irish Security resources? If so, or if you have any ideas on this subject, will you let me see them—in confidence, of course? I remember talking to you on the matter in your room at the House of Commons.[2]

So Morley had been wrong in thinking the financial expert business was a pure blind. Killing two birds with one stone was a favourite sport at Highbury. Harcourt's indiscretion paid off well. 'The extracts from Mr Gladstone's private letter are *most encouraging and most satisfactory*,' wrote Chamberlain. 'I believe that I could accept every word as correctly indicating my position as well as his . . . the outlook is brighter for Liberalism than I could possibly have hoped some weeks ago.' Chamberlain's approval of the letter led him to suggest the extracts be used as a guide by the Committee. They formed a material aid to agreement. Grateful though he was to Harcourt, he was not off his guard. In a second letter that day he went straight to the point:

> in rereading Mr Gladstone's private letter before returning it to you, I am struck by the absence of all reference to the Land Question. I sincerely hope that this was not intentional. The Land Question is of urgent importance—in Ulster as much as anywhere—and no solution of the Irish problem can be other than equivocal which neglects this radical cause of discontent and agitation. I feel bound to make this qualification in my assent to what otherwise seems to me a most admirable statement of the position.[3]

The same tone of guarded optimism characterised his report on

---

[1] Chamberlain to Dilke, 4th January 1887. Dilke Papers, Add. MS. 43888, f. 93.

[2] Chamberlain to Fowler, 4th January 1887. Copy. Chamberlain Papers, JC5/31/10. Hamilton, *op. cit.*, p. 229.

[3] Chamberlain to Harcourt, 4th January 1887, No. 1. Garvin, *op. cit.*, p. 282.

events to Hartington.[1] Having defined what was meant by *modus vivendi*, he once more nailed his colours to the Unionist mast. 'Nothing will induce us to consent to a Parliament in Dublin with an executive dependent upon it. On the other hand Mr G. can hardly be expected to proclaim that he has entirely abandoned what he has declared to be a cardinal principle.' So the land and local government issues will be examined first, and then, and then only, will any '*tetium quid*—any alternative to an Irish Parliament' be sought for. If it were to be found, no 'formal repudiation' of 'previously expressed opinions' would be required from either side. Should Hartington finally decide irrevocably against attending the conference, Chamberlain was anxious to secure from him a statement to the effect that full reports of the negotiations leading up to it had been made to him, that though he 'felt it inexpedient to join at this stage and' was not sanguine as to the result, his genuine wish was for reunion under conditions undamaging to 'the principles' he had 'advocated in Irish Government'.[2] The sunny outlook did not blind him from the need for maintaining both the fact and appearance of Liberal Unionist unity pending the 'failure' of the talks. Afterwards it would be apparent enough.

Hartington was actually not so well informed as his deputy implied. 'I am looking out for the publication of the correspondence,' he stated. 'I suppose it has been sent to you for revision.'[3] That was on 4th January. On the 5th he returned to the point, asking:

> Could you let me see the correspondence between yourself and Harcourt, or others, which bears on the negotiations? I had expected that the published correspondence would have consisted of a letter from Harcourt to Mr G. containing some statement of the basis of the proposed conference, to which Mr G. was to have given some general approval. But all that has been published is a very guarded assent on his part to the desirability of discussion, and nothing like a basis has been laid down. I know that more has passed between yourself and Harcourt than may appear in the correspondence; but ought you not to have something really definite in writing? Altogether without references to the possibility of my giving such a general approval to the conference as you desire, are you not running some risk, if you enter this discussion without a very definite understanding as to the basis on which it is to proceed?[4]

As for participation he had no desire for reunion at all before knowing whether Gladstone was prepared to abandon or postpone Home

[1] Chamberlain to Harcourt, 4th January 1887, No. 2. Harcourt Papers.

[2] Chamberlain to Hartington, 4th January 1887. Chamberlain, *op. cit.*, pp. 243–4.

[3] Hartington to Chamberlain, 4th January 1887. Chamberlain Papers, JC5/22/21.

[4] Hartington to Chamberlain, 5th January 1887. Chamberlain Papers, JC5/22/22.

Rule. Unless the subject was excluded from discussion he would not consider sitting at the 'Round Table'. Not that he envisaged an active hostility to the conference, and he was careful to place on record on the 4th that: 'The *Times* announcements and comments this morning are not in any way inspired by me. I saw Buckle on Sunday, but purposely abstained from any discussion with him on the negotiations with Mr G.'[1] Buckle had thought Hartington had tried to dissuade 'Joe' from negotiating, but Brett soon put him right on this. Hartington had only warned him against 'the wiles of the G.O.M.'. Hartington had no need to worry: 'Joe is too clever to be caught and the climb down is very considerable.'[2] Perhaps in his then mood it was difficult for Hartington to take this cheerful view, for he was said to be anxious and low because of his brother's illness. Writing to Chamberlain on the 5th, Brett showed full awareness of the 'suppressed bitterness' involved in the whole reunion operation.

'After Mr G.'s lukewarm and wily production, plus his letters to the Mayor of Limerick, etc.,[3] would it be dignified or prudent for Hartington to say nothing at all? My view is this. By going into the Conference Morley and Harcourt abandon their position that salvation is alone to be found in their old Bills. Otherwise you abandon yours, which is inadmissible from your recent allusions, while they have said nothing of late to indicate their views. After Hartington's action in inducing Goschen to join the Government, I don't see how he can openly express a wish for reunion until it is more clear than it is what are the bases of the Conference. Does Harcourt's letter to the G.O.M. (not published, and why not?) explain them? In any case there is no hurry. Hartington is extremely suspicious of Gladstone and the real prospects for the conference. You will come out of it unscathed. What about the unfortunate and disunited Liberal party? How will it fare?[3]

All the advice, encouragement and warning left Chamberlain cold. His optimism remained controlled by a highly developed sense of self preservation.

I think the 'Reunion' stands pretty well. All depends on the 'inner mind' of Mr G. and his followers. If they are sick of their position and want an excuse to get out of it, we shall do good business. If they think they hold winning cards, nothing will come of our conference.[4]

[1] Hartington to Chamberlain, 4th January 1887. Chamberlain Papers, JC5/22/21.
[2] Brett to Buckle (Editor of *The Times*), 4th January 1887. Esher Papers. In Esher, *op. cit.*, p. 189, the first words are missing and what remains is passed off as a memorandum. G. E. Buckle (1854–1905) edited *The Times* from 1884 until 1912. He also edited some of Queen Victoria's letters and was part author of the standard biography of Disraeli.
[3] Brett to Chamberlain, 5th January 1887. Copy. Esher Papers.
[4] Chamberlain to Collings, 5th January 1887. Copy. Chamberlain Papers. JC5/18/19.

So he summarised the situation to Jesse Collings—a man more likely than most to be treated with frankness. Amusingly enough he was saying of the Gladstonians what they were saying of him. Both agreed the conference was a cover for a surrender of one sort or another. There was no need for Chamberlain to worry. If his choice evaporated, what matter? The Unionist camp would always be pleased to have him. When Fowler replied by return on the finance point, that choice appeared in quite robust health. As a token of goodwill the *Birmingham Daily Post* of the 4th contained warm praise of the *Daily News* from the pen of the great white chief.[1]

For Harcourt the 4th January posed the problem of how to keep his principal partner firmly behind the matter in hand. Gladstone had been right to regard Morley as basically 'solid on his pins' from a Home Rule point of view.[2] 'Oh thou of little faith! how troublesome you are with your suspicions' was a fitting opening for a letter to him. 'You even attribute the same qualities to others without their deserving it', he went on. 'I enclose a note from Spencer, which I think bears little trace of the fears you suggest'.[3] Nor did it, but time passes, and, as we have seen, Spencer had shifted ground since writing that note. The great man of faith was fighting what would increasingly become a losing battle. He was, however, on stronger ground in dismissing Morley's nightmare of being ultimately isolated at the 'Round Table'. 'I smile at your fears as to being *outvoted*. There is no question of voting at all. If we can't get through without that we shall not get through at all.' An observation even Morley could not question. In case he next seized on the *Birmingham Daily Post* paragraph, Harcourt adroitly forwarded Chamberlain's letter on the subject, and compared the incident to outbursts on their own side.

> I enclose also a letter from J.C., which is meant to appease our alarms as to his Birmingham conversations. We must not take too much notice of these things on either side. There are quite sure to be plenty of good natured friends ready to demonstrate that we have all of us sacrificed honour and everything else for the sake of office.

The fact that Chamberlain might be deceiving him had apparently never crossed his mind, and as far as he was concerned local stuff was for local consumption. As for his own people: 'The ordinary English mind is such a cad of which Stead is a principal type. The only way to deal with them is to pass them by with supreme contempt.'[4] An accomplishment at which, need it be said, its advocate was a past master. Being also a man of much faith he had 'from the beginning

---

[1] *Birmingham Daily Post*, 4th January 1887. [2] Gladstone to Granville, 30th December 1886. Granville Papers, P.R.O. 30, 29, 29A. [3] Harcourt to Morley, 4th January 1887. Copy. Harcourt Papers. [4] W. T. Stead (1847–1912), then editor of the *Pall Mall Gazette*.

a good opinion of the business and mean to persist in that frame of mind until I see some reason to the contrary'.[1] There was no doubt his sight would on occasion be wilfully short. Morley was quite the opposite. He was ever the man for a powerful lens. This held good over people in whom he should have had implicit faith. Even the G.O.M. was not exempt. Commenting on the private letter to Harcourt, he complained: 'Oddly enough, he has not sent me a word on the subject, perhaps his letter has gone wrong.'[2] At times he could be generous and followed this up with congratulations to Harcourt, for if Chamberlain did surrender it would be due principally to him.[3] The interpretation given to paragraph 6 of the Gladstone letter would do a good deal to determine whether this much prayed for event came to pass. On Morley's it seemed distinctly remote.

> I do not read the sentence no. 6 as you do. It is surely obvious that under present circumstances nothing can be done in the way of serious effort. Writing to me this morning in reply to my report on Parnell, as to my hint that Parnell was uneasy as to negotiations, Mr G. says: 'There is no occasion. The national question for Ireland is much too big and heavy for those who have taken it in hand to play pitch and toss with. Atlas might as well conjure with his globe.' So be of good cheer *mon ami;* Home Rule is still the first order of the day.[4]

Powerful stuff—with a sardonic last shot. Morley was in a fighting mood. In a note to Gladstone written at this time he actually made so bold as to describe Chamberlain's original suggestion of Harcourt, Herschell and Fowler for the Gladstonian representatives as a farce![5] Fighting mood or no, Harcourt continued on his determined path. 'I take your word as to the "first order of the day". I have letters from J.C. today, highly satisfied with everything and everybody. I thought the *Daily News* today first rate. It will do great good in the party. I do not see that Labby has yet given tongue.'[6] What could one do with such a man? Morley's very next letter to him, also written on the 5th, appeared at first sight less dyspeptic.[7] He appeared to accept Chamberlain's word over the Birmingham press; but the end revealed the horrible truth. 'By the way, I am sorry I cannot come to you on the 15th, for I must finish my second article in reply to Dicey—and have not an hour to spare. So you must excuse me.' No one was deceived, he simply wished to avoid private contact with Chamberlain after the 'Round Table' sessions of the 13th and 14th January.

---

[1] *Ibid.*
[2] Morley to Harcourt, 4th January 1887. Harcourt Papers.
[3] *Ibid.*   [4] *Ibid.*
[5] Morley to Gladstone, 4th January 1887. Gladstone Papers, Add. MS. 44255, f. 177.
[6] Harcourt to Morley, 5th January 1887. Copy. Harcourt Papers.
[7] Morley to Harcourt, 5th January 1887. Harcourt Papers.

Lewis Harcourt commented: 'This is an excuse.'[1] Perhaps this was scarcely to be wondered at given yet another gyration of the *Birmingham Daily Post*. On the 5th it was virtually back again to the tone of the 3rd, or rather 'Joe' was.[2] In an interview with a reporter, presumably on the 4th, he denied having made 'fresh proposals towards the reunion of the Liberal Party' and claimed the Gladstonians 'were tired of the existing situation and were becoming convinced that Home Rule was impossible'. Actually the opinions had been given before he received news of Gladstone's two letters, but that was hardly the point. He had allowed them to appear in print at a most inopportune time assuming his approach to the conference was sincere. It looked very much as if, finding himself unable to please all the people all the time, he was embracing the Bonapartist principle of pleasing half the people half the time, with regular shifts of favour. If he was playing difficult because of the land question the whole exercise was superfluous. A reassurance was penned by Harcourt that same day, in no way influenced by the interview.

> On the question of land [it ran] . . . I do not wish you to suppose that Mr G. by any means desires to exclude that important branch of the question. He writes to me his views briefly on the question and I have asked for further elucidation before circulating them to anyone else.[3]

A lie, but Harcourt could hardly give any other explanation. If Chamberlain was trying to throw his weight about following the Fowler fiasco, Harcourt did his best to appease by offering thanks for what transpired. If the trouble stemmed from a feeling of being rudely unheeded, Harcourt again threw oil upon the waters by undertaking to try and obtain an 'exposition of Mr G.'s views as I sent them to you, put in a shape in which I can place them before the Conference'.[4] This last was a most unlikely cause, as Harcourt had only just received the request on this subject. If Chamberlain was developing Morley-like suspicions, they should have laid at rest by Harcourt's conclusion. He lied like a hostess determined to get everyone to her

[1] Lewis Harcourt's *Journal*, 6th January 1887. Harcourt Papers. Morley's articles came out in the *Nineteenth Century* for January and February 1887 (Vol. 21) under the title: 'The Government of Ireland's Reply'. At the end of 1886 A. V. Dicey had published his *England's Case Against Home Rule*. It was this rather than Edward Dicey's two articles in the *Nineteenth Century* (Vol. 20) on 'The Unionist Vote' and 'The Unionist Campaign' that he had to answer. Vol. 21 was an interesting issue. It contained an article—a sequel to his earlier contribution, for which see Chapter I, p. 36, note 1—by Matthew Arnold entitled 'The Zenith of Conservatism' and Gladstone's 'Notes and Queries on the Irish Demand'.

[2] *Birmingham Daily Post*, 5th January 1887.

[3] Harcourt to Chamberlain, 5th January 1887. Chamberlain Papers, JC5/38/57.

[4] *Ibid.*

party. 'Morley is in a high state of contentment and all seems for the present to go well.'[1]

Away from the seats of power others were giving vent to deep feeling about what was going on. Wolverton was not one to mince his words. He told Gladstone quite frankly how much he distrusted Harcourt.[2] Of Herschell he had an even worse opinion, judging him neither a true Home Ruler, nor anything like a match for Chamberlain.[3] On the Unionist side Courtney regarded the whole project as 'dubious'. It

> ought to fail because I do not believe G. will budge an inch from his position and reconciliation would therefore mean complete surrender on 'Joe's' part, which would be so unlike him as to be almost incredible. But he may knock under, rather than be out in the cold indefinitely. I don't like this coquetting, as I object to Hartington's joining the Conservatives because I deprecate above all things our public men settling into two and only two parties; so that Liberalism shall mean Home Rule and Anti-Home Rule will mean Conservatism. If that came to pass, Home Rule would soon be passed. I am not sanguine in any case about being able to prevent it permanently. G. has made it terribly hard and the strain upon public virtue is excessive. Not every man will go on fighting a battle he knows to be lost and accepting defeat with a consciousness it means annihilation.[4]

Trevelyan took quite another line. One expected him to. He had readily consented to go on the list of representatives and had wished himself into believing Liberal reunion was probably at hand. To Hartington, as leader and non-participant his language was uncharacteristically restrained.[5] To Chamberlain he was openly enthusiastic.[6] Labouchère and all who thought like him were dismissed as 'surface noise'. 'The general sentiment' of what was 'best in the party was' allegedly 'pretty well expressed by the Midland Railway Guard, who, on parting with' the Trevelyan family at York had 'put his head into the carriage and whispered earnestly that he hoped something would be done to reunite the party'. He was glad Chamberlain was reassured about Gladstone's 'state of mind' and appeared not to entertain any suspicions on the matter himself. 'I am only sorry,' he grumbled, 'about Fowler, whose presence on the Committee is of very real importance, both as one who long ago was very advanced

---

[1] *Ibid.*

[2] Wolverton to Gladstone, 5th January 1887. Gladstone Papers, Add. MS. 44349, f. 223.

[3] *Ibid.*

[4] Courtney to John Scott, 5th January 1887. Gooch, *op. cit.*, pp. 273–4.

[5] Trevelyan to Hartington, 5th January 1887. Devonshire Papers, 340. 2091.

[6] Trevelyan to Chamberlain, 5th January 1887. Chamberlain Papers, JC5/70/22.

about Irish matters, and who now is anxious for reconciliation: and who, whatever opinions he may hold, holds them genuinely and strongly.'[1] Referring to his letter to Hartington, he simply outlines the contents. Quite clearly, writing had merely been an act of politeness. For him, parting with the Whig Liberal Unionists would not be

[1] *Ibid.* On 5th January 1887 H. Cobb, Gladstonian Liberal M.P. for Rugby, sent Chamberlain the following letter. 'I was going to have written to Collings today to tell him how delighted I was to read your speech of 23rd December, and I am still more so to find from this morning's papers that your conciliatory proposal is to have some practical effect. I cannot help remembering that this is not the first time that you have tried to bring about a reunion. In your speech of 9th April you gave up National Councils as not going far enough and said that the key of the position lay in the proposal to exclude Irish members from the House and in another speech (I think in July 1885) you gave the idea that the Irish question was a National and not merely a municipal one. Surely there is very little difference between you and Morley? I have read, I believe, every word you have said about Ireland and am sure that if good temper is shown and personal grievances are forgotten, the conference which you have originated ought to bring about a complete reunion. Long before Home Rule was brought before any Cabinet I had written down my views about it. I am sure that you must be in favour of the principle. There were a great many of the details of the Bill with which I did not agree, but surely you ought to be able to agree upon something? My short parliamentary experience has indeed been unpleasant and sad. I had, when I stood, the expectation of trying, in a humble way, to help the party which I thought you would virtually lead. That I think now may still be so. How can you or I support the present Government? I have always been against Goschen and last night I was reading with pleasure your speeches about him. I think that those who are really Radicals have a kind of right to beg of you to do your best, and if necessary to give way somewhat, to unite our party. I believe that you have had many unpleasantnesses to put up with, but so have others. Mr Gladstone is old and naturally obstinate and I daresay very trying at times. All I ask you is to do your best. I need hardly add that I have protested against the tone of the large type letters in the *Daily News*.' H. Cobb to Chamberlain, 5th January 1887. Chamberlain Papers, JC8/9/2/4.

Even allowing for the fact that the letter is from a West Midlands M.P., who might have wanted to stand well with Chamberlain whatever the result of the parleys, it is still of considerable significance. Cobb was a lawyer, but a genuine Radical of the 'Unauthorised Programme' type, whose skill at pleading would very probably not be used entirely for purely politic purposes in approaching Chamberlain. Any instinct of self-preservation was therefore likely to be mixed with a substantial dose of sincerity. Unlike men of the Labouchère school, Cobb looked back with anguish rather than anger. For him 'Joe' was not a 'Judas'. Hence future cooperation on the basis of acceptance of the Home Rule principle struck him as both desirable and possible. The danger for Chamberlain lay in the ultimate disappointment of Cobb and his like if any 'foxing' became exposed to public view. Doubtless he bore this well in mind.

Labouchère summed up his own attitude extremely well in a letter to Dilke. 'This conference weakens us. The ingenious Chamberlain only wants to get his foot in in order to turn over our weak people. Outside Birmingham he is done, and by the end of the Session, if he acts with the Conservatives, will be smashed. I am sorry, for I like him personally, but in politics business is business.' Labouchère to Dilke, 12th January 1887. Dilke Papers, Add. MS. 43941, f. 1.

a subject for heartbreak. Combined with sincere Unionism was the emotional difficulty mentioned by Courtney. It was eventually to lead him far away from Chamberlain as well, but for the moment ensured the two remained together.

Had Chamberlain persisted in his original intention and made a speech at Birmingham on the 5th, things could either have deteriorated badly or improved mildly. As it was, a slow yet perceptible deterioration, marked by no dramatic events, now set in and continued until the conference met. The more it developed, the more attenuated Chamberlain's choice became. Though it did not really matter to him, his power was that much reduced. He might gaily continue to ply Fowler with friendly comments and financial details.[1] He could safely ask Harcourt to fix the final arrangements for 13th January. Harcourt could ask him to forward data to Trevelyan, give information on when and where for the conference, and say: 'I suppose you will submit to us your Land Scheme as a "pièce de résistance".'[2] He could also press Gladstone to allow extracts of the private letter to be used at the conference by way of a general guide as Chamberlain wished.[3] Nevertheless, the most telling letter of 6th January was Morley's to Harcourt.[4] It more than destroyed any hopes of an easier passage that indefatigable reconciler had based on his impression from the *Pall Mall Gazette* of 'Labby' having swallowed 'the Peace more tranquilly than might have been expected'.

> I am sorry to hear [sneered Morley] that J. Chamberlain is so well satisfied. If you and I do not at the close of the conference leave him thoroughly worsted, we shall produce a worse split in the party than any yet. Be sure of that. Arnold Morley told me yesterday that they had many remonstrants at Parliament Street.[5]

He enclosed a letter from Spence Watson, the chairman of his caucus in Newcastle, extremely hostile to any departure from the pure milk of Gladstonian Home Rule. Not really somebody capable of being treated as 'beneath contempt', since he was 'much the most influential politician in Northumberland and Durham'. Evidently Morley felt the force of the anti-compromise party more and more. 'If we cannot drive or draw J. Chamberlain up to the Leeds resolution before we break up, your handiwork will be a failure',[6] he warned. Of course, there was nothing startling in this. Harcourt himself took

[1] Chamberlain to Fowler, 6th January 1887. Copy. Chamberlain Papers, JC5/31/11. Hamilton, *op. cit.*, pp. 229–30. See also Same to Same, 10th January 1887. Copy. Chamberlain Papers, JC5/31/12. Hamilton, *op. cit.*, p. 230.
[2] Harcourt to Chamberlain, 6th January 1887. Chamberlain Papers, JC5/38/57A. Garvin, *op. cit.*, p. 283.
[3] Harcourt to Gladstone, 6th January 1887. Copy. Harcourt Papers.
[4] Morley to Harcourt, 6th January 1887. Harcourt Papers.
[5] *Ibid.*   [6] *Ibid.*

the same view. What frightened Morley was the possibility of his abandoning it in face of Chamberlainite resistance. Arnold Morley repeated the opinion his namesake held on the original conference personnel proposal to Gladstone at this time. The indirect message being that a lot was expected of the reformed team. Harcourt may have been right in thinking that on the whole the government crisis had ended very well. He was not justified in taking a sanguine line about the Liberal dilemma. 'A real animus of agreement' was not nearly enough widespread. Chamberlain's 'high good humour' evaporated as fast as it came once the Spence Watson party went into open battle array.

Despite the certainty that Unionism would always provide him with a safe home, Chamberlain had to keep irritation at his latest antics within bounds. Otherwise he might be reduced to a position of depending almost entirely on extra-parliamentary pressure centred on his fief in Birmingham. The editor of *The Times* was proving particularly awkward and Brett felt bound to 'put him right'. He reported:

> Buckle is very obstinate, and not so discriminating as he should be. I have written to remonstrate with him again privately. I have pointed out that it is not necessary for him to assume that you are ready to concede everything or anything more than Harcourt or Herschell; that there is some advantage to the cause he advocates in detaching as many Liberals as possible from the extreme party, and that, if the conference fails as it probably will, it must to a considerable extent produce that effect. For many men will think that you were anxious to bring about a reasonable compromise and that the Gladstonians showed themselves unduly stiff.

The very thing Chamberlain planned and hoped for, and Gladstone and Spencer held in such dread.

> On the other hand [Brett continued] it is quite possible that you may capture Harcourt and Herschell, and Morley quite appreciates the danger of his position. I have mentioned that Schnadhorst is violently opposed to the conference on the ground that it will take the heart out of the Gladstone party.[1]

Over Hartington, Buckle was allegedly wrong. He did not disapprove of the conference as *The Times* had maintained, though his recent actions ruled out open sanction of it. Such a move would jeopardise the existence of the government he had just shored up.

> At the same time [Buckle had been told], reconstructed governments . . . are always in a precarious position, and though he may not think so, many of those whose instincts about the House of Commons may be

[1] Brett to Chamberlain, 6th January 1887. Copy. Esher Papers.

trusted think that Goschen is unlikely to succeed in holding his own against the powerful combination sure to form in the course of the session.[1]

Assuming this to be correct, surely it was desirable 'as quickly as possible to create the "cadre" of an alternative administration which is not separatist'? 'Your action,' Brett claimed, 'aims at this, and the more violent partners of Mr G.—more Gladstonian than himself—fear that you may be successful.'[2] Whether Buckle accepted this or not, the fact remained that Gordon's maxim applied and Brett had told him so. This was 'that if you want to keep a man in the straight path, you should not assume that he is likely to wander from it'. Chamberlain was no exception to it.

I think it a great pity [his friend grumbled] that he should apparently underrate your honesty and that he should not altogether appreciate your ability. Heaven knows whether this lecture will have any effect. I think he is in the hands of the leader writers. And they are men very ignorant of all the essentials for forming accurate political judgments.[3]

Chamberlain must have been surprised by Brett's concluding remark: 'Randolph is a great accession of polemical strength to the radical unionist party.' He would have been even more surprised, maybe dismayed, had he seen a letter written that day to Gladstone by Canon MacColl.[4] That is, if his knowledge of Hartington had not caused him to dismiss it as an example of wishful thinking on the Canon's part. The subject matter was a report of a conversation at dinner. MacColl had met Colonel Hozier, Secretary of the Liberal Unionists, at table (metaphorically at least a round one). There arose 'a long talk on the Irish Question' and Hozier asserted 'that Lord Hartington really longed for the reunion of the Liberal party and was still most loyal' to Gladstone. As if that were not enough, he went on to suggest MacColl 'should go and have a talk on the Irish Question with Lord Hartington'. The former objected that he had 'nothing to say', but his companion persisted, saying that if he (MacColl) expressed a wish to see Hartington, mentioning Hozier and a disposition to discuss the Irish question 'in a friendly way', 'some good might come of it'. Wanting to do what was best for Liberalism, the worthy Canon consulted his leader. 'Do you advise me to see Lord Hartington, of course, without committing you?', he asked. 'I told Colonel Hozier that a Statutory Parliament in Dublin under whatever limitations must be the starting point of any discussion.' The G.O.M.'s reply is not preserved, but nothing more was heard of the matter. Perhaps Hozier was indulging in an elaborate legpull. As a highly

[1] *Ibid.*   [2] *Ibid.*   [3] *Ibid.*
[4] MacColl to Gladstone, Malcolm MacColl. Russell, *op. cit.*, pp. 130–1.

placed Whig Liberal Unionist, he must certainly have known Hartington's true attitudes to both reunion and Gladstone personally. Had he not been in such august company, one might have supposed him to have dined a trifle too well.

More to the point was the reply Chamberlain sent to Hartington.[1] Its tone was cold and hectoring. No better illustration could be found of the virtual independence of the Radical Unionists. Headed 'Confidential', it was nothing less than a sustained snub. The opening passages scarcely fell short of an insult.

I consider that the only basis of the Conference is to be found in my speech of 23 December and Mr Gladstone's letter to Harcourt. I have already informed you of the nature of my conversation with the latter. There is nothing in subsequent correspondence of any importance except a private letter of Mr G.'s which has been shown to me, but which I am strictly forbidden to communicate to anyone. It is therefore only interesting to me as indicating Mr Gladstone's personal disposition—in which relation it is satisfactory.

Chamberlain doubtless resented the request to see his correspondence made in Hartington's last letter, for it implied at worst that he had been lacking in candour, and in any case that he had failed to fulfil obligations due to the party leader. His resentment was all the hotter for being founded on guilt. The correspondence with Harcourt was not really suitable for Whig eyes. Apart from politics, there were personal remarks of a private nature. For example, the one about Morley's jealousy. Hartington simply had to be fobbed off. Then, too, there was the 'foxing', and the worse informed the Unionists were about his activities the better.

'I do not think it would be possible or desirable to have any more definite basis for a discussion.' The letter froze on, 'Joe's' sense of his own unreliability making him assert his steadfastness. Of course, he fully intended to remain a Unionist, but the knowledge of how he was going to keep the conference alive seemed to make an asseveration of faith imperative.

I have always been ready to discuss either with friends or opponents the whole of the Irish question, and I do not fear that any Conferences will alter the opinions that I have publicly expressed. I can hardly expect that Mr Gladstone will surrender his opinions either, but it is possible that —admitting his inability to give effect to them now—he may be ready to lay them aside either absolutely or in favour of some substitutes which discussion may suggest. I think, as I always have done, that Land ought to be dealt with first—that there is a possibility of agreement on this branch of the question—and that if it were once settled the Home Rule agitation might be reduced to manageable proportions. It is in answer to

[1] Chamberlain to Hartington, 6th January 1887. Chamberlain, *op. cit.*, pp. 244–6.

a statement to this effect that Mr G. authorises and approves a Conference. Is not this in itself as great a concession as can reasonably be asked
for at this stage? I enclose a statement of my position published in the
Birmingham Daily Post before Mr Gladstone's letter was received.

The only reason for making the enclosure of outdated opinions was
to impress his leader with the toughness shown before Gladstone had
shown himself inclined towards 'goodwill'.

What followed was still more remarkable. Combined with regret
at Hartington's refusal to sit at the 'Round Table' was a veiled threat
of a possible cave in.

I will only add that if you joined the Conference you would immensely
strengthen Trevelyan and myself in limiting the discussion to points on
which agreement is practicable, while if any new proposal—as a substitute for Mr G.'s Home Rule Bill—were mooted, you would be able to
prevent any admission or concession on our part which you thought to
be compromising the Unionist position. If you are not present, we must
do our best under the circumstances; but as we both are probably willing
to go rather further in the direction of Self Government than you are,
there is a danger that—in your absence—we may drift still further apart.
I believe that if you joined Mr G.'s Government we should have been
strong enough to have prevented the introduction of the Home Rule
Bill—and in any case we should have been able to present a united and
concerted opposition without the shades of difference which sometimes
rather embarrassed our joint action.

'Joe' was pulling out all the stops. Talk of drifting 'still further apart'
and 'the shades of difference' spelt 'Be it on your head this time as it
really was last time'. A grave charge and one likely to go home with
considerable force. Chamberlain knew, indeed hoped, that Hartington would not budge from his doctrinal stand. What he wanted was
embarrassment leading to a desire for greater solidarity. A solidarity
leaving the initiative in his hands.

His daring was rewarded. Hartington took it all like a lamb. Whig
aristocrats seldom went beyond personal and social to political pride.
Least of all their current leader, who seldom evinced pride of any
sort. Along with his reply of the 7th came a letter to be published or
not as Chamberlain thought fit.[1] It remained in obscurity. 'I used the
discretion allowed me and did not think it necessary to publish the
letter,' was Chamberlain's comment on it.[2] He did, however, consent
to Hartington's doing so if he wished, knowing he would not. Sincere
in his professions of perplexity, the Liberal Unionist leader did not

see how I can give a more general expression of sympathy with the
proceedings, unaccompanied by such reservations I have made, without

[1] Hartington to Chamberlain, 7th January 1887. Chamberlain, *op. cit.*,
pp. 246–7.
[2] Chamberlain to Hartington, 8th January 1887. Devonshire Papers, 340. 2098.

giving rise to the impression that I am more ready to patch up our differences than I really am, or that I am less convinced than I was of the necessity of keeping Mr Gladstone out while he holds to his Home Rule policy.

By 'our differences' Hartington meant the differences between Liberals, not those between Chamberlain and himself. Insult had aroused in him a mood of self-examination. For the first time some genuine hesitation is apparent. Only something of a highly explosive nature could have shocked him into it. What had been fleeting whimsies now became haunting reflections.

> If, as I expect, you do not think that the publication of the letter would do any good, I do not know what I can do, unless I send it to Buckle, not for publication, but with a request to put in something in this sense, in a conciliatory tone. It has already been stated, I think, that I have been kept informed of the negotiations, but a statement made in a friendly spirit of the reasons which induce me to abstain, appearing in an organ which generally takes my view of the question, may perhaps do something to prevent suspicion and differences breaking out in the Unionist ranks. I hear that the Gladstonians do not much like the negotiations and that Schnadhorst is altogether against them. This is all in your favour and I have little doubt that you will have the best of it. But I think that in the position in which I stand towards the Government it would be too great a risk for me to get myself involved in these negotiations.[1]

Note that his confidence in Chamberlain's ability to keep his end up had increased remarkably. Perhaps Brett had also been at him. The mention of Schnadhorst could be taken to point in that direction. The excuse of great risk is an interesting one. Hartington was no 'fox' and disliked the prospect of a balancing act. Use of the phrase 'get myself involved' indicates that however much his fears for Chamberlain had evaporated, those for himself were quite strong. Indeed, the more confident he was that the Radical Unionists could take care of themselves, the less confident he was likely to be of not being dragged on far beyond his real wishes to a point of no return. Were this to happen the government, and with it Unionism, would probably collapse. At the same time he wanted to keep Chamberlain sweet. Radical Unionism provided the only certain long-term means of retaining and acquiring electoral support among those sections of the electorate which decided the outcome of elections. For Salisbury as well as himself Hartington had to take great care.

The unused letter was a very lukewarm effort. In deciding not to attend the coming conference he denied any lack of general goodwill.

> I need hardly say that I should welcome a successful issue of this Conference on the basis of the suggestions in your speech, not only as re-

[1] Hartington to Chamberlain, 7th January 1887. Chamberlain Papers, JC5/22/24.

uniting the Liberal party, but because it might bring about a solution of some Irish difficulties by the general concurrence of all parties, which I have always earnestly desired. But if there is a disposition to come to an agreement which it would be possible for us as Unionists to accept, my presence is unnecessary and might tend to excite rather than remove differences.

Given his overriding desire for secrecy, Chamberlain was bound to take umbrage at the next paragraph. It hinted at his climb down over the discussion of Home Rule and pointed out the limited nature of any workable compromise.

On the other hand, I do not understand that the basis of discussion which you suggested has been definitely accepted; and I should see but little use in re-opening the discussion on the subject of Home Rule. It may appear, at least to some, that the most probable result of the Conference would be to bring about a partial reconciliation of the party, while the great differences which have divided us still remain. All that I have said at and since the General Election, and the course which I have taken in the last few days precludes me from promoting such a reunion of the Liberal party as would weaken or destroy the existing securities for the Union, until we can feel a greater confidence in the future policy of the party on what we hold to be essential points.

While therefore I think that my presence would do little to promote the substantial agreement which we all desire, it seems to me that it might be open to misconstruction of a nature which I am sure you do not anticipate and would not admit to be reasonable, but which I think it especially necessary for me to avoid.[1]

Small wonder that such sentiments remained far away from the printing works.

Meanwhile the failure to publish the bases of the coming conference agenda had made a deep impression in many quarters. Hartington had been concerned to know what they were. Many had come to believe there were none to reveal. Brett soon got to the stage of asserting this as a fact. Writing to Buckle also on the 7th January, he stated: 'As there are no bases which meet the approval of Mr G.— none really exist. Chamberlain goes in upon his terms and Morley upon his.'[2] Significantly, Harcourt's position was not regarded as worth mentioning. One would have expected Brett to have been better informed since he, Hartington and Chamberlain were showing each other portions of their current correspondence. His ignorance only went to show how cautious Chamberlain could be when he chose. Besides the general initiative brought by discretion, there was Brett's inveterate capacity for sustained gossiping to consider. More-

[1] Hartington to Chamberlain, 7th January 1887. Chamberlain Papers, JC5/22/24.
[2] Brett to Buckle, 7th January 1887. Copy. Esher Papers.

over, that gentleman's position in the Home Rule struggle was not easily definable. Challenged by Buckle as to what his 'game' was, he hastened to explain. 'Why you say that I am not a Unionist I cannot exactly tell. I did not stand for Parliament as a Gladstonian Liberal and I removed my name from the Liberal Association in Parliament Street when I found that their funds were used for Gladstonian Liberal purposes.' Realising this added up to very little and hardly made him a Unionist, he went on to make his excuses.

> It is true that I have joined no other society, but I have reasons for not doing so which I consider adequate. To mention one of them, I think it dangerous to crystalise the sections of the old Liberal party round Gladstone and Hartington for fear that the legitimate opposition in whom lies the reversion of the movement should be wholly separatist. Had I been in Parliament I should have been forced to take up a position which superficially might appear more definite. But should I have done so as it is?[1]

As one not at all desirous of re-entering the Commons he felt there was no necessity. The great aims he was striving for in politics went beyond the Irish question. They were to keep Gladstone out of office and retain Hartington for the Liberal cause. To his way of thinking, Hartington would eventually be ready to implement the policy in his address to the Rossendale electors. Like his Whig predecessors, the Liberal Unionist leader was a practical politician. The impossibility of governing Ireland on the old lines was bound to force his hand. In short, Brett was a man of 'goodwill'. It was all very well to explain to Buckle, but the information was not going to appear in the columns of *The Times*. So he suffered many of the disadvantages of isolation, without any truly solid advantages from independence. Impotent independence, a state common to many men like Brett, was no match for the Schnadhorsts and Spence Watsons of the political world. Without any concerted action they could play very little part. Dale possessed some powerful local influence in Birmingham. Brett's influence was on certain individuals, and even then was not a very powerful one. Gladstone set no store by him and Harcourt and Morley listened, 'but trusted not'. At a time like this he would have served the cause he had at heart much better by taking on an open Unionist label. As it was he carried scant weight. His main contribution was historical, for the sort of information he garnered often illuminates cryptic remarks in other correspondence. Nevertheless, his views were wrong on the basic question, however useful they proved as an illustration of the damage Gladstone's guardedness had done to the belief in his sincerity. The old 'fox' had 'foxed' himself.

[1] *Ibid.*

The men primarily concerned continued their endless exchange of views. Chamberlain told Harcourt that the details of a Land Scheme could only be elaborated in common.[1] He would 'rely much' on the suggestions of the other conference members, but promised to submit 'some ideas and principles as a basis for discussion'. False modesty was a very necessary commodity just then. The last thing he wanted was that his enemies on the Home Rule side should be able to say he was dominating the proceedings. That might lead to a sudden cessation of the whole affair. Then, to make it clear opposition to their activities was not restricted to Harcourt's camp, he went on to note the grumbling *on both sides*, instancing Wolverton, Labouchère, 'etc.' and 'many private letters' from Unionists. But his optimism appeared to persist. As far as he could see, 'all the grumblers are men who for one reason or another desire to keep us apart and fear reunion on any terms honourable to both parties. I believe there is a real sense of relief among the majority of Liberals of all sections.'

Needless to say, Harcourt heartily agreed. Writing to Morley he rebuked him for declining to visit Malwood.[2] 'It is just as essential as going to the play and I think more important than Dicey.' In a second note the rebuke was more severe and the occasion called for it.[3] Replying to his colleague's complaint of Chamberlain's being too pleased with things by half, he left no doubt as to his annoyance.

> I do not at all concur in your desire that anyone shall be 'thoroughly worsted' in our conference. On the contrary I desire that everyone shall have the best of it. This is the essence of 'compromise', as you will find if you attentively study a philosophical work on that subject which I always keep by my bedside. Don't allow the groanings and moanings and snufflings of the sour Noncons. to coagulate the milk of your naturally mild disposition.

The usual banter was there, yet impregnated with an unaccustomed venom. Like Chamberlain he was convinced of the popularity of the conference. Unlike him he really thought something fundamental could be done. 'We may not do all the good we wish, but we shall accomplish some. Depend upon it, whatever the wirepullers may say, the mass of the party are sincerely desirous for a *modus vivendi*.' What he forgot was that this same majority, whatever its opinions, would not throw over Gladstone. In this respect he was as unrealistic as Brett.

Little did he know that Gladstone was composing another master-

[1] Chamberlain to Harcourt, 7th January 1887. Garvin, *op. cit.*, p. 283.
[2] Harcourt to Morley, 7th January 1887, No. 1. Copy. Harcourt Papers.
[3] Harcourt to Morley, 7th January 1887, No. 2. Copy. Harcourt Papers.

piece the overall effect of which was to increase the blurr which inevitably surrounded his opinions.[1] 'I have little to add to my previous letter,' he began. This was ambiguous as things turned out, for there followed a budget of eighteen pages! His first line of approach was that of a political tactician unmoved by the principles at issue.

In your conversations you *3* will represent in one sense 280, and in a fuller sense 195 votes. They *2* will represent 6 or 8? The 195 with firm ground under their feet: the 6 or 8 (if they be so many) floating in the air. While we had better not (I suppose) blazen this inequality, it seems clear that we should say nothing which could seem to show we were not aware of it. Let us for a moment assume that Chamberlain had given no sign. We should have had facing us the hard fact of a hostile majority of 110, and should have had to regulate our conduct in view of that majority and to have made deductions (I do not mean subtractions) from it. I do not at present see what we can say or do in regard to Home Rule, except what we should have said or done if there had been no sign from Chamberlain. It is too early, probably, to fix details; but this seems to *outline* the ground.

In other words Home Rule is to continue as before. There is not even going to be an agreed postponement, or so it would appear. The 'signs' given by angels of the unfallen variety had encouraged the faith and banished the guilt of Hawarden. They were going to continue. On the 6th Wolverton had expressed the fear to Granville that the conference might spoil Gladstone's 'splendid position'.[2] While the G.O.M. was concocting this douche for Harcourt, Wolverton was again beside himself lest the Gladstonians agreed to postpone or modify their Home Rule programme at a time when to him it seemed to be making excellent progress.[3] Further fortified still by the prospects of coercion, Gladstone beat his deputy unmercifully upon the head. 'In a practical aspect, what you have to consider is really I think, what cooperation there can be on matters *outside* Irish policy; or on matters inside it without prejudice to Home Rule.'[4] Practical in terms of what he Gladstone with ultimate control of his party would stomach, yes. Practical in terms of making the conference work, no. Gladstone was now directly taking the line Chamberlain had taken on 30th December, but for exactly the opposite reason. Very relevant to the 'practical' side of politics was the main body of

[1] Gladstone to Harcourt, 7th January 1887. Harcourt Papers. Gardiner, *op. cit.*, p. 26.

[2] Wolverton to Granville, 6th January 1887. Granville Papers, P.R.O. 30, 29, 28A.

[3] Wolverton to Granville, 7th January 1887. Granville Papers, P.R.O. 30, 29, 28A.

[4] Gladstone to Harcourt, 7th January 1887. Harcourt Papers.

the Liberal Unionists. With an ever open eye for the main chance and a yearning for Whig 'ballast' the old party leader was especially keen about any move indicating a possible *détente* with Hartington, the man who held the balance in the Commons.

> In some papers it is said that Hartington in late conferences has reserved the question of a Hartington Ministry. If we ask ourselves what attitude we should hold with reference to such a Ministry, on that subject I am open to be advised, and my feeling would certainly not be one of outright hostility. In a practical view I take it to be impossible.[1]

Impossible, maybe, but later developments were to hinge on whether Chamberlain could bring in Hartington and his men and thus make reunion a 'practical' proposition.

Turning to Ireland and the Irish, Gladstone came out with what he had already told Morley. Though not a surprise to Harcourt it did not become more palatable on a second reading. What followed, however, was altogether new. An addition to the Gladstonian team to attend, the 'Round Table' was suggested. Such a one as to make the Hawarden approach every bit as much of a 'farce' as the first ideas from Highbury. 'As Ireland and the Irish members have behaved well in Parliament for the last 12 months, I take it for granted we shall not lightly do anything to split away from them on the main Irish issue.' Having spoken of Parnell and his men as one would of a senior prefect and boys of a remand home, he switched tones and patronised Harcourt instead. 'Should you want another hand, you might think of Sir C. Russell. As an Attorney-General and planted in the legal line, his position would not be affected by his joining you, like that of a layman outside the (late) Cabinet.'[2] It looked as though Labouchère had lost his bid to be wrecker in chief. Not content with discussing matters germane to Home Rule proper and conference composition, the G.O.M. proceeded to wrest from Harcourt the one hope he had encouraged quite unequivocally. Receiving such a letter must have been like a living nightmare, albeit at the breakfast table. His leader appeared to have attained the acme of bad faith.

> Although one is apt to be too suspicious on these occasions, I think that in the notion of an Irish Local Government Bill, if it is proposed by us, *latet anguis in herba*. The danger would be the acceptance of a Bill which would be taken for and yet did not really constitute a fulfilment of our pledge to Ireland.[3]

[1] *Ibid.*

[2] *Ibid.* Sir Charles Russell (1832–1900), later Lord Russell of Killowen, was at this time Gladstonian M.P. for South Hackney, and had been Attorney-General in the third Gladstone ministry. He defended Parnell before the Special Commission 1888–90.

[3] *Ibid.*

If the commitment to Home Rule was constantly stressed, it is difficult to see how this fear could materialise. The whole idea was, moreover, inconsistent with the general 'expedit' given to things Irish independent of Home Rule earlier on. To wriggle out of this self-contradiction, a mitigating sentence was employed, yet it made no appreciable difference. 'But I do not believe such a danger to be probable; only a thing that we should bear in mind.' It is difficult to understand why Gladstone could seriously have thought this, for acceptance of a Gladstonian Local Government scheme by Chamberlain and Trevelyan was highly probable. Surely the sentence was simply a clumsy device to try and hide what had been said? Though why one says something only to attempt to unsay it is something Gladstone alone could understand. His very next sentence reveals his belief that the Radical Unionists would jump at any opportunity for settlement: 'Chamberlain is under a great necessity of moving—we are not.' Unless he means that Chamberlain will have to provide all the ideas on Local Government and Land. Something Harcourt would not readily agree to and which did not in fact come to pass. Whatever was meant, there was nothing equivocal about the conviction that 'all our necessity is to avoid a reasonably founded charge of overlooking a pacific overture which might have been accepted without compromise of our policy'. 'Foxing' not honesty was evidently the best policy.

To give it greater effect Gladstone gave permission for the use of the extracts as Harcourt had requested.

> I have put in a few words accidentally omitted on the composition of the company. I would advise only having the sentence about Trevelyan. Of course, I took it for granted you would show the whole to your co-adjutor and it would be a comfort to me to know that Morley was not alarmed by anything I have written.[1]

The end gave the key to his whole shift into the open with Harcourt. The 'foxing' was now only for public consumption. 'I have many letters on the coming communications. They are on both sides, but a large majority in the sense of jealousy against undue concessions.'[2] The 'People's William' had often given a bold lead from the front when he had first been led from behind.

The 8th January was an altogether quieter day. Pens were down at Hawarden, Malwood and Elm Park Gardens. Only Highbury carried on in its own relentless way. Apart that is, from the indefatigable Brett. To Hartington, Chamberlain sent a rather nonchalant letter—brief and to the point as ever.[3] It contained the refusal to

[1] *Ibid.* [2] *Ibid.*
[3] Chamberlain to Hartington, 8th January 1887. Devonshire Papers, 340. 2098.

publish his leader's proferred letter and news of the impending discussion of his Land Purchase ideas at the 'Round Table'. He assumed that 'in accordance with' his 'suggestion, the Conference will first deal with this matter'. His general optimism was unabated. The position for him was 'Heads I win, tails you lose'. Signs of impending trouble would hinder, maybe ruin, reunion prospects, but ultimately augment Radical Unionist strength. Hence he could comment in a matter of fact way: 'I need hardly add that if the article in today's *Daily News* is to be treated as inspired, there is not the least probability of our coming to any agreement on Home Rule.' Not mere bravado to suit the Hartington outlook, for the opinion expressed to Dilke, with whom more frankness could have been risked, was imbued with exactly the same spirit. 'I judge from the *Daily News* that Morley is getting frightened at his responsibility and that the Conference will come to nothing.'[1] Had he cared, the paper's denial that concessions had or would be made to him could not have been taken in such a lighthearted way.

Brett's hopes were again boundless.[2] Despite Morley having been his source for the information about Schnadhorst's displeasure he again thought everything appeared to be going very well. Buckle was proving hard to convert to his view of the Chamberlain position, but would doubtless change his tune once 'Joe's' infinite skill had 'captured Harcourt and Herschell'. 'I hope and think there is every prospect of smashing up the Gladstonian party and reuniting the Liberal party': so ran the summary of how he read the situation. Unhappily, caucuses not clubs were trumps and Chamberlain, to whom all this was addressed, could only remain grateful yet unconvinced. Through further correspondence with Buckle, Brett was trying hard to contribute towards the 'capture' and the Gladstonian split that would almost inevitably follow it.[3] Following the advice of the prospective 'captor', he suggested the editor seek to accentuate 'the difference in tone between Labouchère and Co. and H. Fowler and Co.'. Another more direct effort in the cause of reunion had earned him the displeasure of J. D. Leader, editor of the *Sheffield Independent* and right hand man of Mundella. In a letter published in *The Times* he had criticised hostile attitudes to the coming conference.[4] Leader took it as a sneer at the Gladstonians. Willy nilly the fence-sitting days seemed over. There had to be a determined bid to recreate the impression of detached disinterestedness. It took the form of a letter to

[1] Chamberlain to Dilke, 8th January 1887. Dilke Papers, Add. MS. 43888, f. 97. Copy. Chamberlain Papers, JC5/24/236.
[2] Brett to Chamberlain, 8th January 1887. Copy. Esher Papers.
[3] *Ibid.*
[4] *The Times*, 5th January 1887.

the Sheffield editor analysing the situation as seen by a man of 'good-will'.[1]

> I have been sent a cutting from your paper in which you refer in some-what mistaken terms to a letter I sent to the *Times*. My object was not to sneer at any body of good Liberals, but to defend Mr Chamberlain against imputations of meanness which are altogether undeserved. As, however, you seem not to be aware to what a large extent his Birmingham speech received the immediate private response of many Liberals of position, hitherto firm on Mr G.'s policy. I would suggest that you should write privately to him and ask whether it is not a fact that numbers of letters were received by him within a few days of his speech which quite fulfilled the expression I used in my letter.

Whether the tactlessness of suggesting one did not normally see the paper detracted from the general force of the letter must remain a matter of opinion. That the rest constituted an agile piece in self-defence is obvious enough. The only pity was that it appeared in the columns of a journal read widely in only one part of the kingdom. Such readers as there were elsewhere would not, generally speaking, belong to that floating and moderate vote Brett and his like were so eager to collar, but to the 'wire-pullers's' group.

Chamberlain had been wrong about one aspect of developments in the *Daily News*. Morley had had nothing to do with them. Indeed, so sensitive had he been to the likelihood of the affair being fathered on to him that a positive denial was immediately sent off to Malwood, arriving there on the 9th.[2] To Harcourt at least he was prepared to curse the editor's lack of 'goodwill'. All told, editors were receiving more of the politicians' attention than was usual. As Harcourt was consoling himself with Morley's loyalty, Hartington was writing to Buckle in accordance with his offer to Chamberlain.[3] The tone verged at times on the pathetic.

> I endeavoured to ascertain whether any definite basis had been agreed on for the Conference, but so far as I can learn the only basis of discussion are considered to be Chamberlain's speech and Mr Gladstone's published letters. The scope of discussion has been somewhat enlarged in conversation between Chamberlain and Harcourt, but nothing further has been reduced to writing.

What a good thing it was for Chamberlain that Hartington was genuinely friendly when Unionist opinion might have become enraged at his concession over the agenda. The quest for secrecy was

[1] Brett to J. D. Leader, 8th January 1887. Copy. Esher Papers. *Sheffield Independent*, 10th January 1887.

[2] Morley to Harcourt, 6th January 1887. Harcourt Papers.

[3] Hartington to Buckle, Draft, 9th January 1887. Devonshire Papers, 340. 2099.

2. Spencer Compton Cavendish, Marquess of Hartington
    (Later Eighth Duke of Devonshire)

3. Robert Cecil, Third Marquess of Salisbury

proving difficult and the Annual Register for 1887 records this particular development. One of the few really authentic pieces in its
rather garbled account of the 'Round Table' affair. Hartington ended
a description of his latest dealings with Chamberlain over the letter
for publication by hoping that 'in anything' Buckle might say he
would take 'as friendly a line' towards that gentleman as he could.
General trends were maintaining Whig spirits, for although admitting
differences of opinion 'as to the expediency of these negotiations', he
was 'inclined to think that the Gladstonians' had 'more to fear from
them than the Unionists'. His deputy had proved more reliable than
he had dared hope—that much is clear from what followed.

> I am bound to say that so far as I know Chamberlain has not said a
> word which implies any disposition to recede from the position which he
> had taken up on the subject of an Irish Parliament and an Irish Execu-
> tive; and I think that full credit should be given to him for consistency
> in this respect. He says in his letter of yesterday that if the article in
> the *Daily News* is to be taken as inspired, there is not the least prob-
> ability of coming to an agreement on Home Rule.

The situation had its slightly comical side. The more the last ditch
Gladstonians abused Chamberlain and his works, the more popular
with the Unionists he became. The more popular he became the more
he would be trusted. The more he was trusted, the greater influence
he would exercise. The greater the influence he exercised, the greater
amount of progressive legislation the Conservative government
would adopt. The more progressive legislation the government
adopted the less ground the Gladstonians would gain. The less ground
they gained the more remote the chances of putting through Home
Rule became. By spurning Chamberlain the G.O.M. and his friends
were not helping themselves. Coercion was a powerful but overrated
disease. It could weaken Unionism, not lay it low. Perhaps Acton
saw how things would turn out. His advice to Gladstone was not to
overestimate his strength and refuse all concessions. On the other
hand, of course, the more the Conservatives and Whigs had to do
with Chamberlain the less their standstill notions would prevail in the
Unionist parties. Imperialism and Radicalism was the prescription
of the times. 'Joe' was the leader of those who peddled that com-
pound.

Buckle's response to Hartington on the 10th was shrewd and
generous.[1] It coupled telling analysis with a promise of cooperation.
Chamberlain struck him as having

> drawn back somewhat—not so much in his words as in his attitude since
> his first hasty proposal made without reference to you and without even

[1] Buckle to Hartington, 10th January 1887. Devonshire Papers, 340. 2100.

hearing from you. *Then* you thought yourself that he was heading into the Gladstonian camp. I think the criticism his attitude provoked has done good and helped to brace him up and I have no doubt now that he will stick to his guns.

Self-praise and justification apart, there was a strong element of truth in what he said. Admittedly, 'Joe' had never meant to abandon the Union and never thought Gladstone would give up Home Rule. Nevertheless, the degree of Unionist wrath had undoubtedly reinforced his belief in the fighting power of his allies and warned him his 'foxing' would have to be very nicely calculated. The way between the Scylla of majority Unionism and the Charybdis of vital sections of minority Unionism was tortuous in the extreme. That way was his way—and he knew it. What has gone before has shown he wanted it thus. What he wrote to Jesse Collings at that time showed an awareness that a choice of sides was no longer his. 'I am not sanguine about the Conference. The Gladstonians are a bad lot. The Labouchère sections have I think frightened Morley and I expect he will make no concessions.'[1] Bearing in mind he thought Morley the man responsible for the *Daily News* attack there is nothing surprising in this view. Yet however wrong over a detail, he was right in his conclusion. Not that he faltered. The conference retained its usefulness to him and to be gone through with. A note about the technicalities of Land Purchase was sent off to Fowler.[2] But no man likes to feel his freedom of manoeuvre is diminished and when Dilke wrote that 'Willie Bright' had just 'let fall a word which may have meaning in it: "the difficulty is to keep Mr G. in the Gladstonian party" ', he tended to believe it.[3] This was clutching at straws. Dilke also reported Morley as saying he had seen Parnell who 'was *not* uncompromising'.[4] This was 'old hat'. Morley's current thoughts are to be found in two letters to Harcourt, both of the 10th.[5]

The tone of the first was scarcely that of a man very soon to sit at a

[1] Chamberlain to Collings, 10th January 1887. Copy. Chamberlain Papers, JC5/16/20.

[2] Chamberlain to Fowler, 10th January 1887. Copy. Chamberlain Papers, JC5/31/12. Hamilton, *op. cit.*, p. 230.

[3] Chamberlain, *op. cit.*, p. 247. William L. Bright was the second son of John Bright and Gladstonian Liberal M.P. for Stoke-on-Trent. Dilke had added: 'Morley was here today. He repudiates the *Daily News*' attitude. . . . He saw Parnell and' his attitude, 'for which see T. P. O'Connor in the *Liverpool Daily Post* of today, is *not* uncompromising.' Dilke to Chamberlain, 10th January 1887. Dilke Papers, Add. MS. 43888, f. 99. T. P. O'Connor (1848–1929) was Irish Nationalist M.P. for the Scotland division of Liverpool, a prominent member of his party and a prolific writer and journalist.

[4] *Ibid.*

[5] Morley to Harcourt, 10th January 1887, No. 1. Harcourt Papers. Morley to Harcourt, 10th January 1887, No. 2. Harcourt Papers.

reunion conference. Harcourt had suggested dinner on the 12th to discuss plans for the next day. He accepted with 'infinite satisfaction', adding: 'We ought to arrange our lines and get our guns shotted, so no J. Chamberlain, I pray.' One would have thought war rather than peace talks were approaching. Certainly one war meeting was in the offing. On the evening of the 11th St James's Hall would be packed with Gladstonian enthusiasts met together for the express purpose of founding a Liberal Radical Union for London. 'The unwelcome, and in some degree unexpected failure of the Gladstonian Liberals in London and its suburbs set the party managers thinking how the disasters of the past could be repaired in the future.'[1] Messrs. Schnadhorst and Causton considered this new organisation the likely answer. It would try to carry out in the metropolis what the Birmingham Association had achieved in the provinces. Morley was to preside. Strangely enough, he did not seem to have looked forward to platform warfare with the same glee as he did the coming 'conflict' behind closed doors. 'I wish the meeting tomorrow were at the devil. Of course, *I* will try to be as discreet as my nature permits, but the meeting is sure to be strong for Mr Gladstone and Home Rule, and I cannot weep over that.'[2] Even so, as with 'damning' the *Daily News* there is an air of complaisance about what he writes. A refusal to take part would have been more than excusable in the circumstances, but he wished to show Chamberlain that Schnadhorst would now be doing with him what he had formerly done with those now Radical Unionists, notably the great man himself.

The second letter is also slightly unusual. For one thing, it actually criticised Gladstone![3] In fact word from that quarter provided the occasion for writing. Referring to its meaning, he remarked

> If you can make anything definite out of it, it is more than I can do. The main purport of my letter to him was to ask his leave to show the enclosed from his letter of 1st January to the Conference generally. You will observe by comparing these extracts with the original letter that I have omitted those parts of his letter referring to Home Rule and to Land as I thought they might give too much advantage to the enemy, especially the Home Rule paragraph.

Stranger than the hit at Gladstone is the apparent lack of coordination between the two prospective conferenceers. Morley wrote as though he had not acted along with Harcourt in order to ensure a favourable response from Hawarden, but quite independently. The omissions from the private letter of 1st January were the obvious

[1] Morley to Harcourt, 10th January 1887, No. 1. Harcourt Papers.
[2] *Ibid*. Causton was an N.L.F. official.
[3] Morley to Harcourt, 10th January 1887, No. 2. Harcourt Papers.

ones to make. There is nothing suspicious in their both choosing the same. Was it that, jealous of Harcourt because Gladstone had sent the private letter to him, Morley undertook a little initiative of his own? If so, were the criticisms of his leader due to that too? Odder still he then toadied to Harcourt.

> You will see he is very much afraid of you, and the pencil note on the second sheet exhibits the terror of his soul. I have assured him you were quite satisfied with his letter of 1st January. I did not mention to him how I had endeavoured in vain to alarm you on the subject.

Probably his state was one of high excitement and sensitiveness. Still tender on the subject of the *Daily News*, he pointed out that he gathers from Gladstone that 'the telegram from Hawarden on the 7th, was the *causa causans* of the article in the *Daily News*'. Indeed, were one to hazard a guess, this discovery was probably the main reason for writing twice on the same day. Further evidence of a pent-up condition comes from his repetition of the need for 'previous talk before the Conference' followed by a P.S. half suggesting this would not take place, when he knew full well they would be having a whole evening together. 'Remember,' he ended, 'that J. Chamberlain said to me when I recited to him the Leeds resolution: "if it had body or bodies it would have exactly expressed my sentiments".'[1] Why remind Harcourt of anything when he was to meet him before the conference began? Surely because chewing over the whole project in his mind he had worked himself up? Usually he was a most orderly thinker with a knack for writing just the right amount.

Very wisely, Harcourt decided to deal gently with Gladstone's incendiary of the 7th. He approached the knotty points circuitously.[2]

> Many thanks for your letter received today, which I have forwarded to John Morley. I sent him your letter of 1st January with which he appeared quite satisfied. The extracts I sent you were intended to omit such portions of the letter as did not seem prudent to communicate to the *enemy*.

Maybe the last word was used to propitiate the old man. It was not one Harcourt was likely to use in the ordinary way, even in jest. He had not, for example, brought it into any other correspondence dealing with these same extracts. Whatever the case, it was politic to use it now. Entering upon the subject really in hand, he struck another blow for Chamberlain.

> I quite agree that we have the strength of the position and ought to hold it, but we should not, I think, be too chary of the metal of which we

[1] *Ibid.*
[2] Harcourt to Gladstone, 10th January 1887. Gladstone Papers, Add. MS. 44201, f. 24.

construct the bridge for 'Our Joe', if he is willing to retire over it. . . .
Chamberlain did all he could to get Hartington into our Conference
with no success. Chamberlain's personal following is no doubt small and
I think the greater part of the Unionists are Hartingtonians and are
against Home Rule in any shape or form. Still, Chamberlain has a name
in the Liberal party and will never be without influence in the House of
Commons.

With such friends as Harcourt and Dale his influence was sure to
survive. The former now played another card well-calculated to put
the G.O.M. in a spot—the card of historical precedent for which he
had a notorious weakness.

You will remember the part the Stanleyites played in 1835, and the
Peelites subsequently, out of all proportion to their numerical following.
I don't mean to say that Chamberlain's position is the same in degree as
was the case with these sections, but it is *eiusdem generis*. I do not see
how Hartington is ever to form a Government *without* Chamberlain—
the really formidable thing I think would be if he formed a Government
with him.

There was no getting away from this and Gladstone had to remember
that Hartington could only be reached through Chamberlain. Any
chances of doing so were remote, but any hopes of getting the former
without the agency of the latter were ludicrous wanderings.

Chamberlain considered the admonishing of newspaper editors a
very laudable occupation. To judge from his letter to Harcourt on
the 11th press activity was then uppermost in his mind.[1]

Will you consider what is to be done about the Press, damn it? Our
Conference will be worse than a Cabinet and we shall all be pestered to
death. I incline to agree that we might agree on a written paragraph to
be given to all enquirers, and also to refuse absolutely to answer any
questions going beyond this official *compte rendu*. If anything brings our
well-meant effort to grief it will be the newspapers and their persistent
and misleading comments.[2]

Other factors were actually more important. That Dilke's information struck him as 'more promising' is just another proof that the
severely realistic appraisals of the 10th were the result of seeing the
Daily News represented more than itself. Indeed the press generally
reflected more than made opinion. By blaming the newspapers he was
merely making a veiled criticism of the forces behind them—Gladstone, Labouchère, the Schnadhorstian cohorts and most of all,
albeit with some injustice, the 'treacherous' Morley. Unionist opinion
no longer seemed fearful of what the conference would bring. Har-

[1] Chamberlain to Harcourt, 11th January 1887. Harcourt Papers.
[2] *Ibid.*

tington told Henry James that though the government reconstruction did not 'seem to be getting on comfortably', 'the prospects of reconciliation in the Liberal camp don't seem hopeful'.[1] Albert Grey seemed to think the same.[2] Already on the 4th he had invited Hartington to address a meeting of Liberal Unionists in the North-East. Having received encouragement, he had gone ahead and negotiated an actual date with the people on the spot. The event was to take place at Newcastle on 2nd February. Why not make it a singular demonstration of party solidarity after the recent crisis? He therefore suggested that:

> If the 'Round Table' Conference comes to nothing would you like Chamberlain to be invited to attend your meeting. We have several Chamberlainite Unionists in the North and it would please them no doubt if he were to come and speak in your support. Of course, no invitation shall be sent to him unless I get hint from you that you wish it: but if you wish it and Chamberlain were to consent to come, the fact of you and he appearing on one platform would put an end to the belief, which is doing considerable harm, that the Liberal Unionists are not united in their opposition to Home Rule. At present the Northern Unionists have gone no further than to invite Russell and Finlay to come and support you. These two speakers are supposed to represent Ireland and Scotland.[3]

Reading between the lines, Grey appears more worried about Hartington's consent than the possibility that asking Chamberlain might become impossible.

This related to the future. For the present, Morley's meeting had a much greater significance. On the tone and content of his speech would depend the tone and content of the first (and maybe the last) session of the 'Round Table' conference two days later. It was a hotch-potch affair, aimed at several different audiences. To the one before him he promised the continued independence of the local associations. The new Union would simply coordinate their efforts through a federal structure. Switching to the question of mutual confidence he had something for more general consumption. It involved him in telling one of the biggest lies of his lifetime. The greater his experience in politics, he claimed, the less suspicious he became. There was no doubt in his mind that those who differed from him were quite as honest as himself. Doubtless Chamberlain and Harcourt were supposed to lap this up like ambrosia. Still, it was a gesture and must have cost him a lot to make. Last he attacked the

[1] Chamberlain to Dilke, 11th January 1887. Dilke Papers, Add. MS. 43888, f. 100. Hartington to James, 11th January 1887. Lord Askwith, *Lord James of Hereford*, p. 191.
[2] Albert Grey to Hartington, 4th January 1887. Devonshire Papers, 340. 2087. Same to Same, 11th January 1887. Devonshire Papers, 340. 2102.
[3] Albert Grey to Hartington, 11th January 1887. Devonshire Papers, 340. 2102.

government and meant to reach as widely as the press reports could reach. The style was eloquent and amusing.[1]

Mr Morley took credit to himself for having warned the Liberals that they should not say grace for Lord Randolph Churchill's promised banquet of popular measures until the dish-covers had been removed. Already the banquet had become a mere phantom banquet. Though the old Tory pump was fitted with a new Radical handle, the thread of water issuing from it was a very thin one even at first, and now the handle had come off. Mr Goschen's secession to the Government had not, in Mr Morley's opinion, very much altered the level of the Liberal party. An American who wanted to make the most of his successful fishing had boasted that when he got his fish out of the lake, the waters of the lake sank a couple of feet. He did not think Lord Salisbury, after landing his fish, would be able to make a similar boast.[2]

More important than the reference to Chamberlain was the implication that the Liberal Unionists were still genuine Liberals. Goschen had 'seceded' only on joining the government. Prospects for the conference had not worsened. One embarrassment arose, but of a purely domestic Gladstonian nature. The Radicals moved an amendment following a rather feeble seconding speech by Bryce. They deprecated amalgamation with the Liberals lest their cause be weakened and their ability to protest against something like the policy Gladstone adopted over Egypt become hampered. Bradlaugh secured its defeat by an overwhelming majority, but it was an unpleasant reminder to the party leadership that a 'Round Table' conference of another kind might one day be called for. There was, however, a warning for the Gladstonians on the 13th. Too much 'goodwill' might easily provoke a similar outbreak on an infinitely more formidable scale.[3]

On the eve of the conference, Gladstone too showed some sign of renewed friendliness. He sent off to Harcourt a list of 'possible subjects with a view to an honourable and unembarrassing cooperation'.[4] Procedure, Land Laws, Land Taxation (Death Duties 'in which there is room for a big measure'), Local Government (G.B.), Local Government (Ireland), Registration ('to be based on Stansfeld's and James's joint efforts'), and Public Economy—all featured on it. And as he was careful to add, there might be others. Along with this peace offering came two other items of news. One concerned a deterioration in his health. He was anxious to keep his head 'quiet'. The cynic might dismiss this as a device for frightening his deputy into loyalty or, if genuine, the cause of his apparent contrition. Whatever the

[1] *Annual Register*, 1887, p. 6.
[2] *Ibid.*
[3] *Annual Register*, 1887, p. 7.
[4] Gladstone to Harcourt, 12th January 1887. Harcourt Papers.

truth, it meant that during the conference sessions his rôle was more passive than might have been expected. The other dealt with a letter Randolph Churchill had sent to Russell, editor of the *Evening Post*. According to Gladstone it did him 'credit' and might be 'of political importance'. As not a great deal more was heard of it, the G.O.M. was simply mistaken. Not a ripple was raised in London when the letter got there next morning. As arranged, Morley dined with the Harcourts at the Devonshire Club on the 12th to make last minute arrangements for the morrow. After some talk they returned to Grafton Street and finished their business there. It was decided that no communications of the conference proceedings were to be made to anybody outside the conference, with the exceptions of Gladstone and Hartington. Land and local government were to be discussed first, but Harcourt was to try to get on to the legislature question as soon as possible.[1]

The great day began with the arrival at Grafton Street of two letters from Hawarden. The one just discussed, and the other from Mrs Gladstone asking Harcourt not to write much to her husband unless it were absolutely necessary.[2] He was far from well and she repeated the story about his head. Morley came round again before lunch. This time Herschell joined them and a further discussion on proceedings took place. Immediately it was over Harcourt dashed off a note to Gladstone telling of their general agreement.

> You may rely upon it, there will be no surrender of our main positions. I will not trouble you more on this today, as it will probably be too late to write after our Conference and we shall have to compare notes before reporting results to you.

In a P.S. he reported:

> Granville, Herschell, J. Morley and I are all very strongly of opinion that you ought to send out the usual circular as the Head of the Liberal Party

[1] Lewis Harcourt's *Journal*, 12th January 1887. Harcourt Papers.

[2] Lewis Harcourt's *Journal*, 13th January 1887. Harcourt Papers. The *Annual Register*, 1887, states that Herschell acted as president of the conference. The primary sources give no indication that this was so, but see *Annual Register*, 1887, p. 2. (Sir H. Maxwell in *The Life of W. H. Smith, M.P.*, p. 288, also refers to Herschell as chairman.) It is certainly incorrect that Herschell attended to represent 'the Open Mind' and not as a Gladstonian Liberal, though this is asserted in S. H. Jeyes's *Joseph Chamberlain* at p. 191. Nor does the evidence support another of Jeyes's opinions, i.e. that Chamberlain had made a 'great error' in suggesting and entering the 'Round Table' conference. It is far from clear that from his viewpoint he had 'over-rated the importance of Lord Randolph's secession from the Ministry', or that he had 'under-estimated the points of difference between the Home-Rule and Unionist faiths'. *Ibid*. F. W. Hirst in *The Life of William Ewart Gladstone*, edited by Sir Wemyss Reid, at p. 712 also states Horschell took the chair.

to all 'who profess and call themselves' Liberals. They asked through Caine and E. Cavendish to have the 'whip' of the Party sent them and this is the same thing *only less so*. I think the omission of the circular would be interpreted as an admission that we did not regard ourselves as the Liberal Party, or you as its Chief.[1]

Every appearance had to be given of authority, but by showing it in this way the cause of conciliation could simultaneously be served.

[1] Harcourt to Gladstone, 13th January 1887. Gladstone Papers, Add. MS. 44201, f. 28. W. S. Caine (1842–1903), Radical Unionist M.P. for Barrow-in-Furness, a prominent temperance reformer and Liberal Unionist whip. From January 1887 he took over from Lord Edward Cavendish as the chief whip of the party. Lord Edward Cavendish (1838–91), 3rd son of the 7th Duke of Devonshire and brother of Hartington, Liberal Unionist M.P. for West Derbyshire and until January 1887 Liberal Unionist chief whip. From 1887 to 1891 he served as a junior whip.

V

AT THE 'ROUND TABLE': BOUTS
ONE AND TWO

<hr/>

'Can'st thou guide Arcturus with his sons.' Job xxxviii. 32.

A T four o'clock, Morley and Herschell, and Chamberlain and Trevelyan presented themselves on Harcourt's doorstep. Once inside his dining room, they sat down at a round table arranged for the purpose by Lewis Harcourt. First Harcourt read a statement of the circumstances leading up to the meeting and a copy of the extracts from Gladstone's private letter previously sent to Chamberlain. At Morley's particular request, Harcourt was to manage the technical part of the business. Morley and Herschell would devote themselves to the detailed criticism of any plans proposed for consideration. It was then agreed there was an 'absolute necessity of the *strictest secrecy*' in the discussions and proceedings, so that 'if no agreement' was come to 'the whole conversations' could and would be treated as 'non avenues'. During the course of the conference no communication of any kind was to be made to the press, 'except in a *written form*' concurred in by all.[1] The only person to whom the Gladstonians were to forward information was Gladstone himself. 'Chamberlain on his side was to be at liberty (so far as he thought necessary)' to keep in touch with Hartington. Nevertheless, it was understood 'that these communications should be absolutely confined to the persons named and should in no case go beyond them.' The feeling was, nothing would be more injurious to a frank understanding among themselves than 'leakage in the press'.[2] Harcourt then invited Chamberlain to submit his Land Scheme. The 'Round Table Conference' had begun.

The plan was a 'brand new' one. Everyone took rather a fancy to it, especially Harcourt. Though doubtful about the security side he liked the idea of there being virtually no pledging of British credit.

[1] *Ibid.*   [2] *Ibid.*

What pleased him most, however, was the fact that all the risk was to be borne by the landlords. Chamberlain 'pointed out that no absolute security existed for any plan, and this applied whether there was a Home Rule plan connected with the Land Scheme or not'.[1] Mention of Home Rule acted as a red rag to Morley, who straightway weighed in with the argument that only an 'Irish Parliament or Irish central authority' could 'compel fulfilment of obligations'.[2] Battle was joined. Chamberlain replied that 'more control was exercisable over a subordinate local body than over an Irish Parliament, and urged that the Land Scheme was independent of the question of Home Rule which might be reserved. If the Conference could agree on a Land Scheme, it would be possible afterwards either to work it in with an Irish Parliament, or any other form of local authority. In any case there must be some body as a County Board to deal directly with the tenants.'[3] No rancour marred the argument. 'It is sufficient to say,' Harcourt reported to his 'Chief', 'that we all regarded it as a plan well worthy of discussion and consideration.'[4] Copies were circulated and Herschell and Morley undertook 'carefully to examine and report upon it'.[5] Gladstone too was bound to like the minimal pledging of British credit and the dispensing with raising large sums of money. Trevelyan on the other hand appeared to have thrown parsimony to the winds. During the discussion Chamberlain had turned to him on some point and said: 'You agree to that, don't you Trevelyan?' To get the reply: 'Oh yes, I would pledge a hundred millions of British money if it would reunite the Liberal party.'[6] Both Herschell and Trevelyan spoke positively in favour of the Chamberlain scheme. Not that 'Joe' really cared much what Trevelyan said. He despised him and showed it.

From land they passed to the discussion of local government. Rapid agreement was reached on the necessity for County Boards based on the same rules of popular election as were being contemplated for England and Scotland. Harcourt described this section of the session as 'slight',[7] and following out the Gladstonian plan hastened to raise the 'burning question' of Home Rule. He asked Chamberlain whether he was ready to adhere to his letter to Labouchère of

---

[1] Chamberlain, *op. cit.*, p. 248.
[2] *Ibid,*   [3] *Ibid.*
[4] Harcourt to Gladstone, 13th January 1887. Gladstone Papers, Add. MS. 44201, f. 28.
[5] *Ibid.*
[6] Lewis Harcourt's *Journal*, 13th January 1887. Harcourt Papers.
[7] Harcourt to Gladstone, 13th January 1887. Gladstone Papers, Add. MS. 44201, f. 28. An excellent account of the arguments for and against Home Rule and those for and against retention of Irish members at Westminster can be found in Sydney Buxton, *Handbook to Political Questions*, 11th Edition, pp. 130–57.

5th June 1886 and to his speech in the House of Commons 'in which he had professed his readiness to adopt the principles of the Canadian Provincial Legislatures.' 'Certainly,' came back the answer pat—leaving Trevelyan horror stricken and Morley 'in the seventh heaven of delight and surprise'.[5] Chamberlain added that the Canada Act of 1867 'was a very suggestive basis of discussion'.[6] Much pleased, Harcourt then moved on to the Leeds Resolution. Did Chamberlain still subscribe to the view that 'subject to the insertion of the words "legislative authority or authorities" it offered nothing to which he could object'?[1] Once more he got the answer he wanted. 'Very well,' he said, 'let us meet tomorrow to consider an Irish legislature on those lines.' According to Chamberlain, Morley 'seemed to agree'.[2] Had he only known, Morley was delighted.[3] In telling Gladstone about it Harcourt used very vague language. The next session was to discuss 'the condition of an Irish Legislature'. No mention was made of there having been anything more than a reference to 'Joe's' earlier pronouncements. It would never do to commit him before the actual discussion had taken place. Better to err on the side of caution. At seven o'clock the meeting ended. Chamberlain was later to claim nothing had been said about 'a Parliament in Dublin and an executive dependent upon it'.[4] Maybe not in as many words, but by admitting the Canadian provincial model in which the executive was in just that position he had entered upon exceedingly dangerous ground. Had he argued the analogy meant victory for those like Dale and himself who wanted the retention of the Irish members at Westminster he would have stood a much better chance of being believed. On the 13th ambiguity and cross purposes did not matter. Quite a lot had been achieved. The conference members went away in very cheerful spirits. The Gladstonians thinking they were at last catching their fish; Chamberlain that he had a loophole in his qualification of the Leeds Resolution; Trevelyan that Liberal reunion was a fine object in life. The day concluded with a rather curious incident. The Harcourts arrived for dinner at the Devonshire Club to find Trevelyan in the hall. He announced he was to eat there with Chamberlain and could not possibly put it off. So nervous and anxious did his behaviour become that the Harcourts offered to go away. An offer he jumped at, saying he thought it would be much better. They therefore dined at the Oxford and Cambridge Club instead. Hardly an aus-

[1] Garvin, *op. cit.*, p. 286.
[2] Lewis Harcourt's *Journal*, 13th January 1887. Harcourt Papers.
[3] Lewis Harcourt's *Journal*, 13th January 1887. Harcourt Papers.
[4] Chamberlain, *op. cit.*, p. 248.
[5] *Ibid.*
[6] Chamberlain, *op. cit.*, p. 249.

picious development at that particular stage of the talks. The atmosphere was so awkward that even such a wit as Harcourt had not the presence of mind to ask the Devonshire Club management for a round table! What was worse, Trevelyan gave Chamberlain a totally garbled version of what had happened. Telling him there had been 'such a scene in the hall, that Harcourt and "Loulou" *were* coming to dine' at the Devonshire, but that as soon as they found he and Trevelyan were going to dine there they rushed off to the Reform Club.[1] Not exactly the best way to lure 'Our Joe' into admitting the Canadian model meant a legislature with an executive dependent upon it, for, as Morley and W. H. Smith had both remarked, he was an extremely sensitive man.

At noon the next day the five men met again. All the doleful prognostications of the preceding days seemed well and truly confounded. The zeal for reunion had even caught hold of Morley when Chamberlain appeared prepared to live up to his most promising pronouncements of the past.

> If there is a desire to agree [Harcourt had written to Hartington's private secretary], the dullest men will find a way; if there is not the cleverest fellows will fail. As we happen to be all very clever men sincerely anxious to agree, I expect we shall succeed, and the Liberal Party by penny subscriptions will erect a statue to the peacemaker Randolph.[2]

That desire to agree had appeared on the surface at least during the first session. At the second the process went further and deeper, or so any fly on the wall would reasonably have supposed. Lewis Harcourt noted that the 'Conference devoted themselves to the consideration of the Canadian system and succeeded in elaborating an almost complete scheme of Home Rule for Ireland on those lines'.[3] His father told him immediately afterwards that there had been a regular process of Gladstonian take and Chamberlainite give. Harcourt was clearly flushed with excitement, and his story was not substantially true. Also he did not mention that several questions remained untackled. The two main ones were precisely those on which 'Joe' had made his main stand when voting against the Home Rule Bill—Irish representation at Westminster and the fate of Protestant Ulster. Since taking this stand Chamberlain had reverted to the Provincial Councils idea as the furthest he would go. It was therefore something of an achievement to get him to eat his words and go back to the line adopted at the height of the crisis of the previous year. Yet no real persuasion had been necessary. Chamberlain saw quickly enough that if the conference was to last as long as he desired this much had to be conceded.

[1] Lewis Harcourt's *Journal*, 13th and 14th January 1887. Harcourt Papers.
[2] Gardiner, *op. cit.*, pp. 25–6.
[3] Lewis Harcourt's *Journal*, 14th January 1887. Harcourt Papers.

Otherwise there would be no possible basis of discussion and a *modus vivendi* became immediately out of the question. 'Foxing' ordained that he do what he did. Once Home Rule of a meaningful kind had been accepted, the idea of a legislature with an executive dependent upon it followed automatically. The Canadian analogy merely went to underline this point. So it was dishonest of him to claim afterwards that he never agreed to any such idea, but highly politic all the same. Why? Because of his relations with the Unionist parties. Provided the Birmingham left Unionist leaders were satisfied he had tried and been rebuffed, it was vital Unionism as a whole should have the impression he had stood his ground. His local friends could be enlightened in private and the world at large be given an 'authorised version' from his side as to what had happened.

Harcourt may, as he claimed, have gone from point to point, 'pressing Chamberlain when necessary and sometimes leading and sometimes allowing Chamberlain to lead'.[1] Trevelyan may have sat 'horrified and occasionally protesting whilst Chamberlain assented one by one to all our points'.[2] Nevertheless, some of the points assented to were, even if suggested by Harcourt, modifications of the 1886 position in Chamberlain's favour. Just before his resignation on 26th March of that year, he had asked four questions of Gladstone. The first concerned Irish representation at Westminster. The second the power of taxation, including customs and excise. Was it to be given to the Irish Parliament? The third the appointment of the judges and magistracy. Was it to be vested in the Irish Parliament? And the fourth the definition of powers. Should the Irish Parliament be taken to enjoy all authority not specifically excluded by the Act constituting it or not? All the existing accounts of what happened on the 14th January show that, whereas all the answers Chamberlain got ten months before were unacceptable, those given on the same matters that day represented a substantial advance in his direction.[3] 'Foxing' on the vital principle of Home Rule had brought an unexpectedly rapid reward. It looked as though the hooker might yet be hooked. Harcourt's sense of relief had led him into forgetting the Gladstonians had come round to the Birmingham position in several respects. Because Chamberlain agreed to suggestions representing his own views he could hardly be said to be surrendering, but there was this to be said for Harcourt—he was genuinely surprised at the initial ease of bringing Chamberlain back to his Home Rule 'principles'. Hence he stressed that part of the proceedings where it was achieved. As for the rest, plain sailing often seems an

---

[1] *Ibid.*   [2] *Ibid.*

[3] *Ibid.* Chamberlain, *op. cit.*, pp. 249–50. Garvin, *op. cit.*, pp. 286–7. Harcourt to Gladstone, 14th January 1887. Copy. Harcourt Papers.

achievement. Exhilaration hides the fact that the current is favourably inclined.

Summarising the second session for Gladstone, he stated: 'We started with the admitted basis that there should be a *Legislative Body* for Ireland, with an Executive dependent upon it, for purely Irish affairs. Indeed, the Leeds Resolution in principle was frankly adopted,'[1] Chamberlain in his *Political Memoir* merely states: 'Agreed that Provincial Legislature must have some kind of Executive to carry out its work.'[2] Yet he freely admits the discussion was 'founded on the terms of the Act constituting the Federal Constitution of Canada'.[3] With such a foundation the Executive envisaged could only be one dependent on the Legislature. The ambiguity of the 13th had been swept away. His rider to the Leeds Resolution no longer had any relevance once the talks went beyond asking him to what he adhered. Harcourt was undoubtedly acting in the utmost good faith in continuing:

> It was thought convenient to discuss the matter with the Canadian Constitution as a text. There seemed no difficulty upon any side in adopting the powers of the Provincial Legislatures in Canada as an *analogue* for Irish Home Rule. The Imperial Parliament and Government standing to this Irish legislature in the same relation as the Dominion Parliament to the provincial legislatures.[4]

Logically, once Harcourt brought up the Canadian model he was committed to the retention of the Irish at Westminster. Admittedly his commitment was not so clear-cut as Chamberlain's to the Executive point and the principle of Home Rule. The presence or absence of representatives in the central parliament not being so crucial to the nature of the powers governing its relations with the provincial one as the nature of the relationship between executive and legislature to the provincial constitution. Even so, his previous position had become untenable and he was ready to admit it. But that was to come later in the discussion. The second matter settled had been the subject of Chamberlain's fourth question. 'The powers of the Provincial Parliament' were to be 'specifically defined in the statute, a point on which Hartington greatly insists'.[5] A decision precisely opposite to the one insisted upon by Gladstone the year before. Chamberlain did not need much leading into this. 'It was urged,' Harcourt continued,

[1] Harcourt to Gladstone, 14th January 1887. Copy. Harcourt Papers. Gardiner, *op. cit.*, p. 27.
[2] Chamberlain, *op. cit.*, p. 249.
[3] *Ibid.*
[4] Harcourt to Gladstone, 14th January 1887. Copy. Harcourt Papers. Gardiner, *op. cit.*, p. 27.
[5] Harcourt to Gladstone, 14th January 1887. Copy. Harcourt Papers.

that some special machinery should be devised to prevent the Irish Parliament violating or exceeding those powers as is done in the case of the United States and in the provisions of the Dominion Act with regard to Education.'[1] Morley had raised the American analogy, only to be opposed by Chamberlain. To his mind the American rules went too far and therefore should not be followed. The Canadian education case struck him as altogether a superior example to use. This part of the discussion ended well. 'We found no difficulty in assigning to the Provincial Legislature of Ireland, Education, Public Works, and Local Government Board, with a responsible executive to administer these departments.'[2] Had Chamberlain objected to the rôle of the projected Executive Harcourt would not have been able to send Gladstone such a clear-cut statement. Here is just another proof that a man who 'foxes' once can 'fox' again.

Over the police question, Harcourt said

> Chamberlain was willing to give local police to the Irish Government; Trevelyan demurred. We all concurred that there must be a Police force (such as the Irish Constabulary) under the control of the Imperial Government to impose the law so far as it was not within the province of the Irish authority.[3]

According to Chamberlain, though Harcourt omits mention of the subject altogether, judges were 'to be appointed and paid by the Imperial Government as in the case of Canada'.[4] Nor was it stated that Customs and Excise were to remain in London's hands for the time being. This second point neither Chamberlain nor Harcourt include in their accounts. The subject must have come up and there seems no good reason for doubting Lewis Harcourt's account on this point.[5] If it is accurate a significant conclusion can be drawn. Not only had Chamberlain now got a satisfactory answer to question four, but to questions two and three in part as well.

Whether the Irish Legislature should be unicameral or bicameral was left undecided. All were agreed, however, that 'except for military' and naval 'organisation and the Imperial Police, there would be no necessity for any British administrator located in Ireland, but that Irish business, so far as it lay outside the powers of the Irish Govern-

[1] *Ibid.*
[2] *Ibid.*, and Gardiner, *op. cit.*, p. 27.
[3] *Ibid.*, and Gardiner, *op. cit.*, p. 28.
[4] Chamberlain, *op. cit.*, p. 250.
[5] Lewis Harcourt's *Journal*, 14th January 1887. Harcourt Papers. Parnell's desire for protection counted for even less with the Gladstonians at this stage than earlier on. In any case the Irish Nationalists as a whole cared little about it. For Parnell's views on protection see F. S. L. Lyons, 'The Economic Ideas of Parnell' in *Historical Studies II*, edited by Michael Roberts, pp. 60–78.

4. Sir William Harcourt, Kt.

5. Lord Randolph Churchill

ment might be transacted by a Department in London, i.e. by a Secretary of State or other official.[1] Harcourt's account of the talk on Chamberlain's first and most vital question was most garbled, although giving a correct version of the conclusion reached. One would never guess from it that he had come out in favour of allowing the Irish members to remain and vote on all questions. If Chamberlain is to be believed everyone else, including himself, disagreed, considering 'this would be impossible'.[2] Morley still stuck to his original line of exclusion, but found himself alone. What Harcourt did say was not without significance. He dealt with the mood if not the content of the discussion. 'Opinions did not run very strong either way on this point,' he thought, and told his son Chamberlain had not insisted.[3] Later on things were to change, with Morley threatening to leave public life in the event of retention. The mere fact of reservation at this stage pointed to the potentially explosive character of the subject. No realist could afford to regard lightly the fact it was not out of the way.

Severe friction did finally arise on the Ulster issue. Again Harcourt kept his comment to the minimum. Perhaps because of Gladstone's plea as to health. Chamberlain came out hot and strong on this point, sure in the knowledge that no Radical Unionist in Birmingham or elsewhere would take exception to his doing so. On the contrary it was almost certain to win him wide approval in all but the most steadfast Home Rule circles. 'He insisted *very strongly* on the danger and impolicy of forcing "Protestant Ulster" into the arrangement against its will and urged a separate system for Ulster.'[4] Herschell had the idea of the 'separation of certain Irish business and delegations to meet in Dublin for matters in which all Ireland was interested.'[5] Chamberlain himself thought an Ulster excluded from the Home Rule scheme could not remain linked with Britain in the same way as before and therefore proposed it should be given a separate legislature if the population so desired. As then advised he was sure it would be 'satisfied with and even prefer' a Provincial Council for local affairs.[6] One of the Gladstonians then argued that

> some power should be given to Ulster or to some part of Ulster to join the Southern legislature if desired. There might be, for instance, a

[1] Harcourt to Gladstone, 14th January 1887. Copy. Harcourt Papers. Gardiner, *op. cit.*, p. 28.

[2] Chamberlain, *op. cit.*, p. 250.

[3] Harcourt to Gladstone, 14th January 1887. Copy. Harcourt Papers. Gardiner, *op. cit.*, p. 28. Lewis Harcourt's *Journal*, 14th January 1887. Harcourt Papers.

[4] Harcourt to Gladstone, 14th January 1887. Copy. Harcourt Papers. Gardiner, *op. cit.*, p. 28.

[5] Chamberlain, *op. cit.*, p. 250.

[6] Lewis Harcourt's *Journal*, 14th January 1887. Harcourt Papers.

plebiscite of counties to decide whether they would belong to the Northern or Southern Provinces. The plebiscite might be either taken now or at the expiry of a fixed time.[1]

Harcourt maintained that the separation of North and South would involve immense difficulties. Morley proclaimed himself most anxious to consult with 'others' about the whole question. It was therefore put aside for later consideration.

Summing up the achievements of both sessions, Harcourt let his high state of euphoria lead him into a welter of inaccuracy and self-satisfaction.

I think you will be of opinion [he enthused] that in these two meetings we have made very substantial progress. We obtained the admission of all the *principles* for which we have contended. (1) That there is to be a Land Bill which is to transfer the land to the tenant, making an *Irish Local Authority* responsible for collecting and paying the equivalent of the rent to the landlord. (2) That there is to be a 'Provincial Irish Legislature' with an *Irish Executive*, for the transaction of such Irish business as Parliament shall determine, this business being in fact all Irish local affairs, due security being taken that their powers are not exceeded and that the authority of the Imperial Government in matters not transferred shall be respected and enforced. There are many details to be worked out, but it seems to me that we have got a great way in committing Chamberlain to these fundamental propositions (I should say that Trevelyan is far more recalcitrant than Chamberlain). Altogether I am very sanguine of arriving at conclusions which with some modifications you will be able to approve. We do not meet again till Parliament assembles, when we shall be able to consult with you.[2]

The descriptions of the principles were exact enough. What went wrong concerned the point of who gave way to who. Chamberlain had given way on the Leeds Resolution as then interpreted by the three Gladstonian representatives. This was far from the case on land. After all it was his scheme that the conference considered. Then to say details alone remained to be worked out when the question of Irish representation had been left in abeyance after an agreement to differ was just untrue. Nor was all this a specially contrived ploy to impress the G.O.M. Precisely the same sort of story was inflicted on Lewis Harcourt. Statesmen should not allow their 'bleeding hearts to run away with their bloody heads'. Harcourt should have taken a lesson from 'Our Joe'. *He* had not forgotten that part of the Leeds Resolution laying down the necessity of Parnell's approval and had as usual left a deep impression all round. Fear of what he would do next was as profound on his own as on the Gladstonian segment of

---

[1] *Ibid.* Probably Herschell, whose approach would be the most legalistic.
[2] Harcourt to Gladstone, 14th January 1887. Copy. Harcourt Papers.

the 'Round Table'. Pleasure at his being there was powerful on both. Trevelyan had been thoroughly shaken. Announcing his disagreement with what his leader had undertaken, he plaintively preached woe. It would seem to lead to separation 'directly and immediately'.[1] Morley, as 'nervous and suspicious' as ever, thought 'Joe' meant to 'bolt' on the Ulster question and 'break off on that when he wanted an excuse'.[2] Meanwhile the object of all this attention was busily engaged in 'foxing' up a letter to Hartington. In Harcourt's words, it informed him of what had occurred 'so far as' Chamberlain 'thought necessary'.[3] Nothing inaccurate was put down. The exercise came into the category of *suppressio veri, suggestio falsi*. Of the first day nothing was said except what concerned the land question. Local government and the talk about the letter to Labouchère, the Commons speech, Canada and the modified Leeds Resolution went unmentioned. Of the second a great deal on everything discussed except the crucial question of an executive. The word never cropped up once. A fact of which the writer was by no means unoblivious! One piece, while literally true gave an altogether false impression. 'The Constitutions of Canada (internal) and of the U.S.A. formed the basis of the discussion,' it ran, giving Hartington to understand that both had featured equally in the discussion. Whereas, of course, the latter had only cropped up once. The result was that the whole subject became infused with a convenient vagueness. Fuller elucidation was offered *tête-à-tête* at a forthcoming meeting, and the special nature of the extraordinary relationship obtaining between the leading Whig and Radical Unionists, the leader and deputy leader of what passed for one political party, was pinpointed by the last sentences. 'I assume that in no case would you think it necessary to give any information about the Conference to Goschen, I could not otherwise communicate fully with you.'[4] As if communication had been full! And what a tone to adopt! Imagine if Harcourt had told Gladstone 'Communicate with Labouchère and I am very much afraid you will have to remain in ignorance'. True Hartington's views on the definition of powers had weighed heavily with the conference. In effect this signified little, because they also happened to be Chamberlain's. The Liberal Unionist leader cut rather a forlorn figure in this matter. Having rejected the offer of participating, he paid the price. Unlike most of the right and centre of the Gladstonian Liberals and 'the Radical section of the Unionist group in particular', the Whigs and extreme Radicals had

[1] Lewis Harcourt's *Journal*, 14th January 1887. Harcourt Papers.
[2] Gardiner, *op. cit.*, p. 28.
[3] Harcourt to Gladstone, 13th January 1887. Gladstone Papers, Add. MS. 44201, f. 28.
[4] Chamberlain to Hartington, 14th January 1887. Devonshire Papers, 340, 2103.

not looked forward 'with eager anticipation to this Conference'.[1] Rather were they filled with the 'corresponding anxiety' paramount as the rumours proliferated about the goings on in Grafton Street among Conservative supporters.[2] Mundella repeated triumphantly to Leader a message sent him by Arnold Morley, a key doubting figure of the Gladstonian centre minority. 'The fates seem to be conspiring to crush Lord Salisbury and his Government.'[3] Certainly a change of tune. The actual sessions engendered in many a Gladstonian sceptic the sort of blithe enthusiasm Chamberlain's speech had evoked from Harcourt.

Originally Chamberlain had promised to go down to Malwood on the evening of the 14th. Later he changed his mind, thinking it necessary to dine with Randolph Churchill, who produced fascinating plans for making the Ministers' lives a burden to them.[4] Goschen especially had been singled out for attack. So vehement had he been that his guest came to think, or so he said, a little encouragement would induce an actual crossing of the floor of the House. From below the Liberal gangway sniping would be only too easy. Next morning further light was shed on what happened when Chamberlain called to see Dilke. 'Engaging frankness' was all the rage. Apparently, Churchill had gone so far as to ask: 'Shall I come over?' Dilke reported to his friend Chesson:

> Chamberlain had replied that he advised him not to, being afraid that Randolph would play for the lead of the party, and not liking the notion of having him for leader. He had advised Randolph to simulate moderation towards Lord Salisbury, in spite of his anger at the Duke of Norfolk and the members of the Conservative party who, since his quarrel with the Government, had been 'attacking his private character'.[5]

[1] J. Newton, *W. S. Caine*, p. 174.

[2] *Ibid.*

[3] Mundella to Messrs. Leader, 14th January 1887. Mundella–Leader Papers. By 1891 Churchill had rationalised the position so as to be able to tell Asquith: 'When I resigned, I should have beaten Lord Salisbury, as I confidently expected to do, but for their being able to fall back on Goschen.' J. A. Spender and C. Asquith, *Life of Lord Oxford and Asquith*, Vol. I, p. 51. This time Churchill was forgetting W. H. Smith, whom Salisbury had lined up to step into the Chancellorship of the Exchequer if Goschen declined to enter the government, and who did actually take on and make a tolerable job of being Leader of the Commons.

[4] Lewis Harcourt's *Journal*, 15th January 1887. Harcourt Papers.

[5] W. H. Chesson, at one time secretary of the 'Aborigines' Protection Society. Gwynn and Tuckwell, *op. cit.*, p. 267, While at Malwood on the evening of 15th January 1887 Chamberlain merely reported Churchill's feelings without adding any comment of his own, though the tone of Lewis Harcourt's *Journal* for that day suggests Chamberlain might well approve of Churchill's plan. There is, however, Lewis Harcourt's wishful thinking to bear in mind. This may have distorted his presentation of what Chamberlain said.

Not for the last time 'Our Joe' had striven hard to keep his friend in the wilderness. The two had not dined *à deux*. Brett had also been there. His letter to Buckle the next morning revealed how at the very time Chamberlain was advising Churchill to simulate moderation he was simulating belief in the conference and its works. The account ran:

> He was satisfied with the Conference. All the ground was traversed, and there was a complete interchange of views. Nothing was settled, but as the discussion proceeded, it distinctly ran along the grooves of *his* proposals, and not those of Mr Gladstone. There was no question of the old Bills, and there will be none.

A suitably phrased statement for his two particular listeners—optimistic yet vague. More was to come.

> Harcourt cynically throws over the whole scheme; no doubt with a light heart. He is determined to bring about an arrangement, and he is dragging Morley with him in the Conference. No doubt during the intervals of discussion Morley may swing back again under the influence of the Labouchère lot, whom he detests but fears.

Self-satisfied maybe, but devoid of euphoria. Brett had the definite impression that 'Joe' was 'pretty confident' a *modus vivendi* would be found, on the platform of a Land Bill *plus* local government. It might, however, take a little time to arrive at. The 'Round Tablers' were in no mind to hurry. 'Meanwhile, Chamberlain desires to keep the Government in office, and will so arrange that nothing can be settled by the Conference till well on into the session.'[1] Apparently Gladstone was said to be prepared to postpone all question of Home Rule until 1888. The story went he had told this to his friends. Daring to take charge of the conversation for once, Brett had dinned into his companions how unlikely this was to come about. 'I feel certain,' he had insisted, 'that if he sees his way to office, owing to the weakness of the Government, he will throw over the "Round Table" Conference, and go on with Morley, Parnell, and his old allies.' If, on the other hand, he saw no prospect of turning out the government, he would leave Harcourt and Chamberlain 'to settle anything they please'.[2] Meanwhile there was some prospect of a Coercion Act. Quite a lot for Buckle to digest at one go and a clear enough comment on Chamberlain's promise to tell no one but Hartington anything about the inside working of the conference. Once Brett knew, it was only a matter of a very short time before Goschen heard, and a hundred others too. Admonishing Hartington to silence had been superfluous and rendered so by Chamberlain himself.

[1] Brett to Buckle, 15th January 1887. Copy. Esher Papers. Part of this letter is presented as a memorandum in Esher, *op. cit.*, pp. 190–1.
[2] *Ibid.*

Dilke was given what amounted to almost the whole story. Scarcely a cat lurked in a single bag.

> From Chamberlain I heard that his view was to bring about a *modus vivendi* only, under which the Conservative Government was to be turned out on some side-issue. Mr Gladstone would become Prime Minister for the fourth time, if the Irish would consent to take Local Government and a Land Bill first, and to leave Home Rule over. He thought that Mr Gladstone was not unwilling, but that there would be difficulty in getting the Irish to consent. Morley and Harcourt were, according to Chamberlain, friendly to his suggestions, and Hartington hostile, not trusting Mr Gladstone.[1]

Mainly a lot of hot air, for Chamberlain knew full well the Irish Nationalists would put a very large spoke in the wheel when faced with such a proposal. So did Dilke, and realised that his friend was telling him through the bushes that the whole project was a piece of humbug. That knowledge almost amounted to the full story. Once appreciated, precise details about what had been said about the Canadian constitution because so much flotsam and jetsam on the sea of political impossibilities. All the same, Dilke was very probably aware of everything that had been said at both sessions. This is hinted at in the letter to his friend Chesson: 'Chamberlain and Morley were both going to make conciliatory speeches, but . . . nothing had really been done at Harcourt's house, every difficulty having been reserved.' He ventured to think: 'There could be no doubt that several of the five who were there meeting were anxious to keep things open, on the chance of Mr Gladstone not remaining in sufficiently good health to continue to lead the party.'[2] A plausible enough contention, backed by some show of proof. The comment Chamberlain actually made to him on the subject having been recorded. Another extant mention of it from that quarter is in a P.S. to Hartington of the day before: 'I hear that Mr Gladstone's illness is of some gravity.'[3] The significance of this is anyone's guess.

The most revealing part of this 'long and curious conversation with Chamberlain' came towards its end. Speaking through bushes was abandoned. Seldom can there have been such a frank piece of self-revelation in the history of modern party politics. Dilke summed it up:

> He said that the articles which had been appearing in the *Birmingham Post* about his own position were inspired by him—that he and the other members of the Conference were telling the newspapers that everything was going on swimmingly, but that the whole thing was in reality a sham

[1] Gwynn and Tuckwell, *op. cit.*, p. 266.
[2] *Ibid.*, pp. 266–7.
[3] Chamberlain to Hartington, 14th January 1887. Devonshire Papers, 340.2103.

on both sides. Parnell was frightened at Mr Gladstone's declining health, and Mr Gladstone did not wish to end his life by having smashed his party, so that the Conference was willingly continued, although it was doing nothing.

Then came the partial proof of Dilke's hunch. 'It was the wish of all concerned in it to be at the point of an apparent reconciliation whenever Mr Gladstone might become incapacitated, but he, Chamberlain, was firmly decided not to take office under Gladstone.'[1] Bold and to the point though all this was, it characteristically stopped short of revealing all. While saying the conference was a sham on both sides, he gave the reasons motivating one side—the Gladstonian—and both sides, yet made no reference to those peculiar to the Radical Unionists or him personally. To be fair, he pointed to them through the admission of 'foxing' through the columns of his local newspaper. A statement as crystal clear as the bulk of what he had said was nevertheless lacking.

Next he moved on to Devonshire House and had a short interview with Hartington. However much new information was passed on, it included no crucial revelations. Chamberlain had adjusted his tongue to suit the scene. No response 'of a positive character' was evoked, though the 'tone and attitude were not hostile'.[2] The fact was the situation demanded nothing else. All Hartington had to do was wait and see. Given his convictions there was, anyway, nothing else open to him. His deputy enjoyed what amounted to full independence due to the 'Grand Duchy' of Birmingham, and present developments looked like consolidating it whichever way they finally turned out.

Granville's hope for an amicable atmosphere at the 'Round Table' had been fulfilled. Harcourt's for high cordiality at Malwood equally so. Yet with an important difference. The personnel was much reduced—no Herschell, no Morley and no Trevelyan. Only Morley's absence really mattered, but it mattered a lot. 'Joe' continued to play his little game to great effect. Harcourt continued his ready response. How much could it all come to, however, without the imprimatur of a sceptic? At the New Year James had been told how after the conference the 'Round Table' would be going to Malwood, where Harcourt hoped that he (James) would 'one day sit at it to settle the details of Home Rule . . . '. 'Let us both be happy in the belief that we are each right and both about to win'.[3] By the time Chamberlain left on Monday the 17th all this seemed virtually on the verge of coming true. Austen Chamberlain accompanied his father on the

[1] Gwynn and Tuckwell, *op. cit.*, p. 267.

[2] Harcourt to Gladstone, 18th January 1887. Gladstone Papers, Add. MS. 44201, f. 48.

[3] Gardiner, *op. cit.*, p. 26.

visit. The two did not travel down with their hosts, who preceded them by two or three hours. 'Joe' was in high spirits, and full of chaff and good humour. He affected to be intensely delighted at Goschen's having entered the government, ridiculing the idea of his being able to maintain what he termed 'the absurd position of a Liberal in a reactionary Tory Government'. Taking the line of 'in for a penny in for a pound' he actually went so far as to intimate that 'he would not weep if Goschen was beaten at Liverpool'. Even the Harcourts did not swallow that one, thinking it seemed 'hardly possible'. 'Loulou' gave further proof of shrewd judgment in noting that while Austen[1] appeared deeply interested in politics, he did not speak 'as if his father talked to him much of the things of the inner circle'. Either 'Joe' carried the rule of trusting no one right to his fireside, or his son was a chip off the old block, playing canny before an onslaught of aristocratic charm and indiscretion. Keeping one's mouth shut could easily have been a compulsory game in the nursery at Highbury. Probably the former represented the actual situation, Austen had an altogether more open temperament than his father.[1]

On the Sunday the hosts skipped church in deference to the feelings of their guests. After lunch the two proud parents drove out in a pony trap by themselves in order to talk about the conference. Everything was given a thorough going over. Chamberlain carried it off very well, convincing his companion of the absence of self-seeking and solicitude as to his own position in the affair. The fundamental principle of 'an Irish legislature with an Executive dependent upon it, accompanied by specific limitations of its functions with proper securities for the central authority in Imperial affairs' was once more unequivocally accepted. Chamberlain being prepared to face the widespread and bitter attacks from 'his recent allies', particularly 'the Hartington section' which would throw previous pronouncements in his teeth. He was by that time practically inured to avalanches of 'reproach and abuse'. The Gladstonians had given him plenty of experience. Moreover, as Harcourt himself said, he had 'plenty of pluck in such matters'. Not surprisingly, Trevelyan cropped up at this point. Was his dissension on the problem to have any effect? Chamberlain perhaps more than the Gladstonians resented this 'deviation'. First, he disliked and despised 'his coadjutor the

[1] Austen Chamberlain (1863–1937) was not yet an M.P. As is clear from his *Down the Years*, pp. 28-9 he was passing a few months in England at this time between being a student in Paris and one in Berlin. He had gone to Paris after leaving Cambridge in 1885 and left in February 1887 for Berlin. A splendid drawing in Sir Henry Lucy's *Peeps at Politics*, opposite p. 92, brings out the personal and political relationship between the two Chamberlains, father and son, very well, though, of course, it applied to a later period. It would probably be a mistake, however, to regard that relationship as fundamentally different at this early stage.

Baronet'; and second had never wanted him at the conference. Impatient as ever of those striking him as fools, he assured Harcourt 'no attention' would be paid to such 'hesitancy'. Just to make sure his copy book should have no blots, the story of refusing 'to have anything to do with a Hartington–Salisbury combination, with or without Randolph' was trotted out by way of preface to an account of the latest encounter at Devonshire House. The version now produced claimed the land and Home Rule projects were outlined without provoking any 'decided negative'. 'On the whole he did not derive the impression that the Marquis was in a hostile humour, or showed any annoyance at the Conference, and that his sentiments were rather those of weariness than of antagonism.' A most gratifying piece of news to Harcourt, who naturally supposed the dependence of the executive had been included in the 'outline'. Almost equally heartening was the news that James, H. Brand, Caine and Hussey Vivian were 'all strong for accommodation'. A joint examination of the list of the 'principal dissentients' revealed, at least to the satisfaction of those making it, 'only Albert Grey and Courtney and perhaps Craig Sellar' as decisively against it. And they were of little account, being respectively 'an amiable goose', 'a crotcheteer', and 'a cantankerous Scotchman' and therefore to be 'written off'.[1]

Happy at the prospect before them, the pair next 'went over again all the points discussed in Grafton Street'. Chamberlain did not try to back down 'on any of the questions . . . deemed vital'. 'As to Land, he was very reasonable. He declared that he had no *amour propre* which induced him to insist on his own scheme, but was very urgent' that if Herschell and Morley 'could not approve his plan', Morley should 'suggest some other'. Settlement of the question 'somehow or other' was 'of the highest importance'. Common sense strongly supported Harcourt's contention that failure to collect the rents might

---

[1] H. Brand had told for the Liberal Unionists, along with Caine, in the crucial division of June 1886—hence the phrase 'The brand of Caine'. Born in 1841, he had served as Surveyor-General of Ordnance in Gladstone's second ministry from 1883 on. At the time of the Home Rule Bill he had been Liberal M.P. for Stroud, but in the 1886 general election had unsuccessfully contested Cardiff as a Liberal Unionist. His inclination was strongly for Liberal reunion. His father died in 1892 and he succeeded as the 2nd Viscount Hampden. Three years later he went out to New South Wales as Governor, but returned to Britain in 1899. He died in 1906.

Sir H. Hussey Vivian (1821–94) sat for Swansea District as a Liberal Unionist. He proved rather a restive supporter and soon afterwards reverted to Gladstonianism. Although an Anglican he favoured Welsh disestablishment. In June 1887 Gladstone came to his home at Singleton Abbey near Swansea and addressed a mass meeting. The G.O.M. handled the disestablishment issue very gingerly and filled in with a giant panegyric of Welsh nationality.

A Craig Sellar (1835–1890) was Liberal Unionist M.P. for Partick and a party whip 1886–8.

lose the 'Imperial Exchequer' all the taxes paid into the Land Bank bound for the pockets of the landowners. Chamberlain was consequently prepared to give up his idea of 'making the *whole* taxation of Ireland a security for the rents'. It had only been 'adopted at Herschell's instance'. Instead two millions of local taxation 'should be paid in as a collateral security'. The problem of adjusting rents in the event of 'a further permanent fall in prices' was also discussed, Chamberlain again adopting Harcourt's views. These treated the matter as 'Rent Commutation', using methods identical to those employed in 'Tithe Commutation'. The annual payment was to be based 'on an annual produce rent say of three years' prices'. Telling Morley about it two days later, Harcourt appealed to him and Herschell not to be 'too *cassant*' in their criticisms. 'It will be time enough to demonstrate ... weaknesses later, and it is by no means desirable to come to issue upon this part of the business till we have progressed further with the rest.' 'Foxing' so intensively over a long period of time must inevitably have been severely taxing for a man of Chamberlain's type. The talk about land came as something of a relief each time it was raised, requiring nothing more than genuine candour. Honesty is the best policy for the nerves. Moreover, stretches of truth helped give authenticity to the less 'frank' exchanges. With true flexibility of discussion the chances of producing something good largely increased and the resulting satisfaction was bound to soften Harcourt's attitude to his friend.

Home Rule plans remained very much as on the 14th. Chamberlain stood his ground over the Canadian and American education analogy on the problem of abuse of powers for the benefit of a particular class or sect; insisted, Harcourt agreeing, on 'the exclusion of the nomination of judges'; and was willing to reserve the Justice of the Peace issue. Over police matters the two were at one on the local force being controlled by County Boards, but Chamberlain allowed Harcourt to think he was the keener of the two on the necessity for an Imperial force to cope with enforcement of Imperial powers and abuses of provincial ones. They both thought the 'Superior Court' for deciding *ultra vires* cases should be a specially constituted committee of the Judicial Committee of the Privy Council. On the subject of 'Irish Executive Departments dependent upon the Irish Legislature, including an Irish Home Office', the Unionist once more admitted the Home Rule principle. This time, however, he did attempt to introduce 'a disposition to some fixed term of official tenure after the American plan'. Harcourt tried to squash that one, but without success. Chamberlain undoubtedly felt his apostasy had limits, even in a secret discussion. Finance, the Lord Lieutenant and Irish Department in London caused no real dissension. On the second, Harcourt again seemed more Unionist than the Unionist, regarding the post as indispensable to the efficient exercise of British power.

Of the two fundamental questions reserved by the 'Round Table' conference in plenary session, Ulster was far and away the more difficult as between the New Foresters. Indeed the presence of the Irish members at Westminster scarcely provoked an animated argument at all. Chamberlain inclined towards admission generally upon all non-Irish questions '*in parimateria* with the subjects delegated to the Irish Parliament'. The Speaker was to decide as to what came within this category and when the members were to withdraw. Harcourt was in a quandary. Though even more opposed than Morley to their presence in any circumstances, he was for practical purposes prepared 'to admit them without reservation'. 'Goodwill' made him realise some sort of attendance was bound to be inherent in any *modus vivendi* involving Chamberlain. Observation told him considerable sections of the Gladstonian party favoured it. How to apply the precept was the major problem and, failing any satisfactory solution, he was forced back to general admission. Morley alone remained obdurate and he was not at Malwood.

Nothing further was settled about Ulster, but Chamberlain went to some pains to dispel any notion of his wishing to break up the Conference on that question. Nor did he contend that the population should be able to insist upon the *status quo* when the rest of Ireland began to enjoy Home Rule. In fact all he did was to repeat his arguments of two days before. Harcourt was the one to give a little ground. The powerful feeling among Radical Unionists was not lost on him. As with the members there would be no satisfactory outcome to the talks without some concession on the Gladstonian side. The alarm in North-East Ireland, unreasonable though it might be, still had to be appeased.

> It is quite plain [he recounted to Morley] that this strong prejudice must be reckoned with and somehow or other met. Without this there could be no hope of pacifying the Hartingtonians or Scotchmen. I feel all the practical difficulties of the exclusion, in whole or in part, of Ulster from the Irish Legislature, but I feel the force of what Chamberlain says, that if in the present state of opinion we hand them over to a Parnellite Government, there will inevitably be a row à la Randolph. We must therefore strain all our mental resources to find out some *modus vivendi* on this subject.

The difficulty of putting the Chamberlainite partition into operation would, of course, have proved immensely testing. The Irish party had too often been forgotten amidst the varying zests for Liberal reunion. In the pony cart the rural surroundings doubtless revived an acute awareness of that essentially agrarian body. At any rate their likely reactions to the secession of the Ulstermen were at that moment foremost in Harcourt's mind. Optimism did not desert him. He viewed the situation with the conviction that men, Irishmen, were rational beings. A solution was therefore not beyond their devising. 'Mr Parnell would be a greater fool than I take him to be if he preferred to lose nine-tenths rather than compromise as to this question.' The basic supposition and the reckoning of proportions might be open to serious question, but he at least remained confident.

The two companions were sufficiently confident as to discuss what exactly was to be done 'in the event of agreement amongst ourselves'. Both thought it best that Gladstone call the party together with the cooperation of Chamberlain and the Radical Unionists and 'state the general outlines of our agreement'. A more detailed memorandum of the subject matter was simultaneously to be drawn up for the future use of 'Round Tablers'. Chamberlain appeared eager for that meeting to come about at the earliest possible opportunity, but before anything of that sort had time to happen there was the certain prospect of another meeting before him. On the 22nd, he would be speaking at Hawick for Trevelyan. Cancellation was this time quite impossible. The nature of the occasion forbade it. His 'coadjutor's' former constituents in the Border Burghs were to make their defeated member a presentation. In doubt as to what he should say, and out to please, he consulted his companion, telling him his plan was to go into some detail about the land question, leaving Home Rule over until a speech at Birmingham on the 29th. Without hesitation Harcourt pointed out how mischievous this would be to the prospects of the conference. The Gladstonian party would presume the rumours that Home Rule had been dropped were only too true and that would be 'fatal' to its representatives. Better not to enter into details on any debatable issues, later adjustment would be rendered all the more difficult. All-round outline coverage was essential—land, local government and the legislature. Chamberlain assented, saying the motive behind his suggestion had been a desire to avoid putting himself 'in the attitude, by shading out the lines of the Conference, to appear to be laying claim in the future' to having 'originated the "Revised Version"' and having 'imposed it on Mr Gladstone'. He was quite willing to acknowledge all the concessions he had himself made. This Harcourt deemed 'creditable', and either failed, or refused to see how desperately the leader of Radical Unionism was groping about to save himself from a trap largely of his own making. Had Harcourt fallen in with the plan of ignoring Home Rule the incompatibility of being openly an undeviating Unionist and secretly a Home Ruler new style would not have emerged. Now the plan was rejected, Chamberlain had either to break up the conference by adhering to it, or spill some beans of a rather broad variety. The broader the better, because the Home Ruler principle and that of Provincial Councils had to sound like one and the same thing. It had been infinitely easier to carry out that same act the year before. Then there was a definite Gladstonian Home Rule measure before Parliament. The term Home Rule was universally interpreted as meaning that particular brand of Home Rule. Anybody believing in anything else was automatically dubbed a Unionist. For that reason it had been a comparatively simple matter for Chamberlain to skip in and out of a different Home Rule position without changing his label. In 1887 the whole scene had changed. He had promised Hartington no pledge had been given at the 'Round Table' committing Radical Unionism to any form of legislature for Ireland possessed of an executive dependent upon it. That was not the case and Harcourt expected what had transpired to be revealed as far as basic principles went. Unionism had come to exclude Home Rule of any real kind. Provincial Councils were its furthest semi-official limit, and the boundary stones had embarrass-ingly clear inscriptions at the Chatsworth-Rossendale end of the de-marcation line.[1]

Those anxious for the form of Home Rule approved of in Birming-ham at the famous meeting of 21st April 1886 might well find them-selves willy nilly in the Gladstonian camp if the G.O.M. adopted something approaching it. Or, a helpless and unheeded minority in a Unionist camp weakened by their 'deviationism'! The only com-pensating factor would be that they were neither helpless or unheeded on most other issues. Their attraction to the floating voter being enough to carry weight in Whig and Conservative circles alike. Chamberlain's choice of which way he would go—Unionist or Glad-stonian—had been recreated by his antics at the conference. A false move at Hawick and one of three misfortunes might fall upon him, two of them destroying this choice once again. First, the disapproval of both sides might rise to dangerous heights. This would mean any chance of returning to the Gladstonian fold would disappear and the trust placed in him by Hartington become severely attenuated. Rela-tions with the Birmingham Conservatives would be likely to undergo a serious deterioration. A factor never to be discounted, for upon their goodwill or forbearance some of Chamberlain's henchmen depended for their seats in the Commons. Second, the Gladstonians would be angry and third, the Unionists would be; thus creating in each case the relevant part of the situation brought about under hypothesis one.

[1] This account of the Malwood visit is based upon Lewis Harcourt's *Journal* for the 15th and 16th January 1887 (Harcourt Papers) and Gardiner, *op. cit.*, Appendix I, Rossendale was Hartington's constituency in Lancashire.

The chances of escape were further threatened by Harcourt's insistence that 'if he was to say anything on the subject at all, it had better be made conspicuous that he had accepted our principle of Home Rule'. Temporarily caught for the first time the young 'fox' had no alternative but to assent, observing 'very truly' that he 'must prepare his friends for the fact some time or other and might as well do so at once, as if he produced an opposite impression now it would be the worse for him in the future'. His friend was sympathetic. 'It is no doubt a difficult job for him, but he is ingenious enough and will no doubt find his way out somehow or other'.[1] Never was a truer word spoken, but the way out was to be a far less obvious one than Harcourt ever envisaged. 'Our Joe' was to outstrip Delphi and gain himself a breathing space. It was to last a week.

About Churchill becoming a Liberal, Harcourt and his guest saw eye to eye, though not for the same reasons. The Gladstonian feared for his party, not for the effects on his personal advancement. 'May God defend us from such a Coriolanus! He is far more profitable where he is as a thorn in the side of his former friends than he would be in our camp.'[2] On the line to be taken with the press there was complete accord. Everyone was to be given to understand that the whole Irish question had been covered without prejudicing in any way the 'good hopes of a favourable conclusion to the Conference'. Jogging away in that little pony and trap everything seemed so easy. The political world would soon be set to rights with Liberalism triumphant, for with the help of a 'merciful Providence' only 'duffers' could lose the day. For Harcourt that pony seemed the Pegasus and that trap the Chariot of Victory granted by the gods for luring back the brilliant apostate. At breakfast the next morning the task seemed done. 'Well,' said Chamberlain, 'if the Party is reunited and the nett result of last year's Home Rule Bill has been to drive Goschen over to the Tories, I do not feel sure that the game has not been worth the candle'. Afterwards signs of the 'Old Adam' were only too clear to see. When the moment came for signing the visitors' book 'Loulou' jokingly remarked: 'Mr Chamberlain, this is a good opportunity for you to turn over a new leaf.' Back came the answer in a flash. 'I am hanged if I will do anything of the kind.' The great name was then inscribed along the edge of the full sheet. Truly, its owner 'never felt less like surrender'.[3]

Up at Hawarden there had been no joy rides. The G.O.M. had spent the weekend digesting the reports of the conference and writing his impressions to Harcourt. While approving the postponement of

[1] Gardiner, *op. cit.*, Appendix I.
[2] *Ibid.*
[3] Lewis Harcourt's *Journal*, 17th January 1887. Harcourt Papers.

further sessions until the meeting of Parliament, as avoiding embarrassment and 'giving a fresh point of departure', and finding in the 'tone and manner' of the discussions a source of the 'liveliest pleasure', he did not expect much to result from what had or would occur at the 'Round Table',

> Notwithstanding the evident disposition to approximation, I do not venture on so extraordinary an exploit as a treaty, made in opposition, at the present stage, which shall cut all the knots of the Land and Irish Government Bills and carry the late Cabinet, the party and the Irish nation.[1]

A 'friendly attitude' would have to be the sum total of Harcourt's labours. However unridiculous the mice, they could not breed mountains. Two of them in the pony cart had plumped for the G.O.M.'s

---

[1] Gladstone to Harcourt, 16th January 1887. Harcourt Papers. Sir H. Maxwell would have thought Gladstone unduly cautious and modest. His assessment was that in January 1887 'it seemed as if "the old parliamentary hand" was on the point of winning back the allegiance of half the Liberal Unionists.' But then, Gladstone's judgment was so much the better. Maxwell, *op. cit.*, p. 288. Meanwhile Professor Goldwin Smith was lamenting to Milner: 'The people are evidently possessed with the idea that some alternative to Gladstone's scheme must be proposed and the Irish have a real grievance in the necessity of coming to Westminster for all their Private Bill legislation.' He went on, as was usually his custom to suggest a remedy: 'Why not make the Irish members, both in the Lords and Commons, a Grand Committee for Irish Private Bill legislation and let them *sit at Dublin in the recess*, Parliament in the ensuing Session passing the Bills on their report? This, unlike an Irish Parliament however restricted, would be perfectly safe; because as the Committee would be appointed from Session to Session, if it grew factious its existence could be brought to an end by simply omitting to reappoint it. At the same time a sop would be given to the fancy for an Irish Parliament in College Green. The Opposition might fairly be asked to try this limited and practical expedient before launching the country into revolution. As I thought at the time our victory of the summer was a "Quatre Bras", not a "Waterloo": and the "Waterloo" now seems to be at hand.' After an offer to help and be at 'Waterloo', he continued in a postscript: 'I need not tell you how glad I was that Goschen joined the Government. His doing this may really be the saving of the nation. I trust before this reaches you he will be member for Liverpool, though I cannot help fearing the influence of Randolph Churchill. I took that fellow's measure correctly.' (Goldwin Smith to Milner, 15th January 1887. Milner Papers.) Goldwin Smith (1823–1910) had been Regius Professor of History at Oxford, 1858–66. During the United States civil war he had been a great champion of the 'Unionist' North and after a spell at Cornell settled down in Canada in 1871. His Unionism was equally ardent when the United Kingdom stood in danger from Irish Nationalists and this despite his very radical views on domestic policies.

Sir Edward Hamilton was not feeling so complimentary towards Goschen. For him the new minister was a 'Cavendish footman dressed up in Cecil livery'. The peace parleys interested him more. He understood the preliminary exchanges had been 'satisfactory and promising'. At all events nothing but friendliness had been displayed. Sir Edward Hamilton's Diary, 16th January 1887, Add. MS. 48645, p. 83.

calling a party meeting in the event of success, dismissing as premature any attempt then and there to introduce a Home Rule Bill into
Parliament. Until some substantial settlement was made there was
'no chance of Chamberlain, or any of his friends acting with' the
Gladstonians 'so as to disturb the present Government.[1] Gladstone
was more realistic, assessing party strengths with the unerring judgment of 'an old parliamentary hand'.

> But now supposing [he argued] we had got such Bills as would at any
> rate assure the late Cabinet and no breach with Ireland: what should we
> do with them? We should still be a rather small minority of the House.
> Would not the prudent course even then be to see what the Government
> had to produce.[2]

In other words the government could not be disturbed and lacking
the power to overturn it, why should the opposition commit itself?
The Hartingtonians would remain loyal to Salisbury. No amount of
Harcourtian optimism could persuade his leader of the real likelihood
of 'common counsels' between Chamberlain and the Whig Liberal
Unionists, and pending the advent of an opening for real power the
Gladstonians and Chamberlainites, albeit in agreement, would do
better to lie doggo.

The incredulity and common sense underlying these comments did
the Liberal 'Chief' more credit than those he made before the conference met. Then he had created excuses. Now he faced what he
rightly adjudged to be the facts. Sheer accommodation, very welcome
though it was, could well lead to folly. Doubts about the prospective
efficacy of the projected Irish County Boards were legitimate enough
and a natural manifestation of his quest after quality. There was no
carping element marring the honesty of his opinion. As far as he
knew there was now nothing in theory to prevent an entente with
Chamberlain on the principle of Home Rule. Experience simply made
it seem impossible of attainment. If success was potentially possible,
Gladstone was now ready to consider it—coercion or no coercion.
His comments were not all negative by any means. 'The subject of
Land', for example, struck him as being 'in a fair way for effectual
testing, and Chamberlain's acceptance of a 'Statutory Parliament for
Ireland with a responsible Executive' as a 'great point gained'. On
Ulster his views lacked realism in one sense, yet had it in another.
Prejudice in favour of a united independent Ireland led him to an
underestimation of Protestant Ulster's will to fight and be right.
Understanding of Parnell and the National party created in him a

---

[1] Harcourt to Gladstone, 18th January 1887. Gladstone Papers, Add. MS.
44201, f. 48.
[2] Gladstone to Harcourt, 16th January 1887. Harcourt Papers.

6. William Ewart Gladstone

7. John Morley (Later Viscount Morley)

strong conviction partition would not prove an acceptable solution. 'I do not think our agreeing, if we could agree would much advance the matter. Our bid last April for plans of severance had no sequel of any kind and the idea seemed stillborn.' With the conferring of powers problem he adopted what might have been a somewhat disingenuous line, agreeing with Sir Charles Russell that it was all a matter of drafting. That his authority was legal did not rule out the danger of special pleading. The Canadians would not have accepted such an explanation and he knew it, asking whether Chamberlain realised its truth and concluding this could not be so. Had not Harcourt's letter spoken of 'such Irish business as Parliament shall determine' and 'this business being in fact all Irish local affairs'?[1] The G.O.M. was the most wilful of men, liking the idea of Chamberlain conceding to him, yet hating the reverse process. Where he could wriggle back to his particular nostrum he would. On Westminster representation, magistrates and customs and excise he saw no way through. With Ulster and government powers he did. Egoism and genuine conviction combined to impel him forward. At this time more than at any other in the 'Round Table' phase the 'wrecker' outlook was quiescent. For the moment he was actually nonplussed. Cerebrally Chamberlain had 'foxed' him. Intuition alone remained to trouble the serenity of his thoughts. Was 'Our Joe' honest? That went 'to the quick of the text'.

During the pre-conference period Harcourt had stuck to his plans with all the persistence of a limpet. Events had now justified this course and the last thing he had in mind was any abandonment of it. His 'Chief''s' letter did not suggest doing so, but one from Morley, dated the 17th, was anything but encouraging.[2] Gladstone had sent him a copy of the comments on the conference. Oddly enough he found 'some of it less lucid and transparent than it might have been'. Oddly, because it was one of the more simple productions from the supreme Liberal pen. Or perhaps the whole point was to tilt at Harcourt, for there was no mystery about the matter upon which Morley purported to be mystified. County Government in Ireland appeared in both the Chamberlain and Harcourt versions of the first conference session as absolutely common ground. The subject was not one over which either man was prone to get excited or be tempted into distortion, yet Morley now asked whether there had been the unanimous

---

[1] *Ibid.* Ripon was very anxious lest 'Joe' should prevail. Writing to Morley on 17th January 1887 he came straight to the point: 'I hope you are holding firm in your conferences with Chamberlain and Trevelyan; we must not "climb down", as the Yankees say. Liberal reunion is a very good thing, but adherence to principle is much better. I have complete confidence in you, but I cannot say so much for your colleagues.' L. Wolf, *Life of Lord Ripon*, Vol. II, p. 191.

[2] Morley to Harcourt, 17th January 1887. Harcourt Papers.

approval of the scheme the text of the letter implied. He thought not and claimed not to know what exactly had occurred.

> Would you object to telling me what you said on the point? I hope I am not taken to have assented to everything from which I did not openly dissent. Am I taken, for instance, to have agreed to copy exactly the limitations of the Canadian provincial legislatures? I trust not.[1]

Now this was nothing less than downright dishonesty. Morley had not kept silence on other points, Westminster representation for instance, upon which he thought differently from the rest of the team. Why then had he not spoken up on the local government issue in the same way? Surely because he had nothing he felt it imperative to say? In fact, that he concurred in the general recommendation? The conference was a serious bid to reunite the Liberal party. Silence on any subject requiring discussion was dereliction of duty. Here that was not the problem. What then was the explanation? Very probably nothing less than 'follow the leader'. Gladstone had fought shy of County Boards so he did as well. The worry on the Canadian point probably had the same origin. It had been perfectly clear the provincial constitutions were being taken by the conference as an analogy not a model, but the leader hankered after notions of defining the Imperial powers and leaving the residue to the Home Rule administration, and therefore his disciple followed suit. That was not all. Two notes to Harcourt within the next twenty-four hours confirmed this recalcitrant trend.[2] Gladstone's caution would appear to have released all Morley's pent up discontent. The shock of Chamberlain's complaisance had temporarily put him off his stroke. Now the effect was wearing off and the old suspicion and dislike welled up whether he would or not. Things had seemed 'more satisfactory' than he had hoped, or, deep down inside, really wanted, to judge from the rest of the first communication and all the second. A malicious delight dominated his thinking about Chamberlain's plight, backed by the conviction that it would prove too much for him to bear. 'It will, however, tax our good friend's adroitness and resource to get out of his scrape without more humiliation than he will take. The Coercion Bill won't make it pleasanter for him to stay in the Tory camp.' Clearly he expected an explosion at Hawick, for his suggestion was that speaking to the press had better wait until after 'Saturday's speech'. As for coercion without remedial measures, it had to be fought 'with tooth and claw'. Evictions had proved a blessing to the Home Rule cause because through them the system coercion would defend had been and would continue

---

[1] *Ibid.*
[2] Morley to Harcourt, 18th January 1887, No. 1. Morley to Harcourt, 18th January 1887, No. 2. Harcourt Papers.

to be reduced to 'its naked elements'.[1] Paradoxically, during his week-end at Sandringham, the Prince of Wales's good natured enquiries about the conference had drawn from him the remark that it would be 'a great success'.[2] Diplomatic camouflage of the same kind as that in store for the press.

The second dose was a much more considered effort, conceived of during a post-prandial digestive hour. First, he found Harcourt's claim about Chamberlain's disinterestedness quite ludicrous, remaining 'utterly and incorrigibly incredulous' about it. In his opinion that statesman had now found out that 'his egotism, irascibility and perversity have landed him in a vile mess. Those noble qualities' were 'only scotched not killed'. He had 'proved himself to have no wisdom and no temper'. Far from a fair comment in view of the 'sweet reasonableness' 'foxing' had called for and Chamberlain had provided at both conference sessions. To say *c'est fini* of his statesmanship was wishful thinking as much as anything.[3] Not that Morley was failing or intended to fail in his duty. 'I will,' he promised, 'carefully comply with your request to consider his feelings as to the Land Question.' But there were limits and on the appointment of judges he had ideas of his own. 'He insists on the exclusion of the nomination of Judges'—that is by the Irish government to be—'*I do not agree*'. Secure in the feeling that the G.O.M. would be behind him, Morley waxed eloquent on 'the part that the Judges have played in the past bedevilment of Ireland'. The Nationalists would never consent to leaving their appointment in London's hands. And anyway, how would it be done?

> Is the Irish Minister not to choose his own Chancellor? Is the Attorney-General to have no claim to promotion to the Bench? We either appoint Judges in harmony with the wishes of the Irish Government or not. If we do, why not let the Irish Government appoint direct? If not, there will be incessant antagonism between the Bench and the whole array of (nominally) Crown Counsel, etc. Parnell will say, and, in my opinion, will be perfectly right in saying—that no man in his senses would undertake to be responsible for order if he were dependent upon the British Government.[4]

There was no denying this went to 'the quick of the text'. Harcourt must have felt his labours were ending in smoke. Yet no, for in the

[1] Morley to Harcourt, 18th January 1887, No. 1. Harcourt Papers.
[2] *Ibid.*
[3] For a profoundly different appraisal of Chamberlain's character by an even more prejudiced party see Sir Henry Lucy, *Sixty Years in the Wilderness*, p. 252. An appreciation by Austen Chamberlain is to be found on pp. 252–4 of the same work.
[4] Morley to Harcourt, 18th January 1887, No. 2. Harcourt Papers.

next remarks Morley reverted once more to the tone of conciliation. They concerned the need for having a big man on the spot in Dublin, something Chamberlain had eventually agreed to and the whole conference regarded as settled. By way of conclusion he touched upon the two great reserved questions. 'On the . . . points of the presence of Irish members and of Ulster—I can only say that on the first I am open to anything that Chamberlain or anyone else has to propose.' An attitude not adhered to under the stresses and strains of public 'discussion'. 'On the second, I do not as yet see my way to any compromise, nor do I much expect to see it. The more I think of it, the more averse I am to any premature publication of the banns. Let us wait for his deliverance on Saturday.'[1] Unpromising though the overriding sentiment of Morley's pronouncements were, it needed a great deal more to destroy Harcourt's will to win through. He met the latest developments with his usual good humour.

Humour and humouring in fact, impregnating with an appearance of concurrence what amounted to flat contradictions of what Morley had said. On the 18th a letter went off disposing of the first attempted backsliding.[2] It cost nothing to accept the criticism of Gladstone's clarity, particularly when a sly suggestion that the old man had deliberately sought refuge in the opaque could be slipped in. The conference decisions were quite a different proposition. Harcourt was standing for no nonsense.

> What I reported on Local Government was to the effect that having discussed at some length the Land Question (which I said you and Herschell were examining) we went on to Home Rule, passing over Local Government with only slight discussion, as we were generally agreed that Local Government in Ireland must proceed on much the same lines as that in England; viz. County Boards, popularly elected. Was not that a correct account of what occurred?

Having started an effective counter-attack, he pressed home his advantage with a sugary incomprehension.

> I do not understand that anyone was supposed to be bound to the precise limitations of powers in the Canadian Constitution, either more or less, but only that this might be taken as a sort of *analogue* of the relations of the subordinate Legislature. It has the great advantage that it presents a door of escape for J.C. and will help him against his allies who want to pin him to declarations against a separate Legislature with an Executive dependent upon it.

A well handled argument, for it stated no more than the facts, yet indicated a political duty. Morley had nothing positive to go on

[1] *Ibid.*
[2] Harcourt to Morley, 18th January 1887. Copy. Harcourt Papers.

against Chamberlain and Harcourt was allowing no sloppy thinking about constitutions, nor indulgence of personal feelings.

> Please tell me what are the powers you think the Irish Parliament should have which the Provincial Legislature in Canada has not. I remember when I observed on Friday that we had largely contracted the powers of the Irish Parliament as compared with Gladstone's Bill, I was told that was not so and that the Canadian model would give quite as much. Look through the attributions of the Dominion Parliament and see if you think any of them ought to be given to the Irish Parliament.[1]

A capital hit to which Morley had no answer. 'Foxing' was not his forte. Left to the masters it was a potent weapon. In his hands it turned to dust. There was no room in this game for *les renards de l'escalier*.

The next day Harcourt tackled his victim in two stages. The first coped with note one; the second with note two. Both were sent under the same cover.[2] Pleased with the unanswerable case made in the last reply he began by a legpull. He chose to regard note one as 'amusing', and rejoiced in the success of 'the Apostle to the Genteel' at Sandringham. His Royal Highness was 'a capital gossip' and would buzz a sanguine view of the conference abroad in the quarters where it would be most useful. In this relaxed mood a little sarcasm at 'Joe's' expense crept in. The Prince would probably tell Hartington 'a good deal more than he knew before'. As with Gladstone in a difficult phase, so now Harcourt worked round to the nub of the dispute with infinite caution. In condemning evictions and entering into the spirit of Morley's hatred of coercion he managed to slip in a good opinion of Chamberlain.

> We must resist Coercion *pur et simple* and I expect in spite of his loose talk J.C. feels in his inmost heart he cannot support it. Indeed he told me that he had remonstrated against it in his communication with the Government. I expect the near prospect of this question will greatly confirm him in his present disposition.

The likelihood was in other words that he would adhere to his pro-Gladstonian course and cut the ground from beneath the feet of his enemies, among whom Morley was secretly proud to count himself. Through a clever change of emphasis, however, Harcourt conveyed what he knew very well would warm the cockles of that enemy's heart—namely the notion that Chamberlain was being treated as an inferior force. 'I strongly impressed upon him that the success or failure of the Conference in the future will greatly depend on the line he holds next Saturday and that if he plays for his own hand alone he

---

[1] *Ibid.*
[2] Harcourt to Morley, 19th January 1887. Copy. Harcourt Papers.

will lose the game.' He conceded a delay in inspiring the press should be made and confessed the only thing that stuck in his gizzard was 'that indigestable lump of foreign matter—Ulster'. Presumably the great difficulty was that the 'Patriots' wanted to get hold of the Protestant money.

Then note two was brought in and after reading it carefully through Harcourt let fly. Like many a genial man he was prone to short sharp outbursts of temper. This time Morley had got into serious trouble.

> It seems to me as if the genial influence of Sandringham had evaporated and that you were suffering under the fogs of London. Indeed, according to my diagnosis you have contracted a conference intermittent fever and have alternatively a hot and cold fit. To my mind the least helpful part of our business consists in your incurable inveteracy against J. Chamberlain. I believe it to be unjust, but I despair of the task of convincing you of it. I, however, abide by my own opinion and shall not change it till I have some good reason which I do not find at present. All the points on which you dwell in your second letter seem very fairly open to discussion and I do not know that I seriously differ from you on them, except perhaps the Judges.

The storm had gone as quickly as it had come, and while Morley was right to be suspicious he made a false move in using foolish arguments. Only 'some good reason' would convince his colleague and frivolous behaviour opened him to the charge of wrecking the reunion prospects. If Chamberlain was a false friend positive acts of this kind would obscure the fact and possibly enable him to escape scot free from blame. Nevertheless 'Honest John' was on that same day running down the man who had once been his closest friend to a quarter gasping for grounds to justify its feelings. That quarter was, of course, Hawarden.

Already on the 18th a letter had left Malwood bound for Highbury.[1] In it were good wishes and good news. The visit had proved a great success. Whatever had actually been contributed to 'the great objects . . . in view', both guest and host could take satisfaction in mutual goodwill. Comment on Gladstone's response to Harcourt's conference report was disingenuous in a way different from that tried out on Morley. There was no mention of obscurity. On the contrary everything was supposedly crystal clear: ' "The Old Man is Friendly" and is generally quite as favourable to what we have done as I could wish.' Assuming 'could' has its usual meaning in this context the passage is a piece of flannel to encourage the appropriate sort of things to

[1] Harcourt to Chamberlain, 18th January 1887. Chamberlain Papers, JC5/38/60.

emerge on the crucial platform at Hawick four days hence. The element of uncertainty and probable hostility in his 'Chief's' attitude Harcourt dismissed as caution over details, pending further explanations during the coming week. Whether he could continue to 'augur very favourably from the whole tone' of that vital letter would inevitably depend on many things, including Chamberlain's visit to Trevelyan. To suit the moment, convenience demanded something approaching a simplicist mode of argument, and this Harcourt went on to employ. 'I shall be very anxious on the subject of your Hawick speech, for I cannot but feel that the future fortunes of our Conference will greatly depend on the impression you produce by it.' Trevelyan himself was about to return to Highbury a paper on Chamberlain's land scheme handed to him for appraisal by Herschell. The cavalier treatment meted out to him by his fellow Unionist did not seem to have produced a jaundiced view of its merits. His whole tone was infused with friendship and enthusiasm.

> You certainly gave me a very complete 'apercu' of the scheme and I am getting much more hopeful about it. The result of the tremendous strength of the party of authority, which we have not, I fancy, fully tested yet, gives a strong 'point d'appui' for a scheme of this sort. It will give it time to work.[1]

There was no sign here of a waning Unionism. Indeed he went beyond approval of the land scheme to optimism about the popularity of the conference in the North-East, which though the most 'Home Ruly' region in England was said to be 'setting quietly and steadily in favour of it'. If he was right Newcastle was not representative of its hinterland, or Spence Watson and his 'wirepullers' had a good many snapped connections—their hostile sound and fury signifying little. Unhappily for the 'Round Table' idea, he was very probably mistaken.

The reply to Harcourt from Chamberlain was a small masterpiece.[2] The Hawick knot was not to be cut, but carefully and deftly unloosed.

> I share your anxiety as to Hawick [he wrote with greater truth than his 'pen friend' could appreciate], but hope that I have hit upon a line which will completely satisfy you. I shall repudiate warmly any idea of concession of principles by *either* side, and I shall try and show from the public declarations of all parties that there is a general agreement with Mr Gladstone's main principle and that the only difference has been on matters which he has never declared to be fundamental.

[1] Trevelyan to Chamberlain, 19th January 1887. Chamberlain Papers, JC5/70/23.

[2] Chamberlain to Harcourt, 20th January 1887. Harcourt Papers.

This was taking a leaf out of the G.O.M.'s book with a vengeance. Everyone agreed to Home Rule really; the trouble all sprang from some curious and superficial misunderstanding. Fundamentally it was just a semantic challenge easily soluble by the best brains on both, or on all sides. At heart even Goschen was at one with Davitt. Precisely the smooth-tongued method Gladstone had employed to pick his way through the ferocious forests and fever-ridden swamps of Liberal Unionist dissidence. Having given the Gladstonians their principle, Chamberlain denied them the glory of it.

> I shall urge a national rather than a party settlement of the question. This is for the benefit of Hartington and those Liberal Unionists who do not like to 'desert' the Tories. How the Tories will like the idea remains to be seen, but it is strictly on the lines of Mr Gladstone's appeal to them before he took office.

Again the Hawarden line of earlier on was being invoked. This time as a deliberate move to ensure the blockage of a national settlement. When baulked, Chamberlain would be able to plead impracticality as a ground for ratting on the principle the rightness of which he had just so loudly proclaimed. So far the Whig Liberal Unionist leader had greeted reunion projects much in the spirit of Kryler's cook in the fable of his cat Vaska, who 'listened, but went on eating'. The national settlement idea would certainly leave him cold. As for the Conservatives; they would laugh it out of court.

Nor were the Radical Unionists generally so soft as might be supposed. W. S. Caine had returned to Britain on the 11th and straightway set about arranging a meeting in his constituency at Barrow-in-Furness to discuss the current political situation. To it he proposed inviting all the leading Liberal Unionists and Gladstonians, though the latter would not be offered 'much comfort for their souls'.[1] The Conservatives were not to be there, but he intended saying all he could in favour of the government and stating plainly his intention of supporting it until the Cabinet gave 'serious cause for opposition'. Coercion and evictions held no terrors for him. Only war proposals of which there seemed scant likelihood would alienate his support. Discussing the 'Round Table' notion with his association chairman, he declared:

> There is no Liberal reunion possible at present, though we need not say so in public—the Liberal Unionists have such a rooted distrust of Gladstone that I can see no hope myself of our getting together till he is out of the way as an alternative to Lord Salisbury.[2]

[1] W. S. Caine to J. Fell, 20th January 1887. Barrow Election Papers. Lancashire County Records, C.19, DDFe/1. J. Fell was his association chairman.
[2] *Ibid.*

In Birmingham the Dale group hoped for reunion, but only on a Chamberlainite basis. If that was obviously made impossible by the Gladstonian 'rooted distrust' of 'Our Joe', he would be in the clear within his base and could revert to a full scale hostility to Gladstone with impunity. Elsewhere Radical Unionism tended to side with Caine and share his trust in its leader. 'You need be under no apprehension about Chamberlain: *he* won't sell the pass' was the confident opinion he held on the 20th.[1] He proposed to take Hawick in his stride. 'Joe' could speak there knowing his 'give and take away' arguments would not alienate his own particular wing of Liberal Unionism. Given its approval he could remain a fully effective national figure in a way Churchill could not.

Chamberlain's arguments struck Harcourt as 'enigmatical'[2] and in no way allayed his anxiety about the speech. A copy of the letter was sent off to Hawarden and Elm Park Gardens with appropriate comments. Gladstone was told of the dire warnings despatched to Highbury.[3] The text of the speech would provide a commentary on the letter. Morley was informed of how he would place the worst and Harcourt the best interpretation on what was an 'interesting note'.[4] No immediate response on the point came from the 'Chief', but his disciple insisted that, far from thinking the best or the worst, he was enjoying a condition of profound equanimity. An unusual state for him it must be said. Perhaps due to the fact that Parnell, who a week before had apparently expressed himself anxious for an interview with Chamberlain, had ultimately drawn back. Brett thought the reason for this shift was the Irish leader's reluctance to upset Morley, who would undoubtedly have resented any such development. Parnell had made the excuse of 'thinking the matter over', though it was 'clearly ascertained' that his anxiety for a settlement would have led him to 'accept almost anything to which Mr Gladstone' had agreed. There was no doubt in Brett's mind that: 'He [Parnell] knows that if he desires a settlement, he must impress the above fact sternly upon Morley.'[5] Inside information on the Morley–Parnell conversations and correspondence at this time is virtually non-existent, but the former certainly always rushed forward rather gladly with the objections he considered the Nationalists would make, and there is no denying the essential correctness from a long-term view of his judgments. At the same time Parnell himself could temporarily have adopted the attitude of mind Harcourt attributed to

[1] *Ibid.*
[2] Harcourt to Gladstone, 21st January 1887. Gladstone Papers, Add. MS. 44201, f. 55.
[3] *Ibid.*
[4] Harcourt to Morley, 21st January 1887. Copy. Harcourt Papers.
[5] Esher, *op. cit.*, pp. 193–4.

him and decided to opt for 'jam today'. But even had Morley done nothing, withdrawal from that policy was really inevitable once it was apparent important sections of the Gladstonians were opposed to any compromise. The Irish only gave ground for tactical reasons and naturally reoccupied their original position if and when the opportunity presented itself. They would, moreover, have militated against a compromise almost as soon as the ink was dry upon the paper.

Gladstone was certainly convinced the conference would fail because his first Home Rule Bill had itself been on the verge of the 'irreducible minimum', and wrote as much to Morley.[1] The financial side he found especially worrying, because no provisions for this as satisfactory as those previously incorporated in a concomitant Land Bill could be devised without laying hold of all Irish public receipts and making Irish success depend on a surplus. A passion for his own ideas was growing daily. It almost seemed as though he welcomed the prospect of political and technical blockages, and for the same reasons as this particular correspondent. To Harcourt he held different language.[2]

> Your estimate of Chamberlain's temper is fully confirmed by what reaches me through another completely independent and not political channel. I do not, however, venture to wind myself up to the point of *confidently* expecting an immediate agreement upon all the main points which severed us last year from the Dissentient wing.

[1] Gladstone to Morley, Draft, 21st January 1887. Gladstone Papers, Add. MS. 44255, f. 184.

[2] Gladstone to Harcourt, 21st January 1887. Harcourt Papers. One of Milner's correspondents, writing on 21st January 1887 laid great stress upon the need for the government to be prodded into making some very necessary reforms. 'Give Goschen the tip,' he commanded, 'to run the word "integrity"—it is the word for our cause; and if it ends in our being called the 'Grits'—*tant mieux*. Also—my old boy—believe and preach that we are not going to win by standing still. Is there a Criminal Law Procedure Reform Act in preparation? Have the County Courts power to suspend a judgment or have they not? Are they mere Courts of Registry without a discretion? Are they exercising their discretion? Things are 'blue' to my regard just now. Goschen must not be discredited. He must *insist* on the changes which are necessary to make the law just and humane and judgement effective. If I were in power I would enforce the law to the uttermost: for all that it is easy to see that it is uneven and discredited and I would put its reform before anything.' P. W. G. to Milner, 21st January 1887. Milner Papers.

That Gladstone was very much on the *qui vive* is illustrated by the way he scolded Bryce on 21st January for having implied in a piece of written work of a historical nature that the authority attaching to those of his lieutenants like Bright and Hartington, who had rebelled over Home Rule, was as great as that enjoyed by those who had not. See Gladstone to Bryce, 21st January 1887. Bryce Papers. The G.O.M. was determined that no passes should be sold. He was even more determined none should be given away.

A hit directed at the incurable high spirits evinced both at Malwood and in Grafton Street. From that point on the old man seemed to show an eagerness to evade responsibility and slow down the pace of general change. The possible arrival of 'a great Hermaion' through a compromise on Home Rule had awakened the horror he felt at the onset of 'Constructionism'. He had gathered from Harcourt how unwilling Chamberlain was to cooperate with the Gladstonians in promoting measures of Liberal policy until a concordat on Home Rule had been arrived at, or at least that the reverse could not be assumed. If this was so, he raised no complaint as long as there was no other alternative to the Conservative government than the resuscitation of the last Gladstone one. Once more the attractions of Whiggery as a shield from Chamberlain and his 'metropolis of reckless expenditure' had caught hold of his imagination. (The more so as Churchill was now an 'unbound' advocate of the same evil, despite the nature of his resignation.)

> It appears to me, however [he rationalised], that if we suppose such a casualty to have arrived, say from some accidental cause as the downfall of the Salisbury Government, it would be Hartington's duty to try, and the duty of the Tories, especially after what he has lately done, to support him. Had I my choice as to the best course of affairs for an eventual settlement I should like to see the present Government work out its experiment in its own way, and then, on its failure, that the Dissentients should also have a chance. The Dissent has been accompanied with needless animosities, but it has been on a matter of substance hard, tough and big, and it may require a good deal of the teaching of experience to bring *all* the parties whose concurrence is necessary, into such a ripeness of views as may be absolutely necessary in order to enable them to agree.[1]

So, for the sake of the intrinsic merits of the old Home Rule formula and the stoppage created in domestic legislation through the domination of politics by the Irish question, the conference ought to fail, and Hartington become premier should Salisbury fall by the wayside. The 'old Fox' did not on this occasion beat about the bush.

> Another week will probably show us what at the moment is of the utmost importance, namely the shape in which the first issues are likely to be raised. I do not desire a forward policy at once for our party (which R. Churchill may seek to promote) and very much less for myself; but coercion, or the evictions, or other matters, may bring about results not within the circle of our computations.[2]

Actually nothing was more in his computations than these very things. Upon them he relied for the realisation of his great passion and the

[1] *Ibid.*
[2] *Ibid.*

ruin of his great hate. While the Gladstonians were in opposition the new-found predominance of the Radicals resulting from the Whig secession could not break loose. Should they come to power on a wave of indignation about coercion and evictions the way would again be blocked. At all costs therefore, for a man with Gladstone's priorities, the conference had to fail and Ireland hold the stage. All he had to say about the coming events at Hawick was that the 'speech tomorrow will be interesting'. Thus passed the eve of Hawick day.

VI

GYRATIONS GALORE: JOSEPH CHAMBERLAIN PROVOKES AND SOOTHES

'A soft answer turneth away wrath.' Proverbs xv. 1.
'Heap coals of fire upon his head.' Proverbs xxv. 22.
'Hope deferred maketh the heart sick.' Proverbs xiii. 12.

O N the morning of the 22nd an extraordinary diversion from domestic politics arose from the announcement in the *Daily News* that France and Germany were on the verge of war and might well involve the whole continent in their quarrels.[1] Otherwise the meeting that day would have been followed with an even greater attention than in fact it was. The joint appearance of the two Unionist 'Round Tablers' at that point in the reunion proceedings was commonly held to indicate a readiness to sink the known differences between them in their attitude to Gladstonian Home Rule for the sake of a common end. Being the *raison d'être* of the whole affair it was only right that Trevelyan should have spoken first. His speech was predominantly nostalgic, though in it were plenty of lessons for application to the contemporary scene. Unity in the past had brought immense achievements. Now the power of the Liberals for good was temporarily shattered. There was no prospect of things mending until they came to some agreement among themselves.

The public men who dissented from the majority of their party did not go out lightly. They gave up office, seats in Parliament, popularity, old associations, political and social; and, having made this great sacrifice for the sake of honour and conscience, you may be sure that they will never even be tempted to surrender honour and conscience for the sake of getting back what they have lost.

[1] *Daily News*, 22nd January 1887.

237

Brave words, followed by a clear-cut rejection of the idea that anything but a modification of the Gladstonian Home Rule scheme in
'vitally important' particulars would satisfy him, and, he thought,
countless other Liberals. Among these Liberals were large numbers
of those who had voted Gladstonian in the 1886 general election. Of
the loss of Goschen he spoke without regret, regarding his crossing
the floor of the House as an act of 'the most perfect propriety'. The
truest test of Liberalism at that moment was a desire to see the party
reunited. Like Caine he was fully alive to the sentimental attraction
of Irish injustices, but claimed the Irish party made things far worse
through an instrument such as the 'Plan of Campaign'. Towards the
end of his speech he made a point which, a year before, would have
been quite ridiculous. Chamberlain and himself, he claimed, were
representatives of the old Liberal party. The idea of Radical Liberals
of their brands as old Liberals was now sound enough. New Liberals
were to Trevelyan a bad thing by definition, for they were the ultra-
Home Rule Radicals of the Labouchère ilk, whose hatred for Chamberlain and reunion he found so unreasonable and disloyal.

By contrast Chamberlain spoke predominantly about the present
and future, sticking in essence to the plan outlined to Harcourt. No
one was going to forsake fundamental principles.

> There are some [he explained] who say that no compromise can be
> allowed, no settlement take place, unless Mr Gladstone retires from the
> leadership of the Liberal party and confesses the errors he has com-
> mitted. There are others who declare that no arrangement of any kind
> should be listened to unless Sir George Trevelyan and myself are
> sufficiently contrite and humble; and unless we recant our heresy we are
> not to be allowed, we are not to be received into the arms of those
> gentlemen who are generally very sincere politicians. Gentlemen, I shall
> not break any confidence at all when I tell you that no such pretension
> as this by either side has entered or will enter into the deliberations, into
> the proceedings of our friendly discussion.

Fully aware that success at the 'Round Table' meant only half the
task of reunion was accomplished, he nevertheless faced the prospect
of convincing others 'more influential than we are' with confidence.
'May it not be possible even now at this last moment to arrange a
national settlement of what is after all a national difficulty' and put a
stop to Ireland being the sport of parties and politicians? As for the
land question, the answer lay in owner occupation by the peasantry.
The financial risk of any scheme should be borne, not as in Gladstone's
late attempt by the Imperial Exchequer, but by those at present bearing the final brunt of economic hazard—the landlords. Useful though
the Ashbourne Act had been, its voluntary and restricted nature made
it unsuitable for the future.

238

Turning to the central political problem at issue over Ireland, he proceeded to argue that reforming Unionism must inevitably end up by adopting some sort of legislature for Ireland. Conservatives might think the Gladstonian guarantees inadequate. Even so, some measure of autonomy satisfactory to all parties was bound to emerge. 'Every one of the conditions laid down by Lord Hartington would be met by the adoption or by the adaptation of the internal Constitution of Canada.' After discussing the strict delegation of powers and the control of justice by the Federal government, he passed on to ask whether the Nationalist party would accept a proposal of this kind. Parnell had not said he would not, and Justin McCarthy, his deputy, had definitely said he would. Here his self-control weakened somewhat and there followed a searing attack on 'the noisy ranters who have obtained a temporary popularity by abusing us', but the mood soon passed. Under the circumstances outlined he was hopeful a happy family could soon be restored. Should a workable scheme be elaborated after

> full and public discussion (because no man supposes that anything which may be decided in secret conclave can be accepted without the fullest public criticism and public sanction)—if such a plan should be ultimately elaborated, if it should commend itself to the majority of the English and Scotch people, if it should satisfy the demands of patriotic and fair-minded Irishmen,

he hoped that 'the Irish people' would give it 'an impartial and a calm examination'; and if they approved of it he would not allow anybody 'to stand between them and the boon which was so freely offered to them'.[1]

What the speech of 23rd December had begun this one helped quite considerably to continue. One of the commonest mistakes historians tend to make is to neglect the variations of fortune in particular historical processes. Whatever their final outcome, it is all too often assumed everything was developing in that direction the whole time. The essentially erratic nature of so many of them being largely ignored, alarming distortions often come to dominate the assessments arrived at. This whole saga of the attempted Liberal reunion demands a highly developed sense of day to day change. Although Gladstone and Chamberlain did not envisage surrender, one or both of them could have been trapped and forced to recognise

---

[1] *Observer*, 23rd January 1887. *The Times*, 24th January 1887. Justin McCarthy (1830–1912) was deputy leader of the Irish Nationalist party, but a man of mild disposition and marked literary tastes. He sat in the House of Commons for Newry. At the time of the split in the Nationalist party over Parnell's divorce case he led the Anti-Parnellite majority group and continued to do so until 1896. His literary output was enormous.

that the hounds of conciliation were capable of running a 'fox' to earth. The public had been waiting to see what exactly Chamberlain would say with a much greater interest than it had shown just before Christmas. Then he had to comment on a situation made by someone else. Now the situation was one in which he was a prime, and for the moment the prime mover. Once the war scare shock had worn off thoughts were riveted on Hawick.

The speaker himself was anxious to gauge reactions, particularly in that quarter where he knew full well his future would ultimately lie—the Liberal Unionist party. He accordingly wrote off to Hartington on the Sunday morning from Highbury, where he had returned without delay.[1] Both the leader and the 'Grand Duchy' were rapidly to be sounded out. Making the despatch of a copy of his land scheme, lately returned by Trevelyan, the pretext for his letter, he went almost straightway to the matter on which he wanted reassurance.

> I hope you will approve of my speech at Hawick last night. I have tried to say sweet things all round, except to the Parnellites. The audience took my reference to yourself very kindly. I really believe that they think you are a Liberal after all! I knew from Harcourt that the 'Old Man' continues very friendly.

Then, without revealing anything of note he went on to mention developments during the Malwood visit, ending by enjoining a continued secrecy. The change in tone betokened a lessening of self-confidence. Had he convinced others in the ways most necessary to the implementation of his wishes? In a short time the answer would be his. Nevertheless, he tried to elicit a rapid response from the one source prone to delay and to him most vital of all, apart from his 'Grand Ducal' 'subjects'.

A 'vile' report in the *Observer* that day did not obscure from the Harcourts that everything had gone according to plan.[2] Morley was also embarrassed into satisfaction 'as far as the badness of the report allowed him to understand it'.[3] A fortunate thing, for he was due to write the article for Monday's *Daily News*.[4] Harcourt too reserved his comment until Monday, but committed it to his usual personal letter.[5] Sitting in the Reform Club, he could feel a quiet satisfaction that his friend had performed a very difficult task 'with great skill and ability'. The tone had, he thought, been 'well-fitted for the atmosphere of conciliation with one exception', which was to be regretted.

---

[1] Chamberlain to Hartington, 23rd January 1887. Devonshire Papers, 340. 2108.
[2] Lewis Harcourt's *Journal*, 23rd January 1887. Harcourt Papers.
[3] *Ibid.*   [4] *Ibid.*
[5] Harcourt to Chamberlain, 24th January 1887. Chamberlain Papers. JC5/38/60.

8. Farrer Herschell, Baron Herschell

9. Sir George Otto Trevelyan, Bt.

That exception was, of course, the strong language used about 'the Irishmen'. Private enjoyment should not come first when political issues hung in the balance. 'They may deserve it, but it is no good exasperating people who after all must be parties to any settlement which is made and to irritate them is to make a settlement more difficult.' There was no need to tell Chamberlain this. The insult to the Nationalists was just a part of the emotional sop thrown to the Whigs and Conservatives to compensate for the adoption of the self-government idea. What Harcourt missed in his reliance on the words 'internal Constitution of Canada' was the fact that at no stage of the proceedings had the words 'independent legislature with an executive dependent upon it' been used. So adroit had Chamberlain been beforehand, in telling both Gladstonians and Unionists what he would actually be meaning, that everyone, Gladstone and Morley included, gave everything he said the meaning they wanted to find in it. How ironical then that this letter should end: 'Hartington will have a difficult job at Newcastle next Saturday. He will find it hard to agree with you and awkward to disagree. I hear rumours that he is to leave our Bench, but whether for the other side of the House or not I know not.' Difficulty there would be, yet not for the reason Harcourt had primarily in mind. Gladstone was sent a shorter version of the Hawick impressions, though the same points were made.[1] On the subject of Hartington his deputy was quite unable to 'understand' how he could consider 'in any event his formation of an Administration possible', for: 'Who would join it if the Salisbury lot were turned out?' Nobody that he could see except James, Albert Grey and Heneage. 'Hardly a strong Cabinet'. . . . Another matter concerning Hartington and the Liberal unity question cropped up in both letters. The Gladstonians had caused some annoyance in Liberal Unionist circles by sending to all 'Dissentient' members of both Houses a circular announcing the opening of Parliament. Such a response boded ill for a national solution of the Irish issue. Refusal to recognise a formal link with Gladstone was nothing compared with what Chamberlain was asking.

The press was nothing if not generous in the attention given to the occasion. Generally speaking, both in London and Dublin there was a good deal of scepticism about the national settlement idea. Needless to say, loads of positive hostility poured from the Nationalist press, condemning the whole performance. Elsewhere comment almost invariably contained elements of doubt. *The Times* wrote:

> Mr Chamberlain's bias is very strongly on the side of comprehension, and we think that it has led him to overlook or underrate some real

[1] Harcourt to Gladstone, 24th January 1887. Gladstone Papers, Add. MS. 44201, f. 59.

difficulties, and to deal with the subject too much as if human conduct were wholly governed by pure reason. If land is to be first dealt with, we have to reckon with the National League, and the primary problem remains just what it is at this moment—how to make the law respected and to protect the honest and law-abiding. Mr Chamberlain does not refer to this difficulty, or to the divergence of opinion which it excites, yet his programme does nothing whatever to turn it. Mr Chamberlain's programme has only to be taken seriously, and seriously thought out, to bring us back to the old question—Are you going to make imperial law absolute in Ireland or are you not? If that question is answered in the affirmative, then, but not before, we get a basis for Mr Chamberlain's procedure. Unless the National League is put down and the law vindicated Mr Chamberlain's constructive legislation is morally impossible, while Mr Gladstone's destructive legislation is morally easy and nearly inevitable. That is the dominant fact of the situation, which we very seriously commend to Mr Chamberlain's attention.[1]

The *Standard*, 'which all along took a wider view of the duties of England towards Ireland' than Printing House Square, thought:

> Mr Chamberlain is either in pursuit of a shadow, or he is actuated by some *arrière pensée* which it is not expedient to declare. Suppose, for the sake of argument, that the whole body of Scotch and English members could agree upon some Irish measure such as Mr Chamberlain sees in his dreams, and that Mr Gladstone were willing to abandon all his ideas of Home Rule, what would happen? The Bill would be passed. Parties would revert to their original attitudes, and in a little while, perhaps, British parties would be fairly equal, faced by an Irish contingent of sixty or seventy as discontented as ever. We should then have our work to do over again, and have had all our trouble for nothing. We do not, therefore, believe that a compromise on the Irish question would end in any permanent reunion of the Liberals.[2]

Neither of these journals wanted the projected reunion, so their judgments were not likely to be olympian. 'Chamberlain the dreamer' was a new one. Nothing so cosy had been used to describe his support of the more idyllic portions of the 'Unauthorised Programme'. Yet even under the restraint of a partial alliance the Conservative editor went one further and talked of *arrière pensée*. Hawick represented the very furthest anyone could go and still retain the goodwill of the Unionist side. Chamberlain knew this—hence his letter to Hartington; and one to Bunce on the 25th, the day after the splash in the newspapers.[3] The Birmingham editor had approved of what he said, but it was necessary to warn him there might have to be a change of

[1] *The Times*, 24th January 1887.
[2] *Standard*, 24th January 1887.
[3] Chamberlain to Bunce, 25th January 1887. Copy. Chamberlain Papers, JC5/8/89.

tone, and, indeed, of action. Labouchère on one side and the Conservatives on the other would between them facilitate 'Joe's' path towards ending reunion efforts. Bunce and his like had to be convinced. For them the whole 'foxing' operation had largely been staged. This latest small contribution was well up to standard.

> Many thanks for your note. It is most difficult to speak usefully at such a time and perhaps it is almost too much to hope for such a patriotic combination as I have suggested. You see how the matter is treated by Labouchère and *hoc genus omne*. They want confusion and anarchy, and unless the moderate men on both sides speak out boldly and clearly we shall be condemned to a long period of Tory reaction, and I think I shall retire altogether from public life. I have no pleasure in supporting Tories, but I am not going to sacrifice the true interests of the country, even to reunite the Liberal Party.[1]

The appeal to stay in national public life that would inevitably follow could now be answered favourably on the condition that prolonged support of the government should be in order. Bunce was being manoeuvred into a neat little trap.

Morley in the *Daily News* of the 24th had really let himself go and embarked upon a rapturous effusion.[2]

> The past is gone [he trilled] and we are glad to recognise the new tone. The triumph of Mr Gladstone's principle, which Mr Chamberlain declares he never repudiated, and which he now again cheerfully professes, is assured with time. Mr Chamberlain in his speech contributed points to the discussion which deserve consideration. But the most important for the day is his recognition of the impossibility of remaining where we are. We shall soon learn whether Lord Hartington is inclined to take the same line. If not, the speeches at Hawick mark the beginning of the disintegration of Liberal Unionism, and once begun it must inevitably be rapid.

A degree of exhilaration not calculated to obviate 'Joe's' determination to keep in with Hartington.

In Ireland the Nationalists' principal organ, the *Freeman's Journal*, believed:

> Both Sir George Trevelyan and Mr Chamberlain appear to have moved forward since last year. They have not advanced far enough, and we cannot see how the bulk of the Liberal party can accept the terms of reconciliation specified by Mr Chamberlain without abandoning the principles that they have pledged themselves to maintain. It is better that Home Rule should be delayed for twenty years, if needs be, rather than that it should be a farce. We say advisedly that such local autonomy as Mr Chamberlain professes himself willing to concede could never be

---

[1] *Ibid.*
[2] *Daily News*, 24th January 1887.

accepted as a final settlement by the Irish people. If this is his last word, better fight the issue out on the lines laid down if it costs us years of suffering and turmoil.[1]

Nothing could have suited 'Our Joe' better than a fierce onslaught from this quarter. He had, of course, done his best to invite it through abusing the Irishmen and implying they should have what a united British opinion and an Irish minority thought was good for them. With an emotional outrage of such magnitude to overcome it was not surprising the reaction took a strongly hostile form. The mood of indignation led to a narrow interpretation of the ambiguities others saw as generous gestures. Birmingham and the men of 'goodwill' would naturally view the attack as shabby treatment, proving once more the iniquities of the Irish and the unsullied virtues of 'Our Joe'. To gain the plaudits of the *Daily News* and the abuse of the *Freeman's Journal* was something only an exceptional man could have pulled off. It said a lot for the skilful emotional construction of the Hawick speech. At Birmingham on the following Saturday the next thrilling instalment was to consolidate the security of the 'New Machiavelli'.

The two leading Irish Unionist papers differed in their appraisals. One —the *Irish Times* was hopeful.

> Matters at this moment are well controlled by the coalition, and if Mr Chamberlain were to triumph in his undertaking of bringing the Liberal party together again upon a plan of modified local government, a government applicable equally to England, Scotland, and Ireland in its safest form, there would still remain, we believe, sufficient of a coalition in the constituencies and among the public to ensure that the plan would be well considered.[2]

Again an interesting reaction, for it assumed a national settlement would automatically rule out anything so grand as the Gladstonian conception of a legislature with a responsible executive. The other journal—the *Dublin Express* was very much more down to earth.

> In the face of Mr Sexton's declaration that nothing but independence will satisfy the Irish, Mr Chamberlain would be more sanguine and less cool-headed than he is reputed to be if he long indulged in a hope that his compromise would solve the Irish difficulty and be accepted as a final settlement.[3]

Another example of 'Chamberlain the dreamer' approach, couched in more tactful terms.

[1] *Freeman's Journal*, 24th January 1887.
[2] *Irish Times*, 24th January 1887.
[3] *Dublin Express*, 24th January 1887. Thomas Sexton (1848–1932) Irish Nationalist M.P. for Belfast: West.

Replying to Harcourt's congratulations, Chamberlain showed he was very much awake.[1] To Bunce the dangers of the Labouchère gang had been played up. To his Gladstonian friend those of the Conservatives were stressed. 'I am glad you are not dissatisfied. It really is most difficult to speak at all at such a time and I think that you must allow that the comments of the Tory press show that I have leaned as far as was possible in the direction of concession.' Then the attack upon the Nationalists was passed off as self-defence—a natural human frailty.

As to the Irish, please bear in mind that I am only human. The brutes have been abusing and insulting me up to the very last moment and nothing will induce me to turn the other cheek to the smiter. If you want me to be civil to them you must bring pressure to bear on them to treat me with ordinary courtesy.

A difficult answer to counter, whatever its motive, because the essential justice of the main point was beyond dispute. A man of 'good-will' had to admit this, and the request for pressure on Parnell only underlined the fact of Nationalist independence and the very limited effect Chamberlainite restraint could have. The old act of the injured party still had a power in it not to be neglected.

This aspect of the affair caused Harcourt no great worry. About the time when Chamberlain was sending to him, he was forwarding a verbatim copy of his friend's speech to Carlton House Terrace, ready for the G.O.M.'s arrival there at teatime on that day—the 25th. That evening he was able to put into the post for Birmingham a note reporting that at a personal interview Gladstone had expressed himself highly satisfied with the speech, showing how favourably the outlines of the land scheme had impressed him. Apparently the condemnation of the Ashbourne Act had gone down very well and the 'Old Man' was '*most* friendly'.[2] Quite the most significant event since Chamberlain had spoken was not the writing of a letter or the words of a conversation, but the making of another speech. Competing with Hawick for press space it came off badly, the *Daily News* alone giving it much space. On Sunday, at a Gladstonian conference in Cardiff,

[1] Chamberlain to Harcourt, 25th January 1887. Harcourt Papers.

[2] Harcourt to Chamberlain, 25th January 1887. Chamberlain Papers, JC5/38/61. Sir Edward Hamilton's comment on Hawick ran: 'Trevelyan and Chamberlain spoke the other day at Hawick, fresh from the "Round Table" conference. There was evident intention of conciliation. Chamberlain was civil to Mr Gladstone and complimentary to Hartington.' He had apparently forgotten 'his fears of two years ago of being tarred with the Whig brush' and his text had been 'compulsory settlement of the Land Question and a national settlement of the government issue'. 'Is it feasible?' Hamilton asked. Sir Edward Hamilton's Diary, 25th January 1887. Add. MS. 48645, p. 88. He discounted 'rumours of war' launched by the *Daily News. Ibid.*

Mundella had gone out of his way to state that his party would not abandon 'the grand central principle of Home Rule as agreed upon at Leeds'.[1] This more than anything else was the answer to Chamberlain. Labouchère's spite in *Truth* later in the week was so much superfluous verbiage. The answer itself was only necessary for the public. On the 26th Chamberlain made no mention of it to Collings, contenting himself with passing on Harcourt's message about Gladstone.[2]

At eleven o'clock that night the news of Goschen's defeat in the by-election at Liverpool: Exchange became known, not only to Lord Camperdown's assembly of Liberal Unionist members of both Houses gathered together for a preview of the Queen's Speech but to Harcourt at Brooks's, where he and Gladstone had dined together. The G.O.M. had already retired and so missed all the excitement. For his deputy the night was just beginning. Along with an exulting Morley, he 'sallied forth and trampled upon the Whigs', ending up at the 'Cosmopolitan' where a 'gang of Unionists' were 'wailing and gnashing their teeth'. In his view Churchill's resignation and the Liverpool election were the two factors which had changed 'the whole face of politics'.[3] Writing the next morning to R. D. Holt at Liverpool, he thought the Radical Unionist 'Round Tablers' would 'manage to

[1] *Daily News*, 25th January 1887. Mundella had also gone to Cardiff for a prizegiving. See W. H. G. Armytage, *A. J. Mundella, 1825–97*, p. 269.

[2] Chamberlain to Collings, 26th January 1887. Copy. Chamberlain Papers, JC5/16/21. On 26th January Sir Edward Hamilton recorded that Gladstone was in his 'usual confident and buoyant mood', but disappointed by Hartington's support of Goschen at Liverpool. He took it to mean ' "I shall remain outside or go inside the Government, whichever course I think is calculated to thwart Mr Gladstone most effectually" '. On the other hand, the G.O.M. was encouraged by 'Chamberlain's utterances', except for 'his uncompromising allusions to the Parnellites (without whom nothing can be settled)'. Sir Edward Hamilton's Diary, 26th January 1887. Add. MS. 48645, p. 90.

[3] Lewis Harcourt's *Journal*, 26th January 1887. Gardiner, *op. cit.*, p. 30. Besides Gladstone and Harcourt the party included John and Arnold Morley, Welby, Algernon West and Edward Hamilton. Gladstone said that evening he believed Parnell had the Irish party completely in his hands, had been cognisant of the 'Plan of Campaign' and had stepped in to control it when it 'was becoming extravagant'. *Ibid.* The rest of the party remained at Brooks's after Gladstone's departure. When Goschen's defeat was made known Hamilton himself regretted it and hoped the government would survive, but he corroborates Lewis Harcourt as to the 'undisguised glee' with which Harcourt and John Morley received the news. The latter declared all was over with the government. Sir Edward Hamilton's Diary, 26th January 1887. Add. MS. 48645, p. 91. Lord George Hamilton was absolutely amazed by Goschen's defeat. He had been told the seat 'was supposed to be safe' and government supporters had regarded Goschen's impending presence on the Treasury Bench as 'a ray of comfort'. Lord G. Hamilton, *op. cit.*, pp. 54–6. Why the seat was thought safe is far from clear. The Gladstonians had won it in 1886.

console themselves for the disaster of their recent ally'. For Hartington it would be 'a frightful "facer" ', especially as it happened in Lancashire.[1] He was right. At Devonshire House the defeat was treated as 'horrible bad news'.[2]

Parliament met on the 27th. The long respite for the government was over. Chamberlain had been present at the Camperdown meeting, so nothing in the Queen's Speech came as a surprise to him. With coercion and new procedure rules certain, and British local government and Irish land reform mere promises, he had to pick his way forward most gingerly. Gingerly, yet with ginger, for it would have been impossible for him, both by temperament and calculation to have adopted a spineless attitude in the new situation. Radical Unionism needed a big moral fillip. To it, the Queen's Speech rather than Goschen's defeat had been the 'facer'. Progress and the Union had to be proved compatible and those 'bloody heads' put in charge of 'bleeding hearts'. Gladstone had appeared to Hartington as generally moderate in his speech on the government's programme, except in the part on Ireland where he sought to excuse the 'Plan of Campaign'. If others thought the same that might assist Chamberlain in his task of playing the rôle of overmighty friend to a government deeply distrusted by his closest political associates. That was more than could be said for the speech made by Churchill immediately after the notices of motion. 'There were a good many hits at the government which were much cheered by the opposition'.[3] In just two days time Chamberlain had to face this renewed challenge in the town hall at Birmingham. At Hawick the object had been to be all things to all men except the Nationalists. This time the situation demanded a more rallying approach, stressing the value of imperial supremacy. There would be ample room for the use of what Trevelyan termed his 'great and natural original style'. 'Foxing' had its limits and temporarily they had almost been reached. The principles of the 'Round Table' conclusions would have to be upheld, but so too would the government. Order would have to accompany reform. But most of all Radical Unionism had to be justified as a creed, not merely explained as a tactic. The position from which the 'foxing' was carried on had itself to be reaffirmed.

Then again, the Gladstonians felt more confident *vis-à-vis* all forms

[1] Harcourt to R. D. Holt, 27th January 1887. Copy. Harcourt Papers. The Queen telegrammed Salisbury from Osborne asking: 'What will you do for a seat for Mr Goschen? He will have to take a Conservative seat. The Stanleys think people were over-confident about Liverpool and did not work hard enough.' The Queen to Salisbury, 27th January 1887. Windsor Royal Archives, C38/147.

[2] Hartington to the Duchess of Manchester, 26th January 1887. Devonshire Papers, 340. Add. MS.

[3] *Ibid.*

of Unionism, however Liberal or Radical, with coercion in the offing. The choice restored to Chamberlain by the actual sessions at the 'Round Table' might go again and for good. He had therefore to consider even more carefully than usual his relations with the Whig Liberal Unionists and Conservatives. At Hawick he had ridden events more than they rode him. A week later in his 'Grand Duchy' the order was reversed. Nor had the Liverpool election helped, vastly exaggerated though its significance had been. Switching from the national settlement idea, Chamberlain began his speech by claiming Liberal reunion and the settlement of the Irish question were possible, 'if all concerned, Irish as well as English, would bring to the discussion a spirit of moderation and mutual consideration'. Next he sought to raise morale by stating as a fact the steady growth of Liberal Unionist strength to a level well able to cope with an attack upon the integrity of the Kingdom. Both points were meat and drink to the most radical Radical Unionists. On the land issue his contribution was short and to the point.

> My idea is that the true principle of a fair rent is that it could only accrue after the tenant has received a reasonable return for his labour; but when this condition has been fulfilled, then comes in the right of the landlord to a fair rent; and after the fair rent has been established upon this basis, then I say it would not be right to ask the landowner to accept anything less than that fair rent unless you can gradually improve the character of his security. I believe that there are ways, that there are means, of greatly improving the security of the landlord without laying a risk on the British taxpayer.

A popular line to take even in the 'metropolis of reckless expenditure'. More he declined to say, passing on quickly to the key question of Home Rule.

His treatment of it revealed a mind at its liveliest. Coming straight to the vital subject of a legislature, he promptly avoided committing himself. With the aid of that advantageous use of truth only he could fully exploit, the task appeared wellnigh effortless.

> I am asked [he said] whether I am prepared to admit the idea of a legislative authority or authorities [note the inclusion of the plural!] in Ireland—whether I am willing to concede to them a dependent executive. Now I think there is some confusion of ideas upon this subject. At all events, I am not clever enough to define what people mean by a 'dependent executive'.

'Chamberlain the dim wit' might seem implausible, but a vast popular audience seldom fails to warm to an intelligent man who declares himself unclever. Moreover, it gave him the room needed for manoeuvring into the tactic of pondering to himself in public and so blinding his listeners with science. 'Our Joe' was about to unpick a few hems as well.

> If it means [he ruminated] that these legislative authorities—these subordinate authorities—should have a military or a quasi-military force at their disposal, or that they should have the control and the administration of justice, then I say emphatically, 'No'. I believe that such a proceeding, I know that such a proceeding, would be entirely contrary to the precedent of the Canadian constitution to which I refer, and I believe it would be dangerous to the security of the United Kingdom.

Naturally, by ruling out certain powers, he thought the conference had been unanimous in rejecting he was playing extremely safe. Very properly, he judged it safer to say nothing of what such a legislature should have within its province. But there remained the task of definition to get over, and he attempted it by analogy.

> If you take the case of any subordinate local authority—the case, for instance, of the town council of Birmingham—you will find that they have the power to appoint and maintain an executive in connection with their administration. Is that what is meant by a dependent executive? If so, I say you cannot deny it to any legislative authority which you may establish in Ireland. If you were to establish tomorrow a legislative authority in Belfast—a legislative authority in Dublin; if you were to give to them the power of dealing with certain domestic business—with education, with local government, with public works, and similar matters—if you were to transfer to them the administration of Dublin Castle and those Dublin boards which deal with similar subjects, you would have as a matter of course to allow them to appoint an executive to carry out the details of their business, to appoint them, to select them, and to pay them; and if that is what is meant there is certainly no difference upon the matter.[1]

Now he had said so much and yet so little. The analogy with Birmingham reduced the whole conception of a legislature down to Provincial Councils level. The sort of executive he implied there would be reeked of town hall minions—not of the leading politicians of Ireland. In short, he had used Gladstonian language to describe a thoroughly Chamberlainite set-up. As for the form of government, the Irish could decide that for themselves. An extraordinary doctrine had the 'Home Rule' envisaged in his plan amounted to anything substantial. What did it matter in these circumstances if Dublin decided to have a Cabinet with a Prime Minister, and Ministers of Agriculture, Public Works and Education? Most important was the ability of the Imperial Parliament to intervene with effect should abuses arise. Mr Gladstone's Bill had contained no effective provision for such occasions.

[1] *The Times*, 31st January 1887.

'Our Joe' had reverted in substance to his position before the first session in Grafton Street. That satisfied Unionists alarmed at his latest tactics. Nonetheless, by employing terms accepted at the 'Round Table' he also satisfied the reunion zealots in his own flock and rendered any Gladstonian attack upon him very difficult to make. Unless, that is, a spirited defence of his own party was in itself an offence. Following a much interrupted justification of the need to restore law and order to Ireland, he made clear his refusal

> to support what can properly be described as coercive legislation—that is to say, such measures as the establishment of martial law or the suspension of Habeas Corpus, or any legislation generally restricting the liberty of the subject; but if it be necessary, in order that the law should be respected, to amend and strengthen the ordinary law of the country [he was prepared] to give fair and full consideration to any proposals which may be made to that effect.[1]

Reactions from the audience had shown him the extreme delicacy of the position. Objections to coercion rather than a belief in Home Rule was the danger in Birmingham. Illogical though this was, it had to be faced. Hence, while rallying the Unionist forces involved insisting upon some repressive medicine, the progressive sugar surrounding it had to be pressed for at the counter of the government pharmacy. For a time shortage of sugar could be blamed upon the Irish and the government vindicated. This, Chamberlain exploited to the full, but made the most of his opportunity to threaten trouble if the government failed to remedy the position. British reforms 'must not and shall not be indefinitely postponed'.

> The Unionist Liberals have taken their course with a full knowledge of the sacrifices which it might involve; they have staked their seats and they have staked their political fortunes; ay, and we will stake them again in the defence of what we have believed to be the supreme interests of the nation.

The precise direction in which Liberal Unionism of the Birmingham brand would judge the 'supreme interests of the nation' to lie was at that moment only partially sorted out. Only prompt government supply of sugar would ensure the aims Chamberlain had joined in the 'Round Table' to attain were actually fulfilled.

> We have a right [he claimed] to expect from the Government a constructive as well as a negative policy in Great Britain and in Ireland alike. If their legislation for Great Britain is conceived in a liberal spirit, I shall thankfully accept it without reference to the quarter from which it comes; but if it is reactionary, or totally inadequate, the Government must take the responsibility of breaking up the Unionist party, for they know perfectly well that they cannot expect and have not obtained any pledge of unconditional support from any Liberal.[2]

[1] *Ibid.*   [2] *Ibid.*

His insistence was both sincere and tactical. As a Radical he wanted reforms and as a Unionist he desired to assuage the discontents with government policy. To balance matters up and advertise the virtues of Unionism further attacks on the Irish and a sneer at the proceedings of the Leeds conference had he felt been necessary. Anti-Hibernianism was not difficult to work up and the suggestion that the Gladstonians at Leeds had been 'hand-in-glove with their revilers' might do a lot to open Radical Unionist eyes to the dangers too much zest for reunion could lead them into.

Next morning's *Observer* told Harcourt the worst.[1] He immediately sent off a protest to Highbury and a copy of it to Elm Park Gardens.[2] All he wanted was to end the controversy 'without a row' and his language was in no way overbearing. 'For the future the least said soonest mended', though, as he commented to Morley, all the world would soon know how much Chamberlain had conceded.[3] Before lunch Hartington received Harcourt at Devonshire House. Ostensibly the deputy leader of the Gladstonians had sought an interview with the leader of the Liberal Unionists to discuss the new Procedure Rules proposed by the government. The real motive was to find out what Hartington thought of Chamberlain. After half an hour on procedure Harcourt made as if to go, but his host stopped him, saying: 'Well, how are you getting on at your "Round Table"?' Because he was talking to one of the only two men supposed to have received reports on the conference, he was bound to be completely frank. Admittedly he had his suspicions as to Chamberlain's complete loyalty to his chief, but lacked any real proof. Under these circumstances speaking freely was the only sensible course to take. Assumption of ignorance would be insulting; and assumption of knowledge might reveal any gaps in Chamberlain's accounts. Hartington said his deputy had told him something about the land scheme. That something had not been clear enough; he did not understand how it worked. Harcourt's detailed explanation of it evoked the comment: 'There does not seem to be much security for the landlords.' To which he replied: 'No indeed, but then Chamberlain and I do not care about the landlords as much as you probably do,' and went on to say the former had agreed to an Irish legislature. Here Hartington interrupted: 'I did not understand that he had consented to one legislature.' A point well taken in view of the Birmingham speech. Harcourt had to admit this, explaining the plurality in terms of Ulster. Chamberlain, he was sure, believed in having one legisla-

---

[1] *Observer*, 30th January 1887.

[2] Harcourt to Chamberlain, 30th January 1887. No copy of this letter would appear to be extant.

[3] Harcourt to Morley, 30th January 1887. Copy. Harcourt Papers.

ture for the rest of Ireland. After discussing the Ulster difficulty and the anxiety all at the conference had felt for the practical solution no one had yet found, he claimed the Canadian system would give Ireland 'all and more than all' she would have obtained under the Bill of 1886, except the appointment of judges. Hartington listened as if he were genuinely turning the whole matter over in his mind and was not convinced against it. An attitude his companion found most significant. None the less the mission was a failure, for nothing revealing about 'Our Joe' emerged at all. Just before departing Harcourt made one last effort, but in vain. 'You have got to speak at Newcastle this week,' he said. 'Yes,' growled Hartington. 'Damned foolish of you,' he continued. 'Yes, I always think so when it comes to the point,' answered Hartington. 'And you have to say something about "Joe",' he added. 'I suppose so,' muttered Hartington, and the conversation was ended.[1] The Whig leader must have found the Birmingham speech a hopeful sign. Its tone was so much more promising than the two previous efforts of recent months. Even its more concrete proposals were essentially more moderate than he had come to fear. With a strong desire to have his deputy safely back on unneutral ground he was naturally loth to reveal any fault in his loyalty to one on the opposition side with so much to gain from the information and the sheer fact of his having given it. Silence was therefore more than golden.

Even before the Birmingham bombshell, Gladstone had been busy discouraging Harcourt from persisting in his plans. On the 29th before any inkling of what Chamberlain was going to say or had said could have reached him, he wrote:

> With respect to the 'Round Table', I would not interpose any bar to the continuance of your conversations on any point, but it appears to me, 1. That the general Resolution announced by Chamberlain at Hawick represents a fair breathing space for the moment at a real and considerable advance, for which we have to thank (especially) you. 2. That he might very well be encouraged to formulate his ideas upon land which present points of great encouragement, especially with a view to meeting in some simple way any Ashbourne proposals for more extension (as it must now be) of the pecuniary limit set down.[2]

Hypocrisy of the first order, and revealed as such by what followed. Not that that explained all, the Queen's Speech was the main motive power behind it. Coercion and Procedure Rules made wonderful balm for soothing the old man's conscience. Still, the rest of this letter was frank enough.

[1] Lewis Harcourt's *Journal*, 30th January 1887. Harcourt Papers.
[2] Gladstone to Harcourt, 29th January 1887. Harcourt Papers.

Further [it ran], A. Morley seems inclined to believe a good division might be had on a moderate Home Rule motion, possibly one with a majority in two figures, of which he will consider further. *Had we a reasonable certainty of exhibiting a sensible improvement* in the figures of the Election, which showed 110 or so against us, I, though far from anxious to take the issue now, yet if the issue is to be taken, should be less disinclined to join even thus early in a forward step.[1]

And do precisely what Harcourt had wished to avoid before the decisions of the 'Round Table' had been embodied in a definite pact. Arnold Morley was mistaken in thinking a 'breathing space' in the reunion talks could be used for making the government breath its last. Harcourt knew full well Chamberlain would never commit himself at this stage. Did Gladstone? Or did he feel the position was now such that unconditional acceptance of moderate Home Rule would be an earnest of good faith which alone would justify further sessions at the 'Round Table'? There is no means of telling. All that can be said is that Harcourt cannot have derived much pleasure from any of what he read.

An account of the substance of the Birmingham speech in two columns of his Newcastle paper did not alarm Trevelyan. It seemed as acceptable as what had been said at Hawick. A close look at a fuller report would have shattered his dream of 'Chamberlain the peacemaker', but the quixotic streak in him would have made sure he adhered to the belief that it was vital for all parties that the 'Round Tablers' should make the Home Rule wound heal at 'the first intention'. As he said: 'I am prepared for a good deal to do so.'[2] Morley thought differently. He thought he recognised in Chamberlain's latest pronouncements the grounds for the suspicions so lately set aside.[3] The need for finding excuses to undermine the conference had apparently gone. Nevertheless anything to do with Chamberlain was almost bound to annoy him, and this time the fact he had temporarily believed in the man's sincerity aroused more than the usual pique. 'Joe' had an indecent amount of fight in him and would have the cheek to come through unscathed. Just what *The Times* meant when it commented: 'Mr Chamberlain . . . speaks to the electors of Birmingham in tones not at all resembling those of a man who has made up his mind to capitulate to Mr Gladstone, Mr Labouchère and Mr Dillon.'[4] Buckle was on the verge of showing something approaching a proprietary pride in a near prodigal on the way home. Certainly the

[1] *Ibid.*
[2] Trevelyan to Chamberlain, 31st January 1887. Chamberlain Papers, JC5/70/25.
[3] Morley to Harcourt, 31st January 1887. Harcourt Papers.
[4] *The Times*, 31st January 1887.

choice of going to left or right was in a very precarious condition. In fact there were probably enough men in the Gladstonian party so dead against Chamberlain that had it come to the test then he would have met with an opposition strong enough to have forced him to remain a Radical Unionist or leave political life. Whatever the state of the skies above Hawick and Birmingham, there were fewer clouds around the platform of the larger town. Consolidating Unionism inevitably led to Gladstonian resentment.

Morley let off steam twice to Harcourt on the Monday (the 31st). The first time on paper from Newcastle; the second by word of mouth.[1] Clarification of what Chamberlain had said merely aggravated his self-righteous Sabbath wrath. Lewis Harcourt judged the effects correctly:

> Chamberlain's speech in today's papers is, if possible, more unsatisfactory than it was in the *Observer*. I do not see how it will be possible in any way to go on with the Conference as I am sure J.M. will be so angry at the speech that he will have nothing further to do with it.[2]

The letter was couched in terms of mock moderation, yet the burden of it was clear.[3] 'I have read Chamberlain's speech at Birmingham with a feeling of disappointment which must, I should think, be fully shared by you.' A true statement, though the motives for disappointment can hardly have been the same.

> The fact is that he is engaged in what he calls a 'friendly intercommunication of ideas' with you and Herschell and me appears to have been entirely overlooked by him. The hostile tone in which he talks about the Gladstonian Liberals is a singular accompaniment of a serious attempt, undertaken at his own suggestion and request, to arrange a *modus vivendi* with Gladstonian Liberals. His language about the proceedings at Leeds can hardly have been designed to have a conciliatory effect on people like you and me who took an active part in them. Indeed, I do not see how, if we had been in the full heat of controversy, he could have taken a more unfriendly line than that which marks the speech from first to last.[4]

Like Lord George Bentinck, Morley could not bear to be 'sold', especially when he had been thinking his 'Chief' and he himself would soon be 'selling' the present 'seller'. Of course, 'Joe' would have preferred not to make a speech of this type. He had simply obeyed the dictates of circumstances. However skilful a 'fox' may be, there are times when he has to cross open country and leave a powerful scent.

[1] Morley to Harcourt, 31st January 1887. Harcourt Papers.
[2] Lewis Harcourt's *Journal*, 31st January 1887. Harcourt Papers.
[3] Morley to Harcourt, 31st January 1887. Harcourt Papers.
[4] *Ibid.*

The 'earth' too must be secure. If that goes all will be lost. Nor in politics could he 'lie low' for long. The Gladstonians would have argued, had they thought about it, that Unionism was an electoral 'tar-baby' just waiting for 'rabbit' voters. But even if it were, simple waiting was not sufficient. Positive advertisement was only too necessary. There was then a very complicated humour about the rest of what Morley wrote. Perhaps he was trying to fit in with what he thought would go down best with Harcourt. If not, his arguments are singularly lacking in his customary subtlety.

> It seems to me [he grumbled] to indicate a peculiar want of loyalty to the idea of the Conference, though he had himself prepared it. Whoever heard of one of the parties to a friendly discussion of this kind, with the aim of practical cooperation at the end of it, going out at intervals to fire broadsides into those whom he has just left? I say nothing of the good taste, or of the good feeling of such a course. I only submit to you that it tends gravely to lessen the chances of our conference coming to any good issue and adds enormously to the difficulties with which we have to contend. In face of discouraging evidence like this of the frame of mind of our partner at the 'Round Table', I think we shall really have to consider whether it is worthwhile to persevere. What do you say?[1]

To think that Morley considered he had persevered to run the conference! How moving too is his singular concern for it now he thinks it on the verge of petering out! Had he not been genuinely upset himself, Harcourt would certainly have seen the funny side of what he read.

By evening Morley had become much more worked up. Contact in Newcastle and in the Commons lobbies with the professional Chamberlain-haters had proved a powerful stimulant. He dined with the Harcourts in Grafton Street and afterwards put aside all pretence of asking whether the conference be abandoned. The meal over, he launched out quite uninhibitedly, making no bones about his fury. Nothing, he said, would ever induce him to sit again at the 'Round Table' for anything but dinner. Cronies like Spence Watson had urged him on to decide upon attacking Chamberlain in public, first in the Commons on the next Friday (4th February), and then next week when he planned to speak at Newcastle. Nor was that all. He threatened to send Harcourt a letter expressing his views on the situation of which any use whatever might be made. By that he meant it could be shown to Chamberlain if Harcourt pleased.[2]

Not all the Gladstonian leaders reacted in the same way. When the Harcourts did the rounds to gauge opinion they called upon Spencer. His mood was one of only mild dissatisfaction with Chamberlain and

[1] *Ibid.*
[2] Lewis Harcourt's *Journal*, 31st January 1887. Harcourt Papers.

his speech.[1] During a walk together in the Mall all three had bumped into Granville, who was equally indisposed to favour a cessation of the conference and firmly convinced Gladstone was most anxious that it should go on.[2] It looked as if Chamberlain might still enjoy enough 'goodwill' in top Gladstonian circles to receive the benefit of the doubt. A result wholly admirable from his viewpoint, for he would have consolidated Unionism, drawn intensified hostility upon himself and thus increased the sympathy he enjoyed and satisfied others by agreeing to continue with the conference. The Birmingham speech would turn out in the end as an unexpected creator of bonuses on the 'foxing' game.

A temporary diversion from the game was provided that day by Churchill. Speaking in the debate on the Address he enlivened an otherwise 'dull and unexciting evening' by sarcastic comments on the 'Round Table' conference and the whole Liberal Unionist party. An about turn scarcely creditable in one who but lately had seriously contemplated becoming a member of that party in favour of that very conference. Chamberlain's discouragement might have had a souring effect, but in any case Churchill changed like the wind. Lloyd George later on lived for the day. This gentleman lived for the moment. And just then the 'moment' called for being as true to the 'Blues' as possible.

> I notice [he declared] a tendency of the party of the Union to attach too much importance to precarious Parliamentary alliances, which are as transient and uncertain as the shifting wind, and too little to the far more important question how to keep the English people at the back of the party of the Union. When I was in the Government I made it my constant thought and desire to make things as easy as possible for the Liberal Unionists, to introduce such measures as they might conscientiously support as being in accordance with their general principles, and to make such electoral arrangements as might enable them to preserve their seats.[3]

A series of statements true in themselves but telling only half the story. Churchill had used the Liberal Unionists to please himself. They, especially the Chamberlain group, made a most convenient bogey with which to browbeat his standstill or reactionary colleagues.

---

[1] *Ibid.*   [2] *Ibid.*

[3] Churchill, *op. cit.*, p. 284. For a full account of the business of the Parliamentary Session, 27th January to 16th September 1887, see H. Lucy, *A Diary of the Salisbury Parliament, 1886–1892*, pp. 10–13. Just as parliament assembled a number of sprightly younger Conservatives met with the idea of imitating the old 'Fourth Party'. The idea probably originated with George Curzon, but James Lowther was elected chairman. After two meetings, however, the group faded away. See Rt. Hon. Viscount Ullswater, *A Speaker's Commentaries*, Vol. I, p. 189.

'Loyalty' was leading him into some very warped arguments. The tone worsened as the speech went on.

> But I frankly admit that I regarded the Liberal Unionists as a useful kind of crutch, and I looked forward to the time, and no distant time, when the Tory party might walk alone, strong in its own strength and conscious of its own merits; and it is to the Tory party, and solely to the Tory party that I looked for the maintenance of the Union.

An attack giving those with whom he had a lot in common grounds for deep resentment. Hicks Beach might have enjoyed it all, but Chaplin was naturally obliged to belabour him when replying. Most unfortunate of all was the accusation that Chamberlain was pursuing 'an erroneous and mistaken course'. That the Conservative party would never 'follow a line of policy which by any reasonable construction' could create in Dublin 'anything in the nature of an Irish Parliament' was obvious. To tell his friend that it would be well to bear in mind that 'whatever schemes of Home Rule for Ireland may commend themselves to him', they were not, 'under any circumstances, likely to commend themselves to members' on the government side, was nothing short of a gratuitous insult aimed at winning favour with the numerous 'Joe'-hating Conservatives (and Gladstonians).[1] However 'extraordinary' the 'gyrations' in which Chamberlain had and was indulging, Churchill was in no position to denounce them in public. More was to be heard of all this later.

A keen sense of priorities enabled Harcourt to begin the new month by writing soothing letters to both Morley and Gladstone. In the first he found no difficulty in concurring in his colleague's feelings.[2] Nonetheless, the keynote was an appeal to common sense. Certainly 'Joe's' 'onslaught' had been undeserved and unexpected, above all the imputation 'of servility and subserviency' to the dictation of the Parnellites, for he knew perfectly well there had not been 'the slightest

---

[1] Churchill, *op. cit.*, pp. 284–5. It remained to be seen whether Gladstone's prophecy that Churchill's resignation over economy would lead to public saving, but his claim that nationalist Ireland would benefit looked like having a fair chance of proving true if the Liberal Unionists took this speech at its face value. For Gladstone's comments on Churchill's resignation see *Mary Gladstone: Diaries and Letters*, edited by Lucy Masterman, p. 393. A description of Liberal Unionists associating them with gluttony and an indelicate use of toothpicks can be found in the book of a Conservative writer, J. A. Bridges, who entitled his work *Reminiscences of a Country Politician*. See pp. 164–5. For a good summary and assessment of Churchill's career see 'Lord Randolph Churchill' by C. H. D. Howard. *History*, 1940. Although Churchill had been chastened by the tragic death of Lord Iddesleigh (formerly Sir Stafford Northcote) on 12th January the effect would appear to have been ephemeral. Iddesleigh's last months are well dealt with in A. Lang, *Sir Stafford Northcote, 1st Earl of Iddesleigh*, Vol. II, pp. 274–83.

[2] Harcourt to Morley, 1st February 1887. Copy. Harcourt Papers.

trace in any part of our proceedings'. 'Looking at the substance of things, rather than at the form and temper' in which they had been presented, Harcourt felt a very substantial advance had been achieved. The culprit had given public adhesion to the principle of a statutory legislature in Ireland with a responsible executive dependent upon it. With this as a basis a reasonable settlement was not out of the question, despite the 'important matters of detail' remaining to be 'arranged'. He was therefore most unwilling to 'part with this vantage ground' in so great a controversy. A long period in politics had taught him actions made in haste under the influence of irritation, however well justified, were usually unwise. 'Wait and see' should be the watchword, and as the talks had started under Gladstone's sanction, only that sanction could end them. Definitely a contribution to the science of bromides, objects always in short supply at Elm Park Gardens.

Gladstone was given a balanced account of what had occurred.[1] The appeal made was the one most likely to succeed—the appeal to political advantage. There was no attempt to minimise Chamberlain's misdemeanour. To have done so would only have aroused the old man's suspicions. The language of the speech was therefore termed 'highly offensive' and Morley's reaction to it 'red hot indignation'. On the other hand a powerful plea was put in for the continuance of the conference, just though the indignation was. Then as to how the crisis should be handled, Harcourt explained:

> Chamberlain is at present in Birmingham and I hope he is likely to remain there for a day or two, so that we are not forced to an immediate issue with him, but he has unfortunately strengthened the hands of those amongst our party who have from the first been averse to reconciliation with him upon any terms.

This he very deeply regretted because that much-hated man had already conceded almost all that had been required of him. A quarrel now was therefore deeply to be regretted, and a great deal would depend on the *manner* in which 'this unfortunate business' was handled. He felt very strongly that the 'Round Table' Gladstonians should have their leader's 'countenance and support in whatever course is now determined upon'. Gladstone's authority had started the conference, only that same authority could end it. Consultation with him was earnestly desired by both Harcourt and Morley. As he was staying at Cambridge and was intending a return to Hawarden a journey via London would be perfectly possible. This Harcourt enjoined him to make.

[1] Harcourt to Gladstone, 1st February 1887. Gladstone Papers, Add. MS. 44201, f. 64.

During the course of the day Lewis Harcourt found Spencer in the peers' gallery of the Commons and took him round to meet Morley and Harcourt senior and have a talk in Gladstone's room behind the Chair.[1] Morley remained extremely stubborn, telling Spencer exactly what he had said at the Harcourts' house the night before and adding a threat to produce all the 'ransom' and 'natural rights' quotations when he next spoke. A short time before he had encountered 'Joe' in the lavatory of the Commons. The great man had shown not the slightest trace of embarrassment, stalked up to him and asked: 'Well, Morley, when are you coming to see me to discuss my Land Bill?' Much taken aback, and not fancying to say bluntly that he would not come at all, Morley compromised. 'Well, Chamberlain,' he replied, 'after your Birmingham speech I do not see that it would be any use, but if you like I will come to see you in a friendly way, but not in any way that can be considered official.'[2] After that reminder of how powerful a personality the man he hated was, any immediate chances of calming him down no longer existed. All Spencer's efforts in that direction were without effect.

That chance encounter illustrated very well the line Chamberlain proposed taking to avoid nemesis. Brazening it out in the *pissoir* was no spontaneous aberration. He intended to brazen the whole thing out and pretend the Birmingham speech had never been made. After all, if he was cheerful and cooperative Harcourt and those of his persuasion would have their hands strengthened. He realised his chief Gladstonian friend would be almost frantic not to throw away newly won advantages and therefore take a severely reasonable view of what had happened. Perhaps arguing to Gladstone and Morley that it had only been for consumption within the 'Grand Duchy' and so both understandable and excusable. Anyway it was worth a try and meeting Morley enabled him to practice his technique on one of the toughest subjects. 'Joe' always enjoyed a challenge. He had not remained at home as Harcourt had hoped, but there was going to be no 'immediate issue' with him—simply smiles all round from his side and a mixture of relief and gradual cooling down among Gladstonians. In a note of the next day Brett encouraged this line of thinking.

The offending passage is the reference to the Leeds Conference. I have not looked it up, but the *fact* of the resolutions quoted by you is denied. The offence given is mainly to the Chatterer of the Lobby. I don't think Harcourt really feels it much, though apparently he does a little. *Why* they should object to be told they are bound hand and foot to Parnell I can't imagine. But they do. A little patience will mend all.[3]

[1] Lewis Harcourt's *Journal*, 1st February 1887. Harcourt Papers.
[2] *Ibid.*
[3] Brett to Chamberlain, 2nd February 1887. Chamberlain Papers, JC5/6/7.

Good advice, however wrong on details and lacking in perception on one point of Gladstonian psychology!

Chamberlain's fixed rule, according to Garvin, was 'never to take any blow without retaliation'.[1] Not as 'fixed' as all that, for Churchill got away with his escapade very lightly. Polite remonstrance from a wounded friend was the limit of the 'retaliation'.

> Why will you insist [he bewailed] on being an Ishmael—your hand against every man? Why did you go out of your way on Monday to attack me? You know that I am the mildest of men, but I have a strong inclination to hit out at those who strike me, and my experience teaches me that no private friendship can long resist the effect of public contest. You and I have plenty of enemies. Is it not possible for us each to pursue his own way without coming into personal conflict? Surely we shall have our hands fully occupied without tearing out each other's eyes?[2]

Like the shrewd warrior that he was, 'Joe' generally knew when not to bite off more than he could chew. War on one front was enough, and why start an extra Randolph one during what amounted to an armistice? Churchill would be a useful ally in the struggle Chamberlain was to reopen at the point circumstances dictated or designated opportune. Within twenty-four hours a reply had come.[3] Announcing his departure for southern climes, Churchill explained how tired and worn out he was. He had anticipated his friend's annoyance with 'the chaff of the "Round Table" business'. His justification was that he had 'to think of the future of the Tories', which was being 'damnably compromised'. The 'Round Table' conference aimed at reuniting the Liberal party. The reuniting of the Liberal party was for the object of turning out the 'Tory' party. While this was going on Hartington was able to 'pose as a patriot', to patronise the 'Tories', lend them a man or two, 'lull them to sleep and cause them to lose all vitality and independence'. He concluded:

> My warning, which I gave the Tories to look out and to try and stand by their own strength, will turn out—before long—to have been well-timed, and it was only to illustrate that warning that I referred to the 'Round Table'. Therefore do not think that I said anything which ought to ruffle even our private friendship, which, though it may be of a paradox to say so, is to me one of the chief and few remaining attractions of political life.[4]

Without doubt Churchill was sincere in what he wrote. Though the Harcourts said all along the offending speech had been 'to the address

---

[1] Garvin, *op. cit.*, p. 291.

[2] Churchill, *op. cit.*, pp. 286–7.

[3] Churchill to Chamberlain, 3rd February 1887. Chamberlain Papers, JC5/14/29.

[4] *Ibid.*

of Goschen', Chamberlain not Goschen had been singled out by name and his activities attacked bitterly and at considerable length.[1] The Harcourt diagnosis was only half the story, for Churchill resented any weakening of the Unionist alliance just as much as the pollution of pure 'Toryism' by Goschen's appointment to the Chancellorship of the Exchequer. The difference was that he had repented the personal side of the attack on Chamberlain and badly wanted him to remain Unionist. Hostility to a friend on the wrong road could pass, but hatred of an enemy on the right one was to remain unabated. One way or the other it did not make an iota of difference. Out of sight, Churchill almost passed from the mind of politics and had no influence on the final outcome of the Liberal reunion bid. When next he returned to the scene his friend was firmly in the Unionist camp, albeit on its leftmost edge.

Through bad eyesight Gladstone misdirected his note agreeing to meet Harcourt and consequently waited for him at Euston Station in vain. Communications therefore sped fast and furious between them, giving posterity details of their thoughts which might otherwise have passed through a few feet of air into oblivion. First Gladstone offered 'a few words, rather at a venture' from the station waiting room.[2] He thought any deliberate breaking off of the conference by a formal act would be a mistake. Everything indicated they should wait for the government proposals, or at any rate the first of them. Innate caution and experience made him draw back from the thing he wanted most, even when coercion and new procedure rules were bound to come. He knew well how easy it was to overestimate the damage a good weapon could inflict, and had, moreover, heard of boomerangs. The talks might still turn out to be useful, whatever their particular result. About a success the old man still thought the same.

> In no case could signal or telling good have proceeded from any conclusion of an alliance with Chamberlain at this moment. Caine's conduct seems to show that he has few, if any, followers, and I think we may have to wait for the influence of our old friend as well as enemy—Time.

Caine's recent pronouncements certainly made it seem he was spurning his section leader.[3] Yet, as we have seen, his judgment was that that leader was only playing a game. With no local Dales and Bunces at Barrow-in-Furness he therefore saw no reason to participate in it. None the less, he was a Chamberlain man. Gladstone's appraisal was correct from his viewpoint, but belied the crucial facts.

[1] Churchill, *op. cit.*, pp. 284–5.

[2] Gladstone to Harcourt, 2nd February 1887. Harcourt Papers.

[3] At Barrow-in-Furness (his constituency) on 1st February 1887. *Ulverston Advertiser*, 2nd February 1887. See Gladstone to Harcourt, 2nd February 1887. Harcourt Papers.

No wonder when he still mistook 'foxing' for sincerity. Whig repentance alone could have reconciled him to Chamberlain's negotiated return, and of that there was no sign. Until there was, prejudice tallied with fact. The Radical Unionist leader would certainly not bring back more than a handful of M.P.'s to the true church.

The advice and guidance of the G.O.M. would have been most useful to his deputy just then. Things were certainly difficult with Morley, who remained 'very stiff' and resolved 'to break off the Conference in spite of all that Spencer, Granville and S. Whitbread' could say to the contrary.[1] Of course, admitted Harcourt, responding to the Euston note, Chamberlain was not so important as he thought himself, but his quitting the Unionists would throw confusion and breed suspicion among them, and he was a man in any event whom it was better to have with than against them.[2] A contention which surely needed no proof bearing in mind the effectiveness of the Birmingham attack on the 1886 Home Rule Bill and the panic Churchill's resignation had occasioned? 'However,' he complained, 'we conduct ourselves as if we had an overwhelming majority and could do just as we pleased and when we please. We are like the Italians *fara da se*, though they never did anything by themselves and little for themselves.' The nearest he ever came to a direct criticism of either Gladstone or Morley in the whole of this long-drawn-out tragi-comedy. On the 3rd the former wrote again, hoping Harcourt would 'arrange with J. Morley not to perform any *act* of rupture. Neither the need nor the advantage present themselves to me and I am sure he could not act from feeling.' Clearly 'feeling' was troubling the air at Hawarden, for next came the indignant claim that it was 'little less than an insult to the main body of the party to call them "Gladstonian Liberals" '.[3] But, as was admitted, they were used to it, because of the clear insult of calling them 'Separatists'. Time would be a great rewarder.

> I think that if we have a little patience [wrote Harcourt to Morley], the proposals of the Government will open out Chamberlain, who if not very near us does not seem very near to Hartington. My feeling has always been that the battle was for the present mainly out of our hands, but that it would be fought *for us* by experience of Ireland, and partly by the proposals and errors of the Government.[4]

In short, events would force Chamberlain to revert to full Unionism or unconditional surrender, and work for the government's destruction. The days of guilt had gone, very probably for ever. Plied with

[1] Harcourt to Gladstone, 2nd February 1887. Gladstone Papers, Add. MS. 44201, f. 70.
[2] *Ibid.*
[3] Gladstone to Harcourt, 3rd February 1887. Harcourt Papers.
[4] *Ibid.*, and Gardiner, *op. cit.*, p. 31.

these arguments Morley gave way, adopting a much more conciliatory mood towards Chamberlain and actually thanking Harcourt
for the part he had played in soothing him down.[1] Pressing home this
newly won advantage, the deputy leader actually read a little lecture
on avoidance of personal attacks to his prickly colleague and ex-
tracted promises that nothing untoward would be said at Newcastle
on the 9th.[2]

During the debate on the Address Colonel Saunderson painted the
picture of 'the very remarkable structure which the right hon. member
for Midlothian had erected on the twin piers of British Radicalism
and Irish-American Fenianism, with Mr Gladstone as corner-stone,
and Mr Labouchère and Mr Conybeare as ornamental gargoyles'.[3]
In essence the charge was an old one and naturally Gladstone was
anxious not to appear to justify it. When Parnell planned an amendment to the Address Morley told Harcourt he would speak and vote
for it.[4] Harcourt then told Gladstone he was prepared to follow suit.[5]
All the amendment said was that Home Rule and Land Purchase,
not coercion were the remedies for the Irish situation. A straightforward avowal of the very line of action the Liberal leader favoured
with all his heart and soul. Nevertheless, he 'gathered' 'no advantageous motion' could be made on Parnell's initiative and 'supposed'
Harcourt would not emphasise his support of it. 'It would, I think,
be rather a misfortune,' he thought, 'for us to be in the way when it
comes on.'[6] Parnell 'deve fara da se'. Events turned out otherwise,
but the drift of Gladstone's evasion of blame is here for all to see. His
aides were in bolder spirits. Winterbotham, the Radical Unionist
member for Cirencester, expressed the strongest possible objection to
coercion on the evening of the 3rd and they drew no small encouragement from any straws in the current wind.[7] Also, the restive mood of

[1] Lewis Harcourt's *Journal*, 3rd February 1887. Harcourt Papers.   [2] *Ibid.*
[3] Hansard, 3rd Series, Vol. CCCX, Col. 181. Colonel E. J. Saunderson (1837–
1906) was Conservative M.P. for North Armagh and leader of the Irish Unionists
in the Commons. His biographer thought the 'Round Table' conference 'a crisis
for Unionism'. Had it succeeded he thought the history of Unionism over the next
twenty years would have been very different. The anti-Home Rule side would have
been bereft 'of some of its most valuable assets'. Some weeks earlier, at the annual
meeting of the Irish Loyal and Patriotic Union, Saunderson had said he regarded
the government as safe while Gladstone lived. 'If his party should come under the
leadership, as it probably would, of Mr Chamberlain . . . it would be a more
doubtful matter.' See R. Lucas, *Colonel Saunderson, M.P.*, pp. 192–4.
[4] Harcourt to Gladstone, 2nd February 1887. Gladstone Papers, Add. MS.
44201, f. 70.
[5] *Ibid.*
[6] Gladstone to Harcourt, 3rd February 1887. Harcourt Papers.
[7] Hansard, 3rd Series, Vol. CCCX, Cols. 596–602. A. R. Winterbotham, was
49 years old and on the point of rejoining Gladstone. See Chapter VIII, p. 354,
note 6.

the extreme Gladstonians demanded a well-aired militancy. With Professor Stuart describing the 'Round Table' conference as a 'compromise which would enable a few men sitting on the fence to salve their consciences at the expense of a country's rights', they had to demonstrate their impeccable reliability.[1]

The previous evening Newcastle had seen a formidable Liberal Unionist rally. No Chamberlain graced its platform, but Hartington was well-flanked by Finlay and T. W. Russell, and delivered an excellent speech, couched in calm and unspectacular language. Everything was treated with a touching and unaggressive frankness conducive to a lowering of the political temperature. For a noted foxhunter he showed singularly little bitterness against the 'foxes'. The Irish struggle would, he believed, be very protracted. When the Unionist Liberals had decided to work with the Conservatives the likely cost had been counted. There would be no coalition, because his party could best exert its influence from a position of independence. Equally there would be no desertion. Goschen's position in the Liberal party had been unusual in that he differed on many points from great numbers of his colleagues. His joining the government had the complete concurrence of the speaker.

Instead of trying to tuck away the subject of Liberal reunion into the recesses of a defence of government policy, Hartington stuck to his usual transparent honesty and dealt with the 'Round Table' next. Chronology dictated that he should!

> Lord Herschell and Mr Chamberlain had suggested the bases of a conference which might examine the points of agreement existing among various shades of Liberals, might define the points of difference, and might, if possible, eliminate and remove such points of difference.

With the Hawick speech as his text he discussed the bare bones of the situation, regretting the sad tale that emerged.

> Mr Chamberlain [he began] has gone even further, and he has hinted at the possibility of arriving at a national, as opposed to a party settlement of this great question. I need not say how thankful and happy I should be if it were possible to arrive at a national settlement of this great question. I think that I have said as much as any man in favour of treating this not as a party, but as a national question. But I am afraid that the time has hardly yet come. There has been scarcely a sufficiently clear

[1] Hansard, 3rd Series, Vol. CCCX, Col. 596. 'Lord Hartington,' he declared, 'was keeping the pass at the new Thermopylae'. 'The Irish people was being treated by a physician at a distance.' 'No amount of consulting round a "Round Table" would ever change' the belief in a parliament for Ireland and an 'Executive proceeding from that Parliament' held by the 'Radical party'. They were determined 'to adhere' to it. *Ibid.* (R. B. Finlay was Liberal Unionist M.P. for Inverness District. An enemy of Church disestablishment, he had begun his career as a doctor and then turned to the Bar).

definition of the views of parties upon this subject to admit of such a settlement as that which I would gladly see. I wish well to these well-meant endeavours which are being made to arrive at a settlement and a reunion of the Liberal party, if that settlement can be made without sacrifice to principles on either side. I do not conceal from myself that there are some dangers in any such attempt as is now being made.

There then followed an account of the dangers. The unerring objectivity purged what was said of any power for giving umbrage to the Unionist 'Round Tablers'.

These dangers would be great if the negotiations were conducted by men less able, less clear in their opinions, less firm in upholding them, than my friends Mr Chamberlain and Sir George Trevelyan. There would be danger if these negotiations were entered into with any disposition to exaggerate points of agreement, to put into the background or to slide over points of difference. There would be danger if they were approached from the point of view of detail and not of general principles, if both parties did not clearly understand the point of view from which this subject was to be approached; but I believe that in the hands in which they are these negotiations are without danger.

As for himself, he had judged his place to be that of the man who stays at home to guard the position already occupied and keep watch upon the movements of the enemy. Over the actual Irish question his suggestions proved him far from negative. He had always, 'while opposing the Nationalist demands for an Irish parliament, admitted there was a ground, which was a strong one, upon which some change should be urged and recommended'. That ground was 'the growing incapacity of Parliament to deal with the wants and requirements not only of Ireland, but of the whole of the United Kingdom'. He believed his deputy wished to extend to Ireland, and indeed to other parts of the kingdom, something in the nature of enlarged municipal government. Approached from this angle the problem could be considered without endangering imperial interests, but if there were to be any question of taking into account the 'so-called national aspirations of the Irish people' problems of an insoluble and difficulties of an inescapable nature would be encountered. So too with thrashing about in masses of details, or collecting together for comparison 'various schemes of self-government, founded either upon the government of Canada or any colony'. If there was ignorance as to how much one side was willing to concede and the exact objects the other was aiming at the confusion would only increase and render a solution still more difficult to reach. For the immediate future, some form of Home Rule was preferable to anarchy and contempt for the law. To cope with Ireland's real difficulties restoration of law and order was the paramount consideration.[1]

[1] *The Times*, 3rd February 1887.

'You do manage somehow,' commented his sister, Lady Egerton, 'to speak out so clearly and truly and yet keep clear of personal bitterness.'[1] And so he had, making play with objectivity to an extent unattained by many in the academic and legal fields. Sometimes the honesty which was its principal motive force led him into boredom and consequent dullness. On this occasion nothing could have been more suitable. He was interested and obviously enjoyed picking his way through the minefield Harcourt had so gleefully predicted would cause him trouble. His father judged the performance 'capital', and like Lady Egerton was right.[2] Churchill took it as a 'striking confirmation for all except the blind of the accuracy and justice' of his remarks 'anent the temporary character of the usefulness of the "crutch" ', but only an exceptional egoism such as his could have warped the evidence in this way.[3] True to his convictions, Hartington had rejected anything in the nature of a desertion of the Conservatives; accepted the ideal of Liberal reunion while rejecting the present as an occasion for it; accepted the need for changes in Irish government, but rejected Home Rule or anything approaching it; and gone all out for coercion. There could be no mistaking what staying at home to guard the position already occupied involved for him. Praise of Chamberlain went along with the refusal to join him at the 'Round Table'. Adoption of his local government motions preceded the disapproval of his Canadian constitutional analogy. Tact and frankness are not often easy bedfellows. Under Hartington's guidance they were married with distinction.

Chamberlain's bargaining position *vis-à-vis* the Gladstonians was inevitably reduced by what had been said. Gladstone found comfort in the passages as to the timing of reunion talks and discomfort in the bald revelation of Whig intransigence. Both factors would aggravate his already strong opposition to the further pursuit of a *modus vivendi* drawn up on 'Round Table' lines. Harcourt and Morley stood more or less where they had, but it was their leader's wishes that would ultimately count, even had they both been at one on reunion matters. Nor would Granville, Spencer and their like manage to alter his convictions. Schnadhorst, his 'wirepullers' and Labouchère could rejoice. Yet Chamberlain really had the laugh on them, for Hartington wanted him badly and there was a good chance discontents

[1] Lady Francis Egerton to Hartington, 3rd February 1887. Devonshire Papers, 292. 252.

[2] Diaries of the 7th Duke of Devonshire, 3rd February 1887. Devonshire Papers. The 7th Duke of Devonshire (1808–91) was a highly intelligent and successful man of affairs. The death of his wife at a comparatively young age had deterred him from entering politics.

[3] Churchill to Chamberlain, 3rd February 1887. Chamberlain Papers, JC5/14/29.

among the anti-coercionist Radical Unionists in Birmingham would be kept within bounds, even if things got tough in the reunion negotiations. The great question was—would they? However unwilling Gladstone and Morley were to continue, Harcourt and the men of 'goodwill' and Chamberlain himself prevented them from risking a breach. Unless an excuse was conveniently provided by the Radical Unionists it looked very much as if the conference would have to drag on—alive in death. Stalemate would prevent any progress, but equally public opinion would prevent any going back. The reduction of bargaining power was therefore without significance for Chamberlain. He wanted a continuation of the conference and would get it. On the Unionist side Hartington was not the only leader to want his company. Salisbury invited a call at his house in Arlington Street on the 4th and was 'gladly' obliged.[1] Dilke noted that day: 'Chamberlain very sore against Labouchère and others.'[2]

Hartington himself was in the depths of despair and genuinely amazed at the approval with which his speech had been greeted. 'I thought I made a very bad speech: I am sure that it was quite wretched in delivery and form and I was afraid that I had not said what I intended.' As for parliament, he intended to say nothing there until the debate on Parnell's amendment, and then to make it brief. 'I was awfully long the other day at Newcastle.'[3] A conversation with Goschen and other members of the government had done nothing to raise his spirits. 'I can't see how they are ever to pass a Coercion Bill, and if they fail there must be either a dissolution or the Grand Old Man must come back. It is a bad look out, but Parliament is in such a rotten state that I can't see how it is to be helped.'[4] Other Whig Liberal Unionist leaders had more fight in them and gave ample evidence of it at a conference of the party at Manchester on the 5th. James presided, reading out a most outspoken letter from Lord Derby. The gist of it was that there were but two alternatives to choose

---

[1] Chamberlain to Salisbury, 3rd February 1887. Salisbury Papers.

[2] Gwynn and Tuckwell, *op. cit.*, p. 267. He also remarked that 'Chamberlain was very rude and vindictive against Labouchère and others' and feared 'all this split has spoilt Chamberlain and that he will be very difficult for all men to work with in the future. He and Randolph' were 'now like rogue elephants'. Diary of Sir Charles Dilke, 4th February 1887. Add. MS. 43927. Very probably the first item is a watered-down version of the second.

[3] Hartington to the Duchess of Manchester, 4th February 1887. Devonshire Papers, 340. Add. MS.

[4] *Ibid.* On 5th February 1887 Sir Edward Hamilton recorded that Hartington at Newcastle had shown 'no sign whatever of yielding' and had, on the contrary, 'put his foot down more firmly than the most Tory of Tories'. On the 6th he thought it worth while to note that the Duke of Westminster had decided to sell his portrait of Gladstone by Millais. Sir Edward Hamilton's Diary, 5th and 6th February 1887. Add. MS. 48645, pp. 101–4.

between—'either to maintain the Union or to let Ireland go'.[1] In his own inaugural address the president made a most vigorous onslaught on Home Rulers, Gladstonians and Nationalists alike. Apart from some lawyer-like points against the 'Plan of Campaign', the speech consisted of an attack on the Gladstonians for their silence on this subject and the dangers of putting power into the hands of those hostile to Britain. 'It did not improve your control over a somewhat unruly horse to take the bit out of his mouth, and sit on the box with only the reins in your hand; yet that was what' Britain had been asked to do 'as regarded Irish obedience to the central authority'.[2] Nothing in the proceedings gave the slightest evidence of support for the Chamberlainite policies of 23rd December and after. Hartington had spoken for the vast majority of the Liberal Unionist party. Bright left Chamberlain in no doubt as to his position. At the instance of his brother, Arthur Chamberlain wrote to Bright requesting he contribute an introduction to a volume of speeches made by Chamberlain on the Irish question, beginning with those delivered in the Commons when the Home Rule and Land Bills had been under discussion the previous year and ending with the Birmingham affair of a few days before.[3] The book was to be published by the National Radical Union in a cheap edition, as it was thought 'the constituen-

[1] *The Times*, 7th February 1887.

[2] *Ibid*. See Appendix 2. See also Wolf, *op. cit.*, pp. 191–2 for Ripon to Morley, 7th February 1887 and Morley to Ripon of the same date. Ripon in his letter still adhered to his mood of 1st February. 'I hope,' he warned, 'that in your negotiations with Chamberlain you bear in mind that it is not impossible, in attempting to heal one breach, to produce another. To my mind the essence of the position is that we must carry the Irish representatives along with us in anything that we may agree to. We need not refuse concessions to Chamberlain which they are willing to accept. But it would be impossible for us, consistently with the principles which we have steadily laid down, to attempt to "settle" the Irish question without the concurrence of the Irish leaders. Personally, I should care very little if the round table were, as Illingworth said, to be "put up for sale". I should be glad to see Liberal reunion if it can be got without a sacrifice of the Irish cause, though I have no great desire to see the Party once more inundated with the cold stream of Whig country gentlemen. But it would be both foolish and wrong to abandon any portion of our essential principle in order to snatch a hasty junction with men who have forfeited the confidence of the overwhelming majority of the party in the country. We can afford to wait; they cannot. I would give them much in matters of form; nothing in matters of principle.' Morley replied post-haste, full of hope and bounce. Chamberlain, he claimed, had already made important concessions, especially over a Home Rule scheme based on 'the Canadian Federal precedent'. 'Don't think,' Morley continued, 'we should have screwed him up to this point without the temptation of the Round Table. *We* are exactly where we were. He will carry off not a single scrap of substance from us.' But as Wolf adds: 'A few days later Chamberlain slipped through Morley's fingers, carrying with him all his contemplated concessions, and the Round Table collapsed.' Wolf, *op. cit.*, p. 192.

[3] Arthur Chamberlain to Bright, 9th February 1887. Copy. Chamberlain Papers, JC5/7/55.

cies' were 'in a more receptive condition than they were during the period of the last election and inclined to consider calmly proposals that they scouted during the Gladstonian fury'. The letter made quite clear Bright need not in any way commit himself to the opinions expressed. All that he had to do was give his own reasons for opposing Home Rule. The day after receiving brother Arthur's request, 11th February, Bright replied in the negative. The letter had 'rather disturbed' him and he was 'very unwilling to accept responsibility for what is on the pages of a book' by someone else.[1] 'Joe' had known full well how little his fellow Birmingham member shared some of the opinions contained in the speeches, but had entertained the hope of getting what he wanted by telling his brother to insist no responsibility would be implied. Of course, Bright did not fall for that one. He was old, not senile. To a second attempt, on the 13th, he sent the same reply.[2] That little piece of manoeuvring had failed. The only things actually singled out as being quite unacceptable had been ideas on Federation and the analogy of the Canadian constitution. In themselves a clear enough answer to the question of where Bright stood in relation to the Conference.

Arthur Chamberlain gave away the real reason behind the whole move at the end of his second appeal. Bright being somewhat out of the controversy would carry great weight with many people, especially in Birmingham. It therefore seemed 'natural' to the Chamberlains to ask for a token of broad support 'in this crisis'. Necessary rather than 'natural', because the result did not surprise 'Joe'. Birmingham conditions made even a scintilla of Bright's support worth its weight in gold. The speech of 29th January had proved to have been a temporary solution.

Originally, the idea had been for another session at the 'Round Table' once parliament had met and the government's policy produced. Bad feeling had intervened to prevent its realisation. Trevelyan arranged to see Harcourt on the 6th February and was told how Chamberlain's public utterances 'had appeared to other members of the conference as inconsistent with friendly negotiation'.[3] At the same time, as Chamberlain had himself made similar complaints, 'some steps should be taken to prevent the conference falling through'.[4] Those steps Harcourt induced Trevelyan to undertake.

[1] Bright to Arthur Chamberlain, 11th February 1887. Chamberlain Papers, JC5/7/56.

[2] Arthur Chamberlain to Bright, 13th February 1887. Copy. Chamberlain Papers, JC5/7/57. Bright to Arthur Chamberlain, 15th February 1887. Chamberlain Papers, JC5/7/58. Of course, Bright's Radicalism had by this time lost a lot of its bounce. See J. T. Mills, *John Bright and the Quakers*, Vol. II, p. 323.

[3] *Annual Register*, 1887, pp. 17–18.

[4] *Ibid.*

He invited all five 'Round Tablers' to dinner at his London house on the 14th.[1] That morning Morley had been thinking along lines proving how very much 'steps' needed taking. Reflection had made him change his mind over meeting Chamberlain in private. The situation in the Commons' lavatory had not been conducive to clear thinking.

> You can have no assurance [he told Harcourt] that it would be kept private; and if you could, I don't know that it would really affect the difficulties of the conference. What I suggest is that the matter should wholly stand over until the end of the very difficult week in front of us. I have two speeches to make. J. Chamberlain will pretty certainly speak on Parnell's amendment and I will bet twenty to one that *you* are dragged in. If you feel bound to say anything to J. Chamberlain, you might say that his offensive speech has thrown things back and has irritated our friends; perhaps the coming week's work may bring some good counsel to the front again.[2]

Fortunately for the men of 'goodwill', Harcourt was one ahead of him. Before much of that 'difficult' week had passed Trevelyan's invitation lay on Morley's desk. Nor did Chamberlain oblige by speaking in parliament, disappearing as he did to the far north to woo the crofters of the Highlands and Islands. For, as he informed his brother,

> the local leaders of the crofters tell me that they will put their case wholly into my hands and will shut up any Scotch or other member who presumes to interfere with my authority. They seem to be thoroughly in earnest and frankly say they would rather have my assistance than that of all the Scotch members put together. As you know, I am much interested in the question, but independently of this, it seems a good move to take the leadership as it is an absolute answer to the men who declare that I have no longer any influence, or any right to call myself a Radical.[3]

His plans were well up to standard. Deeds spoke louder than even his words. It would not be easy, even for Labouchère, to declare him a humbug. Domestic Radicals had called him in to deal with a domestic Radical matter. He had accepted the call. Gladstone and Morley would find it harder still to break off with him and Trevelyan's invitation acquired an enhanced importance.

Despite what Gladstone had advised, his party supported Parnell in the debate on his amendment. The proceedings lasted five nights,

[1] Gardiner, *op. cit.*, p. 32. Trevelyan was still convinced reunion was 'thoroughly attainable'. See F. W. Hirst in *The Life of William Ewart Gladstone*, edited by Sir Wemyss Reid, at p. 712.

[2] Morley to Harcourt, 6th February 1887. Harcourt Papers.

[3] Chamberlain to Arthur Chamberlain, 8th February 1887. Chamberlain Papers, JC5/11/16. For the general situation at this time in Highland politics see D. W. Crowley, 'The Crofters' Party, 1885–1892', *Scottish Historical Review*, 1956.

beginning on the 7th. Morley spoke with great venom[1] on the 8th and Harcourt with moderation on the 11th.[2] Hartington made a powerful contribution on the 10th,[3] but no major minister took part. In Harcourt's words, the government relied upon 'twopenny-half-penny lawyers', yet the outcome, the first division of the session, gave the government a majority of 106.[4] No fewer than 68 Liberal Unionists of all shades were included in it. The knowledge was widespread that many Liberal Unionists were keener than the ministry on a tough policy in Ireland. The 11th must have seemed a magic day to Salisbury, for some hours ahead of the division the Irish Court of Appeal had decided the 'Plan of Campaign' was illegal, and parties involved in a fraudulent concealment of property, guilty of an act of bankruptcy. Yet to Hartington it all appeared useless. 'We have been talking for a fortnight and not a single thing done', was his moan to the Duchess of Manchester. 'I hope,' he went on, 'that Goschen, now that he has got into the House, will wake' the government

up a bit; but anyhow, I don't see what is to be done. The evictions and all that is said about jury packing in Ireland makes a good deal of impression here, and they will *never* carry a Coercion Bill. There is a sort of passive resistance in Ireland now, which seems to grow in proportion to any attempt to put it down, and there seems to be nobody strong enough to deal with it. I get more and more hopeless about it all every day, but I shall go on fighting as long as it is of any use.

There then followed one of the most startling things Hartington must ever have committed to paper. It could only have figured in correspondence with someone as intimate as a trusted mistress. 'I almost hope something may come of Chamberlain's negotiations, though I have not given him any encouragement, as I really believe that if it does not succeed, we shall have Mr G. and his mania back again before long.'[5]

[1] Hansard, 3rd Series, Vol. CCCX, Cols. 898–914. In particular he quoted what Chamberlain had said in 1885 about the need for landlord reciprocity and how excessive rents were in fact the 'confiscation of life savings'.

[2] Hansard, 3rd Series, Vol. CCCX, Cols. 1308–28. This is not to say Harcourt was meek and mild. He accused the Liberal Unionists of having as their fundamental principle, not only the neglect of Irish opinion and Irish wishes, but the denial of them. Nor did he let Goschen off lightly. Why, he asked, if Goschen was 'the champion of his country', as he had claimed at Liverpool, had he put on Conservative ministerial uniform?

[3] Hansard, 3rd Series, Vol. CCCX, Cols. 1113–34.

[4] Hansard, 3rd Series, Vol. CCCX, Cols. 1471–4. J. W. Barclay, M.P. for Forfarshire, was the only Liberal Unionist who voted with the Gladstonians and Parnellites.

[5] Hartington to the Duchess of Manchester, 11th February 1887. Devonshire Papers, 340. Add. MS.

Chamberlain's tactic of 'evade and rule' had not worked a complete transformation of the scene. The negotiations upon which Hartington had at last come to set some store became seriously compromised because of events at Newcastle. Having spoken in the Commons, Morley too made for the north, but only to his constituency. There his second pronouncement of the week was to be made on the 9th.[1] True to his promise to Harcourt and the spirit of the Trevelyan invitation, he kept resentment against Chamberlain within bounds. Indeed, there was only one oblique allusion to him.

> The Chairman [he said] referred to a Canadian settlement. Now I am one of those who think that if you are in a conference there is some delicacy in treating in public matters which are there dealt with more or less privately. It is a matter of taste and good feeling, but that is the way in which my taste and my good feeling point.

Had this been all Chamberlain would still have been angered and thus helped to spoil the effect of his own latest tactic. As it was, there was much more. Spence Watson, who presided, was almost a professional 'Joe'-hater and practised his 'skill' with uninhibited abandon. Almost the first words he used in opening the meeting admonished his *bete-noire* to keep a civil tongue in his head if he was anxious for an arrangement. As if that was not enough, he added that the sole factor making the conference tolerable to the Newcastle Radicals was the fact of having a reliable representative in Morley.[2] To add insult to injury, the two newspapers with which Morley had closest contact adopted a renewed tone of unmitigated hostility.[3] Both were actually indulging in a modicum of *fara da se*, but Chamberlain presumed the worst.

As usual, Harcourt, receiver-general of complaints, had to hear the details of Chamberlain's displeasure.

> You will not be surprised to hear that the tone of Morley's speech at Newcastle is personally most offensive to me. However, I do not intend to allow private feeling to interfere with negotiations which have been dictated by considerations of public policy, and I shall say no more on the subject either to you or to him, although I reserve my right to make a full public reply at the first convenient opportunity.

If his self-control held out, there was a chance of this particular incident passing off, but it had done no good to make a fuss even to

[1] *The Times*, 10th February 1887.
[2] *Ibid.*
[3] *Daily News*, 10th February 1887. *Newcastle Leader*, 10th February 1887. See also *Northern Echo*, 10th February 1887. For a general disclaimer by Morley about the Newcastle paper: Garvin, *op. cit.*, p. 291.

Harcourt. The picture of being too occupied with real Radical work to notice lesser nonsense was spoilt.

Right at the end was a sentence couched in mysterious terms. 'Since I saw you, a point of the highest importance has arisen on which I wish to consult you: please give me five minutes at the opening of the sitting today.'[1] Those words were written on the 10th. During the course of the 11th Brett sent Chamberlain a note very probably bearing on the same subject. The wording makes it quite clear both sender and recipient had discussed what was in it at some time in the very recent past. Indeed, Chamberlain says in his *Memoir* that Brett had raised the matter in a letter of the 8th.

> I find [explained Brett] that I am not at liberty to mention the intermediary's name, owing to 'the relation in which he stands to the Gladstonian party', but I may say that 'he is not an Irishman'. I should suggest caution, but not an absolute refusal to try and find a rough line of agreement. Discussion of details through a third person commits no one, and though it may have no good result can do no harm.[2]

Before the debate on his amendment Parnell had been insisting on retaining the judiciary and the magistrates for any prospective Irish government. The debate itself had dealt with current questions and had not called for expositions of attitude towards an accommodation. Nor would the Irish leader have obliged with any truly frank version of his thoughts on the subject. Brett's message, nevertheless, referred to a willingness on his part to hold an interchange of views with Chamberlain. This much is proved by subsequent correspondence from the same source. Why should such a move have been contemplated just then? The whole affair is shrouded in mystery. Nothing is known of what had gone before or what Chamberlain and Harcourt had to say to one another at their meeting before the sitting. That they would have discussed this development cannot, of course, be proved. Still, Chamberlain got to hear of it shortly before the 11th and there is no trace in any source of any other exciting political development, though trouble was threatening on Parnell's domestic front. Everything was clearly very tentative, but the knowledge of the possibility of by-passing Gladstone and Morley must have appealed to Chamberlain's sense of power, not to mention his sense of humour. It altered the possible course of events at Trevelyan's house and undermined the argument that the Nationalists would never countenance any compromise.

[1] Chamberlain to Harcourt, 10th February 1887. Harcourt Papers. Garvin, *op. cit.*, p. 291.
[2] Brett to Chamberlain, 11th February 1887. Chamberlain Papers, JC5/6/9. See also Appendix 2.

At the end of Brett's letter the question was raised as to who had written the 'London Letter' of the *Newcastle Leader*. Chamberlain had sent his friend a cutting for inspection and was clearly bent on a spot of detective work. Far from letting Newcastle slip from his memory, he had determined upon finding out whether or not Morley was the bitter and secret enemy he suspected him to be. The extraordinary degree of self-righteousness he could muster is staggering, given the fact of his having 'foxed' those friendly to him. Few people want to have their cake and eat it twice. Salisbury had been right. He was as 'implacable as Juno and as touchy as a schoolgirl'.[1] Any attack of any kind rankled deeply and he had never learned to take the cut and thrust of political controversy. For him the only permitted opposition was that he himself was good enough to sanction. Hardly an occasion passed without his raising the matter. MacColl told Gladstone of a dinner party a few days before at which Chamberlain had first expressed anxiety to rejoin the party without appearing to surrender, but then passed on rapidly to lay into Labouchère's attacks upon him.[2] Why, he asked, had not the rank and file and some of the leaders publicly disassociated themselves from them? Naturally, Gladstone could not be expected to say anything, but some of the minor leaders could have. Now it is conceivable that the anger was simulated to gain advantage. Nevertheless, there is evidence of genuine annoyance in sending the cutting to Brett and in his behaviour on the 14th on meeting Morley at Trevelyan's.[3] The truth is that he was able to use real resentment against actual enemies to an end complementary to his 'foxing'. With MacColl he scored a hit. The poor innocent was lured into proposing a dinner party on the 21st for Chamberlain, Trevelyan, Spencer, Morley and the G.O.M.[4] Curiously enough, something came of it, and though precluded by the Birmingham barbed wire entanglement from repudiating the conference, Morley was extremely down in the mouth when he called in to see Dilke on the 13th. The whole affair was in his opinion hopeless, although there was another meeting planned to follow the one due the next day.[5] 'Both sides are very cross, and each side asks, "What is

---

[1] Salisbury to A. J. Balfour, 29th March 1886. B. E. C. Dugdale, *Arthur James Balfour*, p. 101.

[2] Russell, *Malcolm MacColl*, p. 131.

[3] Gardiner, *op. cit.*, p. 32.

[4] When approached, Chamberlain offered 21st February, 22nd February and 4th March 1887 as possible dates. MacColl was engaged on the 22nd and asked Gladstone to choose one of the remaining dates. Russell, *Malcolm MacColl*, p. 131. Gladstone plumped for the 21st. The company ate at the Devonshire Club and Gladstone recorded in his diary: 'Much conversation with C., who was very friendly.' J. L. Hammond, *Gladstone and the Irish Nation*, p. 568.

[5] Gwynn and Tuckwell, *op. cit.*, p. 267.

to become of the other?".'[1] That same day, P. A. Chance, a Nationalist lawyer M.P., told Dilke that O'Shea was 'going forward with his divorce case against Parnell, and that Parnell had no defence possible'.[2] Why nothing came of the plan at that stage is impossible to explain. Perhaps O'Shea felt both private gain and political expediency had a higher priority. He was a great 'patriot'.

[1] *Ibid.* According to Dilke, Morley told him that on the 11th February, while Harcourt was speaking in the Commons, Chamberlain was 'sitting jeering next to him, and when Harcourt said "principle" Chamberlain exclaimed "his principle". The "Round Table" business is hopeless, but they meet at dinner tomorrow at Trevelyan's and meet once again after that.' Diary of Sir Charles Dilke, 13th February 1887. Add. MS. 43927.

[2] Gwynn and Tuckwell, *op. cit.*, p. 268. P. A. Chance was Irish Nationalist M.P. for South Kilkenny. He was born in Chelsea in 1857, but had been educated in Ireland at University College. The information he referred to may have a direct link with the letters mentioned by Chamberlain to Dilke in his letter of 29th December 1886. See Chapter III, p. 125, note 2.

VII

AT THE 'ROUND TABLE' AGAIN: BOUT THREE AND ITS AFTERMATH

———◆◆◆———

'Great men are not always wise.' Job xxxi. 37.

'Ye are spies; to see the nakedness of the land ye are come.'
Genesis xlii. 9.

'Who made thee a prince and judge over us.' Exodus i. 14.

'Am I a dog that thou comest to me with staves?'
Samuel xvii. 43.

EVENTS *chez* Trevelyan began most inauspiciously. Not much love was lost, despite it being St Valentine's Day. Chamberlain arrived first and used language of such violence about Morley that the host feared a personal altercation would break out upon their coming face to face. He was not far wrong, for 'Chamberlain was so cold and almost insulting to Morley' that it looked as though the latter would have left the house. Happily, just at the critical moment, Harcourt turned up wearing an enormous orchid.

> There was a burst of laughter at the apparition, and Harcourt, with mock solemnity, said, 'When the ambassadors of the contending powers meet it is the custom of the plenipotentiaries to wear the favour of the opposing sovereigns.' The jest warmed the atmosphere and the dinner passed off with so much success that the formal resumption of the Conference seemed possible.[1]

The resumption was friendly, yet only superficially so, for a great deal of the time was spent in going over what had already been decided, or reserving what had already been reserved. First, Harcourt asked for 'explanations on certain points' of Chamberlain's land scheme.[2]

---

[1] Gardiner, *op. cit.*, p. 32.
[2] Garvin, *op. cit.*, p. 287. Chamberlain, *op. cit.*, p. 251.

During the following discussion the principles involved in it were never once challenged. Then came another argument about Home Rule, especially the Ulster and administration of justice questions. As usual, Chamberlain insisted upon separate treatment for the northern Protestants, Harcourt and Morley objecting that Parnell would never agree to sabotaging the concept of Irish nationality and the 'financial position of the Dublin authority'. When Morley 'proposed as a compromise that the Crown should have veto for ten years on the nomination of judges', Chamberlain refused his consent. Over the Lord Lieutenancy issue, everyone except him thought that office or some equivalent should continue 'to represent the Executive authority of the Crown'. Coming back to the land problem a happier note was struck when all agreed Morley and Herschell should continue their examination of Chamberlain's scheme with special reference to the questions reserved in his draft, and deputed to Harcourt the task of preparing a Home Rule scheme based on the Canadian model, 'leaving as reserved questions the points on which no agreement had been as yet arrived at'.[1] The situation was summed up by Harcourt: 'We never were on more cordial terms or nearer an agreement', but serious trouble was in store.[2] Irish representation at Westminster had only been touched upon in casual conversation and Morley had taken the opportunity of announcing that though he would accept retention in conference, he would have to 'consider his own position afterwards and might probably have to retire altogether'.[3] He felt his previous statements on the subject had been so strong in a contrary sense that honesty precluded him from the promotion of any scheme going against them. This, Chamberlain regarded as an excuse to cover hostility to the continuance of the conference.

Gladstone was abroad at this time. Before leaving Britain, however, he had written a letter, published in his absence, laying all the blame for the postponement of Liberal legislation, including Welsh Disestablishment, upon the Liberal Unionists.[4] This gave Chamberlain an opportunity to hit out in defence of the whole dissentient party and expose for the benefit of restive Radical Unionists in his 'Grand Duchy' just how unfair and malignant the G.O.M. himself really was. Doubtless the hostile tone of many Gladstonians and much of their press had done a great deal to convince him a counter-attack was called for. He has himself described the situation as 'extremely difficult' for him.[5] Whatever he did, a grave risk was involved over Birmingham. The main problem lay in judging the right moment to abandon the 'foxing'. Local sympathy was the craft in which he

[1] *Ibid.*
[2] Newton, *op. cit.*, p. 175.
[3] Chamberlain, *op. cit.*, p. 252.
[4] Chamberlain, *op. cit.*, p. 252.
[5] Chamberlain, *op. cit.*, p. 252.

hoped to float to safety. Gladstone's letter, coming on top of the *Daily News*, *Truth* and provincial papers like the *Newcastle Leader* seemed to clinch his decision that the time for a break had arrived. Whether Morley or Stead was guilty of the attacks in the last-mentioned journal was immaterial in the last analysis. The attitude they represented was sufficiently widespread to help the plea of persecution and lack of 'goodwill' go home at the west midland fire-sides. Nor was there much time. Soon the government would be proceeding with a Coercion Bill and before that the people of the 'Grand Duchy' had to be convinced such a course was inevitable. If possible it had to be blamed on Gladstone! A bold course had been necessary on 29th January. By mid-February it had become very much more so. The Birmingham Liberal and Radical Association had remained unsplit in 1886. Then the fact was a blessing, now it had become a veritable curse. An active minority of its membership owed allegiance to a 'foreign power' and had constantly to be watched. Their presence gave an added importance to men of the squeamish school like Dale and Harris and a 'father-figure' like Bright. Having got the friendship of the former, Chamberlain had naturally been eager to exploit the influence and authority of the latter, as we have seen, without success. For security both were needed at his side and in a terrible crisis Bright would be obliged to commit himself. The conference had strengthened Chamberlain; so had the hostility to it. Circumstances both invited and dictated what he now undertook.

Arthur Chamberlain was informed on the 18th that the third conference session had been 'satisfactory'.[1] That was all. The local situation occupied top place in 'Joe's' mind. 'This old man is not friendly,' he complained of Bright.[2] The occasion for the comment was the book fiasco, but added proof of perfidy was found in the description of the 'Round Table' as 'a piece of impudence'.[3] The special article in the *Birmingham Daily Post* had dealt with the whole reunion issue in

[1] Chamberlain to Arthur Chamberlain, 18th February 1887. Chamberlain Papers, JC5/11/17. W. T. Stead (1849–1912) was currently editor of the *Pall Mall Gazette*.

John Bright had met Gladstone in the street on 17th February 1887. He recorded: 'Walking along Piccadilly, I met Mr Gladstone—had not seen him since the defeat of his Irish Bill last year. We stopped and shook hands. I remarked we had been far apart for some time. He said: "I hope we may before long be nearer together again", which I doubted or feared we might not be.' Bright asked after the G.O.M.'s family and was told all about Herbert's visit to India. Bright added: 'Mr Gladstone took his glove off to shake hands with me as indicating more cordiality of feelings.' G. M. Trevelyan, *The Life of John Bright*, p. 460. On 18th February 1887 Dilke was informed by Chamberlain that the conference was progressing 'favourably'. Chamberlain to Dilke, 18th February 1887. Dilke Papers, Add. MS. 43888, f. 103.

[2] *Ibid.*   [3] *Ibid.*

a thoroughly useful way, but there had been some difficulty with Collings. That faithful but slow moving friend had been finding difficulty in understanding the new situation and accepting his master's way out of it. Lengthy discussion had not entirely convinced the master that his voice had prevailed, but he was quite hopeful that it had. 'If,' he told his brother, 'you can secure Vince and Harold Carter, I think the Committee will be safe. If not, we must pack the public meeting on the 11th of March'.[1] The ground was being well-prepared for the counter-attack.

As the tussle with Collings implies, the specific nature of 'Joe's' remedy was by then decided upon. Fortune played into his hands when one, F. H. Stockwell, editor of the *Baptist*, invited him to reply to Gladstone's fusillade. About the time of the letter to Arthur he went so far as to tell Lewis Harcourt when they met at Lady Dorothy Nevill's of what was in store. He had, he said, written 'a letter on disestablishment in poor little Wales which will make your hair curl'.[2] While on a visit to Chamberlain in Prince's Gardens, to talk about prospects following the latest talk, Caine had actually been allowed to see the text of it. A single reading was enough to throw him into consternation. The contents were bound, he was sure, to 'prove an apple of discord among the approaching sections' and therefore begged his host not to publish. 'Throw it in the fire,' he urged.[3] A reaction like this proves how tiresome Chamberlain must have found some of his fellow Liberal Unionists. Here was a Radical, who had taken especial pains to give public support to coercion plans and avoid pronouncing in favour of the 'Round Table' talks, now getting cold feet at the prospect of a decisive attack upon Gladstone and a likely end to those talks. How could a man like this, full of assurances that his section leader would not 'sell the pass', maintain any pretence of consistency? Probably the strong emotional pull which was ultimately to take him back to Gladstone was already intermittently at work. On the 15th, Gladstonian hostility at a temperance meeting had certainly left its mark. Nevertheless, 'Joe's' efforts, however 'foxlike' he had suspected them of being, had afforded him a vicarious pleasure.

Had the committee of the Ulster Liberal Unionist Association been admitted to the secret and told what a *modus vivendi* would have

---

[1] *Ibid*. W. B. Vince (1861–1890) was then assistant editor of the *Birmingham Daily Post*. His father, Charles Vince, was minister of the Baptist Chapel in Graham Street, Birmingham, and the family gave Chamberlain its powerful support at the time of the split. Vince junior had been a lecturer for the N.L.F. He died comparatively young from typhoid fever. Harold Carter was another prominent Liberal Unionist in Birmingham.

[2] Gardiner, *op. cit.*, pp. 32–3.

[3] Newton, *op. cit.*, p. 175.

involved, wild shouts of approval would have ensued. On the 14th it had passed the following resolution:

> That this committee representing the Liberal Unionists of Ulster cordially sympathises with Mr Chamberlain's programme for reunion of the Liberal party—viz. to deal effectively with the questions of land reform and local government, but expresses its emphatic conviction that no reunion of the Liberal party is possible on terms which would involve consent to the establishment of an Irish legislative body, or an executive not responsible to the Imperial Parliament, or which would propose the abandonment in any degree of loyal Irishmen to the rule of the Nationalist local majority.[1]

Nothing less could have been expected from that quarter. Others of the same party were hoping against hope for some magic formula to turn Home Rule into reforming Unionism without anyone, even Labouchère and Parnell, noticing. MacColl, ever zealous in reporting movements of opinion among leading political figures, had noticed how very ardent Trevelyan was for the reunion cause. On the several occasions when the two had met in recent weeks, the latter had been most friendly 'towards Home Rule Liberals' and Gladstone personally. Indeed, had given the impression of wanting the reunion to take place at the first possible moment.[2] In the belief that Home Rule was inevitable he wanted, apparently, to remain outside parliament until the matter was settled and therefore craved for a rapid solution. Being a 'Round Tabler' would have satisfied many men, but Trevelyan went further, acting sometimes with others and sometimes alone. At the very time Chamberlain was encouraging the foundation of the Liberal Union Club he embarked upon an extra piece of window-dressing for the 'Round Table' by suggesting the Devonshire Club restart its 'House-dinners', suspended since the party split. Once the idea was adopted it was decided Trevelyan should preside at the first and Campbell-Bannerman at the second.

Trevelyan, however, was aiming at higher things. Being a 'peacemaker' involved more than talking at a table in a conference or at dinner. Quite rightly he saw what the biggest achievement could be and straightway made a bid to bring it off. On 16th February, only two days after his dinner party, he made his way to Devonshire House and there spent an hour and a quarter with Hartington. Like Harcourt he fell into one of the traps Hartington had enumerated at Newcastle and let his wish for reunion lead him to minimise what were actually wide divergences of opinion. Even so, the time chosen for this foray was happier than he could have guessed on setting out, for, as we have seen, the Whig leader was in a very unhappy frame of

[1] *Northern Whig*, 15th February 1887.
[2] Russell, *Malcolm MacColl*, p. 131.

mind and had come to regard the 'Round Table' with far from a jaundiced eye. But, allowing for this, it is hardly credible that the noble lord's view of the situation was 'essentially the same' as that held by Chamberlain, Harcourt and Trevelyan himself. On the other hand there is no doubt that the impression that the same noble lord was 'much interested in the prospect of seeing' the first of these three was absolutely correct.[1] Harcourt greeted Trevelyan's news on the first score with open incredulity, declaring: 'I have found him, though amiable and civil in talking on these subjects, very stiff and dour on the essentials.' He was, none the less, only too ready to be convinced to the contrary by good evidence, 'because, unless we carry Hartington with us, we shall do little to heal the rent in the Party. I am not sure that I agree with you that the more haste the best speed.' Very sensibly, he argued that while knowing 'very well the agencies at work to break us up to which incompatibilities much contribute', success, if it came, would be due to there being in 'the body of the Party' a real desire for reunion. Time alone could develop this. In practice he acted as though the best time was the present, inviting Trevelyan round the next morning to give a full account of his 'impression of Hartington's mind'.[2]

There was, however, no chance of converting Trevelyan to fabian tactics. 'There is great danger in delay,' he thought.[3] Like Chamberlain, he had been keeping an eagle eye upon the antics of those Gladstonians inimical to reunion. Research had revealed to him the extent of Irish Nationalist penetration into some seemingly English provincial agencies. For example, there were 'the clever, amusing letters, full of theatrical and literary gossip, which the correspondent of the *Northern Echo*' wrote daily. 'Notice,' he warned Chamberlain, 'how under the guise of an English Radical the author is running down the Conference.'

> I am told [he went on] that he is T. P. O'Connor, and that he corresponds for all the North Country Liberal papers. This is only a specimen of what the enemies of Union are doing in every corner of the country, and, as long as our efforts are in secret they have the field to themselves. What is done ought to be done as soon as Mr G. gets to London.[4]

That was exactly what MacColl had planned. Apart from stray references, information about his dinner party is non-existent. In his letter to Chamberlain of the 17th, Trevelyan expressed deep pleasure that

[1] Trevelyan to Chamberlain, 17th February 1887. Chamberlain Papers.
[2] Harcourt to Trevelyan, 17th February 1887. Copy. Harcourt Papers.
[3] Trevelyan to Chamberlain, 17th February 1887. Chamberlain Papers, JC5/70/26.
[4] *Ibid.*

his section leader was going to meet Gladstone.[1] But it was not to be on the 22nd as Trevelyan stated, but the 21st, for Harcourt, writing on the 19th, mentioned how very interested he would be 'to learn the outcome of your Monday's dinner'.[2] Monday was the 21st and Gladstone had just returned from abroad. The reference is clearly to an occasion concerned with reunion. 'Whom the cause has joined together, let no man put asunder,' joked Harcourt, adding, 'For my part, I am patient and hopeful.'[3] Once more he stressed the importance of a cumulative effect. 'It is a bad thing to hurry any man's cattle. You must have time to heal wounds and the main element in the operation is to get rid of the "proud flesh".'[4] Undoubtedly a hit at Chamberlain and Morley alike.

Advising patience was all very well, but fresh wounds were being inflicted during the period of uncertainty. Trevelyan had been thinking of the whole spectrum of public activity before becoming so excited. Liberty, Equality and Fraternity at the Devonshire Club was being largely undone by the developments at Brooks's, where the 'door was slammed, on political grounds, in the face of several most eligible candidates'. Within a week Lewis Harcourt, Sir Henry Primrose, Lord Wolmer and Sir Horace Davey were blackballed. Then, too, came the the foundation of the Liberal Union Club. Harcourt was stung into commenting tartly on this, telling Chamberlain:

> I thought your letter to the Liberal Union Club not as bad as might have been expected. I should very much like to have seen a list of the *60*. I fancy that if you had scratched them you would find a very good Tory underneath—at least if Stalbridge is to be taken as the type.

After this attempt to alienate his friend from the whole project on doctrinal grounds, he turned to arguments of expediency.

> I don't think this is a favourable moment for undertaking a deliberate organisation avowedly hostile to Mr Gladstone and purporting to stereotype the differences in the party. Action of that kind would of course indicate a final abandonment of any desire for reunion, which, I feel confident is not your state of mind. After all the great convert we have to make is Hartington.[5]

Primed with Trevelyan's report, he asked Chamberlain for his views on the possibilities of conversion. Now while Harcourt's argument added up to something akin to 'Comme il est méchant, quand l'on attaque il se défend', there was no denying the aid and comfort to the Labouchère school of thought the Club's foundation afforded. A

---

[1] *Ibid.*

[2] Harcourt to Chamberlain, 19th February 1887. Chamberlain Papers, JC5/38/62. In any case see Chapter VI, p. 274, note 4 for reference to Hammond, *op. cit.*, p. 568., and Chapter VII, p. 284, note 1.

[3] *Ibid.*   [4] *Ibid.*   [5] *Ibid.*

better organised Liberal Unionism would logically appear to have a stronger bargaining position, but such reasoning took no account of the increased resentment behind those with whom the bargain had to be struck. The French adage fairly summarised the majority view among Gladstonians about the 'dissentients' and their rights.

On the 18th Chamberlain had sent off to Harcourt a scheme of Irish Home Rule propounded by Cooper of the *Scotsman* as suitable in principle for application later on to Scotland.[1] All Irish legislation was to 'lay on the Table' of the House of Commons at Westminster, a feature Chamberlain deemed neither necessary nor expedient. Statutory conditions would suffice; in the case of education to secure liberty of conscience, and in those of civil rights and property to prevent confiscation and ensure no preferential legislation should be passed in favour of classes or individuals. Should the conditions be broken the legislative power of the 'Imperial Parliament' would thereby be revived as in the Canadian analogy. Harcourt had not expected Cooper to turn out as 'the Gamaliel at whose feet I should desire to sit' and one look at the scheme convinced him its author was 'a bad Cooper', whose cask would not hold water. 'He commits the greatest of all blunders, that of discrediting beforehand by his ungracious phrase the boon he wishes to confer'.[2] The beneficence was of a provocative character. Chamberlain replied with spirit, saying Harcourt had mistaken the intention and importance of the whole idea. Scotland not Ireland was in question. If the scheme were to be accepted, it could then have its scope 'magnified' for the benefit of the Irish.[3] A very lame answer by any standards.

With all these cross currents and the introduction of the federal concept on a broader front there was going to be plenty to talk about at MacColl's. Collings interpreted the situation as one in which Gladstone meant 'mischief'.[4] Brett also was less sanguine, writing to Lewis Harcourt that the conference was still far from 'hopeless collapse',[5] but Chamberlain, of course, was in fighting mood. Four days after meeting the G.O.M. at dinner the bombshell was due to burst in the *Baptist*. As if to match the tentative feelers from Parnell,

[1] Chamberlain to Harcourt, 18th February 1887. Harcourt Papers. Cooper was editor of the *Scotsman*.
[2] Harcourt to Chamberlain, 20th February 1887. Chamberlain Papers JC5/38/63.
[3] Chamberlain to Harcourt, 21st February 1887. Harcourt Papers. The Gladstonian gain in the Burnley by-election (for which see below, pp. 346–47) had just occurred. Sir Edward Hamilton commented that the majority had exceeded 'sanguine expectations'. Sir Edward Hamilton's Diary, 21st February 1887, Add. MS. 48645, p. 112.
[4] Collings to Chamberlain, 22nd February 1887. Chamberlain Papers, JC5/16/22.
[5] Brett to Lewis Harcourt, 22nd February 1887. Copy. Esher Papers.

the Irish in parliament had not been in their usual cracking form. Discussion of the new Procedure Rules had begun on the 17th, and while they were being dealt with at a very slow rate, the opposition was far from unanimous in its attitude towards them. Commenting on the first bout, Brett remarked: 'The Irish made a mess of it last night. They seem to be much cowed. Has the American money stopped and are they afraid of being put on half pay?'[1] Arrangements had been made on the 14th to secure Gladstone's views on what the conference had so far agreed upon. Close contact with the G.O.M. would put a severe test to the 'foxing', all the more so as the finale would begin on the 25th. What actually happened will always remain a mystery, but at any rate no really new developments arose, or else Gladstone would have mentioned them to Harcourt in the letter he wrote him on the 24th. The promised memorandum was drawn up in the presence of the three Gladstonian 'Round Tablers' on the 25th ready for presentation to Chamberlain and Trevelyan on the morrow! Irony was having a fine season. It had started on 23rd December.

The letter was something approaching an encomium of Chamberlain's land scheme.[2] Praise on that score could be showered on him without hurting the true cause, for any Gladstonian government of the future could filch it from him were the Conservatives to satisfy themselves with something modest and inadequate.

Chamberlain's plan for Irish Land [Gladstone began] appears to be in the highest degree comprehensive, and it must have cost him much labour. It involves a large number of principles, each requiring to be weighed and sifted with care and to be accepted by a sufficient number of men of authority in the confidential sphere to render their acceptance beyond that sphere probable. I feel indebted to him particularly for the emphatic repudiation it implies of such use of the public credit as is involved in the Ashbourne Act; and for the manner in which he has opened the very large question. Is it possible to frame a good scheme of

[1] *Ibid.* On 22nd February 1887 Sir Edward Hamilton noted that Gladstone had returned to London the day before and that he had been round to see him that very morning, finding him extremely well and 'quite up in his stirrups'. The Burnley by-election was seen as the turning of the tide. Hamilton went on: 'He had met Chamberlain at a dinner last night given by MacColl. He was pleased with Chamberlain's mood; found him very amenable and ready to discuss at length about the Irish Land Question. I expect they kept clear of Home Rule. I impressed upon him the necessity of not haranguing Chamberlain. Mr Gladstone declared he was quite alive to this.' It appeared that Gladstone intended to take Lord Aberdeen's house at Dollis Hill for the time being. His head was full of a land scheme which, he claimed, it was possible 'to implement without imperilling British credit'. Sir Edward Hamilton's Diary, 22nd February 1887, Add. MS. 48645, pp. 114–17.

[2] Gladstone to Harcourt, 24th January 1887. Harcourt Papers.

Land Purchase *without any use whatever of Imperial Credit*? I confess to having received from his paper new lights upon this vital portion of the subject; and am almost prepared to answer in the affirmative the question I have just put. My 'almost' really has reference to an old habit of mine, which indisposes me to final acceptance of a proposal purely financial until I have had the advantage of testing it in conjunction with experts. The acceptance of this principle when final would open a large space of ground which we should occupy in common with Chamberlain.[1]

The idea of saving money was very attractive, but there might be snags in the scheme.

With respect to the plan as a whole, I do not find any computation to show that the debit and credit accounts will balance—as at present advised, I do not see from whence the local authority could pay in perpetuity, or until redemption the 56 million pounds per annum, which the landlord is to get out of each 100 million pounds of fair rent. Progress with such a scheme cannot be rapid, but if the principle of non-liability can be held, the progress thus achieved would be real and large.[2]

Perhaps the conciliatory tone employed was the result of some well-deployed Highbury charm at the MacColl party, or the dictates of expediency, for the general memorandum too seemed more flexible in approach than the old man's previous pronouncements and his usual reaction to even a superficial glance at something like the *Baptist* letter would have led anyone to expect. At the 'Round Table' he thought, certain supposed differences on Home Rule had been exposed as being no differences at all. Even the genuine ones were not so profound as to put hopes of an eventual agreement out of court. Of course, he as one man could not sanction or reject any projected alteration in the party's plans, nor could his colleagues. A contention many would have thought too modest, if taken in its broadest sense. But moving on from that he argued that long experience had taught him ground for cooperation could be supplied by general confidence until the time for actual legislation arrived. Any immediate attempt to settle too much legislative detail would be dangerous, and he was not confident the conference could do a great deal more just then. The burden of further initiative was firmly pushed on to Chamberlain's shoulders. At his instance Gladstone promised to call his colleagues together and ascertain their general views on whether and how far negotiations could be continued beyond what had already been done. At the end one major concession was made—a concise

[1] *Ibid.*

[2] *Ibid.* See Appendix 3. See also H. G. Hutchinson, *Life of Sir John Lubbock*, p. 252, for a list, published in the *Pall Mall Gazette* on 24th February 1887 and based on the preferences of its readers, of men considered suitable to form a British equivalent of the French Academy of Letters. Gladstone headed the list, having received the most votes.

repetition of what he had said about Land Purchase in the letter to Harcourt. Fair words indeed, but for all that, the full effect was bound to be dampening because, assuming Chamberlain to have been in good faith, he would be reluctant to risk a complete rebuff at the hands of a majority of the Gladstonian leadership. Harcourt himself would probably have resisted such a development. Had Chamberlain invited a decision his own desire for reunion would have become suspect. The G.O.M.'s offer was an empty one. Moreover, it ignored all three questions Chamberlain held vital—Ulster, how the Irish parliament was to be guaranteed, and whether or not the powers of that parliament were to be enumerated. The only real message of the memorandum, land being a secondary issue, was 'Basta, Basta!'. The conference might well have ended over that, not suddenly with an undignified break-up, but through a gradual petering out. Round and round the table the talk would have gone until the quantity of words uttered induced a resigned exhaustion.

Chamberlain decreed otherwise and never got what had been in store for him. Rumours that his surrender was impending had simply strengthened the motives behind the decision to launch the counter-attack in the columns of the *Baptist*.[1] The first salvo went straight on to the target.

> If the Welsh constituencies intend to show their approval of Mr Gladstone's Irish policy, and to support his contention that no legislation for Scotland or Wales can be undertaken, or even contemplated until the Irish question has been settled on his lines, then they have no right whatever to complain of the delay in their hopes, and they must wait patiently until the country has changed its mind, and is prepared to hand over the minority in Ireland to the tender mercies of Mr Parnell and the Irish League.

The second was of a higher explosive; the conversion of the country to Home Rule might be, and probably would be, slow and protracted, taking up to ten or twenty years. There might be no conversion at all.

> But whether the process occupies a generation or a century 'poor little Wales' must wait until Mr Parnell is satisfied and Mr Gladstone's policy adopted. They will not wait alone. The crofters of Scotland and the agricultural labourers of England will keep them company. Thirty-two millions of people must go without much-needed legislation because three million are disloyal, while nearly six-hundred members of the Imperial Parliament will be reduced to forced inactivity because some

[1] *Baptist*, 25th February 1887. For Gladstone's little known and rather unspectacular reply see *Baptist*, 3rd March 1887. Like Chamberlain, E. Strauss in his *Irish Nationalism and British Democracy*, at p. 193, stresses the blockage of British reforms by the Irish question. His explanation for it, however, is profoundly different. See Strauss, *op. cit.*, p. 175.

eighty delegates, representing the policy and receiving the pay of the Chicago Convention are determined to obstruct all business until their demands are conceded.

Were the Welsh nonconformists, he asked, prepared to tolerate such a situation? Hitherto they had supported Gladstone's Irish Bills without much examination 'under the impression they were thereby promoting the cause of Disestablishment in Wales'.

So long as the majority of the Liberal Party is committed to proposals which a large section of Liberals and Radicals firmly believe to be dangerous to the best interests of the United Kingdom, unjust to the minority of the Irish people, and certain to end in the disintegration of the Empire, so long the party will remain shattered and impotent and all reform will be indefinitely postponed.

He next reminded these same Welsh nonconformists that 'some of the best and most earnest friends of Disestablishment were in the Liberal Unionist ranks and were now branded by the leaders of Welsh Dissent as traitors and deserters'.

The only wise and prudent course for Welsh Nonconformists is to press on their leaders the absolute necessity for reuniting the Liberal party, so that this great instrument may once more be brought to bear with unimpaired efficiency to secure the reforms on which Liberals are practically agreed. The plans are methods for settling the Irish Question, which have been rejected, must be set aside and some alternative must be found which will take account of the objections conscientiously entertained by so many good and consistent Liberals. The breach which has been made must be repaired, and this can only be done by conciliatory action, and not by threats of expulsion on charges of treachery. . . . Some of the former leaders of the Liberal party are now engaged in this necessary work of reconciliation. They require, and they ought to have, the support and sympathy of all those who desire that remedial legislation should be at once resumed. The issue of the Round Table Conference will decide much more than the Irish question. It will decide the immediate future of the Liberal party, and whether or no all Liberal reform is to be indefinitely adjourned.

Garvin claimed the publication of this letter gave the Gladstonians a 'flaming chance for retaliation'.[1] Yet surely the truth was that Gladstone's letter had given Chamberlain just that chance? To say that the latter misjudged the effect of what he had written is contradicted both by what he said to Lewis Harcourt and the way he always learned from experience. Reaction to the Birmingham speech could have left him in no doubt as to what was likely to occur, especially as it would be the second 'offence'. He realised the G.O.M. was keen

[1] Garvin, *op. cit.*, p. 293.

for Home Rule and scented victory. He knew a *modus vivendi* based on his land and local government schemes alone would never come about. He saw the necessity of rallying the Radical Unionist forces to uphold the Conservative government and felt circumstances allowed him to do so safely because of the vicious attacks upon him. Righteous indignation was going to be his tack. Why should he be silent under the impact of insult and everyone on the Gladstonian side be given *carte blanche*? It had of course been the intention of enemies like Labouchère and Stead to bring about just such an outburst. But the fact of it suiting them did not mean it did not suit him even more. When verbatim reports of the *Baptist* letter along with lengthy leading articles filled the columns of the press, he was invariably a gainer. Support strengthened him with the Conservatives, Whig Liberal Unionists and docile Radical Unionists in the country and in his 'Grand Duchy'. Attack strengthened him with these same people, plus many restive Radical Unionists, above all those in the town of Birmingham. The two later contacts with Gladstone do not prove anything about his intentions in the period preceding and including 25th February. The situation was fluid and some Radical Unionist reactions to government policy and Gladstonian propaganda after that date made him regret what he had done. Hence the description of the letter as 'indiscreet' to Dilke does not mean he had been mistaken as to its effect, but mistaken as to the direction events generally would take.[1] Expediency apart, he was, as a vehement Radical, much troubled by the difficulty of reconciling his creed with backing Salisbury during the first half of 1887. The offer and acceptance of the American mission were together a recognition of his dilemma.

The whole of the correspondence from 25th February to 8th March illustrates clearly how Chamberlain was ready to end all pretence of continuing the conference and how the Gladstonians were not, thus supporting the view that the *Baptist* letter was intended as its ruination. Nevertheless, unwilling though they were to incur the *odium* of ending the talks, the latter apparently made it clear the Home Rule reins should remain firmly in their hands. On the 22nd, the morning after meeting Gladstone, Chamberlain had received a note from Brett, telling him, 'Parnell has drawn back'.[2] The reason was his fear that Morley might resent a Radical Unionist-Nationalist interchange. Though he was described as 'thinking the matter over',[3] there could be little doubt the idea would be heard of no more. Brett thought Chamberlain had profited to the extent of discovering the Irish would

---

[1] Gwynn and Tuckwell, *op. cit.*, p. 268.
[2] Brett to Chamberlain, 21st February 1887. Chamberlain Papers, JC5/6/10.
[3] *Ibid.*

accept almost anything Gladstone accepted. Maybe, but Gladstone was not going to accept anything. He also ventured to say Parnell now knew that if he desired a settlement, Morley had to have the fact sternly impressed upon him. Again, maybe, but Parnell was, on Brett's own evidence, afraid of crossing Morley. There was to be no dealing other than between the 'Round Tablers'. Later on, Chamberlain took steps to ensure he was not by-passed by Gladstonian bids to sweeten Hartington.

Just as it had been Morley's, now it was Chamberlain's turn to endure the rough side of Harcourt's nature. Confessing to deep feelings of annoyance, verging on despair, he wrote much regretting what he termed 'your allocution to the Welsh'. It could only be regarded as 'a studied and irritating attack on Mr Gladstone and his party and an attempt to put them in an odious light as the obstacles to Liberal reform'. Herschell had just made a 'considerate and conciliatory' speech, which made the offensive 'tone and temper' of Chamberlain's pronouncement all the harder to bear. Such 'an outbreak of spleen' could but produce the worst impression. Certain of the sincerity motivating his moves towards reunion, Harcourt presumed his friend incapable of judging the effects upon others of what he said and did. Why, after admitting the bad results of attacking the Irish at Hawick, had the whole performance been repeated 'if possible in a more offensive form'? The sole consequence was bound to make it still less likely that 'the Irish people should accept any compromise' in which Chamberlain was supposed to have had any hand.

Moving on from manner to matter, Harcourt claimed the whole of the offending document could be condensed into a single sentence:

> Gentlemen, if you will only pronounce that from first to last Mr Chamberlain has been wholly in the right and Mr Gladstone mischievously in the wrong then you may have disestablishment or anything you please, but until you humiliate Mr Gladstone and place Mr Chamberlain on the pinnacle which is his due neither your objects nor any other Liberal measures shall be allowed to advance.

Such a line made any amount of private negotiation 'of no avail'. If the Gladstonian party as a whole suspected the negotiations had been going on with a basis of that kind, it would regard its three representatives as disloyal to Mr Gladstone. 'I feel,' he wrote, 'that we are engaged in the work of Sisyphus. As soon as we have with great labour rolled the stone up the hill, you in an outburst of temper dash it down again to the bottom.'[1] It was all very well for Chamberlain to complain of the bitterness against him. Why did he not consider how much of it he had himself provoked? Now things would be much

[1] Harcourt to Chamberlain, 25th February 1887. Chamberlain Papers, JC5/38/64. Gardiner, *op. cit.*, pp. 33–4.

worse. Maybe this letter would be resented, but Harcourt felt justified in what he was doing. 'I am conscious of having played quite fairly by you, and I should do no good unless I spoke my mind plainly and frankly as to proceedings which can only wreck the objects you profess to have at heart.'[1]

These were first thoughts, written on the morning of the 25th without consultation with a single soul. Before sending them off a passage through the lobbies left him in no doubt as to the authenticity of his fears.

> The effect of your letter is worse even than I anticipated [he added in a P.S.]. I can only describe the feeling as one of universal indignation, and that of the Welsh M.P.'s as one of fury. Even those who are most anxious for reunion are led to believe you are resolved to make it impossible. But it is a melancholy thing that it should go off, not on principle but on temper.[2]

Of course, there was a deal of unfairness in Harcourt's strictures and in the anger of the Gladstonians in the lobbies. The sentence said to contain the message of the *Baptist* letter could easily have been applied with adjustments as to names to Gladstone's preceding contribution. The G.O.M. was second to none in arrogating truth unto himself. His 'tone and temper' were certainly more restrained, but knowing 'Our Joe' to be a fighter, it was stupid to expect him to criticise without considerable zest. The greater the truth, the greater the libel. The greater the libel, the greater the annoyance. The Gladstonians feared what he said would go home. The Welsh M.P.'s had horrible visions of reduced or destroyed majorities. The 'wirepullers' began to fear their work had been in vain. At bottom Harcourt's anger was that of a man who feels the ground shaking beneath his feet. Chamberlain had played into the hands of the very groups he had almost succeeded in holding at bay. The Sisyphus sentence is the key to the letter. Disappointed men are often unfair. Nevertheless, Chamberlain had spoken out, realising the inequitable conditions in which circumstances had placed him. Feeling not logic ruled the roost. Certainly there had been a lack of discretion in risking the allegation of desiring a break up, for it would inevitably reach home and be exploited by Schnadhorst's 'stoats and weasels'.

Gladstone was slow to move into action. As a matter of fact, he had actually received a copy of what had gone off to Highbury before doing more than glance at the text of what Chamberlain had written. His habit was to read the papers thoroughly late in the day. The land question was still uppermost in his mind and the note commenting

[1] Gardiner, *op. cit.*, p. 34.

[2] Harcourt to Chamberlain, 25th February 1887. Chamberlain Papers, JC5/38/64.

on Harcourt's action began: 'I am glad you approve of my letter, in which my endeavour was to put everything in the mildest form. It was seen by Granville and A. Morley.'[1] What followed was scarcely a helpful guide as to what to do next.

> You have certainly told Chamberlain the whole truth. In reading your expostulation and rebuke I hope he will know, in order to do you justice, that you have been fighting his battle among your colleagues and stirring to obtain for him favourable construction and fullest fair play. This last letter is one of his greatest mistakes.[2]

Harcourt would not at that time have welcomed the note of caution so characteristic of the 'old parliamentary hand', and little knew it was partly due to ignorance. But ignorance apart, 'the whole truth' was something uncongenial to the subtle civilisation of Hawarden, even when its prime exponent was resident in Carlton House Terrace.

There was a humorous side to this latest upset. The prime exponent had the meeting that evening for drawing up the memorandum without even Morley daring to question his unconcern at what had happened. Later the fine copy was made with the awful truth lying around him in his newspapers and Harcourt's letter on his desk! Having this task hanging over his head, his time on the papers had been cut short to perform it. The advance in his understanding of what had occurred between writing to Harcourt and going to bed had not been appreciable. In his own words:

> I wrote out according to our intentions last night what I thought might be taken as a result of our conversation to be communicated to Chamberlain. But I had then only cursorily perused his letter to the *Baptist*, and had taken it as mere personal censure on me (with a side stroke at the Irish) for having given the opinion that the Irish question blocked the way. But I have this morning (i.e. the 26th) read it carefully and it is a denunciation of the 'policy' and the 'proposals' in a mass. I also find it has been widely noticed and has excited much not unjust indignation. Viewing its actual character, I am inclined to think we can hardly do more now than to say we fear it has interposed an unexpected obstacle in the way of any attempt at this moment to sum up the result of your communications which we should otherwise hopefully have done; that on the other hand, we are unwilling that so much ground apparently gained should be lost; that a little time may soften or remove the present ruffling of the surface; and that we are quite willing that the subject should stand for resumption at a convenient season.[3]

Chamberlain had told Gladstone to go on his knees before him. Now Gladstone was insisting the opposite take place and until

[1] Gladstone to Harcourt, 25th February 1887. Harcourt Papers.
[2] *Ibid.*
[3] Gladstone to Harcourt, 26th February 1887. Harcourt Papers.

naughty 'Joe' complied and decided to be a good boy he was to go into a corner. The *Baptist* letter had been written to gain prestige. A lesson had to be inflicted upon its perpetrator for indulging his 'proud flesh'. Full comprehension did not lead the G.O.M. into forsaking caution. A rash reaction under provocation might lead the public into supposing he was the true author of collapse.

For once Harcourt took it all without a murmur of protest. In his letter to Gladstone on the 26th the tone is one of acquiescence and sorrow. 'I was quite prepared,' he admitted, 'for the view which you take of Chamberlain's recent publication. I entirely concur in the judgement you pass upon it and the method in which you propose to deal with it.' On the 25th it is conceivable he was telling Chamberlain indirectly he suspected he had been 'foxing'. To his leader he was quite explicit.

> There is no one who feels more deeply his conduct in this matter, or has more reason to complain of it than I have. I have been the direct organ of communication with him and from first to last we have treated him *uberrime fide*. He has held to us in private the most reasonable and conciliatory language to suit one object and has thought fit to denounce us in public to serve another. I am not surprised that our friends should dislike and distrust negotiations conducted on such a basis.

Then came the question of tactics. If the negotiations were to end, as seemed probable, the Gladstonians should 'take care to put an end to them on grounds from which he can derive no advantage. If they are suspended on the ground of his overweening temper, it will do him much good with the Party and the Country.'[1]

Without waiting for a reply from Birmingham, which, the 26th being a Saturday, could not possibly arrive until the 28th, Harcourt sent off another packet of recrimination couched in even plainer and franker terms. 'I find that the results of your paper have proved this morning even more grave than I had anticipated,' ran his opening rebuke. He then dangled before Chamberlain the picture of a missed opportunity. Of how Morley, Herschell and himself had come together with their leader the evening before, when 'the force of the blow' which had been 'struck at the party of conciliation had not been fully felt', and how, when the discussion was over, Gladstone had drawn up a memorandum upon the points dealt with at the conference table with the express intention of authorising him to communicate it to the Radical Unionist representatives. There was no doubt in his mind 'that it would have afforded a satisfactory basis for further proceedings'. Now all was changed. In a most uncharacteristically schoolmasterish manner, he continued: 'The flood tide of

[1] Harcourt to Gladstone, 26th February 1887. Gladstone Papers, Add. MS. 44201, f. 77.

what seems to me a very just indignation at the manner in which you have treated Mr Gladstone and his friends in the midst of what was supposed to be friendly negotiations is running too high at this moment to make it possible to stem it.' Time had therefore to be taken to consider what could be done to remedy the situation thus created, and a meeting was necessary when Chamberlain returned to London. Having expounded the views of the G.O.M. ('really the most placable of men') and concurred in his hope that the ground gained should not be lost, he appealed for an end of pulling Gladstonian noses in public. Otherwise nothing could come of efforts to patch things up. The parting shot was one of high explosive.

> I learned with great surprise that Hartington had derived from you the belief that the question of an Irish legislature and a responsible Government had never been entertained by the conference, and that you and we had never agreed to anything but a strictly *municipal Government*. It is a very bad job, and I wish I saw my way out of it.[1]

Avoiding serious wounds was going to tax all Chamberlain's 'fox-like' qualities to the utmost. Giving Harcourt the lie would not work as he could immediately have recourse to Hartington and the risk of full exposure loom all too large. Keeping his leader in the background and, if not in the dark, then in the twilight had always been Chamberlain's aim from the very beginning of his phoney reunion activities. A total revelation now was the last thing his position allowed of. Bluff alone remained to him as a mode of escape.

To the first Harcourt attack he returned a reasoned and skilful reply, containing not an iota of apology. The whole business would drag on still longer under conditions of *toujours la politesse*. He agreed with Harcourt that their task was 'almost impossible', there being 'so much sensitiveness and feeling *on both sides*' as to make the difficulties wellnigh unsurmountable. The Gladstonian, and indeed Harcourt's attitude towards his position infuriated him. Why should he be expected to ignore or overlook all the offensive remarks about himself and the 'repeated asseverations' that no concessions whatever would be forthcoming from the Gladstonian side? It was extremely trying to be told constantly that he would be allowed back within the true fold only after 'sufficient and complete acts of submission and penitence'. Not only had men like Morley, Stansfeld, Campbell-Bannerman and Sir Charles Russell, and organs like the principal journal of the party—the *Daily News* acted in this way, but Gladstone himself, 'in recent letters and speeches', had made clear he adhered 'to the whole policy' to which the Liberal Unionists objected and was not prepared to make 'the slightest concession'. Something of an

---

[1] Harcourt to Chamberlain, 26th February 1887. Chamberlain Papers, JC5/38/65. Gardiner, *op. cit.*, p. 35.

exaggeration, but not appreciably wide of the mark. It was certainly true that, as Chamberlain next pointed out, the Gladstonian press was unanimously of the opinion there were going to be no concessions and wrote of a Birmingham 'cave in' as the sole chance of reunion. The *Newcastle Leader* had had the audacity to suggest Chamberlain was 'furtively preparing for surrender'.[1] Morley and Newcastle having been so prominent in the list of critics gave him a splendid excuse for a counter-attack, for a fellow 'Round Tabler' was a suitable person against whom to have a 'tit for tat'. Strong too was the argument that Gladstone spoke as no one else did for the majority Liberal party and could not be discounted. 'Joe' had Harcourt in a fix, and seeing his advantage pressed home the attack with a piece of chronic unfairness.

> From first to last [he stormed] there has never been the slightest indication on the part of any Gladstonian of an intention to make the slightest concession of any kind in order to meet the advances which I have openly made. What is the result? I get letters daily urging me not to sell the position and declaring that if I do the Unionists will not follow me.[2]

This was to ignore the vast numbers of the men of 'goodwill' and the way their leaders had exerted themselves upon his behalf. One can only conclude he was trying to manoeuvre himself into the position of being able to claim the discussion had been one in which the Gladstonians had stuck to Home Rule while the Radical Unionists had been peddling Provincial Councils. Doubtless it was true numerous Unionists had written in the vein he described. None the less, most of the letters were inevitably from Whigs and few well-informed people had ever supposed they would ever follow Chamberlain back to Gladstone. Radical Unionist views were divided and their leader had to mind his 'p's' and 'q's'. The side to which he finally inclined was determined by the balance of forces in the home base. On 26th February he was still confident of breaking up the conference and simultaneously appearing a martyr to Gladstonian 'bigotry and malice'. 'I must point out to you,' he patronised, 'that a compromise is one thing, but an abject surrender such as is attributed to me is another, and I cannot afford to give colour to such an accusation.'[3] Afford in what way? It was, of course, not impossible that if it came to the pinch, most of Birmingham Liberalism would have 'caved in' with him. Bright was very powerful, yet not all-powerful. A combination of energetic men like the Chamberlain clan, Bunce, Dale and Harris, backed of course, by the Gladstonian minority, might have overcome the influence of a man whose physical faculties were considerably sapped and zest for battle seriously diminished. But pride

[1] Chamberlain, *op. cit.*, pp. 254–6. Gardiner, *op. cit.*, pp. 34–5.
[2] *Ibid.*   [3] *Ibid.*

too undoubtedly stood in the way of 'affording' and 'Joe' was one of the proudest of men, and at bottom the whole point was an excuse as well as a complaint. 'Home opinion' was and is one of the commonest explanations, genuine or false, employed in external relations. The 'Grand Duke' could sometimes fabricate besides heeding opinion within his domain.

In discussing the *Baptist* letter itself, Chamberlain sought to fix the blame for any rupture in the reunion talks fairly and squarely upon Gladstonian shoulders. There is more than an element of the disingenuous about the way he explained things. First, he would not admit the interpretation Harcourt had given to the letter was at all justified. His view was and always had been that the 'Round Tablers' were substantially agreed about 'principles and objects', while differing about 'methods'.[1] What constituted a principle and what a method? Those were the crucial questions. The laws of semantics allowed the term 'Home Rule' to mean very different things to different men. So when Chamberlain proclaimed himself prepared to accept the Gladstonian principles he was not really being very precise. He would be able to say Provincial Councils were but a brand of self-government if the need arose. At that moment, of course, he was stressing how very much he had conceded by agreeing to discuss what was usually understood by 'Home Rule' at all, and meant Harcourt to understand as much. Having made the great sacrifice of accepting as a basis of the talks something he himself had advocated in the past, he appealed to his friend for a putting aside of 'old methods'. New methods, 'less open to objection and equally consistent with the principle' could surely be found? Were Harcourt and Gladstone to give assurances on this, there would not be reason again to complain 'of the form of' his 'justification or explanation'. A safe enough promise to give, for he knew the Ulster and Westminster representation problems would not be lightly settled in his favour after all the fuss made at the 'Round Table' about reserving them. A threat followed hard upon the promise. 'But if it is not your intention—if you mean to stick to old methods and continue to give everyone the impression that you are immovable and that every sacrifice must come from me—then we have mistaken each other and we had better retire from an impossible position.'[2] In other words—surrender to me, or else the conference must end. This sort of attitude had very little relevance to the idea of keeping his end up. Provided any settlement had included land scheme and local government victories for him, his return to the Liberal majority could not have been depicted as an 'abject surrender'. Had Westminster representation been agreed to, then defeat on Ulster alone would have appeared excusable. No,

[1] *Ibid.*   [2] *Ibid.*

'Joe' was engaged in wrecking and therefore demanded complete and immediate satisfaction. A rapid cessation was necessary for his plan to work.

Coming down to details, he claimed everything in the letter had simply been intended as an answer to Gladstone's charges about the blockage of reform levelled at the Liberal Unionists. Blockage would be obviated through Liberal reunion and that could be achieved by one thing alone—mutual concession. The phrase 'poor little Wales' had been taken amiss. He just could not see why the Gladstonians had interpreted it as a sign of 'malignant spite'. Then the idea of calling it a day was repeated. 'We look at all this from such different standpoints that agreement is almost impossible and the attempts to secure it only produces misapprehension.' The situation was 'very grave'; party feeling had never run higher and 'a large section of politicians' were 'apparently willing to run any risks, to accept any policy' which could embarrass their opponents and 'make the government of the country impossible'. Nothing would induce him to sympathise with such tactics, and if the 'future programme of the Liberal party' was to include 'Plans of Campaign, Obstruction, and Heaven knows how many wild theories of revenge or destruction', he would be obliged to 'stand aside . . . or resist them'. 'The avowed object of the Gladstonians,' he was convinced, was to identify Gladstone's original Home Rule Bill with Liberalism and 'force out of the Party everyone' who would not swallow it. Then the aim was 'by purely party tactics to get rid of the Tory Government and take their places.'[1] For 'Gladstonians' read 'Gladstone and a large section of his party' and Chamberlain was right, but it was a pity Harcourt had to be the one to take this particular knock. Not satisfied with moving for an end to the talks, Chamberlain drew to a close with yet another threat. It made quite clear how he expected future events to go.

> I have hitherto done my best to prevent Hartington from joining a Coalition and I have always rejected the possibility of my doing so. But if things continue on their present footing I must either go out of politics altogether—or assist in forming some third Party that will strenuously resist the new Programme of Labouchère and Co., while ready to give effect to the older policy of Constructive Liberalism. In any case, let us remain friends—even if it is out of the question that we should be allies.[2]

'Out of the question' was a most definite phrase. Chamberlain's policy was going to be a building up of Radical Unionism as *the* pressure group the government needed for survival. A counter attack could then be launched against the Gladstonians in good conscience, for the potential of the pressure group as an offensive weapon would

[1] *Ibid.*   [2] *Ibid.*

wring from the Conservatives legislative concessions of a distinctly 'Constructive Liberal' kind. The argument that the government would give little if the votes of the group in parliament were small in number and certain on major issues would no longer hold. The future had to be thought of and, with such a fundamental and lasting threat as Home Rule on the political menu, by-elections during the current parliament and the next general election were things never to be lost sight of.

On receipt of what he termed the second 'lecture', Chamberlain sent Harcourt a note which was clearly intended to finish off the good work of disentanglement begun the day before. So far as he was concerned, the history books would record 27th February as the day when disingenuousness from the Gladstonians had obliged him to call for an official conclusion to what their persecution had ruined. Harcourt's reference to the misinforming of Hartington had cut to the quick. As argued above, bluff was the only way out.

> You are *quite* wrong about Hartington as I could prove to you in two minutes if it were worthwhile. But is it worthwhile? Your lecture this morning has pretty well completed the work which your lecture of yesterday commenced, and if it is your intention to abandon the conference and the hopes raised by it, I shall receive your decision with something approaching a sense of relief.[1]

Evasion and counter-charge, attributing to an opponent the precise path to be followed by oneself was the neatest way Chamberlain could find of extricating himself. As bluff it was not bad, for if the talks ended there would be no need to consider whether Hartington should or should not have joined them, or what he should or should not have been told. But evading was one thing, catching another, and Chamberlain had not yet lured Harcourt into the snare set to trap the Gladstonians into bringing reunion prospects to a full stop.

Much emerged too as to how very coolly he had surveyed the power balance in relation to the talks.

> It seems to me [he hectored] that you must have entered on the negotiations with a totally wrong idea. You appear to have thought it possible for me to remain absolutely silent and passive while the Gladstonians, high and low, were doing everything by organisation, by speeches, by letters, by articles in the newspapers and by proceedings in the House of Commons to strengthen their position. This would have been a very one-sided armistice, and if the conference failed it would have left me in an entirely defenceless position.

His view had been that, until an agreement was arrived at, each side was at liberty 'to fortify itself against the possibilities of the future'.

[1] Chamberlain to Harcourt, 27th February 1887. Harcourt Papers. Gardiner, *op. cit.*, pp. 35-6.

Despite the constant assertions by men inside as well as outside the conference that it was merely intended to cloak his capitulation as a compromise, he had made no direct answer, restricting himself to statements intended to clarify the position. Such statements the Gladstonians had immediately treated as 'mortal offences'. There had not been the slightest concern for his plight. Two letters from Wales waiting for him in London both spoke of the immense effect produced by the Gladstonian allegations against Unionism over the delay in disestablishment. If the conference had been supposed to seal his lips, while leaving Gladstone's free, the sooner the conference was 'speedily abandoned the better'. Backing up what was by any test a capital hit with a snatch of self-pity, 'Joe' confessed himself 'deeply wounded' by Harcourt, whose letters had gone 'altogether beyond the limits of friendly remonstrance'.[1] The correspondence could not continue if couched on the latter's side 'in such arbitrary terms'.

'Foxing' had paid off excellently so far. The ice had often been uncomfortably thin and no more so than on 27th February, with Harcourt in a singularly aggressive mood and indecently interested in Hartington. The Gladstonians had therefore to be caught out before any damage was done.

> If it be, as I understand it is [wrote 'Joe'], your intention to bring negotiations to a close, I hope we may be able to agree on the form in which this decision is to be announced. It is, of course, clearly understood that the proceedings of the conference will remain secret, and that both sides are perfectly free to pursue any policy they may see fit in the future, and are not to be held committed by anything that has passed in confidential intercourse. I am afraid the political future is dark, but the responsibility does not rest with me.[2]

[1] *Ibid.*

[2] *Ibid.* Sir Edward Hamilton jotted down that Lord and Lady Pembroke were of the opinion that Churchill would 'go for Home Rule and smash up the Unionist party before two years were up'. Sir Edward Hamilton's Diary, 27th February 1887. Add. MS. 48645, p. 118. On the same day Herschell wrote to Chamberlain, apologising for having omitted to have coupled his name with those of James and Trevelyan when discussing some aspects of Liberal reconciliation, but scolding him soundly for the 'Baptist Letter'. 'As I am writing,' he remarked, 'I cannot help expressing the regret with which I read your letter to the Welsh paper. I have never said anything to embitter the existing situation and I cannot help feeling that you might have said all that was necessary from your view to establish your point, if it were necessary to establish it, without introducing matter so calculated to give offence. It is hard enough under any circumstances for those who desire moderate counsels to hold their own, but I assure you, that such a letter as yours makes the task almost impracticable. It makes me in my position an object of suspicion and vastly adds to the difficulty of concessions of any kind. You have always evinced so friendly a spirit towards me that I am sure you will not misunderstand the spirit in which I write this, or doubt its friendliness.' Herschell to Chamberlain, 27th February 1887. Chamberlain Papers, JC5/42/5.

In the renewed role of active Radical on the Unionist side, he was going to use Provincial Councils as the answer to Parnell. He wanted no doubts raised as to whether they were a serious proposition. Security all round was best for 'Our Joe'.

Sunday the 27th was not a day of rest for either Harcourt or Morley. The former composed a letter to *The Times* on the Land Commission Report and coercion.[1] The two had talked the matter over on the Saturday evening, agreeing that the latter should check through the facts, figures and logic, without in any way taking on any responsibility 'as to the expediency of the publication'.[2] Given Chamberlain's determination to back coercion, the spirit of enterprise Harcourt showed in furthering the anti-coercion campaign made nonsense of going on with the 'Round Table'. Expediencey apart, there was no common ground on the most urgent Irish question. The leading Gladstonian 'Round Tabler' thought it 'of the first importance to possess the public mind as soon as possible of the salient points as to the policy of coercion'. He was willing to take all the consequences of doing so on to himself. 'The government,' he was certain, found itself 'in a position from which there is no escape.' 'The moment of *Sedan*' had arrived for them and they 'should be smitten hip and thigh'.[3] Morley scrutinised the text carefully, but could find no fault. 'Nothing but good could come of it. *Habent, habent*, and they well deserve it'.[4] Harcourt was making up for a very long period of restraint and now shared with his leader the view of coercion as the great political weapon with which to purloin power. Yet risks had to be minimised and the enemy should not be gratuitously strengthened. Chamberlain should still be prevented from profiting from the way the conference ended, assuming his faith to have been bad. And, if it were not, then no chance of attaching him, when coercion was smashing up the Unionist combination and his bargaining power became almost nil, should be lost.

On the 28th, therefore, instead of falling for his friend's wiles, Harcourt returned a soft answer. Dealing first with the issue of injured feelings was comparatively easy.

> If I have written rather warmly on this subject, you must ascribe it to the acuteness of my disappointment at the increased frustration of an object for which I have so earnestly and so honestly laboured and at the collapse (I trust temporary) of hopes which seemed just on the point of fulfilment.

Chamberlain's wish that the two remain friends he heartily recipro-

---

[1] *The Times*, 28th February 1887.
[2] Harcourt to Morley, 27th February 1887. Copy. Harcourt Papers.
[3] *Ibid.*
[4] Morley to Harcourt, 27th February 1887. Harcourt Papers.

cated. The one point singled out for challenge was the claim that the Gladstonians had never given the slightest indication of being prepared to make concessions of any kind. What Chamberlain had put about principles and methods he accepted as fair and accurate, and nothing Gladstone or anyone 'having authority to speak in his name' had since the commencement of the conference said 'anything inconsistent with this position'. The 'chatter of insuperable frivolity' was quite another matter and Chamberlain paid too much attention to it. Here Harcourt delivered a masterstroke, putting an end to all the dreams of a clear-cut termination to what Morley termed the whole 'fruitless episode'. He admitted Gladstone had been willing to revise method and offered the one boon implicit in Chamberlain's complaints and the one boon past humbug forbade him to accept—publicity.[1] Not a fit diet for a 'fox'. His own last specific request to Harcourt had been for secrecy. Without publicity Chamberlain had, according to himself, to make speeches like that of 29th January and write articles like the *Baptist* letter. With it he might be ruined as a national and badly damaged as a local politician. Just then, that is. Yet here was a promise being handed to him on a plate. 'I think you are quite entitled to have it publicly known that we have proceeded throughout on this basis [i.e. revision of method]. I should have had no difficulty myself if you had expressed a desire on the subject.'[2] But was there any need? To Harcourt the matter had long been clear for Gladstone had said so in a published letter approved of by none other than Chamberlain. Here was the rub with him. He could truthfully say that on the most fundamental matter the Gladstonians had not budged one iota, but they could say with equal accuracy that once he gave way on it their attitude on certain 'methods' and related matters like land and local government had been flexible. Sorting out what Gladstone had meant in relation to all this in the letter would have involved Chamberlain's undoing in the eyes of Hartington, Salisbury and almost all the Unionist camp. Certainly, they might not have wanted further truck with him. He desired a grievance and what he cherished, publicity and explanation would destroy. Harcourt's offer and the existence of the Gladstone letter therefore put paid to a quick release. There were going to be no martyr scenes to kindle fires in the bellies and revenge in the hearts of the Birmingham citizenry.

Two days before the publication of the *Baptist* letter, Herschell, notorious for his 'goodwill', had delivered a speech at Manchester.[3]

[1] Harcourt to Chamberlain, 28th February 1887. Chamberlain Papers, JC5/38/66.

[2] *Ibid.*

[3] 23rd February 1887. *The Times*, 24th February 1887. Extracts from the speech were sent by Harcourt to Chamberlain and are to be found among the Herschell–Chamberlain correspondence in the Chamberlain Papers, JC5/42/5.

In it, thought Harcourt, he swept away all grounds for asserting the Gladstonians were intransigent.

> In speaking of the conference, Herschell [took] the very line which you complain we have not followed. Certainly no man had a better right than Herschell to expound the spirit and the principles upon which our section of the Round Table were acting and in the House of Commons on Thursday last, you expressed yourself to me as completely satisfied with what he had said.[1]

To clinch matters, Harcourt enclosed an extract which to him seemed a complete fulfilment of Chamberlain's conditions for good behaviour. Not unnaturally, the accident of timing made the letter appear like a specific answer to Herschell and the reaction to it among 'goodwill' Gladstonians had therefore been all the more hostile. A comparison between the two productions, made by any impartial person, would, Harcourt was sure, leave no doubt as to which was the more calculated 'to secure the ends of reunion'.[2] He was all for continuing exchanges of opinions with an eye to reopening the conference. As conversations went more smoothly than correspondence and did not leave behind them a mounting irritation, the next step should be a meeting. Having neither the intention nor authority to bring negotiations to a close, he was eager to place Gladstone's views before Chamberlain at the 'earliest opportunity',[3] if the latter would suggest a time and place. Needless to say, Chamberlain had probably been harking back to the very opening of the conference when talking of lack of concessions. Although suspicious of his intentions towards reunion, Harcourt had not realised this and very reasonably regarded Herschell's speech as the perfect answer. Perfect or not it served the purpose of putting Chamberlain in a corner superbly well. Trevelyan's ever augmenting enthusiasm for reconciliation protected him from a revelation of the whole truth to the pundits of Great George Street. Nothing, however, could help him with the ructions likely to arise in the 'Grand Duchy' were the blame for breaking up the conference to be brought to his door. 'Foxing' had its 'Sisyphitic' side.

'Sweet accord' and 'divide and rule' were the weapons he brought into play for breaking free again. His letter to Harcourt on the 29th accepted all assurances of friendship and concentrated upon an exposé of the difficulties with which he was beset.[4] Herschell's speech had had an 'admirable' tone and spirit, but, of course, the *Baptist*

[1] Harcourt to Chamberlain, 28th February 1887. Chamberlain Papers, JC5/38/66.

[2] *Ibid.*   [3] *Ibid.* See Appendix 3.

[4] Chamberlain to Harcourt, 29th February 1887. Harcourt Papers. Liberal Unionist headquarters were in Great George Street.

letter had been written long before. The wind would have been taken out of Harcourt's sails altogether had he been able to claim efforts had been made to cancel its publication. One can be sure that if they had, he would not have let the fact pass without attempting to scoop the maximum credit for such a noble deed. Nothing was said! Instead came the old tack of 'my supporters'.

> You cannot know [he claimed] how I am bothered by Unionist correspondents to express an opinion or make some reply whenever any attack is made on us. Undoubtedly, the result of Mr Gladstone's utterances was to produce the impression that the Unionist Liberals were directly and primarily responsible for delaying Welsh Disestablishment, and it was to meet this special aspect of the case that I wrote.[1]

Having gained all the confidence pertinacious repetition could yield, he next counter-attacked by enclosing two extracts from the morning's newspapers. One was from a speech of Bryce at Liverpool, repeating the 'No Surrender' line so offensive to the Chamberlainites.[2] The other was more important, coming as it did from the pen of the correspondent who had anticipated 'exactly and verbatim' the compromise suggested by Morley at Trevelyan's on the 14th about the appointment of judges.[3] Chamberlain regarded it as curious and argued that if not inspired the writer was uncommonly well-informed. There could be no doubt that he had stated correctly the 'calculations' of a 'section of the Party'.[4] These 'calculations' envisaged an altogether more militant policy towards Liberal Unionism and those in the Gladstonian fold 'soft' on it. 'I have heard of it from many sources,' he confided, 'and also . . .'. There followed his first bid to undermine Harcourt's trust in his colleagues. A desperate effort to inflict the maximum damage upon the group he was sure would remain his principal opponents for the remainder of his political life—long or short. He went on: 'and also of a project in the same quarter to displace you from the Deputy Leadership in favour of Morley. These plans are not likely to succeed, but their enunciation by Morley's friends in the Lobbies and in the press makes people uneasy and suspicious.'[5] Nothing was more fitted to carry 'calculations' than the *Newcastle Leader*, but the 'project' was hardly likely to penetrate to its columns in the same way. Still, the story was extremely plausible, given Harcourt's behaviour and the discontent with it evinced in certain circles. It also served as a reminder that all was not united and

[1] *Ibid.*
[2] Delivered on the 26th February 1887. *The Times*, 28th February 1887.
[3] *Newcastle Leader*, 28th January 1887.
[4] Chamberlain to Harcourt, 29th February 1887. Harcourt Papers.
[5] *Ibid.*

secure in the Gladstonian party and something of a revenge for the pumping of Hartington. The young 'fox' had strong teeth.

With this friendly warning off his chest, Chamberlain returned to the subject of his own plight and told of the total discouragement and despair that periodically descended upon him. Skating on very thin ice was 'more than difficult',[1] yet the traps set for him could be by-passed solely by means of that dangerous sport. As for allegations that he had intended a personal attack upon Gladstone, nothing could be further from the truth. The slightest disrespect had never been meant. Indeed, the old man enjoyed his 'unbound admiration',[2] and any way in which this could be made clear he would readily adopt. Tomorrow would be a good time to meet and talk over the whole business.

During the involuntary reflective period imposed upon him by a violent cold, 'Joe' had ample opportunity to ponder the question of traps. The thought of Harcourt inveigling Hartington into a deal behind Radical Unionist backs, especially his own, kept crowding into his mind. Had the Gladstonians this plan up their sleeves, Harcourt's impetuosity in hinting at it proved a liability. Suddenly, it struck 'Joe' that the only sensible thing to do was to acquaint his leader with 'the why's and wherefore's' of the 'Round Table' discussions on Home Rule. He would then have strengthened his links with Devonshire House before his enemies went into action. Or so he hoped, for there was no time to lose. Reliance on continued secrecy would be tempting fortune too far. Provided the wording was carefully drafted no harm would be done by revealing his special brand of responsible government for Ireland. On 23rd January a draft land scheme had gone to Hartington. Later, more details of the government question had been promised. What better time was there than the present for fulfilling that longstanding obligation? The covering note sent with the memorandum was drafted in suitably flexible terms.

> I send you, according to promise, a rough draft of a Home Rule Bill such as I could accept and such as I hope the conference may be induced to adopt. It is incomplete, of course, but it will enable you to make criticisms and suggestions, and to say whether you could treat on such a basis.[3]

The package went off soon after breakfast on 1st March and Chamberlain then prepared himself to meet Harcourt. He must have changed his original intention of a talk at the House of Commons because of his cold and suggested Prince's Gardens as an alternative, for when no Harcourt had appeared by late that evening, he began a

[1] *Ibid.*   [2] *Ibid.*
[3] Chamberlain to Hartington, 1st March 1887. Devonshire Papers, 340, 2112.

letter to him: 'I suppose that you have been detained at the House tonight.'[1] Whatever reason prevented the call, after what Chamberlain had written in his letter of the day before caution must have appeared very necessary. It was perhaps as well no conversation took place that day. With his rear probably secured, Chamberlain was in a much more perky mood and felt his battle against continuance of the talks could be reopened. Such a change could best be broken on paper. By the time they met Harcourt would have got used to the shift in emphasis and worked off any resentment alone, or with his pen. At times like this, the tongue was mightier than the pen so far as private contacts were concerned. The more written, therefore, the soonest mended.

The rights and wrongs of Harcourt's last letter Chamberlain left on one side until their talk took place. The vital question, which had to be put was: 'What is to be your next step?' Well aware that Gladstone and the overwhelming majority of his party leadership were for a delay in reunion activities, he suggested immediate action unless the Gladstonians wanted an end to the idea.

> I gathered from the earlier letters of this correspondence that you were inclined to give up the conference. From a later letter I find that this was a wrong impression. I am ready to accept either view, but if you are going on, I am clear that the matter must be carried through quickly. I was not of this opinion at first, but I see that the situation is too strained to last.

Naturally, he was willing to appear complaisant when one 'view' alone would and could find favour in Harcourt's mind. Anyone reading between the next lines would have had no doubt Chamberlain entertained a hearty wish that the Gladstonians would break off diplomatic relations and take the odium of disunity upon themselves.

> I am bothered every day [he grumbled]—almost every hour—for some expression of opinion. If I give it—no matter what pains I take—I am sure to offend you and your friends. On the other hand, everything your friends say or do offends me, although you think it perfectly justifiable. In these circumstances we are always on the edge of the volcano; let us close the business one way or another. We have all the conditions of the problem before us, and we ought to be able to say whether the members of the Round Table Conference can, or cannot agree. When we have settled this point, the situation will be clear.[2]

So far an extremely riling communication for anyone in Harcourt's position and state of mind to receive, but there was some solace to be found at the end.

[1] Chamberlain to Harcourt, 1st March 1887. Harcourt Papers.
[2] *Ibid.*

Even if we think it desirable not to allow our agreement to be known, the fact that it exists would justify me and others in a policy of silence, which we cannot observe so long as it is possible that we may once more have to fight for our lives. And, if we must fight, the sooner it will be over, and the less chance of misapprehension and ill-feeling.

Solace of a totally impractical kind, however, for while Harcourt might like to fall in with such a plan, giving way to Chamberlain on Ulster and Westminster representation, Morley would have found the whole notion anathema. In any case, of what real value would an agreement kept secret be?

There was not long to wait before Hartington spoke his mind. That very day he composed one of his most detached pronouncements. Its cool objectivity put even Dale into the shade. As was evident from what he wrote, the subject of Irish government had been on his mind a good deal of late. Endeavouring a comparison of the 'Responsible Government' and 'Municipal' ideas had yielded him no 'satisfactory conclusions'. His initial impressions of Chamberlain's scheme were strictly fair. The aim was clearly to show up the particular faults rather than give an interim solution to a fundamental question as yet unresolved in his own mind. Quite rightly, he pointed out how Chamberlain had not adopted 'Responsible Government' *in toto*. The Lord Lieutenant would have two sets of duties were this scheme to be adopted. There would be those relating to reserved matters like the 'employment of the Constabulary without the advice of his Irish Ministers, where his sole responsibility would be to parliament'; and those relating to all other matters within 'the competence of the Irish Legislature' in which he could 'only carry on the government of the country through Irish Ministers professing the confidence of the Irish Legislature'. In circumstances 'where as an Imperial Minister' he were to do something disapproved of by the majority of his legislature, his ministers might resign and be found unreplaceable. If, for example, he were to send the Irish constabulary to quell riots in Belfast or Cork, 'this might very probably happen'. Hartington explained it all with his inimitable crystal clear simplicity. 'Although the Ulster or Dublin Ministers would not be responsible for what he had done, the Ulster or Dublin Legislature might very probably compel the ministry to put this pressure on him. And I do not see the issue from this deadlock.' Moving on to the 'Municipal' system he was careful not to claim too much for it, but inclined to think that if 'a difficulty in a similar case' arose under it, different considerations of a less formidable character would be involved.

The Lord Lieutenant would only, under such a system, be responsible for that portion of the government which was reserved to him by the statute. The duty of carrying on the other functions of the government would no longer rest directly upon him. The Belfast and Dublin Municipal Councils would have directly assumed them.

In the case he had instanced 'the Councils would only mark their displeasure by a sort of strike and by throwing up duties they had undertaken'. This struck him as less likely to happen than the constitutional refusal described in relation to 'Responsible Government'. He concluded on a kindly note. 'My impression is that you will have to look more in the direction of the precedent of municipal government. I shall see you tomorrow evening, if not before.'[1] There was no more than an apparent need for such arguments. The converted needed no preacher, least of all Chamberlain, with his long record of municipal achievement and advocacy of Irish Provincial Councils. Acceptance or rejection of the draft had not, anyway, been the object of the exercise. Provided his leader would no longer be in a position to find information had been withheld and accepted the fact of the discussion and adoption of 'Responsible Government' by him at the 'Round Table' he would be satisfied. Hartington had obviously responded well and he could relax. The highly objective attitude, plus the tactful assumption that Chamberlain would probably change his mind, plus the cheerful mention of an immediately impending tête-à-tête—all showed how fair the Cavendish barometer was set.

The Chamberlain–Harcourt conversation did not come off until late on the 2nd March. In the meantime the latter sent two letters, one on the 1st, answering the former's arguments of the 29th February, the other early on the 2nd, disagreeing with his 'make haste' demand of the day before.[2] The attempt to 'divide and rule' had clearly brought out a certain awkwardness in Harcourt. Although glad the personal trouble with his friend had been set to rights, he tended to carp about the *Baptist* letter on the 1st, warning against judging participants in the 'Round Table' conference by 'the action and language of irresponsible outsiders', complaining no chapter and verse had been provided for the complaints against Gladstone and condemning the assurance Chamberlain had given to his supporters that a clean sweep of Gladstone and his policies from the field would be a condition precedent of reunion. Unlike Herschell, Chamberlain had shown not a trace of conciliation in his language and had thus gone back on the Hawick speech. Nor had he stated the differences were those 'of method and not of policy or principle'. There could be no doubt of the vote given in the Commons, 'practically for the post-

[1] Hartington to Chamberlain, 1st March 1887. Chamberlain Papers, JC 5/22/25.
[2] Harcourt to Chamberlain, 1st March 1887. Chamberlain Papers, JC5/38/67. Gardiner, *op. cit.*, pp. 36–7. Harcourt to Chamberlain, 2nd March 1887. Chamberlain Papers, JC5/38/68.

ponement of Welsh disestablishment', having caused profound offence 'to the Nonconformist and Radical Party'. But it was just one of the examples, of which there would probably be many, of 'Radicals voting against Liberal measures in order to support a Tory Government' and thus perplexing the intellects and distressing the 'conscience of the Liberal Party'.[1] Continued scolding was scarcely calculated to achieve what Harcourt had in view—the cooperation of 'Joe' in renewed talks. One bout was really one too many. A third was revelling in it—the consequence of fresh irritation on receipt of the 'divide and rule' pronouncement. All the reward he got from this needling over the *Baptist* was a weakened position. 'Joe' would be able to justify himself so much more easily and claim persecution and high handedness had once again been inflicted upon him.

The extracts had not cut much ice with Harcourt, or so he said. All Bryce had done was to explain the Gladstonians' Irish policy was one of 'self-government and responsibility'; that these principles had been embodied in the 1886 Home Rule Bill; and that the party would 'always remain faithful'[2] to them. What was there to object to there, or in the statement denying any hard and fast retention of details was involved? The whole cutting contained 'an accurate exposition of the basis of the conference'.[3]

As to the London correspondent of the Newcastle paper I pay no attention to what he says. That J. Morley has many friends and admirers who look forward to his eventually taking the first place in the Liberal Party I have no doubt is perfectly true, and seems to me quite natural. I dare say they would prefer him to either you or myself, and it is certainly not for me to say that they are wrong. For my part I have no desire to force myself into any position which is not voluntarily accorded, and I have no views whatever except to do for the time being what may appear most advantageous to the Party to which I belong. No newspaper correspondence or lobby gossip will induce me to suspect J. Morley of any underhand proceedings either towards myself or anyone else. His good faith is transparent, and he appears to me always to be the soul of honour. If he has any defect in the high position he occupies in the party it appears to me to be a somewhat excessive distrust of his own powers and claims, and I never saw a man less disposed to be jealous of others or egotistically eager to urge his own pretensions.[4]

[1] Harcourt to Chamberlain, 1st March 1887. Chamberlain Papers, JC5/38/67.
[2] *Ibid.*
[3] *Ibid.* On 1st March 1887 Sir Edward Hamilton noted: 'Trevelyan appears to be on the verge of returning to the Gladstonian fold, if one may judge from the report of a speech he has made at the Devonshire Club. But I do not attach much importance to it. He is very impulsive and changeable. Moreover, he only speaks for himself: he carries no one with him.' Sir Edward Hamilton's Diary, 1st March 1887, Add. MS. 48645, p. 119.
[4] Gardiner, *op. cit.*, pp. 36–7.

A classic instance of protesting too much, especially over Morley's character. 'Little John' was ambitious and diffident—a combination tending to the jealousy and distrust of other more powerful figures so evident in these pages. No immediate danger was threatening Harcourt's position and so magnanimity was an easy enough tactic to employ. There were too the practical needs and good of the Liberal party to consider. Any ill-considered criticism of a colleague could well form a potent weapon in the armoury at Highbury and be brought out when the need arose. However uncomfortable it was to have tongue in cheek, there it had to remain. The fine art of implication would not be lost on Chamberlain. Harcourt therefore brought it into play most adroitly to bring home the mutual closeness between himself and Morley.

> He desired me last of all distinctly to assure you with reference to the article of the Newcastle Correspondent to which you referred so pointedly at Trevelyan's, and to which you again revert in your letter of today, that he knows nothing whatever of it, that he did not inspire it and that he had not even read it. . . . He tells me that he is in no way responsible for any inspiration of the Newcastle papers.[1]

Had the two Gladstonians been comparing notes? That in fact was what was implied, and shed a very unpleasant light on the sanctity of private correspondence, if Harcourt was in earnest. More likely he had discussed Chamberlain's complaints about the Gladstonian press yet again with his colleague on receipt of the latest charges, without going so far as to reveal what tricks had been tried on. Common sense dictated such a course, for, with a deep desire to continue the conference at the first possible moment, he would not really have wanted to bring Morley up to boiling point and implant in his memory still more grudges against Chamberlain. Temporary annoyance was bound to be caused by raising the subject of the Newcastle press, but loyalty to the party would enable Morley to curb his displeasure. With the bigger question things were much less predictable.

Bismarck at this time was suffering from his almost perpetual 'cauchemar des coalitions'. In this respect at least 'Joe' was his spiritual brother. What he, in the full efficiency of his deviousness, had in mind for, or practised against others, was, he suspected and feared, actually being or about to be applied against himself. Harcourt knew him well enough to realise this and his parthian shot was almost as deadly as the reference to Hartington on 26th February had been. A capital hit!

> Having said this [i.e. about Morley and the Newcastle press] I should be very glad if you would in like manner place me in a position to assure him and his friends that you were not in any way privy to the com-

[1] *Ibid.*

munication which appeared some days ago in the *Birmingham Post* on the subject of the conference, and which contained a bitter personal attack on J. Morley contrasting his conduct very unfavourably with that of his colleagues at the Round Table. I now should be pleased to have your authority to remove the painful impression which your supposed sympathy with the language of that communication has produced upon many of Morley's friends.[1]

It was Harcourt's turn to wriggle out of a difficulty on the 2nd. Chamberlain had returned to direct attack. Mounting a counter offensive which has to grind to a halt on reaching the point where the enemy began his advance is neither simple nor safe. Yet it was just this that Harcourt was called upon to perform. Pushing back Chamberlain was never an enjoyable occupation. Too much blood was lost in the process. Now the task was, if anything, more difficult than usual, for he had the moral advantage—the desire for a clarification of the future of most Liberals and almost all Radicals. Not to push him back too far and afford room to the pose of martyrdom required a master plan. Harcourt began by apologising for their failure to meet on the 1st and promised to 'try to come to you between the rising of the House and the Speaker's dinner'. Procrastination through non-comprehension was the weapon he next chose to employ.

> Meanwhile [he continued], in case I should not find you, I must say that I do not myself follow your change of opinion as to the need or wisdom of precipitating. I don't think it is at all necessary that things should be 'strained', nor do I see anyone who wishes 'to strain them'. I feel confident you will succeed in your effort to give expression to your opinions without offending us, and I do not feel the least on the 'edge of a volcano'. On the contrary, I think Herschell's speech and Trevelyan's letter have shown a 'sweet reasonableness' (as Mr Arnold calls it) and have done much to clear the air. Indications of approximation on a still more important question are not wanting. I am therefore in favour of cultivating the greatest of all political virtues. I mean patience.[2]

A moderate form of operation without tactical nuclear weapons, it succeeded in putting things back just about where they had been. But not for long.

[1] *Ibid.*

[2] Harcourt to Chamberlain, 2nd March 1887. Chamberlain Papers, JC5/38/68. Guinness Rogers was far from being completely estranged from Chamberlain. On 2nd March 1887 he sent him a most friendly letter. The attempted 'rapprochement' had heartened and Labouchère's behaviour disgusted him. The great influence of Irish Nationalist M.P.s and journalists on the contents of local newspapers had struck him forcibly as he travelled round the country. The hostility to Chamberlain's moves had, he said, baffled him. He offered to write to the press expressing his views. Guinness Rogers to Chamberlain, 2nd March 1887. Chamberlain Papers, JC6/42/13.

At the interview Harcourt reintroduced the subject of Hartington, saying the Gladstonians could and would proceed no further 'unless they were satisfied as to' his 'attitude'.[1] 'This,' as Chamberlain was quick to grasp, 'was a new point.'[2] What end was it intended to serve? The most obvious was delay. The next most obvious the deflation of 'Joe'. In Garvin's opinion, getting Hartington to the 'Round Table' would have been as easy as bringing down the man in the moon and he was most very probably correct.[3] None the less, beginning with the Trevelyan episode, there had been a growing volume of reports that the Whig leader 'was favourable to a liberal scheme of Local Government of Ireland'.[4] Gladstone straightway jumped at the idea of reuniting the whole party and bringing back the right wing ballast on domestic affairs. The great puzzle was—had the noble lord given a false impression? Only a probe would reveal the truth and upon this the G.O.M. now determined. The motives were therefore mixed, aiming to serve both the long and short interests of the Gladstonian party. Any immediate prospect of realising motive two had been stymied by 'Joe's' own promptitude. Harcourt should have kept silent until after feelers had been made to, or contacts actually established with Devonshire House before telling the very man a successful outcome was bound to discomfort one way or the other. (Knowledge is power and 'Joe' was adept at its exploitation.) Instead, he first revealed a conversation which had obviously gone to the root of the whole Irish question and then told how serious approaches were going to be made before so much as a finger had been lifted to set things in motion. Had Chamberlain done nothing on the first warning signs, he would still have had plenty of room for manoeuvre. At lunch with Dilke, some hours before meeting Harcourt, he had revealed much about the failure of the conference.[5] To him it was as dead as the dodo. If the Gladstonians delayed consent to its burial much longer the corpse would begin to stink. With Hartington in the know and friendly to boot, nothing Harcourt said alarmed him. He did the sensible things, quietly requesting Hartington to prepare a statement of his views to be submitted to the Gladstonians via him, and returning to the attack with Harcourt. *Sine mora* would have made him a good motto had he ever deigned to enter the peerage. Never was its appropriateness more apparent.

An important event on 3rd March was bound to harden both Chamberlain and Harcourt in the attitudes they had taken up. Hicks Beach's resignation as Irish Secretary was commonly regarded at first as just another sign of the government's chronic weakness. A

---

[1] Chamberlain, *op. cit.*, p. 258.   [2] *Ibid.*
[3] Garvin, *op. cit.*, p. 293.   [4] Chamberlain, *op. cit.*, p. 258.
[5] Gwynn and Tuckwell, *op. cit.*, p. 268.

feeble front bench would become feebler by his absence and though health not policy differences had caused it, there was no denying he had represented a more liberal outlook on Irish matters than many of his colleagues. A successor was likely to be sterner of opinions, if not of stuff. The Radical Unionists necessarily took alarm at both sides of this prospect. The Gladstonians saw it as an added opportunity. The moral for the former was a rallying round and the maximum pressure on Salisbury to make reform the concomitant of coercion. That for the latter, to step up the pressure in an attempt to provoke another and perhaps decisive crisis. The chances for bringing down the ministry and installing themselves in office had to be used and ruthlessly used. Were the ministry to fall, the attachment of Hartington might prove easier to bring about. But Unionism could not be unbuilt in a day. Time became even more valuable. The Whigs moved slowly and without their accession Chamberlain would be immovable. Were it achieved he would have to conform. Meanwhile, he had to be kept at bay.

The prospects for this were poor. 'Joe' was not the man to give respite. In his determination not to be the 'fall guy' of the crisis he was prepared to sacrifice anything getting in the way. Just now delay in a final rupture was his prime worry. Having carefully considered Harcourt's view of the situation, he sent word to him on the 3rd, again urging haste, despite the Gladstonians' refusal to proceed.[1] The two months devoted to reunion discussions had 'disclosed a broader basis of agreement' than either of them had ventured to anticipate. Vital differences of opinions had been reduced to 'one or two points', but such was the fullness of information available upon them that a decision could certainly be come to as to whether or not the conference would be able successfully to accomplish its task. Maybe the divergences were too serious to be bridged over. Here 'Joe' again put Harcourt in a spot; 'I understand that Mr Gladstone has prepared a memorandum which was to have been shown to me and which would throw light on this question'.[2] He had taken out a metaphorical writ of 'Habeas Corpus'. Should the request be granted and the memorandum be produced, the G.O.M. would have eaten humble pie, albeit for nothing. Should it be refused, 'Joe' would have a reinforced grievance against the Gladstonian party forming strong evidence of its having ruined fine peace prospects.

Next he relied on the firm alliance with Hartington to dare the 'enemy' to enter into relations with him. They wanted to satisfy themselves as to the Whig attitude, by all means let them go ahead. What time was better than the present? 'I think you are right,' he

[1] Chamberlain to Harcourt, 3rd March 1887. Harcourt Papers.
[2] *Ibid.*

enthused, 'in attaching the utmost importance to his adhesion. If he can be induced to accept a basis of settlement which satisfies Mr Gladstone, the gain both to the Liberal party and to the Irish question would be immense.'[1] Hypocrisy was not in it, and what followed was worse. It was one 'fox's' field day!

Since I first entered on the conference, my efforts have been continuously directed to this result and I have been recently hopeful of success. If you think that more could be done by direct negotiation with Lord Hartington, I shall be delighted to support any effort with this object. I suggest that you should arrange for an *immediate* meeting of the Conference to receive Mr Gladstone's communication and that you should invite Lord Hartington to join. I do not know whether the objections he previously entertained to taking part in such a meeting still exist, but I shall be very glad to find that they have been removed.[2]

Harcourt had really asked for this. How could he answer, except by a blank refusal to proceed? By flaunting his proprietary interest in his leader and showing a most obliging willingness to act as an intermediary, Chamberlain had completely countered the move to freeze him out and generally 'reduce him to size'. His appraisal of how things stood led him to produce something little short of an ultimatum.

In any case [he insisted] I do not think that I could consent to an indefinite delay in the proceedings of the conference. I feel now very much embarrassed as to my public utterances. Before I go to Scotland I ought to know whether our labours are to be fruitless or not. In the former case, it is my intention to put forward my own plan for a solution of the Irish question, of course, on my own responsibility; in the second case, it will be my duty to maintain and defend the Plan of the conference whatever it may be. But I ought not to float like Mahomet's coffin between Heaven and earth, with the certainty that everything I do will be misconstrued and misrepresented.[3]

What was heaven and what earth did not emerge in the body of the letter, but in a P.S. there was an excellent indication.

I note your statement in the *Times* today that my leading principle as a person 'who calls himself a Unionist' is to discard the opinion of the representatives of Ireland and to regard exclusively the interests of the Irish landlords. And then you complain of my letter to the 'Baptist' and consider that the situation is not strained. If this is peace, frankly I prefer war.[4]

War he was determined to have.

[1] *Ibid.*   [2] *Ibid.*   [3] *Ibid.*
[4] *Ibid.* Sir Edward Hamilton commented for the 3rd March: 'Dined last night with Chamberlain—a large man's party. Hartington, Bright, F. Rothschild, Camperdown, Sir F. Leighton, Buckle, R. Brett, Hurlburt, J. Collings, R. Chamberlain, etc. Hartington and Chamberlain had much talk together. They seem the

In his reply the next day Harcourt was scarcely polite.[1] He thought he had made it clear that an immediate meeting of the conference such as Chamberlain had suggested was 'not at present practicable'. 'You desire it for the purpose of discussing Mr Gladstone's communication, but I have mentioned to you in a former letter that upon the appearance of your letter to the *Baptist* newspaper that communication was withdrawn and I have not seen it, nor am I cognisant of its purport.' The 'naughty boy be quiet' line had been revived again, and revived with a lie, for Harcourt had been at the discussion where the 'purport' of the document had been discussed and had seen a copy of what Gladstone committed to paper the next day. What was odder than the untruth was the revelation of it a few lines further on. To avoid what he termed 'fear of any misapprehension', he thought fit to quote Gladstone's letter to him of 26th February, and, of course, the composition meeting was mentioned. The 'convenient season' Gladstone had referred to would, hoped Harcourt, arrive 'when we are able to ascertain Hartington's mind'.[2] Meanwhile there was nothing more that could be done. During the few days' lull that followed Chamberlain was active at Devonshire House. Lord Hartington's 'mind' was ascertained at break-neck speed by the standards of the noble lord and the world he lived in.[3] And on the 6th a full blown statement reached Prince's Gardens. Could Harcourt still delay, when his condition was satisfied? Or would he find some other reason? Or would he simply tell Chamberlain to do as the G.O.M. told him? The answer was soon to be revealed.

Trevelyan had been left out of all this, content to leave to his section leader the doubtful honour of senior wrangler. Working on his own account, he had behaved as though the *Baptist* letter had never been written. During the course of February he had declined to stand as a Radical Liberal Unionist at the Burnley by-election caused by the death of Peter Rylands. Pending reunion he preferred

closest of friends now. The Radical takes the tarring of the Whig brush most complacently. I did not succeed in having much talk with Chamberlain, who is always very cordial. He professed to be full of political keenness again. His *ennui* had passed away. He was strong against the present state of things in the House of Commons.' Admittedly, he said, Churchill had led the way over obstruction, but there had been no need for the Gladstonians to have followed suit. Bright was very anti-Gladstonian, but there was a feeling that Liberal Unionists were beginning to say that 'if Ireland cannot be governed, she should govern herself'. It would appear, thought Hamilton, that the government were 'getting into a tight place'. . . . 'Liberal Unionists say their alliance with the Conservatives was made to get law and order. Where are they?' Sir Edward Hamilton's Diary, 3rd March 1887. Add. MS. 48645, pp. 119–23.

[1] Harcourt to Chamberlain, 4th March 1887. Chamberlain Papers, JC5/38/69.
[2] Harcourt to Chamberlain, 4th March 1887. Chamberlain Papers, JC5/38/69.
[3] Chamberlain, *op. cit.*, p. 258.

to remain a free agent. On 28th February he wrote to Chamberlain about a collection of papers relating to Land Purchase, used in 1886 by the Liberal ministry, a draft of the Bill based upon them, and a 'very curious letter from Hamilton'.[1] Not even a mention was made of the turn events had taken since the 25th. Burnley had not been the first, nor the last invitation he received to be adopted as a candidate for parliament. Gladstonians as well as Liberal Unionists had sought and were seeking him out. Declining the offer of the Aberdeen Liberal Unionist Association on 1st March, he wrote the letter Harcourt had referred to as the complement of Herschell's speech of the 23rd in his letter to Chamberlain on the 2nd March.[2] Earnest as ever in his endeavours to compose party differences, he gauged the situation as one in which

> the Irish question must be dealt with promptly and thoroughly—thoroughly, radically and remedially; and it could only be so dealt with by a reunited Liberal party. The events of the last eight or nine months in Parliament and Ireland had conclusively shown that such was the case. For that reunion on terms honourable to all concerned he believed the moment to be ripe. The opinions on the practical points of the problem held by leading Liberals with whom he was acquainted were such as, he was satisfied, admit of their working together without any of them losing their respect for each other or themselves.[3]

Clearly, he was praying that Gladstone's 'convenient season' was just round the corner and entertaining the hope that his optimism about Hartington had not been illusory. The very next day, he was presiding at a practical contribution to 'peace and understanding' at the Devonshire Club—the eagerly awaited reconciliation dinner.[4]

His speech left no doubt that the enthusiasm he entertained for reconciliation with Gladstone was every bit as great as Harcourt's had been for an arrangement with Chamberlain at the outset of the 'Round Table' cycle.

> The point on which we are agreed [he averred], the point on which, as far as I can see, we are in diametric opposition to the Conservatives—is that the condition of Ireland is past correctives and palliatives, and that it should be treated radically and remedially. The points upon which we are disagreed were contained within the two great Bills of last Parliament (strange language from a Liberal Unionist, however zealous for an accommodation); and, to use the words of their author, those Bills are now dead (perhaps he was applying the maxim 'de mortuis nihil nisi bonum'); and dead and buried with them are, or should be, all bitter

[1] Trevelyan to Chamberlain, 28th February 1887. Chamberlain Papers, JC5/70/27.
[2] *Annual Register*, 1887, p. 28.
[3] *Ibid.*
[4] *Annual Register*, 1887, pp. 28–9.

words that were spoken with regard to them, and every regrettable action to which the election gave rise.

A very fond hope in view of what had been raging in the press and on the public platforms, but there was no denying the validity of most of what came after.

> With regard to the further scheme for future relations between Great Britain and Ireland we have a clean sheet, and those of us who have been endeavouring to write upon that sheet have at any rate discovered this, that in the mind in which the so-called sections of the Liberal party are, if we cannot agree on our Irish policy as a united party, and support it as a united party, and carry it out as a united party, the leaders and prominent men in the Liberal ranks will indeed be deeply responsible. If the public spirit and personal magnanimity which we have a right to ask from British public men do not fail, if those to whom the destinies of our great empire are entrusted look to facts and substance instead of to old worn-out war-cries of a General Election which is now over, and which never should have taken place, the breach in our ranks might be healed tomorrow, and it is high time that it should.[1]

Yet another of the ironies of this whole story was the conversion by 'Joe', in his capacity of 'foxing' preacher, of his fellow Radical Unionist. The first moves towards the Birmingham brand of Home Rule at the 'Round Table' had left Trevelyan dumbfounded and protesting. Gradually the magic had begun to work. Instead of loneliness and recrimination he found friendship and praise—for himself at least. Though a scholar, there was nothing of the cold calculating intellectual about him. His heart was all that of a biographer of Charles James Fox should have been. The atmosphere opened his mind to Chamberlain's arguments. What the principal acted, the assistant came to accept with sincerity. His interview with Hartington must have been largely an exercise in cross-purposes and Chamberlain never took alarm at it. None of the nuances of difference on responsible and municipal government systems can have come through the mass of verbiage contained in the appeals for Whig participation at the 'Round Table'. Moreover, if Hartington had run anything like true to form, his pronouncements in conversation would have been laconic to the point of obscurity. While there were certain doubts in his mind at the time of meeting Trevelyan, we know they were but passing fancies probably confided to his mistress alone. There is, for instance, no mention of them in his father's private diaries. He would never have told Trevelyan anything kept back from his parent. Still, the former was in the state of mind where everything seems encouraging and 'Joe' had been the prime mover in its creation!

Coming down to brass tacks at the Devonshire Club, Trevelyan

[1] *Ibid.*

set out to define what he meant by saying the Liberal party was essentially united in principle. First and foremost, he considered it united in the belief that 'before any other question' could 'be satisfactorily settled the condition of Ireland' would have to be tackled. The Irish question and the peace and happiness of everyone in Ireland must inevitably remain unsettled, until Liberals had 'the outward and visible sign of the agreement' he was satisfied existed in 'the minds' of their leading figures 'in the shape of a carefully matured scheme for the government of Ireland, and the settlement of the land question on very different lines from Lord Ashbourne's Act'.[1] A virulent cold prevented his reporting the event immediately to Chamberlain, but on the 4th he wrote that it had gone off 'capitally'.[2] The audience had been 'largely mixed of both sections', yet all had been smooth and hearty, Fitzmaurice and Finlay saying just what they 'ought' to have said. The only cloud on the horizon as far as he could see was Hartington's intention of attending Goschen's dinner, an act certain to give great pain 'to a great many'. On personal grounds he felt a deep repugnance at seeing someone like Hartington swelling the triumph of a man who was 'his infinite inferior and the worst possible counsellor'. Meanwhile he was preserving his purity for the reunion cause and had just declined two offers 'from different parts of Birmingham' to adopt him as a parliamentary candidate.[3] He had

[1] *Ibid.*

[2] Trevelyan to Chamberlain, 4th March 1887. Chamberlain Papers, JC5/70/28.

[3] *Ibid.* Great stirrings broke out on 4th March because the Irish Secretary, Sir Michael Hicks Beach, resigned. The government could not really take much comfort from the fact that Gladstone got lost in the fog near Stanhope Gate on his way out to Dollis Hill. Sir Edward Hamilton's Diary, 4th March 1887, Add. MS. 48645, p. 123. On the 5th March Trevelyan dined out (at the Hayters': for whom see Chapter VIII, p. 348, note 3). Hamilton reported: 'He is keenness itself about reuniting the Liberal party, but one's fear is that he will be making the pace too hot. The Liberal Unionists will not and cannot be hurried. Time, time, time is the proper political *mot*.' The Queen had just had a small party of Gladstonians to Windsor. The Gladstones, Herschells and John Morley had been summoned to her table. Sir Edward Hamilton's Diary, 5th March 1887, Add. MS. 48645, p. 126. Herschell had sent Chamberlain another letter on the 4th March, principally about the question of the sacrificing of principles. He denied that the Gladstonian leaders deserved the strictures as to conduct Chamberlain was pouring out against them. 'Mr Gladstone has not spoken at all, nor has Harcourt, and John Morley did not speak until after both you and Hartington.' Charges of provocation were therefore false. It seemed to Herschell that the best course would be a complete reticence as to the views held by 'Round Tablers' during the course of the negotiations. The past should be avoided in public pronouncements as much as possible. 'You must remember,' he appealed, that 'there are extreme and unreasonable men on our side as well as yours, who do not want any concession made and who rejoice at anything that seems to render it impossible. I am sure you will not wish to play into their hands.' Herschell to Chamberlain, 4th March 1887. Chamberlain Papers, JC5/42/6.

drifted into a kind of neutralism. The sort that tends to assume ex-enemies have a better case than ex-friends.

At Willis's Rooms the next day, Salisbury gave his 'Politics are Ireland' speech and brought the country's full attention back to the practical side of the Home Rule issue.[1] Liberals—Gladstonians and Unionists alike—had been devoting a vast proportion of their time and energy to *their* internal problem. The actual situation in Ireland had been heeded mainly from this angle and the coming of coercion seen as a blessing to the British domestic scene. The prime minister's attempt to recreate a proper perspective met with no instantaneous success, despite the fact that the burden of his speech, had it been absolutely true, would have represented the triumph of Gladstone's dearest wish—that his latest 'cause' had come to outstrip all else in importance. Nevertheless, importance was different from influence and the paradox of that in this context lay in the fact that this distinction was a blessing to all forward-looking Liberals, Radicals and Socialists. For had Ireland really become the whole of politics for the British electorate, Gladstone's sun would straightway have set. Patriotism would have ousted the cause of reform and sympathy for the underdog, and 'Tory Democracy' come into its own.

With a keen eye for priorities, Chamberlain had already seen the pressure of conditions in Ireland would soon set up a tendency for events to move towards this very thing. How soon and how far depended on a great many factors, but Gladstone's prestige and the popular majority for reform were two of the largest blocking the way. The first would not, could not, last for much longer and the second could be obviated to some extent by dovetailing Unionism and reform. 'Tory Democracy' would then mean more than making the 'democracy' Tory. All brands of Unionism appeared to be losing ground in the country. Before the dovetailing counter-attack could be launched, Unionist unity had to be thoroughly recemented. Before that could take place the conference notion had to be blown sky high. Yet if Chamberlain was the obvious artificer of this, his chances of surviving to direct his counter-attack might be seriously prejudiced. The work of extrication had therefore to be pressed on with, and quickly. Ideally the finale should include a public embrace between Chamberlain and Hartington, followed by each murmuring assertions that Unionism meant reform as well as order, the recipe of the true Liberalism.

Hartington drew up on the 6th a lengthy memorandum giving his views on the questions discussed at the three conference sessions.[2]

[1] *The Times*, 6th March 1887.
[2] Hartington to Chamberlain, 6th March 1887. Chamberlain, *op. cit.*, pp. 258-61.

Nothing of major importance not in his election address at Rossendale the year before and the speech of 2nd February was in it.[1] To some extent he begged the question by arguing there was nothing in the way of proposals emanating from the 'Round Table'—simply exchanges of views. All he could do was comment on these as reported to him by Chamberlain. On land purchase he accepted the principle, but hoped the landlords would obtain a fair deal. There was no doubt he wanted the issue out of the way. 'I should have no objection to a plan which would, if optional, give such inducements to landlords and tenants as would make its general adoption likely, or if compulsory, would give to the landlords fair compensation both as to terms and as to security.'[2] On local government he accepted the conditions Chamberlain had made, but proceeded to dilate upon the necessity of any scheme offering

> a reasonable probability of being a practical one, having regard to the circumstances of Ireland and the temper of the leaders of the Irish people. It would not be very difficult to devise several schemes for the extension of local self-government in Scotland which might be tried without much risk, because the demand in Scotland, such as it is, is on the part of the vast majority, really limited to local self-government. But in Ireland the demand is, on the part of a large section at all events of the people and their leaders a demand for national recognition; and it is certain that unless the provisions for the maintenance of the authority of the Imperial Parliament and Government are made strong, simple, and effective, the concession which may be made will be used for the purpose of extorting complete separation and independence.[3]

In arguing that the spirit behind the working of the law was more important than its letter, he was in effect retracting in practice the Chamberlainite arguments he had just accepted in theory. This way of going about the issue preserved a united front in Unionist doctrine, yet placed an insuperable obstacle to any positive achievement were he to consent to sit in at the 'Round Table'. However moderate the

> necessity of looking at any scheme from the point of view of distrust as well as of confidence, and of bearing in mind the danger of assuming that a scheme which might work admirably in the case of a people which desires Union would be prudent in the opposite of a people who have been taught to desire the largest possible measure of separation—

this was diametrically opposed to the 'Union of Hearts' principle, based on risking trust, entertained so vehemently at Hawarden.[4] The

[1] For the election address see: Holland, *op. cit.*, pp. 158–9. The speech is dealt with above in Chapter VI on pp. 264–65.

[2] Hartington to Chamberlain, 6th March 1887. Chamberlain, *op. cit.*, p. 259.

[3] Hartington to Chamberlain, 6th March 1887. Chamberlain, *op. cit.*, p. 259.

[4] Hartington to Chamberlain, 6th March 1887. Chamberlain, *op. cit.*, p. 261.

Gladstonians would never consent to admit the Whig leader to any conference with the condition precedent on his side that the Canadian analogy was ruled out. In making a move towards him they had, if sincere, assumed he had undergone a change of heart. The homily on distrust proved the exact opposite. For all practical purposes they might as well have been back on 8th June 1886.

From Chamberlain's point of view nothing could have suited his immediate plans better. It would oblige Harcourt to speak out, probably in the sense of ending the conference. Much would then be in the bag. As soon as he could on the 7th 'Joe' despatched to Grafton Street a rather imperious communication, trenchant to the point of rudeness. The days of flowery civilities were definitely over.

> In my letter of March 3rd [he began], I pointed out to you why it was impossible for me to consent to an indefinite postponement of our negotiations. In your reply you put forward two pleas for delay: First, that you want to satisfy yourself as to Hartington's attitude. I am glad to tell you that this obstacle to progress has now disappeared, since Hartington has written a letter which I am authorised to show you at the proper time, and which contains the conditions on which he thinks it necessary to insist. Until he knows that these have been assented to, he will certainly decline to join our discussion.[1]

Behind the peremptory 'tone and temper' lurked the feeling of triumph so resented by his enemies. It had the cocksure touch of a businessman writing to his bankrupt rival, or a solicitor with an open and shut case attacking some ne'er-do-well. The treatment meted out on point two was so cheeky as to excite admiration. Harcourt's last letter had made it quite clear that continuance of conference sessions no longer hinged on the *Baptist* letter, but on Hartington. There was no second plea for delay. A complaisant Whiggery would be able to undo the evil spell of 25th February. This did not suit 'Joe', who dragged it back as a plea in order to indulge in a little more self-justification.

> Your second reason for delay was the publication of my letter to the *Baptist* in which Mr Gladstone sees a condemnation of his Irish policy. It appears to me that Trevelyan in his speech at the Devonshire, reported in the *Daily News* this morning, has repeated the same condemnation and I confess that I thought the foundation of our conference was that this policy was dead and that we were to seek an alternative policy which would meet the objections of the Liberal Unionists, while giving effect to the main principle on which Mr Gladstone has always insisted.[2]

He was out to score a total victory in the matter of his notorious letter through making the Gladstonians' objections to it seem both silly and perverse.

[1] Chamberlain to Harcourt, 7th March 1887. Harcourt Papers.
[2] *Ibid.*

If I am mistaken [sarcasm was ever a strong point with him] and if the condition of the conference is that we should accept the policy of the Bills of 1886, which was the cause of the rupture and which I thought had now been laid aside, I can only say that this affords ample ground—not for postponing—but for finally abandoning the attempt at agreement. There may be reasons for breaking up the conference—there can be none for delay, and if you are still unwilling to continue the discussion and to see how far it is possible to conciliate the views of Mr Gladstone, Lord Hartington and the parties to the conference, I must assume that our well-meant efforts are at an end and that we have all recovered our entire liberty of action. I confine myself to the main point and reserve for conversation any further reference to the side issues in your letter.[1]

Liberty of action, that was what he wanted and was determined, come rain come storm, to get. The conclusion was an indirect question in form—a virtual declaration of war in fact. The P.S. gave still more proof of his irritating arrogance. 'I hope you have seen the further curious letter of the well-informed correspondent of the *Newcastle Leader*'.[2]

Much satisfied with having worked all that off his chest, he wrote to Hartington.[3] The first step to take was to see 'how far Mr Gladstone and his late colleagues assent to the fundamental conditions on which' the two Liberal Unionist leaders 'alike insisted'. 'Alike insisted'—this was a 'flexible' interpretation to say the least. There had been no equivocation about his repeated acceptances of the Canadian analogy, yet here he was aiding and abetting its rejection. And ultimately, Hartington had known anyway of his espousal of it at the conference. Here was the 'fox' not bothering to 'fox' the man with whom he felt fate had involved him. There were no distortions in the account of what had been written to Harcourt. Of course, he did not say he hoped his request for a meeting at once 'to consider Mr Gladstone's memorandum on our discussions and you letter' would be refused.[4] In the circumstances of agreeing on principle with Hartington it was hardly necessary, for what could come of any meeting held to consider two such mutually contradictory documents but the final dashing of current reunion hopes?

Within a few hours Harcourt's rejoinder was at Prince's Gardens. Length rather than originality was its main feature. Deprived of the shelter of waiting for Hartington's 'mind' to become known, he resurrected all the grievances about the *Baptist* letter, 'refusing either to break off the conference or to go on with it at once'.[5] There was no real choice open to him because of what Gladstone and the Gladstonians generally felt. Being caught out by Chamberlain

[1] *Ibid.*   [2] *Ibid.*
[3] Chamberlain to Hartington, 7th March 1887. Chamberlain, *op. cit.*, p. 261.
[4] *Ibid.*   [5] Chamberlain, *op. cit.*, p. 262.

was just one of the prices he had to pay for the sake of the party. Nor were relations with the Radical Unionists confined to their leader. In two days' time he would have to reply to a toast proposed at a dinner to Schnadhorst by Dale of all people. Now to blame the delay in proceedings privately or publicly on Chamberlain when in contact with that influential divine would have been quite impossible. The opinion was sure to be passed on to the alleged culprit within less than twenty-four hours. So far as the Birmingham Radical Unionists, signed up or not, were concerned, 'Joe' was to be judged by the works they could see for themselves. No stories against him would wash, even if they came from Harcourt. Unrest in Birmingham was rife among the Gladstonian minority, but it would take a great deal to turn those of the Dale way of thinking to schemes for unhorsing the town's leading figure. Obviously any speech Harcourt might make had to tackle the reunion issue. No mention could be made of it without bringing in Chamberlain.

In doubt as to what exactly should be said, he had consulted Morley in conversation and mooted the desirability of papering things over by talking about the responsible executive outlined in the Hawick and Birmingham speeches. On reflection, Morley wrote him a note advising against 'specific reference' to these particular 'deliverances'. To do so would 'bring us to details more or less explicit and details are exactly what we shall do well to avoid, for the sake of Hartington on the one hand and the Irish on the other'. The sad truth was, too, that 'the very worst recommendation to any plan or detail of a plan, in the eyes both of the Irish and of our own left is that it can be supposed to proceed from or be approved by J. Chamberlain'. And to emphasise his point: 'Be sure of that.'[1] The chance to hit hard at his enemy seemed too good to miss, the more so as there was a considerable amount of evidence to justify a Gladstonian in doing so. He therefore tendered some rather tough positive advice. Chamberlain had managed 'to make his name and personality odious and irritating'. 'It is that which makes the Party regard the Round Table with such restless distrust and suspicion. If I were speaking I should *leave him out altogether*. You won't forget that though one speaks of the left, the left means the main body of our modest army.'[2]

Trevelyan, thought Morley, was quite a different case. His speech at the Devonshire Club had certainly been 'rather remarkable'. But the main thing to be done was not primarily concerned with him.

A word or two might usefully be said to disarm and quiet the real dislike of sensible fellows such as Samuelson to settling the Irish question in your parlour—independently of the past, etc. Of course, we never meant

[1] Morley to Harcourt, 7th March 1887. Harcourt Papers.
[2] *Ibid.*

Y
321

to do anything of the kind, nor had we power. But there might be good in saying so. Forgive me for troubling you with this.[1]

Fortunately, Harcourt had some hours to mull all this over before being called upon to commit himself. Chamberlain's intervening acts helped make up his mind.

The first of these acts was the brusque breaking off of the 'diplomatic relations' kept up by Harcourt to facilitate further meetings at the 'Round Table' when the G.O.M. thought fit. Being what Sir Maurice Powicke would have termed 'a man to be reckoned with', Chamberlain acted with swiftness and decision once he saw the way clear. Harcourt's tergiversations over Hartington, plus the general abuse continually showered upon him—'The Judas from Birmingham'—seemed to afford him more than adequate excuses with which to satisfy the Dales, Bunces and Harrises of his flock. On the morning of the 8th a note with no mean sting to it was sent round to Grafton Street. After making quite clear he had not meant to convey the impression of agreeing with all Trevelyan was reported as having said, but merely that part of the speech condemning and treating as dead the Bills of 1886, he maintained there was a clear distinction between 'principles and policy', arguing that it was open to him to condemn the latter even if he were prepared to accept the former. He said 'so much to avoid misapprehension', but felt it was useless to continue their present conference.

> I gather clearly from your last letter [he announced] that you do not look to the conference for any further results in the direction of the reunion of the party. The reasons you give appear to me of so little weight, especially since your reference to Hartington's attitude has been completely disposed of, that I am forced to the conclusion that you have other and stronger grounds for declining to come to an issue on the points raised, or to communicate to me the memorandum prepared for Mr Gladstone with that object.[2]

Faced with such behaviour there was nothing for it but to accept Harcourt's decision, and to express the hope that the settlement he assumed was still desired would be 'arrived at by some other means'.[3] The second act was one of direct retaliation—a refusal to let Harcourt see Hartington's memorandum. Understandable enough, and most convenient, since the Gladstonians in their ignorance might well suppose themselves to blame for having lost a fine opening to the greatest goal. Yet essentially unfair, for while Gladstone had personally ordered the withholding of his document, Hartington had

[1] *Ibid.* Sir Bernard Samuelson was Gladstonian M.P. for Banbury.
[2] Chamberlain to Harcourt, 8th March 1887. Harcourt Papers. Garvin, *op. cit.*, p. 294.
[3] Chamberlain to Harcourt, 8th March 1887. Harcourt Papers. See Appendix 2.

done no such thing. In fact he showed it to Harcourt himself a little over three months later.

Early on the 9th, some hours prior to Harcourt's speech, Chamberlain took another step towards finalising proceedings. As events had shown, Trevelyan had been taking off on his own, and his leader and fellow 'Round Tabler' was naturally anxious to inform him of what he had done and ascertain his exact state of mind. There was no shilly-shallying. The letter serving these purposes was well to the point. The 'Round Table' had come to an end so far as he—Chamberlain—was concerned. This had resulted from a long correspondence with Harcourt, which Trevelyan was more than welcome to see, had he the time and inclination. While it had been going on Chamberlain had been pressing for a resumption of negotiations and the handing over to the Radical Unionist representatives of Gladstone's memorandum. Excuses of extremely doubtful validity had been produced time and time again and he had been forced to the conclusion that 'having ascertained our views, Harcourt and his friends' now shrank from 'committing themselves to any opinion on them'. Note the omission of any mention of the dual nature of Chamberlain's demand—to go on forthwith, or cease then and there—and the eagerness to arouse in Trevelyan also a feeling of having been slighted. If Trevelyan eventually read the letters he would see the full facts for himself, but meanwhile it would be useful to inflame him as much as possible and thus counteract any tendency to be 'soft' on the Gladstonians. Chamberlain proceeded to enumerate the reasons adduced by Harcourt. First the Hartington red herring, then the *Baptist* letter, and last, what he considered the true explanation of Gladstonian conduct, the argument that time was working on their side. Trevelyan's own recent pronouncements, 'Hartington's more conciliatory attitude' and the general weakness of the government had convinced them of this. Repeating the tactics practised on Harcourt, he now put an 'either or' poser to Trevelyan in a most take it or leave it manner. As Harcourt had declined to fix any time for resuming the discussions, he argued, and seemed to think he could keep the two of them in the ante-chamber 'until his present mood of exultancy gives place to a new fit of depression', he now intended 'to act independently and without further reference to the conference'. Harcourt's conduct had been neither 'loyal' nor 'wise'.[1]

The night before, a meeting of the Liberal Unionist parliamentary party had taken place. A 'fighting humour' had prevailed, but doubts had been expressed about Trevelyan.[2] Considerable unease had been

---

[1] Chamberlain to Trevelyan, 9th March 1887. Copy. Chamberlain Papers, JC5/70/29.
[2] *Ibid.*

felt because of Gladstonian comments upon his recent activities. Chamberlain had been reassuring, insisting there 'was no cause for anxiety, or reason to suppose' a change of views. Nevertheless, it was perfectly clear from what came at the end of his letter of the morning after that he was troubled with similar misgivings. He pressed home the 'either or' treatment still more, contending that for Trevelyan's own sake 'and in view of such statements as that in the *Daily News* leader' of that day, It would be highly desirable were he, 'by letter to the *Times*, or otherwise, to make' his position clear.[1]

When it came to the point, Harcourt came very near to following Morley's advice. In replying to a toast by Dale, he kept things as vague as possible. And so, while adhering to the Morley line, avoided its 'tone and temper'. The matters on which the representatives of the two sections agreed, he stated, were 'many and great', while those on which they differed were 'small and few',[2] or as he put it later to Professor Stuart, 'secondary and few'.[3] By studiously ignoring Chamberlain's *démarche*, Harcourt put a spoke in the former's wheel, because explaining the situation to Dale and company was thereby made doubly difficult for him. Had Harcourt made a rumbustical witty attack upon Chamberlain's conduct and even temporarily contributed to the 'Joe-hating' cult, the prospect would have been clear. As things were, caution had hastily to be reintroduced into the 'fox's' repertoire. Climatic conditions in Birmingham strongly reinforced the need to castigate the Conservatives and emphasise the essential radicalism of Radical Unionism. They also dictated the public endorsement of the principle of Home Rule, originally adopted by the Liberal and Radical Association on 21st April 1886. The opportunity to try and set the course fair was waiting him in the form of the meeting he was to address on 12th March. He seized it with both hands.

Neither the letter to Harcourt on the 8th, nor that to Trevelyan on the 9th had brought Gladstonian reconnaissances to a halt. Early in the second week of March Trevelyan had a three-quarters of an hour interview with Gladstone himself. Granville reported to Spencer on the 10th that the G.O.M. had found it very amiable, 'but you cannot get out of a box more than is in it'.[4] A day or two later, Herschell had

---

[1] *Ibid.*   [2] Dale, *op. cit.*, p. 469.

[3] Harcourt to Professor Stuart, Draft (never sent), April 1887. Harcourt Papers.

[4] Granville to Spencer, 10th March 1887. Spencer Papers. On 10th March 1887 Goschen warned the Queen about possible Liberal Unionist desertions on the government's new coercion proposals for Ireland. Goschen to Queen Victoria, Windsor Royal Archives, B38/37. He repeated his warnings the next day, quoting James as sharing his fears. Goschen to Queen Victoria, 11th March 1887. Ed. Buckle, *op. cit.*, p. 284.

sought out Hartington for a long talk and mistakenly gained the impression he was changing his opinions.[1] Chamberlain had therefore to combine sweetness of 'tone and temper' over Gladstonian policy with a fierce defence of the Radical Unionist position *vis-à-vis* Conservatives and Gladstonians alike. So while Morley was wrong in swallowing the Herschell story and misguided in passing it on to Spencer on the day Chamberlain was due to speak, he was correct in the assumption that his foe was in a scrape.[2]

[1] Morley to Spencer, 12th March 1887. Spencer Papers.
[2] *Ibid.*

VIII

A RADICAL UNIONIST FOR RADICAL UNIONISTS, OR 'THE DARK WAYS' OF 'OUR JOSEPH'

———◆◆◆◆———

'Saying peace, peace, when there is no peace.' Jeremiah vi. 14.
'Now there arose up a new king over Egypt, which knew not
Joseph.' Exodus i. 8.

THE second Birmingham speech of this period was by a Radical
Unionist for Radical Unionists. Harcourt's immediate reaction, that of thinking a renewed bid for reunion would now be possible, was certainly mistaken. Suspense was widespread as Chamberlain began to speak, but the audience did not have to suppress its excitement for long. Tension dropped among the hostile sections as the Home Rule principle was openly and freely accepted. What worried some, encouraged most and relieved others were the conditions and safeguards attached to the acceptance. Irish representation at Westminster was to be maintained. An Irish parliament was to be subordinate, not co-ordinate, and its powers 'strictly defined and limited'. The maintenance of law and order was to remain under the control of the imperial authority. Ulster had to receive separate treatment and British credit was not to be pledged for the benefit of Irish landlords. There could be no question but that Gladstone's financial proposals would have to be abandoned. Likewise his scheme for two orders and plurality of voting. Chamberlain, taking an entirely different attitude to the proceedings of the conference from Harcourt, revealed how the first five points had been adopted by the Radical Unionists there and claimed the remaining three were merely nothing more than 'concessions consequential upon the adoption of the original terms.' Without these concessions, taken as a whole, Liberal reunion would be absolutely impossible. The great complication involved in this would be the impossibility of getting the Conserva-

tives to support Liberal candidates, with whom, in any case, they were agreed only on one great issue. The solution, he maintained, lay in the determination of Radical Unionists throughout the length and breadth of the land to organise themselves as a separate party. Were they prepared to run candidates in every constituency where a triangular fight seemed desirable and undertake that 'in all such cases no Unionist was prevented from polling by the fact that he had not a candidate with whom he could agree upon all points as well as upon one',[1] untold things might well be theirs. Was this a genuine call to arms, when the prime aim motivating his whole strategy, apart from his desire to survive as a national politician, was the defence of the Union through the Salisbury government? Would not attacks in the constituencies at key by-elections go some way towards defeating that purpose? Surely, it was sincere enough up to a point? Sincere as a bid to prise out of the government a legislative programme congenial to the Birmingham tradition, for Chamberlain saw it as his 'business to guide social' and all other measures.[2] A desperate game to play, maybe, yet the best one in the circumstances.

The remainder of the speech suggested this was his object, particularly the very next point. Fair exchange would be no robbery, and in return for a firm support to government action directed against outrage and intimidation there had to be an end to landlords' abuses of their rights and 'one more great effort to deal with the land question', and 'root of all the evil' to be banished from Ireland.[3] Then came a long passage on the report of Lord Cowper's Commission, the inclusion of which was directly due to the intervention of Dale. Such was the extent of his influence on the local scene, and Chamberlain acknowledged it in a note to him on the following day. Like his friend he disapproved of the Commissioners' recommendations, though not cavilling at their facts. Perpetual tampering with the 1881 Land Act struck him as dangerous because judicial rents would cease to enjoy the sanctity statutory enactment usually gave. The law would appear no more permanent than a gentlemen's agreement. What was required, and what he hoped the government would introduce was a large measure with some chance of finality. It would have to make the tenants virtual owners of the lands they cultivate. 'If they take this course I am quite certain that Liberal Unionists will give to them a sufficient and a loyal support, and in that case there will be no early appeal to the country.'[4] The sudden change of tune from the independent candidatures threat could hardly have been made had it been

[1] *Annual Register*, 1887, pp. 26–7. *The Times*, 14th March 1887.
[2] *Ibid*.
[3] *The Times*, 14th March 1887.
[4] *Ibid*. The Cowper Commission had been set up by the Salisbury government to enquire into the Irish land question and suggest possible reforms. Lord Cowper

meant in a sense other than the one suggested above. Certain though it was that the Gladstonians too had been in Chamberlain's mind, that did not affect his message to the Conservatives one iota. In fact it strengthened the challenge, for a man dangerous to the G.O.M. was worth his weight in gold to Salisbury as a stabiliser, bringer in of abstainers and converter of the 'infidel'.

Apart from Dale's interest in the point, Chamberlain was seriously opposed to the recommendations of the Cowper Commission.[1] Two things besides his friend's influence emerge from the note of the 13th. One was a keenness to impress him with the fact that he held a view in common with Gladstone—'I disapprove of the recommendations of the Cowper Commission and *Mr Gladstone agrees with me.*' The other, an apparent certainty that the government would bring forward some sort of substantial proposals not envisaged by the Commission—'I hope and believe that the government will make remedial proposals, but not in this direction.'[2] The speech brought a considerable reward in the form of Dale's approval of coercion, provided it was accompanied by remedial measures. Actually he had not himself been thinking so much of the recommendations of the Report as the statement in it that a large proportion of the judicial rents were excessive. Much of the violence stemmed from this parlous state of affairs and unjust evictions should be halted. Immediate action was necessary and the vagueness of Chamberlain's language on the prospective reforms and the definiteness of his comments on Home Rule, was bound

was a Liberal Unionist and Lord Spencer's predecessor as Viceroy. The proposals brought forward did not include one for an all-out drive for making the tenants owner-occupiers. According to his biographers, James Stansfeld made one of the best speeches of his life when attacking the government for failing to implement the Cowper recommendations. It was in the debates on the 1887 Coercion Bill. J. L. and B. Hammond, *James Stansfeld: A Victorian Champion of Sex Equality*, p. 283.

[1] Chamberlain to Dale, 13th March 1887. Copy. Chamberlain Papers, JC 5/20/59. According to Sir Edward Hamilton's Diary the Prince of Wales disliked what he termed the government's 'flabby policy' in Ireland. Writing of the Birmingham speech, Hamilton described it as 'dextrous'. He was nevertheless careful to remark: 'Chamberlain's position is becoming a difficult one, for, as Schnadhorst said the other day, if the leaders cannot reunite the party will. So the Liberal Unionists will have to mind what they are about. Otherwise they will find themselves knocked out of time altogether. The leaders will be without a following: the shepherds without sheep. At the same time, notwithstanding Chamberlain's recalcitrance, people will be very foolish if they try to rid themselves of him. I met a typical Gladstonian M.P. this afternoon. The line he held was "Blow Chamberlain, we can get on very well without him. He has forfeited for good and all the confidence of the Liberal party." I venture to think such language is a mistake. The Liberal party cannot afford to dispense with Chamberlain's services. He is too big a man.' Sir Edward Hamilton's Diary, 13th March 1887, Add. MS. 48645, p. 127.

[2] *Ibid.*

to create anxiety. All the more so because of his 'natural clearness and rigour of speech'.[1] Clearly, Dale wanted 'cash on delivery' for his support.

> Prospective remedial measures [he insisted] do not satisfy the exigencies of the case. At present, to put it roughly, the tenant who is called upon to pay an excessive rent is protected by the menace of outrage: in suppressing this outrage the law will leave him without protection. Or, what is worse, the ingenuity of the men who run the National League will probably discover other, and possibly worse, methods, if they can be worse, of holding their present power over the country.[2]

Unrelenting pressure on the government was therefore imperative to preserve enthusiastic Unionism among its leftmost adherents. Coercion was going to be hard to stomach on hard practical grounds such as Dale's, besides the theoretical objections to restrictions upon the liberty of the subject. However much the majority of Birmingham Liberals and Radicals disliked Parnell and all his works, social injustice could easily influence them temporarily to desert the Union. Until the Union brought basic justice to Ireland they could not give unwavering loyalty to a government they knew was secure in its parliamentary majority. The Whig Liberal Unionists enabled them to indulge their radical principles without Gladstone actually coming to power. Unfortunately for him, Chamberlain and his entourage had their future threatened in the process.

Also on the 14th, Trevelyan at last ventured a note to his section leader. It was in no way, except by implication, a reply to the letter of the 9th. The recent speech enabled him to ignore everything that had gone before. 'It certainly is much more satisfactory, at a time like this,' he prattled, 'when one gets people's views before the public in their own words.' He had liked the reference made to him and considered 'it was important to have said it'. The nearest approach to frankness came in the last sentence. 'I thought a great deal in the *Daily News* this morning very reasonable.'[3] Relations between the two were evidently no longer at all close. Not that they ever had been so far as Chamberlain was concerned, but Trevelyan's failure to

---

[1] Dale to Chamberlain, 14th March 1887. Chamberlain Papers, JC5/20/81.
[2] *Ibid.*
[3] Trevelyan to Chamberlain, 14th March 1887. Chamberlain Papers, JC 5/70/30. In conversation with one Robinson, manager of the *Daily News*, Sir Edward Hamilton gleaned some very interesting information. He recorded it: 'He told me they were always being pulled by the Party (i.e. Liberal) leaders in different directions about Chamberlain. The ostracism of Chamberlain is a very foolish game. The *Daily News* very properly will not make an enemy of him.' Hamilton urged Robinson to give less prominence to Labouchère, only to learn that he would be surprised to learn just how much interest that gentleman's speeches aroused. 'So much the worse,' grumbled Hamilton. Sir Edward Hamilton's Diary, 15th March 1887, Add. MS. 48645, p. 131.

mention his meeting with Gladstone indicated this attitude was now reciprocal. One of the Unionist 'Round Tablers' had become a kind of Radical Goschen. Goschen's Liberalism was scarcely distinguishable from Conservatism; Trevelyan's Unionism now appeared to be Gladstonian Home Rule under another name.

If the 'Joe-hating' *Daily News* was at all 'reasonable', it was only to be expected that Harcourt would be more than that. He was. The *Observer* report of Chamberlain's speech struck him as 'so important as to require serious consideration'. Or at least, that was what he wrote to Gladstone on the 13th.[1] Perhaps, as he had the conference axe to grind, he was making as much as he could out of something less distinctly anti-Gladstone and anti-Gladstonian to persuade his 'Chief' to repent over the memorandum. For with that produced, Chamberlain would find it difficult not to reopen the whole affair. More likely, he did feel the pleasure he expressed, but determined all the same to profit to the maximum from the drop in tension. Chamberlain had capped his acceptance of the responsible government principle with the comment: 'that being the case, where is the hitch and why are we not all agreed?'[2] Harcourt, of course, blamed him for the hitch, yet found in his latest pronouncement ample atonement for it. Being very human, he must have found some pleasure in the well-founded supposition that the 'fox's' own cubs had coerced him. 'He has evidently spoken under strong pressure from his friends to pursue the path of conciliation and has made certainly the largest advance in that direction which he has yet done.'[3] Gladstone certainly relished not only this, but the wishful thinking which succeeded it. 'His speech will, I think, spread confusion into the ranks of the Ultra-Unionists, but I imagine it has a good deal of Hartington in it, and very likely contains the gist of Hartington's note which he was instructed to show us.'[4] On the threat of Radical Unionist candidacies, Harcourt missed the point, regarding 'Chamberlain's own "plan of campaign" by way of menace at the close of his speech' as a 'mere silly *brutum fulmen*'.[5] The picture of a 'coerced' Chamberlain having his own 'plan of campaign' was an accurate one, but to dismiss anything he did in that way was to ignore the whole of his political method. He just was not the man to indulge in pointless threats.

During the next two days Gladstone, Harcourt and Morley were mainly taken up with concerting plans for the debate on the second

[1] Harcourt to Gladstone, 13th March 1887. Gladstone Papers, Add. MS. 44201, f. 81.
[2] *Annual Register*, 1887, pp. 26–7. *The Times*, 14th March 1887.
[3] Harcourt to Gladstone, 13th March 1887. Gladstone Papers, Add. MS. 44201, f. 81.
[4] *Ibid.*   [5] *Ibid.*

reading of the Coercion Bill, which was to begin on the 22nd, shortly before parliament adjourned for the Easter recess. Their minds were, nevertheless, ever watchful on the 'dissentient' position and the reunion issue in general. Harcourt wanted Morley, as the leading Gladstonian spokesman on the Irish question, to move an amendment.[1] Gladstone had demurred at first, preferring Harcourt, but eventually, on the 15th, gave way ('About Morley, I readily agree').[2] The news did not reach Morley until the 16th, and he had meanwhile sent off to Grafton Street a token of his ruffled feelings.[3] Further proofs of the grave personal defects in this key Gladstonian representative at the 'Round Table'. If he was so jealous of Harcourt, how much more did he resent Chamberlain and fan the flames of the hatred felt for him by Labouchère and the Schnadhorstian 'wirepullers'. Thinking a final decision had been made against him, he wrote:

> You told Mr Gladstone last night that you thought it would be best for me to move the amendment. So it would have been, because it would have left the duty of replying to Hartington or J. Chamberlain to you, who are a very powerful debater, instead of to me, who am a very unhandy debater. Mr Gladstone decided otherwise. So be it. As you know, I always seek the background rather than otherwise.

Worse was to come.

> But on these terms I'll be hanged if you shall not do the outdoor work too. Therefore I propose to tell Schnadhorst and H. Fowler that I will not go to Wolverhampton for the great function on April 19th and they must ask you. So be prepared.[4]

Before this self-pitying rubbish arrived, Harcourt had sent to say there were distinct hopes of reversing the decision and that he did not 'care a pin' about when he had to speak or to whom he had to reply.[5] The next day, the 16th, after announcing the reversal of rôles, he gave Morley a piece of his mind.

> Why do you and J. Chamberlain [he asked] always think it necessary to conclude the exposition of your views with menaces? Have you found me unreasonable in meeting your wishes? If not, why threaten me? I assure you it is unnecessary, as I have nothing more readily at heart than to co-operate with you in the manner which is most agreeable to you.[6]

The comparison with 'Joe' must have hurt. It was none the less a

[1] Harcourt to Gladstone, 15th March 1887. Gladstone Papers, Add. MS. 44201, f. 85. Harcourt's original request had been made verbally on the 14th.
[2] Gladstone to Harcourt, 15th March 1887. Harcourt Papers.
[3] Morley to Harcourt, 15th March 1887. Harcourt Papers.
[4] Ibid.
[5] Harcourt to Morley, 15th March 1887. Copy. Harcourt Papers.
[6] Harcourt to Morley, 16th March 1887. Copy. Harcourt Papers.

sound thrust, and brought results. An immediate and grateful reply, marred only by an attempt to justify the Wolverhampton suggestion.[1] With Hartington speaking on the 16th, retaliation by Harcourt would have been appropriate he thought. Was it really surprising that Harcourt's life had been so difficult during the past two and a half months with Chamberlain and Morley to manage? The 'Round Table' could have been the name of an opera school.

On the more important matter of the wording of the amendment Gladstone and Harcourt settled things between them. The former felt strongly that 'words which would include (if not name) Irish Government' were required by the party's position and would probably be insisted upon by the Irish members, with whom some communication would presumably be necessary.[2] Harcourt hastened to point out that were Home Rule put into the amendment, they would deprive themselves of 'all the votes of the Liberal dissentients, who would be compelled to go with us into the Lobby on the question of unjust evictions'. They would, moreover, 'ride off upon the Home Rule issue and treat the other as subordinate, and so justify their support of the government'.[3] Again he got his way and the Nationalists had to lump it. The 16th was a day of accord in the party.

At Liskeard the Liberal Unionists had a red letter occasion. Much to the interest and surprise of their opponents, Trevelyan carried out his promise to participate in a ceremony arranged in honour of Courtney by his local supporters. Caine accompanied him and both spoke. The guest of honour no less than almost everybody else was intrigued as to what reunion zeal would lead the worthy baronet into saying.

> Sir George [he recorded in his journal] is apparently seized with such a passion for Liberal reunion that he talks about the differences that separate Gladstonians and Liberal Unionists being purely imaginary. One would like to know how the situation has changed since he left Mr Gladstone last year. The secrets of the Round Table must be well kept if there is so much change as all that in the views held by the guests. We are rather nervous about what he will say at Liskeard at our demonstration. Will he be a second Balaam?[4]

Many of the numerous local Home Rulers rubbed shoulders with the Liberal Unionists to do honour to Courtney's absolute consistency. Trevelyan would not therefore have found the audience absolutely hostile had he pursued his latest line unabashed. Instead he devoted most of what was, as it turned out, the principal speech of

[1] Morley to Harcourt, 16th March 1887. Harcourt Papers.
[2] Gladstone to Harcourt, 15th March 1887. Harcourt Papers.
[3] *Ibid.*
[4] Gooch, *op. cit.*, p. 274.

the evening to stressing how much his views coincided with those of the local member. To the delight of the Unionists and consternation of their foes, he opened with an impassioned assurance that he would never care to sit in parliament again if it did not 'represent in equal proportions all parts of the United Kingdom, and if it did not control every other body and authority, and to which every citizen could look for the safety of his life and for the maintenance of his personal rights'. Odd phraseology, yet undoubtedly very well meant. He continued: 'The greatest misfortune which could befall either the country or the party is that the great number of the brave, honest, full-spirited, and responsible-minded politicians should be permanently excluded from the Liberal ranks.' Courtney was to remark afterwards on the signs of his coming change the speech displayed, and there is certainly something in the tone to support such a view. His words implied he was with but not of the Liberal Unionists. At times they were distinctly patronising coming from him. As for example:

It is difficult to conceive how anybody who has watched the proceedings in Parliament during the last session and this session can doubt that the non-recognition by the Liberal party of Lord Hartington, Sir Henry James, Mr Chamberlain and Mr Courtney, as leaders to whom they look for guidance in the lobby and for advice in debate, is not only a great misfortune to the Liberal party, but it is a great national danger. It is better, far better, that these men should stay outside the majority of the party unless they can re-enter on honourable terms; and if the Liberal party can be reunited on these terms, it is a result at which every good Liberal and every good patriot will rejoice.

Passing on to his attitude to Home Rule, he explained how he accepted the principles subscribed to by the majority of Liberals while rejecting the details of dead Bills.

My own position about Home Rule is still sufficiently unmistakable. [Did he fear that would soon cease to be the case?] I advocated very extensive changes in the relations between Great Britain and Ireland, and when the Bills were brought before the House of Commons I indicated great and grave and numerous objections, and these objections not being met as they should have been met, I left the Government and voted against the Bills. But as soon as a scheme is agreed upon by the Liberal leaders of all sections, as I am sanguine there will be; if such a scheme is agreed upon, then I shall vote for it.

After a short sharp retort to Salisbury that Liberal unity alone could lead to a solution of the Irish question, he defined what he considered the present duty of the Liberal Unionists. Being more or less at one with the Gladstonians on every 'pressing question' except Ireland, two things had to be borne in mind.

333

First, to be very clear indeed on the points on which we must insist before we come to any agreement whatever. I have never departed by one word from first to last from the points on which I should insist, and I shall insist on them again. But our duty likewise is to try to understand the present position of our adversaries, and to use towards them the most courteous and conciliatory words.[1]

In a second speech, later on in the evening, he expanded upon and clarified the duties point, arguing the need for firmness in insisting upon certain conditions. These should be:

That the Parliament shall have a real control over the business of the empire; that it shall have the supreme management of the finances of this country, so that in case of any great war the whole of the country—not only England, Scotland, and Wales—shall be made to contribute to it; and, above all, the rights of the minority shall not be protected by mere paper guarantees; that the rights of every body of citizens shall be protected, that the men of Ireland shall feel as comfortable as they felt before Home Rule was talked about two years ago.

Nor must the British Treasury be burdened 'after the manner which Mr Chamberlain described'. In conclusion he discussed coercion, singling out the Conservative overthrow of Spencer and himself in 1885 as the greatest of political errors. Despite it, the decided duty of Liberal Unionists was to 'strengthen the hands of the Government in dealing with order in Ireland'.[2]

Courtney also spoke twice, addressing himself in particular to those Liberal Unionists who seemed to shrink from the consequences of having revolted. Fine phrases and catch expressions should not, he believed, be allowed to cloud the issue. Any Home Rule would really amount to separation. Nothing of the kind would come if his party did its duty 'to their consciences, regardless of the immediate consequences'. The union had lifted up and would lift up still further the standards of the Irish people, 'infusing them with new and correct ideas, reforming the whole course of their lives, and recreating the nation'. Any legislation, Land Acts included, would fail unless this process was continued 'by association and connection with ourselves'. Unionists need not fear the future, however great the anxiety. Ultimately, 'the popular voice will insist that the Unionist idea must be upheld', and he therefore had no hesitation in believing that those who, 'under the influence of a great name and under the specious influence of a gifted leader', had been seduced into following an exciting new policy would see their mistake and 'rejoin what was the faith of their fathers'. Meantime the Liberal Unionists should reorganise themselves into a body to which they could be welcomed.

[1] *The Times*, 17th March 1887.
[2] *The Times*, 17th March 1887.

The orthodox circles of his party found these words a fund of refreshment; fighting words most apposite to a most testing time. It was one thing to block the Nationalists; quite another to aid and abet the Conservatives in repression, albeit accompanied by reform. The *Spectator* enthused:

> It is a pleasure in this flabby generation to read such words. We have sometimes thought and occasionally said that Mr Courtney was too confident in his own judgement; but there are times when that capacity for being certain is the necessary condition of resolution to do one's duty. It is manliness not without its touch of stubborn defiance that Unionists now require.[1]

Caine spoke out in a very similar vein. 'Full-blooded', Courtney termed it.[2] There were no signs of wavering such as the discerning espied in Trevelyan's 'peace' homilies. Underneath, his mood was a complicated mixture of hope and apprehension. For the reasons worrying him when the *Baptist* letter was impending, no one was more anxious for reunion, provided the terms were good. Once rumour had it that Hartington was likely to join the 'Round Table' talks an enormous weight was lifted from off his mind. Without the Whigs' support he knew any *modus vivendi* would have involved 'selling the pass'. Hence he had hoped for a failure of Chamberlain's initiative in his mind, judging it to have been tactical, yet yearned for its success in his heart. All he asked for in a practical way from his section leader was a tactful rupture throwing the onus of renewed hostilities upon the G.O.M. and his minions. If full Liberal unity and the preservation of the Union were simultaneously possible, then head and heart could act in unison. Five days after his speech, in another letter to his constituency chairman, Fell, he pronounced the 'Round Table' to be looking 'very healthy' and was hopeful it would end in a compromise acceptable to Hartington. Catching on to the 'national settlement' concept, first mooted by Gladstone to Balfour in 1885, and lately resurrected at Hawick by Chamberlain, he insisted the 'Tories' would be great fools to reject something the Whigs had swallowed and refuse to 'come in too and *do it*'. Labouchère's fulminations in the Commons' smokeroom about Gladstone's 'dying to rat' provided a final comfort.[3] At Liskeard 'full-blooded' Unionism seemed compatible with 'goodwill' towards the Gladstonians. The whole occasion provided a much needed tonic to a party badly demoralised since Churchill's resignation. A tonic to the whole party,

---

[1] *The Times*, 17th March 1887.

[2] Gooch, *op. cit.*, p. 275.

[3] Caine to Fell, 21st March 1887. Barrow Election Papers, Lancashire County Records, C.19. DDFe/1.

not like the Hartington and Chamberlain contributions, pick-me-ups for the right or left sections. Coercion prospects might prove, and, indeed, looked like proving a severe electoral handicap, but had not led to any disintegration of the Liberal Unionist party's membership. With time, the country might well view the whole issue differently and turn increasingly to non-Home Rule Liberalism. This was 'Joe's' gamble and the one Gladstone deeply feared. With the 'dissentients' intact no immediate prospect of a parliamentary coup presented itself. Siren noises had therefore to be repeated and pride pocketed. Trevelyan at least had to be lured into the snare to discomfort 'Joe' and improve the chances of acquiring the whole Radical vote.

At least a day before the Liskeard demonstration, Gladstone had become so impressed with the staying power of the Hartington–Chamberlain combination and the persistence of its following that he decided upon a conciliatory course towards the erring sheep. The occasion for its application came on the 17th. The Gladstonian members from Yorkshire were holding a dinner in London at which he was due to speak. Harcourt was assured he had every intention of saying something 'in a quiet and . . . quieting way'.[1] A great comfort to his deputy, ever a glutton for punishment in the reunion cause. But now reunion was not his sole concern. 'Joe' had to be brought to book and this was the best way of doing it. In reply he laid stress on the desirability of repudiating 'Chamberlain's dictatorial tone of ultimatum' *and* the need for 'a kindly word' from the party leader indicating his readiness 'to discuss and reconsider' the particulars of the 'Home Rule plan of last year', while in no way abandoning 'its objects and principles'. 'Many among our friends and still more among those who desire to return to the fold' were heartily craving for it. By this means 'the stock misrepresentation by the Chamberlain party to the effect that we obstinately adhere to every tittle of the Bill of 1886' would be set at naught. At present it was used with great effect by its author 'amongst the weak-kneed dissentients'. Detail was neither desirable nor necessary, 'but a frank statement of openness of mind to modifications would do a great deal of good'. At this particular dinner an allusion to the 'Leeds platform (viz. an Irish Legislative body for the transaction of purely Irish affairs upon such conditions as Parliament might impose) would perhaps be appropriate'. Chamberlain's declaration against pledging British credit for Irish land should be specifically taken up and adopted as 'necessary after what has occurred'. The advantages likely to stem from such a declaration would certainly prove considerable, especially just at that moment when the government, with Hartington's support,

[1] Gladstone to Harcourt, 15th March 1887. Harcourt Papers.

were probably contemplating 'a great extension of Ashbourne's Act'.[1]

Gladstone was as good as his word. His opening remarks were entirely given over to relations with the 'dissentients'. What attitude, he asked, should 'austere' Liberals maintain towards them? This was no more than a rhetorical question to which he intended to provide the relevant answer. Nothing should be done to wound or embarrass them, and Schnadhorst's warning, that a failure by the leaders to settle this whole matter among themselves in the Liberal party would lead to the people doing so, had constantly to be borne in mind. There could be no greater misfortune, however, than if, by a hasty acceptance of formulae not thoroughly understood, they should 'profess that an agreement had been arrived at when, in point of fact, only a form of words had been agreed to, which on examination proved to be without value'. He was making sure the giving had still to be on the Liberal Unionist side, whatever the pains taken to protect its feelings. Forms of words had always been a particular fad of his when trying to entice Hartington into the Home Rule net. It was therefore not without humour that he of all men should admonish anyone for that particular failing. A whole-hearted invitation to a compromise like the one partially arrived at between the 'Round Tablers' would have been quite beyond him. Quiet and quieting as he had been, the undying desire to dominate was just as apparent as ever. So was the unquenchable self-righteousness and conviction that the future lay with him. Those like Salisbury, who talked of the nightmare of the Irish question, were, he assured the Yorkshiremen, more than half persuaded that Home Rule must come. It would be no more use 'trying to touch any other great question' till Ireland was out of the way 'than it would to move on a train till the debris of a collision had been removed from the line on which the train was placed'.[2] Had not Chamberlain been justified in attacking such a view, whatever the motive for doing so? 'Tone and temper' aside, blaming Home Rule for the blockage of domestic legislation was an obvious and useful argument for any Unionist worth his salt to pursue. To single out Gladstone for a personal attack was equally reasonable, for who else could have commanded the loyalty of the Liberal majority to that order of priorities? There was no group in the party capable of foisting it upon him. Outside, Parnell could have been disowned and the Hawick line tried out. A united British front could have legislated without reference to the Nationalists, who would have been cutting off their noses to spite their faces had they afterwards

[1] Harcourt to Gladstone, 16th March 1887. Gladstone Papers, Add. MS. 44201, f. 87.
[2] *Annual Register*, 1887, pp. 83–4.

given up working with the Liberals, and anyway, a long-term alliance with the Conservatives would have been out of the question. Besides sticking to his nostrum, the G.O.M. indulged in the very word game he was simultaneously condemning in others. Phrases covering no more than the approach to Irish issues were made to imply goodwill could achieve all. 'Tone and temper' were passed off as the substance of the problem.

On land he was more yielding. Yet again he was demonstrating the knack for abandoning what circumstances would not let him get away with. Home Rule was one thing, the land issue quite another.

> Of all the points which caused out defeat in the last General Election, and certainly of all the points which constituted—as far as I know—the difficulty among our best friends, the most important and the most dangerous was this—that we had to propose to make a very large use of Imperial credit for the purpose of buying out the Irish landlords.[1]

Not even a sixpence would have been in danger of loss, but that did not decide the case. His late proposal had represented the furthest point the Liberal government had been willing to go on the landlords' behalf. Two reasons had been responsible for this generous attitude. The first, the desire to offer the best inducement for a speedy and thoroughgoing settlement of a great problem. The second, the feeling it was wrong suddenly to round on those who had lately been 'the petted children of England'.[2] Now he believed Land Purchase could be carried through without British credit, provided 'a real Irish Government able to speak and act for Ireland' was straightway created.[3] 'Without that I do not see how to stir a step towards the adoption of such a plan.'[4] A Chamberlainite land scheme could only flourish at the cost of sacrificing the main Chamberlainite political policy on Ireland. The words *modus vivendi* had, whether he wished it or not, temporarily fallen out of Gladstone's vocabulary. They had been replaced by *modus dicendi*, the means highly likely to win over some Radical Unionist support and thus destroy 'dissentient' solidarity. Trevelyan would be a rich prize, not in himself, but as a symbol. After such a speech the 'woodcock' was almost bound to be 'near the gin'.

In parliament the Gladstonians determined to fight the coercion proposals tooth and nail. The decision was welcome among all sections of the party. Even MacColl's charitable inclinations had dried up by this time. A letter of his to Gladstone on the day of the Yorkshire speech struck an almost bitter note.

> The Liberal Unionist 'Knights of the Round Table' appear to have coolly come to the conclusion that it is your business to cast aside your

[1] *Ibid.*   [2] *Ibid.*   [3] *Ibid.*   [4] *Ibid.*

own Bible in toto and set to work drafting their ideas into a Bill. They have both declared that they do not abate a jot of their ideas. The concession is to be all on your side. And what do they mean by accepting your 'principle'?[1]

Trevelyan's apparent about turn at Liskeard had been too much for him and was clearly the immediate occasion for the reinforced vehemence on this occasion.

Courtney last night [he fumed] repudiated all idea of anything like an Irish Parliament and Executive, and he claimed as on his side, not only Lord Hartington and Sir Henry James, but also Chamberlain and Sir George Trevelyan, who was present and tacitly accepted the position assigned to him by Courtney.[2]

His remedy was drastic, but fell upon welcoming ears.

I hope there will be no more Round Table Conferences. The only result will be to confuse the people. Any idea that you are going back from the main principles of your Bill will take the heart out of the Liberal party. Of course, you are doing nothing of the kind. But I can see already that some very good Liberals are getting bewildered.[3]

By the time the month was out any confusion and bewilderment were to be scattered to the winds. 'Very good Liberals' of all shades were to have a much clearer idea of where exactly they stood. As the coercion battle approached, the Gladstonian front bench gloried in the opportunities for slashing at the government. Harcourt was second to none in militancy, telling Gladstone on the 19th, how vital it was that they rely on their own merits. In his view 'a strong point in this case' was the fact that this would be the first occasion, 'certainly for half a century', when a Coercion Bill had been prepared 'without the substantial assent of the regular Opposition'. They had therefore to make their own precedent. It being their intention to take the lead in opposition to the Bill, he considered that lead should be asserted at the earliest possible moment. There was no use in throwing it in the first instance 'into Parnell's hands, only in order to resume it later'. The proper course would therefore be for Morley to move the party's amendment 'upon the very first motion, whatever it may be, which the Government make in furtherance of their Bill'.[4] Quite correctly, he foresaw this would be a motion to postpone the Orders of the

[1] Russell on MacColl, *op. cit.*, p. 132.
[2] *Ibid.*   [3] *Ibid.*
[4] Harcourt to Gladstone, 19th March 1887. Gladstone Papers, Add. MS. 44201, f. 91. Lord Castletown, an Irish peer, wrote to Chamberlain on 23rd March 1887 reminding him of his promise to reveal the exact kind of Irish land scheme he backed once the 'Round Table' conference was over. Castletown to Chamberlain, 23rd March 1887. Chamberlain Papers, JC8/6/3A/3.

Day so as to bring on the notice for the introduction of the Bill and maintained this would enable the argument for using the Commons' valuable time in discussion of the remedial Land Bill to be powerfully made. Three days later W. H. Smith put forward the motion Harcourt had envisaged and the fight was on. In accordance with his own dearest wish, Morley led off for the Opposition, but Gladstone spoke on the 24th. By the time the division was taken early on the 26th, after an all-night sitting, Chamberlain and James had made major contributions to the government's case. A government majority of eighty-nine was eminently satisfactory in the circumstances.

Within thirty-six hours Hartington had penned an account to his mistress, holidaying on the continent.[1] A month before, on the day the *Baptist* letter had been published, the Duke of Devonshire recorded his son's spirits as being by no means 'high' about 'Parliamentary matters'.[2] Much had happened since then and, allowing for Hartington's proverbial pessimism, there were signs of greater hope. 'The division the other night,' he wrote, 'was as good as I expected. Most of our men came up well and Chamberlain seems very straight. The Conservatives did not come up quite as well as they should have done, and two or three stayed away on purpose.' The week had been stormy and unpleasant and getting the Bill through would be 'tremendous work'. Although the opposition intended to contest every stage with all their might and were elatedly forecasting it would never pass, too much use of the closure would not be wise 'on this sort of question'. Perhaps he felt there was nothing like dishing out one's opponents a plentiful supply of rope, for Gladstone was pronounced 'more Jesuitical and hair-splitting than ever', and Harcourt described as having so spoken that 'you would imagine he had been a Parnellite all his life'. Balfour commanded his unwavering confidence, but he feared that 'even if the Fenians don't shoot him' overwork would have the same effect. He himself was in no such danger. Back in 1886 the threat to the Union had been real. In a flash the aristocratic torpor held to have been part of his fundamental make-up was cast aside. Its return was surely an index of how he judged the situation? 'I did not take part in the all-night sitting,' he confessed, 'as I did not know it was coming on; but I was down at the House at nine o'clock in the morning and found them all in a very dirty and disorderly state.' Nor was this all: 'I got off speaking on Morley's amendment to the Coercion Bill, as I got Chamberlain and H. James to speak and they both made capital speeches.' Curiously enough he regarded himself

[1] Hartington to the Duchess of Manchester, 27th March 1887. Devonshire Papers, 340. Add. MS.

[2] Diaries of the 7th Duke of Devonshire, 25th February 1887. Devonshire Papers.

as chronically overworked, commenting: 'I am afraid that this week they will want me to speak; but when I am to find time to get anything ready I don't know.'[1] Writing again on the 29th, he claimed not to have had a spare moment during the past four days. With committee, company, and party meetings immediately in the offing, plus the need to speak in the Commons, prospects did not look like improving. 'I feel rather seedy,' he complained, 'and if this sort of thing goes on much longer I shall get quite knocked up.'[2] What did he suppose was happening to an old man like Gladstone, or near contemporaries like Chamberlain and Harcourt? It is, of course, conceivable that he was out to impress a jealous woman with the impossibility of his having, as Balfour once put it, met any 'mice' while the 'cat' was away. Yet there is present an element of genuine indignation arising from the fact that he should be put about. Really it boiled down to annoyance at having the ways in which his waking hours were used dictated to him.

Balfour had the day before moved for leave to introduce the 'Criminal Law Amendment (Ireland) Bill' and the Nationalists at last came into their own. The day following, Hartington worked off one of his chores by addressing the inaugural dinner of the Liberal Union Club. The speech was a vigorous defence of Liberal Unionist support for coercion.[3] Finlay and Dicey spoke too, and while Chamberlain was absent, an article by him appeared in the new 'Liberal Unionist' weekly just started under the editorship and control of St Loe Strachey, the first number of which each diner found on his plate.[4] Morley made the highlight of his day an attack upon 'Radical Coercionists' at a meeting of the Liberal Reform Union.[5] Chamberlain was well to the fore against his enemies. They could now attack him without fear of criticism in their own party.

Greater confidence had not led Hartington into vast prophesying about the future in his private correspondence. 'I can't tell you much about political prospects yet'—was his line in the letter of the 29th to the Duchess of Manchester. But he did venture to think his 'people' would support the Coercion Bill, despite their dislike for the clause making possible the removal of Irish trials from Ireland to England.[6] Not a very daring forecast after the vote on the precedence motion!

[1] Hartington to the Duchess of Manchester, 27th March 1887. Devonshire Papers, 340. Add. MS.
[2] Hartington to the Duchess of Manchester, 29th March 1887. Devonshire Papers, 340. Add. MS.
[3] *The Times*, 31st March 1887. Liberal Unionist, No. 2, 6th April 1887.
[4] *The Times*, 31st March 1887. Liberal Unionist, No. 2, 6th April 1887.
[5] *The Times*, 31st March 1887.
[6] Hartington to the Duchess of Manchester, 29th March 1887. Devonshire Papers, 340. Add. MS.

His main worry was understandably the effect the coercion issue was going to have in the British constituencies. 'From Mr Gladstone's speech,' he mused, 'there will be the most determined opposition to every line of the Bill; and I should think that they will try to get up an agitation against it in England.' This was obvious enough. About the outcome he was non-committal. 'I think that a great deal depends on whether they succeed or not, as I doubt the possibility of carrying the Bill if there is a very strong feeling against it in England.'[1] Taken with the feeling about his party this speculation becomes less of a genuine puzzle. He was probably mildly confident the government would prevail.

Be that as it may, the Leader of the House was leaving nothing to chance. Knowing as he did that the Club dinner was to be followed by a meeting of the Liberal Unionist parliamentary party, the chance of rallying it to the immediate demands of the cause seemed too good to miss. Accordingly, on the 30th, a letter was sent round to Devonshire House containing the request that the situation should be explained to the Liberal Unionists 'in plain language'. 'We cannot,' it claimed, 'carry our measures without the active help of the Liberal Unionists; as active as if they were, for the purposes of these Bills (Coercion and Land Purchase) amalgamated with us.'[2] M.P.s had to be for or against coercion. Their constituents would not swallow abstention. The moment for Radical Unionists was one of acute anxiety and embarrassment, for the whole reunion question had been cruelly thrust aside by circumstances not even Schnadhorst and his 'wirepullers' were really able to control. At best the N.L.F. could exploit a situation created by the Irish peasantry and elaborated upon by the government. Immediately the only sort of union possible on fair terms was with the Conservatives. The Liberal majority could only be rejoined on its own particularly hard conditions. In the words of Smith:

We are entering upon a most serious struggle in which all ordinary Parliamentary understandings and courtesies as between parties may be suspended and divisions may be taken with or without notice, as may suit the Opposition. It is therefore essential that arrangements shall be made during the continuance of the fight we shall always be secured of a majority in the House. Our own friends will do their part, but the strain is excessively severe upon them, as it is not their practice in ordinary times, as it is that of the Gladstonian–Irish party, to live in the House; and I therefore hope we may rely on the organisation of the Liberal Unionists to assist the Conservative party to prevent the possibility of a surprise.[3]

[1] *Ibid.*
[2] W. H. Smith to Hartington, 30th March 1887. Devonshire Papers, 340. 2116.
[3] *Ibid.*

The practical parliamentary battle faced those genuinely of the centre of the spectrum created by the Home Rule issue with only one effective future—one away from the centre. Whether it was to be to the left or right of it was in their hands, but being Unionists, that is against Gladstonian Home Rule, their road seemed pretty clearly marked to the right, unless they hurriedly reordered the political priorities which had activated them since last June at the latest.

The 31st was packed full of activity. The principle of remedial measures accompanying coercion got practical recognition with the introduction of the Irish Land Bill in the Lords. The practice looked like being well-below the standards of reform expected by Radical Unionists and Chamberlain had written to Balfour only the day before expressing dissatisfaction. Reading through the draft had convinced him the scheme was 'thin porridge' for keeping his 'section of the Liberal Unionists in heart'.[1] The government had not consulted him about their Irish policy and the advice proferred them by Hartington only went to show how little the two had in common, apart from a deep hostility to Irish nationalism and Gladstonian Home Rule. The absence of provisions for revising judicial rents and the nature of the bankruptcy places was certain to upset Ulster Radical stalwarts, let alone the 'bleeding hearts' in Birmingham, although these were Chamberlain's immediate concern. An uproar was brewing in his capital and the band of anti-coercionist lieutenants were more restive than usual. Dale was finding the ordering of his priorities a severe tax on his considerable hair-splitting capacities. Many of Chamberlain's section had misunderstood his motives over the 'Round Table' conference and he stood badly in need of some thick porridge.

Unfortunately for him, Hartington was unable to tell the Liberal Unionist parliamentary party, assembled that day at Devonshire House, of any government abandonment of the 'change of venue' clause in the Coercion Bill. Instead the leader insisted upon the necessity for the Bill and announced his party should be prepared to make any sacrifice to get it on to the statute book.[2] Chamberlain was far from happy. The porridge would still have to become thicker and more plentiful. While concurring in general with what had been said he was at pains to make clear the continued support of the government by Liberal Unionism would be conditional upon 'the sufficiency of the remedial measures to be proposed by the Government'.[3] The absence of land purchase clauses in the Land Bill, was quite a smack in the eye for Radical Unionism. At this stage no mention was made

---

[1] Chamberlain to Balfour, 30th March 1887. Balfour Papers, Add. MS. 49733, f. 42. Copy. Chamberlain Papers, JC5/5/42. Garvin, *op. cit.*, p. 304.

[2] *The Times*, 31st March 1887.

[3] *Ibid.*

of it among the parliamentarians, but eagle eyes throughout the land had noted the fact. Simultaneously, the Conservative members of the Commons had been meeting at the Foreign Office, where Salisbury had also spoken of the need for sacrifice. As Hartington had noted, certain elements of deliberate backsliding had already become apparent in their ranks.[1] When an encouraging response broke forth, Goschen was deputed to report the unanimous sense of the meeting to Hartington and the Liberal Unionists.

Gladstone was scenting victory and decided to try and inflict a grievous blow upon the Unionist cause. He so demeaned himself as to initiate feelers towards 'Joe' through Lady Hayter and Lord Thring, who reported how much the G.O.M. regretted the failure of the conference and how glad he would be to talk over the political situation with him, provided everything could be kept discreetly private and non-committal.[2] 'Joe' agreed—readily as it happened, for 'foxlike' considerations alone dictated the need to lose no opportunity of tackling Gladstone, especially when the whole 'Round Table' effort stood in danger of coming to naught in respect of the most important thing it had been aimed at achieving—security in the 'grand ducal' capital. One of the many others puzzled as to the true state of affairs resulting from the 'Round Table' conference had been consulting Brett as to what he should do. He was Lord William Compton.

> Why don't you write to Gladstone [Brett urged] and ask him categorically whether all idea of excluding the Irish members from the House of Commons is definitely abandoned? It is upon that point that everything hinges. Hartington's and Chamberlain's 'conditions' follow as a matter of course. Cannot you 'draw' the old man?[3]

Before the various exchanges and enquiries could get under way, the 'old man' had to endure the division on the first reading of the Coercion Bill. The government majority rose in comparison with that on the precedence motion to 108. Gladstonians and Nationalists had to take comfort in the fact of it being All Fools' Day. Hartington reported on 2nd April:

> We had a great scene last night on closing the debate. Mr Gladstone was tremendously excited and is furious with the Speaker. Nobody knows what he will do next, but his walking out afterwards in the midst of the

[1] Hartington to the Duchess of Manchester, 27th March 1887. Devonshire Papers, 340. Add. MS. W. H. Smith to Hartington, 30th March 1887. Devonshire Papers, 340. 2116.

[2] Chamberlain, *op. cit.*, p. 262.

[3] Brett to Compton, 31st March 1887. Esher Papers. Lord William Compton (1851–1913) had been Liberal M.P. for Stratford-upon-Avon 1885–6, was a supporter of Home Rule and returned to the Commons in 1889 as a Gladstonian, following a by-election at Barnsley.

cheers and shouts of the Home Rulers was intended as a protest against the action of the Speaker, and he is evidently ready to go to any lengths. They will try to get up a great agitation in the country and perhaps they may succeed. There is to be a great meeting in Hyde Park on Easter Monday and we are sure to have some very stormy times before long.

Not so stormy, however, as to provoke the noble lord into any frenzied activity.

I had awful hard work all this week, though I got off making a regular speech on the 1st Reading. I suppose I shall have to speak on the 2nd Reading, and I shall try to get it off Thursday, so that it may perhaps not be necessary for me to come back for the meeting of the House, which will be, I expect, on the Tuesday in Easter week.[1]

From what specific data had the G.O.M. drawn so much encouragement? How could he be so sure the tide was flowing his way?

The answer is to be found in large part by looking at the by-election results during the first months of 1887. They created a rosy picture for the Home Rule side, particularly in relation to the electoral staying power of Liberal Unionism. Back in mid-February, Caine had told Fell he was anxious about his party's organisation, as the offices at Spring Gardens did not appear to be doing their work. Apparently Colonel Hozier was spending only half an hour a day there; insufficient time, even for an exceptional man like him. Since then, Courtney's agent had been brought in to help and a young and able peripatetic barrister sent off on organisational forays into the constituencies. The great aim was not a series of public meetings, but solid laborious work creating associations and committees, according to the numbers involved. There would then come into being by degrees in every division 'a body of men who could bring their influence to bear at election times and in close contests their votes would have a considerable market value and secure large concessions'. The great aim should be 'a Gideonlike policy' of concealing numbers by plenty of show and vigour. 'A determined knot of influential men' could still, thought Caine, 'exercise a big influence over an election'. Behind the new moves was a small organisational committee, consisting of himself, Arthur Elliot and Henry Hobhouse. Nevertheless, the prospect of reconciliation and the 'Round Table' negotiations had hindered the process of rigorous Liberal Unionist self-assertion. Settlement one way or the other had been longed for in Spring Gardens long before it occurred and the whole move towards reunion was viewed by Caine as 'premature'.[2] Whatever the rights and wrongs of

[1] Hartington to the Duchess of Manchester, 2nd April 1887. Devonshire Papers, 340. Add. MS.
[2] Caine to Fell, 14th February 1887. Barrow Election Papers, Lancashire County Records, C.19. DDFe/1.

that, there could be no doubt by-elections were 'premature' for the Liberal Unionists early in 1887. When Chamberlain had threatened three-cornered fights in his speech of 12th March it was to the future he was referring, but by-elections had an unpleasant habit of cropping up in the present and that was just where the party came to grief.

It was generally agreed in all but the most blindly Unionist circles that such evidence as there was suggested the strong general attachment of the Liberals to Gladstone. Many who had voted Liberal Unionist or Conservative, or abstained in the general election of 1886 now found little or no difficulty in supporting Gladstonian candidates. Of course, they were almost certain the ministry would weather the storm and many only hoped to goad it into necessary reform. Given the weaker Gladstonian position in January, the failure of Goschen to capture Liverpool (Exchange) was a genuine setback for Unionism, despite the drop in the Home Rule vote. Admittedly, its candidate was by no means a paragon for progressives, but his sheer ability and the effort put into the fight should have more than outweighed that. When the Radical Unionist member for Burnley, Peter Rylands, died in February, his local supporters straightway asked Trevelyan to contest the seat. He refused, and when H. G. Crook, Secretary of the Lancashire Liberal Unionists had no bright ideas, they were forced back into accepting a Conservative candidate, one C. J. Thursby, scion of a prominent Anglican and coal-owning family. The excuses offered were that the arrangement was only for this election and that Thursby had promised unconditional support for Hartington—'a somewhat dubious check on his outright Conservatism' according to one source,[1] but however valuable it was or was not, there were no grounds for accepting the argument that Radical Unionists could relax and be cheerful. The Gladstonian, L. J. Slagg, a Manchester merchant and chairman of the National Reform Union, was bound to attract a good deal of sympathy from them, leading in numerous instances to positive support. Support given on Gladstonian terms, for as Caine was quick to notice, there was scant yielding in the letter the G.O.M. sent his candidate. Nor was there any kindly reference to Rylands, who had been his devoted follower for sixteen years. For this Caine abused his ex-leader, calling him a 'heartless old man' and a 'thoroughly unforgiving vindictive old sinner'.[2] Great was his

[1] Trevelyan had first been asked to stand as a Liberal Unionist and on his refusing H. G. Crook, Secretary of the Lancashire Liberal Unionists, had felt compelled, failing any other likely names in his hat, to turn to the Conservatives. See E. P. M. Wollaston, *The Flowing Tide, 1886–92: A Study in Political Meteorology*, p. 1 (Gladstone Memorial Trust Essay, 1959).

[2] Caine to Fell, 14th February 1887. Barrow Election Papers, Lancashire County Records, C.19. DDFe/1.

chagrin when Slagg succeeded in converting a Radical Unionist majority of fifty-three to a Gladstonian one of five hundred and forty-five. 'Burnley is a bad blow and will make the Gladstonians cocky',[1] he lamented, but by the end of March he had hit upon a rationalisation sufficiently respectable to publish in the first issue of the *Liberal Unionist*.[2] Apparently the whole defeat could be explained away by the assertion that exactly the same would have happened in 1886 had the Unionist been a Conservative.[3] There was something in this, especially as the margin of Rylands' victory had been so narrow. Nevertheless, true or false, it was no real consolation for a defeat at such a time. The enemy had another parliamentary seat, and that was all the country as a whole would notice. The local excursion to Hawarden had every reason to rejoice. Temperance rather than Home Rule had carried the day, though doubtless T. W. Russell and Saunderson on one side and T. P. O'Connor on the other influenced certain coteries. Those who believed in temperance usually disliked coercion, so the domestic and Irish issues in their immediate form combined to favour Slagg. But Home Rule itself was not the great weapon Gladstone supposed it to be. Not that that would matter, of course, if other matters put in a government pledged to carry it. However Burnley was regarded, the Gladstonians had a right to be 'cocky'.

A third contest at Ilkeston probably provided a good indication of what might happen to the abstainers of 1886. The contest in 1885 had resulted in a Liberal majority of 1,987 (L. 5,780. C. 3,793); that of 1886 in one of 828 (GL. 4,621. C. 3,793). These figures make it very clear that those Liberals in Ilkeston who had not been able to bring themselves to vote Home Rule had refused to vote for a Conservative and abstained to the number of almost 1,200. During the last week of March the electors had again returned a Gladstonian, this time with an increased majority (GL. 5,512. C. 4,180). Discounting changes in the register, the increased poll indicated the abstainers of the year before had now divided into 800 voting Gladstonian and 400 Conservative. Caine was not surprised as the average elector never took to disenfranchising himself, even in the gravest crises, and few would do so twice. To him the 800 extra Gladstonians were simply the lost sheep of Liberal Unionism, whose action had resulted from want of mutual support and encouragement. With education and organisation they could be retrieved, because the Gladstonian

---

[1] Caine to Fell, 21st March 1887. Barrow Election Papers, Lancashire County Records, C.19. DDFe/1.

[2] *Liberal Unionist*, No. 1, 31st March 1887.

[3] *Ibid.* For a detailed account of Unionist affairs in Burnley at this time see: Papers concerning Conservative–Liberal Unionist relations deposited in the offices of the Burnley Conservative Association.

had secured their votes by playing on domestic issues like local option, disestablishment and the general desire for radical change.[1] Much of what he claimed was true, though the way of putting it could well be criticised as tending to the subjective. The 800 were part of the new floating vote, the more radical group. The 400 too were floaters, of the less radical sort. In the race for the votes of the uncommitted the Unionists were, in Ilkeston at least, falling badly behind. It looked as though Gladstone was right in thinking the pattern would become national and it was therefore high time an assertive policy should be pursued by the Liberal, and even more the Radical Unionists. Potential support was being thrown away while Spring Gardens bumbled along. With activity at top speed there would be a chance of making progressive Unionism a real force, and once it was that, the political climate of the country would ensure it went from strength to strength. Chamberlain had always seen the only real way to sustained success lay in organisation. Now he saw that for Radical Unionism survival was largely bound up with it outside his capital and its environs. Fighting on two fronts in different ways is a tall order for any party. The Radical Unionists, with diminishing forces, had three fronts to face—the Gladstonian, the Conservative and the Whig. Chamberlain did not intend meeting Gladstone with cap in hand, yet wearing it took courage.

The G.O.M. had made it a condition of talking that the initiative should appear to come from Chamberlain.[2] Accordingly, an approach was made through Mrs Gladstone and answered by letter on 3rd April.[3] 'Foxes' have to play-act, not always in the fashion they would prefer! It was on that day that Dilke received a full Chamberlain account of the rights and wrongs of the 'Round Table', including the admission that the *Baptist* letter had been 'indiscreet'.[4] Certainly, the days of talk at Grafton Street and Malwood must have appeared palmy beside current events and made 'Joe' regret his earlier plan, emotionally at least. Writing from Lord Aberdeen's house at Dollis Hill, Gladstone was at his most patronising and expressed himself ever 'willing and gladly willing to see any old colleague or friend' who believed that 'an interview might bring about a removal or mitigation of differences'.[5] Was it that his colleagues had not been friends and vice versa? The Burnley letter raises doubts about the genuineness of

[1] *Ibid.* Between the general election of 1886 and the dissolution of 1892 the Gladstonians made 22 gains and suffered 1 loss.

[2] Chamberlain, *op. cit.*, p. 262.

[3] Chamberlain, *op. cit.*, pp. 262–3. Lady Hayter and Lord Thring had separately done Mrs Gladstone's bidding. The first was the widow of Sir W. G. Hayter, Liberal–Whig Chief Whip, 1850–8.

[4] Gwynn and Tuckwell, *op. cit.*, p. 268.

[5] Chamberlain, *op. cit.*, 262–3.

feeling towards both. He thought that while 'considerable progress' had been made 'on the subjects of Irish Land Purchase and Government', coercion and closure had come in 'to widen the breach'.

> I observe [he condescended] that you have maintained your freedom of action on Coercion for the coming stages, but I do not know the state of your mind about it so as to be justified in taking any initiative as to conversation upon it, though gladly willing to converse as I have stated above.

Moving on to the closure question he understood Chamberlain to have said he was 'ready and desirous to remove this most unhappy intervention of the Chair' and hoped 'a ground' had been laid 'for a useful cooperation which would aim at the removal of a very serious mischief. I should certainly wish to converse on the subject with my friends, which however I know could not be done tomorrow; and you might have heard further from me on the subject.' He closed much in the mood of his opening: 'If you think progress can be made, I then *desire* the conversation, in which we might try . . . . My impression is that, on the point I have last named, you have before you an opening, without loss of freedom, for a great public service.'[1] The stress had all been on the new coercion and closure points, but Chamberlain did not let matters rest there in his letter of the 4th.

Knowledge of Gladstone's mind would, he maintained, be most useful to him in 'the present very grave situation'. Meanwhile a few sentences about 'the position in which I am placed by recent events' would enable a judgment to be formed as to whether, 'under the circumstances, such an interview as has been suggested should take place'. At the last meeting of the 'Round Table' conference, held at Trevelyan's house on 14th February, it had been the unanimous opinion of all present that 'great advances had been made towards agreement, and that there was good reason to hope that a little further discussion might enable all of us to concur in the main lines of proposals intended for the settlement both of the Irish Land and Irish Government questions'. Harcourt had himself said publicly some time later that the 'points of agreement were many and important and that the points of difference were secondary and few'. What then had been the difficulty in arranging 'a satisfactory settlement'. Had it been clinched then and there there would have been a strong possibility of Hartington's adopting its main drift. 'In this case, either the Government would also have to accept it, or they must have lost the support of the Unionist Liberals and have given place to others.' Harcourt's constant refusal to follow up the achievements of 14th February, despite 'pressing entreaties', had been a cause of grief and

[1] Chamberlain, *op. cit.*, pp. 264–5.

surprise to him. So too had the withholding of information about Gladstone's views on 'the new situation brought about by our discussions'. It would only have been a matter of accepting or rejecting a policy the exact nature of which was known. Clarification would have settled the reunion issue and governed the attitude the Liberal Unionists were to adopt over the Conservatives. Even though the crisis had taken a new turn through the introduction of the coercion issue, there was still time to make amends. Most Liberal Unionists, indeed the vast majority, were practically pledged to supporting the second reading of the Crimes Bill—'in default of an alternative policy to which they could give their assent'. Nevertheless, were such a policy to be arrived at, albeit at this eleventh hour, 'our future action would be a matter for the gravest consideration'. Of course, the unfortunate delay had created 'the most serious obstacles to immediate cooperation' and had 'tended to harden and widen the differences which we all deplore'. The more so because of its interposition at such a critical stage. Over the 'recent operation of the Closure Rule and the intervention of the Speaker' he felt in complete accord with Gladstone and was ready and willing to take any step necessary to obviate 'a condition which seems likely to affect inuriously the authority of the Chair'. For the moment the only practical suggestion he had to make was one made to him the previous night by Churchill. In face of the difficulty of changing the rule passed in the present session, there 'should be a Conference between the leaders on both sides as to the future course of the debates on the Crimes Bill'. The government 'should concede to the Opposition any reasonable terms that the latter' might insist on, with respect to 'the dates for proceeding with the stages of the measure and the time that' might 'fairly be asked for each important discussion'. By this means 'all further necessity for a resort to Closure might . . . be avoided'. Later the new rule itself could be tackled.[1]

According to Dilke, Chamberlain was convinced Gladstone was going to use their interview, fixed for the 5th at Dollis Hill, pumping him for his proposals.[2] Things turned out rather differently and, characteristically, the old 'fox' did quite as much talking as the young, who got no real satisfaction. What remorse and fear of blame the former had felt after the failure to reunite in February had almost completely disappeared with the full resurrection of the coercion bogey and the leftward trend in by-elections resulting in part from it. The G.O.M. began by airing his grievances on the latest bee in his, the most formidable of bonnets. Were Chamberlain to propose the abrogation of the Speaker's veto, both the prospects for success and

[1] *Ibid.*
[2] Gwynn and Tuckwell, *op. cit.,* p. 268.

reunion would be weightily served. To show a spirit of cooperation on matters of agreement would do a power of good. Chamberlain neatly countered this by pointing out the intervention of the Speaker had first been proposed by a Liberal government against his will and how much better the present rule was than its Liberal predecessor, though he was careful to add that his disapproval was none the less very real for all that. Moreover, the government was unlikely to take his advice on the point, while 'recent action by Liberals' made him sceptical about Liberal approval of his intervention. Obviously embarrassed, the patriarch hastily 'repudiated for himself any such feeling, but said he would enquire of A. Morley and see if it existed among his friends'. As pure a piece of fustian as ever was seen. Hawarden may have offered detachment, but never the remoteness such ignorance would have required, and, anyway, he had been in the south for some time. Dollis Hill too, was a mere rendezvous for a secret meeting and in no sense a suburban Varzin. While pleased with Churchill's suggestion, he doubted whether his 'party generally would approve of negotiation or agree to arrangements as to the course to be taken in future discussions on the Crimes Bill'.

Only then did the conversation turn to the subject of the 'Round Table' conference and its failure. Gladstone steered clear of any 'specific points of difference, except with regard to Land Purchase, as to which he said that he accepted the idea of employing Irish credit in any such operation in lieu of resorting on a large scale to British credit'. The essential conservatism of his outlook emerged in the opinion that 'a very extensive or complete scheme embracing all the land of Ireland might be found to be unnecessary'. Parnell, he thought, had not received detailed accounts of the results of the talks, but anyway, Hartington would not swallow anything the Irish leader could consider. 'In fact . . . Lord Hartington was going back in his public utterances on the (Irish) question.' When Chamberlain raised Harcourt's statement about points of difference and reiterated the argument about its confirmation, the old man swept it aside with the remark that he was not inclined to cry over spilt milk. 'Coercion having now intervened, it filled all the space and nothing else could profitably be considered.' This spurred on Chamberlain to ask whether he was to understand Gladstone to believe that the coercion question had to 'be fought out in the House and the Country before it could be profitable to make any further attempts at agreement on the main question of the Government of Ireland'. Although claiming forty-eight hours for reflection prior to giving a categorical answer, the old man managed to say 'that was his present impression' and how he supposed Chamberlain shared it. The latter did no such thing and complained of the delay once more, blaming upon it the present condition with its likely consequences of a widened breach and permanent weakening of the Liberal party.

The G.O.M. then added insult to injury by simply urging a return to the fold by the whole Liberal Unionist party, and when told this was impossible pending a compromise, advised Chamberlain to publish his alternative plan for devolution, saying it might well offer a basis for such a settlement. Again pure fustian, or possibly old-world courtesy, but his companion would have none of it, insisting Parnell would reject anything he produced and would thereafter be estopped from accepting it at Gladstone's hands. At this the patriarch protested he had meant a Liberal Unionist rather than Chamberlain's personal plan, and thus left the latter little alternative but to admit the impossibility of this. Rather oddly, the Radical Unionist leader went on to give the G.O.M. a boost to his morale. His confidence must have been all the greater because of what Chamberlain admitted about the Liberal Unionists' loss of ground, the possibility of their right wing joining the Conservatives and his own likely retirement from politics if this came about.[1] Why he said all this remains something of a mystery. Perhaps he wished the G.O.M. to know he realised the difficulties yet stuck to Unionism; that there was no chance of his surrender. Winterbotham, the Radical Unionist member for Cirencester, had already defected to Gladstone on the coercion issue. If hopes of a wider defection had been entertained, this interview went far towards dashing them. For Chamberlain the information garnered was useful. He had the impression firmly in his mind as to just how confidently Gladstone counted on the unpopularity of coercion 'to bring about an early appeal to the country and to secure a decision in his favour'. The old man neither wanted to proceed further with conciliation, nor believed that his party would let him. He and his Gladstonians were the willing prisoners of each other. Almost three weeks later, Chamberlain revealed the secret of the interview to Dale, commenting: 'It was very discouraging and although Mr Gladstone is personally friendly, he abstained from giving the least hint of any practical advances towards reunion and I inferred that he relied on the unpopularity of coercion to secure him a majority without yielding anything to the Unionists.'[2] Yet was he truly discouraged? He had never wanted reunion and the letter was probably tailored to suit its recipient. To the end he had 'foxed'. With only minor lapses en route from 23rd December he had maintained the pretence of wanting reunion. Gladstone had ultimately let the mask drop. Though the 'wirepullers' were to score an occasional success in Birmingham,

[1] Chamberlain, *op. cit.*, pp. 266–8.
[2] Chamberlain to Dale, 25th April 1887. Copy. Chamberlain Papers, JC5/20/60. Garvin, *op. cit.*, p. 318.

always in Chamberlain's absence, the Liberal and Radical majority stuck to him, however beset by doubts. To this the 'foxing' contributed in no small way. The picture of 'Our Joe' the rejected and wronged had gone over well. Not that sympathy and pride were the sole factors. Bright and *The Times* played their part with a vengeance.

From first to last in the series of events ending at Dollis Hill, Chamberlain had been the central figure of efforts for reunion. From Gladstone's refusal to retire after failing to carry Home Rule in 1886 stemmed the need temporarily to try and divert the flow of events and present politics to the electorate in a new light. It had not been easy for Chamberlain to give the public the impression that being against Gladstone did not involve being fully with Salisbury and Hartington. His first attempt to escape from the dilemma at the 'Round Table' failed because the sort of tortuous behaviour it involved convinced only those with an already deep respect for him. Birmingham was survival, not success. There were, however, two other bids to cut loose about to begin. One, the concept of a 'National Party' had been broached by Churchill on 3rd April, but never stood the slightest chance of success.[1] The other—moving towards the Conservatives— he had played simultaneously with the first, though *sotto voce* until the *Baptist* letter. Ultimately, it was to flourish, but for the immediate present was wellnigh ruined by certain aspects of the government's tough Irish policy. Back on 18th December Morley told Gladstone how Chamberlain was hoping against hope coercion would not be brought on.[2] Now it was an unpleasant reality. The second reading of a Crimes Bill began the very evening after the Dollis Hill encounter. Earlier that day, Hartington had written: 'It has been very quiet here this week after all the row on Friday, but I suppose it will all break out again soon.'[3] How right he was. As the debate raged to and fro tempers got heated. In conversation on the 10th April Morley charged Chamberlain with having ruined the 'Round Table' project by his 'masterful demeanour' in the 'Baptist' letter and the speeches. In other words, through being a 'one man band', conciliator and self-defender combined. To be fair, Morley also blamed Hartington, who had, he said, made it impossible for himself (Hartington) and his friends to desert the government and Goschen.[4] Bright was asked to speak in the debate, but declined, fearing his relations with Glad-

[1] Garvin, *op. cit.*, pp. 313–16. Churchill, *op. cit.*, p. 349. Gwynn and Tuckwell, *op. cit.*, p. 268.

[2] Morley to Gladstone, 18th December 1886. Gladstone Papers, Add. MS. 44255, f. 146.

[3] Hartington to the Duchess of Manchester, 5th April 1887. Devonshire Papers, 340. Add. MS.

[4] Morley to Gladstone, 10th April 1887. Gladstone Papers, Add. MS. 44255, f. 191.

stone would be finally ruined.[1] Nevertheless, his being a Liberal Unionist alone was enormously useful to Chamberlain in the base.

On the 13th Chamberlain arrived in Ayr for the first speech of a Scottish tour destined to last into May. One of his constant themes was that Gladstone had terminated the reunion discussions by refusing to entertain any modification of the 1886 Home Rule Bill.[2] Morley countered on the 19th at Wolverhampton, right in the heart of the 'Joe' country, by openly asserting the breakdown of the 'Round Table' idea had been due to the irreconcilable language used by Chamberlain outside.[3] Meanwhile, the second reading of the Coercion Bill had been passed without a division, after a Gladstonian amendment had been rejected by a majority of 101, and on the morning of the same day—the 18th—there had appeared in *The Times* a facsimile of a letter purporting to have been written by Parnell to one of his associates in the Land League after the Phoenix Park murders of 1882 conniving at the deed.[4] A denial in the Commons immediately preceded the second reading vote, but neither there nor outside was it believed by a very large number of people. Certainly enough mud stuck to help Chamberlain at home and nothing Gladstone said at the 'Eighty Club' on the 19th scraped it off. 'The constitutional Irish party', as he termed it, might well never have been 'individually' associated with the commission of crime in Ireland.[5] Who, however, was going to believe it—the majority of electors? The rest of his speech was principally an attack upon the Liberal Unionists of a particularly unfair kind, given their Unionism. He blamed them for maintaining the government at all costs, even those of accepting delays in reform and the rigours of coercion.

What coercion had begun to do for the Gladstonians, *The Times* began to do for Unionism. Electors might still be fickle, yet the Liberal Unionist politicians as a whole acquired a new *élan*. Ten of them were absent unpaired on the 18th, including Chamberlain and Collings away in Scotland, but only three—Talbot, Vivian and Winterbotham—voted for the Gladstonian amendment.[6] Their party was no Jericho for Arnold Morley's trumpets. It is certain that the pre-

[1] Hartington to Bright, 9th April 1887. Bright Papers, Add. MS. 43387, f. 254. Bright to Hartington, 13th April 1887. Devonshire Papers, 340. 2119.
[2] Chamberlain, *op. cit.*, p. 270.　　　[3] *The Times*, 20th April 1887.
[4] *The Times*, 18th April 1887. For the most recent and best account of the Phoenix Park murder crisis and its final denouement see C. C. O'Brien, *Parnell and his Party, 1880–1890*, p. 82 sqq. and p. 232. See also F. S. L. Lyons, *The Fall of Parnell, 1890–1891*, Chapter I.
[5] *The Times*, 20th April 1887.
[6] Of the three rebels only A. R. Winterbotham, M.P. for Cirencester, defected then and there to the Opposition. However, C. R. M. Talbot, who sat for Mid-Glamorgan, eventually followed suit and Sir H. H. Vivian was a full Gladstonian by that summer.

dominant mood Gladstone entertained over reunion was expediency. He only regretted the split in so far as he might be blamed or lose influence through it. The men of 'goodwill' had been powerless to prevent the launching of a Home Rule campaign in which they had little or no belief. The G.O.M. had had the prestige to capture the N.L.F. from the Chamberlainite clique. Only he could enable the men of 'goodwill' to proceed with reunion talks in the face of the strong disapproval of Labouchère and the Schnadhorstian 'wire-pullers'. The 'new' Radicals and the Nationalists were an excellent excuse for the party leader to play with against Harcourt, Herschell and their like. Actually he had the authority to impose a good deal upon both. He was the king-pin and his assessment of the situation would govern the party's policy on the reunion issue. He was less determined than Chamberlain that nothing should result. The latter was more sure of himself and confident of bringing off his trick. For Gladstone, it would depend. When coercion and domestic issues seemed to help him, it 'depended' against continuance of reunion talks.

The conference idea was not invented in the post-split period. Francis Channing, the Liberal M.P. for East Northants and an advanced Radical, had suggested on 1st June 1886 that the quarrel be coped with something like the Redistribution Bill—a conference should evolve a 'working compromise'.[1] He had written to Chamberlain on the subject. Many sceptical of such a move in the summer of 1886 were ready for it by December, and some saw in it a good instrument ruined by the personnel at the 'Round Table'. One such was Sir Alfred Pease, who wrote:

> If instead of Chamberlain Hartington, and instead of Morley Rosebery, had been there, something might have come of it; as it is nothing (and nothing did). Though Hartington is more decidedly against Home Rule than Chamberlain and Rosebery for it, but not enthusiastic, these two are both full of cool common sense, and put the 'general good' first. The other two I regard as quite hopeless and of peculiar and divergent mentalities.[2]

Such men made the talks 'a stupid affair'. Others thought them entirely abortive.[3]

[1] Channing to Chamberlain, 1st June 1886. Chamberlain Papers, JC5/76/37.

[2] A. E. Pease, *Elections and Recollections*, pp. 152–3. Sir Alfred E. Pease was at that time Gladstonian M.P. for York. The view of another important Gladstonian backbencher on the conference was more typical of the centre of the party. Jeremiah J. Colman, M.P. for Norwich and a mustard magnate, declared: 'Even if it does no good in the sense of any further outward step towards union being taken, I think it is pretty clear it won't do any harm, but will tend towards a better understanding in the House itself.' Helen C. Colman, *Jeremiah James Colman, A Memoir*, p. 316.

[3] For example, Morley. See p. 354, note 3.

Hartington had remained stolid to almost all external appearances throughout the crisis. Memories of the famous theatre meeting and the presence of Chamberlain told him to go no further than alliance with the Conservatives and to work that with caution. Such waverings as he had had towards the conference were the result of a misapprehension. April found him in the same position that he had come to occupy by December 1886. So too with the Gladstonians. Immediately the secession of the 'dissentients' took place, the centre of gravity of the Liberals shifted markedly to the left and the N.L.F. came much nearer to being a reflection of average party opinion. The journey to the Newcastle Programme had begun before the Leeds conference. In December the pattern was already clear. Home Rule for 'Constructionism' was the exchange Gladstone made with the Radicals. How different was the case of Chamberlain and the vast majority of his Radical Unionist following. While the Hartingtonians stood still, he and his henchmen steadily came to reconcile Unionism and Radicalism, ending up as men of the left centre on the right-wing side of the Irish battle. Less faddist than their Gladstonian ex-comrades, they tended to concentrate on more truly national issues in the spirit of the 'Unauthorised Programme'. As the 'Round Table' conference faded into oblivion, except for periodic wrangling as to what had actually happened at it, Radical Unionism found itself firmly aligned with Whig Unionists and Conservatives. Chamberlain had not changed his policies, merely the way of pursuing them. Throughout his public career he was a man who pursued the priority of the moment without in any way seriously betraying any basic principle once genuinely held or restricting himself to a narrow view of politics. As a municipal leader he had still been interested in the wider issue of national education, indeed in the full spectrum of affairs, foreign and colonial matters included. As a Radical leader he had never neglected his town, or entertained 'Little Englandism' in its true sense. As a Radical Unionist, from 1886 to 1895, he fought for the Union without sacrificing any of the other causes, particularly domestic reform. After 1895 he was at last able to think beyond survival to the great problems of the maintenance and expansion of British wealth and power and the raising of the standard of living. Making his Scottish tour, he pulled no punches at the iniquities of highland landlordism and advanced the Unionist cause for his pains.

Trevelyan had said nothing since Liskeard, but all the time his feeling that 'imperialism was more distasteful than Home Rule'[1] grew in strength. Gladstone was not without his worries, but he was able to turn them to good account. Harcourt continued to 'harp' on the

[1] G. M. Trevelyan, *Sir George Otto Trevelyan: A Memoir*, p. 119.

desirability of reunion. After two conciliatory speeches of Gladstone's at the end of April and the beginning of May, stating that he did not insist on all the details of his 1886 Home Rule Bill, but simply on its underlying principles, Trevelyan made friendly overtures, first at the 'Eighty Club', and then at the Manchester Reform Club. Immediately, Harcourt began to insist that Gladstone should make a specific announcement as to what lines a new Home Rule Bill would take, especially over the vexed question of the retention of the Irish members. While quite unwilling to fall in with this, Gladstone was anxious to isolate Chamberlain from the main streams of Liberalism still more, and after consultation with some of his closest associates asked Trevelyan to come and see him. When this resulted in an unconditional surrender on the latter's part Harcourt certainly had the tables turned upon him. Trevelyan and Winterbotham were not serious losses to Radical Unionism on any but a symbolic level. But this is to anticipate where the former was concerned and the fortunes of 'Our Joe' should command more immediate attention.

The 25th February must be taken as the day on which he openly threw in his lot with Salisbury and Hartington, and though the Schnadhorstian menace in the west midlands had led him into a few diversionary tactics, the *Baptist* letter was never disowned. On 22nd April events in Birmingham took a serious turn from a Chamberlain viewpoint. The '2000' voted against coercion.[1] The 'enemy' had taken advantage of his absence to sway enough of those 'bleeding hearts' to carry the day. As he told Dale, the decision had 'pained and distressed' him. The meeting had been a 'disgrace to Birmingham' and only a sense of the responsibility resting upon him prevented a glad departure from politics.[2] Unlike the Gladstonian men of 'goodwill', he was not impotent before a popular body. For the time being he avoided an open battle with Schnadhorst. 'Joseph the Peacemaker' would stand an infinitely better chance of ultimate victory. With Bright and 'Parnellism and Crime'[3] working for him and the possibility of pressure on the government, accompanied by lurid accounts

[1] Garvin, *op. cit.*, p. 318.

[2] Chamberlain to Dale, 25th April 1887. Copy. Chamberlain Papers, JC5/20/60. Garvin, *op. cit.*, p. 318.

[3] The letters of 18th April 1887, referred to above (see p. 354, note 4), were the climax of a series of articles entitled 'Parnellism and Crime' published in *The Times* from 7th March on. When they began, Mrs O'Shea hid *The Times* from Parnell until he had eaten a peaceful breakfast. K. O'Shea, *Charles Stewart Parnell: His Love Story and Political Life*, Vol. II, p. 129.

Three articles, those of the 7th, 14th and 18th March had appeared before A. J. Balfour, the new Irish Secretary and Salisbury's nephew, gave notice of his Coercion Bill on the 22nd March. 'The Bill was read for the first time in the beginning of April, and on the last day of the debate on the second reading, 18th April, *The Times* published its "piece de resistance"— what has since

of the danger in Birmingham, yielding results, it paid to let the Gladstonians attack and eventually overreach themselves. Neither the government nor the Whigs could afford to let him lose his base. The more Gladstonian attacks there were, the more reforms he would be able to obtain. A successful Unionist Radical was a lesser evil in the eyes of Chatsworth and Hatfield than a triumphant Home Rule Radicalism. Still, there was no denying the minority in his capital had been capable of inflicting a humiliation upon him. Something like that could get out of hand and was not solely something to be exploited. Loss of prestige alone could prove serious and unnerve wavering Radical Unionists. The time would arrive when Schnadhorst's defeat would be imperative. That time would be when the choice between action and inaction no longer rested with Highbury. This time waiting was possible. And the attack brought results. On the 30th Hartington told a meeting of the Liberal Unionists at Devonshire House that the change of venue clause was no more.

The real losers in these months had been the Gladstonian men of 'goodwill'. Above all Harcourt, who had striven manfully to bring about the 'working compromise' Channing had wanted so badly in 1886. So, in a less spectacular way, had Herschell and Fowler, supported by many lesser lights of the party in spirit at least. They longed for the pay-off with Parnell that actually came in 1890 and 1891, but it was quite impossible until feeling in the N.L.F. had swung round to their position. Only then would the situation prove too much for the G.O.M. In the spring of 1887 this was far from being the case, and then too, there was the complicating factor of the hatred and distrust felt for 'The Judas from Birmingham'. One not so relevant to 1890, when his return to the fold had become an almost impossible proposition. The quest for unity had forced the Harcourt school to welcome the speech of 23rd December. The need for Gladstonian solidarity had obliged them to resent the *Baptist* letter and fall in line once more at a nod from their 'Chief'. Most of them liked Chamberlain personally, just as Gladstone, Morley, Labouchère, Schnadhorst

become known as "the facsimile letter".' A. Thorold, *The Life of Henry Labouchère*, p. 326. Thorold also comments: 'It is very certain that all Liberal Unionists, and even a few of the more educated Tory statesmen, realised that the articles were merely theatrical appeals to the contracted imaginations of those armchair politicians, whose ways of influencing voters in rural districts were all-powerful, but it was not to be expected that the man in the street could understand them as such. On him they made a profound impression. *Ibid.* Although a strongly partisan statement the piece about 'the man in the street' was undoubtedly true. What C. C. O'Brien termed the men of the 'Fairyhouse Tradition' —the almost invariably indifferent—were shocked and gulled by the 'facsimile letter'. The phrase is, of course, used here in a general sense and not in the particular context of Ireland in 1916. For that see C. C. O'Brien (Editor), *The Shaping of Modern Ireland*, p. 14.

and the luminaries of the N.L.F. did not. This he exploited in the great 'foxing' feat he ran in those months. And feat it was, whatever the moral judgment the deeds merited. In contrast to the unfailing openness of Harcourt at the outset, he gave his whole confidence to no one. What he wanted has to be pieced together bit by bit. The complete picture is complicated, yet so very logical. More than any other character on the political stage he prayed to the great god reason. But whereas the mind was clear, Courtney was right in believing that 'The ways of our Joseph were dark'.[1]

[1] Gooch, *op. cit.*, p. 272. Summing up his impressions of the conference one biographer of Chamberlain confessed himself baffled. 'Mystery has continued to surround his (i.e. Chamberlain's) motives at the period of the conference, and the view which politicians take of his conduct in suggesting it and subsequently writing to the *Baptist* are influenced in many cases by preconceived notions.' A. Mackintosh, *Joseph Chamberlain: An Honest Biography*, p. 139.

In an interview with Chamberlain at the Colonial Office, on 15th February 1898, R. Barry O'Brien was told the Radical Unionist leader had 'never' been 'near' to being 'converted to an Irish Parliament' in 1886 and that 'the national councils' had been his 'extreme point'. 'What is more', added Chamberlain later in the conversation: 'I revived my National Councils scheme at the Round Table Conference. They asked Parnell. Parnell would not have it, and that of course made an end in the matter. They thought they could turn him round like Trevelyan, but found they were mistaken.' R. B. O'Brien, *The Life of Charles Stewart Parnell*, Vol. II, pp. 140–2. As the pages above tell the true story no further comment on Chamberlain's words are necessary! O'Brien's question which led to the comment on the 'Round Table' conference had been occasioned by a statement allegedly made by S. H. Jeyes to the effect that Chamberlain had been on the verge of conversion to Home Rule during the reunion talks. For an account of the main developments in the controversy as to what actually happened at the 'Round Table' Conference see Appendix 4.

EPILOGUE

◄►✦◄►

'But the end is not yet.' St Matthew xxiv. 6.

'Behold a greater than Solomon is here.' St Matthew xii. 42.

REUNION between the Gladstonian Liberals and the Liberal and Radical Unionists never came. Indeed, in some respects the split became severely aggravated, especially after Schnadhorst's surprise capture of the hitherto nominally united Birmingham Liberal Association in 1888 during Chamberlain's absence in the United States obliged the Radical Unionists to fight back hard in the organisational field or perish.[1] The agony of uncertainty was well and truly over.

Chamberlain himself had been responsible for a good deal of the apparent fluidity in politics, but gradually, as Gladstonian strength had mounted, his almost frantic changes of front had had to be brought to an end. Some time after the 'Round Table' conference was over when the dissentient Liberals seemed able, albeit to a limited extent, to influence the general shape of government legislation, he had tried out moving towards the Conservatives. In December 1886 Middleton, their Chief Agent, during a passing moment of lucidity, had realised well enough that Chamberlain 'alone could influence the classes from which Ld. Randolph brought us strength', and stressed that while

[1] See Hurst, *Joseph Chamberlain and West Midland Politics, 1886–95*, and Hurst, *Joseph Chamberlain, the Conservatives and the Succession to John Bright, 1886–89*, both *passim*. Granville's biographer summed up the situation: 'There was no pacification; not even "a truce of God", and only fresh recriminations were the result.' Fitzmaurice, *op. cit.*, p. 491. For a Whig Liberal Unionist comment on the 'Round Table' conference see Elliot, *op. cit.*, pp. 114–15. For a Gladstonian one see Morley, *op. cit.*, pp. 363–8. In his own *Recollections*, Vol. I, pp. 297–310, Morley rejects the view put round by Harcourt in private—that the Chamberlain–Morley quarrel had ruined all. P. Stansky, *Ambitions and Strategies: The Struggle for the Leadership of the Liberal Party in the 1890's* gives a very clear account of the difficulties caused by Harcourt, Morley and Rosebery once the G.O.M. lost the 'hardihood' and prestige rightly stressed in Sir Wemyss Reid's *Memoirs and Correspondence of Lord Playfair* at p. 392. Things worsened still more when Rosebery became prime minister. It would appear that Chamberlain was far from alone in his irascibility during the 1890s. That he was not in the 1880s is clear enough from what has gone before.

'these are merely electioneering considerations' they were none the less vital to survival when the government next faced the electorate.[1] The impact of this opinion was bound to be ephemeral because in parliament it was Hartington who counted and upon him the government could always rely in the last resort. The prospect of a general election and the need for Chamberlain were therefore far from immediate—that is, for those whose innermost desires inclined them to favour the course involving least change and to calculate as though the present alone mattered. Salisbury and most of his Ministers had just that outlook and, over Irish policy, where they realised Hartington was least likely to be difficult they tried on negative or even reactionary lines unthinkable in a purely British context. Both the Land and Coercion Bills had undergone modification under Liberal and Radical Unionist pressure and Chamberlain had consequently felt able to decide on a closer alignment with the government.[2] Their alignment with him was quite another matter though, and he had underestimated the toughness they could muster when having their own way struck them as imperative. Despite the unfavourable trend of by-elections Salisbury had decided upon the proclamation of the National League, without so much as a word to Hartington, let alone Chamberlain, who did not get to know about it until ten days before the public was told.[3]

Rumours forecasting a Hartington coalition had flown about

[1] Capt. R. W. Middleton to A. Akers-Douglas (Conservative Chief Whip), 30th December 1886. Chilston, *op. cit.*, p. 104.

[2] Hurst, *Joseph Chamberlain, the Conservatives and the Succession to John Bright, 1886–89, passim.* The complaints of numerous Conservatives that Salisbury had gone too far to meet the wishes of Liberal Unionists were mentioned by H. D. Traill in his short biography of the Conservative prime minister. 'There are some,' he writes, 'who think that he [i.e. Salisbury] has already yielded too much to those whose one idea of the true policy of a Conservative party in a democracy is to give larger promissory notes than the demagogue—whether with or without design, not long since recommended to them, of subsequently repudiating their signatures.' H. D. Traill, *The Marquis of Salisbury*, p. 218. But as Arthur Elliot pointed out in his biography of Goschen: 'the majority of the Liberal Unionist Party were moderate Liberals, and with some of them undoubtedly the Liberalism had become so "moderate" that a political microscope would have been necessary to distinguish them from Conservatives born and bred.' Elliot, *op. cit.*, p. 120. Chamberlain was clearly the force the rightists feared and disliked. At the end of August 1887, however, 'Lord Hartington, having consulted Sir Henry James, communicated to Goschen the substance of Mr Chamberlain's proposals [i.e. for Ireland], with the comment that, although he did not like the scheme, he considered that Goschen and Lord Salisbury would do well to ponder carefully whether Home Rule could be permanently resisted on present lines; that is, without its opponents offering any alternative system beyond the mere extension to Ireland of local county government.' Elliot, *op. cit.*, p. 115. Small wonder that some Conservatives were in a constant state of nervousness.

[3] *Ibid.*

during the Conservative climb down over the Land Bill.[1] Under the impact of this new and calculated snub, Chamberlain had neither awaited any possible repetition of these rumours, nor taken any positive steps to raise Cain within the Unionist fold. Instead, he had collared John Morley and attempted a second 'go' at the G.O.M.[2] A speech of Gladstone's at Swansea on 4th June had seemed to offer ground for a true compromise.[3] It had appeared that the Gladstonians were now prepared to envisage the retention of the Irish representation at Westminster as part of their Home Rule plan. Dale's comment had been: 'If Mr Gladstone's speech had been made before the Home Rule vote, no split would have occurred.'[4] More telling perhaps as an indication of the effect of the speech upon Dale than as a statement about 1886, but, nevertheless, important to Chamberlain in his quest for political security. More pertinent still was the fact that Gladstone had spoken thus because of pressure from Harcourt during the latter half of May. The deputy leader of the Gladstonians had by that time become willing to accept Chamberlain's four-point programme of the full supremacy of the Imperial parliament, retention of the Irish members, protection of the minorities and the separate treatment of Ulster, and the right of London to legislate for Irish law and order, as a basis for reunion.[5] By May 1887, however, there was not the slightest chance of Gladstone leaving the Gladstonians in the lurch as William Bright had feared in January.[6] He had come to appreciate very well how little Harcourt's views on Chamberlain were now echoed in the Liberal party. Even so, a concession on the easiest point had shown great prudence and a keen sense of political realities. Actually going further and sending positive word to Chamberlain via Morley was an entirely different kettle of fish. Delay had been the keynote of the response. Delay to ensure a favourable response among Gladstonian Liberals and Unionist Liberals alike. By 20th August it had been perfectly clear nothing would result and Chamberlain had addressed a Radical Union garden party at Highbury with some trepidation.[7] The one really bright spot on his

---

[1] *Ibid.* [2] Garvin, *op. cit.*, pp. 310–13.

[3] *Annual Register*, 1887, pp. 106–7. [4] Dale, *op. cit.*, p. 470.

[5] Harcourt to Gladstone, 27th May 1887. Gladstone Papers, Add. MS. 44201, f. 127.

[6] Gwynn and Tuckwell, *op. cit.*, p. 267. It was in May 1887 that the uneasy truce broke down at the Liberal 'Eighty Club'. For the secession of the Liberal Unionist members see Elliott, *op. cit.*, pp. 116–17.

[7] Garvin, *op. cit.*, p. 318. On 11th June 1887 Chamberlain had written to Austen Chamberlain in Germany: ' . . . I think that matters are coming to a crisis here. Gladstonianism is becoming more sectional and more irreconcilable and I do not want to reunite with such a party—or faction controlled by Labouchère . . . and Co. I see the possibility of a strong Central Party, which may be master of the situation after Mr G. goes. Meanwhile Unionism in the country is de-

political horizon at that moment had been Collings' success in wring-
ing out of the government a modest Labourers' Allotments Bill. The
audience had not been unsympathetic, but when the six Radical
Unionists voted against proclaiming the League on 26th August they
voiced a deep feeling prevalent among their west midland backers.[1]

Chamberlain had been one of the six, although Hartington, Bright
and forty-five other Liberal Unionists had stuck to the government,
despite widespread discontent and misgivings. Driven from the Conservative pillar to the Gladstonian post. 'Joe' had found no comfort.
Accordingly, he had changed front yet again and acted as though the
'National' party, lately mooted between Churchill and himself had
become a reality. But the final positioning had been created by forces
beyond his control, though its nature corresponded with what under
certain conditions he had come to prefer. First had come Salisbury's
invitation for him to head the British delegation destined to try and
settle a fisheries dispute with the Americans.[2] Then Schnadhorst's
aggression after acceptance of the mission had taken him across the
Atlantic.[3] His future lay with the Conservatives whether he liked it
or not—that is unless he caved in over Home Rule or fled the political
field. 'Our Joe' was not the man to do either and, on balance, liked
what fortune had decreed.

The first fruit of his latest and last position was organisational; the
second a policy statement entitled 'A Unionist Policy for Ireland'.[4] It
was published entirely on his own responsibility, for Hartington had
declined his cooperation, and appeared in the columns of the
Birmingham Daily Post without any signature, although the whole
world immediately guessed the author's identity. Many of its proposals, particularly those relating to public works, land purchase and

cidedly making progress and Mr G.'s Welsh speeches have not done him any
good.' About a month later, on 16th July 1887, Chamberlain wrote to Austen
about having him adopted as Liberal Unionist candidate for Trevelyan's old seat
in the Border Burghs. Chamberlain Papers, AC1/4/5/12 and AC1/4/5/13. Sentiments such as those expressed in the first letter led those deeply hostile to Chamberlain into comparing him with Becky Sharp in *Vanity Fair* when she remarked:
'But oh! Mr Osborne, what a difference eighteen months' experience makes!
Eighteen months spent—pardon me for saying so—with gentlemen.' See J.
McCarthy, *The Story of Gladstone's Life*, pp. 336–7.

[1] The six consisted of Joseph Chamberlain himself and five others: Richard
Chamberlain (Islington West), brother; Jesse Collings (Birmingham: Bordesley);
William Kenrick (Birmingham North); Powell Williams (Birmingham South); and
Sir B. Hingley (Worcestershire North). For an excellent account of Unionist
versus Gladstonian in the last constituency see A. G. Gardiner, *Life of George
Cadbury*, pp. 71–90.

[2] Garvin, *op. cit.*, pp. 322–6.

[3] Garvin, *op. cit.*, p. 345. Hurst, *Joseph Chamberlain and West Midland Politics,
1886–95*, p. 45.

[4] Chamberlain, *op. cit.*, pp. 281–3.

local government, were subsequently 'adopted in principle' by the Conservative and Liberal Unionist parties. At the end of June 1888, letters reached Chamberlain from MacColl and Childers. The former stressed Gladstone's approval on seeing the first *Daily Post* article and reported how he had said: 'If Mr Parnell were to ask my opinion of it—which he is not likely to do—I should say "Accept it by all means".'[1] The latter went further, for after approving of the programme 'as a stepping stone', he actually asked 'whether something could not be done to approximate the two sections of the Liberal Party.[2] But wishful thinking and grasping at drawing room straws were not for a man such as 'Our Joe'. Less than a month later the government appointed the Parnell Commission. The future was still going to be very difficult for Chamberlain, yet it was something to have a properly fixed position. To have made nothing of it would have been totally uncharacteristic of him.

In fact, of course, he made amazing strides. The man who in 1885 had been thought of as the potential leader of the Liberal party was by 1900 the most powerful single man in the Unionist parties. Before he had split these parties in 1903 on the protection issue their leadership had been within his grasp, but preferring reality to appearance, he chose to exercise the maximum power possible from safe ground rather than venture upon the bog of a leadership deeply resented by influential and socially elevated minorities. This was typical of him. So was his espousal of tariff reform. Provided the Birmingham base was safe he almost invariably waged a sharp ideological war of one sort or another throughout his career. Like the G.O.M. he worked for what he considered crying national needs rather than for the sweets of office. Like the G.O.M.'s, his sense of timing was often imperfect. Clear vision can mislead as to the distance an object is away and the difficulties involved in getting to it. Yet error of this sort is at once the mark and the drawback of statesmanship. So is the hubbub of controversy which seldom left either of these men alone. Both in turn got their reward. First Gladstone, then Chamberlain was acclaimed by the majority of the British electorate.[3]

[1] MacColl to Chamberlain, 28th June 1888. Chamberlain, *op. cit.*, p. 282.

[2] Childers to Chamberlain, 30th June 1888. Chamberlain, *op. cit.*, p. 282.

[3] Writing just after the results of the 1895 general election had become known Beatrice Webb deemed Chamberlain 'the man of the moment'. B. Webb, *Our Partnership*, p. 125, The 'Squalid Argument' of imperialism and social reform had temporarily come out on top. See B. Semmel, *Imperialism and Social Reform*, pp. 83–97. Nevertheless, though acknowledged as a charming conversationalist, Chamberlain never really took the palm from the G.O.M. as a great holder forth. See J. McCarthy, *Reminiscences*, Vol. II, p. 401. Writing to Sir Algernon West in June 1886 Chamberlain had remarked: 'What a pretty smash our Chief has made of it! It is not often given to the leader of a party twice to bring his followers to utter grief by an unexpected *coup-de-main*.' Sir Algernon West, *Recollections*,

The most vital contrast between them as public figures arose from the consequences of different responses to a changing world, due in turn to profoundly different temperaments, social backgrounds, educational experiences and generations. Gladstone came to Liberalism slowly, gradually casting off an initial bigotry, and able, because of contemporary circumstances, to stay in public life without much trouble while the change was in progress. In things like methods of administration and the scope of government activity his views did not develop a great deal. His major preoccupation was with the concept of liberty in all its applications. Chamberlain, on the other hand, never had, nor felt he had the time to take his time at any time. Starting at a provincial level, he worked and grew his way up to the top, constantly adjusting himself to new facets of existence. Gladstone could respond more quickly than most to the demands of Irish nationalism because its cause fell within his special liberty groove, but fell down badly in other spheres. The highly educated all-rounder failed, where Chamberlain the rather narrowly educated business man scored time and time again. In his 'League of Nations mentality' Gladstone was a visionary.[1] In general he remained a democratic

1832–1886, Vol. II, p. 286. He would have echoed the views of Hartington when he proclaimed that Gladstone had the defects of Napoleon, mistaking will for judgment and preferring the conferment of power 'by the inarticulate cries of a multitude' to that 'sanctioned by the deliberate judgment of a senate'. Yet was Chamberlain so different? Was it not 'given' to him to bring his followers to 'utter grief'—once at exactly the time he said that Gladstone had done so and again in 1903? See *Edinburgh Review*, July–October 1886 for the report of Hartington's speech. As late as August 1892 R. B. Haldane told Sir Algernon West of how Chamberlain was 'clearly looking forward to leading the Liberals' and of how he had said 'his position in keeping a Tory Government in was very different from that of supporting them when out'. *Private Diaries of Sir Algernon West*, p. 45. Very probably Chamberlain, though having a hankering after leading the Liberals, had no real hopes of doing so. Perhaps he was just sounding out one of the leading young imperialistically inclined Liberals. For Haldane's association with H. H. Asquith and Edward Grey see D. Sommer, *Haldane of Cloan: His Life and Times, 1856–1928*, p. 67. More to the point of political realities was an acrid comment Chamberlain made on Rosebery, who had been the G.O.M.'s pet and like a good many 'favourites' a bitter disappointment to his sponsor. In April 1887 Rosebery had reaffirmed his 'unlimited belief in Gladstone' (T. F. G. Coates, *Lord Rosebery, His Life and Speeches*, Vol. II, pp. 534–5), but ultimately his imperialism proved too much for his leader to swallow. When the time for his retirement arrived he had come to favour Spencer as his successor, but the Queen in her turn had decided to back Rosebery. The former Hawarden favourite therefore went on up the ladder of promotion to become prime minister in 1894. Gladstone had no chance to push Spencer because he was not asked for an opinion. After some months of his premiership that passed Chamberlain commented to A. J. Balfour on 8th December 1894: 'What a pricked bubble the Rosebery is!' How right he was.

[1] See Sir P. Magnus, *Gladstone*, passim and R. Deacon, *The Private Life of Mr Gladstone*, passim. A full discussion of Gladstone the political visionary can

Peelite. Chamberlain was always modern, often ahead of his time, but never up in the clouds. In the history of the 'Round Table' conference we see the two at their most cunning. Each followed an idea with perseverance and subtlety, calculating every move to the last detail. The younger man had the more difficult task, the older less energy for the game. Which came off the better will never be agreed upon, but the fact remains that once Chamberlain again reached a firm fighting position Gladstone's star began to wane. Some even said: 'Behold a greater than Solomon is here.'

be found in *Essays in Honour of Gilbert Murray*, edited by J. A. K. Thomson and A. J. Toynbee. The relevant piece is by J. L. Hammond and entitled *Gladstone and the League of Nations Mind*. For estimates of the influence of Chamberlain and Gladstone on the course of events, see R. C. K. Ensor, 'The Evolution of Joseph Chamberlain', *Spectator*, 3rd July 1936, and B. Miller 'Chamberlain and Gladstone', *Twentieth Century*, Vol. CLIII, 1953. In his 'Some Political and Economic Interactions in Later Victorian England' Ensor explains most of the basic political developments in terms of the Irish question. For this article see *Transactions of the Royal Historical Society*, 1949.

BIBLIOGRAPHY

A. MANUSCRIPT COLLECTIONS

This book is based very substantially upon the materials listed below. To their owners and custodians I owe my best thanks, especially to Her Majesty the Queen, by whose gracious permission the Royal Archives at Windsor were thrown open to me. Such collections as are not referred to directly in the text were, nevertheless, extremely useful in its preparation.

The Alfred Austin Papers in the library of the National Liberal Club, London.

The Bagshawe Papers in the Sheffield Central Public Library.

The Balfour Papers in the British Museum, London.

The Barrow Election Papers in the Lancashire County Record Office, Preston.

The Bright Papers in the British Museum, London.

The Bryce Papers in the Bodleian Library, Oxford.

The Campbell-Bannerman Papers in the British Museum, London.

The Courtney Papers in the London School of Economics.

The Cranbrook Papers in the East Suffolk and Ipswich County Record Office, Ipswich.

The Joseph Chamberlain Papers in the library of Birmingham University.

The Austen Chamberlain Papers in the library of Birmingham University.

The Chilston Papers in the Kent County Record Office, Maidstone.

The Dale Papers in the library of Birmingham University.

The Devonshire Papers at Chatsworth House, Derbyshire.

The Dilke Papers in the British Museum, London.

The Esher Papers at Watlington Park, Oxfordshire.

The Gladstone Papers in the British Museum, London.

The Herbert Gladstone Papers in the British Museum, London.

The Goschen Papers in the Bodleian Library, Oxford.

The Granville Papers in the Public Record Office, London.

The Hambledon Papers, temporarily in the keeping of the National Register of Archives, London.

The Edward Hamilton Papers in the British Museum, London.

The Harcourt Papers at Stanton Harcourt House, Oxfordshire.

The Milner Papers in the library of New College, Oxford.

The Monk–Bretton Papers in the Bodleian Library, Oxford.

The Mundella Papers in the library of Sheffield University.

367

BIBLIOGRAPHY

The Mundella–Leader Papers in the library of Sheffield University.
The Ripon Papers in the British Museum, London.
The Royal Archives at Windsor Castle, Berkshire.
The Salisbury Papers in the library of Christchurch College, Oxford.
The Spencer Papers at Althorp Park, Northamptonshire.
The St Aldwyn Papers at Williamstrip Park, Gloucestershire.
The H. J. Wilson Papers in the library of Sheffield University.
The H. J. Wilson Papers in the Sheffield Central Public Library.
The Papers concerning Conservative–Liberal Unionist relations in Burnley at the offices of the Burnley Conservative Association.

B. PRINTED DOCUMENTS

Documents Relating to the Irish Central Board Scheme, 1884–5, Editor C. H. D. Howard, Irish Historical Studies, Vol. VIII, 1953.
Letters of Queen Victoria, 2nd and 3rd series. Edited G. E. Buckle, London, 1926–1932.
Political Correspondence of Mr Gladstone and Lord Granville, 1876–86, Editor Agatha Ramm, Oxford, 1962.
Select Documents XXI. Joseph Chamberlain, W. H. O'Shea, and Parnell, 1884, 1891–2, Editor C. H. D. Howard, Irish Historical Studies, Vol. XIII, 1962.

C. NEWSPAPERS AND PERIODICALS

1. Newspapers
    Baptist
    Birmingham Post
    Daily Chronicle
    Daily News
    Dublin Express
    Freeman's Journal
    Irish Times
    Leeds Mercury
    Liberal Unionist
    Newcastle Leader
    Northern Echo (*Darlington*)
    Observer
    Pall Mall Gazette
    Scotsman
    Sheffield and Rotherham Independent
    Standard
    St. James Gazette
    The Times
    Ulverston Advertiser
2. Periodicals
    Edinburgh Review
    Fortnightly
    Nineteenth Century
    Quarterly
    Spectator

BIBLIOGRAPHY

D. WORKS OF REFERENCE

BATEMAN, J. *Great Landowners of Great Britain and Ireland*, 4th Edition, 1883.

BOASE, F. *Modern English Biography*, Truro, 1892–1921.

Burke's Landed Gentry.

Burke's Peerage, Baronetage and Knightage.

Debrett's Peerage.

Complete Peerage.

Debrett's Baronetage.

Dictionary of National Biography.

Directory of Directors.

Dod's Parliamentary Companion.

Hansard.

MACCALMONT, F. H. *Parliamentary Poll Book of all Elections*, Nottingham, 1910.

Newspaper Press Directory.

Whitaker's Almanack.

Who Was Who.

E. THESES AND PRIZE ESSAYS

No quotations have been used from the theses. Their main function for me has been as a check on my own researches. Several minor mistakes of fact were avoided through consulting their pages and following up discrepancies.

GOODMAN, G. 'The Liberal Unionist Party, 1886–95', University of Chicago, PhD, 1956.

LINDSAY, J. K. 'The Liberal Unionist Party Until December 1887', University of Edinburgh, PhD, 1957.

SAVAGE, D. C. 'The General Election of 1886 in Great Britain and Ireland', University of London, PhD, 1958.

WOLLASTON, E. P. M. 'The Flowing Tide, 1886–92: A Study in Political Meteorology', Gladstone Memorial Trust Prize Essay, 1959.

F. LEARNED ARTICLES

ARMYTAGE, W. H. G. 'The Railway Rates Question and the Fall of the Third Gladstone Ministry', *English Historical Review*, 1950.

BEALES, H. L. 'Revisions in Economic History. 1. The Great Depression', *Economic History Review*, 1934–5.

BLEWETT, N. 'The Franchise in the United Kingdom, 1885–1918', *Past and Present*, 1965.

CROWLEY, D. W. 'The Crofters' Party, 1885–92', *Scottish Historical Review*, 1956.

DUNBABIN, J. P. D. 'The Politics of the Establishment of County Councils', *Historical Journal*, 1963.

DUNBABIN, J. P. D. 'Expectations of the New County Councils, and Their Realisation', *Historical Journal*, 1965.

ENSOR, SIR R. C. K. 'Some Political and Economic Interactions in Later Victorian England', *Transactions of the Royal Historical Society*, 1949.

BIBLIOGRAPHY

FRASER, P. 'The Liberal Unionist Alliance: Chamberlain, Hartington, and the Conservatives, 1886–1904', *English Historical Review*, 1962.

GOODMAN, G. 'Liberal Unionism: The Revolt of the Whigs', *Victorian Studies*, 1959.

HOWARD, C. H. D. 'Lord Randolph Churchill', *History*, 1940.

HOWARD, C. H. D. 'The Parnell Manifesto of 21 November, 1885 and the Schools Question', *English Historical Review*, 1947.

HOWARD, C. H. D. 'Joseph Chamberlain and the "Unauthorised Programme" ', *English Historical Review*, 1950.

HURST, M. C. 'Joseph Chamberlain, the Conservatives and the Succession to John Bright, 1886–9', *Historical Journal*, 1964.

KELLAS, J. G. 'The Liberal Party and the Scottish Church Disestablishment Crisis', *E.H.R.*, 1964.

MOODY, T. W. 'Michael Davitt and the British Labour Movement, 1882–1906', *Transactions of the Royal Historical Society*, 1953.

ROSTOW, W. W. 'Investment and the Great Depression', *Economic History Review*, 1937–8.

SAVAGE, D. C. 'Scottish Politics, 1885–6', *Scottish Historical Review*, 1961.

SAVAGE, D. C. 'The Origins of the Ulster Unionist Party, 1885–6', *Irish Historical Studies*, Vol. XII, 1961.

THOMPSON, A. E. 'Gladstone Whips and the General Election of 1868', *English Historical Review*, 1948.

THOMPSON, P. 'Liberals, Radicals and Labour in London, 1880–1900', *Past and Present*, 1964.

THORNLEY, D. 'The Irish Home Rule Party and Parliamentary Obstruction, 1874–87', *Irish Historical Studies*, Vol. XII, 1960.

WILLIAMS, P. M. 'Public Opinion and the Railway Rates Question in 1886', *English Historical Review*, 1952.

G. BIOGRAPHIES AND AUTOBIOGRAPHIES

This section of the bibliography is not exhaustive. Only those works I found especially useful are listed. Most of them are referred to at some point in the text.

ALEXANDER, H. *Richard Cadbury of Birmingham*, London, 1906.

ARGYLL, EIGHTH DUKE OF. *Autobiography and Memoirs*, 2 Vols., Edited by the Dowager Duchess of Argyll, London, 1906.

ASHBY, M. K. *Joseph Ashby of Tysoe, 1859–1919*, Cambridge, 1961.

ASKWITH, LORD. *Lord James of Hereford*, London, 1930.

ASQUITH, EARL OF OXFORD AND. *Fifty Years of Parliament*, 2 Vols., London, 1926.

BALFOUR, A. J. *Chapters of Autobiography*, London, 1930.

BASSETT, A. TILNEY. *The Rt. Hon. J. E. Ellis, M.P.*, London, 1914.

BEACH, LADY V. A. HICKS. *Life of Sir Michael Hicks Beach (Earl St. Aldwyn)*, 2 Vols., London, 1932.

BONNER, H. B. *Charles Bradlaugh: A Record of his Life and Work*, 2 Vols., London, 1895.

BRIDGES, J. A. *Reminiscences of a Country Politician*, London, 1906.

BRYCE, J. *Studies in Contemporary Biography*, London, 1903.

370

BIBLIOGRAPHY

CECIL, LADY G. *Life of Robert, Marquis of Salisbury*, 4 Vols., London, 1921–32.

CHAMBERLAIN, SIR A. *Down the Years*, fifth edition, London, 1935.

CHANNING, F. A. *Memories of Midland Politics, 1885–1910*, London and Edinburgh, 1918.

CHILDERS, LT.-COL. SPENCER. *The Life of the Rt. Hon. C. E. Childers*, 2 Vols., London, 1901.

CHILSTON, VISCOUNT. *Chief Whip*, London, 1961.

CHILSTON, VISCOUNT. *W. H. Smith*, London, 1965.

CHURCHILL, SIR W. S. *Lord Randolph Churchill*, 2 Vols., London, 1906.

COATES, T. F. G. *Lord Rosebery, His Life and Speeches*, 2 Vols., London, 1900.

COLLINGS, J. and GREEN, SIR J. L. *Life of Jesse Collings*, London, 1920.

COLMAN, H. C. *Jeremiah J. Colman: A Memoir*, London, 1905.

CRESWICKE, L. *Joseph Chamberlain*, 2 Vols., London, 1904.

CREWE, THE MARQUESS OF. *Lord Rosebery*, 2 Vols., London, 1931.

DALE, A. W. W. *The Life of R. W. Dale of Birmingham*, second edition, London, 1899.

DEACON, R. *The Private Life of Mr Gladstone*, London, 1965.

DE BROKE, LORD WILLOUGHBY. *The Passing Years*, London, 1924.

DUGDALE, B. E. C. *Arthur James Balfour*, 2 Vols., London, 1936.

ELLIOT, HON. A. D. *Life of Lord Goschen*, 2 Vols., 1831–1907, London, 1911.

ESHER, VISCOUNT. *Extracts from Journals, 1880–1895*, Printed for Private Circulation, Cambridge, 1914.

FITZMAURICE, LORD EDMUND. *The Life of Lord Granville, 1815–91*, 2 Vols., London, 1905.

FLETCHER, C. R. L. *Mr. Gladstone at Oxford, 1890*, London, 1891.

GARDINER, A. G. *Life of George Cadbury*, London, 1923.

GARDINER, A. G. *Life of Sir William Harcourt, 1827–1904*, 2 Vols., London, 1923.

GARVIN, J. L. and AMERY, J. *The Life of Joseph Chamberlain*, 4 Vols., London, 1935–51.

GATHORNE-HARDY, A. E. (Editor). *Gathorne Hardy, First Earl of Cranbrook: A Memoir: With Extracts from his Diary and Correspondence*, 2 Vols., London, 1910.

GLADSTONE, VISCOUNT, *After Thirty Years*, London, 1928.

GOOCH, G. P. *Life of Lord Courtney*, London, 1920.

GREGORY, B. *Sidelights on Conflicts in Methodism*.

GWYNN, S. and TUCKWELL, G. M. *The Life of the Rt. Hon. Sir Charles Dilke*, 2 Vols., London, 1917.

HALDANE, R. B. *An Autobiography*, London, 1929.

HAMILTON, LORD G. *Parliamentary Reminiscences and Recollections, 1886–1906*, London, 1921.

HAMILTON, R. *The Life of Henry Hartley Fowler, First Viscount Wolverhampton*, London, 1912.

HAMMOND, J. L. and HAMMOND, B. *James Stansfeld: A Victorian Champion of Sex Equality*, London, 1932.

HOLLAND, B. *Life of the Duke of Devonshire, 1833–1908*, 2 Vols., London, 1911.

BIBLIOGRAPHY

HOWARD, C. H. D. (Editor). *Joseph Chamberlain: A Political Memoir*, London, 1953.

HUTCHINSON, H. G. *Life of Sir John Lubbock*, 2 Vols., London, 1914.

JAMES, R. R. *Lord Randolph Churchill*, London, 1959.

JAMES R. R. *Rosebery*, London, 1963.

JEYES, S. H. *Joseph Chamberlain*, 2 Vols., London, 1903.

KENNEDY, A. L. *Lord Salisbury, 1830–1903: Portrait of a Statesman*, London, 1953.

LANG, A. *Sir Stafford Northcote, First Earl of Iddesleigh*, 2 Vols., London, 1890.

LECKY, E. *A Memoir of W. E. H. Lecky*, London, 1910.

LEVESON-GOWER, SIR G. *Years of Content*, London, 1940.

LEVESON-GOWER, SIR G. *Years of Endeavour*, London, 1942.

LONDONDERRY, MARCHIONESS OF. *Henry Chaplin: A Memoir*, London, 1926.

LUCAS, R. *Lord Glenesk and 'The Morning Post'*, London, 1910.

LUCAS, R. *Colonel Saunderson, M.P.*, London, 1908.

LYTTELTON, E. *Alfred Lyttelton: An Account of his Life*, London, 1917.

MACKAIL, J. W. and WYNDHAM, G. *Life and Letters of George Wyndham*, 2 Vols., London, 1924.

MACKINTOSH, A. *Joseph Chamberlain: An Honest Biography*, revised and enlarged edition, London, 1914.

MAGNUS, SIR P. *Gladstone*, London, 1960.

MALLET, C. *Herbert Gladstone: A Memoir*, London, 1932.

MARRIS, N. M. *Joseph Chamberlain: The Man and the Statesman*, London, 1900.

MAXWELL, SIR H. *Life of W. H. Smith*, new edition, London, 1894.

MCCARTHY, J. *Reminiscences*, 2 Vols., London, 1899.

MCCARTHY, J. *The Story of Gladstone's Life*, London, 1907.

MCCLELLAND, V. A. *Cardinal Manning: His Public Life and Influence, 1865–92*, London, 1962.

MELLY, G. *Recollections of Sixty Years—(1833–1893)*, Coventry, 1893.

MILNER, VISCOUNT AND OTHERS. *Life of Joseph Chamberlain*, London, 1914.

MORLEY, J. *Life of Gladstone*, 3 Vols., London, 1903.

MORLEY, J. *Recollections*, London, 2 Vols., 1917.

MOULTON, H. F. *The Life of Lord Moulton*, London, 1922.

NEWTON, J. *W. S. Caine*, London, 1907.

NEWTON, LORD. *Lord Lansdowne: A Biography*, London, 1929.

O'BRIEN, R. B. *The Life of John Bright*, London, 1910.

O'BRIEN, R. B. *The Life of Charles Stewart Parnell*, 2 Vols., London, 1899.

O'BRIEN, R. B. *The Life of Lord Russell of Killowen*, London, 1901.

O'CONNOR, T. P. *Memoirs of an Old Parliamentarian*, 2 Vols., London, 1929.

O'SHEA, K. *Charles Stewart Parnell: His Love Story and Political Life*, 2 Vols., London, 1914.

PEARSON, H. *Labby: The Life of Henry Labouchère*, London, 1936.

PEASE, SIR A. E. *Elections and Recollections*, London, 1932.

PONSONBY, A. *Henry Ponsonby: His Life from his Letters*, London, 1942.

BIBLIOGRAPHY

REID, T. WEMYSS. *Memoirs and Correspondence of Lord Playfair*, London, 1899.

REID, T. WEMYSS. *The Life of William Ewart Gladstone*, London, 1899.

ROGERS, J. G. *Autobiography*, 1903.

RUSSELL, G. W. E. *Fifteen Chapters of Autobiography*, London, 1915.

RUSSELL, G. W. E. *William Ewart Gladstone*, London, 1913.

RUSSELL, G. W. E. *Malcolm MacColl: Memoirs and Correspondence*, London, 1914.

RYLANDS, L. G. *Correspondence and Speeches of Peter Rylands, M.P.*, 2 Vols., Manchester and London, 1890.

SIDGWICK, A. and E. M. *Henry Sidgwick: A Memoir*, London, 1906.

SOMMER, D. *Haldane of Cloan*, London, 1960.

SPENDER, J. A. *Life of Sir Henry Campbell-Bannerman*, 2 Vols., London, 1923.

SPENDER, J. A. and ASQUITH, C. *Life of Lord Oxford and Asquith*, 2 Vols., London, 1932.

ST HELIER, LADY (MARY JEUNE). *Memories of Fifty Years*, London, 1909.

STRACHEY, J. ST LOE. *The Adventure of Living: A Subjective Autobiography*, London, 1922.

STEPHENS, W. R. W. *The Life and Letters of Edward A. Freeman*, 2 Vols., London, 1895.

THOROLD, A. *The Life of Henry Labouchère*, London, 1913.

TRAILL, H. D. *The Marquess of Salisbury*, London, 1892.

TREVELYAN, G. M. *The Life of John Bright*, London, 1913.

TREVELYAN, G. M. *Sir George Otto Trevelyan: A Memoir*, London, 1932.

TUCKWELL, REV. W. *Reminiscences of a Radical Parson*, London, etc., 1905.

ULLSWATER, VISCOUNT. *A Speaker's Commentaries*, 2 Vols., London, 1925.

WEBB, B. *My Apprenticeship*, Pelican edition, London, 1938.

WEBB, B. *Our Partnership*, London, 1948.

WEST, SIR A. *Recollections, 1832–86*, 2 Vols., London, 1899.

WEST, SIR A. *Private Diaries*, London, 1922.

WHIBLEY, C. *Lord John Manners and his Friends*, 2 Vols., Edinburgh and London, 1925.

WOLF, L. *The Life of Lord Ripon*, 2 Vols., London, 1921.

YOUNG, K. *Arthur James Balfour*, London, 1963.

H. OTHER PRINTED BOOKS

This section of the bibliography is also not exhaustive. Only those works I found especially useful are listed. Most of them are referred to at some point in the text.

ARMYTAGE, W. H. G. *A. J. Mundella, 1825–97*, London, 1951.

ARNSTEIN, W. L. *The Bradburgh Case: A Study in late Victorian Opinion and Politics*, London, 1965.

ASHWORTH, W. *An Economic History of England, 1870–1939*, London, 1960.

AUSUBEL, H. *The Late Victorians*, New York, 1955.

BICKLEY, F. *The Cavendish Family*, London, 1911.

BLUNT, W. S. *The Land War in Ireland*, London, 1912.

BIBLIOGRAPHY

BRETT, M. V. *Journals and Letters of Reginald, Viscount Esher*, 4 Vols., London, 1934.

BRIGHT, J. *Diaries*, Foreword by P. BRIGHT, London, 1930.

BUCKLE, G. E. (Editor). *Letters of Queen Victoria*, Third Series, 3 Vols., London, 1930.

BUXTON, S. *Handbook to Political Questions*, eleventh edition, London, 1903.

CHAMBERLAIN, J. *The Radical Programme*, London, 1885.

CLAYDEN, P. W. *England under Coalition*, London, 1892.

COLLINGS, J. *Land Reform*, London, 1906.

CONDURIER DE CHASSAIGNE, J. *Les Trois Chamberlains*, Paris, 1938.

COUPLAND, SIR R. *Welsh and Scottish Nationalism*, London, 1954.

CURTIS, L. P. *Coercion and Conciliation in Ireland, 1880–92. A Study in Conservative Unionism*, London, 1963.

DICEY, A. V. *England's Case Against Home Rule*, London, 1886.

DICEY, A. V. *Law and Opinion in England*, second edition, reprint, London, 1948.

DICEY, A. V. *A Leap in the Dark: A Criticism of the Principles of Home Rule as Illustrated by the Bill of 1893*, second edition, London, 1911.

DILKE, SIR C. W. *The Present Position of European Politics*, London, 1887.

ENSOR, SIR R. C. K. *England, 1870–1914*, Oxford, 1936.

FOX, J. A. *A Key to the Irish Question*, London, 1890.

GILL, C. and BRIGGS, A. *History of Birmingham*, 2 Vols., London, 1952.

GLADSTONE, W. E. *The Irish Question*, London, 1886.

GREGORY, B. *Sidelights on the Conflicts of Methodism during 1827–1852*, London, etc., 1898.

GWYN, W. B. *Democracy and the Cost of Politics*, London, 1962.

HERTZ, G. B. *The Manchester Politician, 1750–1912*, London, 1912.

HAMMOND, J. L. *Gladstone and the Irish Nation*, new impression, London, 1964.

HAMMOND, J. L. and FOOT, M. R. D. *Gladstone and Liberalism*, London, 1952.

HANHAM, H. J. *Elections and Party Management: Politics in the Time of Disraeli and Gladstone*, London, 1959.

HARDIE, F. *The Political Influence of Queen Victoria, 1861–1901*, second edition, London, 1938.

HURST, M. C. *Joseph Chamberlain and West Midland Politics, 1886–95*, Oxford, 1962.

JACKSON, J. A. *The Irish in Britain*, London, 1963.

JAMES, SIR H. (LORD JAMES OF HEREFORD), *The Work of the Irish Leagues*, London, 1890.

JOLL, J. *Intellectuals in Politics: Blum, Rathenay, Marinetti*, London, 1960.

LANGER, W. L. *European Alliances and Alignments*, second edition, New York, 1950.

LOWE, C. J. *Salisbury and the Mediterranean, 1886–96*, London, 1964.

LUCY, H. W. *A Diary of the Salisbury Parliament, 1886–92*, London, 1892.

LUCY, H. W. *Nearing Jordan*, London, 1916.

LUCY, H. W. *Peeps at Parliament*, second edition, London, 1904.

LUCY, H. W. *Sixty Years in the Wilderness*, London, 1909.

LYONS, F. S. L. *The Fall of Parnell, 1890–91*, London, 1960.

LYONS, F. S. L. *The Irish Parliamentary Party, 1890–1910*, London, 1950.

MARRIOTT, SIR J. A. R. *Modern England, 1885–1945*, London, 1946.

MASTERMAN, L. (Editor). *Mary Gladstone (Mrs. Drew). Her Diaries and Letters*, London, 1930.

MCDOWELL, R. B. *British Conservatism, 1832–1914*, London, 1959.

MCDOWELL, R. B. *The Irish Administration, 1801–1914*, London, 1964.

M'GRIGOR, A. B. *The British Parliament, Its History and Function*, Glasgow, 1887.

MILLS, J. T. *John Bright and the Quakers*, 2 Vols., London, 1935.

MORGAN, K. O. *Wales in British Politics, 1868–1922*, Cardiff, 1963.

O'BRIEN, C. C. *Parnell and His Party, 1880–90*, Oxford, 1957.

O'BRIEN, C. C. (Editor). *The Shaping of Modern Ireland*, London, 1960.

O'CONNOR, SIR J. *History of Ireland, 1798–1924*, 2 Vols., London, 1926.

O'DONNELL, F. H. *A History of the Irish Parliamentary Party*, 2 Vols., London, 1910.

O'LEARY, C. *The Elimination of Corrupt Practices in British Elections, 1868–1911*, Oxford, 1962.

REID, A. (Editor). *Why I am a Liberal*, London, 1885.

ROBB, J. H. *The Primrose League, 1883–1906*, New York, 1942.

ROBERTS, M. *Historical Studies Two*, Papers read to the Third Conference of Irish Historians, Cambridge, 1959.

ROBINSON, R. and GALLAGHER, J. with DENNY, A. *Africa and the Victorians*, London, 1961.

RUSSELL, SIR C. *Speech Before the Parnell Commission*, London, 1889.

SCOTT, J. W. R. *The Story of 'The Pall Mall Gazette'*, London, 1950.

SEMMEL, B. *Imperialism and Social Reform*, London, 1960.

SEYMOUR, C. *Electoral Reform in England and Wales*, New Haven, 1915.

SHANNON, R. T. *Gladstone and the Bulgarian Agitation, 1876*, London, 1963.

SOUTHGATE, D. *The Passing of the Whigs, 1832–86*, London, 1962.

STANSKY, P. *Ambitions and Strategies: The Struggle for the Leadership of the Liberal Party in the 1890's*, London, 1964.

STIRLING, A. M. W. *Victorian Sidelights*, London, 1954.

STRAUSS, E. *Irish Nationalism and British Democracy*, London, 1951.

TAYLOR, A. J. P. *The Struggle for Mastery in Europe, 1848–1918*, Oxford, 1954.

THOMPSON, F. M. L. *English Landed Society in the Nineteenth Century*, London, 1963.

THOMSON, J. A. K. and TOYNBEE, A. J. *Essays in Honour of Gilbert Murray*, London, 1936.

THORNTON, A. P. *The Imperial Idea and its Enemies*, London, 1959.

THORNTON, A. P. *The Habit of Authority: Paternalism in British History*, London, 1966.

TREVOR-ROPER, H. R. (Editor). *Essays in British History*, London, 1965.

TSUZUKI, C. *H. M. Hyndman and British Socialism*, Oxford, 1961.

WOODWARD, E. L. *The Age of Reform, 1815–1870*, second edition, Oxford, 1961.

YOUNG, G. M. *Today and Yesterday*, London, 1948.

YOUNG, G. M. *Victorian England: Portrait of an Age*, second edition, London, 1953.

APPENDIX I

Henry Labouchère to Herbert Gladstone, 9th July 1886. Herbert Gladstone Papers, Add. MS. 45990, ff. 93–5.

We have not had speeches enough in the local meetings and lying has been triumphant. This I judge because every day I have had dozens of telegrams asking me to go down to this or that place, which I have been unable to do, as in winning my seat I entirely lost my voice, it being the unpleasant habit in Northampton to shout politics in the Market Place. What I want you to do is to implore your father not to resign. I enclose a statement of the position from the Gladstone Radical standpoint. We want some of the *saevus animus Catonis* just now. I am getting letters from all parts of the country in this sense. Schnadhorst writes to me today: 'The immediate and urgent necessity is to induce Mr G. to hold on. Unless the Tories are in an absolute majority of the whole House he ought not to resign, and I am almost disposed to say even then after only a great debate. The country has confidence in Mr G. in all other matters and no party can attempt to deal with Ireland for some months. I see no reason why the Govt. should be handed over to the Tories – there are very few of the L.U.'s. who desire to see Mr G. resign and everyone is very anxious that these few should be disappointed. The Elections have gone worse than I expected, but I did not expect the leaders of the revolt would have carried their hostility to such grievous lengths. I have been very dissatisfied with the management of things here. We have lost ground in consequence. Had I consulted my own comfort and reputation I should have kept out of it. I have stayed here as a matter of duty, but there must be a change.' What Schnadhorst says about the management is quite correct. It lacked centralisation, the Parliament St. place was a fifth wheel in the coach and the whole thing ought to have been placed in the hands of an 'old electioneering hand' like Schnadhorst.

We can and we will win if only Mr G. will stand to his guns. So soon as the Radicals realise how near they have landed us with a Tory Govt. by their silly abstentions and so soon as they are given a Radical programme, they will awaken to their folly. As for Chamberlain, I do not believe that he has influenced a dozen votes out of Birmingham, whilst Hartington's friends had already gone over at the previous election.

Do therefore urge on your father not to sentimentalise, and not to commit the fatal mistake of either urging or precipitating action. With time and with a clear definite plan of campaign we will turn the tables before Easter.

Enclosure. 45990, ff. 96–9.

Election Lost because:

1. No thorough centralised organisation.
2. Dislike of Radicals to Land Bill.
3. The Irish Govt. Bill not being before the country in a definite form.

4. Justice to Ireland not being accompanied by some radical sops for England.

5. So many artisans having changed their residence since last Registration.

The result of all this has been that, whilst the Conservatives voted, many Liberals and Radicals sulked, and did not come up to the poll.

The Future

The Tories and Unionists will have (probably) between them a majority. If so, I protest against Mr G. either resigning, or having an Autumn Session. Either course would be fatal. The plan that is so often advocated of marching out of a fortress and letting the enemy establish itself in it, has always seemed to me weak, contemptible and unpractical. I would suggest: that Mr G. calls Plt. together at once to vote the Estimate and wind up for the year. Everyone wants repose just now, therefore this can easily be done. Not one word about Ireland should be said.

Next year Plt. should come together early. The Queen's Speech should announce: 1. An Irish Bill. 2. An English County Govt. Bill. 3. A Bill with a 'Three Acre and a Cow' tendency for the agricultural labourers. 4. That the duties will be taken off tea and coffee for artizans and the poor voters generally.

It would be almost impossible for the Tories and Unionists to unite on an amendment against this, particularly if Plt. be told that they will only know what the Irish Bill is when they see it. The Address having been voted, all these Bills should be brought in. If we are defeated (as is possible) on the Irish Bill, there ought to be a dissolution on the ground that no party has a working majority. But if this be deemed too strong a measure then the Tories must come in. By a determined and drastic opposition of the Irish and the Radicals, their Govt. might be made impossible, and they might be forced to resign before Easter. In either case, therefore, there would be an election almost immediately and the country would be consulted, not on the Irish issue alone, but on a full Radical programme.

If we are well-organised, I am sure that we shall win—the masses care very little about Ireland, but would be glad to have the question settled—they dislike the idea of giving anything to the landlords and they like to know exactly what they are voting for in regard to the future Govt. of Ireland. But justice to Ireland does not arouse their enthusiasm, unless it be wrapped up in what they regard as justice to themselves. Mr G.'s estimate of human nature is too high and he has not sufficiently realised how slow Englishmen are to take in a new idea.

But to win a battle like this there must be no kid glove fighting and no divided councils. If any of Mr G.'s colleagues hang back they should be cashiered. With the exception of one or two they have no individuality and the electors do not care a brass farthing for them. It is not in the House of Commons that we have to win, but in the country. There we can win, if Mr G. will throw himself upon the Radicals. The Radical flag must be nailed to the mast. Ireland must be sandwiched between a few Radical measures for England. We must have a better organisation, and having once laid down a plan of campaign we must stick to it.

APPENDIX II

Mrs. Dilke's Diary, 7th and 11th February and 8th March 1887.
Chamberlain Papers, JC8/2/1.

Monday 7th Feb. 1887.

Our Dinner party on Saturday was most interesting, it was also the best dinner I ever *saw*. I cannot say *tasted*, for I never can eat when I am interested & excited—Mother of course went in with the American minister, Mr Phelps—he sat on her right, & Rustem Pasha, the Turkish Ambassador on her left but mother went down with old Rustem the Turkish Ambassador, as Charlie thought Turkey took precedence of America! Perhaps the 'Sick Man' not having long to live deserved the privilege. There was Mr Buckle—The Trevelyans Sir Arthur & Lady Hayter—Louisa, Lady Ashburton—Mr Mackinnon etc. and Mr Chamberlain, and as I wanted to sit near him I just hocussed the people—& got him for myself—I had much interesting talk with him—he looked as cheerful and smartly decided as ever. One thing is clear to me in conversing with him—that no subject really has any interest for him that is not *connected* with politics—and nothing interests him so much as talking of *his* connection with politics and his attitude. When he is an older parliamentary hand this will modify & pass and merge into the greatest outlook.

His conversation, however, is never egotistical—rather he charms you by his frankness & his clearsightedness, for he knows what he can do, & means to do, and as his game is to be a great one & for a great end, he speaks of himself, I might almost say 'historically', as a man who is to be 'lifted high'—and become a conspicuous object, in the Nation's eye. If there is no humility about Mr Chamberlain, there is no arrogant assumption, and I must confess, his confidence, & his tenacity of purpose, impress me very greatly.

If I feel that a becoming diffidence is rather *wanting*, this is made up for by what seems calm prescience and consequent decision making him as a man who *must* win in the long run.

I propose now to note down as well as I can, some of the things Mr Chamberlain said to me. I don't say they are very deep—or very remarkable words—in themselves, but somehow coming from Mr Chamberlain they have some special significance.

Speaking of the extension of Great Britain's possessions, the acquiring of fresh territories, he said that he *had* been in favour of annexing Kilimanjaro, but that he had no great land appetite. He thought we had enough to protect & administer.

Mr Mackinnon (Sir William afterwards who founded the British West African Co) said that it was not so much for the *sake* of acquiring fresh territory that we ought to plant the British flag especially in Africa, but because, if *we* do not, other countries—particularly Germany, will take possession of all she can possibly get, and *shut us out*. When Germany comes on the scene our trade is completely wiped out. Germany will not allow England to trade in German territory—Mr Mackinnon thought it highly important that England should now take all she can, *whilst* she can.

I remarked to Mr Chamberlain that I had heard that since Lord Randolph Churchill had left the Cabinet, Lord Salisbury had reverted to a dangerous foreign policy—Mr C. only replied he did not think Lord Salisbury would be so 'silly'.

Mr Chamberlain then said that it was a great question whether modern democracies would in future countenance war. 'The Greek Republic, we know', continued Mr Chamberlain, 'was a conquering Republic, taking, & expanding by conquest, but I believe that the modern republics will set their face against war, that fighting can never again be *popular* with the people, with the masses.'

'Do you not think,' I replied, 'that when it becomes a question of *sentiment*, when once people are stirred up to fight—let us say the Russians, who might march on India, that then our imagination quickened, & our sentiments roused the people of England will be eager to fight.'

'The army may—but not the people,' said Mr C. 'I believe that spirit is past & the democracy is & will remain opposed to war.'

Mr Chamberlain then spoke very bitterly of Mr Gladstone.

'Who could have foreseen that Mr Gladstone, at the end of his life, would have created such confusion, would have broken up parties and given shape to proposals so monstrous and absurd that they could never have been seriously entertained had any other man but Gladstone brought them forth? It proves to me, if I ever needed proof, that a man should not hold responsible office, should not direct a great party, and certainly should not be Premier after 70.—He cannot have in full vigour, the faculty of judgment, his intellect must be on the wane, he may serve effectually as a consultative agent, but, after 70, a man cannot and should not *direct*. A great surgeon would not practice much after 70. He would not probably care to undertake any delicate or dangerous operation, but, he would still be valuable as a consultant, his experience would be of assistance to the operation, and so it is, said Mr C. with Politics a man cannot be trusted, much after 70, to undertake duties which require the full flash and energy of a man at his prime.'

I instanced Lord Palmerston. 'Well—Lord Palmerston, his last years of office were weak drivelling years, it would have been far better if he had retired before.'

'And you yourself? If you were Premier at an advanced age,' I asked, 'would you then think it admirable to withdraw, because of your on-coming years?' 'I might possibly desire the sweets of office, but, if I desired it, and would continue as Premier, it would not, for all that, be a happy thing, or a good thing for the country, without being in my dotage, I might still be very harmful, because as I said before I should, in reality, be in-capable of directing the great and complicated affairs of the country.'

'If Mr Gladstone died,' I asked, 'do you believe the Home Rule cry would die out?' 'I believe that Ireland would see and understand that she must accept something less and other than Home Rule, that Gladstone gone, the English Home Rulers would rapidly crumble away. There is not an honestly convinced man amongst them,' continued Mr C. very sweepingly and very assuredly.

'I learnt this year what men are, how little reliance is to be put in them. I never before realised what abject cowards men can be. Why, there is only a handful of men with any moral courage in the whole House of Commons. I repeat, there is not one English Home Ruler who is so from conviction.'

But surely—you do not include John Morley and Mr Bryce in this denunciation? 'Yes I do,' said Mr Chamberlain almost fiercely. 'Even John Morley—Why. I have known him intimately for nine years, we have talked together in private of our dearest hopes and dreams & desires and plans, and never has Home Rule been breathed or thought of. John Morley, is only a Home Ruler of yesterday, like all the others. He has *not* been panting for years to right the wrongs of Ireland by giving Home Rule.'

'Did he not,' I asked, 'write about Ireland in the "Pall Mall"?'

'Certainly he did, but you cannot twist a sentence here and a sentence there into meaning that he wanted Home Rule granted to Ireland, he did not write in ink the other in sympathetic ink which would, under certain conditions become legible—and then show that he was in favour of Home Rule. No, Morley never shaped his thoughts into the grant of Home Rule before the year 85, and I don't believe in all this burning desire to avenge the wrongs of Ireland by Home Rule. As for Bryce,' he continued, 'he is as bad as the others, he is just a *snivelling professor*, who turned Home Ruler because he found that Aberdeen would have it so, and that there was the chance of office.'

'You know nothing of James Bryce if you say that, he has a high moral character and he would never condescend to anything of the kind.'

'Ah well, I think very little of his moral nature or of his intellect as a statesman. I believed in such men once, now, I despise them. Look at Stansfeld, Why. I was completely ignorant of the man's nature till last year. I had a sort of respect for him until the other day. Now, I will give you an illustration of what the man is worth, and he is only an instance of many, and you shall tell me what you think of such Home Rulers.'

He then proceeded to tell me about Mr Stansfield's conduct, I have not time tonight as it is past nine, so I must continue 'in my next'.

Friday 11 Feb. '87.

I must not forget that I have my talk with Mr Chamberlain yet to tell. I must make haste and dispose of it, for last week's history is almost ancient history in these past whirling days. Mr Chamberlain was denouncing the English Home Rulers, saying that there was not an honestly convinced man amongst them, one instance in point he gave. When Mr Stansfeld was appointed President of the Board of Trade in Mr Chamberlain's place, Mr Chamberlain called upon his successor, for whom he had always had a great respect, not to say admiration. When he saw Mr Stansfeld Chamberlain said, 'I am come to express my satisfaction at seeing you fill this office, I feel how admirably you will fulfil all the duties. I could not desire to see any other here but yourself etc. I am only sorry that we are so radically opposed on one single point, and that you come in on the question which forces me to resign.'

Mr Stansfeld looked at me with puzzled astonishment. 'Radically opposed?' he repeated interrogatively. 'What! is it possible that you are under the impression that . . . that . . . I differ from you?'

'Certainly', rejoined Mr Chamberlain, puzzled in turn. 'I certainly am under that impression, but there is some misunderstanding. I meant that our point of difference is Ireland.'

'But I do assure you,' persisted Mr Stansfeld, 'that I am quite of your way of thinking about Ireland. I agree with you about National Councils and Local Government for Ireland. I am entirely of your opinion, don't you remember, I wrote (or spoke) to that effect, endorsing all you said, some months ago.' 'But then,' said Mr Chamberlain, and he described a sudden feeling of deep repulsion for the man.

'But then,' speaking frigidly, 'I am at a loss to understand how you come to be in Mr Gladstone's cabinet.'

'Oh! well, well, well, don't you see. I have been so long out of office, that if I had not accepted this, I should probably never be invited again. I should certainly be overlooked, but although I am in the Government, I am nevertheless quite of your way of thinking,' 'and,' added Mr Chamberlain, 'this man is actually going about the country today speaking of Home Rule as the salvation of Ireland, & blaming the Unionists for not upholding Gladstone's schemes, and this man, before he was offered a place in the Government, on the first reading of the Home Rule Bill went about the lobbies crying "This won't do—this will never do"—I call such conduct *vile*,' said Mr Chamberlain with explosive vehemence, 'and he is only one of many. I do assure you that the only men for whom there is a good word to be said, are the Irish members, they are convinced and consistent. The worst charge against them is that they are all paid, not one man is the poorer for being a Nationalist, that feature of the case certainly taints their patriotism. I don't believe that there is any other instance in history of a great National Movement being kept up by *paid* agitators. The Great French Revolutionists were pure, as regards that charge, but though I feel no sympathy for or interest in these Irish members, they are not like our English Home Rulers—contemptible men'.

So much, I vividly remember, regarding Home Rule, Mr Chamberlain said this, and more, but nothing is amplified or altered, if not absolutely word for word, it is very nearly so, and exactly the purport of what he said.

He spoke confidently of himself. 'Of course I shall be Premier, there is nothing more certain, and I can assure you that I will *rebuild* the fortress. I will *re*form the Party, so rudely torn asunder by Mr Gladstone. He has done a great deal of mischief, but there is nothing irremediable. We shall not have Home Rule, we shall have improved Government in Ireland, there shall be great Reforms throughout Great Britain and Ireland, but it shall never come to granting Home Rule—take my word for it.

'I won't say that Gladstone has *not* shaken down the edifice I so proudly, with others, contributed to build up, but—given health, given time, I shall conquer. I never have doubted the power of will and determination, if you only know how steadfastly I am purposed to be Leader. . . . I remember when I had just come into the House, Mr Rathbone, who was rather addicted to giving fatherly advice, he said to me, "Well, now, be careful, do this and do that, don't say this and don't attempt that." I replied, "Well I am resolved what *I* mean to do. I have determined what I shall be." "And pray what is that?", enquired Mr Rathbone. "Why, I mean to be Prime Minister. I have come to the House of Commons with that intention, and it is to be Prime Minister that I am here today a member of Parliament." Of course my saying so now, does not sound in any way surprising because, as everyone must acknowledge, I am in the runnings, but it rather astonished Rathbone, coming from a new fledged M.P.'

Mr Chamberlain spoke contemptuously of Mr Goschen. 'He is of no use to any party—he is not a statesman. I quite agree with some news paragraph which described him as a man who was neither a candid conservative nor a frank liberal. He can never serve for any purpose.'

I asked him whether he looked forward to some day imposing a progressive income tax. 'It would in my opinion be a fair thing, but it cannot be done, it would be quite impossible in England, it might be harmful too, as its effect would be to drive capital out of the country. No, I do not think it would be possible.' He then talked about wealth, the little pleasure he derived from money. 'I think the only expensive taste I have, and would like more lavishly to indulge in is orchids, but as for fine houses, carriages etc. I do not care for or desire any of these things. I am not really a rich man, I might have been if I had stuck to my business and left politics alone, but I find so little pleasure, in mere money making and in what wealth affords, that business offered me but little inducement to continue in it.'

Mr Chamberlain spoke with convincing sincerity. No one can possibly talk to Mr Chamberlain without being impressed and attracted by his directness and earnestness.

March 8th. '87.

On Saturday I met Prof. Stuart M.P. in St James Park. We walked round the lake together: he gave me a lecture on Home rule. He is a fanatical Home Ruler—he explained his views, feelings & hopes at great length. Home Rule he solemnly declared, *must come*. He, for his part was ready to 'Tarry for God's Time'. He then told me of Sir Michael Hicks Beach's resignation as Chief Secretary for Ireland and the appointment of Arthur Balfour. 'Hicks Beach can no longer stand the awful strain and now that coercion is likely to be enforced, a Secretary's life is in great danger.— A thrill is passing through every man in the House and the time is at hand when a man must range himself on the side of Coercion & Conservatism or Home Rule & Liberalism. I was impressed by Mr Stuart's enthusiastic convictions, or rather I was impressed by his enthusiasm, but his arguments did not convince me. I am willing to recognise that when a great tide rises, a man, however, unwillingly, must give up walking & take to swimming.

There *is* a great change taking place in opinion, so I suppose the tide is rising. Well—may be a lot of members of parliament will be drowned.

APPENDIX III

An extract from Lord Herschell's speech at Manchester on 23rd February 1887, sent by Harcourt to Chamberlain on 28th February 1887. For the whole speech see The Times, *24th February 1887, but this is the portion which Harcourt obviously considered crucial. Chamberlain Papers, JC5/42/5.*

'You must remember that a great many Liberals, followers of Mr Gladstone, who voted for the second reading of his bills, were nevertheless not satisfied with some of the provisions contained in them, and consequently at the time of the vote on the second reading and at the time of the General Election, Mr Gladstone emphatically declared that he took the opinion of the country, *not upon the particular details embodied in his bill, but only on the general principle which it sought to carry into effect. Those details therefore will remain for further consideration.* It is obviously essential that we should *try to make those details as satisfactory as we possibly can and that we should endeavour to obtain in support of them the greatest amount of consent that we possibly can.* The greater the area of consent that you can get to the measure the better for the measure itself; yes and for the Irish people and the success of the measure afterwards. *The more of these people you can bring into harmony with the measure and into satisfaction with it the better for the Irish as well as for us.* It gives the measure a better chance, a better hope, a better prospect of success; and therefore *I think those are mistaken who desire that we should limit in any way the number of those who can be satisfied with the measure which has to be brought forward.* My desire on the other hand would be to make the area of satisfaction as vast as I possibly could. It is surely to the interest of all of us that this great question should be settled; and I think we may appeal to all Liberals and I would extend my appeal even beyond their ranks, to all who have arrived at the conviction that some change must be made, to abandon their negative attitude of mere criticism and *to give us the aid of their constructive faculties, to devise when safeguards, in their view, are needed, or at least to endeavour to devise such safeguards as seem to them most sufficient.* If all were thus to cooperate I should not despair of seeing this different and momentous problem, which has perplexed and may well perplex the greatest of statesmen, brought to a solution which would be satisfactory to all reasonable men. It is not a party question. Surely, it is one worthy of the efforts, the best efforts, of every individual, of every Liberal, of the entire people?'

APPENDIX IV

The story of the 'Round Table Conference' has already been told. There were, none the less, several echoes later on which ought to be mentioned before closing the subject.

When Sir G. O. Trevelyan finally decided to stand for parliament once again it was in the Bridgeton division of Glasgow, where a by-election took place in the summer of 1887. He was, of course, the Gladstonian Liberal candidate. Against him was ranged that unluckiest of Liberal Unionists— Evelyn Ashley, for whose use Chamberlain sent off on 27th July 1887 a letter giving his version of the part he had played in the attempt at Liberal reunion. It was published for the electors' enlightenment, but failed to command universal acceptance! Chamberlain claimed in his 'Memoir' (at page 268) that Ashley embroidered the story somewhat and went further than he was justified in attempting to 'sell' the Radical Unionist position and down Trevelyan. Broadly speaking, however, Chamberlain accepted as true Harcourt's allegations that up to 14th February 1887 the subjects agreed on were important and numerous and those remaining bones of contention less important and few. That the *Baptist* letter had wrecked proceedings he denied vehemently, pointing out that at the banquet to Schnadhorst on 9th March 1887 Harcourt had maintained his optimistic tone. What had really ruined prospects, claimed Chamberlain, was the refusal by the Gladstonians to make clear when the crucial moment arrived just what, if anything, they were willing to concede in order to conciliate Liberal Unionists. Speculating as to the causes of Gladstonian perfidy he ventured the suggestions that either Gladstone and those holding the initiative in their party had refused to allow Harcourt and Morley to make the necessary concessions, or that the prospects of a Coercion Bill convinced the Gladstonians generally that events would play totally into their hands and ruin the Liberal Unionists and the Conservatives alike. Harcourt replied to this onslaught in a letter of his own to Trevelyan, on 29th July 1887, denying that Gladstone had delayed his approval of what had been settled prior to the publication of the notorious *Baptist* letter and once more claiming the whole calamity was due entirely to Chamberlain. The letter had not after all been the first offence. Had not the Birmingham speech of 29th January had to be smoothed over on 14th February 1887? The memorandum drawn up by Gladstone on what the Gladstonian 'Round Table' representatives wanted had never seen the light of day because the *Baptist* letter had been published just at the time when it was ready for use.

Naturally enough, Chamberlain itched to reply, but on reflection desisted. The lengthy and often personal nature of the correspondence made him doubt the wisdom of going the whole hog. He did, nevertheless, taunt Harcourt, challenging him to publish the Chamberlain memorandum on land, and ultimately both agreed all their mutual correspondence over the conference could be published if either individual so wished. Nothing transpired.

Some time later on, in 1889, the subject of publication came up again. Early in February of that year the 'Round Table Conference' was mentioned in the House of Commons. Following a statement by Rosebery that Harcourt was about to bring out his version of what had transpired, Chamberlain proposed an agreed joint 'protocol'—an idea Harcourt rejected out of hand, justifying his proposed initiative on the ground that some speeches made by Chamberlain in Scotland on the 13th, 15th and 16th February had made it imperative to speak out. At Glasgow Chamberlain had said publication of his 'Round Table' Land Scheme would show how nearly agreement had been reached on Irish land purchase and that there was no reason why the Conservative government should not put such a scheme into effect with the blessing of the Liberal Unionists and Gladstonians and without any recourse to Home Rule. In his speech at Dundee he had gone out of his way to laud his National Councils solution for Ireland, adding that it would suit Scotland too. To get the proportion of developments properly in focus, it should be pointed out that these Scottish speeches had served him as a vehicle for propagating his new advanced Unionist programme. The Conservatives found to their chagrin that Free Education was now something it would be wellnigh impossible to avoid implementing. Even so, the past interested Harcourt as much as the future and he did not consider the replies of Morley, Rosebery and Trevelyan to Chamberlain's campaign as sufficient in themselves. 'Our Joe' had to be taught a lesson. Rosebery's speech had contained the warning referred to, but what was a warning to Chamberlain! As usual, 'Joe' claimed he had not forced the pace as Harcourt claimed. Morley's jokes about what he (Chamberlain) had known at the 'Round Table' and the malicious criticisms of 'A Unionist Policy for Ireland' had surely started the process? That was his line on 21st February 1889 and it did not change as further letters flew back and forth. But Harcourt was not having any and spoke out at Derby on 27th February. Chamberlain knew it would do more harm than good to prolong this argument in public and like the Brer Fox he was 'lay low'. Even in his 'Memoir' the explanation is somewhat lame: 'Harcourt gave his account which did not appear to me to require elaborate correction so that I again allowed the matter to drop.' Very convenient—but anyway the past was the past to Chamberlain. His new counter-attack upon the Gladstonians was well on and required all his energy. For him the great thing was not to be 'right', it was to be successful.

For the sake of completeness the relevant parts of Harcourt's speech are reproduced below. It was not a pussyfooting performance and Chamberlain can hardly have found it his favourite reading that week.

Sir William Harcourt's Statement of the Proceedings at the Round Table Conference in his Speech at Derby, 27th February 1889.

I entered into a pledge some time ago to speak on another matter. (Cheers.) It is a very prosaic story I have to tell. It had not for its object to traduce the character of any man. (Laughter.) It had for its object—I am sorry to be obliged to class it among the failures of good intentions—it had for its object to reunite the members of the Liberal party. I speak of the Round Table Conference. (Cheers.) I observe that Mr Chamberlain— (groans)—in his recent pilgrimage to Scotland, where he met with his usual success, as was seen at the East Perthshire election, when the only satisfaction they had was in capturing my friend Mr Carew, upon the day of the poll—has chosen to revive the buried corpse of the Round Table—I thought it had now returned to its original use, that of entertaining my friends in my country home. (Laughter.) I thought it was ancient history, and that nobody would care to hear anything more of it again. However, it formed the main part of Mr Chamberlain's speech in Scotland. I suppose he casts a longing lingering look to the days that are no more. (Laughter.) I call them the days that are no more, because after the manner in which Mr Chamberlain has conducted himself I do not think it is likely that the Liberal party are going to enter into conference with him again—(cheers)— for the settlement of the Irish question. He demands the publication of the proceedings. Well, as a general rule when men meet upon confidential terms under a pledge of secrecy I think it is better under all circumstances to observe it, because the notion that it might in time be divulged restricts freedom of intercourse; but if Mr Chamberlain desires we have nothing to be ashamed of, and by daring us to a disclosure he makes the publication necessary, so let him have it. (Laughter and cheers.) It sometimes happens that a man in his latter years looks back with a sort of longing to the memories of the innocence of his youth—(laughter)—and he is glad to get his old friends to testify to what he once was. I suppose it is some feeling of this kind which induces Mr Chamberlain to desire to obtain from his old friends and colleagues at the Round Table a testimonial to show what an excellent Home Ruler he was both in principle and in detail two years ago. (Cheers). Well, I am happy to say that no political differences have ever altered the mutual regard which exists between myself and Mr Chamberlain. (Hear, hear.) I make a point of never quarrelling personally with my political opponents, and, therefore, I cheerfully render to him the services which he desires. (Loud laughter.) I can most cordially concur in the opinion which he expressed in Scotland, and which I myself have often affirmed, that at that conference we were substantially agreed, and that people would be astonished, as I think you will presently be astonished, to hear how small were the points of difference between us. That which I regret, and which I confess I cannot understand, is why he should now so vehemently differ from us as to principles on which we were then agreed; and why he thinks it necessary every day to denounce us as enemies of our country for entertaining and maintaining opinions in which he then fully concurred. (Hear, hear.) Now I must ask you to bear with me with patience —I would hardly try it upon anybody but my constituents—if I tell you a story, which cannot be very short, which must be very dull. You must forgive me, for you must remember that I am paying a debt at his request to the memory of a departed friend—(laughter)—a friend to whom I might apply a touching epitaph, and say: 'When I think of what he is and what 'he ought to was, I can't but think he's throwed hisself away without 'sufficient cause.' I have confidence that I can state the circumstances with accuracy, because what I shall say is taken from memoranda made at the time and from reports of our proceedings made to Mr Gladstone and my colleagues from time to time.

The Round Table Conference

I have submitted the statement I am now about to make to the consideration of Mr John Morley and of Sir George Trevelyan; Lord Herschell being unfortunately abroad. It has been verified and confirmed by them, and if any errors or omissions occur Mr Chamberlain will correct me. The origin of the Round Table Conference may be simply told. Immediately upon the resignation of Lord Randolph Churchill in December, 1886, Mr Chamberlain made a speech in Birmingham which appeared couched in so conciliatory a tone that, taking advantage of our personal friendship, I wrote to him expressing my satisfaction and my sincere desire to co-operate in any attempt which might lead to the reunion of the Liberal party. I received from Mr Chamberlain on December 27th a letter cordially responding to my sentiments, and suggesting a meeting between himself and some others of our party to discuss the Irish question. I met Mr Chamberlain on December 30th. His disposition originally was to confine the discussion principally to the Land question and that of Irish Local Government, but I pointed out to him that it was impossible for Mr Gladstone and his friends to enter upon any discussion for the settlement of the Irish question which excluded the consideration of a Legislature and Government for the transaction of Irish affairs, and I stated that of course the nature of that Legislature and its attributes might be left entirely for further discussion. To this Mr Chamberlain assented, and we agreed that if this discussion were entered upon it should embrace Irish land, Irish Local Government, and a plan for the Irish Legislature also. The proposal for the conference was submitted to Mr Gladstone, and sanctioned by him. It was understood that the conference pretended to no binding authority, that its objects were to ascertain what common ground existed between us, and to reduce points of difference to a minimum. As far as we were concerned it was understood that the whole discussion should be conducted under the auspices and the instruction of Mr Gladstone, and finally referred to his judgment. As I am aware that Mr Chamberlain was in communication at the time with Lord Hartington, I presumed that the latter was cognisant of the proceedings throughout. It was finally settled that Lord Herschell, Mr John Morley, and myself should represent the Liberal party, and Mr Chamberlain and Sir George Trevelyan should represent the Dissentients, that the transactions of the conference should be strictly secret, subject to the communication of the proceedings to Mr Gladstone and Lord Hartington. The conference met on the 13th January. Mr Chamberlain proposed an elaborate and ingenious plan for land purchase in Ireland. It involved too much detail to be discussed on the spot, and it was referred for further examination to Lord Herschell and Mr John Morley. It is impossible for me now to enter into the details of the scheme. I don't pretend to be a great authority on such matters, but I confess the plan seemed to me to be more ingenious than practical. It had, however, one great merit in my eyes.

Mr Chamberlain and the Ashbourne Act

The fundamental principle was to exclude the pledging of British credit for Irish land purchase, for at that time no man more vehemently denounced the principle of the Ashbourne Act than Mr Chamberlain in public and private; and if, as it should seem, Mr. Chamberlain is still willing to run his plan against the Ashbourne Act, I can see no reason why he should not submit it to the public judgment, and, indeed, I fancy that he had already done so in the *Birmingham Daily Post*. Indeed, as to this land plan, when the conference closed no absolute conclusion had been arrived at in the matter, though my impression was that Mr Gladstone was not unfavourable to the principle of the plan, and that is all I need say about the land question. The conference did not expend much time upon Irish Local Government, for it was expected that the principles which it was assumed would be adopted in England would also be applied to Ireland. Then we came to that which constituted the principal subject of the discussions of the conference, namely, the establishment of an Irish Legislature. I shall state what passed at these meetings from a report I wrote to Mr Gladstone on January 13th and 14th, and from my own notes. Having referred to the terms of the Leeds resolution, viz., 'that the only plan which will satisfy either the justice or policy of the case is that of an Irish legis- 'lative body for the management of what Parliament shall decide to be 'distinctively Irish affairs,' and having referred, also, to Mr Chamberlain's letter to Mr Labouchère on June 5th, 1886, in which Mr Chamberlain said: 'We are ready to accept as a principle the expediency of establishing 'some kind of legislative authority in Ireland subject to the conditions which 'Mr Gladstone has laid down,' and also to Mr Chamberlain's speech in the House of Commons, in which he professes himself ready to adopt the principles of Canadian provincial legislatures, it was agreed that we should on the next day, that is on January 14th meet to discuss the conditions of the Irish Legislature. On January 14th I wrote as follows to Mr Gladstone: 'Since writing the above, we have held our second meeting, 'of which I must say the omens were favourable beyond expectation. We 'started with the admitted basis that there should be a legislative body for 'Ireland, with an executive dependent upon it for purely Irish affairs.' (Cheers.)

The Leeds Resolution Adopted

'In fact, the Leeds resolution in principle was frankly adopted. It was 'thought convenient to discuss the matter with the Canadian Constitution 'as a text. There seemed no difficulty upon any side in adopting the powers 'of the provincial legislatures in Canada as an analogue for Irish Home 'Rule. The matters which are granted exclusively to the provincial legis- 'latures by the Dominion Legislature Act are as follows.' Now mark what Mr Chamberlain was willing to give to an Irish Parliament. 'The exclusive 'powers given to the Provincial Legislatures in Canada are these:— 1st. 'The power to amend the constitution of the province except as to the

'Lieutenant-Governor. 2nd. Direct taxation within the province and 'borrowing powers. 3rd. The establishment, appointment, and payment of 'provincial officers. 4th. The control of prisons. 5th. Municipal. institu- 'tions. 6th. Licences. 7th. Local public works. 8th. Marriage laws. 9th Property and civil rights in the province. 10th. The administration of 'justice. 11th. The imposition of punishments for breach of laws relating 'to above matters. Lastly. Education with special provisions to prevent 'sectarian injustice.' Now, gentlemen, those powers to which Mr Chamberlain agreed were powers more extensive than those which Mr Gladstone's Bill proposed to give to the Irish people. (Hear, hear, and cheers.) I go on with my report. 'We agreed that the powers of the Irish Legislature should 'be especially defined in the statute. It was suggested that some special 'machinery should be provided for restraining the Irish Legislature from 'violating or exceeding those powers as in the case of the United States and 'of Canada. We discussed but did not determine the question of one or two 'chambers, and also, whether, when the Irish Legislature was established, 'Irish representatives should sit and vote at Westminster. On this latter 'point opinions did not run very strong either way. As to the police, 'Mr Chamberlain was willing that the local police should be under the 'control of the Irish local authorities. It was, however, considered that 'there should be also an Imperial police for executing in Ireland the 'authority of the Imperial Government in matters not conceded to the 'Irish Legislature and Executive. At the close of the meeting Mr Chamber- 'lain raised the difficult question of the separate treatment of Ulster, a 'matter which you had spoken of in 1886 as an open question. The 'difficulties of this subject were recognised on all hands, and the matter 'was postponed for further consideration.' Now, that was our second sitting. In concluding the report to Mr Gladstone, I said, 'I think you 'will be of opinion that we have made very substantial progress. We have 'had the proposal of a Land Bill resting exclusively upon Irish credit. We 'have agreed to the establishment of an Irish Legislature with an Irish 'Executive for the transaction of such Irish business as Parliament shall 'determine, this Irish business being in fact all Irish local affairs, due 'security being taken that those powers are not exceeded, and that the 'authority of the Imperial Parliament in matters not transferred shall 'be respected and enforced. There are many details yet to be worked out; 'but it seems to me that we have got a very great way in establishing these 'fundamental propositions.' (Cheers.)

A Plan of Home Rule

Now, gentlemen, you will see that practically speaking, with certain modifications, our plan of Home Rule was thoroughly adopted. It was an Irish Legislature for Irish affairs, and an Irish Executive dependent upon it. On Saturday, the 16th, I had a further opportunity of discussion with Mr Chamberlain on most of the unsettled points. I was enabled to report to Mr John Morley on the 17th when I wrote to him: 'Nothing could be 'more frank and explicit than Chamberlain's acceptance of our funda- 'mental principle, namely, an Irish Legislature with an Executive dependent

'upon it, accompanied by specific limitations of its functions and with
'proper security for the central authority in Imperial affairs. Chamberlain
'and I went over all the points we discussed in Grafton-street, and I found
'no flinching on his part on any of the questions which we deemed vital.
'As to the Home Rule chapter, matters stand very much as they did.
'Chamberlain definitely and distinctly accepts an Irish Legislature, with the
'Canadian provincial powers specifically defined. He desired, while con-
'ceding authority over civil rights and property there should be special
'provisions to prevent abuse of these powers against classes or sects,
'something after the fashion of the United States Constitution, and the
'provisions of the Dominion Act in respect of education. He wishes the
'nomination of the judges to be reserved to the Imperial Government; as
'to the justices of the peace he was willing to leave that over to future
'discussion; on the head of police he adopted my view that the local
'authorities, that is, the County Board, not the Irish Executive, should have
'a police under their control for enforcing what lay within the scope of
'their authority. He seemed more indifferent than I expected on the subject
'of an Imperial police, which, however, I thought quite necessary in order
'to enforce matters lying outside the provincial authority, and if necessary
'to restrain the excesses and abuses of that authority—for instance, the
'enforcement of the decisions of the supreme court on the question of
'*ultra vires*. The supreme court which is to keep the Irish authority within
'the limit of its power to be a special constitution of the Judicial Committee of the Privy Council. He quite accepted the idea of a regular Irish
'Executive dependent upon the Irish Legislature, with regular departments,
'including an Irish Home Office. As to finance, the Irish Executive would
'have the administration of all the funds now expended on Ireland. Of
'Imperial establishments in Ireland, there would then only remain the
'military and the Imperial police; the revenue establishments, of course,
'remaining as they are, a Lord-Lieutenant or Lieutenant-Governor
'representing the Imperial Government in Ireland. Chamberlain seemed to
'think this last might be dispensed with, and the powers relating to
'Ireland not delegated to the provincial government might be administered
'by an Irish department in London. I did not agree to this, as without
'some channel for information or action, I did not see how the Imperial
'authority could be maintained in Ireland. On all the above points there
'seemed to be very little practical difficulty.

Two Hard Nuts to Crack

'There remained only two hard nuts to crack: First, the presence of
'the Irish members at Westminster. Chamberlain was disposed to admit
'them generally, excluding them upon all non-Irish questions *in pari materia*
'with all subjects delegated to the Irish Parliament. We discussed over
'and over again the great Ulster stumbling-block. We both fully recognised
'the expediency of doing something, if possible, to satisfy the Ulster
'people. I pointed out all the difficulties of a separate treatment, and
'insisted specially on the fact that the majority of Ulster, geographically
'and in its representation, was in favour of Home Rule. Chamberlain fully

'admits that the Ulster people cannot be allowed to say they will remain 'as they are whilst a system of self-government is given to the rest of 'Ireland. But he suggested that they should be told that whilst they are not 'to be subject to the Irish Government they must accept some form of local 'government of their own to perform the same functions, whether it be 'called a provincial legislature, or whether, as he thinks, they might accept 'and prefer some more modest machinery of provincial councils. This is 'all no doubt very difficult, but ought not to be insoluble.' We were not very far off from one another then, gentlemen. Two speeches were made that very week by Mr Chamberlain—one at Hawick, the other at Birmingham—in which, though not disclosing that these were resolutions of the conference, he himself argued in both these speeches in favour of the adoption of an Irish Legislature and an Irish Executive. (Cheers).

On Saturday, January 22nd, Mr Chamberlain had to speak at Hawick in company with Sir G. Trevelyan, who was his colleague at the Round Table. His original intention had only been to deal with the Irish Land Question, but I pointed out to him that such a course might produce the impression that the conference had shelved Home Rule. He therefore agreed to present an argument in favour of the acceptance by all parties of the principles of Mr Gladstone's Home Rule on the lines of that which had been practically agreed at the conference. Anyone who takes the trouble to read this speech will see that though general in its terms it conforms to what I have above stated. It is an elaborate and careful argument on behalf of the establishment of an Irish Legislature.

In that speech, having pointed out what was Mr Gladstone's position, viz., that 'his object was to establish some kind of legislative authority in 'Ireland for the transaction of domestic business,' and having stated that 'that was Mr. Gladstone's main principle' and that that principle, apart from the Home Rule Bill, was 'one to which no reasonable man could 'object,' he proceeded to point out that even the Conservative party 'were not averse to large and drastic changes in the Government of 'Ireland. They are prepared for a reform in the system of Local Govern-'ment. They are prepared to consider and review the whole of the irritating 'system of administration which is known as Dublin Castle, but if they 'come to this they will be compelled, if they have not already done so, to 'accept the principle, the main principle, of Mr Gladstone's Bill. They will 'have to substitute for the administration of Dublin Castle some kind of 'legislative authority, subject to the guarantees which Mr Gladstone has 'laid down, and this will be the case, though they have rejected Mr Glad-'stone's plan as dangerous and his guarantees as inadequate.'

He then referred to the four conditions 'which in Lord Hartington's 'opinion were essential to the establishment of any legislative authority in 'Ireland', and after enumerating them he says: 'I hope you will have 'already observed that there is nothing in any one of these four conditions 'which is inconsistent with the main principle which alone Mr Gladstone 'considers fundamental.' And he finally 'expressed his own opinion that on 'the lines of the Canadian Constitution a plan might be found which' would 'give to Ireland such a measure of local autonomy as would satisfy all just and reasonable desires.'

And in a later speech at Birmingham, March 12th, Mr Chamberlain, speaking of himself and Lord Hartington, said that though they were opposed to Mr Gladstone's scheme 'they were willing to agree in the 'future to the creation of some legislative authority in Dublin in accordance 'with Mr Gladstone's principle.'

Now, after reading the first speech at Hawick, I observed he had fully maintained the doctrine of the Irish Legislature; but I pointed out to him that he had said nothing about the Irish Executive, and in deference to my suggestion, when he spoke at Birmingham, on January 29th, he definitely though not very graciously declared in favour of an Irish Executive. He says: 'You must allow them'—that is, the Irish Legislature under Home Rule—'to organise some form of government'. 'What the exact form of 'government is to be is a matter which in my judgment concerns them much 'more than it does us. I should think if they were anxious to be economical 'and business-like they would have as little red tape and form as possible; 'that they would be satisfied with a standing committee, with a council and 'permanent officers of some kind or another.' Now mark this passage.

Mr Chamberlain's Ideas of Home Rule

'But if they thought that they could be better served by imitating the 'cumbrous forms of our Parliamentary government, if they desired to have 'a Ministry—a Prime Minister, a Minister of Agriculture, a Minister of 'Public Works, a Minister of Education, and a Cabinet, and to imitate on 'a small scale everything that goes on at Westminster and in Parliament 'street and at Whitehall—all I can say again is that that seems to me to 'be a matter entirely for their discretion, with which I at all events have 'no desire to interfere.' (Cheers.) Well, is it possible for a man to be a sounder Home Ruler than that? ('No,' and laughter.) He is ready to give them an Irish Parliament, he is ready to give them an Irish Cabinet; he is ready to give them an Irish Prime Minister and an Irish Home Secretary. It will be found that in neither of these important speeches did he say much on the Ulster subject, except by reference to the expression of Mr Gladstone's willingness to consider the question. It was no doubt, as Mr Chamberlain himself felt, very inconvenient that he should be called upon to speak in public during the pendency of the conference. As to the substance of his declarations, I felt that there was no ground for complaint as they contained an explicit adoption of an Irish Legislature and an Irish Executive—declarations which spread much dismay in the Unionist camp. Well, unfortunately, this speech was accompanied—I cannot think why— by most ungracious attacks upon Mr Gladstone and his supporters, as well as upon the Irish members. Why this tone should have been adopted by Mr Chamberlain, being, as it was, entirely at variance with the friendly and confidential spirit in which we were acting, I have never been able to understand, and it finally ruined the accord that promised so well. This bitter and discordant note in the last Birmingham speech produced great irritation in the Liberal party, and gave rise to much distrust of the conference by our friends outside, as people could not understand how men could be *bona fide* agreeing in private while they were denouncing one another in public. This led to some difficulty, which I am not disposed how to recall, and delayed further the meeting of the conference till February 14th, when at my instigation the members met at dinner at Sir George Trevelyan's. All the unsettled points were again discussed. The result of this meeting has been thus described in a speech of Sir George Trevelyan at the Bridgetown election: 'We afterwards sat for several hours and the nego-'tiations, which had been in a very advanced state previously, were brought 'into a condition which left in my mind no doubt whatever that the union 'of the party was thoroughly attainable.' It will be remembered that at the time of this dinner Sir G. Trevelyan was acting with Mr Chamberlain as the representative of the views of the Dissentient Liberals, and it was because he was satisfied, as he thus stated, 'that the union of the party was 'thoroughly attainable,' that, as I am glad to say he found it consistent with his convictions to return to our camp. I am convinced that at that time such was also the opinion of Mr Chamberlain.

Mr Chamberlain Stultifies Himself

On 29th January, a fortnight before, when the points of difference had not been as far settled as they were on the 14th February, Mr Chamberlain said in his speech at Birmingham: 'All I want to tell you is this, that as far 'as I have seen there is nothing in any of these objections which raised 'questions which need divide us or be an obstacle to re-union.' The only anxiety at that time on the part of Mr Chamberlain and Sir George Trevelyan was, that the whole matter having been so far ripened should be brought as early as possible under the judgment of Mr Gladstone. Mr Chamberlain seemed to have an idea that we had some sinister motive for postponing the bringing of it before Mr Gladstone. That is an error. Mr Gladstone was away, and returned on February 21st, and I saw him on the 22nd and 23rd. The whole question was placed before him by Lord Herschell and Mr John Morley—(cheers)—and myself on February 25th. After hearing all that had passed Mr Gladstone undertook to draw up on the next day a memorandum of his own views upon all points agreed to, and left open at the conference to be communicated to Mr Chamberlain. Unfortunately, on that very day Mr Chamberlain published a letter in *The Baptist* newspaper. I have no desire to revive unpleasant recollections. I have said all I have to say on the subject—which it is necessary I should say—in the letter I addressed to Sir George Trevelyan on July 29th, 1887, during the Bridgetown election. Everybody felt that it was impossible to proceed with an amicable conference under the sting of such an attack. Its publication was hailed by the whole Unionist Press at the time as a proof that all negotiations had failed, and that open war had broken out between us. And no wonder. Mr Gladstone, however, was indisposed finally to break off the conference, though he felt it necessary to suspend it for a time, and, in that placable and conciliatory spirit which he has displayed throughout this controversy towards his opponents, and for which he has received a very sorry return, wrote to me on the 26th February telling me that he had drawn up a memorandum, but that the circumstances made it impossible to communicate at that time further with Mr Chamberlain. He said:— 'Viewing its actual character'—that is *The Baptist* letter—'I am inclined to 'think we can hardly do more now than to say we fear it has interposed an 'unexpected obstacle in the way of any attempt at this moment to sum up 'the result of your communications which we should otherwise hopefully 'have done, but on the other hand we are unwilling that so much ground 'apparently gained should be lost, that a little time may soften or remove 'the present ruffling of the surface, and that we are quite willing that the 'subject should stand for resumption at a convenient season.' Is it possible for a man to have written a more moderate or a more conciliatory letter with a view to the reunion of the whole party upon a more sound and solid basis? It was my duty, thereupon, to inform Mr Chamberlain that the meetings of the conference and the communication of Mr Gladstone's judgment, must be suspended for a time. A long correspondence took place during the ensuing fortnight, in which, while I expressed my strong sense of the mischief wrought by the course Mr Chamberlain had pursued in this publication, I also indicated my opinion that it would be advisable to ascertain more fully the views of Lord Hartington. I thought, indeed, it was no use going on unless we knew that Lord Hartington was with us, and that we could not treat Mr Chamberlain as the representative of the Dissentient Liberals. (Laughter.) Whilst stating our inability on account of what had occurred to proceed at once with the conference, I did all in my power to induce Mr Chamberlain to accept the proposal of Mr Gladstone, and that after a sufficient interval the conference should be resumed. This, however, he declined; and the conference came to an end by Mr Chamberlain refusing to take any further part in it. It seems strange enough that during all this interval, Mr Chamberlain had not communicated a word of what was passing to his colleague, Sir George Trevelyan. Of course I did not, because I was acting with Lord Herschell and Mr John Morley. It was for Mr Chamberlain to have told his own colleague what he was about. When I spoke at the banquet to Mr Schnadhorst on March 9th I had still hopes that Mr Chamberlain would accept advice and go on, after a temporary suspension. It seems, however, that at the moment I was speaking Mr Chamberlain informed Sir George Trevelyan that he would have no more to do with the conference, and Sir George Trevelyan at the Bridgetown election on July 26th said this: 'When I came 'home' (this was on March 9th) 'I found a letter in which Mr Chamberlain 'told me he should not return to the Round Table Conference. I was never 'more surprised in my life than by the news I heard that night. Sir William 'Harcourt afterwards showed me the correspondence, from which it was 'evident that the failure of negotiations was due to the conduct of Mr 'Chamberlain, and that its failure was greatly regretted by the other parties 'to the conference. When I contrasted its result with Mr Chamberlain's 'personal assurance to me if I joined the conference it should be for the 'purpose of renewing the amicable relations with our old party, I felt deeply 'hurt personally, and greatly pained and disappointed on public grounds.' (Cheers.) Now you know the reasons why Sir George Trevelyan returned to the Liberal party—(cheers)—because his honest doubts had been satisfied by our conference, and you also—if you can understand them, which I cannot—know the reasons why Mr Chamberlain finally left the Liberal party. (Cheers.) Now, that is a simple and, I believe, accurate account of the beginning and the end of the Round Table Conference. Mr Chamberlain wished it to be revealed, and I have revealed it. (Cheers.) I leave you to judge it. It was not broken off owing to any difference of principle or even to any insuperable difference of detail. There was every reasonable hope that an understanding might and would have been arrived at on the unsettled points. It was not broken off because Mr Gladstone or his representatives at the conference were unwilling to come to a common understanding upon points of difference. They were from the beginning to the end sincerely desirous of an accommodation if it could be had upon honourable terms, consistent with the principles that they had laid down; and, in my opinion, those terms were found in that conference. (Cheers.) It was not broken off owing to any dissent or remonstrance from Mr Parnell or anyone else. I think it necessary to state this explicitly, because suggestions have been insinuated to that effect. It came to an end solely and simply because we could not accept the situation that Mr Chamberlain should, in spite of repeated remonstrances, continue vehement attacks upon Mr Gladstone, his friends, and his policy, whilst he was conducting these friendly negotiations. We offered Mr Chamberlain that if he would abstain from this course in the future we would renew the conference after a temporary suspension, and endeavour to bring it to a satisfactory conclusion; that offer Mr Chamberlain declined, and finally took leave of us and of the Liberal party. (Cheers.) Sir George Trevelyan, who, like Mr Chamberlain, had recognised that no real difference of principle divided us, and not thinking it necessary to quarrel with us in public whilst he agreed with us in private, resumed his place in the party of which he is so great an ornament. (Cheers.) I am glad to think that that is the course which has been taken as appears from recent elections, by the great majority of the Liberals who dissented from our policy in 1886. Throughout the country the majority of the Liberal Unionists of 1886 have followed Sir George Trevelyan and have refused to follow Mr Chamberlain.

Mr Chamberlain's Reasons

It is not for me to judge Mr Chamberlain. He has taken his own course, and he is responsible for it. I never have been able to comprehend why, having suggested and joined the conference, he broke it off by the conduct which I have described. What we have a right to complain of is that having two years explicitly accepted our principles in the main, and in great part in detail, and having substantially adhered to Mr Gladstone's policy of Home Rule, he should have occupied himself for the last two years in going up and down the country denouncing us as the enemies of our country for following a course which he himself had agreed to. Having agreed to a Legislature for Ireland—I leave out of the question for the moment the treatment of Ulster—with powers as extensive as those which Mr Gladstone proposed—by what right does he vilify us as Separatists because we propose an Irish Parliament which he now says must necessarily lead to separation? If so, why did he agree to it? He knew then as well as he does now that in such a Parliament as that to which he agreed the Nationalist party must and would be supreme. Yet he was perfectly prepared to consent to give, at least in three provinces of Ireland, the conduct of the domestic affairs of Ireland to the Nationalist party. He is very great indeed now in the protection of what he calls the loyal Protestant minority. In all other provinces except Ulster what did he propose for the Protestant loyal minority? Nothing at all. He left them to the Irish Legislature subject to the provisions I have mentioned. The great staple of his speeches now is abuse of Mr Parnell and the Irish party. But when he agreed to the Irish Executive, who did he expect would be the Irish Executive? When he agreed to an Irish Prime Minister, did not he know who would be the Irish Prime Minister? (Cheers.) Well, he knew and intended it would be that party which he says ought never to be trusted and ought never to be spoken to; with whom he now says it is a shame to consort, the tools of the Chicago Convention, &c., &c. He was ready to give them the Executive of Ireland. By what right does he denounce us for handing over Ireland to the enemies of law and order? He agreed that the police should be in the hands of the local authorities in Ireland. He knew that no man has a possibility of being elected for any public authority in Ireland unless he is a Nationalist, and yet to them he was ready to commit the charge of law and order in Ireland. I say he saw no difficulty in advising separate treatment for Ulster, and was prepared for the separation of Ulster as well as the rest of Ireland from English administration. He saw no difficulty in that then, but now he says it is not to be heard of. As to the presence of Irish representatives in Westminster, he had no difficulty in reconciling that with the plan for an Irish Parliament; but now he says that is impossible. In short, if you examine any one of the heads of the flaming orations which he delivers in every part of the country denouncing his old friends and his old party, you will find they consist in attacks upon the very things to which he then agreed, or in things which are the necessary consequences of the principles in which he concurred. That is a thing we have a right to complain of. He has a perfect right to his own opinions, but he has no right to denounce us as Separatists and enemies of our country for maintaining that which two years ago he thought perfectly reasonable. If he said then, as he does now, we were so nearly agreed, how comes it he denounces our conduct as monstrous, ruinous, and revolutionary? We have not budged one inch from our position at the conference—(cheers)—when, as he said, we were so nearly in accord. He made a solemn appeal in Scotland to what he called his Gladstonian friends—(laughter)—to tell him what is our policy. When I get a civil question put to me I try to give it a civil answer. His question being asked in Scotland, I will give it a Scotch answer by asking another question. I say to Mr Chamberlain: What is your policy? In January, 1887, you were in favour of an Irish Legislature. Are you in favour of it now? If so we are agreed. In January, 1887, you were in favour of an Irish Executive. Are you in favour of it now? If so again we are agreed. Mr Gladstone has agreed that the powers of the Irish Parliament shall be defined in the Act, and he has agreed that the Irish members shall be retained at Westminster, and that being so, let Mr Chamberlain tell us what is the difference between us which justifies him in holding us up to execration as destroyers of the Empire and enemies of our country. What is the root of this bitterness with which he assails the Liberal party and its leaders, and which has finally thrown him into the arms of the Tories, who absolutely and wholly reject each and all of the proposals to which he has assented? That is my answer to Mr Chamberlain's questions. (Cheers.) Now I have trespassed upon you most unconscionably by a task which was imposed upon me by others, but if I touched this subject at all I was bound to deal with it in fairness to all parties and fully. I could not make a less or or shorter statement upon a matter in which such deep interests, national much more than personal, are involved. Though it is an old story it still contains a useful lesson. There are many men who had doubted the wisdom of this policy, which unquestionably, and I have never denied it, was a new policy which took many people by surprise, but I want to show you that when men met together in a fair and intelligent spirit to discuss the question they found the difficulties were not insuperable. So I believe it will be found by Liberals who have doubted throughout the country. I find the history of that in every election.

INDEX

All persons referred to below are given the descriptions applying to them in the years dealt with by this book, or, when not contemporaries, those now usually employed for them.